CODE RED

The Secret Communist Takeover of America

★ ★ ★

Cynthia F. Hodges, JD, LLM, MA

Auriga Books, LLC
Edmonds, Washington

DESCRIPTION

Code Red: The Secret Communist Takeover of America is an exploration of the present-day challenge posed by communism to the core values of the United States. This intellectually stimulating book delves into the historical backdrop, ideologies, and societal impacts of communism, revealing the imminent perils and driving factors behind its resurgence. It uncovers its influence within education, media, and politics, undermining the pillars of liberty and equality under the guise of "equity."

Offering an analysis of the infiltration of Marxist ideology into American society, *Code Red* delves into historical contexts, methodologies, and consequences of this subversive trend. It provides readers with an understanding of the threats to American values, institutions, and freedoms. Through a historical lens, this book explores the communist resurgence, dissecting past instances of communism worldwide and drawing parallels to the current political landscape. This juxtaposition enhances readers' comprehension of potential consequences of progressive policies under the current regime. Beyond a historical reflection, *Code Red* serves as a critical roadmap for the future, empowering readers to identify warning signs, engage in enlightened discourse, and safeguard America's republican heritage. By exposing concealed agendas that jeopardize the fundamental principles upon which America was built, this book prompts readers to scrutinize the motives behind policies and actions, fostering an environment of critical analysis and contemplation.

By offering a comprehensive examination of the evidence, the book invites readers to question motives behind policies and actions, make well-informed judgments regarding the nation's destiny, and engage in meaningful dialogues. Serving as a source of inspiration for concerned citizens, policymakers, and individuals who cherish American ideals, *Code Red* compels them to confront ideological hurdles and preserve a future where liberty flourishes. It reminds readers that the struggle for freedom is ongoing, enlisting them to safeguard the American dream for future generations. Emphasizing unwavering vigilance, discerning thought, and collective action, this book confronts the escalating wave of communism, ensuring a future in which freedom and prosperity prevail.

CONTENTS

"Communism is a hateful thing, and a menace to peace and organized government."

~ President Grover Cleveland ~

INTRODUCTION

The Looming Specter

In 2022, a poll revealed that almost half of Americans feel estranged in their own country, viewing the government as corrupt and even hostile.[1] This discontent spans political affiliations, with stronger alienation among Republicans, Independents, and conservatives, although some Democrats also feel disconnected. The poll showed that over a quarter contemplate armed action against the government, depicting substantial discontent, polarization, and mistrust in government, political parties, and media. While not the sole cause, Marxism's influence significantly contributes to the disconnection and disillusionment among the American populace. The presence of socialism in discourse and policy discussions exacerbates divisions, amplifies polarization, and further intensifies the discontent evident in the poll.

---

[1] 56% of respondents perceive the government as rigged against everyday people. Democrats are the only group where disagreement slightly outweighs agreement. Additionally, 28% of Americans support the idea of armed resistance against the government, particularly among conservatives, Republicans, Independents, and gun owners. Even 19% of self-described Democrats see the potential necessity of armed resistance. The poll also highlights a lack of trust and mutual dislike between supporters of major political parties. Republicans view Democrats as "bullies" imposing their views and generally being untruthful, while Democrats likewise hold negative perceptions of Republicans. "Number of Americans willing to take up arms revealed." *RT*, 1 Jul. 2022, www.rt.com/news/558193-americans-arms-against-government/.

Communism's impact in America has been intricate and far-reaching, finding resonance among intellectuals, activists, labor unions, and left-wing political circles from the late 19th century to the present day. This ideology has significantly shaped American political and social discourse.

Communism emerged as a response to the growing social and economic disparities exacerbated by the Industrial Revolution and the initial expansion of capitalism in the 19th century. It sought to address the perceived inequalities ingrained within capitalism by prioritizing resource allocation based on need rather than the accumulation of individual wealth. As economic gaps widened during industrialization, disillusionment with capitalism grew, prompting an exploration of alternative ideologies, notably communism. The perceived exploitation of workers served as a catalyst for the adoption of Marxist principles, gaining ground within the early 20th-century labor movement and trade unions.

Labor movements became influential platforms that effectively mobilized the working class and shaped national conversations. Communists advocated for labor rights, fair wages, and improved working conditions by amplifying workers' grievances. Through collective actions such as strikes and protests, they disrupted established economic norms to advance their revolutionary goals. By harnessing worker discontent, socialists deliberately introduced instability into societal and economic structures, aiming to pave the way for a classless society.

The oppressive working conditions and widespread exploitation, coupled with widening wealth disparities between social classes, fueled discontent, particularly among the working class. Over time, labor movements and unions coalesced around leftist ideologies, drawing inspiration from communist principles to champion societal equality and assert laborers' rights.

The emergence of these movements was epitomized by the radical labor union, the Industrial Workers of the World (IWW), founded in 1905, advocating for worker unity and the collective ownership of production. Despite a waning influence over time, the IWW's legacy endured within the American labor movement, shaping the development of labor laws and practices related to workers' rights and collective bargaining. Its impact left an indelible mark on the socio-political landscape.

Following the 1917 Bolshevik Revolution in Russia, communism surged in visibility. The establishment of the Soviet Union captivated American leftists and intellectuals, initiating a growing intrigue with communism. It magnetized those dedicated to social justice, uniting varied movements under its ideological umbrella. At its core was an emphasis on class conflict and a sharp critique of capitalism, alluring passionate individuals striving for significant social and economic transformations.

During the Cold War, the United States opposed communism, a sentiment epitomized by the McCarthyism wave of the 1950s. The rivalry between the United States and the Soviet Union, based on capitalism versus communism, defined international relations for decades. This period was marked by fervent anti-communist zeal and decisive actions led by Senator Joseph McCarthy (R-WI) and the House Un-American Activities Committee (HUAC). They conducted aggressive campaigns to eliminate communist influences across sectors such as Hollywood, government agencies, education, and labor unions. Fear of communist infiltration fueled suspicion, resulting in widespread blacklisting and severe consequences for suspected sympathizers. The Cold War era encompassed more than a mere geopolitical standoff; it encapsulated an intense ideological clash between the United States and the Soviet Union, rooted in opposing ideologies of capitalism and communism, dominating global relations for decades.

The fervent opposition to communism reached its peak during the McCarthyism wave of the 1950s, a time when anti-communist sentiments soared to unprecedented levels. Senator Joseph McCarthy and the House Un-American Activities Committee (HUAC) emerged as emblematic figures spearheading the battle against communist threats. Their initiatives extended across various sectors of American society.

Hollywood, an emblem of American entertainment and culture, was not exempt from the anti-communist fervor. The entertainment industry faced intense scrutiny, with accusations of communist sympathies leading to the blacklisting of artists, writers, and filmmakers. Numerous individuals found themselves ostracized and unable to work due to suspicion about their political beliefs.

Government agencies encountered similar scrutiny, with allegations of communist infiltration resulting in purges and investigations. The nation was gripped by the fear of subversion, leading to a climate of suspicion and rigorous loyalty tests for many public servants.

The education sector and labor unions did not escape scrutiny either. Educators and union leaders suspected of leftist leanings faced inquiries, often resulting in dismissals or exclusion within their respective fields.

The Communist Party USA (CPUSA) faced hurdles that thwarted its ascent as a significant political force. The party grappled with fierce competition from other ideologies, while its own radical image hindered widespread acceptance. The prevailing disdain for communism in the United States cast a shadow over the party, deterring broad-based support. Government crackdowns during the Red Scare and the era of McCarthyism severely restricted CPUSA's activities and expansion. Despite advocating for social justice and labor rights, internal rifts and struggles in connecting with the broader public limited its overall impact. These combined challenges stifled the CPUSA's growth, preventing it from emerging as a prominent political entity, although its influence persisted in shaping political discussions and championing workers' rights.

The collapse of the USSR in 1991 had a seismic impact on global politics, reshaping how communism was viewed within the United States. This pivotal event resonated worldwide, reshuffling perspectives on the viability and desirability of communist ideologies.

The dissolution of the Soviet Union marked a significant milestone, casting doubt on the effectiveness of a state-controlled economy and authoritarian rule. The aftermath of the Soviet collapse—a tumultuous mix of economic decline, political turmoil, and social disarray—laid bare the inherent flaws and weaknesses of the communist system. This spectacular fall of a superpower punctured the myth of the invincibility of a centrally planned economy, highlighting the failures of totalitarian governance. It underscored how excessive government control stifled progress, leading to discontent and eventual collapse.

Moreover, the USSR's demise reverberated globally, serving as a stark lesson about the deficiencies of collectivist ideologies. It discredited the communist model, showcasing its incapacity to sustain economic growth, ensure social stability, or safeguard individual freedoms. This profound event amplified the narrative on the pitfalls of state control and reinforced the virtues of free-market economies and democratic governance.

The collapse of the Soviet Union reinforced the prevailing view in the United States: capitalism stood as the preeminent global economic and political system, effectively discrediting communism. This discrediting led to a waning appeal of communist ideology within American society. Additionally, the disappearance of the USSR removed its role as the primary adversary around which anti-communist sentiment in the US rallied. This absence lessened the urgency to confront communist influence, causing a reduced emphasis on it within American politics and culture.

Despite the diminished influence of communism after the Soviet Union's collapse, interest in Marxist ideas persisted, particularly among intellectuals, activists, and those dissatisfied with certain aspects of capitalism, such as income inequality, healthcare disparities, and social injustices.

Recently, a resurgence of interest in communist ideologies challenging the fundamental principles of the nation has emerged. This revival actively critiques capitalism, income inequality, and social injustices while offering alternative solutions. The reappearance of communism in America is evident across diverse societal domains. The acceptance of socialist policies has notably broadened, with concerns such as wealth inequality, healthcare access, and free education assuming paramount importance in political discussions. This surge in socialist ideology within specific segments of the population indicates a notable shift in the American political landscape. Moreover, prominent political figures such as Bernie Sanders and Alexandria Ocasio-Cortez, known for advocating Marxist ideologies, signify a wider embrace of such concepts within mainstream discourse.

Furthermore, communist ideologies have made substantial inroads into academia and cultural institutions, shaping prevalent narratives and values. The influence of Marxist theories, critical race theory, and left-leaning perspectives in media and entertainment underscores the significant impact of communist ideas on steering public discourse. This influence has sparked ongoing debates and raised concerns about the ideological trajectory of educational and cultural platforms.

The ascent of far-left movements, notably groups such as Antifa and Black Lives Matter, adds another layer to this resurgence. These movements advocate for revolutionary change and challenge capitalism while promoting communal ownership and collective action. They aim to dismantle capitalism and establish collectivist structures akin to communism.

The resurgence of communism's influence within American discourse signifies a substantial shift, affecting policy debates, social movements, and cultural narratives, amplifying existing societal tensions and divisions. This renewal triggers concerns about its potential impact on core American principles such as individual liberty, free-market capitalism, and limited government intervention. The historical association of communism with totalitarian regimes heightens fears regarding the erosion of individual freedoms and human rights. Skeptics question communism's methods for achieving equality and social justice, especially those who advocate for meritocracy and individual responsibility. The ascent of communism implies an expansion of government authority, sparking worries about increased government control over people's lives, businesses, and personal freedoms, particularly concerning proponents of limited government intervention.

The growing prominence of communism in the American context has bred discontent among certain segments of society. Rooted in principles of collective ownership and a classless society, communism diverges from fundamental American values of individualism and free-market capitalism. Concerns stem from the idea that immigrants from countries where communism prevailed are challenging the established American way of life. There are fears about potential erosions of personal freedoms and property rights, particularly among those who prioritize self-reliance and individual responsibility.

Moreover, worries persist about communist ideologies undermining the democratic framework, as the emphasis on collective ownership and centralized planning risks compromising personal liberties and the ethos of free enterprise—both integral components of the American identity. This resurgence has led some to perceive these ideologies as threats to democratic values, individual liberties, and the deeply ingrained free-market capitalism in American society. There are concerns that romanticizing communist ideals may overshadow historical atrocities linked to their past implementation, fueling worries about potential impacts on human rights.

Code Red delves into communism's historical context, theoretical underpinnings, and its impact on American society, aiming to shed light on its increasing influence in the US and the potential threats it poses to cherished values such as freedom, individualism, and republican governance. Through an analysis of historical events, ideological frameworks, and current societal shifts, the book uncovers the catalysts behind communism's resurgence. It emphasizes the importance of vigilant awareness, critical thinking, and the protection of democratic principles.

Communism, Marxism, and socialism share commonalities while exhibiting distinct characteristics. Marxism, shaped by Marx and Engels, focuses on resolving class conflict toward a classless society. Both socialism and communism prioritize shared ownership and government involvement to promote equality. Socialism allows various degrees of private ownership alongside state intervention, seeking parity through shared ownership and state participation. In contrast, communism envisions a society devoid of private ownership and government structures, emphasizing collective resource sharing for a stateless society grounded in shared ownership principles.

Marxism acts as a comprehensive framework encompassing socialism and communism, addressing societal class conflicts. Within Marxism, socialism and communism offer distinct paths toward a classless society. Positioned between capitalism and communism, socialism permits some private ownership while incorporating state intervention. Its mechanisms include welfare programs, progressive taxation, and state-regulated industries, maintaining elements of private ownership to mitigate inequality.

Conversely, communism takes a more radical stance, envisioning a society without private ownership and government structures. It emphasizes communal resource ownership, striving for a classless, stateless society. In this idealized concept, communism follows the principle of equitable distribution based on individual abilities and needs.

The spectrum between socialism and communism represents variations in government involvement, private ownership, and the envisioned path toward a stateless society. Marxism serves as the encompassing umbrella for these ideologies. Socialism and communism, differing in economic and governmental structures, offer varied approaches to achieve the ultimate Marxist goal of a classless society. Despite technical differences, for simplicity in understanding and discussion, this book will occasionally interchange these terms.

Serving as a comprehensive guide to the present political landscape, *Code Red* calls upon citizens, policymakers, and advocates of American values to confront ideological challenges, safeguard liberty's future, and uphold core republican principles. It urges a careful evaluation of historical events, ideological shifts, and contemporary developments while stressing the need to draw wisdom from history's lessons. By revealing the imminent dangers to these foundational values, the book underscores the urgency for action and serves as a rallying cry to persevere in the struggle for freedom. In navigating these challenges, preserving American values and nurturing informed discourse remains paramount for fostering unity amidst diversity. Together, united in purpose, we can preserve the American dream and ensure a future where liberty thrives.

Chapter 1

The Rise of Communism

In this chapter, we examine communism's origins and principles to understand the current situation. We explore Marx and Engels' influential works that shaped Marxist theory. We also give an overview of political ideologies such as communism, socialism, and capitalism, analyzing their core principles. This sets the stage to comprehend today's ideological landscape.

Throughout history, the majority of individuals endured lives marked by desperate poverty and seemingly insurmountable hardships. However, the 19th century witnessed an extraordinary transformation, particularly in Western societies. This change can be attributed to intellectual movements such as the Renaissance and the Age of Reason, which emphasized values such as rationality, individualism, and the pursuit of knowledge. These principles laid the foundation for the eventual emergence of capitalist ideologies.

The 19th century stands as an era of profound intellectual advancement, deeply rooted in the Renaissance and the Age of Reason. During this period, Aristotelian philosophy's enduring influence paved the way for an unprecedented economic system tightly interwoven with principles of political liberty: capitalism. Aristotle's emphasis on reason, logic, and individual fulfillment seamlessly integrated with the prevalent intellectual climate, giving birth to a capitalist economic structure that valued individual initiative and creativity. This epoch exemplified the zenith of evolving intellectual movements, highlighting the significance of rational self-interest and individual rights as essential pillars necessary for the prosperity of capitalism.

Capitalism, as an economic framework, is fundamentally rooted in the principles of individual rights and private property ownership, driven by the dynamics of free markets and competition. It champions economic prosperity, individual autonomy, and the advancement of society as a whole. Through effective resource allocation, the fostering of innovation, and the empowerment of individuals, capitalism has unequivocally demonstrated its efficacy.

Capitalism incentivizes individual initiative through various mechanisms. At its core, capitalism is driven by the concept of private ownership, free markets, and competition.

Firstly, the profit motive is fundamental. Capitalism hinges on generating profits, motivating individuals or businesses to innovate and offer goods or services that consumers demand. This drive enables them to earn financial rewards for successful ventures, encouraging the initiation of new businesses or product lines.

Competition, another critical aspect, pushes individuals to excel and innovate. In capitalist markets, competition is the norm, fostering creativity, efficiency, and the drive to improve goods or services to attract consumers. Those who stand out among competitors are rewarded for meeting consumer needs effectively.

Moreover, capitalism celebrates entrepreneurship. It allows individuals to create businesses or startups, encouraging risk-taking and initiative. Successful entrepreneurs are rewarded with profits and the potential for growth and expansion, promoting the spirit of innovation and enterprise.

Additionally, capitalism often operates as a meritocracy, where success is based on merit and effort. People are rewarded based on their contributions and skills, fostering motivation to improve productivity and skills to succeed.

Furthermore, capitalism fosters an environment conducive to innovation. In a competitive market, there is a continuous drive for improvement and innovation to create better products or services. This encourages individuals to take risks, experiment with new ideas, and invest in research and development to stay ahead.

Lastly, wealth accumulation is possible in capitalism through successful ventures or investments. This accumulation can serve as a reward for individual initiative, providing the means for individuals to pursue further opportunities, invest in new ventures, or contribute to societal development. Overall, capitalism's structure, emphasizing competition, entrepreneurship, innovation, and rewards for success, serves as a powerful engine to incentivize and reward individual initiative within the economy.

Capitalism, deeply rooted in principles of individual rights and private property ownership, has been a driving force behind upward mobility and economic expansion while boasting a well-documented history of poverty alleviation and as a cornerstone for both cultural and political freedoms. The ascent of capitalism during the 19th century ushered in a transformative shift within Western societies, significantly enhancing the overall well-being of the masses as newfound prosperity gradually trickled down to ordinary individuals. The emergence and dissemination of capitalism played a central role in elevating living standards, drawing inspiration from earlier intellectual movements, notably the Renaissance, which was deeply influenced by Aristotelian principles. This evolution marked a pivotal juncture in the trajectory of human progress, improving well-being and shaping the modern world.

Throughout America's history, capitalism has consistently stood as the fundamental foundation, continuously generating wealth while steadfastly upholding the core tenet of freedom—a principle intricately interwoven into the nation's identity. The nexus between capitalism and political freedom is paramount, highlighting the innate connection between the economic structure and political liberty. Capitalism's emphasis on private ownership, competition, and market-driven outcomes resonates harmoniously with the ideals of individual freedom. This synergy between the economic and political spheres defines the transformative landscape of the 19th century.

Capitalism and freedom from excessive government intervention are closely linked through core principles that define this economic system. One crucial aspect is the notion of limited government involvement in the economy. In a capitalist setup, the government's role is typically restricted, granting market forces the primary authority to govern economic activities. This translates to minimal interference in business operations, pricing mechanisms, and individual economic decisions.

Property rights are fundamental in capitalist structures. People have the right to own property, including assets, land, and businesses. This ownership grants autonomy in managing these assets without intrusive government involvement.

Free markets, a foundational element of capitalism, facilitate voluntary transactions between individuals and businesses with minimal government control. The determination of prices, production, and distribution of goods and services rests on market forces such as supply and demand, fostering economic freedom for both buyers and sellers to engage in transactions based on their preferences.

Capitalism also champions the concept of free enterprise. It encourages entrepreneurship and competition by enabling individuals to establish businesses, innovate, and compete freely within the market. This competition cultivates economic dynamism and allows individuals the liberty to pursue their economic ambitions without facing extensive bureaucratic hurdles.

Moreover, capitalism stresses individual responsibility and self-reliance, aligning with the idea of personal freedom. It encourages people to take charge of their economic destinies, make choices regarding employment, investments, and consumption, free from excessive government influence.

In a capitalist system, the concept of freedom from government welfare is interlinked with the belief in self-reliance and individual responsibility. Capitalism emphasizes personal empowerment and financial independence through hard work, innovation, and entrepreneurship. It places importance on individuals leveraging their skills, talents, and efforts to generate income and support themselves without substantial dependence on government aid.

Fundamentally, capitalism promotes the idea that people are accountable for their economic outcomes. It advocates for the notion that through initiative and diligence, individuals can enhance their economic status, achieve financial autonomy, and provide for themselves and their families.

Additionally, capitalism encourages personal savings and investment to secure future financial stability. It fosters a culture of financial prudence and independence, aiming to reduce reliance on government assistance during financial hardships.

While capitalism may endorse self-reliance, safety nets and social programs can still exist within its framework. However, the focus within capitalism typically centers on empowering individuals to create their economic opportunities, lessening reliance on extensive government welfare programs, and nurturing personal responsibility for financial well-being.

Communism, as a socio-economic ideology, stands as the antithesis to capitalism, representing a complete ideological opposition in economic principles and societal organization. Communism strives for a classless society by advocating for collective ownership of the means of production, with the ultimate goal of achieving fair wealth distribution and social equality. This ideology sharply contrasts with capitalism, which hinges on the concept of private ownership of factories, machinery, land, and other production assets. In a communist system, the emphasis shifts from private ownership to collective or governmental ownership and oversight of property, means of production, and commercial channels.

Central to Marxist principles is the dissolution of class distinctions, aiming to eradicate social hierarchies prevalent in capitalist societies. By advocating for collective ownership, communism seeks to eliminate the ownership and control of production by a specific class, thereby erasing the disparities between the bourgeoisie (the owning class) and the proletariat (the working class) observed in capitalist structures.

Unlike capitalism's reliance on profit-driven markets, where production decisions are made based on individual profit motives, communism proposes a planned economy, where the state or collective entities decide the allocation and distribution of resources based on societal needs. This planned economy is meant to ensure equitable distribution of goods and services, intending to eliminate wealth disparities and provide for the welfare of all citizens.

Marxist ideologies often entail extensive government involvement in economic affairs, where the state acts as the primary owner and administrator of resources and enterprises. The aim is to shift economic power from private entities to the government or collective bodies, purportedly to prevent exploitation and ensure fair treatment of all individuals.

However, criticisms of communism center on the concentration of power within the government, often resulting in authoritarian regimes that curtail individual freedoms, limit dissent, and suppress personal initiative. Additionally, the lack of market-driven competition in a planned economy can lead to inefficiencies, resource misallocation, and a diminished incentive for innovation, which are often cited as drawbacks of communist systems.

Communism, socialism, and Marxism are connected ideologies, each with distinct features that define their approaches to socio-economic structure and governance. Both socialism and communism prioritize collective ownership and governmental intervention as tools to achieve equality, yet they diverge in their perspectives on ownership and the role of the state.

Socialism encompasses a range of ownership systems, allowing varying levels of private ownership alongside governmental intervention. This ideology accommodates cooperative enterprises, state-run industries, and mixed economies. In contrast, communism envisions a stateless society where private ownership is entirely eradicated in favor of collective ownership of all resources. Its goal is to establish a society free from social classes and hierarchies.

Marxism, serving as the foundational theory for both socialism and communism, advocates for the abolition of private property and the establishment of a centrally planned economy. Its aim is to create a more equitable distribution of wealth through collective ownership of the means of production. At the core of Marxism lies an analysis of class struggles within societies, advocating for the creation of a classless society liberated from divisions.

While communism and socialism differ in their approaches to ownership and the role of government, they share a common objective of reducing socio-economic disparities and fostering more egalitarian societies. Marxism, being the ideological bedrock, investigates societal classes and suggests transformative measures toward a society liberated from class divisions and characterized by collective ownership.

The intellectual origins of communism find their roots in the seminal works of Karl Marx and Friedrich Engels, pivotal figures who wielded significant influence in shaping and disseminating communist ideologies. These two thinkers laid the theoretical foundation for communism, presenting a critical assessment of capitalism as an inherently exploitative system that concentrated wealth and power in the hands of a privileged few while subjecting the majority to adversity. Collaborating on several influential texts, most notably *The Communist Manifesto* (1848) and *Das Kapital* (1867), Marx and Engels established a theoretical basis for communism.

Karl Marx, a Jewish philosopher in Germany, stands prominently as the progenitor of communism. He introduced the concept of historical materialism, which asserts that societal and economic evolution is propelled by the struggle between classes and the inherent conflict between the bourgeoisie (the capitalist class) and the proletariat (the working class).

Friedrich Engels, a close collaborator of Marx, expanded upon these notions and contributed supplementary analysis and support. Engels placed a premium on understanding the material conditions of society and claimed that capitalism perpetuated inequality and exploitation. He made considerable contributions to the maturation of Marxist theory, particularly with regard to the intricacies of historical and dialectical materialism.

Karl Marx's vision encompassed a future marked by freedom and abundance, a transformation he believed would require the dismantling of the capitalist system. He advocated for socialism as an alternative framework, a crucial step toward achieving his vision. At the heart of Marxist ideology lies a conception of a society where a strong central government oversees the means of production.

Communism, as envisaged by Marx, embodies the ultimate utopian ideal—a society free from class divisions and government, where private property is eliminated. In this scenario, goods are produced and distributed based on the principle of "from each according to their ability, to each according to their needs." This vision proposes a society where the state gradually fades into obsolescence, viewed as unnecessary for regulating social relations.

Marxist thought propounds the eventual dissolution of societal hierarchies, rendering the government obsolete as social harmony and equity prevail. The concept encompasses a harmonious existence where the need for a governing entity diminishes as collective ownership and communal cooperation flourish. This transformative view anticipates the emergence of a self-regulating society where individuals contribute based on their capabilities and receive based on their necessities, fostering an idyllic state of egalitarianism and communal cooperation.

Marx's critique of capitalism centered on the concept of private property, which he perceived as a catalyst for self-centered pursuits that functioned as an "alien power." While advocates of private property assert its role in fostering responsible resource management, critics emphasize its potential to exacerbate societal inequality by restricting access for certain groups.

Communists argue that capitalism, driven by private ownership of the means of production, inherently perpetuates a lopsided distribution of wealth and authority. They underscore the exploitation of the working class, known as the proletariat, by the capitalist class, or bourgeoisie, to generate profits and accumulate wealth. This exploitation widens the economic gap between a prosperous minority and a financially disadvantaged majority.

At the core of their critique lies the assertion that the bourgeoisie benefits from the labor of the proletariat in what they view as an inherently exploitative relationship. Marxists claim that the bourgeoisie profit from the labor of the working class while providing insufficient compensation in return. This exploitative cycle perpetuates enduring economic inequality, where the affluent amass wealth while the working class struggles to meet basic needs.

Socialists emphasize the significant disparities perpetuated by capitalism, highlighting the profound divide between the affluent and the less privileged. The resources and privileges accumulated by the capitalist class starkly contrast with the limited access to essential necessities and opportunities for the working class. According to their perspective, this pronounced division undermines social cohesion, obstructs upward mobility, and fosters an environment where the economically marginalized face barriers to meaningful progress.

Critics often overlook the positive outcomes of capitalism, which involve fostering innovation, driving economic growth, and motivating individuals, all while contributing to improved living standards. One key advantage of capitalism compared to socialism is its inherent accountability to the free market. Capitalist economies, shaped by consumer demands, prioritize addressing crucial issues such as pollution, sustainability, and profitability.

The expansion of capitalism has revolutionized production, consumption, and global interconnectedness through technological and communicative advancements, liberating individuals from geographical constraints. Through innovation and job creation, capitalism generates wealth, propelling progress and societal advancement.

Capitalism's alignment with human nature and survival instincts is often juxtaposed with socialism, seen as incompatible with individual competitiveness and prone to failure in accommodating these human traits. Author Ayn Rand argued that capitalism, rooted in self-interest and competition, resonates with rational human behavior, fostering individual survival and preserving justice. In contrast, socialism contradicts competitive human nature and carries inherent flaws. Capitalism encourages innovation, productivity, and progress, aligning with human instincts, while socialism's emphasis on collective ownership and central planning suppresses individual initiative and ambition, fundamentally conflicting with human nature. Rand's perspective suggests that the diversity and competitive drive among individuals find better alignment with the principles of capitalism, fostering a society where personal achievements are celebrated, and individuals can thrive based on their merits. According to Rand, attempts by socialists to enforce artificial equality will unravel due to innate individual diversity.

In *The Communist Manifesto*, Marx conceded that capitalism marked the onset of an era characterized by unparalleled wealth generation and the expansive reach of markets, facilitating the accumulation of essential capital for societal advancement. Karl Marx acknowledged capitalism's profound impact, attributing to it the reformation of societal frameworks and the impetus behind the pursuit of prosperity and civilization. He emphasized capitalism's revolutionary influence on economic relations, methods of production, and global interconnectivity, acknowledging its capacity, fueled by innovation, technology, and industrialization, to prompt unprecedented societal transformations. Marx outlined how capitalism dismantled feudal structures, disrupted traditional economic systems, and ignited significant technological advancements, fostering rapid industrial growth and the sprawling expansion of urban areas.

This economic model propelled increased productivity, generating surplus wealth crucial for the proliferation of cities, the rise of industries, and the development of vital infrastructure. While recognizing capitalism's transformative capability in generating wealth and advancing progress, Marx chose to focus on its perceived deficiencies and alleged flaws.

Despite the lofty ideals upheld by communism, historical evidence vividly illustrates its significant drawbacks. The pursuit of centrally planned economies within communism encounters stumbling blocks, including inefficiencies that hinder progress, impede innovation, and grapple with bureaucratic hurdles. The heavy reliance on state control inherent in communism often limits freedoms, obstructs economic advancement, and paves the way for authoritarian rule.

Societies governed by domestic socialist regimes often promise to provide necessities free of charge. However, the implementation of government-provided resources and welfare programs, dubbed as "government cheese," triggers concerning consequences. While these programs aim to address immediate needs, they foster a culture of dependence on the government. This gradual erosion of self-sufficiency stifles individual initiative and dampens the drive for innovation.

From an economic standpoint, the implementation of central planning and state-controlled economies within communist systems frequently results in stagnation. This inertia primarily stems from the absence of market-driven mechanisms, healthy competition, and incentives for innovation. Critics of this approach emphasize how centralized resource control engenders inefficiencies, leading to stagnation and shortages. This, in turn, diminishes incentives for innovation and individual productivity. The absence of personal gains for exceptional efforts dampens creativity and entrepreneurship, directly impeding progress and hindering technological advancement.

Moreover, when individuals lose their incentive to work due to everything being provided for free, it inevitably leads to a significant reduction in production levels. This decrease subsequently triggers shortages in essential goods and services, adversely impacting various facets of society. Consequently, inefficiency, resource misallocation, and reduced productivity become pervasive issues, leaving nations following socialist principles struggling to keep pace with the more dynamic growth seen in market-driven economies.

Despite the intentions underlying these progressive policies, they frequently unravel into unintended consequences. Critics consistently underscore the emergence of inefficiencies and bureaucratic controls within centrally planned economies. The absence of market mechanisms for resource allocation often results in misallocated resources, hindering economic growth and stifling innovation. Central planning, often unable to adapt to changing consumer demands and technological advancements, frequently grapples with shortages, surpluses, and operational inefficiencies, further undermining the potential for sustainable growth and progress.

Throughout history, communist regimes have often grappled with inefficiencies and struggled to uphold adequate environmental stewardship, primarily due to centralized control. At its theoretical core, communism aims to address the "tragedy of the commons," intending to collectively manage resources based on needs rather than individual gain. This concept signifies the overuse of shared resources propelled by self-interest, resulting in depletion due to the absence of clear ownership or regulation.

The environmental deterioration observed in communist systems frequently stems from the lack of individual responsibility and accountability. This deficiency is compounded by centralized decision-making, often resulting in inadequate resource management and subsequent environmental harm. The absence of individual ownership and accountability in these systems can diminish personal investment in environmental preservation, contributing to an overall decline in stewardship.

Under communist paradigms, the collective ownership and control of resources might theoretically offer an egalitarian approach. However, in practical terms, this centralized control can create a disconnect from ecological consequences at the individual level. The absence of a direct correlation between one's actions and the environment's well-being might foster negligence or disregard for sustainable practices.

Moreover, the concentration of decision-making power within the central authority often results in a lack of flexibility in responding to environmental challenges. Bureaucratic hurdles, slow decision-making processes, and an absence of diverse perspectives can hinder timely and effective measures to address ecological issues. The rigid structure of centralized control may impede adaptive and innovative approaches necessary for sustainable environmental management.

In essence, while communism theoretically aims to address collective management of resources, its practical application has often led to environmental shortcomings. The absence of individual responsibility, coupled with centralized decision-making, creates a challenging environment for effective resource management and environmental preservation within these systems.

The market-driven accountability within capitalism often leads to a responsiveness in addressing societal issues —a characteristic frequently lacking in socialism, as evident in the environmental catastrophe of the Aral Sea.

Once a vast inland sea between Kazakhstan and Uzbekistan, the Aral Sea's decline began in the mid-20th century due to Soviet irrigation projects. Central planners redirected the two major rivers, Amu Darya and Syr Darya, crucial sources feeding the Aral Sea, to irrigate vast cotton monoculture and other agricultural crops. This diversion significantly reduced the sea's inflow, swiftly depleting its water levels and volume.

The Soviet Union's 20th-century irrigation projects aimed to bolster agriculture in Kazakhstan and Uzbekistan's arid regions. However, this approach overlooked the long-term environmental consequences and sustainability of extensive water diversion. The priority was meeting production quotas, overshadowing considerations for preserving the ecosystem and the Aral Sea's health.

The ecological impact of the sea's decline included the exposure of salt flats and heightened salinity levels, releasing toxic chemicals previously trapped in the seabed. This environmental disruption devastated local flora and fauna, leading to the extinction of various species and the collapse of the once-thriving fishing industry that sustained local communities.

Moreover, the impact extended to human health, as the desiccation of the sea bed contributed to the formation of dust storms carrying salt and toxic residues. These storms had adverse effects on the health of nearby populations, causing respiratory issues and various health problems among those living in the region.

Economically and socially, the disappearance of the Aral Sea brought about severe hardships for local communities. Fishing villages lost their livelihoods, agricultural productivity declined due to increased salinity in the soil, and unemployment surged. The region experienced economic decline and social upheaval as people struggled to cope with the loss of their traditional ways of life.

Soviet central planning played a pivotal role in the catastrophic decline of the Aral Sea. The absence of comprehensive environmental assessments and checks within the centrally planned system overlooked the impact of diverting such substantial water volumes away from the Aral

Sea. The plan neglected the delicate balance required to sustain the sea's water levels and ecological equilibrium. As a result, the Aral Sea began to shrink rapidly, leading to its eventual depletion.

The centralized decision-making process, characteristic of Soviet planning, lacked flexibility and mechanisms for feedback or adjustments based on environmental concerns. It emphasized meeting predetermined targets without considering the far-reaching ecological repercussions of diverting massive water resources for agriculture.

Moreover, the lack of local autonomy and input in decision-making prevented the incorporation of regional knowledge and expertise, which might have highlighted the potential ecological devastation. This top-down approach inhibited the ability to adapt policies to local environmental conditions or heed warnings from scientists and experts about the consequences of diverting water away from the Aral Sea.

Unfortunately, efforts to revive the Aral Sea have been only marginally successful. Attempts to redirect some water back to the sea and conservation initiatives have faced an uphill battle against the extensive damage caused over several decades. This environmental disaster demonstrates the consequences of a centrally controlled economy lacking the corrective mechanisms found in a free market. Centrally controlled economies lack the corrective incentives found in capitalism, resulting in reduced responsiveness and adaptability to changing circumstances.

Evidences gleaned from past socialist endeavors paint a picture where attempts at economic harmonization fail to invigorate prosperity. Rather than fostering equality, socialism tends to consolidate wealth within an exclusive elite, leaving the masses with diminished resources. The core aim of socialism is to achieve equality through wealth redistribution and centralized governance. However, historical experiences with Marxism often reveal a stark reality of widespread impoverishment, as these systems often favor a select ruling class. Citizens surrender their wealth for government-led redistribution, a process rife with susceptibility to corruption and coercion.

Alexis de Tocqueville, acclaimed for his influential work, *Democracy in America*, identified a crucial paradox inherent in communism. While communism strives for collective ownership to eliminate private property and ensure fair distribution, the elimination of private property raises concerns about the likelihood of heightened government control. This situation presents a complex dynamic where individuals might become dependent on the state for necessities, rendering them vulnerable to political manipulation. The potential for centralized authority prompts deep concerns about possible abuses of power and encroachments on individual liberties.

In essence, the eradication of private property in communist ideals intends to create a more egalitarian society by sharing resources equally among all individuals. However, this path to equality raises a significant challenge: the concentration of control in the hands of the government. The absence of private ownership might inadvertently lead to an increased reliance on the state, potentially enabling authorities to wield substantial influence over citizens' lives. This scenario creates a delicate balance between the collective welfare sought by communism and the preservation of individual autonomy.

Tocqueville's insight into this paradox illuminates a fundamental tension within communist ideologies. The pursuit of equality through collective ownership risks a trade-off with individual freedom, as extensive government control could potentially infringe upon citizens' rights and subject them to the whims of political authorities.

Marxism tends to consolidate power, curtail individual freedoms, and incubate corruption. Contrary to the ideal of wealth redistribution, it often facilitates a scenario where a select few luxuriate in opulence while the majority endure poverty, manifesting an alarming disparity. Critics contend that communism, in practice, can culminate in a dichotomy where an elite relishes opulence while the masses grapple with poverty. Socialism, in its practical application, benefits a privileged minority at the cost of reduced prosperity for the broader populace.

The allure of socialism often rests on promises that frequently obscure the true trajectory of this ideology: The consolidation of government power, ultimately leading to the erosion of individual rights and property ownership. These enticing pledges, often manipulated to maintain control by the ruling elite, mask the harsh realities experienced under such systems.

In historical contexts, the pursuit of leaderless, egalitarian communism has frequently involved the forceful seizure of private property. Leaders, designated as the "vanguard of the proletariat," have often led lives of opulence reminiscent of royal courts under a monarch's rule. The journey toward communism typically traverses a path marked by coercive property seizures and a steadfast reluctance to relinquish power once it has been attained.

Sadly, Marxist regimes bear a dark and troubled history overshadowed by authoritarianism and egregious human rights abuses. The concentration of power among the elite commonly results in widespread corruption and exploitation, lacking the essential checks and balances crucial for upholding democratic principles. This environment stifles freedom of expression, subjecting dissenters to censorship, incarceration, and even execution, thereby nurturing an atmosphere of fear that undermines egalitarian values.

The manipulative allure of socialism, promising equality and justice, often serves as a façade for the centralization of power, leading to the subjugation of individual rights and property. Historical examples demonstrate how the pursuit of socialist ideals has frequently entailed forceful property seizures and a reluctance to relinquish power, fostering an environment ripe for exploitation and severe human rights abuses. The concentration of power within a select elite has tragically led to a climate of oppression, curtailing freedoms and silencing dissent in the name of maintaining control.

Historically, every communist regime has resorted to punitive measures such as establishing labor camps and deploying execution squads to suppress opposition and maintain control. Chairman Mao Zedong of China openly acknowledged that "Political power emerges from the barrel of a gun" and affirmed that "Communism is a tool for crushing the enemy."

Instances such as the reign of Nicolae Ceaușescu in Romania and the perpetuation of power by the Kim family in North Korea vividly underscore this trend. These leaders luxuriate in grandiose palaces and opulent lifestyles while ordinary laborers struggle with meeting the most basic needs. Their primary focus revolves around consolidating and perpetuating their power structures, heavily investing in internal security measures for self-preservation, rather than prioritizing the collective welfare of the nation.

Consider the case of communist Yugoslavia under Marshal Tito's rule, where he controlled a staggering number of at least 34 villas, each designated as his "homes," despite their official categorization as state property. Many of these opulent residences were seized from the nation's former royal family, the Karađorđevićs. Following the pattern observed in other communist regimes, Tito not only expropriated these properties but also embraced the lavish lifestyle reminiscent of his predecessors. To ordinary Yugoslavs, the communists seemed as, if not more, brutal than the royals they had replaced. This stark contrast served to magnify disillusionment among the populace.

The cases of Ceaușescu, the Kim family, and Tito in Romania, North Korea, and Yugoslavia, respectively, highlight a recurring pattern among communist leaders. These leaders, while advocating for collective equality, often indulge in extravagant living and the consolidation of power at the expense of the populace's well-being. Their opulent lifestyles, in stark contrast to the struggles of ordinary citizens, contribute significantly to disillusionment and resentment toward the ruling elite. This stark disparity between the leaders' luxurious lifestyles and the everyday hardships faced by the masses amplifies the sense of betrayal and disillusionment, undermining the credibility of the proclaimed egalitarian principles.

Communist regimes often perceive the educated and prosperous middle class as a direct threat to their authority.

This segment of society, equipped with critical thinking skills, inherently challenges the regime's control and ideology. Consequently, such regimes frequently resort to violent means to maintain their grip on power, manipulating the population through instilling fear as a means of control.

A profoundly chilling illustration of this phenomenon is evident in Pol Pot's rule in Cambodia from 1975 to 1979, where the communist Khmer Rouge executed a harrowing campaign. This brutal regime forcibly relocated millions of people from urban areas to the countryside, leading to extensive suffering and catastrophic loss of life. It is estimated that approximately two million people, constituting a quarter of the population, succumbed to starvation, disease, and systematic executions.

Under Pol Pot's despotic regime, individuals symbolizing education and intellect, often identified by the simple act of wearing glasses, became special targets for execution. This intentional targeting aimed to systematically eradicate potential sources of opposition and enforce rigid control. The ruthless eradication of the educated class reflected the regime's fervent drive to eliminate any dissenting voices that could challenge their authority.

This tragic episode in Cambodian history underscores the extreme measures to which communist regimes can go in their quest to retain control and suppress opposition. The deliberate targeting of intellectuals and educated individuals, symbolic of dissent, represents a grim testament to the lengths to which such regimes will go to safeguard their power, even at the cost of incalculable human suffering and loss.

Communism advocates for collective resource ownership and centralized control over production and distribution. Theoretical communist ideals highlight equal access to resources, particularly concerning food. However, chronic food shortages stem fundamentally from economic planning failures, misguided policies, and severe resource mismanagement. These factors contribute significantly to scarcity, with governmental control over distribution becoming a tool for totalitarian regimes to wield and perpetuate their political dominance. Moreover, international food aid provided to communist regimes can inadvertently bolster their power structures by fostering dependency and reinforcing authoritarian rule.

Critics argue that communist regimes systematically exploit food systems for political gain. Figures such as Henry Kissinger, who was of Jewish descent, have acknowledged the potency of food as a tool of influence, equating its control to governance over entire nations and populations. His famous quote, "Control oil and you control nations; control food and you control people," encapsulates this perspective. Manipulation of food availability can take nefarious forms, including obstructing cultivation, destroying harvests, disrupting transportation, or contaminating supplies. Historical evidence strongly supports claims of communist regimes weaponizing food, with glaring instances in the Soviet Union, Maoist China, and North Korea.

Under Joseph Stalin's leadership, agricultural collectivization policies in the Soviet Union resulted in widespread famine, notably the Holodomor in Ukraine. Similarly, Maoist China's Great Leap Forward precipitated a catastrophic famine. Accusations also extend to North Korea, suggesting the regime exploits food as a means of control and manipulation. These tactics have inflicted dire consequences, fostering severe poverty and famine, with an estimated 60 million deaths occurring in the USSR alone.

All of these regimes share a defining characteristic: Prioritizing the group over the individual, a stark departure from Enlightenment principles that championed individual sanctity. Enlightenment thinkers emphasized the state's role in safeguarding individual rights, considering them inherent and beyond the control of any earthly authority. Philosopher John Locke encapsulated this belief, stating that these rights are "free from any superior power on earth, and not subject to the will or legislative authority of man."

Notably, Josef Goebbels, the National Socialist propaganda minister, famously remarked, "Socialism is sacrificing the individual to the whole," encapsulating an ideology that contrasts sharply with the Enlightenment's emphasis on individual rights and autonomy.

Former Arkansas governor, Mike Huckabee, vehemently criticized communism, pointing out its consistent practical outcomes of corruption, tyranny, poverty, and widespread death. Despite its promising theoretical underpinnings, Marxism's real-world applications tend to yield oppressive regimes, economic impoverishment, and severe human rights violations. Huckabee underscores how communism's emphasis on collective ownership and centralized control stifles individual initiative, impeding progress and fostering authoritarianism and economic struggles. His stance starkly portrays communism's darker historical aspects, depicting it as a system that inflicts suffering and oppression. Ultimately, he asserts that the consequences of communism far outweigh its theoretical allure.

Margaret Thatcher, the former Prime Minister of the UK, viewed democratic socialism as a contributing factor to the UK's decline. She is famously quoted as saying,

"Socialist governments traditionally do make a financial mess. They always run out of other people's money." According to her perspective, socialism has the potential to stifle entrepreneurship, hinder innovation, and impede economic growth.

Thatcher underscored the core tenets of socialism, highlighting its focus on state ownership, government control, and the pursuit of equality, often at the cost of individual opportunity. She said, "Socialism places paramount importance on state ownership over private property, government oversight of individual enterprise, and the pursuit of equality, sometimes diminishing opportunities for all and marginalizing the individual."

She argued that socialism led to poverty, conflict, oppression, and contributed to the staggering loss of up to 100 million lives in the 20th century. Thatcher's perspective, encapsulated in her statement, "Communism seeks the domination of the state over the individual...It suppresses the rights of the individual," reflects her fundamental belief in the suffocation of individual liberties under socialist regimes.

Thatcher's assertion, "Socialists cry 'Power to the people' and raise the clenched fist, but in reality, they seek power over people, power to the State," embodies her critique of the deceptive rhetoric of socialism. She believed that despite the outward appearance of championing people power, socialism ultimately aimed at consolidating power within the state apparatus rather than empowering individuals. Her contention was that the proclaimed empowerment was a façade masking an insidious agenda of state control, ultimately stifling individual freedoms.

Thatcher's staunch opposition to socialism centered on its encroachment on individual freedoms. She argued against the suppressive nature of socialist ideologies, asserting that they purported to champion the people while, in reality, subjugating them to the dominance of the state.

Her beliefs encapsulate a profound skepticism toward socialist rhetoric, highlighting the divergence between socialist ideals and the realities of centralized state control.

Conservative commentator, Bill O'Reilly, challenged the concept of "equity," suggesting that its pursuit within centralization may result in unintended negative consequences. O'Reilly argued that an excessive focus on equal distribution, without accounting for initiative and merit, could lower living standards and ultimately lead to equal misery. He cautioned that prioritizing uniform outcomes over individual potential could impede progress and hinder innovation.

Former Prime Minister of the United Kingdom (UK) Winston Churchill's quote, "Capitalism's vice is unequal blessings, socialism's virtue is equal miseries," captures the essence of the competing economic systems. Capitalism generates wealth but fosters disparities due to innovation and individual ability. On the other hand, socialism aims for equity through redistribution and collective ownership, dampening innovation and leading to authoritarian suppression.

Yeonmi Park, a defector from North Korea, explained the dynamic: "The definition of socialism means giving all the power to the government – they decide the means of production. They despise every aspect of our lives...In North Korea, they say, 'Okay, we're going to make sure everybody is equal...So give us all your land.' So we gave the regime all the land, so they abolish[ed] private property. Nobody could own anything. State owns it. And that is when they took everything, did not give anything back to us. And then when we gave all our rights, they didn't give anything back... That's a reality of socialism...There is a playbook for this elite...to seize power from people. And this brainwashing is a seed of that like making sure that everybody [is]...

brainwash[ed] to believe this is a way to get to that paradise. And the paradise doesn't exist."[2]

Communism, often sought by those disillusioned with capitalism, envisions an idealistic world but falters in practicality. Its ambitious goal of achieving economic equality by eliminating private property and instituting collective ownership encounters substantial hurdles. A fundamental critique of communism is its disregard for individual incentives, overlooking humanity's inherent drive for personal progress and achievement.

While communism may appear appealing to those disillusioned with capitalism due to its promise of absolute economic equality, its implementation often falls short of idealistic promises. This exclusive focus sidelines individual incentives, resulting in economic stagnation and limited opportunities for progress. Additionally, the inherent power structure within communism stifles innovation and personal ambition, constraining freedom and perpetuating reliance on authority figures.

The absence of competitive markets and innovation incentives within communism frequently leads to economic stagnation and a scarcity of diverse goods and services, severely limiting choices for individuals. State-controlled economies and centralized planning breed inefficiencies that hinder innovation, dampen ambition, and curb entrepreneurial spirit. Furthermore, the lack of private property rights and limited free markets diminishes individual motivation for advancement.

---

[2] Grossman, Hannah. "North Korean Defector: I Am Terrified of the 'Massive Indoctrination Coming from the Left' in Public Schools." *Fox News*, 15 June 2022, www.foxnews.com/media/north-korean-defector-i-am-terrified-of-the-massive-indoctrination-coming-from-the-left-in-public-schools.

Practical communism's centralized control over resources suppresses individual innovation and initiative, perpetuating inefficiencies entrenched in bureaucratic structures. The bureaucratic framework hampers innovation and individual drive, fostering inefficiencies that impede societal progress and development.

Communist propaganda serves as a potent tool in upholding the allure of communism by stifling critical thinking and fostering an environment of unwavering conformity. Yet, as time progresses, the assurances of Marxism begin to unravel, revealing their inherent emptiness.

Marxism tends to consolidate power, curtail liberty, and often leads to impoverishment. The practical application of communism consistently culminates in the concentration of power and the erosion of individual rights. This system contradicts liberty, entangling individuals in a cycle of reliance on authority and hindering their ability to challenge the entrenched privileges held by a select few.

Individuals gradually find themselves ensnared in dependence on the government, rendering them incapable of challenging the entrenched power structures. Marx's ideological framework, though aiming for societal equality, lays the groundwork for an unchecked and oppressive state that fundamentally undermines liberty.

The antagonistic relationship between Marxist regimes and religious institutions is a recurring theme in history, born from the Marxist leaders' deep-seated apprehension towards any power structure not subservient to their ideology. These regimes have systematically targeted religious entities, viewing them as formidable adversaries and impediments to the consolidation of their socialist or communist agendas. Such actions find their origins in the concerted efforts of socialist regimes to diminish the influence of religious establishments historically associated with the ruling elite, aligning with broader ambitions to remodel society in accordance with their totalitarian ideals.

This ideological divergence forms the crucible of a simmering conflict between communist factions and religious institutions, with the church often at the forefront of this contentious battle. The communists' disdain for religious autonomy manifests in their relentless efforts to erode and suppress the influence of faith-based institutions. They view these institutions not as bastions of moral guidance and community support but as impediments to their pursuit of absolute state control.

The Marxist narrative aims to undermine the principles of religious freedom by subordinating the individual's right to worship to the omnipotent authority of the state. Through legislative overreach and cultural coercion, they seek to replace the moral compass of religious faith with the absolutism of state ideology, effectively erasing the distinction between faith and allegiance to the state.

This ideological collision threatens not only the autonomy of religious institutions but also the foundational fabric of a pluralistic society. It exemplifies the coercive tendencies of Marxist ideologies, which, in their relentless pursuit of power, demonstrate a flagrant disregard for the cherished principles upon which free societies are built.

Karl Marx, who was born into a Jewish family but later adopted atheism, is renowned for coining the phrase "religion is the opium of the people." He argued that religion stemmed from societal and economic conditions manipulated by the ruling class to legitimize their control over the working class. Marx viewed religion as a tool that obscured class exploitation and mirrored societal disparities and alienation. Eliminating religion was, in his view, crucial for the liberation of the working class, and he wove these ideas into his critique of capitalism and his vision of socialism.

According to Marx, religion served as a means of social manipulation, and its removal was a pivotal step in freeing the working class.

Communism, at its core, envisions a societal paradigm devoid of class distinctions, fostering collective ownership as a counterpoint to the individualistic ethos often espoused by religious institutions. In many instances, certain communist regimes have not merely sidelined religion but actively promoted atheism as a surrogate doctrine, prioritizing allegiance to the state above all forms of faith.

This fervent advocacy for a classless society manifests in communists' advocacy for sweeping control over resources, wealth, and means of production. Such governance hinges on an overarching state apparatus that micromanages economic and political domains under the guise of ensuring fairness and equity. However, in practice, this centralized control burgeons into a behemoth that stifles innovation, initiative, and personal freedoms.

Communism's disdain for religion emanates from multifaceted origins. Firstly, the ideology champions materialism and atheism, lambasting religion for allegedly perpetuating societal control mechanisms and diverting attention from genuine societal change. Communists contend that religious institutions serve as vehicles for perpetuating existing power structures and inequalities by inculcating unquestioning obedience among their adherents. The invocation of rights purportedly originating from a higher power poses a direct challenge to state authority, conflicting with the communists' pursuit of a uniform, state-dominated society free from hierarchical influences.

Central to the critique is the claim that religious organizations maintain hierarchical structures that sow divisions within the working class, all while emphasizing spiritual concerns that, according to socialists, distract from the material realities of societal transformation. Marxists argue that these institutions manipulate their followers into supporting policies that uphold existing power structures.

Moreover, communism fears that religion might undermine the urgency of class struggle and revolutionary fervor, diverting attention from immediate pursuits of justice and equality. The rejection of private property intrinsic to Marxist ideology fuels criticism against wealthy religious institutions, which are perceived as formidable barriers obstructing the grandiose objective of social and economic metamorphosis.

The vehement opposition to religion by communist entities transcends mere theological differences; it reflects a strategic maneuver aimed at consolidating absolute control, subverting dissent, and erasing competing allegiances in the ruthless pursuit of a monolithic, state-driven society. In their quest for absolute dominance, communists often bulldoze individual freedoms and pluralistic values, perpetuating a coercive apparatus that erodes the very fabric of a diverse and free society.

In the United States, a bastion of constitutional liberties, the sanctity of religious freedom clashes with the dogmatic inclinations of the far left. This clash does not merely represent a disagreement over policy; it epitomizes an ideological chasm rooted in fundamentally divergent beliefs regarding the origin and nature of rights. While individuals of faith attribute rights to an inherent, divine source, communists staunchly centralize authority within the state, subjugating all facets of society to the dictates of the ruling regime.

Historical accounts consistently reveal the propensity of communist regimes for authoritarianism, systematically infringing upon individual freedoms and perpetrating extensive human rights violations. Instances of communism often culminate in authoritarian governance, concentrating power within a select few and undermining professed ideals of equality. This concentration not only fosters oppressive regimes but also contradicts the claimed egalitarian values, evident through widespread human rights abuses, restricted political freedoms, and suppression of dissent. The historical implementation of socialism highlights its innate tendency toward authoritarian control, characterized by centralized power and resource control by an elite ruling class, resulting in the erosion of individual freedoms and stark contradictions with its proclaimed egalitarian principles.

Dana Loesch, radio and TV host, charged that "Communism isn't just a failed system, it's an evil ideology that murdered millions and was created by a dirty, grifting racist [Karl Marx] whose only contribution to earth was to feed the worms after he went to hell."[3]

Dana Loesch's statement touches on valid historical points regarding the atrocities linked to communist regimes and the foundational figures of the ideology. Communism, as practiced in various countries, has been associated with regimes responsible for the deaths of millions. The regimes under figures claiming adherence to communist ideology, such as Stalin and Mao, orchestrated brutal purges and policies resulting in immense suffering and loss of life.

Marxist theory posits that capitalism carries within itself the seeds of its own demise. Marx foresaw capitalism's downfall occurring through a proletarian revolution that would pave the way for a classless society, characterized by communal ownership of production.

Marx identified a core conflict within capitalist systems between the bourgeoisie (the capitalist class) and the

---

[3] T, Brett. "Squad, Bernie hardest hit: President Biden denounces communism, says socialism isn't a very useful substitute." *Twitchy*, 15 Jul. 2021, twitchy.com/brett-3136/2021/07/15/squad-bernie-hardest-hit-president-biden-denounces-communism-says-socialism-isnt-a-very-useful-substitute/.

proletariat (the working class). He foresaw that capitalists' unrelenting pursuit of profit would deepen the exploitation of workers, escalating class conflict. According to Marx, this conflict would climax in a proletarian revolution, where the unified working class, acknowledging their collective power, would overturn the capitalist system. This revolution aimed to usher in socialism, characterized by collective ownership of the means of production and the establishment of a dictatorship of the proletariat.

Marx envisioned socialism as a precursor to communism, the ultimate utopian ideal. This view aligns with Vladimir Lenin's perspective, seeing socialism as a bridge to communism. Expanding on Marx's concepts, Lenin championed socialism as an essential phase on the path to achieving communism. He introduced the notion of a vanguard party, representing the proletariat's interests and guiding the transition from capitalism, through socialism, ultimately aiming for the envisioned communist utopia.

The United States is currently navigating a landscape where ideologies, particularly those stemming from the left, are actively attempting to redefine societal norms and influence public sentiment. Among these, socialism emerges as a notable challenge to American values, sparking concerns about its potential impact on the foundational principles of the nation's republican governance.

At the heart of the American economic system lies capitalism, serving as its cornerstone and advocating for individual liberties while propelling innovation and fostering wealth accumulation. Its essence thrives within a free-market structure, championing concepts such as private ownership, healthy competition, and an entrepreneurial spirit—values intricately interwoven with the ideals of personal freedoms, free enterprise, and the pursuit of happiness and prosperity. These values have long been deeply ingrained in the fabric of American society.

However, there is an increasingly audible call for an economic paradigm shift—one that prioritizes equity and addresses persistent issues such as inequality and social welfare. This evolving narrative seeks systemic changes within the existing economic framework, aiming to establish fairness, sustainability, and an augmentation of social welfare measures. This movement challenges the traditional notions of capitalism, advocating for adjustments to ensure a more balanced and inclusive society.

Russian President, Vladimir Putin, recognized that the current model of capitalism, which has been instrumental in driving progress, faces opposition: "Everyone is saying that the current model of capitalism…has run its course and no longer offers a solution to a host of increasingly tangled differences."[4]

In her 2023 commencement address at Boston's Northeastern University, Deputy Prime Minister of Canada Chrystia Freeland raised a significant question: "Is capitalist democracy still effective?" She expressed concerns about whether parents can rely on capitalist democracy's promise to secure a more prosperous future for their children, a perspective shaped by her 2014 book, *Plutocrats: The Rise of the New Global Super-Rich and the Fall of Everyone Else.*

The belief in communism as a viable alternative to capitalism disregards the harsh realities within such systems. These encompass severe constraints on personal freedoms, decreased economic incentives leading to lowered productivity, and a significant hindrance to individual innovation due to the absence of competitive markets.

---

[4] Zukerman, David. "Putin's Remarks About 'Woke' Culture Deserve Serious Consideration." *American Thinker*, 31 Oct. 2021, www.americanthinker.com/blog/2021/10/putins_remarks_about_woke_culture_deserve_serious_consideration.html.

Additionally, many who view socialism as a potential substitute for existing systems often overlook or lack accurate information about its historical track record. This record reveals systemic failures, severe human rights abuses, and economic stagnation.

Communism, characterized by centralized control and collective resource ownership, has a historical track record marred by economic inefficiency, stagnation, and pervasive human rights abuses. Emphasizing the collective good over individual rights, progressive ideologies advocate for a centrally planned economy, frequently imposing restrictions on personal freedoms.

The economic shortcomings of communism are apparent, given its reliance on centralized control and state ownership. This approach leads to inefficiencies, shortages, and a lack of innovation. The absence of market-driven competition and incentives hinders economic progress, resulting in stagnant economies and an inability to adequately meet people's needs.

The theoretical ideals of equality and collective ownership inherent in communism often collide with the practical realities of implementation. Marxist regimes have repeatedly fallen short in meeting their citizens' basic needs, resulting in recurrent shortages of essential goods and services, restricted consumer choice, and an overall diminished quality of life for the majority. Previous attempts to establish communist systems led to authoritarian regimes characterized by the suppression of individual freedoms, censorship, and political repression.

Historical attempts to implement socialist systems led to authoritarian regimes that restricted individual freedoms and hindered innovation. The documented histories of countries under communist rule—such as the Soviet Union, China, North Korea, and Cuba—paint a picture of dire socio-economic conditions, a deprivation of basic freedoms, and enduring struggles with poverty and scarcity. This pattern shows the impracticality and inherent problems of communism as a viable alternative to established economic models.

The core principles of communism, advocating for collective ownership and centralized resource control, starkly contrast with the foundational tenets of American capitalism. While capitalism may have flaws, it has shown adaptability, fostering innovation, and driving economic growth. It champions individual freedoms, competition, and the potential for upward mobility. The pursuit of profit within a capitalist framework fuels innovation, enhances living standards, and creates diverse opportunities for individuals in society.

Ayn Rand complained, "The flood of misinformation, misrepresentation, distortion, and outright falsehood about capitalism is such that the young people of today have no idea...of its actual nature."[5] Her frustration with the misunderstood nature of capitalism, particularly among youth, underscores concerns about the accurate grasp of its core principles.

Presenting communism as a viable alternative to capitalism disregards the harsh realities experienced under past socialist regimes. Those viewing communism as a feasible substitute might lack information or purposely overlook historical realities in favor of an idealized vision. This ignorance of Marxism's track record could stem from a lack of understanding regarding the experiences of individuals under such regimes or could be fueled by

---

[5] Geller, Pamela. "Pelosi Says Capitalism Has Not Helped US Economy, Argues 'We Have To Correct That.'" *Geller Report*, 18 Sept. 2021, gellerreport.com/2021/09/pelosi-says-capitalism-has-not-helped-us-economy.html/?utm_source=dlvr.it&utm_medium=facebook.

ideological fervor that conceals the failures and human costs associated with past attempts. Essentially, advocating for communism often arises from a lack of awareness or a misguided perception of its history and its detrimental impacts on societies.

Justo Antonia Triana, a Cuban student who arrived in the United States in 2019, was taken aback by the "distorted idea" his peers at Syracuse University held about socialism in Cuba. He lamented that they primarily saw the positive aspects such as palm trees, free healthcare, and education, while overlooking the harsh realities of ongoing political indoctrination, suppression, and government control. Triana pointed out that some were fixated on the idealized imagery, while others parroted the typical justifications used by the international left to justify the Cuban regime: "free healthcare, free education, American embargo." He further disclosed the limited awareness about the daily mental siege experienced by Cubans, which encompassed political indoctrination, enforced reverence for leaders, widespread communist propaganda via media, severe restrictions on individual thought, and extensive government control over people's' lives.

Triana said, "Many could only think of the palm trees on a beach, but the first impulse of others was to repeat the magic words with which the international left justifies the tyranny: 'free healthcare, free education, American embargo.' Nobody knew about the constant mental siege in which Cubans survive: the strong political indoctrination and the forced cult of the personality of the leaders, the communist propaganda thrown at us by all the media, the absolute repression of individual thought, the impudence with which the government dictates and controls everything in our lives."[6]

Renowned Russian writer and dissident, Aleksandr Solzhenitsyn, observed, "For us in Russia communism is a dead dog. For many people in the West, it is still a living lion." Solzhenitsyn's statement starkly contrasts the perspectives of those who endured communism firsthand and those who view it from a distance. In Russia, communism is a "dead dog," indicating that it is both inviable, and at the same time, reflecting its destructive impact on society. In the West, communism's allure endures despite historical failures.

Solzhenitsyn's critiques of socialism, shaped by his harrowing experiences under the Soviet regime, stand as profound warnings. Imprisoned for challenging the government, his work, *The Gulag Archipelago*, laid bare the horrors of Soviet forced labor, revealing the regime's callous disregard for human rights. Solzhenitsyn's apprehensions about socialism stem from his insight into its potential to concentrate power and stifle freedoms. He argued that despite its promise of equality, socialism could erode autonomy and responsibility, fostering conformity over individuality. Crucially, he cautioned against the dehumanizing effects of communist systems, where ideological pursuits could lead to oppression, surveillance, and suppression of dissent.

The presence of socialism within the USA is viewed by some as a precursor to an imminent revolutionary transformation. Evidences of ideological infiltration and influence are noticeable across various sectors of American society, spanning academia, media, and political discourse.

---

[6] Aitken, Peter. "Recent Cuban immigrant and college student shocked by peers' perception of socialism, seeks to dismantle it." *Fox News*, 19 Jan. 2022, www.foxnews.com/us/recent-cuban-immigrant-college-student-shocked-perceptions-socialism.

Critics emphasize initiatives, policies, and movements aligned with communist principles, suggesting a deliberate effort to redirect the nation's trajectory. Proposals advocating universal healthcare, universal basic income, wealth redistribution, and improved labor rights often echo socialist ideals, raising concerns about increased government intervention in citizens' lives. Similarly, movements advocating for police defunding, racial justice, and income equality spark suspicions of a broader socialist agenda aiming to reshape fundamental structures in the US. These trends prompt critics to caution against veering from free-market capitalism and individual liberties, fearing the potential consequences of a more centralized government and diminished economic freedom.

The ongoing ideological friction in the United States, spanning capitalism, communism, Marxism, and the looming shadow of totalitarianism, transcends a mere economic or political confrontation. This contest illuminates the threat that centralized control and constraints on personal liberties pose to the treasured democratic and republican ideals of the nation. It embodies a clash of values—a profound conflict between individual freedoms and collective control, challenging the foundational principles of American governance and societal convictions.

Ideologies such as communism and Marxism stand diametrically opposed to the fundamental principles of freedom and democracy upon which the United States was built. They undermine the notion of private property rights and the belief in inherent individual rights. Of particular concern is that communism directly contradicts crucial aspects of the US Constitution, including private property rights, individual freedoms, limited government, free markets, democracy, and the rule of law.

Communism's advocacy for the abolition of private property and the establishment of a centrally planned economy presents a significant challenge to American ideals and its deeply ingrained political identity rooted in liberal democracy. Furthermore, communism's rejection of nationalism in favor of international working-class solidarity could erode American national identity and patriotism, potentially fragmenting the unity and shared values that have historically bound the nation together. The advocacy for a strong central government, extensive economic control, and potential limitations on democratic processes and political participation by Marxists starkly contrasts with the constitutional framework of the United States.

Alexis de Tocqueville distinguished between democracy and socialism, highlighting that democracy values individual freedom while socialism curtails it. In his view, democracy aims for equality within liberty, whereas socialism pursues equality through control and subordination. He wrote, "Democracy extends the sphere of individual freedom, socialism restricts it. Democracy attaches all possible value to each man; socialism makes each man a mere agent, a mere number." Democracy seeks equality while upholding liberty, while socialism seeks equality through restraint and servitude.

In socialism, politicians take charge of daily life, fostering dependency as everything is provided for free. State actions might be misconstrued by a lazy, ill-informed electorate as uplifting the "disenfranchised" at the expense of the "oppressors." For instance, politicians such as Joe Biden advocate for the wealthy to contribute their "fair share" to support government programs, raising questions about individual responsibility versus government assistance.

However, framing entitlements as rights does not signify freedom; instead, it parallels provisions for subjugated individuals, akin to provisions for livestock.

Tocqueville's perspective on "rights" within socialism is stark: "[T]he 'right' to education, the 'right' to healthcare, the 'right' to food and housing. This isn't freedom; it's dependency. These aren't rights; they're the allocations of slavery — sustenance and shelter for human cattle." Tocqueville's insight resonates with the potential dangers of excessive state intervention and dependency, cautioning against eroding individual liberty and self-reliance.

Government welfare programs, designed to offer essential support, can impact individual freedom in several ways. Firstly, prolonged dependency on welfare might erode the motivation for individuals to pursue employment or personal development opportunities. This reliance can create a cycle where initiative wanes, potentially affecting one's overall contribution to society.

Moreover, these programs often come with bureaucratic regulations and administrative procedures. Adhering to these regulations can significantly limit choices and decisions for recipients. Requirements such as income thresholds, household compositions, or behavioral standards imposed by these programs can curtail autonomy, constraining the freedom to make personal choices.

Additionally, conditions attached to government assistance can dictate how recipients use aid, further restricting their decision-making abilities. Limits on the utilization of aid, such as food stamps or housing vouchers, may undermine individual autonomy by controlling choices and preferences.

Furthermore, extended dependence on welfare may impede social and economic mobility, trapping individuals in cycles of poverty. Structural barriers and limited resources can hinder the transition out of welfare programs, making it challenging for individuals to improve their circumstances.

Despite their role in offering support, welfare programs' structures and conditions can limit individual freedoms, presenting a challenge in balancing aid provision and preserving personal autonomy.

Alexis de Tocqueville, a keen observer of democratic societies, voiced grave concerns about the potential encroachment of socialism into the American Republic. He cautioned against a shift in the country's fundamental principles, particularly highlighting the danger of deviating from the core values of democracy and republicanism.

The core duty of the American government is to safeguard self-reliant and industrious citizens from oppressive and tyrannical governance. Tocqueville predicted a potential path wherein the government, particularly Congress, might progressively extend its reach by furnishing public benefits financed by taxpayer funds. This trajectory would signify a departure from the quintessence of the American Republic. He feared that such a shift could corrode the fundamental bedrock upon which the nation was founded, imperiling the principles of individual liberty and self-governance that formed the very heart of its inception.

His warning was not merely a critique of economic policies but a broader apprehension about the philosophical and societal implications. Tocqueville believed that embracing socialist tendencies could potentially weaken the fabric of American society by diminishing the spirit of individual initiative and fostering dependence on the government. He was concerned that such a shift might lead to a loss of personal freedoms and an erosion of the vibrant civic engagement that had characterized the nation.

For Tocqueville, the adoption of socialism was not just an economic choice but a perilous ideological shift. He cautioned that aligning too closely with socialist principles could undermine the revolutionary ideals that had inspired the nation's birth. In doing so, America might risk diluting the very essence of its exceptional experiment in democratic governance.

In essence, Tocqueville's concerns were rooted in the belief that a move toward socialism in America could signify a departure from its foundational values of liberty, self-reliance, and democratic governance, ultimately endangering the unique spirit that defined the nation.

Sergey Naryshkin, Director of the Russian Foreign Intelligence Service, has raised the alarm about a concerning lack of awareness among the American population regarding a swift movement toward a totalitarian regime. His assertion gains traction when considering the observable erosion of civil liberties in recent years. This erosion emerges from policies and laws encroaching upon civil liberties, such as expansive surveillance programs, limitations on freedom of expression, and the broadening of government powers under the guise of national security. These measures collectively contribute to a gradual erosion of individual freedoms, often escaping full recognition by citizens, as the true extent of these changes remains elusive.

Totalitarian shifts frequently unfurl gradually, with each individual change appearing inconsequential when observed in isolation. People tend to miss these incremental alterations in governance, particularly when they do not immediately disrupt their daily lives. Instead, pressing concerns such as economic stability, healthcare, and education tend to dominate their attention.

It is the collective view of these seemingly minor adjustments that reveals a larger, interconnected pattern, significantly influencing personal freedoms. Yet, this cumulative effect often escapes widespread notice, allowing these changes to blend into the background, especially when they occur gradually and subtly over time.

This lack of immediate impact can lead to a lack of awareness among the general public until these changes coalesce into a substantial alteration of the societal fabric. By the time the broader implications become evident, it might be too late to reverse or challenge these shifts effectively.

This chapter delved into the origins and principles of communism through the lens of Marx and Engels. In addition, we explored diverse political ideologies including socialism, capitalism, and democracy. The next chapter explores the impact of global communism, showcasing historical instances and consequences. Case studies of the Soviet Union, Mao's China, Cuba, Venezuela, and North Korea highlight the devastating effects of communist rule. It emphasizes learning from history and protecting democratic values, freedom, and individual liberties.

Chapter 2

From Revolution to Repression

In *The Communist Manifesto*, Marx and Engels predicted the downfall of capitalist society, foreseeing a scenario where the proletariat, the working class, would revolt against the bourgeoisie, the middle-class property owners. A fundamental principle of Marxist ideology revolves around eradicating the bourgeoisie, seen as the embodiment of exploitation. Karl Marx advocated for a strategy aimed at dismantling capitalism by stoking class conflicts, fostering animosity, and ultimately precipitating societal breakdown. These forecasts of socialist uprisings were realized in Russia, where the Bolsheviks toppled Czar Nicholas II, leading to a dictatorship that purported to act in the name of "the people."

Numerous communist regimes strayed from their original ideals, resulting in egregious instances of abuse of power. Despite advocating for collective ownership and equality, the stark reality in many cases was the concentration of authority within the state or a privileged ruling elite. Paradoxically, the pursuit of a classless society often birthed a new ruling class, exacerbating the very inequality that communism purported to abolish. This consolidation of power frequently bred authoritarianism and the ruthless suppression of dissent, as these regimes aimed to stamp out opposition and perpetuate their dominance. Reports of restricted free speech, information censorship, and grotesque violations of basic human rights were rampant under such regimes.

The failures in attaining economic prosperity and the suffocation of individual freedoms brewed widespread disillusionment and discontent among the populace. Economic stagnation, shortages of goods, and the absence of political liberties significantly contributed to the downfall of numerous socialist states, notably the Soviet Union and Eastern Bloc countries. These collapses exposed inherent vulnerabilities and shortcomings in these systems, vividly underscoring the insurmountable challenges of sustaining a centrally planned economy and an oppressively controlled society over the long term.

Marxism, as an ideology, has caused profound and catastrophic impacts on various regions. The relentless pursuit of dismantling capitalism, obliterating free markets, and erasing private property has culminated in tragic outcomes, marked by mass deportations, the establishment of forced labor camps, state-sponsored terror, and widespread starvation. The consequences of communism stand as a grim tally, accounting for the loss of at least 65 million lives since 1917.

This chapter delves into the case studies of several countries, notably the Soviet Union, Mao's China, Cuba, Venezuela, and North Korea, illustrating the ruinous effects of communist rule. These case studies serve as stark reminders of the far-reaching and devastating impacts of communism on societies and the immense toll it exacts on human lives. The hope is that readers will glean lessons from history and reflect on whether similar patterns can be identified in the United States.

USSR

In Russia, the Bolsheviks, spearheaded by figures such as Vladimir Lenin and Leon Trotsky (also known as Lev Bronstein), both of whom were of Jewish descent, emerged from the Russian Social Democratic Labour Party and wielded significant influence during the 1917 Revolution. Their primary objective was to institute a communist society, advocating for a stringent, centralized party apparatus to guide the working class in overthrowing capitalism.

Their vision entailed a forcible shift towards communism, emphasizing the need for a disciplined vanguard party to steer the proletariat towards seizing power from the bourgeoisie. This aspiration for a revolutionary overthrow of the existing social order led to significant turmoil. The Bolsheviks championed an ideology that centralized authority in the hands of a select few, breeding a system that prioritized the party's dominance over individual freedoms and democratic principles.

Their implementation of communist ideals resulted in a totalitarian regime marked by state control over all facets of life, curtailed civil liberties, and the suppression of dissent. The consolidation of power under figures such as Stalin led to a brutal authoritarianism that trampled on human rights, perpetuated political purges, and instilled fear and oppression throughout the populace.

The Bolsheviks' ambition to establish a communist society led to a tragic legacy marred by repression, economic hardship, and the sacrifice of individual liberties in favor of an authoritarian state. The consequences of their revolution profoundly altered Russia's trajectory, leaving behind a legacy of suffering, suppression, and the perversion of noble ideals into a repressive regime that marginalized and oppressed its own citizens.

Prior to the actual communist coup, a series of calculated provocations unfolded, including orchestrated riots and demonstrations staged against the existing government. These events were meticulously designed to incite chaos, often culminating in armed clashes that lacked clear objectives and resulted in casualties. The deliberate intention behind these actions was to sow discord and exploit the resulting unrest for propaganda purposes, strategically aiming to sway public sentiment against the established government and towards the Bolshevik cause.

The Bolsheviks manipulated these moments of turmoil through a meticulously crafted propaganda campaign. They skillfully projected themselves as the saviors of the nation, positioning their party as the only viable solution to the chaos and promising to bring stability and prosperity. The population, bombarded with persuasive messaging and imagery, was systematically convinced of the Bolsheviks' role as the beacon of hope amidst the tumultuous landscape.

This calculated use of orchestrated upheaval, coupled with an astutely crafted narrative, aimed not only to undermine the existing government but also to mold public perception in favor of the Bolshevik agenda. By capitalizing on unrest and leveraging it for their propaganda machine, the Bolsheviks capitalized on the vulnerabilities of a fractured society, ultimately propelling themselves to power through a campaign that manipulated emotions, exploited chaos, and distorted the truth.

The Russian Army found itself targeted for subversion by the Bolsheviks. The Bolshevik agenda involved a systematic campaign to undermine the State by infiltrating and influencing the military apparatus. Their strategy was focused on persuading the armed forces, especially the generals and commanding officers, to pivot their allegiance toward Lenin's ideology. The concept of loyalty to "Mother Russia" was supplanted by allegiance to Lenin's vision of a communist state. Any dissent or opposition within the ranks was swiftly eradicated, ensuring a unified front in favor of the Bolshevik cause.

Consequently, the regiments of the Petrograd Garrison, a crucial stronghold, became bastions either fully aligned with the Bolsheviks or sympathetic to their cause. This strategic alignment within the military power structures greatly bolstered the Bolsheviks' position, providing a formidable base of support within the armed forces, which proved pivotal in solidifying their grip on power.

In 1917, the Bolshevik Party ascended to power despite securing only 23% support in elections, marking a pivotal historical shift. Lenin's strategic maneuvering, coupled with the tactical prowess of Bolshevik troops, facilitated a relatively unchallenged seizure of power. They strategically targeted vital installations, notably the Winter Palace, the seat of the Provisional Government, orchestrating a swift takeover. Following Tsar Nicholas II's abdication in February 1917, Russia established a Provisional Government dominated by liberal and moderate socialist figures. However, grappling with challenges from World War I, economic instability, and widespread discontent, the Provisional Government failed to effectively address these pressing issues, resulting in a loss of public support.

Exploiting this discontent, the Bolshevik Party, under Lenin's leadership, capitalized on grievances, overthrowing the Provisional Government in October 1917 and instituting Soviet rule.

The Bolsheviks' success was not solely due to military might but also cunning tactics. Infiltrators disrupted the palace's infrastructure, plunging it into darkness and effectively sapping the defenders' morale. The absence of a strong defense from the generals and commanding officers, combined with the lack of organized resistance from any regiment in support of the democratic principles of free and fair elections, played into the Bolsheviks' hands.

The brutal execution of the Romanov family in 1918 stands as a tragic chapter in history. Following the upheaval of the Bolshevik Revolution in 1917, Tsar Nicholas II, along with his family, was detained and held captive. As the country grappled with the tumultuous civil war, the Bolsheviks feared that the presence of the Romanovs could potentially galvanize counter-revolutionary forces, posing a threat to their newfound rule.

In a harrowing turn of events in July 1918, the Bolshevik authorities sanctioned the execution of Tsar Nicholas II, his wife Alexandra, and their five children— Olga, Tatiana, Maria, Anastasia, and Alexei. The family faced a brutal fate at the hands of Bolshevik soldiers in the confines of the Ipatiev House's basement in Yekaterinburg.

The Romanov family's murder starkly symbolizes the Bolsheviks' ruthless tactics in eradicating threats to their rule. It represents their use of violence to secure power, revealing their callous disregard for human life in pursuit of ideology. This act remains a haunting testament to the extremes the

Bolsheviks would go to eliminate challenges to their authority, leaving a tragic legacy in history.

Following the Bolsheviks' success in the October Revolution, their establishment of a new government marked the inception of what would evolve into the Communist Party of the Soviet Union. This leadership spearheaded profound changes across Russia, sparking significant social, political, and economic transformations that culminated in the birth of the Soviet Union.

Communism's origins in the Soviet Union can be traced back to the aftermath of the Russian Revolution led by the Bolshevik Party and Vladimir Lenin in 1917. Following the revolution, the Bolshevik Party, under Lenin's leadership, established the Soviet government. However, the formal consolidation of several Soviet republics into the Union of Soviet Socialist Republics (USSR) occurred in 1922, marking the official establishment of the Soviet state. While policies and movements toward communism commenced shortly after the revolution, the formal creation of the USSR took place in 1922.

The Bolshevik Revolution, led by Vladimir Lenin and the Bolshevik Party, marked a pivotal moment in history. It aimed to dismantle established imperialist and capitalist structures, paving the way for a societal overhaul rooted in socialist ideology. This shift centered on the collective ownership of production means and resources, profoundly influencing the revolution's trajectory and subsequent governance.

At its core, the revolution sought to construct a socialist state, progressively moving towards communism by abolishing class divisions and eradicating private ownership. Initial efforts were concentrated on implementing socialist policies, promoting collectivization, and driving industrialization. However, these endeavors faced fierce opposition, particularly from the peasantry, presenting substantial obstacles to the realization of these ambitious objectives.

Following the revolution, the Soviet government, under the Communist Party's guidance, initiated radical policy changes to restructure the economic and social landscape in line with communist ideals. Industries underwent nationalization, transferring ownership and control of major enterprises to the state, purportedly aiming to shift power away from capitalist elites and towards the broader populace.

Simultaneously, agricultural collectivization emerged as a critical strategy. Small private farms were amalgamated into larger collective entities, purportedly seeking communal utilization of land and resources. This restructuring aimed to divert focus from individual gains to the collective benefit of society, although it often resulted in significant hardships for many farmers and disrupted agricultural productivity.

Moreover, the government implemented wealth redistribution policies, intending to curb the accumulation of wealth within the privileged class through property and asset redistribution. The overarching goal was to ostensibly narrow economic disparities, advancing the communist vision of a classless society. However, these measures often led to economic stagnation, inefficiency, and widespread hardship for citizens.

The pursuit of socialist ideals, envisioned to create a fairer distribution of wealth and authority, faced substantial hurdles in practice. The consolidation of control within the state machinery, allegedly intended for societal improvement, veered away from the initial goals of fostering a more egalitarian society.

The transition towards socialism led by the Bolsheviks sparked a profound overhaul of societal norms and economic structures. Yet, rather than empowering the masses, this transformation centralized power within the state apparatus. Instead of elevating the working class, a new class of state officials emerged, reaping the benefits of seizing assets from capitalists. This redistribution of wealth and resources ultimately enriched a privileged group entrenched within the state hierarchy, creating a disparity that contradicted the intended equality.

Despite the lofty ambitions, the execution of these policies encountered significant challenges. Resistance emerged from diverse societal factions, and inherent logistical issues plagued the implementation process. The pursuit of communist ideals often resulted in authoritarianism, economic inefficiency, and a suppression of individual freedoms.

The initial aspirations of equitably distributing resources and power for the collective good gradually transformed into a system where control and privilege were concentrated in the hands of a select few.

The Soviet government instituted a repressive regime that wielded total control over public and private life. This control manifested in severe political oppression, rampant human rights abuses, and a stifling grip on individual freedoms. The consequences were dire, leading to widespread political repression, economic inefficiencies, scarcity of goods, and impoverished living conditions for many.

After Lenin's death in 1924, Joseph Stalin ascended to power and swiftly instituted transformative Five-Year Plans aimed at accelerating industrialization and bolstering military capabilities. While these plans did spur progress, they came at a staggering human cost, marked by harsh conditions, the proliferation of labor camps, and the imposition of forced labor on a massive scale.

The centrally planned economy of the Soviet Union, despite its initial ambitions, grappled with chronic inefficiencies that perpetuated enduring scarcities of vital goods and dismally low living standards for a significant portion of the population. These economic deficiencies played a pivotal role in the eventual collapse of the USSR in 1991, highlighting systemic flaws within the model. The failure to prioritize and sustain crucial sectors essential for citizen welfare ultimately eroded the system's viability, contributing significantly to its downfall.

The government's prioritization of heavy industry and substantial allocations to military expenditures significantly impacted the availability of essential necessities such as food, housing, and healthcare. This focus diverted resources away from sectors crucial for the well-being of the populace, amplifying the hardships faced by ordinary citizens. The repercussions of this policy became starkly evident during the 1930s collectivization efforts under Stalin's regime.

The push to consolidate individual farms into collective units disrupted agricultural practices, leading to a reduction in output and exacerbating food shortages. The loss of ownership and control over land demoralized farmers, further exacerbating the crisis. Simultaneously, the disproportionate emphasis on heavy industry and military buildup resulted in a significant oversight of sectors essential for sustaining the population's basic needs.

The consequences of these economic decisions were profound, perpetuating humanitarian crises and neglecting the fundamental requirements of the populace. Shortages in food, inadequate housing provisions, and limited access to proper healthcare became grim realities for many citizens. The government's skewed priorities, favoring industrial and military sectors over essential social and welfare sectors, significantly contributed to the suffering experienced by a large portion of the population.

Forced collectivization, a policy imposed by Stalin, triggered the devastating Holodomor famine of 1932-1933 in Ukraine, a catastrophic event that unfolded due to Stalin's rigid directives. Ukrainian peasants opposed collectivization, prompting severe repression by the Soviet government, which included confiscation of grain. This resistance sparked a cascade of tragic events. Beyond the acute food shortages, the famine became a tool for Stalin to tighten his grip on power, using it as a means to suppress dissent while prioritizing arbitrary production quotas over the well-being of the Ukrainian people.

The regime's actions during this period led to an estimated 3.9 to 7.5 million deaths from starvation and its related consequences, inflicting unfathomable suffering on the Ukrainian population. What compounded this tragedy was the deliberate denial of the famine's existence, a denial that exacerbated the anguish and firmly cemented this catastrophe as a significant genocide in history. The regime meticulously controlled information, both domestically and internationally, to conceal the true extent of the suffering, perpetuating a veil of silence over the harrowing reality faced by the Ukrainian people during those devastating years.

In his 1937 book, *The Revolution Betrayed*, Leon Trotsky, a prominent Jewish Bolshevik, outlined how scarcity was cynically manipulated within the Soviet bureaucracy to tighten its grip on power. Trotsky argued that the bureaucratic rule in the Soviet Union thrived on the impoverishment of society in terms of consumer goods. When resources were abundant, individuals had some semblance of freedom in their purchases without excessive control. However, in times of shortage, queues for basic necessities became the norm, necessitating police intervention to maintain order.

Trotsky viewed this orchestration of scarcity as a calculated ploy by the Soviet bureaucracy. He saw it as a deliberate tactic to mold behaviors, foster allegiance, and create a reliance on the state for fundamental needs. This deliberate fostering of scarcity aimed to consolidate the government's authority, coercively shaping the population's dependence on the state for essentials. By exploiting shortages, the regime not only controlled access to basic goods but also controlled the lives of its citizens, suppressing any dissent by keeping them reliant on state channels for survival. This cynical use of scarcity starkly highlighted its role as a means of enhancing government control, stifling individual freedoms, and subduing opposition, revealing yet another manipulative facet of communist governance.

The Soviet regime employed a combination of censorship and propaganda as potent tools to exert control over information flow and mold public sentiment, effectively stifling the fundamental freedoms of speech, expression, and assembly to silence any form of dissent. Criticism directed at the government incurred severe repercussions, ranging from imprisonment and forced labor to outright execution. Dissenters faced harsh punishment through imprisonment in gulags, often enduring horrendous conditions, or even met their fate through calculated murder.

The Bolsheviks displayed an absolute intolerance towards any divergent opinions, ruthlessly silencing voices that deviated from their own narrative. This intolerance was woven into the very fabric of governance, perpetuating an environment where challenging the established ideology or expressing dissenting views was met with brutal suppression.

The iron-fisted control over information and the systematic squelching of opposing opinions formed the cornerstone of the Soviet regime's strategy to maintain power. Censorship and propaganda were not merely tools; they were the means by which the government curtailed any form of dissent or opposition, ensuring a near-monopoly on public discourse and perpetuating a climate of fear and silence among its populace.

During the Soviet era, strict controls over citizens' movement within the USSR were deeply embedded in the government's policies, serving multifaceted purposes. Primarily, these restrictions were a means of political control. The Soviet regime aimed to limit the exchange of information and curb potential dissent by restricting travel, particularly to areas considered politically sensitive or along borders. The objective was to prevent the spread of anti-government sentiments or ideas that opposed communist ideology, thereby maintaining the ruling party's authority and ideological purity.

Economically, travel restrictions were instrumental in the government's centralized planning efforts. The Soviet

Union regulated the movement of its citizens to control labor allocation and maintain stability in various regions and industries. Free movement could potentially lead to labor shortages in crucial sectors or regions, undermining economic targets set by the state. As such, restrictions were imposed to ensure a steady supply of labor and maintain the status quo in key economic areas.

State security was also a significant concern. The Soviet authorities were apprehensive about espionage, dissent, and attempts by citizens to escape the country. By controlling movement, the government sought to prevent defections and limit the risk of citizens fleeing to Western countries, which was perceived as a threat to the state's stability and image.

Moreover, the Soviet government's centralized planning system tied nearly every aspect of a citizen's life, including housing, education, and healthcare, to their place of residence. This made it challenging for individuals to relocate freely. Access to these basic necessities was often contingent upon where one lived, reinforcing the control exerted by the state over its populace.

Travel within the USSR necessitated official permission and internal passports. Citizens were required to obtain authorization to move between cities or regions, with strict penalties for attempting to leave the country without permission. The consequences for unauthorized travel, especially attempts to flee the country, were severe, often resulting in imprisonment or forced labor.

In essence, the limitations on citizens' travel within the USSR were a methodical strategy employed by the Soviet authorities to maintain political control, regulate the economy, ensure state security, and tightly manage nearly every aspect of citizens' lives, all in line with the principles of communism and the preservation of the regime's power.

The Communist regime instigated a systematic expansion of secret police organizations aimed at identifying, apprehending, and often executing individuals labeled as "class enemies." Any political ideologies or parties diverging from the prescribed communist doctrine faced severe repression and suppression. The overarching goal was the eradication of opposition forces and the preservation of stringent ideological control throughout society.

Under the ruthless reign of Stalin, Lavrentiy Beria, the chief of the NKVD secret police, epitomized the regime's relentless pursuit of control. Beria boasted of his ability to incriminate even the innocent by fabricating evidence, arrogantly asserting, "Show me the man and I'll show you the crime." This declaration underscored the pervasive use of manufactured charges to justify persecution, showcasing the arbitrary and oppressive nature of the regime's actions.

These draconian measures were integral to the functionality of communist regimes, ensuring a climate of compliance while ruthlessly quelling dissenting voices. The systematic expansion of secret police forces, coupled with a manipulative use of fabricated charges and intimidation tactics, served as a grim reminder of the lengths to which the regime would go to ensure conformity and suppress any form of opposition. Ultimately, these actions perpetuated an environment of fear, mistrust, and coercion, cementing the regime's control over society through systematic repression and the elimination of perceived adversaries.

An illustrative instance of the draconian censorship and suppression of dissent lies in the story of Alexander Solzhenitsyn, a celebrated Russian writer and Nobel laureate.

Solzhenitsyn's literary works shed light on the grim realities of existence under Soviet governance, particularly highlighting the atrocities pervasive within the Gulag labor camps. His unflinching portrayal of these horrors challenged the Soviet regime's narrative, leading to the banning of his works and subjecting him to severe censorship.

Solzhenitsyn's case stands as a poignant testament to the ruthless measures taken by the Soviet regime to muzzle dissent and control the narrative. The regime aimed to uphold its grip on power by silencing voices that dared to expose the truth about life under its rule, both to its own citizens and to the wider world. By banning Solzhenitsyn's works and subjecting him to censorship, the regime sought to suppress the dissemination of critical information that could undermine its authority and reveal the bleak realities of its governance.

The persecution faced by Solzhenitsyn serves as a stark reminder of the regime's determination to maintain a façade of control and perpetuate a sanitized version of its narrative, shielding the populace from the harsh truths of life within the Soviet Union. The suppression of Solzhenitsyn's powerful narratives reflects the lengths to which the regime went to ensure that dissenting voices were silenced, reinforcing its stranglehold on power and preventing the world from fully grasping the harrowing realities endured by its citizens.

In the USSR, the ruthless use of political murder stood as a chilling hallmark of the Soviet regime's tactics to eliminate perceived threats and opposition. Spearheaded by influential figures such as Lenin and Stalin, the Bolshevik government wielded brutal force to establish and consolidate power by aggressively quashing dissent, often resorting to executing anyone deemed as an enemy of the state. This grim practice remained a terrifying feature throughout the Soviet regime's existence.

Stalin's rule was characterized by totalitarianism, epitomized by severe censorship, the brutal eradication of dissent, and a succession of devastating political purges. The notorious "Great Purge" of the late 1930s led to the deaths of millions, encompassing not only party members and intellectuals but also ordinary citizens and military personnel.

Under Stalin's rule in the 1930s and 1940s, the distressing impact of the Great Purge unfolded, resulting in the execution of thousands, including high-ranking officials, military figures, intellectuals, and common citizens labeled as "enemies of the people." This merciless implementation of political murder and purges became emblematic of the regime's extreme measures to suppress any form of opposition or dissent. The peak of this terror emerged in 1937 and 1938, witnessing an alarming wave where an estimated 750,000 individuals faced execution without due legal process. The Soviet secret police orchestrated mass shootings, leading to the tragic demise of hundreds of thousands within an incredibly short timeframe.

Stalin's era of paranoid purges and crackdowns on military officers posed a significant threat to the readiness and efficiency of the Red Army. The relentless purges instilled a climate of fear and distrust, devastating the leadership ranks and impairing the army's operational capabilities.

The manipulation of military allegiance, coupled with ruthless purges to ensure compliance, underscored the Bolsheviks' willingness to assert dominance, regardless of the dire repercussions for the integrity and fighting capability of the Red Army.

A haunting example of the regime's callousness unfolded on December 12, 1937, as Stalin and Vyacheslav Molotov personally approved the death sentences of 3,167 individuals before casually attending a cinema. This dark episode epitomized the regime's complete disregard for human life, showcasing their unflinching pursuit of control through fear and intimidation tactics.

The Soviet regime's deployment of political murder as a tool to assert dominance underscored the depths of its brutality and the lengths it would go to maintain an iron grip on power. This grim legacy of terror and suppression serves as a somber reminder of the regime's utter disregard for basic human rights and its ruthless pursuit of control through coercion, fear, and brutal repression.

The Soviet regime's aggressive suppression of religion stemmed from the Communist ideology's ambition to forge an atheistic state. Organized religion posed a direct ideological challenge, prompting the government's zealous efforts to eradicate its societal influence. This led to a series of stringent measures aimed at stifling religious practices, targeting religious leaders, and controlling expressions of faith.

Under Soviet rule, religious suppression manifested in multifaceted ways, ranging from the persecution of clergy members to the closure and repurposing of religious sites. Religious leaders were systematically targeted, often enduring imprisonment, exile, or execution. The campaign extended across diverse religious groups; mosques, synagogues, and churches of various denominations faced closure or repurposing for secular uses. Holidays and religious practices were discouraged, with religious leaders encountering severe restrictions on their activities. Places of worship were either demolished, repurposed, or monitored under state supervision. Additionally, propaganda campaigns aimed to dissuade adherence to religious beliefs.

In the 1920s and 1930s, the Soviet government launched an extensive anti-religious campaign involving the closure of churches, seizure of religious assets, imprisonment of clergy, and the propagation of atheistic doctrines through education and propaganda. This concerted effort aimed to eradicate religious influence and enthrone atheism as the dominant ideology, leading to the persecution of thousands of clergy members and the suppression of religious teachings.

A poignant example of religious suppression unfolded within the Soviet campaign directed at the Russian Orthodox Church, an institution deeply intertwined with Russia's cultural and historical essence. The Church's existence posed a substantial obstacle to the Communist Party's relentless pursuit of absolute ideological dominance.

A pivotal episode in this crusade manifested in the demolition of the Cathedral of Christ the Savior in Moscow, a grand Orthodox edifice commemorating Russia's victory over Napoleon in the early 19th century. Its destruction in 1931, ordered by the Soviet government, epitomized a decisive moment. The site was earmarked for the construction of the Palace of Soviets, envisioned as a testament to Soviet achievements. However, this ambitious endeavor remained incomplete, and the area was repurposed into an open-air swimming pool. This act symbolized the regime's systematic endeavor to eradicate religious symbols and institutions. It showcased their readiness to substitute historical and cultural landmarks with manifestations of Communist ideology, creating a void within Russia's cultural landscape. This deliberate erasure sought to diminish the influence of religious institutions, emphasizing the regime's determination to supplant faith-based symbols with representations aligned with Communist doctrine.

The regime's fervent pursuit of eradicating religious influence aimed to establish a society devoid of religious allegiances, replacing them with allegiance solely to the Communist Party and its ideology. This stringent suppression, enforced through coercion and control, aimed not only to restrict religious practices but also to weaken the societal bonds formed through faith-based communities. The measures taken by the Soviet government underscored its determination to enforce ideological conformity and eliminate any perceived challenge to its authority, leaving a profound and lasting impact on the religious landscape of the Soviet Union.

Religious adherents faced widespread discrimination in the Soviet Union, affecting their access to education, employment, and government roles. The regime actively sought to undermine religious practices, promoting atheism through educational programs and pervasive propaganda campaigns that targeted all levels of society. In schools, atheistic principles were mandated, excluding religious teachings from curricula and indoctrinating students with anti-religious ideologies. This led to ostracism, social stigma, and academic challenges for children from religious families.

Professional opportunities were likewise constrained by one's religious beliefs. Those practicing faith encountered barriers in securing jobs, promotions, and governmental positions due to the perception of ideological nonconformity with the state's atheistic agenda. Openly expressing religious beliefs often led to employment discrimination, hindering career advancement and societal acceptance.

In governmental roles, being openly religious posed significant obstacles. Strict measures discouraged religious participation in public office, viewing religious adherence as conflicting with the state's secular principles. This limited individuals from holding influential positions, impeding their contributions to governance and fostering prejudice and exclusion.

The regime's active suppression of religious practices went beyond disapproval; it was systematically enforced through relentless propaganda campaigns. Media, cultural events, and public gatherings were used to disseminate anti-religious messages, discrediting religious beliefs and promoting atheism as the sole acceptable worldview. These campaigns aimed to sway public opinion and suppress religious sentiment.

The Soviet regime's efforts to discourage religious adherence had far-reaching impacts, permeating individuals' educational, professional, and civic lives. Discrimination against religious believers affected societal structures, limiting opportunities for those openly practicing their faith. The state's endorsement of atheism and suppression of religious expression profoundly shaped Soviet society, creating an environment where openly embracing religious beliefs often hindered societal integration and professional progress.

The Soviet government's suppression of religion left an indelible mark on religious life within the USSR. Although certain religious practices persisted clandestinely or in private settings, the state's systematic endeavors to obliterate religious influence notably diminished its societal impact throughout the Soviet era. The concerted efforts to eradicate religion from public life left a lasting impact, significantly weakening its presence within Soviet society.

The reign of terror during Bolshevism's rule in the USSR plunged the nation into a frightening period marked by extensive loss of life and an overarching sense of fear and mistrust, even within close circles, owing to the government's ruthless strategies. This oppressive regime established an iron-fisted totalitarian grip over the Soviet state, leaving behind a grim legacy characterized by widespread repression and egregious human rights abuses. The forcible collectivization of farmlands and the ruthless elimination of intellectuals and dissenters through brutal labor camps exacerbated shortages of vital resources and provided the state with an enhanced means of exerting control over the populace. These tactics not only resulted in severe deprivation but also consolidated the government's power, fostering an environment of despair and helplessness among the people.

Following Stalin's death in 1953, the USSR witnessed a series of contrasting periods: the "Khrushchev Thaw" under Nikita Khrushchev's leadership, characterized by relative openness, juxtaposed with subsequent repressive phases under successive leaders. Despite maintaining its stature as a global superpower, engaged in a tense ideological and military rivalry with the United States throughout the Cold War, the country struggled with persistent problems such as economic inefficiencies, bureaucratic corruption, and a dearth of political liberties. By the 1980s, economic stagnation had set in, fueling widespread discontent among Soviet citizens.

The year 1991 marked a seismic shift in history as the Soviet Union formally dissolved, signaling the conclusion of its communist era. This dissolution precipitated the independence of several former Soviet republics, while the Russian Federation emerged as the USSR's successor state.

The legacy of communism in the Soviet Union stands as a stark reminder of the perils of unchecked state control, the erosion of individual liberties, and the devastating human toll exacted by authoritarian regimes in the pursuit of ideological ends. The heavy imprint of substantial human rights violations, pervasive repression, and formidable economic hurdles speaks to the pitfalls of governance models fixated solely on centralized control and ideological uniformity. This legacy underscores the challenges inherent in implementing Marxist ideologies on a vast scale, emphasizing the complexities and limitations of such endeavors. The Soviet experience serves as a cautionary tale, offering profound lessons on the dangers inherent in systems that prioritize ideological conformity over the well-being and freedoms of their citizens.

China

Communism has played a central role in sculpting China's political, social, and economic landscape over the past century. The inception of the Communist Party of China (CPC) in 1921 laid the foundation for a monumental shift in the nation's trajectory. Yet, it was not until 1949, following the resolution of the Chinese Civil War, that the CPC, led by Mao Zedong, assumed authority and initiated a new era in China's history.

Mao Zedong's leadership signaled a monumental shift in China's history. The Communist Party of China's ascent to power heralded an abrupt transformation, plunging the nation into an era of communist rule. Mao's vision of communism aimed to overhaul every aspect of Chinese society, advocating for collectivization of agriculture, industrialization, and a reshaping of societal norms in adherence to communist doctrines.

During Mao's reign, China experienced seismic shifts: from land reforms to the calamitous Great Leap Forward and the tumultuous Cultural Revolution. These endeavors aimed to thrust China toward a socialist ethos, emphasizing communal ownership of land and resources. However, they proved fraught with difficulties, yielding severe economic setbacks, social turmoil, and extensive human suffering.

The Great Leap Forward, a pivotal initiative launched in 1958, sought rapid industrialization and modernization. Yet, its policies, including the aggressive mobilization of agricultural resources and the establishment of small-scale furnaces for steel production, led to catastrophic outcomes. Economic mismanagement resulted in a devastating famine, claiming the lives of millions.

During Chairman Mao Zedong's ill-fated Great Leap Forward, China was plunged into a brutal famine, estimated to have caused the deaths of a staggering 45 to 50 million people due to starvation. In the late 1960s, the Guangxi region witnessed horrifying instances of cannibalism, where hundreds of individuals became victims of this gruesome act. Official records document 137 individuals consumed, but the actual toll is believed to be far higher. Wuxuan County alone recorded at least 38 incidents of cannibalism, earning it the chilling distinction of being the site where "more people were eaten than anywhere else in China," as chillingly declared by one participant in the Guangxi massacre.

Under communist rule in China, religion faced severe suppression as the Communist Party aimed to institute an atheistic state. Much like the Soviet Union, the Chinese Communist Party (CCP) perceived religion as a potential ideological threat and sought to eradicate its influence within society. This suppression was multifaceted, employing strategies to regulate religious practices, stifle religious institutions, and propagate atheism through educational campaigns and propaganda. These measures significantly constrained religious freedoms, hindering the practice of faith nationwide. As a result, ethnic and religious minorities, notably Muslim Uyghurs in Xinjiang nd Tibetan Buddhists, encountered relentless persecution. Distressing accounts surfaced, detailing surveillance, forced labor, attempts at cultural assimilation, and arbitrary detentions in "re-education" camps targeting these marginalized groups.

In May 1966, China was thrust into a tumultuous period as Mao Zedong launched the Cultural Revolution, a political movement aimed at purging perceived adversaries of communist ideals while promoting revolutionary values. Mao's fervent accusations of high-ranking officials as "counter-revolutionary revisionists" set off a fervor that unleashed profound societal upheaval. The ambitious campaign sparked widespread unrest, leading to a wave of political persecution and violence that swept through educational institutions, cultural bastions, and deeply rooted traditions.

During the Cultural Revolution from 1966 to 1976, a pivotal wave of religious suppression unfolded as Chairman

Mao Zedong orchestrated an ambitious campaign to eradicate the "Four Olds," encompassing ancient customs, culture, habits, and ideas. This zeal for ideological purification targeted religious practices and cultural artifacts associated with China's pre-revolutionary heritage.

Religious institutions bore the brunt of this ideological fervor. Temples, churches, and mosques faced closure or repurposing, their sacred spaces transformed for secular use or completely shuttered. Texts and artifacts integral to various faiths encountered widespread destruction, while religious leaders found themselves subjected to public scorn, persecution, and imprisonment. The Communist Party's objective was clear: to forge a society stripped of what they considered superstitious beliefs, fostering allegiance solely to the Party's authority.

One poignant example of this relentless suppression occurred at Mount Wutai, a revered site in Chinese Buddhism boasting UNESCO World Heritage status. The mountain, adorned with ancient temples, became a tragic casualty of the Cultural Revolution. These sacred sites, revered for centuries, fell victim to looting and desecration, their spiritual treasures plundered during this tumultuous period. Buddhist monks and nuns faced coercion to forsake their monastic lives, enduring severe restrictions on religious practices and facing the dismantling of their spiritual homes.

The obliteration of Mount Wutai's Buddhist temples and the coercion imposed on its devoted practitioners stand as a stark testament to the broader religious suppression and cultural upheaval of that era. The Cultural Revolution epitomized the Party's unyielding resolve to reshape China's societal fabric in strict adherence to its ideological framework, leaving a profound and lasting impact on the country's religious landscape and social ethos.

During the Cultural Revolution, intellectuals, artists, and officials faced severe persecution, plunging the nation into an era marked by unprecedented brutality, moral decay, and even instances of cannibalism. Local Red Guard factions, comprised of zealous students and communist officials, unleashed unparalleled levels of violence upon their perceived opponents. Shockingly routine were "Struggle Sessions," infamous for public humiliation, torture, and horrifyingly, instances of cannibalism.

The cannibalistic episodes in Guangxi during the late 1960s stood out for their sheer depravity. Unlike the famine-induced acts of cannibalism during the Great Famine, those during this period could not be solely attributed to starvation, as food supplies had significantly recovered by then. This grim reality painted a harrowing picture of the extremes to which ideological fervor and political persecution had spiraled during the Cultural Revolution, culminating in acts of unimaginable horror.

The ghastly events at Wuxuan Middle School in 1968 epitomized the depths of depravity witnessed during China's Cultural Revolution. Fueled by fervent ideology, students committed unthinkable acts of violence, killing a teacher and grotesquely extracting organs from another for consumption —a grotesque distortion of humanity.

Even more chilling was the participation of senior Communist Party members in what were termed "flesh banquets." These influential figures engaged in cooking human organs such as hearts and livers, mixing them with pork and spices. Shockingly, individuals such as Wang Wenliu developed disturbing tastes, acquiring a preference for preserved male genitals. This macabre practice extended beyond the elite, but lower-ranking party members were limited to consuming only certain body parts.

The horrors of Guangxi during this era transcended mere cannibalism. The violence escalated to unimaginable levels, involving beheadings, beatings, live burials, stonings, drownings, boiling, group slaughters, and more—every form of atrocity seemed acceptable.

Historian Frank Dikötter revealed widespread torture and summary killings resulting in two to three million deaths. Extreme punishments for minor offenses, such as burying a boy alive for stealing grain, were reported. Dikötter noted in *Mao's Great Famine*: "It is not merely the extent of the catastrophe that dwarfs earlier estimates, but also the manner in which many people died: between two and three million victims were tortured to death or summarily killed, often for the slightest infraction…"[7]

This harrowing chapter in history serves as an unsettling reminder of the unchecked fervor and brutality that engulfed Chinese society during the Cultural Revolution. It starkly portrays the descent into inhumanity fueled by unwavering ideological zeal, culminating in a level of cruelty and violence that defied rational understanding. The accounts of persecution, betrayal, and ruthless suppression vividly illustrate the depths to which societal upheaval can plunge.

The far-reaching effects of the Cultural Revolution resonated deeply within China, leaving an indelible mark on its social structure and institutional foundations. It carved a

---

[7] Kotkin, Stephen. "Communism's Bloody Century." *The Wall Street Journal*, 3 Nov. 2017, kickthemallout.com/article.php/ Communisms_Bloody_Century.

profound scar into the fabric of society, etching the trauma of widespread fear and distrust that persisted long after the movement's official conclusion. The enduring legacy of this era cast a shadow over Chinese society, shaping its cultural landscape and fostering a lingering sense of caution and wariness in interpersonal relations and public discourse.

After Mao Zedong's death in 1976, China faced the limitations of socialism and embraced capitalist elements, led by Deng Xiaoping. Operating as "capitalism with Chinese characteristics," the government allowed controlled capitalism for property ownership, free enterprise, and wealth generation, alongside continued authoritarianism. Post-Mao, Deng Xiaoping guided China into a reform era, marked by market-oriented changes, foreign investment, and private entrepreneurship, resulting in a shift to a market-based economy, rapid growth, and improved living standards for many Chinese.

China's remarkable economic growth in recent decades has elevated it to global economic prominence. Nevertheless, this progress has been accompanied by challenges and trade-offs, particularly related to labor rights, environmental conservation, and income equality. Despite economic successes, China's human rights and political situation continue to face international scrutiny and apprehension.

Working conditions, notably in the manufacturing sector, have drawn rightful criticism due to excessive hours, inadequate pay, and unsafe surroundings. Some companies have prioritized production quotas and cost reduction, neglecting worker well-being, which has resulted in fatigue, burnout, and safety risks.

The electronics manufacturing industry offers an example of these difficulties, with reports of subpar labor conditions and rights violations. The surge in demand for consumer electronics has driven sector expansion, raising concerns about labor exploitation and restricted worker rights.

Moreover, China's economic growth has taken a toll on the environment. The push for industrialization and mass production has brought about significant pollution and environmental degredation. Air and water quality have suffered, impacting public health and the sustainability of natural resources.

While economic reforms boosted prosperity, China remains under one-party rule with limited political freedoms and human rights. The government tightly controls media and suppresses dissent. The Communist Party's grip has led to concerns about rights violations and privacy breaches.

Freedom of expression in China is heavily restricted, with the government controlling the media and internet. Independent journalism is limited, and online content undergoes extensive censorship. Social media platforms and messaging apps are closely monitored to prevent the spread of dissenting views. The Chinese government's censorship and surveillance practices extend to the digital realm, with the Great Firewall blocking access to foreign websites and social media platforms. Internet users face restrictions on their online activities, and concerns about privacy are widespread due to extensive government surveillance.

Political freedom in China is severely limited, with dissenting voices systematically suppressed. The government maintains a monopoly on political power, preventing the formation of opposition parties and limiting political pluralism. Activists, human rights defenders, and those advocating for political reforms face persecution, imprisonment, and censorship.

Under President Xi Jinping's stewardship, the Chinese Communist Party (CCP) has reinforced its grip on religious affairs, intensifying regulatory measures and oversight. Religious groups face stringent mandates, necessitating registration with the government and adherence to rigid regulations. Activities conducted outside this framework are deemed illegal, inviting punitive measures. The scrutiny extends to religious leaders and practitioners, subjecting them to continuous surveillance, while religious materials and teachings undergo extensive censorship.

This resurgence of control echoes a historical pattern where the state exerts formidable influence over religious life in China. The government's stance toward religion reflects a concerted effort to assert ideological dominance and neutralize potential challenges to its power. This tyrannical approach encompasses various faiths, aiming to shape and monitor religious practices, beliefs, and institutions according to the state's directives.

The overarching consequence of this control is a profound shaping of religious life within China. The state's assertive stance results in a landscape where religious freedoms are curtailed, and adherence to state-sanctioned norms becomes imperative. The government's objective remains rooted in maintaining a firm grip on ideological narratives and ensuring that religious entities align with the authority of the CCP.

The Communist Party's stronghold on China's governance has been an unyielding force, shaping the nation's policies, ideologies, and societal structures for the better part of a century. From its inception in 1921 to the establishment of the People's Republic of China under Mao Zedong's leadership in 1949, the country underwent profound transformations, all aimed at crafting a socialist society grounded in Marxist-Leninist principles.

Communism, as a guiding ideology, spurred rapid industrialization and economic growth. Yet, its implementation also bore the heavy weight of human rights violations, political repression, and stifling constraints on individual freedoms. The tumultuous episodes of the Great Leap Forward and the Cultural Revolution serve as stark, haunting reminders of the catastrophic repercussions inherent in imposing sweeping communist policies on a massive scale.

While subsequent years witnessed a shift toward market-oriented reforms, the Communist Party has maintained an iron grip on power. The CPC's centralized authority extends beyond politics, permeating into the social and economic spheres, effectively molding life across the country.

Even amid economic reforms and opening up to the global market, the CPC retains a formidable hold on China's governance. Its enduring legacy continues to cast a shadow over modern China, underscoring the enduring, often adverse, influence of communism on the nation's historical narrative and ongoing trajectory.

Cuba

Communism under the Communist Party of Cuba (PCC) has created a repressive framework curtailing political freedoms and violating human rights. The Cuban government stifles freedom of expression, impinging on political liberties. Human rights abuses, economic struggles, and brain drain compound challenges for the populace, straining international relations and prompting concerns about rights violations and economic stability.

Communism's enduring impact on Cuba's political landscape spans more than six decades, originating with the seismic Cuban Revolution of 1959. Spearheaded by Fidel Castro and Che Guevara, the revolution toppled the autocracy of Fulgencio Batista, ushering in a new era characterized by socialist ideals and Marxist-Leninist principles.

The leadership within the regime has faced allegations of amassing considerable personal wealth while a significant portion of the population grapples with economic hardships. Fidel Castro, the iconic figure at the helm of the regime, was purported to have accumulated a substantial fortune estimated to range between $500 million and $900 million. Similarly, his brother, Raul Castro, was reported to possess personal wealth totaling around $100 million.

Such disparities in wealth were starkly evident through instances such as Fidel's son, Antonio, who was photographed indulging in a lavish vacation aboard his yacht in the Aegean Sea in 2015. These glimpses of opulence contrasted sharply with the dire economic conditions endured by the majority of Cuban citizens, struggling to subsist on a meager monthly income of around $20. The glaring incongruity in living standards between the ruling elite and the general populace paints a disconcerting picture of inequality and disparity under communist rule in Cuba.

This stark contrast in lifestyles underscores the egregious wealth gap within Cuban society, accentuating the profound inequality perpetuated under the regime's governance. While a privileged few within the leadership enjoyed luxurious lifestyles and amassed considerable personal fortunes, the vast majority of Cubans grappled with financial hardships and lived in conditions characterized by economic struggle and deprivation. This stark reality unveils the harsh disparities and entrenched inequality that persisted despite the rhetoric of egalitarianism espoused by the communist regime.

Castro's ascension to power marked the establishment of a socialist state aligned with the Soviet Union during the intense geopolitical tensions of the Cold War. Under his leadership, Cuba embarked on a transformative journey, enacting socialist policies that encompassed the nationalization of industries, comprehensive land reforms, and the implementation of a centralized planned economy. The overarching objective was to eliminate socioeconomic disparities, prioritize literacy, healthcare, education, and foster societal equity.

During the early years of Castro's rule, his ambitions appeared to yield positive outcomes, notably in education and healthcare. Cuba's initiatives seemingly made strides in reducing illiteracy and improving public health, garnering international acclaim for achievements in sports and the arts. However, these accomplishments were often highlighted while overlooking the broader socio-economic challenges and human rights concerns that persisted under the regime.

Cuba's post-revolutionary path was deeply intertwined with its alliance with the Soviet Union, significantly impacting its economic and geopolitical landscape. Following the Cuban Revolution in 1959, Fidel Castro's government solidified a robust alliance with the Soviet bloc, which proved instrumental in shaping Cuba's trajectory.

Economically, the Soviet Union played a pivotal role in supporting Cuba. This assistance included financial aid, preferential trade agreements, and subsidies for key Cuban exports, particularly sugar and nickel. Becoming a primary market for Cuban goods, the USSR provided vital resources essential for the island nation's economic stability, cementing Cuba's heavy reliance on Soviet support.

Beyond economic aid, the Soviet Union supplied Cuba with military resources, including weapons, equipment, and advisors. This military assistance was evident during the Cuban Missile Crisis in 1962, amplifying Cuba's defense capabilities and leading to a tense standoff with the United States.

Additionally, the Soviet Union offered technical expertise across various sectors, spanning agriculture, industry, and infrastructure. This support aimed to advance Cuba's developmental initiatives by providing critical resources and knowledge for essential projects.

However, this dependency on Soviet aid left Cuba vulnerable to external factors. Fluctuating global commodity prices and the persistent impact of the U.S. embargo strained Cuba's economy. The collapse of the Soviet Union in 1991 triggered the "Special Period," a profoundly challenging phase marked by acute economic crisis, shortages, rationing, and widespread hardship.

The abrupt loss of Soviet support forced Cuba to navigate economic upheaval, prompting the country to seek alternative strategies for survival and stability. The termination of economic subsidies and trade agreements compelled Cuba to initiate reforms and explore new avenues for economic sustenance.

Despite facing challenges, Cuba has staunchly adhered to socialist principles, offering free education and healthcare to its citizens. While these initiatives aim to provide essential services and rights to the populace, they have been overshadowed by severe limitations on political dissent and the stifling of opposing voices. The stranglehold on political freedoms by the Communist Party remains unrelenting, perpetuating a climate of suppression and restricted expression.

The commitment to socialist ideals in providing education and healthcare has been a cornerstone of Cuba's governance. However, this dedication has been marred by the heavy-handed approach to dissent. Political freedoms are significantly curtailed; dissenters face harsh repression and systematic suppression under the control of the Communist Party.

Cuba's regime has faced human rights criticism for suppressing dissent and curbing freedoms. While lauded for universal healthcare, concerns about quality, shortages, and healthcare professional emigration exist. The Communist Party's omnipresence in governance has effectively snuffed out any form of political opposition, solidifying its dominance as the exclusive political force. This control extends across all facets of governance, maintaining an iron grip on power and systematically quashing any challenges to its authority.

The centrally planned economy in Cuba has wrought significant economic hardships upon its populace. The government's overarching control over the economy, coupled with the dearth of private enterprise, has cultivated an environment marred by inefficiencies, stifled innovation, and economic inertia. Consequently, the livelihoods of Cubans have borne the brunt of these challenges, resulting in a scarcity of essential goods, restricted access to quality healthcare and education, and paltry wages.

One glaring manifestation of these adversities is the chronic scarcity of basic goods experienced by Cubans. The government's grip on production and distribution, as dictated by the central planning system, perpetuates shortages of vital items such as food, medicine, and everyday necessities. This chronic scarcity has left many Cubans struggling with inadequate supplies, enduring lengthy queues, and navigating rationing systems that impose further hardship.

Furthermore, the absence of competition and limited private enterprise in Cuba's economy has stifled innovation and efficiency. With businesses bereft of incentives inherent in a market-driven economy, the impetus for improving productivity and fostering technological advancements remains woefully lacking. Consequently, economic growth stagnates, leading to a static job market and minimal prospects for increased wages or professional advancement.

The state's monopolistic control over key economic sectors has also exacted a toll on access to essential services such as healthcare and education. While Cuba's healthcare system is often lauded for its emphasis on preventative care and universal coverage, it grapples with severe constraints due to resource scarcity and constrained funding. Similarly, the education system, despite prioritizing high literacy rates and educational access, contends with antiquated facilities and inadequate resources, compromising the overall quality of education afforded to students.

The economic ramifications extend farther, manifesting in the form of depressingly low wages. The absence of competitive pressures and limited opportunities within the state-controlled economy result in meager compensation for workers. Many Cubans grapple with the harsh reality of insufficient income, facing substantial financial hardships due to the constricted earning potential within this centrally planned system.

In recent times, Cuba's cautious step toward introducing limited capitalism within its socialist framework speaks volumes about the shortcomings of socialism. The emergence of small private enterprises and the embrace of foreign investment signify an implicit acknowledgment that pure socialist models have failed to deliver sustainable economic prosperity.

These economic reforms, while cautiously implemented, represent a recognition of the need to adapt to global economic realities. They reflect a fundamental understanding that rigid adherence to socialist principles has hindered Cuba's economic growth and stability. The shift towards allowing small private businesses and foreign investment is a tacit admission that the traditional socialist model has been inadequate in fostering robust economic development.

The very essence of these reforms underscores the necessity of departing from strict socialism to navigate the complexities of the global economy. Cuba's pragmatic approach acknowledges that the rigid constraints of a purely socialist system have led to stagnation and inefficiency. These changes aim to strike a balance between acknowledging the failures of socialism and preserving certain foundational principles, albeit within a more adaptable economic framework.

While safeguarding elements of socialist identity, these reforms inherently imply that socialism alone is insufficient to meet the economic demands of a rapidly evolving world. The need for economic liberalization within the socialist framework demonstrates an understanding that clinging to an outdated model is counterproductive. Instead, Cuba's measured approach signifies an acknowledgment that socialism, in its traditional form, has not yielded the desired economic outcomes and needs to integrate elements of capitalism to survive in the modern global landscape.

In Cuba's communist system, the landscape for political diversity is barren, and the notion of fair elections remains a distant dream. The exclusive dominion of the Communist Party of Cuba (PCC) over the political realm effectively quashes any semblance of opposition or dissent. Independent journalists, activists, and political dissidents challenging the government's authority face a daunting reality characterized by harassment, imprisonment, and stringent limitations on their activities.

Under the grip of communist rule, Cuba has become synonymous with a repressive regime that systematically tramples on human rights and quells any whisper of dissent. Political dissidents, human rights advocates, and independent civil society organizations are frequent targets of government crackdowns, enduring relentless harassment, imprisonment, and severe curtailment of their basic rights to express themselves and assemble peacefully.

The plight of the Ladies in White (Damas de Blanco) stands as a poignant testament to the repressive nature of the Cuban government. Comprising wives, mothers, and relatives of political prisoners, these peaceful advocates tirelessly demand the release of their loved ones and champion human rights. Despite their nonviolent stance, they face consistent persecution—harassment, intimidation, and arbitrary arrests orchestrated by Cuban authorities. Their peaceful gatherings are disrupted, and members endure assaults, house arrests, and arbitrary detentions, starkly highlighting the regime's determination to suppress any form of opposition, even from individuals advocating for political freedoms and human rights.

Moreover, the restrictions imposed on independent journalists and civil society organizations in Cuba are stifling. Any form of critical reporting or dissent against the government can swiftly lead to censorship, imprisonment, or relentless harassment. Independent media outlets operate under severe constraints, with journalists covering narratives that deviate from the official government stance facing heightened risks of persecution and suppression. This pervasive atmosphere of fear and censorship underscores the oppressive tactics employed by the regime to muzzle any form of dissenting voices and maintain an iron grip on power.

Under communist rule in Cuba, religious freedom remains tightly constrained as the government maintains strict control over religious institutions and practices, viewing religion as a potential rival to communist ideology and seeking to diminish its societal influence. This translates into rigorous oversight, limitations, and, in some instances, persecution of religious activities.

In the initial years following the Cuban revolution in 1959, the government implemented stringent policies aimed at reducing the prominence of religion in public life. Fidel Castro declared atheism as the state's official stance, sparking tensions with religious entities. Catholic schools were nationalized, eroding the Church's educational role, while Catholic clergy faced harassment and constraints, discouraging public displays of religious devotion.

The suppression of the Catholic Church vividly exemplifies the regime's efforts to diminish its influence. Before the revolution, the Church wielded considerable influence, prompting communist ascendancy to weaken its authority. Numerous Catholics, including priests and nuns, encountered persecution and imprisonment for their religious convictions and activism. Father Manuel Rodriguez, known for advocating social justice and aiding the marginalized, notably faced imprisonment in 1961 for challenging the government.

In subsequent years, the government softened its stance on religion, amending the Constitution in 1992 to eliminate atheism as the official ideology. However, religious practices in Cuba continue to face constraints, with stringent government oversight imposed on religious groups and activities. These groups must register, and their leaders are subject to strict regulations and oversight.

Despite enduring hurdles, Cuban religious communities persistently cling to their faith, showcasing remarkable resilience in the face of ongoing restrictions and historical suppression. Their steadfast commitment to their beliefs serves as a testament to their resilience, navigating through the challenging landscape of religious limitations imposed by the government.

Cuba's communist regime has fueled a significant brain drain, with skilled professionals such as doctors and engineers seeking opportunities abroad. The allure of better career prospects, higher incomes, and expanded personal liberties outside the confines of communism prompts these individuals to explore opportunities in other nations. The stifling environment, limited career paths, and restricted freedoms drive many skilled Cubans to seek new horizons elsewhere, often in capitalist nations where they can escape political suppression and freely express their beliefs.

The appeal of economic prospects, personal freedoms, and the ability to engage in activism in more liberal societies often serves as a powerful draw for Cuban communists seeking to leave their homeland. The desire to break free from the limitations imposed by the communist regime propels many to seek asylum abroad, where they can explore diverse perspectives and enjoy greater personal and professional liberties.

The United States particularly beckons Cuban communists with its promise of personal and professional growth, robust political liberties, and a thriving Cuban-American community. The benefits provided by the Cuban Adjustment Act serve as an additional incentive, offering avenues for resettlement and support upon arrival. These factors coalesce to compel Cubans to escape communism and seek refuge and opportunities in the U.S., drawn by the prospect of a more promising future and the chance to flourish in an environment that embraces their aspirations and beliefs.

Maximo Alvarez, who fled the island in 1961, recounted that rights evaporated quickly under the communist leader, Fidel Castro. The empty promises "under any communist regime [are]: 'Free education, free healthcare, defund the police, trust a socialist state more than your family and community...'"[8] "I can never forget all those who grew up around me,...who suffered and starved

---

[8] Smith, Justin O. "Willing to Risk Everything for Freedom: All Eyes Are On Cuba and America." *The Blue State Conservative*, 15 Jul. 2021, thebluestateconservative.com/2021/07/15/willing-to-risk-everything-for-freedom-all-eyes-are-on-cuba-and-america/.

and died because they believed those empty promises. They swallowed the communist poison pill."[9]

In 2021, Cuba witnessed significant turbulence as thousands of citizens took to the streets on July 11, 2021, rallying in San Antonio de los Banos and along Havana's Malecon promenade to protest food shortages and soaring prices. Their impassioned cries for freedom and an end to the communist dictatorship laid bare the deep-seated frustration accumulated over 62 years of oppression and impoverishment, which had been promised as a utopian vision under Fidel Castro's regime. The disillusionment stemmed from unfulfilled promises, leaving the populace fatigued by enduring endless breadlines and grappling with subpar socialized healthcare, ultimately igniting a fervent call for the cessation of communism and its suffocating governance. These protests were fueled by chronic shortages of basic necessities that had become an entrenched norm in Cuban society.

Cuba's State Police and military were swiftly deployed to quash the dissent. This heavy-handed approach resulted in the tragic use of force against unarmed protesters, with reports of shootings and numerous arbitrary arrests, leaving many others unaccounted for and disappeared.

Amidst the chaos, voices from political figures in the United States echoed in support of the Cuban protesters. Florida Lieutenant Governor Jeanette Nunez (R) emphasized

---

[9] Brown, Jon. "Cuban Refugee Warns Americans Have Already 'Swallowed' Communism's 'Poison Pill.'" *DailyWire.com*, 28 Apr. 2021, www.dailywire.com/news/cuban-refugee-warns-americans-have-already-swallowed-communisms-poison-pill?utm_source=facebook&utm_medium=social&utm_campaign=ben shapiro&fbclid=IwAR3kjrRIjG_8OHDL9eWaAWcdsA_5BXCjE_gv7gOiAphiv9VXzJhBx0mAruI.

that the widespread images from the island depicted an outcry driven by severe shortages of vital commodities. Senator Mitch McConnell (R-KY) acknowledged the bravery exhibited by the men and women who boldly sought freedoms long denied to them.

Senator Marco Rubio (R-FL) used social media to underscore the significance of the Cuban people's protest, linking it directly to 62 years of socialism, tyranny, and enduring suffering. He emphasized that socialism, as a system, has consistently led to catastrophic consequences.

Senator Ted Cruz (R-TX), drawing from personal ties as the son of a Cuban immigrant, forecasted the fate awaiting the current regime, destined to be consigned to the dustbin of history due to its relentless brutality and the sustained denial of freedom to generations of Cubans. Cruz highlighted how this oppression had led numerous families to flee their homeland in search of a better, freer life.

Communism has profoundly marred Cuba's path, leaving a lasting and grim imprint on its history and developmental landscape. The ideology's implementation has brought about economic hardships, severe political repression, and a stifling suppression of individual freedoms. Despite Cuba's unwavering adherence to socialism, recent years have shown feeble attempts at economic reforms. The nation finds itself at a critical juncture, wrestling with the burdensome legacy of communism while striving to find stability and evolve politically, all while clinging tightly to socialist ideals.

The resolute longing of the Cuban populace for freedom and an escape from oppressive governance resounded forcefully in the 2021 protests, laying bare the enduring discord between the state's entrenched communist regime and the people's yearnings. This tension underscores the ongoing clash between the regime's iron grip of communism and the population's aspirations for autonomy and liberties.

Amidst internal challenges and shifting global dynamics, the prospect of communism in Cuba appears increasingly uncertain. Economic strains, worsened by a decline in tourism, compound an already complicated situation. Efforts to court investments and diversify the economy clash with an unyielding commitment to socialist principles. The nation grapples with a precarious balancing act between these ideals and increased demands for expanded political freedoms and human rights.

Cuba finds itself in a fragile balancing act between ideology and public dissent, standing at a pivotal moment fraught with demands for change while struggling to maintain the foundational pillars of its socialist ideology. The future direction hinges on a complex interplay between economic adaptation, potential political reforms, and the fervent desires of a populace yearning for greater liberties within the constraints of its historical legacy.

North Korea

The imposition of communism in North Korea has forged a repressive regime centered around the unwavering authority of the Kim family. A distinctive feature of North Korean society is the pervasive personality cult meticulously crafted around the ruling Kim dynasty. These leaders are elevated to near-divine status, their actions and pronouncements considered beyond reproach. Citizens are indoctrinated from an early age to display unswerving allegiance and reverence to the ruling family. Within this system, human rights violations, economic hardships, pervasive propaganda, and restricted access to information have become entrenched realities.

The administration's governance is characterized by egregious human rights abuses and a tight grip over both public and private spheres, quashing any form of opposition and violating fundamental human rights. Basic liberties such as freedom of speech, expression, and assembly are severely restricted, leaving no space for political diversity or dissenting opinions. A plethora of testimonies from international organizations and defectors corroborate harrowing accounts of human rights violations. These include instances of forced labor, arbitrary detentions, systemic torture, public executions, and the existence of political labor camps.

The state's omnipresent control extends to virtually every facet of life, perpetuating a climate of fear and surveillance. The Kim regime's iron-fisted rule has created a society steeped in propaganda, fostering an environment where dissent is met with severe punishment. The regime's stranglehold over information flow and the isolationist policies further contribute to the populace's limited exposure to external perspectives, reinforcing the government's narrative and maintaining an iron grip over the population's thoughts and actions.

Communism's hold on North Korea has been entrenched in the nation's political fabric since its inception in 1948. At the helm of this ideological framework stands the doctrine of Juche, formulated by the nation's founding figure, Kim Il-sung. The Democratic People's Republic of Korea (DPRK) staunchly upholds this ideology, advocating for self-reliance, nationalist fervor, and the cultivation of a robust socialist state. Under Kim Il-sung's guidance, North Korea embraced a centralized approach, imposing state control over every sphere of society, including the economy, media, and cultural domains.

The regime established an exclusive single-party system, placing the Workers' Party of Korea (WPK) at the apex of political authority. This authoritative structure vehemently suppresses any form of political opposition or dissent, employing ruthless measures such as imprisonment and execution for those perceived as threats to the regime's stability. The stranglehold on political power is further reinforced by a network of surveillance and coercion that leaves no room for opposing ideologies or alternative political affiliations. This iron-fisted grip has solidified the party's monopoly on governance, effectively eradicating any challenges to its authority.

The North Korean economy operates under the framework of state-owned industries and collective farming, but it contends with persistent inefficiencies, mismanagement, and a stark disconnect from the global market. Adding to these challenges are the crippling effects of international sanctions imposed as a response to North Korea's nuclear and missile initiatives, which exacerbate the country's economic woes.

The economic landscape of North Korea vividly portrays the consequences of a state-controlled economy fixated on military spending and nuclear ambitions. This approach has led to widespread economic mismanagement and dire humanitarian crises. Under the rule of the Kim family, North Korea's economic agenda has revolved around bolstering military capabilities and advancing nuclear programs, neglecting crucial sectors such as agriculture and social services. This lopsided resource allocation perpetuates poverty and chronic shortages of essentials, contributing to prevalent malnutrition and hunger, necessitating heavy reliance on international aid.

Moreover, crucial investments in essential infrastructure and public services such as healthcare, education, and sanitation have been sidelined in favor of prioritizing military and nuclear pursuits. Consequently, the well-being and quality of life for many North Koreans have been significantly compromised. The stark contrast between the regime's priorities, which favor opulent lifestyles and massive investments in military and nuclear ventures, and the harsh living conditions endured by ordinary citizens vividly underscores the repercussions of economic mismanagement and the relentless pursuit of nuclear armament. While the leadership indulges in lavish lifestyles and channels substantial resources into military advancements, ordinary North Koreans struggle to meet their basic needs, emphasizing the profound disparities perpetuated by the regime's economic strategies.

In the confines of communist North Korea, the regime exerts rigorous suppression over religion, considering it to be a potential competitor for the absolute loyalty of its citizens. The government perceives religion as a formidable threat to its authority and meticulously strives to eradicate any semblance of challenge to its rule. The state exercises strict control and surveillance over religious activities, deeming them a potential conduit for dissent. Practitioners of Christianity and other religious faiths endure severe persecution, arrest, and torture simply for exercising their religious beliefs.

The government's overarching objective is to foster absolute allegiance to the ruling Kim family and the ideology of Juche. This fervent loyalty is expected from all citizens, and any divergence from this mandated allegiance is met with severe repercussions. Religious adherents, seen as potential dissenters, face relentless persecution in an effort to eliminate any perceived threat to the regime's authority. The regime's measures to monitor and suppress religious practices underscore its determination to maintain control over the beliefs and loyalties of its populace, demanding an unwavering commitment to its authority above all else.

The North Korean government relies heavily on propaganda and indoctrination to bolster its authority, crafting a narrative that glorifies the ruling regime while suppressing dissenting voices. The flow of information and access to technology are severely restricted, with limited internet availability and pervasive censorship. The regime exerts tight control over media outlets and communication channels, creating a state of isolation that obstructs the free exchange of information within the nation.

Information access in North Korea is rigorously governed, with strict censorship of media and stringent controls on internet usage. State-controlled media serves as a powerful tool for propaganda, disseminating the regime's ideology while maintaining a firm grip on public perception. The government manipulates these platforms to portray a carefully curated image of the leadership and its policies, discouraging any form of dissent and reinforcing unwavering loyalty to the regime. This control over information flow not only sustains the regime's narrative but also reinforces its authority by stifling alternative viewpoints or criticisms.

An example of free speech suppression in North Korea is embodied by the case of Song Byeok. Previously a propaganda artist for the North Korean government, Song's work glorified the regime and its leaders. Yet, upon fleeing to South Korea, he harnessed his artistic prowess to illuminate the realities and hardships faced by North Koreans. Song's artwork portrayed their harsh living conditions, poverty, and oppression, juxtaposed against the glorification of the ruling Kim family through public portraits. His potent creations garnered global attention, shedding light on human rights abuses and the absence of freedom within North Korea. Yet, this courageous act of dissent via art carried substantial risks. The North Korean regime perceives any criticism as a severe threat to its authority. Despite the peril, Song persisted in his artistic endeavor, showcasing the resilience and determination of those who courageously challenge the regime's control and suppression of free expression.

Human rights abuses in North Korea have garnered extensive documentation from international human rights organizations and defectors, shedding light on a grim reality of systemic abuses. These violations encompass a spectrum of atrocities, including the existence of forced labor camps, instances of torture, public executions, and pervasive surveillance that casts a shadow over the population's daily life. The regime enforces stringent constraints on fundamental freedoms, severely limiting freedom of expression, religion, and movement. Citizens exist under constant surveillance, living in perpetual fear of severe repercussions for even the slightest perceived deviation from loyalty to the state.

The North Korean regime maintains an iron grip on power by fostering an atmosphere of intimidation and suppression that permeates every facet of society. Citizens live in constant fear, as the regime utilizes a web of control mechanisms to quell any form of dissent or opposition. This tight control extends across various domains of life, coercing obedience and demanding unwavering allegiance to the state. The regime's systematic violations of human rights serve as stark reminders of the severe realities faced by North Korean citizens under its tyrannical rule.

Despite enduring isolation and economic hardships, the regime adeptly reinforces its dominance through a blend of political suppression, pervasive propaganda, and the cultivation of fear among the populace. The seamless transitions of leadership within the Kim family dynasty— from Kim Il-sung to Kim Jong-il and later to Kim Jong-un— have significantly strengthened the family's authoritative rule over the nation.

The regime's adeptness in consolidating control lies in its sophisticated employment of tactics such as stringent censorship, pervasive surveillance, and severe reprisals against dissenters. Simultaneously, an extensive propaganda apparatus glorifies the Kim family, fostering loyalty and reinforcing the regime's narrative of absolute authority. This relentless propagation of the family's cult-like veneration aims to instill unwavering obedience and devotion among the populace.

The successive transitions of power within the Kim family lineage have further fortified the regime's authority, solidifying the family's dynastic rule. These smooth successions have bolstered the regime's stability, projecting an image of unity and perpetuating the legacy of the Kim family as the unchallengeable protectors of the realm.

In recent times, North Korea has shown subtle signs of initiating limited economic reforms while attempting diplomatic overtures to engage with the global community. However, the regime remains steadfast in its commitment to its socialist ideology, maintaining a firm grip on authoritarian control. This unwavering dedication to communism has shaped North Korea into an insulated and repressive regime, characterized by stringent state authority.

At the core of North Korea's governance lies the adherence to the Juche ideology, intricately interwoven with an extensive personality cult centered around the Kim family. This amalgamation has resulted in severe curtailment of personal liberties and widespread human rights violations. The regime's tight control, coupled with enduring international sanctions, has posed substantial obstacles to the nation's economy. Additionally, the pursuit of nuclear capabilities has further complicated North Korea's interactions within the global community.

As North Korea charts its course within the confines of communism, the international community remains apprehensive about various critical aspects, including its track record on human rights, the advancement of its nuclear program, and the overall stability of the region. These concerns stand central in global discussions and negotiations concerning North Korea, underlining the complexities and uncertainties surrounding the nation's communist trajectory.

Vietnam

Communism's influence in Vietnam has profoundly shaped the nation's political, social, and economic landscapes. After the 1976 reunification under the

Communist Party of Vietnam (CPV), the country embarked on a socialist path, aspiring to create a classless society. Yet, this communist governance has also given rise to a suppressive regime that restricts political freedoms and quashes opposition. The CPV's firm grip on power has led to a lack of political pluralism and a notable absence of multi-party elections, severely limiting the avenues for diverse perspectives and dissenting voices.

The CPV's control extends across the political spectrum, leading to a significant constriction of political liberties. This dominance stifles the formation of alternative political ideologies or parties, effectively monopolizing political power and stifling any semblance of genuine political diversity. Consequently, the political landscape remains highly centralized, with a singular ruling party dictating policies and agendas, leaving little room for dissent or varied viewpoints.

The scarcity of multi-party elections further underlines the restrictive nature of the political environment in Vietnam. The absence of competitive elections limits the opportunities for alternative political parties or independent candidates to participate in shaping the nation's governance. This entrenched system reinforces the CPV's dominance, perpetuating a political structure that diminishes pluralistic representation and constrains the democratic process.

As a result, Vietnam's political sphere operates within a framework largely dictated by the Communist Party, fostering an environment where divergent opinions struggle to find expression, and dissenting voices face considerable challenges in being heard within the political discourse.

Economically, Vietnam's state-controlled system, deeply rooted in socialist principles aiming for equitable resource distribution, has encountered challenges resulting in inefficiencies and limited avenues for economic progress. The predominance of state control in crucial industries presents significant hurdles for the private sector, including bureaucratic complexities, restricted access to resources, and challenges in navigating a system that often fosters corruption. These barriers contribute to income disparities despite economic growth.

The focus on substantial military expenditures and nuclear programs has strained Vietnam's economic resources. This allocation of funds, while intended to bolster national security, has led to widespread poverty, food shortages, and a lack of essential infrastructure and public services. The prioritization of these endeavors over socio-economic development has hindered progress in improving the living standards of many Vietnamese citizens.

In the pursuit of economic advancement, environmental sustainability has often been sidelined, resulting in adverse consequences. Vietnam's drive for economic growth has come at the cost of the environment, leading to issues such as deforestation, pollution, and the depletion of natural resources. This neglect of environmental concerns poses long-term risks and challenges for the country's ecological well-being and sustainability.

Within the governance of the Communist Party, both freedom of expression and press freedom in Vietnam face profound limitations, manifesting in stringent governmental control over the media landscape. This control has fostered an environment where fear and self-censorship prevail among journalists and bloggers, hindering access to unbiased information and reinforcing the government's ideological dominance in shaping public discourse. The pervasive atmosphere of fear restricts the free flow of information, discouraging individuals from expressing dissenting opinions or reporting on topics deemed sensitive by the authorities.

The government's meticulous management of freedom of expression extends to the manipulation of media channels to suppress viewpoints that challenge or diverge from the party's agenda. This control inhibits the proliferation of independent journalism, resulting in a scarcity of diverse perspectives and objective reporting accessible to the public. The lack of independent and critical journalism diminishes the availability of nuanced and unbiased information, limiting citizens' ability to engage in informed discourse and form well-rounded opinions on socio-political issues.

As a consequence, the media landscape in Vietnam operates within strict confines set by the authorities, impeding the open and free exchange of ideas. This controlled environment fosters a narrative that aligns with the government's objectives, constraining the populace's access to a wide range of perspectives and hindering the free flow of information crucial for an informed and democratic society.

Human rights abuses in Vietnam have been widespread, encompassing arbitrary detentions, limitations on religious freedom, and severe restrictions on civil society organizations. The historical period of land reform spearheaded by communist leader, Ho Chi Minh, in the late 1950s to the early 1960s marked a tumultuous chapter in Vietnamese history, marred by grave allegations of a class genocide targeting affluent farmers and landowners. This initiative, aimed at redistributing land to the rural poor, led to widespread human rights abuses and a tragic loss of life.

The land reform campaign was rife with violence, coercion, and brutality as it targeted people deemed to be wealthy landowners or part of the bourgeoisie. Accusations of collaboration with colonial powers or exploitation of the rural populace were often used as grounds for persecution. Tragically, this period resulted in mass executions, arbitrary arrests, and the forced displacement of individuals from their lands.

The repercussions were devastating, creating an atmosphere of fear, distrust, and profound instability within Vietnamese society. Families were torn apart, communities fractured, and livelihoods destroyed, leaving a deep scar on the social fabric of the nation. The trauma and collective memory of this period continue to resonate within Vietnamese society, shaping perceptions of justice, governance, and the protection of human rights.

Activists championing various causes, be it human rights, democracy, or environmental concerns, frequently face government harassment and unwarranted imprisonment. Civil society organizations and individuals advocating for these causes encounter systematic repression from the government. Those involved in activities perceived as challenging the state's authority often become targets of intimidation, legal persecution, and arbitrary detention.

These measures aim to quash dissent and curtail the emergence of a robust civil society crucial for fostering societal progress and advocating for marginalized communities. The use of arbitrary detentions serves as a means to suppress opposing voices and restrict freedom of expression. Individuals expressing dissenting opinions or engaging in peaceful protests contrary to the government's stance risk arbitrary arrest, instilling a pervasive atmosphere of fear and intimidation among activists and citizens hesitant to voice their opinions.

The Vietnamese government perceives certain religions as potential threats for various reasons deeply rooted in historical, political, and social contexts. One significant aspect is the historical backdrop, marked by foreign influences and periods of conflict. Some religions might have historical associations with movements or entities perceived as challenging governmental stability or authority. Past engagements or affiliations of specific religious groups with uprisings or movements against state control contribute to this perception.

Political control and stability stand as paramount objectives for the Vietnamese government. Religions or religious groups operating independently, outside government oversight, might be viewed as potential sources of dissent or opposition. There is a concern that these groups could challenge the government's authority or serve as platforms for organizing movements against government policies, posing a threat to stability.

Moreover, religious beliefs or practices sometimes conflict with the ideologies promoted by the government. This misalignment raises concerns about the potential impact on societal values, norms, or behaviors, prompting the government to perceive certain religions as threats to its control over shaping societal ideologies.

Additionally, ties to international organizations or entities by certain religions may heighten the government's wariness. If these connections are perceived as conflicting with national interests or sovereignty, the government might view these religions as threats to its authority or national security.

The government's desire to maintain control over information dissemination and societal narratives is another factor. Religions with independent networks or communication channels may challenge the government's monopoly on information, posing a threat to its ability to shape societal discourse.

Lastly, competition for influence within society plays a role. State-sanctioned religions are often perceived as more aligned with government objectives. In contrast, independent or newer religious movements might be viewed as competitors for followers, potentially undermining established power structures and thus considered as threats to governmental control.

In Vietnam, state-sanctioned religions are those officially recognized, approved, or regulated by the government. These religious institutions, such as Buddhism, Catholicism, Protestantism, Islam, Hoa Hao, and Caodaism, operate within established boundaries set by the state and are subject to government oversight. They enjoy certain benefits such as legal recognition, access to resources, and some protection from interference or persecution.

However, independent religious groups, which operate outside this recognized framework, face considerable challenges. They lack official recognition, leading to restrictions on their activities, limitations in legal status, and heightened scrutiny from authorities. Consequently, practitioners within independent groups often struggle to practice their faith openly due to the absence of government approval and support.

This distinction shapes Vietnam's religious landscape, impacting the freedom of worship and expression for various communities. Those within the state-sanctioned system experience a different level of freedom compared to independent groups operating outside the government's approved religious framework.

These constraints manifest in several ways. Firstly, there is constant surveillance and monitoring of religious activities conducted beyond state-sanctioned institutions. Authorities closely watch gatherings and ceremonies, often resulting in harassment or intimidation of practitioners.

Secondly, independent religious groups encounter hurdles in the registration process, facing strict regulations that make gaining legal recognition challenging. Without official registration, these groups face increased scrutiny and limitations on their activities, hindering their ability to operate openly.

Moreover, instances of direct interference in religious practices occur, with some groups reporting disruptions in their ceremonies or gatherings by authorities who pressure them to comply with state regulations or disband.

Arizona state representative, Quang Nguyen, a refugee from war-torn Vietnam, strongly voiced his opinion on communism's impact on the Vietnamese people. He emphasized that communism was responsible for grave atrocities during the Vietnam War, resulting in the loss of hundreds of thousands of lives. He cited specific examples, such as the drowning of 250,000 Vietnamese in the South China Sea and the execution of 86,000 South Vietnamese during the fall of Saigon, attributing these tragedies to communism. His personal experiences, including the loss of his cousins and family members, drive his belief in the destructive nature of communism. Rep. Nguyen's statement reflects the perspective shared by many Vietnamese refugees who have experienced the consequences of communism firsthand, urging awareness about its historical impact and advocating for a recognition of the threat posed by this ideology. Rep. Nguyen said, "I just recently heard somebody say that...communism is not the enemy, but white nationalism [is]...White nationalism didn't drown 250,000 Vietnamese in the South China Sea. Communists did. White nationalism did not execute 86,000 South Vietnamese at the fall of Saigon. Communists did. White nationalism did not put me here. Communism did...I lost most of my cousins, my family members due to communism."[10]

Communism's entrenched presence in Vietnam has left a deep and lasting impact, a legacy marked by a mixed bag of outcomes—some ostensibly positive, yet overwhelmingly overshadowed by a slew of detrimental consequences. Undoubtedly, the country has witnessed strides in economic growth, lauded by proponents of the regime. However, beneath this façade of progress lies a grim reality steeped in severe challenges that afflict the nation.

The regime's iron grip on power has birthed a repressive governance model, suffocating political liberties and stifling dissenting voices. It is a system where expressing contrary political opinions comes at great personal risk, a haunting reminder of the suffocating grasp of authoritarianism. This suppression of fundamental freedoms

---

[10] Saunders, Joe. "Survivor of Communism Slams Down Democratic Rep for Claiming 'White Nationalism' Is More Dangerous than Communism.' *The Western Journal*, 30 Jun. 2021, www.westernjournal.com/survivor-communism-slams-democratic-rep-claiming-white-nationalism-dangerous-communism/?ff_source=mewe&ff_medium=westernjournalism&ff_campaign=manual post&ff_content=2021-07-07.

has created a culture of fear, where speaking out against the government is met with swift and severe repercussions.

Moreover, the regime's track record on human rights remains appalling, marred by consistent abuses that violate the basic dignity of humans. Instances of censorship, arbitrary arrests, and silencing of opposition voices are rampant, painting a bleak picture of a populace deprived of essential rights and liberties.

The environmental toll of Vietnam's communist policies is equally distressing. Pursuit of rapid economic growth at the expense of environmental sustainability has led to widespread degradation. Irresponsible industrial practices, unchecked pollution, and environmental mismanagement have resulted in severe ecological damage, imperiling both the natural world and the well-being of the populace.

As Vietnam trudges forward under the shadow of communist rule, the pressing need to confront these deep-rooted issues looms large. The nation's progress and the well-being of its citizens hinge on addressing the egregious human rights violations, fostering genuine political freedoms, and undertaking sustainable environmental practices. Failure to reckon with these critical challenges threatens to impede the country's holistic development and undermines the very fabric of its societal health and prosperity.

Cambodia

The impact of communism on Cambodia, notably during the Khmer Rouge regime led by Pol Pot from 1975 to 1979, remains an indelible scar on history. The Khmer Rouge zealously pursued the establishment of a radical agrarian communist society, labeling it Democratic Kampuchea and claiming adherence to Marxist-Leninist principles. Unfortunately, their pursuit of this idealistic vision birthed one of the most harrowing genocides recorded in history.

Upon seizing power, the Khmer Rouge swiftly undertook a ruthless overhaul of Cambodian society, obliterating any vestiges of the past and enforcing an extreme communist ideology. Their paramount objective was the creation of an agrarian utopia, achieved through the forced relocation of urban residents to labor camps in the countryside. Urbanites were branded as counter-revolutionary, perceived threats to the regime's envisioned pure communist state, and were thus systematically uprooted and marginalized.

The Khmer Rouge's authoritarian grasp plunged Cambodia into an unfathomable abyss, a descent marred by an inhumane campaign characterized by forced labor, appalling executions, and unrelenting torment. Under their ruthless regime, the Cambodian populace witnessed a horror unfurled upon intellectuals, professionals, and dissenting voices—a meticulously orchestrated purge aimed at the systematic obliteration of minds and spirits.

Their chilling objective sought not just the physical eradication of individuals but the annihilation of their essence, the extinction of diversity in all of its forms. The regime's terrifying blueprint aimed to carve out a homogenized society, devoid of any trace of perceived capitalist or bourgeois tendencies—a ruthless endeavor to strip Cambodia of its multifaceted cultural, social, and intellectual tapestry.

The Khmer Rouge's methods were shockingly precise, meticulously calibrated to extinguish lives and erase the vibrancy of Cambodia's identity. The sinister machinery of this regime silenced voices that resonated with knowledge and wisdom, snuffing out the flames of intellect and enlightenment. Their actions were not just executions; they were an assault on the very soul of a nation, tearing apart the fabric of its cultural heritage and splintering the mosaic of its social diversity.

Amidst the orchestrated chaos, Cambodia's societal harmony was shattered, replaced by a bleak landscape where fear, suffering, and desolation reigned supreme.

The Khmer Rouge's policies plunged Cambodia into a catastrophic cycle of famine by forcibly uprooting urban populations and disrupting established agricultural practices. Their ill-conceived initiatives, aimed at reshaping society, wreaked havoc on the nation's agricultural landscape. The abrupt relocation of city dwellers to rural labor camps disrupted agricultural productivity.

This upheaval proved disastrous as those resettled lacked the necessary farming expertise to sustain themselves adequately. The regime's directives, fueled by ideological fervor rather than practical knowledge, exacerbated the crisis. The harsh conditions prevailing in the labor camps, coupled with meager resources and an absence of proper agricultural techniques, worsened the plight of the people.

Cambodia's once-thriving agricultural sector, disrupted by this turmoil, struggled to produce food. The forced labor camps became hotbeds of hunger and malnutrition, with inadequate food supplies failing to meet the basic needs of the populace. The widespread hunger that ensued was not just a consequence of food scarcity but a grim reminder of the mismanagement and disruption inflicted upon the country's agricultural backbone.

The haunting legacy of the Khmer Rouge regime is starkly embodied in the notorious Killing Fields, a site steeped in unfathomable tragedy where the echoes of unspeakable horrors still reverberate. This event stands as a gruesome testament to the atrocities committed, where the lives of thousands of innocent souls were callously extinguished, their bodies thrown into mass graves.

The horror inflicted by the Khmer Rouge regime resulted in a staggering loss of life. Estimates paint a devastating picture, suggesting that approximately 1.7 to 2.2 million Cambodians perished during this dark chapter in the country's history. This death toll accounted for nearly a quarter of Cambodia's population at that time—a devastation that scarred the nation for generations to come.

The Killing Fields symbolize a heart-wrenching tale of unimaginable suffering, a place where the fabric of humanity was torn asunder by the ruthless machinery of an oppressive regime. Each unmarked grave holds a story untold, a life brutally cut short, a family shattered, and dreams violently extinguished. The sheer scale of loss, the magnitude of grief, and the brutality inflicted upon the innocent souls etch a haunting reminder of the depths of human cruelty and the tragic consequences of unchecked power.

These numbers, while staggering, are not just statistics; they represent the anguish and profound loss that scarred Cambodia's collective soul. The Killing Fields serve as a poignant memorial, a sacred ground bearing witness to the immense tragedy inflicted upon a people, and a somber reminder of the imperative to ensure that such horrors are never repeated.

The dire situation was a tragic testament to the disastrous repercussions of forcibly altering established systems without understanding their intricacies. The Khmer Rouge's misguided policies not only displaced countless lives but also sowed the seeds of a devastating famine that ravaged a nation already reeling from the brutality of their rule.

The downfall of the Khmer Rouge in 1979, orchestrated by Vietnamese forces, marked the beginning of a tumultuous period for Cambodia. The aftermath witnessed the nation descending into a state of protracted civil unrest. In the wake of the Khmer Rouge's ousting, Cambodia found itself grappling not just with political instability but also the immense task of reconstructing a shattered society scarred by the ghastly and tragic past.

The dark years under the Khmer Rouge's radical communist rule left an indelible mark on Cambodia's collective psyche, casting a shadow that continues to loom over the nation. The legacy of devastation and despair wrought by this era persists as a haunting reminder of the unparalleled human suffering and egregious violations endured by the Cambodian people. The wounds inflicted upon the social fabric of the nation continue to resonate, serving as a poignant testament to the enduring resilience and perseverance of its people in the face of unimaginable adversity.

The catastrophic consequences of unchecked radical ideologies, vividly exemplified by the Khmer Rouge's reign of terror, stand as a chilling cautionary tale. This period remains a stark reminder of the perilous depths to which unrestrained power can plunge a society, offering a grim reflection on the vulnerabilities of the human spirit when subjected to unbridled tyranny.

Amidst the arduous journey of rebuilding and healing, Cambodia endeavors to reclaim its narrative from the horrors of its past. The scars left behind serve not only as painful reminders but as marks of resilience, embodying the nation's determination to forge ahead and build a future that stands in stark contrast to the darkness it once endured.

Today, Cambodia maintains its status as a one-party state, firmly held under the sway of the Cambodian People's Party (CPP), wielding substantial control that permeates the nation's political terrain. The lingering shadow of communism continues to cast its influence, shaping the intricate fabric of Cambodia's political and social spheres. However, the legacy of this ideological stronghold manifests in a dichotomy, perpetuating a complex landscape where issues pertaining to human rights and political liberties persist as critical points of concern.

The dominance of the Cambodian People's Party (CPP) underscores the enduring legacy of its historical roots, steeped in the principles of communism. This party's stronghold on the political apparatus retains significant control over governance, fostering an environment where dissenting voices face hurdles in expressing opposition or advocating for alternative ideologies.

Despite Cambodia's strides toward economic development and modernization, concerns surrounding human rights and political freedoms persist. The suppression of dissent and limitations on fundamental rights continue as disconcerting realities within the country. Instances of censorship, restrictions on the media, and the silencing of opposition voices exemplify the challenges faced by those seeking to exercise their rights in this political landscape.

Communism's lingering legacy looms ominously over Cambodia's political and social landscape, perpetuating a precarious balance between advancement and the perpetuation of oppressive centralized control. The nation's future direction remains entangled in a web of woes, where confronting these enduring problems becomes imperative to overcome authoritarian rule and protect basic human liberties. As Cambodia treads its uncertain path ahead, the formidable obstacle lies in reconciling the remnants of its communist past with the yearnings for a society that upholds inclusivity and prioritizes individual rights.

East Germany

The German Democratic Republic (GDR) was an era fraught with oppressive measures, characterized by the imposition of pervasive surveillance and stringent control mechanisms that stifled the freedoms of its populace. Under the guise of socialist ideals, the Socialist Unity Party of Germany (SED) established the GDR in 1949, purportedly striving to forge a utopian socialist society rooted in communist principles. However, the reality starkly deviated from the envisioned ideals, plunging the nation into the clutches of an authoritarian regime that manipulated power to suppress dissent and trample on basic human rights.

The GDR operated under a centrally planned economy that, in its initial stages, exhibited signs of growth. However, as time wore on, this economic model unraveled, plagued by inefficiencies, a dearth of innovation, and a labyrinth of bureaucratic hurdles. The ostensibly planned system, which aimed to steer the nation toward prosperity, eventually stumbled under the weight of its own limitations. The stifling bureaucracy blocked entrepreneurial spirit, hampering adaptability and impeding the economy's ability to evolve and compete on a global scale.

The promise of a socialist utopia in the GDR quickly devolved into a suffocating environment where citizens endured constant monitoring, restrictions on movement, and severe limitations on free expression. The regime ruled with an iron fist, wielding absolute control over all facets of life and using surveillance as a tool to suppress any form of political opposition. Dissidents and those expressing contrary views were met with relentless harassment, intimidation, and imprisonment, perpetuating an atmosphere of fear.

Far from embodying the ideals of equality and freedom envisioned by communism, the GDR epitomized a stark reality—a regime that wielded unchecked power to quash individual liberties and maintain its stranglehold on authority. The Socialist Unity Party's monopolistic control extended beyond governance; it entrenched itself as a suppressive force, exploiting communist principles to justify its tyrannical rule and perpetuate a system that prioritized control over the fundamental rights and freedoms of its citizens.

During the GDR, the Ministry for State Security, infamous as the Stasi, wielded a pervasive and menacing presence, resulting in the severe restriction of individual liberties for citizens. Core freedoms, including the rights to speech, press, and assembly, were systematically undermined under the unrelenting gaze of this oppressive apparatus. The Stasi's sprawling network of surveillance and intimidation operated as a suffocating shroud, encumbering the populace's ability to express dissenting opinions or organize against the regime.

The GDR's media landscape bore the unmistakable imprints of the Stasi's omnipresence, becoming a tool manipulated to perpetuate the government's narrative while silencing dissenting voices. Information flowed under tight control, meticulously curated to align with the regime's prescribed ideology. Access to independent sources of information was severely restricted, leaving the populace starved of alternative viewpoints or critical perspectives. The Stasi's stranglehold on media and information created a formidable barrier, curtailing the citizens' right to access diverse and uncensored sources of news and opinions.

The Stasi's encroachment on personal freedoms was not merely a suppression of individual liberties; it was a calculated effort to stifle any semblance of free thought and independent expression. This pervasive surveillance state did not just restrict actions but instilled a chilling atmosphere of self-censorship, where citizens lived under constant threat of reprisal for any divergence from the prescribed narrative. The Stasi's overbearing presence corroded the very foundations of democratic principles, perpetuating a society where the notion of free speech and access to unfiltered information remained a distant dream for the oppressed populace.

Within the GDR, intellectuals, artists, and writers who dared to challenge the regime's narrative were met with harsh censorship or compelled into self-censorship to evade persecution. The stifling grip of the regime's oppressive policies extended beyond overt suppression, seeping into the psyche of the intelligentsia, suffocating their ability to freely express thoughts or ideas that deviated from the state-sanctioned ideology.

The specter of censorship loomed ominously over the intellectual landscape, coercing many creative minds into a chilling silence. Those brave enough to confront the status quo risked facing the wrath of a regime intolerant of dissent. Their works were subjected to relentless scrutiny, often censored or suppressed if they dared to challenge the established norms or expose the regime's failures.

This repressive environment fostered an atmosphere of fear and distrust among citizens, utterly contradicting the GDR's façade of being a "Democratic Republic." The supposed democratic principles were nothing more than a hollow proclamation, undermined by a system that quashed intellectual freedoms and stifled any semblance of open discourse.

The pervasive climate of fear permeated every aspect of creative expression, fracturing the foundation of artistic freedom and intellectual exploration. It was not merely a battle against censorship; it was a psychological struggle against an oppressive regime that sought to muzzle critical thinking and subjugate individual liberties under the guise of a so-called "Democratic Republic."

The construction of the Berlin Wall in 1961 stood as a tangible embodiment of the stark division between the communist Eastern Bloc countries and the capitalist Western nations during the height of the Cold War. More than just a physical barrier, it became an ominous symbol of the ideological chasm that clove Europe. Ostensibly built to deter East Germans from fleeing to the comparatively affluent West Germany, this formidable structure effectively imprisoned citizens within the confines of the GDR.

The consequences of attempting to breach this fortified barrier were severe. Desperate attempts by East Germans to escape were met with draconian penalties, including imprisonment or even death, highlighting the extreme measures undertaken by the regime to enforce its oppressive hold on its populace. The inner German border, transformed into a heavily fortified zone, stood as a grim reminder of the oppressive regime's determination to quell any aspirations for freedom or escape from its citizens.

Communists in East Germany were deeply apprehensive about dissent owing to the inherent threat it posed to their authority. Dissent within a communist regime stood as a challenge to the fundamental tenets of the ruling party's ideology. Given the sanctity attached to communist principles, any questioning of the party's doctrine was perceived as a direct affront to their legitimacy and power.

Moreover, dissent was viewed as a catalyst that could rapidly escalate into widespread social unrest or potential revolution. Historical precedents underscored the potential danger posed by dissent, showcasing how it could quickly transform into movements capable of challenging the very foundations of the ruling party's control. This fear of dissent evolving into a larger, uncontrollable force drove the regime's relentless efforts to suppress any opposing voices.

The purity of communist ideology was paramount to the ruling party. Any deviation from the established party line was considered an insidious threat to the core principles and values espoused by the regime. Dissenters were perceived as a contamination that could undermine the ideological coherence of the communist ideals, potentially eroding the support base crucial for the regime's sustenance.

Control over information and narratives was pivotal for the survival of the communist regime. Dissent challenged the party's monopoly on shaping public opinion and controlling the flow of information. This challenge to the party's narrative threatened the regime's ability to maintain a stranglehold on the dissemination of information, a critical aspect of ensuring compliance and support from the populace.

Additionally, the fear of dissent being influenced by external forces, particularly from the Western world, intensified the regime's fears. Dissenters were often seen as potential collaborators with Western powers, raising concerns about threats to the regime's independence and sovereignty. The regime's stringent measures, including pervasive surveillance, censorship, and harsh repression, were orchestrated to neutralize dissent and fortify the regime's hold on power. Dissent, in the eyes of the communist authorities in East Germany, posed not just a challenge to their authority but a threat to the entire socio-political framework that they had painstakingly constructed.

The Berlin Wall's erection was not merely a physical division; it was a manifestation of an ideological schism that scarred a nation and symbolized the authoritarian oppression inflicted upon those yearning for liberty and a better life beyond the confines of the GDR.

The monumental event of the Berlin Wall's fall on November 9, 1989 heralded the dawn of an era signaling the demise of communism in East Germany. The resounding echoes of mass protests reverberated across the country, fueled by fervent demands for political reforms that reverberated far beyond the confines of Berlin. These demonstrations were not merely calls for change; they were seismic waves of discontent that undermined the foundations of the Socialist Unity Party (SED) government.

The relentless pressure from the populace, amplified by mounting dissent and a fervent desire for freedom, gradually eroded the SED government's grip on power. These protests crescendoed into a political upheaval that ultimately proved insurmountable for the regime. The collapse of the SED government marked a seismic shift in the course of history, paving the way for a new chapter in the annals of Germany.

The domino effect of these revolutionary movements cascaded swiftly, culminating in the reunification of Germany in 1990. This historic milestone was not just the stitching together of a divided nation; it represented the triumph of the collective will of the people, who yearned for liberty and unity. The reunification was a reclamation of shared identity and an affirmation of the enduring spirit of a nation no longer bound by the shackles of division.

Romania

During Nicolae Ceaușescu's tenure, Romania descended into a period characterized by a relentless and oppressive regime, marked by pervasive political repression, stringent censorship, and egregious human rights violations.

The origins of communism in Romania trace back to the aftermath of World War II when the reins of power fell into the hands of the Romanian Communist Party, helmed by Gheorghe Gheorghiu-Dej. However, it was under the protracted and authoritarian rule of Nicolae Ceaușescu, spanning from 1965 to 1989, that communism in Romania reached its apex of brutality and oppression.

Ceaușescu's reign was defined by his zealous pursuit to consolidate absolute authority, fashioning a cult of personality around himself that became a hallmark of one of the most draconian dictatorships in Eastern Europe. His regime orchestrated a calculated assault on individual liberties, imposing stringent controls over the media and ruthlessly quashing any hint of political dissent. Policies enacted during his rule severely curtailed freedoms, instilling an atmosphere of fear and suppression that suffocated the populace.

Under Ceaușescu's iron-fisted rule, Romania's Securitate, the notorious secret police, operated an extensive web of informants. This clandestine network ensured that any semblance of opposition or dissent to the regime was swiftly identified and silenced, employing tactics of intimidation, coercion, and imprisonment to eradicate any dissenting voices. The Securitate's omnipresence instilled a terror among the populace, compelling many to censor their thoughts and actions out of fear of reprisal from the state.

Ceaușescu's despotic regime perpetuated a culture of repression, where the mere expression of independent thought or dissenting opinion was met with severe repercussions. The pervasive control exerted by the government stifled free expression and perpetuated an environment of subservience and fear, suppressing any flicker of opposition and perpetuating an era of unrelenting tyranny and oppression in Romania.

During Ceaușescu's tenure, the Romanian government embarked on an ambitious campaign focused on forced industrialization and the consolidation of agricultural lands. Initially, these policies yielded a modicum of economic progress, showcasing short-term signs of growth.

However, the long-term ramifications of these measures were profoundly detrimental, inflicting enduring hardship on the populace and precipitating a series of socio-economic crises that plagued Romania for years.

The push for rapid industrialization and the consolidation of agricultural resources were pivotal components of Ceaușescu's grand vision for modernizing Romania. This vision, however, was marred by fundamental flaws in execution and planning. The forced industrialization drive aimed to propel Romania into the ranks of industrialized nations, but it came at a tremendous cost, both economically and socially.

While these policies showcased initial signs of success, including spurts of economic growth and limited industrial advancements, their sustainable viability was questionable. The forced collectivization of agriculture, in particular, disrupted the traditional farming practices and upended the agricultural landscape. This upheaval led to a downturn in agricultural productivity, exacerbating food shortages and laying the groundwork for widespread poverty.

The repercussions of these policies were severe and far-reaching. Romania grappled with rampant poverty as the standard of living plummeted for the majority of its citizens. Food shortages became a distressing reality for many, compounding the already challenging economic conditions. The once-promising economic growth sputtered, giving way to a deteriorating quality of life for ordinary Romanians, further aggravated by a shrinking access to basic necessities.

Ceaușescu's ambitious industrial and agricultural policies, while initially showcasing glimpses of progress, ultimately resulted in a stark decline in the overall standard of living for the populace. The short-term gains failed to offset the long-term consequences, leaving a legacy of economic distress, widespread poverty, and social hardships that continued to afflict Romania for years beyond his rule.

Within Ceaușescu's regime, flagrant human rights abuses marred the fabric of Romanian society, constituting one of the most reprehensible facets of his rule. The regime's iron grip on power translated into egregious violations against political opponents and dissenting voices, perpetuating a climate of fear and repression that cast a dark shadow over Romania.

Individuals who dared to voice dissent or challenge the regime's authority were ruthlessly targeted. Arbitrary arrests became commonplace, with dissidents subjected to harrowing ordeals that included torture, unjust imprisonment, and various forms of physical and psychological abuse. Ceaușescu's government displayed an utter disregard for the most basic human rights, employing a brutal crackdown on any perceived opposition.

The regime's ruthlessness extended to extreme measures, including extrajudicial executions, where numerous individuals were executed merely for expressing dissent or attempting to flee the country in pursuit of freedom. The callous disregard for human life underscored the regime's determination to squelch any form of opposition, employing terror tactics to intimidate and silence dissenting voices.

Ceaușescu, despite presiding over an oppressive regime, meticulously crafted an image of Romania as a purportedly successful and independent socialist state. His staunch refusal to seek financial aid or loans from Western countries was a cornerstone of this narrative. Additionally, he prioritized the repayment of Romania's foreign debt, projecting an image of financial self-sufficiency and determination, even if it came at the expense of the citizens' well-being.

However, this carefully cultivated façade starkly contrasted with the harsh reality experienced by the Romanian populace. Ceaușescu's dogged determination to repay the nation's foreign debt and assert Romania's independence resulted in dire socio-economic consequences for ordinary citizens. A stringent austerity program was imposed, inflicting severe hardships on the population, including food and fuel shortages, decrepit living conditions, and a crumbling infrastructure.

The relentless hardships faced by the Romanian people under Ceaușescu's communist regime reached a tipping point, sparking a groundswell of discontent and dissatisfaction. The simmering discontent erupted into mass protests that initially occurred in Timișoara in December 1989. These demonstrations swiftly spread across the country, echoing the collective cries for an end to Ceaușescu's authoritarian rule and the regime's oppressive policies.

The government's response to these burgeoning protests was marked by brutal repression, employing the full force of the state apparatus to suppress dissent. However, far from quelling the uprising, the heavy-handed tactics fueled further outrage and intensified the protests. The resilience and determination of the protesters grew as they united in their fervent demand for an end to Ceaușescu's rule and the oppressive communist regime.

The mounting pressure from the relentless protests eventually reached a crescendo, culminating in a pivotal moment in Romanian history. Ceaușescu's grip on power crumbled as the protests escalated and spread throughout the country, leading to his eventual overthrow.

On December 25, 1989, Nicolae Ceaușescu and his wife, Elena, faced a swift and dramatic downfall. They were captured, promptly subjected to a hasty trial, and were executed by a firing squad. The death of the Ceaușescus served as a chilling denouement to their tyrannical rule, symbolizing the abrupt and decisive end of Ceaușescu's despotic regime.

The uprising in December 1989 remains an indelible symbol of the Romanian people's unyielding determination, a pivotal moment that signaled the downfall of Ceaușescu's communist regime and steered the nation toward democracy. This monumental shift not only marked the regime's demise but also heralded the collapse of communism within Romania's borders, initiating an era of profound political metamorphosis and expansive democratization.

Subsequent to the collapse of Nicolae Ceaușescu's regime, Romania started on an arduous path toward embracing the tenets of capitalism and democracy. The nation embarked on a multifaceted journey of comprehensive political and economic reforms, designed to dismantle the centralized, state-controlled economic structure erected under communism.

This transformative journey involved economic restructuring, such as privatizing state-owned enterprises and embracing market liberalization, steering Romania from a planned to a market-oriented economy. Concurrently, political reforms were enacted, introducing multiparty elections, establishing democratic institutions, and nurturing a legal framework conducive to democratic governance.

Yet, this transformation was fraught with challenges. Romania struggled with the complexities of adapting to market forces, addressing socio-economic inequalities, combating corruption, and instituting significant institutional changes. Despite these hurdles, the nation made considerable strides toward a capitalist economy and democratic governance. Its integration into international organizations, notably the European Union in 2007, represented a pivotal milestone, affirming Romania's position within the broader European community.

However, the pall of communism's legacy persists in Romania, echoing through the scars of repression, human rights violations, and economic hardships. While the nation embarked on a journey of democratic reforms post-Ceaușescu, the shadow of its communist past lingers over its political and social landscape. Ceaușescu's rule fostered a pervasive climate of fear, suffocating free expression and eroding the fundamental rights of the Romanian people. The regime's systematic assault on human rights left an enduring impact, a haunting legacy of brutality and oppression that endured well beyond Ceaușescu's downfall.

Ethiopia

The emergence of communism in Ethiopia took shape in the 1970s, propelled by the ascent of the Derg, a Marxist-Leninist military faction that seized power in 1974 by toppling Emperor Haile Selassie. Spearheaded by Mengistu Haile Mariam, the Derg envisioned reshaping Ethiopia into a socialist state rooted in the principles of communism. During the reign of the Derg military junta, Ethiopia plunged into a harrowing era marred by severe human rights abuses, relentless political purges, and widespread massacres.

Under the iron fist of the Derg's governance, Ethiopia underwent sweeping and radical transformations across its political, economic, and social landscape. The government initiated a wave of nationalizations, taking control of major industries, and executed land reforms aimed at redistributing land to rural farmers, with the goal of eradicating entrenched feudal structures and fostering a more equitable society. Concurrently, efforts were made to institute a centrally planned economy, aiming to diminish reliance on foreign aid and external investments, thereby asserting Ethiopia's autonomy and self-reliance.

Under the constraints of the centrally planned economy, Ethiopia grappled with immense economic challenges, marked by chronic food shortages and widespread hardships for its populace. The mandated collectivization of agriculture encountered vehement opposition from farmers, resulting in diminished agricultural productivity and exacerbating the scarcity of food. This, coupled with mismanagement of resources and pervasive corruption within the government, compounded the nation's economic woes.

The year 1984 marked a tragic chapter in Ethiopia's history as the country confronted a devastating famine that drew global attention and humanitarian efforts. This catastrophic famine, intensified by severe drought and exacerbated by government policies, precipitated a humanitarian crisis, leaving hundreds of thousands of people on the brink of starvation. The plight of the populace reached staggering proportions, sparking international aid initiatives in an attempt to alleviate the harrowing effects of the crisis.

The Derg's implementation of communist policies encountered staunch resistance and internal strife. The era witnessed heightened armed conflicts between the government and various ethnic and regional factions aspiring for self-determination, notably the Eritrean and Tigrayan liberation movements. These confrontations escalated, leading to egregious human rights abuses, including massacres and coercive resettlement initiatives imposed by the government.

Throughout the reign of the Derg, Ethiopia contended with relentless political repression and flagrant human rights violations. The regime aggressively stifled freedoms of speech, press, and assembly, clamping down on dissenting opinions with severe reprisals. In a bid to maintain a firm grip on power, the government resorted to imprisoning or executing thousands of political dissidents, journalists, and intellectuals. This coercive strategy aimed to silence opposition voices, perpetuating an atmosphere of fear and subjugation across the country.

In 1991, the Ethiopian People's Revolutionary Democratic Front (EPRDF) assumed power after a coalition of rebel factions ousted the Derg, signifying a pivotal shift in Ethiopian history. This transition marked a departure from the country's communist past, steering towards a different economic framework. The EPRDF embarked on an economic trajectory emphasizing more market-oriented strategies, aiming to revamp Ethiopia's economic landscape while upholding a notable presence in the political sphere.

Following the Derg regime's overthrow, Ethiopia initiated a shift from its communist roots toward a more market-driven economy under the EPRDF's leadership. This transition involved implementing economic reforms geared towards liberalizing certain sectors, encouraging private investments, and fostering market-based strategies. These changes introduced elements of a market economy, yet Ethiopia did not adopt a purely capitalist system. The government retained significant involvement in shaping economic policies and retained ownership over key industries and sectors. Consequently, Ethiopia's economic structure blended aspects of market-driven approaches with elements of state control, reflecting a hybrid economic model.

The lasting impact of communism remains a significant obstacle for Ethiopia's economic advancement and political equilibrium. The legacy of the Derg regime, marked by a history replete with human rights violations, economic mismanagement, and extensive political oppression, significantly shapes Ethiopia's present-day political and social framework. The enduring repercussions of this tumultuous era persist as a formidable challenge, necessitating extensive efforts to surmount the ramifications of past abuses and systemic mismanagement, and chart a course for Ethiopia's development.

Venezuela

Venezuela stands as the latest example of a nation that endeavored to forge a socialist utopia, only to experience a profound collapse. Helmed by Hugo Chávez and later succeeded by Nicolás Maduro, Venezuela embarked on a path of socialist policies, which, instead of prosperity, precipitated a tumultuous series of events. The country witnessed a steady erosion of its democratic institutions, coupled with rampant economic mismanagement, plunging the nation into social unrest, widespread human rights abuses, and pervasive corruption. These adversities collectively marked a catastrophic turn from the initial aspirations of a utopian vision to the harsh reality of a nation in profound distress.

Not long ago, Venezuela basked in its abundant oil reserves and resources, enjoying a period of prosperity and a notably high standard of living. However, the country's trajectory took a drastic nosedive, plunging its citizens into a grim reality of dire scarcities in essential resources such as food and medicine, rampant corruption, and an omnipresent climate of fear. The implementation of socialist policies by the Venezuelan government became a harbinger of severe economic mismanagement, triggering a chain of disastrous consequences. The nationalization of industries, imposition of price controls, and excessive government intervention shackled productivity and deterred investment, heralding an era of profound economic crisis. Over-reliance on oil exports rendered the economy highly vulnerable to global oil price fluctuations, culminating in hyperinflation, acute shortages of vital goods, and a staggering decline in living standards. The once-thriving oil sector now lies in ruins, while President Maduro's introduction of the "petro" currency remains overshadowed by the rapid deterioration of Venezuela's oil industry.

The profound economic crisis and societal breakdown in Venezuela have endured for more than a decade, beginning around the mid-2000s and persisting to the present day. The severe disintegration and widespread famine, including acute shortages of food and medicine, hyperinflation, and a significant decline in living conditions, became pronounced in the latter part of the 2010s and extended into the 2020s. This period revealed a gradual but distressing deterioration over time.

The severe starvation crisis gripping Venezuela is a result of a multifaceted interplay of factors intricately tied to the government's implementation of socialist policies. These policies, adopted under President Nicolás Maduro's regime, have significantly contributed to a dire humanitarian crisis characterized by acute food shortages and widespread hunger. This crisis stems from a combination of economic mismanagement, corruption, and an extensively controlled state-run economy. The repercussions have led to a grim reality where a considerable number of Venezuelans struggle to access fundamental necessities, notably food.

Central to the issue is the government's overbearing control over the economy, resulting in inefficiencies across production, distribution, and supply chains. Price controls and interventions in industries have discouraged private investment and production, causing a decline in agricultural output and reliance on food imports. This dwindling production, coupled with hyperinflation, has rendered essential goods, especially food, increasingly unaffordable for the populace.

Furthermore, the expropriation of private farms and agricultural businesses, often without adequate compensation, has severely disrupted the agricultural sector. Consequently, there has been a notable decline in domestic food production, exacerbating dependence on food imports. However, economic mismanagement, currency devaluation, and international sanctions have significantly hampered the country's ability to secure sufficient food imports.

The crisis has been further compounded by inefficient distribution networks. The government's oversight of imports and distribution has fostered corruption, favoritism, and a lack of transparency in allocating food resources. This uneven distribution has led to unequal access to food, with those connected to the government receiving preferential treatment, while ordinary citizens grapple with severe shortages of basic necessities.

The profound economic crisis in Venezuela has triggered a mass departure of skilled professionals, including farmers, seeking more promising prospects abroad. This substantial emigration, often referred to as a "brain drain," has notably impacted agricultural productivity, aggravating the already dire food shortages gripping the nation.

The departure of skilled farmers and agricultural workers, among other professionals, has significantly depleted the labor force crucial for sustaining agricultural output. These individuals possessed expertise vital for maintaining and enhancing agricultural productivity. Their absence from the workforce has led to a depletion of knowledge, skills, and experience in the agricultural sector, contributing to a decline in overall output.

The consequential reduction in agricultural productivity, compounded by other factors such as government policies, disruptions in the farming community, and resource shortages, has exacerbated the severe scarcity of food. The absence of skilled professionals within the agricultural sphere has hindered innovation, technological advancement, and efficient farming practices, further intensifying the challenges faced by the agricultural sector and deepening the country's food crisis.

Communism's influence in Venezuela has significantly corroded the bedrock of democratic principles and institutions. The government's consolidation of power has systematically sidelined political opposition, undermining the checks and balances essential for a robust democratic system. Elections, once a beacon of democracy, have been marred by accusations of fraud and irregularities, casting doubt on the credibility of the electoral process and the government's legitimacy.

Corruption has been pervasive within the communist regime, fostering a climate of embezzlement, nepotism, and the misallocation of public funds. These rampant misappropriations of state resources have worsened the economic crisis, exacerbating the struggles of ordinary Venezuelans by impeding the delivery of essential services. The widespread corruption not only undermines public confidence in the government but also amplifies the myriad challenges confronting the Venezuelan population, further compounding their hardships.

The impact of the socialist regime in Venezuela has been marked by a concerning suppression of free speech and religious freedom. Through a series of measures, the government has striven to control information and silence dissenting voices. Strict regulations on media, censorship, and targeted harassment of critical journalists and media outlets are employed to control the narrative and suppress viewpoints conflicting with official stances. Independent media entities have been forced to shut down, while journalists face threats, intimidation, and imprisonment.

Additionally, the regime has exerted control over the internet and social media, restricting access to platforms critical of the government. Online dissenters and activists expressing alternative views have encountered persecution, creating an environment that stifles free expression in the digital realm.

Religious communities in Venezuela have faced challenges under this regime. Despite constitutional guarantees of religious freedom, instances of government interference and limitations on religious activities have arisen, especially when religious figures or institutions critique governmental policies or advocate for political change. Religious groups viewed as opposing the government have encountered bias and mistreatment. The government's influence has led to the manipulation of religious institutions and leaders, causing polarization and politicization within these communities. Moreover, cases have emerged where religious figures and practitioners expressing views contrary to the regime's ideology have been targeted. Certain religious groups have faced allegations of involvement in activities labeled subversive, leading to increased surveillance and scrutiny.

This suppression of free speech and religious liberties has cast a pall over civil society, dampening open discourse and dissent. These actions have triggered concerns among human rights organizations and the international community about the erosion of democratic principles and the violation of fundamental rights within Venezuela.

Under President Nicolás Maduro Moros' socialist administration in Venezuela, a distressing pattern of human rights violations and the suppression of political dissent has been pervasive. Amnesty International has documented these abuses, shedding light on unjust trials and the arbitrary detention of political activists, journalists, and healthcare workers. With President Maduro's explicit support, the military has resorted to draconian measures to suppress opposition voices, severely restricting freedom of expression, assembly, and of the press. Journalists, activists, and opposition figures have faced harassment, incarceration, and censorship. Numerous international human rights bodies have raised alarms about extrajudicial killings, instances of torture, and arbitrary arrests, often traced back to the country's security forces. These reprehensible actions have led to a concerning erosion of democratic values and the protection of basic rights and freedoms in the nation.

Venezuela's painful experience with socialism stands as a cautionary tale, starkly portraying the immense obstacles the nation faces in forging a sustainable path toward economic stability, political freedom, and societal well-being. The aftermath of communism in Venezuela serves as a stark warning, underscoring the profound dangers and complexities entangled in radical ideological experiments, accentuating the critical need to avoid extremist measures.

Amid the country's ongoing upheaval and its search for a viable direction, the lessons learned from its bout with communism will help shape its future trajectory.

In this chapter, historical examples have shed light on the unfavorable outcomes often associated with socialism and communism—namely, impoverishment, oppression, and the concentration of wealth among ruling elites. By delving into real-world instances from countries such as Venezuela, the USSR, China, and Cuba, we witnessed how these ideologies led to repressive regimes and the suppression of basic human rights.

In nations that embrace Marxist ideologies, a consistent pattern emerges—a sequence of economic hardships, famine, and systematic violation of human rights. While Marxism espouses equality and social justice in theory, its application consistently leads to dire economic consequences. The establishment of state-controlled economies tends to breed inefficiencies, stifle innovation, and provoke a decline in productivity. This mismanagement triggers scarcities, food shortages, and, in extreme cases, famines due to disruptions in supply chains and agriculture.

Moreover, Marxist regimes have a historical track record of suppressing fundamental human rights. Centralizing power within the state constrains individual freedoms, silences dissenting voices, and undermines democratic institutions. Political opposition is routinely quashed, resulting in censorship, imprisonment, and persecution of journalists, activists, and intellectuals challenging the ruling regime.

Countries adhering to Marxist principles have often experienced recurring cycles of economic stagnation, food crises, and severe constraints on civil liberties. The emphasis on centralized control often sidelines the importance of a free-market economy, individual liberties, and the innovation necessary for societal advancement. The detrimental impact of communist ideologies on both the economy and human rights underscores a concerning trend seen throughout history.

The history of socialism serves as a stark reminder of the perils of radical ideological experiments, showcasing the potential for severe human rights abuses, starvation, and loss of life when taken to extremes. This ideology, with its aspirations for global revolution and tyrannical governance, has been linked to oppressive regimes, economic stagnation, and the curtailment of individual freedoms, posing a significant threat to fundamental principles of freedom, prosperity, and human dignity in various societies.

Throughout history, a consistent pattern emerges in communist countries where individuals seek to escape to capitalist nations rather than the reverse. This phenomenon is rooted in the stark differences between the socio-economic and political systems of communism and capitalism.

In communist regimes, people often endeavor to flee to capitalist countries due to a myriad of reasons. Firstly, economic factors play a significant role. Communist systems have historically struggled with economic stagnation, scarcity of goods, and limited opportunities. Citizens may seek better economic prospects, higher living standards, and more opportunities for personal and professional growth in capitalist societies, where free-market economies foster innovation, job creation, and higher standards of living.

Secondly, political oppression and restricted freedoms in communist states drive individuals to seek refuge in capitalist nations. Communist regimes tend to suppress dissent, curtail civil liberties, and wield tight control over citizens' lives. The lack of political freedom, censorship, and persecution of those opposing the ruling ideology can compel individuals to seek asylum in countries that uphold democratic principles, respect human rights, and provide freedom of speech and religion.

Moreover, the allure of individual liberties and personal autonomy that characterize capitalist societies serves as a powerful motivator for those seeking to escape the constraints of communist rule. Fundamental rights, including freedom of movement, speech, and religion, are often more robust in capitalist nations, attracting individuals seeking to lead lives free from excessive state control.

The pattern of individuals fleeing communist countries for capitalist ones underscores the inherent differences in socio-economic structures, governance, and the quality of life between these two ideological systems. The pursuit of economic prosperity, personal freedom, and a better quality of life often drives individuals to seek refuge in countries that embrace capitalism's principles of free markets, individual rights, and democratic governance.

The examination of historical cases in this chapter aimed to provide insights into the potential impacts of such ideologies on a nation's socio-economic fabric. The legacy of communism serves as a poignant warning against substituting communism for capitalism.

The next chapter examines Marxist strategies of demoralization, infiltration, and subversion as potent tools used to undermine capitalist societies from within, ultimately aiming to pave the way for socialist ideologies. It delves into their profound impacts on societal structures and democratic principles, specifically focusing on their implications for the United States.

Chapter 3

Ideological Subversion

In this chapter, we confront the looming threat posed by the communist movement to the United States, uncovering its detrimental impact on the nation's core principles and social fabric. Rooted in socialist ideology, which centers on concepts such as economic control, wealth redistribution, and opposition to free-market capitalism, this movement directly challenges the bedrock values that have long defined the nation's identity. Our exploration navigates the ongoing ideological conflict between Marxism and the Western world, particularly focusing on its cultural dimensions. We delve into the profound influence of communist movements during pivotal junctures in American history, such as the impactful 1960s Cultural Revolution, dissecting its lasting effects.

This analysis delves into the infiltration of Marxist ideologies within American institutions, exposing the tactics employed to subvert traditional values, enforce ideological conformity, and manipulate public discourse. Scrutinizing the concepts of Cultural Marxism and the Frankfurt School, we unravel their roles in fostering societal fragmentation and eroding vital elements such as the family and religious institutions. Moreover, our examination looks into the encroachment of communism into crucial areas such as education, media, and politics, highlighting the imminent threat it poses to fundamental American values.

Through insights into the methods employed by communist movements to incite revolutions, we emphasize the critical need for vigilance in safeguarding democratic values and protecting individual rights. This chapter underscores the importance of understanding communist strategies to comprehend the potential consequences should these ideologies gain more ground in the US. By shedding light on covert tactics and their implications, it opens a pathway for discussions, critical thinking, and a comprehensive grasp of potential societal transformations. Moreover, by raising awareness, this chapter aims to empower readers to identify key indicators, engage in informed discussions, and ultimately safeguard American liberty and prosperity.

The United States boasts a rich heritage deeply rooted in the preservation of freedom, democracy, and individual rights—an ethos woven into its founding principles. American culture thrives on the tenets of capitalism and individualism, cherishing personal liberty, entrepreneurial spirit, and minimal government interference. These deeply entrenched values naturally serve as impediments to the widespread acceptance of Marxist ideologies.

At the heart of the nation's governance lies a robust democratic system, meticulously crafted to embody essential principles of checks and balances, citizen engagement, representation, and the safeguarding of individual liberties. This system's inherent strength poses considerable barriers to the proliferation of Marxist ideals. The intricate web of checks and balances ingrained within the government serves as a formidable defense against potential threats to democracy, ensuring power remains vested in the hands of the populace. This robust framework not only fortifies the nation's resilience, but also empowers the government to address emerging challenges while remaining responsive to the needs and aspirations of its citizens.

The bedrock of the United States' resilience against subversive threats lies in its foundational document, the U.S. Constitution, and the robust institutions it established. Crucially, the Constitution safeguards essential freedoms such as free speech, assembly, and of the press, fostering an environment for the open exchange of ideas. These protections form a bulwark against the encroachment of ideologies seeking to undermine the democratic fabric.

Central to the Constitution's design is the separation of powers, a critical defense mechanism against the influences of ideologies such as communism and the dangers of unrestrained authority. This principle of separation of powers allocates distinct roles and authorities to each branch of government—executive, legislative, and judicial— ensuring a system of checks and balances. This framework serves multiple purposes, ensuring transparency in governance, holding authorities accountable, and, significantly, preventing the concentration of excessive power in any single branch.

Moreover, the concept of federalism, enshrined within the Constitution, delineates authority between the national and state governments. By dispersing power across multiple levels of governance, federalism prevents the centralization of authority, fostering a diverse governance landscape rooted in democratic principles. This decentralized approach not only upholds local autonomy but also provides a safeguard against the consolidation of power that could potentially threaten the democratic foundation of the nation.

The Bill of Rights, an integral component of the U.S. Constitution, stands as a cornerstone of American society, embodying the nation's commitment to individual liberties and justice. Drafted by James Madison and formally ratified in 1791, these first ten amendments delineate and defend specific rights and protections afforded to every American citizen.

The Bill of Rights serves as a potent shield against encroachments on personal freedoms, government overreach, and as a sturdy barrier against tyrannical tendencies. It stands as a testament to the nation's dedication to preserving freedom and preventing any erosion of democratic principles by oppressive regimes.

At its core, the Bill of Rights is designed to safeguard individual liberties while imposing constraints on federal government authority. It guarantees essential rights such as the freedom of speech, religion, the right to bear arms, protection against unlawful searches and seizures, the right to a fair and speedy trial, and safeguarding against cruel and unusual punishment. These rights are intrinsic to the very essence of democratic principles, constituting the bedrock upon which American civil liberties are built.

For instance, the First Amendment, a pillar of the Bill of Rights, guarantees the freedom of speech, press, assembly, and religion. This crucial freedom enables open discourse, facilitates the questioning of ideologies, and serves as a potent tool against censorship, countering the pervasive influence of communist ideologies while steadfastly upholding democratic principles.

Preserving the freedom of speech is paramount for nurturing diverse perspectives, fostering intellectual growth, and promoting informed discussions. However, the delicate balance between this freedom and public safety presents a complex challenge. While this freedom encourages robust debates and dissent, it can also be exploited to facilitate subversion of established norms—a subject that will be discussed later in this chapter.

The Second Amendment safeguards the right to keep and bear arms, serving as a defense against potential government tyranny and authoritarian control.

The Fourth Amendment protects against unreasonable searches and seizures, preserving individual privacy and limiting the state's ability to conduct surveillance on citizens.

The Fifth Amendment guarantees the right to due process of law, protecting against arbitrary detention or punishment without a fair legal process, preventing double jeopardy, and safeguarding individuals from political persecution or unjust treatment.

The Sixth Amendment ensures the right to a speedy trial by an impartial jury, protecting against unfair trials and ensuring justice is served fairly.

The Eighth Amendment prohibits cruel and unusual punishment, safeguarding individuals from torture or excessive penalties commonly used in communist regimes to suppress opposition.

The Tenth Amendment asserts that powers not expressly granted to the federal government or prohibited to the states by the Constitution are reserved for the states or the people, serving as a safeguard to maintain balance between federal authority and state autonomy within the constitutional framework. By establishing limits on federal power, it prevents the government from overreach and maintains this balance, acting as a crucial defense against authoritarianism on a national scale.

The historical opposition of the United States to communism is deeply rooted in fundamental ideological disparities and concerns centered around the protection of individual freedoms. This longstanding conflict emerges from the stark clash between the principles of individualism and collectivism, representing a profound divergence in societal beliefs. At its core, this ideological confrontation is grounded in the intrinsic values that have shaped the American identity: a staunch adherence to capitalism, a commitment to democratic governance, and an unwavering emphasis on individual autonomy and liberty.

The divergence between the American ethos and Marxism lies in their contrasting visions for societal organization. The U.S. champions a capitalist system that celebrates free-market dynamics, entrepreneurial spirit, and individual initiative. This system fosters competition, rewards innovation, and champions personal success while encouraging diverse viewpoints and fostering a culture of self-reliance and freedom.

Conversely, communism, as an ideology, espouses collective ownership, equal distribution of resources, and centralized control over the means of production. It prioritizes the collective good over individual achievement, aiming to create a classless society devoid of private property. However, in practice, this centralized control often leads to limitations on personal freedoms, stifled innovation, and a curtailment of individual autonomy.

Capitalism and communism stand in stark opposition, reflecting fundamentally divergent principles in their approach to economic and social organization. Capitalism, with its cornerstone elements of individual ownership, free markets, and private enterprise, contrasts sharply with communism's focus on collective ownership and centralized planning. The principles of capitalism champion individual ambition and incentivize innovation, nurturing entrepreneurial endeavors and driving societal progress. In contrast, communism prioritizes the common good through centralized decision-making and collective ownership, aiming for an egalitarian society.

Capitalism's emphasis on private property acts as a catalyst for innovation, fostering a competitive environment that stimulates creativity and productivity. In contrast, communism's collective ownership structures often encounter challenges in incentivizing individual initiative, potentially leading to inefficiencies inherent in centralized planning and distribution.

The United States' commitment to democratic principles and the protection of personal freedoms stands in direct contrast to communism's historical tendencies toward repression and authoritarianism. This commitment forms the ideological bedrock of the nation's opposition to socialsim. The U.S. prioritizes the protection of individual rights, free speech, and democratic governance, all of which stand as fundamental counterpoints to the centralized control and limited freedoms often associated with communist regimes. This steadfast commitment to democratic ideals underscores the stark contrast between the two ideologies and forms the basis of the historical opposition between the United States and Marxism.

The clash between these ideologies is emblematic of a broader global struggle, echoing the tension between collective welfare and individual liberty. The United States, as a bastion of democratic principles and individual rights, has historically stood against communism, viewing it as a threat to the cherished values that underpin the nation's identity and way of life. This opposition is not merely a political stance but a reflection of the deeply ingrained values that define the American ethos.

Following World War II, the world plunged into the Cold War, pitting the Western capitalist bloc, spearheaded by the United States, against the Eastern communist bloc, led by the Soviet Union. This tense era was marked by conflicts, proxy wars, and the dangerous escalation of nuclear tensions, as the US advocated for democracy and capitalism while the Soviet Union championed communism.

The intensification of hostilities during the Cold War witnessed a fierce rivalry between the United States and the USSR. In 1956, Soviet leader Nikita Khrushchev made a bold declaration, expressing his firm belief in the eventual triumph of communism over capitalism. While often remembered for the phrase "We will bury you," the Russian wording he used, "Мы вас похороним!" ("My vas pokhoronim!"), translates more accurately as "We will outlive you." Khrushchev's words were widely interpreted as a veiled threat to America and its way of life, sparking concerns about potential communist infiltration and subversion within American society and institutions. These words stoked fears and contributed to a climate of suspicion and vigilance against perceived communist threats.

Communists perceive the capitalist-democratic system as perpetuating inequalities and oppression. Their objective involves dismantling capitalist structures through political activism. Socialists employ subversive methods to challenge the capitalist-democratic system in the U.S., seeking to destabilize democratic institutions and diminish public confidence in democratic processes. Their ultimate goal is to dismantle traditional Western values and systems through radical social and economic reforms, not just limited to the West, but aspiring to establish alternative systems worldwide.

The process of a communist revolution encompasses a spectrum of strategies spanning ideological, social, and political realms. Tactics include infiltrating institutions, propagating alternative ideologies, and inciting social unrest when conventional methods face resistance within existing systems. For instance, American workers resist communism due to the tangible benefits provided by capitalism, such as financial stability, technological opportunities, job markets, private property ownership, autonomy, and entrepreneurial success.

Marxists engage in Fourth Generation Warfare (4GW), a disruptive form that blurs the line between state and non-state actors, merging military and political objectives. This approach extends beyond military victory, employing unconventional tactics, information warfare, propaganda, and psychological operations. Central to 4GW are decentralization, ideological and cultural aspects, mass mobilization, and infiltrating institutions to effect change internally. Its primary goal is to instill a sense of futility within the target population through psychological and ideological means.

Ideological subversion is a systematic strategy aimed at undermining a society from within. This tactic gradually erodes the foundations of a society to create conditions conducive to a communist revolution. It involves a deliberate effort by one faction to undermine the societal, cultural, and political frameworks of a country by influencing its ideological values and beliefs. In the context of communism versus capitalism, ideological subversion involves skillfully manipulating the perceptions, attitudes, and behaviors of capitalist adversaries, as seen in the United States, to align with communist objectives.

Marxist groups often uphold free speech as a means to challenge existing power structures when they lack control, emphasizing its role in amplifying marginalized voices and fostering discourse aimed at achieving equality. However, a noticeable change occurs once these groups attain power. Their focus shifts toward stifling dissent, aiming to consolidate authority, suppress anti-revolutionary sentiments, and fortify their ideological dominance. This shift—from promoting free speech to curbing it—highlights their lack of commitment to democratic principles and individual liberties once they assume control. It underscores the opportunistic nature of their approach, utilizing free speech as a tool for advancement while undermining it once in positions of authority.

Yuri Bezmenov, a former KGB agent turned defector, exposed the strategies of ideological subversion orchestrated by the Soviet Union during the height of the Cold War. Working as a propagandist for the Novosti [News] Press Agency, he was involved in deploying disinformation and manipulation tactics to undermine foreign nations, advancing Soviet interests. Following his defection and resettlement in Canada, Bezmenov advocated vigilance against subversive activities, using his writings and lectures to shed light on the critical nature of this ideological threat.

His revelations peeled back the layers of covert and protracted ideological subversion, which aimed to corrode target societies from within by exploiting divisions and molding public sentiment. Bezmenov's warnings resounded, emphasizing the paramount importance of protecting democratic values and institutions. He urged societies to exercise discernment in evaluating information and fortifying themselves against manipulative tactics. His insights stand as a timeless testament to the calculated techniques used by formidable adversaries to subvert and weaken targeted nations.

Bezmenov notably delineated four methodical stages employed by the Soviets to weaken adversaries systematically: demoralization, destabilization, crisis, and normalization. Each stage represented a strategic blueprint for gradually eroding societal values and stability, setting the groundwork for radical transformation. His delineation of these stages provided a framework to comprehend the subtle yet profound progression employed to undermine targeted societies.

The process of ideological subversion follows a strategic sequence of stages, each designed to weaken the foundations of a targeted society. The initial phase, known as demoralization, strategically spotlights the shortcomings and vulnerabilities within the existing capitalist system. This phase operates as a calculated strategy aiming to sow seeds of doubt and disillusionment among the populace. Its primary objective is to weaken the psychological and ethical bedrock of the society, subtly nudging the public toward ideologies influenced by Marxism.

Demoralization aims to gradually erode a nation's core values and ethical foundations. Through tactics such as propaganda, subversive agents challenge fundamental principles such as individual rights and liberty, fostering discontent and nudging public sentiment toward alternative ideologies promising societal revolution.

In tandem with this psychological campaign, communists strategically target essential societal institutions such as family, religion, and cultural norms. Their fervent advocacy for radical social policies directly challenges traditional values, sparking cultural upheaval and unsettling the prevailing status quo. This calculated approach aims to disrupt and undermine the established societal framework, paving the way for ideological change.

The subsequent phase, known as destabilization, marks a deliberate exploitation of existing divisions, societal tensions, and economic disparities by communist forces. This stage involves actively promoting radical movements and intensifying societal conflicts to amplify chaos and undermine the stability of the established order. Its primary aim is to create an environment of unrest and uncertainty, shaking the public's confidence in their societal structures.

During the destabilization phase of ideological subversion, antagonistic actors intentionally induce disorder within the targeted society. Their goal is to erode institutions, sow discord, and exploit vulnerabilities, thereby fostering an atmosphere conducive to radical transformation. This strategy often manifests through activities conducted by groups such as Antifa and Black Lives Matter, where protests escalate into violence, exacerbating social turbulence and polarization. By leveraging legitimate grievances, these subversive elements incite chaos, weaken societal bonds, diminish institutional trust, and deepen societal divides, ultimately fostering discontentment with the existing order. Destabilization strategies encompass a range of tactics, including economic disruptions, political maneuvering, and the exacerbation of social conflicts, all aimed at escalating tensions and undermining the foundations of stability.

As prevailing systems falter under the weight of instability, crises inevitably arise, presenting communists with a strategic opportunity. They capitalize on these crises, positioning their ideologies as solutions to the perceived shortcomings of the existing system, effectively advocating for radical change. This phase becomes pivotal in framing their ideologies as credible alternatives and gaining traction among disillusioned segments of society.

During the crisis phase of ideological subversion, the system becomes susceptible to internal and external pressures that threaten its stability. These vulnerabilities allow subversive forces to exploit opportunities and advocate for radical change. Factors such as social unrest, ideological shifts, and political dynamics create an environment conducive to the emergence of a revolution, spanning economic, social, and political dimensions. Ongoing discussions about this phase reflect the intensifying polarization in political discourse, marked by competing ideologies and narratives clashing in the public sphere. The ascent of populist and radical movements challenging the traditional political establishment deepens societal divisions, fueling speculation about the possibility of a transformative revolution.

Political dynamics significantly contribute to this phase. Escalating polarization and gridlock within the political system hinder effective governance, eroding public trust in institutions and elected representatives. These conditions provide a window of opportunity for subversive elements to exploit vulnerabilities. Joseph Stalin's assertion, "You cannot make a revolution with silk gloves," underscores the aggressive nature of communist movements that resort to force and violence to dismantle prevailing social, economic, and political structures.

The final phase of ideological subversion, normalization, signifies communists' concentrated efforts to cement their dominance and institutionalize their ideologies as the new order. They position themselves as saviors capable of guiding society toward their envisioned utopia, reshaping its core values and embedding their influence for the long term.

Post-revolution, the normalization phase initiates substantial transformations across a society's social and economic frameworks. Its primary aim is the dismantling of existing political systems and hierarchies, facilitating the transition toward collective ownership and resource management. Industries and economic activities undergo restructuring to align with the new ideological framework, paving the way for a revamped socio-economic landscape. Yet, normalization is not merely about restructuring; it seeks to instill acceptance and routine, portraying the new government as legitimate. This phase is critical for ensuring stability, with media playing a pivotal role in solidifying the narrative of acceptance.

Central to the normalization phase is the establishment of institutions reflective of Marxist principles, often through social welfare programs ensuring equitable resource distribution. Economic stabilization and reconstruction take precedence to counter potential disruptions post-revolution. The focus lies on revitalizing infrastructure and industries in accordance with communist ideals, consolidating the revolution's transformative impact. This phase navigates the transition from upheaval to stability, embedding socialist ideologies and structures into the fabric of society for lasting influence.

Ideological subversion operates by infiltrating key cultural, educational, and political institutions to shape public opinion and steer societies towards a desired ideology. Communists employ "entryism" to penetrate establishments such as academia, media, and government, aiming to disrupt and overthrow existing governance structures. Through covert orchestration, like-minded individuals are strategically placed in influential positions within these institutions. This clandestine maneuvering subtly influences public discourse, guides policy directions, and manipulates alliances to consolidate power.

In environments dominated by mainstream ideologies, subversion creates alternative platforms for marginalized viewpoints. By doing so, it weakens opposition and allows unconventional ideas to permeate societal values and narratives held by cultural, media, and educational realms.

This method integrates communist ideals into mainstream discourse, spotlighting themes such as class struggle and equity while critiquing capitalist frameworks. Communists exploit existing societal rifts to intensify tensions, amplifying discord and undermining the fabric of society. The objective is to engineer a transformation within societies, gradually paving the way for a successful communist revolution from within.

Growing concerns surrounding deliberate ideological subversion in the United States stem from observed cultural shifts, ideological divides, and societal transformations. Critics highlight the changing values, the rise in secularism, and deepening ideological rifts as indicative of a calculated demoralization strategy. This orchestrated demoralization is viewed as a deliberate attempt to weaken the moral fabric of society by challenging established norms and values, fostering disillusionment, and promoting alternative ideologies.

One notable aspect contributing to these concerns is the erosion of trust in various societal institutions and media outlets. There is a pervasive sense of skepticism and suspicion regarding the accuracy and impartiality of information provided by traditional sources. Universities, in particular, have faced allegations of promoting left-wing ideologies and suppressing dissenting views. These allegations underscore a broader concern about educational institutions becoming breeding grounds for one-sided ideological indoctrination rather than fostering critical thinking and open discourse.

In academia, there is a concerted effort by radicals to infiltrate educational systems, aiming to instill anti-American sentiments and indoctrinate generations with collectivist ideologies. These individuals who are sympathetic to the cause strategically assume roles as professors and researchers, leveraging their positions to integrate Marxist narratives into curricula, fund research aligned with their progressive ideology, and emphasize narratives of capitalist exploitation. They interpret various subjects through the lens of class struggle, all while creating an environment that fosters a receptive audience for Marxist viewpoints among students.

Education becomes a powerful tool for communists to propagate and entrench their radical ideology. They tailor the curriculum to endorse their ideas, incorporating concepts such as class struggle, historical materialism, and the pursuit of a classless society. These notions are presented as frameworks for understanding societal dynamics, historical progression, and the purported path toward a communist utopia. The educational systems are manipulated to ensure ideological conformity, promote unquestioning loyalty to the state, and cultivate future generations committed to embracing socialism.

This infiltration and manipulation of academia represent a troubling trend, exploiting the realm of education to mold young minds and indoctrinate them with ideologies that subvert American values. It is a methodical and calculated strategy aimed at reshaping perceptions, fostering discontent with the existing system, and grooming a generation ideologically aligned with communism.

Marxists place a high priority on targeting children for indoctrination, understanding the profound impact it can have on shaping the future of a society. They recognize that children, with their impressionable minds and limited critical thinking abilities, are highly susceptible to absorbing and internalizing ideological beliefs. This susceptibility becomes a strategic advantage for communists seeking to instill their principles at an early age.

Indoctrinating children serves multiple strategic purposes. Firstly, by introducing communist ideologies to children, it aims to ingrain these concepts into their core perspectives on society, politics, and economics. This early exposure intends to mold their foundational beliefs, making it more likely for them to carry these ideologies into adulthood, influencing the societal landscape as they mature. Secondly, communists view targeting children as an investment in the future, recognizing that influencing young minds can have enduring effects on the direction of a society for generations to come.

The quote often attributed to Adolf Hitler, "He who owns the youth controls the future," encapsulates the profound idea that shaping the beliefs and values of the younger generation significantly impacts the trajectory of a society. It underscores the significance of controlling education, culture, and the narratives young people are exposed to. This control is pivotal as it recognizes the vulnerability of the youth to new ideas and their lack of historical context, making them particularly susceptible to ideological influence and manipulation.

Communists strategically prioritize indoctrinating children to lay a strong foundation for their ideologies, envisioning a lasting influence that extends into adulthood. Their aim is to shape young perspectives early on, ensuring the perpetuation of their vision for societal transformation and securing control over the trajectory of society. This process involves instilling in students a critical view of capitalism, interpreting historical events through a Marxist lens, fostering allegiance to the state, and cultivating empathy toward the struggles of the working class.

The targeting of children by communists serves the purpose of reshaping cultural narratives and molding societal norms to align with their ideological agenda. They understand that modifying cultural beliefs can profoundly impact the collective consciousness of a society. To achieve this, socialists work to undermine traditional family values that might oppose their ideology, recognizing that such values are often instrumental in transmitting intergenerational beliefs. Disrupting this transmission of values is crucial for communists as they endeavor to reshape societal norms and ideologies to reflect their own.

Marxist governments exert tight control over the education sector, employing various methods to shape historical narratives favorably and reinforce the legitimacy of their regime. This manipulation of history serves to create a collective identity centered around communism, instilling a sense of unity and shared purpose among citizens. By crafting the curriculum, these regimes aim to ensure that an active citizenry participates in the state's objectives.

The educational system under communist regimes is carefully structured to propagate and fortify their ideology within society. The curriculum is tailored to align with their principles, molding citizens' beliefs to ensure ideological conformity and perpetuate their rule. Manipulating historical accounts, controlling the curriculum, and suppressing dissenting perspectives are all tactics employed to shape a generation dedicated to communist principles and actively engaged in advancing their envisioned utopia.

Beyond imparting knowledge, communist education aims to nurture a revolutionary spirit and an unwavering commitment to the cause. This comprehensive approach ensures that each aspect of education serves as a vehicle for reinforcing Marxist ideals and securing the continued allegiance of the populace to the cause.

Supporters of cultural Marxism aim to influence societal perspectives by reshaping cultural norms, institutions, and values to align with their preferences. They actively challenge traditional Western values and institutions, prioritizing collective "safety" and "equity" over individual liberties. Their overarching goal is to destabilize established social orders and pave the way for the acceptance of socialist ideals through cultural and societal transformations.

Central to their strategy is the elevation of education as a pivotal tool in challenging prevailing ideologies and fostering leftist academic pursuits. Rooted in Marxist principles, their aim is to confront dominant ideologies, particularly capitalism, significantly impacting fields such as sociology, philosophy, and political science. This strategy is a deliberate attempt to undermine and destabilize cultural values in order to advance the agenda of communism.

Antonio Gramsci played a pivotal role in formulating the concept of cultural Marxism, particularly with his theory of cultural hegemony. His ideas underscored the influence of cultural norms and institutions in perpetuating societal inequalities and forms of oppression, highlighting that societal control goes beyond explicit coercion. According to Gramsci, the dominant group establishes its ideology as the norm through cultural institutions such as education, media, and language. The process involves legitimizing the dominant ideology as "common sense," obtaining consent without overt coercion, and using cultural avenues to reinforce this dominant narrative.

Gramsci differentiated between "traditional" and "organic" intellectuals, the latter challenging the prevailing hegemonic order by presenting alternative perspectives and contesting the existing status quo. His concepts significantly influenced disciplines such as political science, sociology, and cultural studies. The idea of cultural hegemony has been applied extensively to analyze media representations, identity politics, and power dynamics across diverse contexts. It sheds light on how cultural institutions bolster dominant ideologies, shaping public discourse and societal norms.

This understanding has fueled various progressive intellectual movements that challenge established norms and values. These movements aim to promote social justice and equality by effecting cultural and societal changes over time. Gramsci's theories continue to inform critical perspectives that seek to dismantle ingrained power structures and address alleged societal inequalities through cultural transformation.

Strategically embedding themselves within educational institutions provides Marxists a platform to influence the narratives and ideologies imparted to students, effectively disseminating socialist and communist ideals. The Frankfurt School's legacy highlights its emphasis on using education and intellectual influence to upend existing societal structures. Within academic circles, they propagated the idea of education as a tool for confronting established norms, paving the way for the ascent of radical intellectual movements.

Communists use critical theory to pick apart and condemn established social, political, and economic systems, singling out perceived injustices, inequalities, and power imbalances. Operating by undermining cultural narratives, language structures, educational models, and media portrayals, critical theory serves as a tool to spotlight what it deems to be systemic injustices deeply embedded within society. While purporting to advocate for equality and fairness, this approach fundamentally challenges traditional values and institutions, aiming to overhaul societal norms, beliefs, and practices. It often involves discrediting prevailing narratives and identities, amplifying marginalized viewpoints, and advocating for what it claims to be social justice and collective welfare.

Their criticism of capitalism primarily aims to discredit the system by highlighting its flaws—inequality, conformity, and alienation—neglecting to consider its strengths or complexities. This lopsided analysis attributes societal issues solely to capitalism, dismissing the multitude of factors that contribute to the dynamics of society.

The Marxist strategy deployed within academia revolves around manipulating education to challenge conventional narratives and steer students toward alternative ideologies, particularly communism. Cultural Marxists mold curricula to highlight perceived social inequities, effectively steering students toward a predefined worldview. Encouraging skepticism towards established norms without providing a balanced discourse exposes students solely to revolutionary ideas, undermining critical thinking and fostering a narrow ideological view.

Proponents of Cultural Marxism wield their influence over academia through strategic faculty appointments and educational administration, crafting an environment that suppresses dissenting opinions. This approach ensures that academic settings exclusively endorse socialist and communist ideologies, ultimately hindering intellectual diversity and impeding critical inquiry.

Their manipulation of educational content, notably in textbooks and resources, serves as proof of Marxists actively molding educational materials to align with their ideological stances. This includes injecting partisan viewpoints and advocating interpretations deeply rooted in socialist principles.

Moreover, Marxists extend their reach to teachers' associations, significantly impacting the training and professional development of educators. By permeating teaching methodologies and content with their ideologies, they effectively mold the broader educational narrative and the perspectives imparted to students. This systematic influence skews educational discourse and limits the exposure of students to a diverse range of ideas and perspectives.

The infiltration of socialist and communist ideals within educational institutions has become conspicuous, seen through contemporary instances of communist propaganda interwoven into educational materials. This integration aligns with the objective of shaping future generations to embrace Marxist ideologies.

Observable changes in curricular content underscore a notable shift away from traditional values and historical perspectives. This shift appears to be in line with the Marxist agenda of advancing socialist and communist principles, reflecting a conscious pivot toward narratives rooted in these ideologies.

Educators harboring leftist or progressive leanings actively propagate these perspectives within the American education system. Employing methods of persuasion, indoctrination, and even vilification of opponents, they work towards undermining core Western values. Their influence spans across various educational tiers, from Kindergarten to higher education. Critics raise concerns that certain segments of American public education have been reconfigured to nurture individuals inclined towards dismantling societal structures.

Instances abound where educators openly endorse radical ideologies, exemplified by a self-professed Antifa-supporting teacher who admitted to dedicating his workday to cultivating young communists, stating, "I am in the business of creating young communists" — and he has seven hours every day to do it.[11] This influence extends beyond

---

[11] Green, John. "School's Out – For the Marxists." *American Thinker*, 9 Oct. 2021, www.americanthinker.com/articles/2021/10/schools_out__for_the_marxists.html.

academia, infiltrating workplaces, seminaries, and media platforms. Notably, this effort garners financial backing from corporate entities and philanthropic organizations not aligned with American values or religious beliefs. An example of this could be the Open Society Foundations, associated with George Soros, who comes from a Jewish background.

The broader concern revolves around the potential impact of manipulated education, which could steer society towards dependence on the state, nurturing ideologies deeply rooted in collectivism. Communist educational frameworks tend to prioritize conformity and collective values over individualism and independent thinking. Consequently, students are often molded to adhere strictly to particular ideological principles and narratives. This narrowing of perspective limits their exposure to diverse viewpoints and discourages critical inquiry or dissent against the dominant ideology. The result is a culture steeped in political correctness, which effectively stifles any dissenting or divergent perspectives.

The inclusion of Critical Race Theory (CRT) in educational frameworks has ignited debates. CRT, framing societal issues through the prism of oppressor-oppressed dynamics along racial lines, draws sharp parallels with divisive strategies similar to those seen in communist ideologies. This tactic historically utilized to destabilize democratic societies raises concerns about CRT's approach, with critics likening it to a method of "divide and conquer."

Communist proponents have historically employed similar strategies, exploiting societal divisions to advocate for significant change. CRT's emphasis on recognizing victimhood holds the potential to foster grievances and rifts among racial communities. Critics fear this emphasis might be exploited by opportunistic forces to galvanize support, uniting marginalized groups against perceived common adversaries.

Rooted in European Marxist critical theory, CRT examines historical racial influences on societal structures to address alleged systemic racial disparities and encourage conversations about social justice. It emerged in legal studies and extended to fields such as education, driven by scholars such as Derrick Bell and Kimberlé Crenshaw. As racial discussions grew, academia elevated CRT, influencing its integration into schools amid diversity awareness. Educators saw CRT as a tool to address disparities, and advocacy groups and activists pushed for curricula changes, incorporating discussions on race, racism, and social justice. Educators received CRT training and integrated it into classrooms for dialogue on racial issues, privilege, and discrimination, aiming to address achievement gaps and reform unequal practices.

Similar to critical theory used by communists, Critical Race Theory (CRT) scrutinizes racial dynamics to challenge established systems, claiming that systemic racism is deeply ingrained within U.S. social, political, and economic systems, resulting in racial inequalities. At its core, CRT asserts that White individuals receive advantages based on their racial background, and "White guilt" is a term often discussed within the context of CRT as a means to address historical disparities.

Critics raise concerns about bias and division in CRT, particularly due to its focus on systemic dynamics, identities, and racial issues. This approach might foster division and oversimplify complex matters, potentially hindering open discourse by disproportionately emphasizing identity over individual agency. Specifically, they worry about the attribution of historical injustices solely to Whites, the potential divisiveness of "White privilege," and its risk of fostering an "us versus them" mindset. This emphasis on systemic racism and oppressor-oppressed dynamics within

CRT has raised concerns about the deliberate cultivation of animosity and victim mentality, ultimately eroding solidarity.

Furthermore, CRT, historically associated with leftist ideologies, is criticized for exacerbating division through oversimplified racial categorizations in education. The intense focus on systemic racism and oppressor-oppressed dynamics is believed to escalate tensions among students, parents, and educators, further dividing communities. CRT's focus on oppressors and the oppressed, coupled with its distinctions among racial groups, could deepen societal divisions, potentially undermining Western unity. Concerns also extend to CRT's emphasis on victimhood and historical grievances, which could be manipulated to incite social unrest and hinder cohesion within Western communities. Additionally, the focus on collective remedies for racial disparities might be viewed as discriminatory, potentially worsening divisions and undermining the foundations of Western culture and institutions. Some critics argue that the ascent of CRT indicates an anti-white agenda, with concerns that this approach may expedite the deconstruction of dominant culture, including elements of White dominance.

Critical Race Theory (CRT) can be seen as a variant of the class struggle theme inherent in communist ideology. While traditional Marxism focuses on class struggle between the proletariat (working class) and the bourgeoisie (capitalist class), CRT shifts the focus to racial dynamics and power imbalances within society. This shift does not abandon the Marxist concept of oppressor-oppressed relationships but instead applies it to racial divisions.

In classical Marxism, the struggle is framed as an economic conflict between those who own the means of production and those who labor for them. CRT extends this notion, asserting that society's fundamental conflict is not only about economic disparity but also about racial dominance and subordination. It contends that systemic racism perpetuates and reinforces power imbalances akin to the class struggle in Marxist theory.

CRT analyzes society through the lens of oppressor groups and oppressed groups, mirroring Marxist ideas of exploiting and oppressed classes. It identifies racial minorities as the oppressed group, drawing parallels to the proletariat, while the dominant racial majority, often perceived as the oppressors, bears resemblance to the bourgeoisie.

Moreover, just as traditional Marxism seeks to dismantle the capitalist system to achieve equality and societal change, CRT advocates for deconstructing systemic racism embedded within societal structures to address racial disparities and promote social justice. This aligns with the Marxist aim of dismantling capitalist structures to establish equality and fairness.

Under the banner of Critical Race Theory (CRT), proponents strategically introduced terms such as "white fragility," "systemic racism," and "intersectionality" into societal discourse. These terms, used as ideological tools, aim to dissect and challenge prevailing understandings of racial dynamics. They seek to disrupt traditional perceptions by emphasizing perceived systemic injustices faced by marginalized communities. However, this deliberate integration serves a broader agenda—manipulating and reshaping racial conversations to sow division and magnify grievances rather than seeking genuine resolution.

For instance, "microaggressions" spotlight subtle discriminatory behaviors contributing to broader racial disparities, shedding light on inadvertent actions perpetuating inequality. "White fragility" targets defensive responses to racial discussions, highlighting how these reactions stifle constructive dialogue. These concepts, touted by CRT, ostensibly aim to uncover unconscious biases perpetuating inequality. Yet, this intentional focus on specific racial, ethnic, or social identities is a divisive maneuver. Instead of uniting diverse groups, it fosters animosity and division. This emphasis on identity, seen as a calculated strategy, threatens to erode solidarity within dominant societies, potentially deepening societal fractures rather than fostering inclusivity.

In current discussions within the United States, a growing perception termed the "anti-White agenda" has gained attention. This perception revolves around a movement influenced by communist ideologies seeking to disrupt established societal norms. This movement is often linked with ideologies and trends found in Critical Race Theory (CRT).

Advocates of the "anti-White agenda" argument assert a deliberate intent to dismantle the existing social fabric. They draw parallels between this movement and concepts within CRT, particularly its emphasis on systemic racism and the focal point placed on racial dynamics. Critics of CRT frequently tie its principles to a broader movement challenging traditional cultural and societal norms, specifically those associated with White identity.

The association of CRT with the "anti-White agenda" has sparked contentious debates, with critics expressing deep concerns about the potential fallout of adopting CRT in societal discourse. They argue that CRT's emphasis on systemic racism and its tendency to classify social groups into oppressors and oppressed could heighten societal divisions and foster animosity among various racial factions. This critical perspective amplifies fears that CRT feeds into the narrative of an 'anti-White agenda,' exacerbating societal fractures instead of promoting genuine fairness and inclusivity.

One example illustrating concerns linked to CRT comes from Lilith Sinclair, an activist advocating for the abolition of the United States. Sinclair's viewpoints underscore certain apprehensions associated with CRT. She openly asserts that White individuals are inherently racist and actively participate in the oppression of people of color.

This assertion echoes a fundamental aspect of CRT, which identifies the dominant racial group—Whites—as inherently privileged and complicit in perpetuating systemic racism. This narrative mirrors the class struggle notion in communism, where the bourgeoisie (the dominant class) is portrayed as inherently oppressive, benefiting from and maintaining the exploitation of the working class.

This framing leads to the demonization of an entire racial group and promotes the idea of collective guilt based on skin color. This fosters division and resentment among racial groups, essentially labeling one group as the "oppressor" similar to the class struggle concept within Marxist ideology. Critics also highlight the potential for such rhetoric to polarize societies and undermine unity, which is a prerequisite for dismantling the dominant culture.

Prior to President Obama's election, the United States was making strides toward a society less defined by racial divisions. However, this trajectory shifted as certain factions within the political left and specific interest groups impeded this progress, fostering a resurgence of racial tensions for their own interests. This setback was notably influenced by the adoption of concepts such as Critical Race Theory (CRT) and the restorative justice agenda in public schools.

The era during Barack Obama's presidency was marked by a "race-centered conflict," a deeply concerning trend due to its inherently divisive nature. This period witnessed the manipulation of identity politics and the exploitation of racial issues to further certain agendas and gain political leverage. This approach polarized discussions around race, detracting from the momentum towards a society beyond racial distinctions that had been previously observed.

CRT and the restorative justice agenda introduced in schools were intended to address systemic inequalities and foster social justice. However, these initiatives, rather than unifying communities, exacerbated divisions by framing societal issues through a primarily racial lens. The emphasis on race and identity politics led to a decline in educational standards and concerns about the ideological bias within academic settings.

This manipulation of racial tensions for political gain and the integration of CRT into public discourse not only hindered the progress made against racism but also heightened societal divisions. It led to a culture where discussions on race became politically charged and further deepened existing divides, detracting from the collective goal of fostering a more inclusive society.

Author and professor, Dr. Carol Swain, explained, "Racism was dying in the United States before President Barack Obama was elected...At that time, the country was portrayed by legacy media as being a post-racial society. I think that because we were making so much progress, the political left and those that benefit by racism and keeping us divided...they had to act. This was the time when the racial tensions, which divided people, restarted and when standards in classes, especially in public schools, were lowered owing to CRT and the restorative justice agenda being pushed."[12]

Glenn Beck has posited a theory that associates the widespread adoption of Critical Race Theory (CRT) in education with deliberate actions tied to the Obama administration's policies. According to Beck, these actions were intended to provoke a "race war" and promote the idea

---

[12] "Critical Race Theory may violate Civil Rights Act, the Constitution: Dr. Carol Swain." *Natural News*, 23 June 2021, www.naturalnews.com/2021-06-23-critical-race-theory-may-violate-civil-rights.html.

of "equity," particularly in wealth redistribution. His argument suggests that the incorporation of CRT into educational curricula was part of a broader strategy influenced by Obama's policies, aimed at perpetuating the concept of systemic racism so as to foster racial division.

Beck's assertion implies that there was a calculated effort to introduce CRT into educational systems as a means to create discord and reinforce the narrative of inherent racial inequality.

The "1619 Project," despite not being explicitly aligned with Marxism, functions as a tool to challenge established historical narratives. Introduced by The New York Times in 2019, it reimagines American history by placing a spotlight on 1619, when enslaved Africans arrived in Virginia. While aiming to address systemic racism, the project faces criticism for historical inaccuracies and its potential to sow divisiveness. The convergence between the "1619 Project" and Critical Race Theory (CRT) accentuates racial oppression, potentially undermining national unity and diluting a shared American identity.

By emphasizing historical injustices and systemic racism, both the "1619 Project" and CRT challenge the traditional American historical narrative. Their goal is to reshape societal perceptions and values, primarily highlighting the plight of marginalized groups, notably African Americans. While they are not explicitly aligned with Marxist ideology, their emphasis on systemic inequalities aligns with the Marxist objective of dismantling existing structures and cultural norms perceived as oppressive.

These initiatives contribute to the denigration of traditional American values by asserting that the dominant culture—often associated with White, Western values—is accountable for historical injustices and ongoing systemic racism. This narrative parallels Marxist ideology, which aims to challenge and deconstruct the dominant culture deemed oppressive. By redefining historical narratives and amplifying systemic inequalities, they seek to erode the legitimacy of the dominant culture, fostering a cultural shift that aligns with their ideological goals.

Justo Antonia Triana is concerned about a growing sentiment among some students who view "the United States itself is nothing more than a symbol of racism and oppression that must be destroyed in the name of social justice – only later to become a communist dystopian hell."[13] Justo Antonia Triana's apprehension over the emerging sentiment among certain students, which envisions the United States as a symbol of racism and oppression necessitating destruction for the sake of social justice, and the possible consequent shift towards a communist dystopia, could be interpreted as a consequence of Marxist subversion within education. This viewpoint aligns with the broader modern discourse about the nation's historical narrative and its societal frameworks.

The "divide and conquer" strategy fosters discord among different societal factions or groups, aiming to attain control over a population, weaken resistance, and consolidate power by exploiting existing rifts or creating new ones.

Identity politics, at its core, has the potential to exacerbate these societal divisions. By placing emphasis on specific social identities—whether racial, gender-based, or cultural—identity politics tends to centralize discussions and actions around these distinct group identities. While the initial intentions may revolve around addressing historical

---

[13] Aitken, Peter. "Recent Cuban immigrant and college student shocked by peers' perception of socialism, seeks to dismantle it." *Fox News*, 19 Jan. 2022, www.foxnews.com/us/recent-cuban-immigrant-college-student-shocked-perceptions-socialism.

injustices or disparities, the outcome often deepens fractures among various groups.

While the premise of identity politics is to acknowledge and confront the unique challenges faced by different identity groups, its execution often results in heightened societal fragmentation. When identity takes precedence, communities can become polarized, escalating tensions and obstructing collaborative efforts necessary for addressing broader societal issues.

Instead of uniting individuals under a common cause, identity politics reinforces group segregation. This prioritization of group identity over a shared identity can provoke conflicts and impede cooperative endeavors crucial for tackling larger societal challenges.

Marxism operates by exploiting societal divisions, manipulating discontent, and leveraging existing grievances to advance its agenda. It capitalizes on inherent class struggles, highlighting disparities between the working and capitalist classes, fostering resentment among those economically marginalized.

Moreover, contemporary Marxist tactics extend beyond economic divisions, delving into identity-based fractures such as race, gender, and ethnicity. This expansion into identity politics aims to mobilize marginalized groups against what is portrayed as an oppressive majority, instigating conflict and nurturing an "us versus them" mentality. This approach intensifies societal discord and impedes efforts toward genuine unity and progress.

The insidious tactics of Cultural Marxists mirror the manipulative language techniques depicted in George Orwell's dystopian novel *1984*, perpetuating what can only be described as a linguistic siege. These ideologues cloak their ambitions in the guise of progressiveness and justice while cunningly wielding language as a weapon to mold societal perceptions.

Their grandiose mission supposedly revolves around challenging established power structures and instigating societal transformations, all under the deceptive veil of inclusivity and redefined terms. This cabal seeks not merely to encourage gender-neutral language or alter derogatory expressions but to hijack and dominate discussions regarding social justice, inequality, and power dynamics.

Consider, for instance, the distortion of terms in totalitarian regimes such as North Korea, where the concept of "equity" becomes a grotesque charade, manipulated to justify preferential treatment for an elite few at the expense of the oppressed masses. This linguistic sorcery perpetuates an illusion of fairness while the reality starkly contradicts the foundational principle of equal treatment.

North Korea's communist overlords take this manipulation to odious extremes, wielding "equity" as a fig leaf to maintain their stranglehold on power. They perpetuate a rigid class system that eviscerates any notion of equality, exercising draconian control through censorship, forced labor camps, and rampant human rights abuses. The cult of personality around the leadership further obscures these disparities, entrenching authoritarianism while shrouding resource imbalances.

In the United States, Cultural Marxists employ a similar lexicon of deceit. They deftly inject economic terms such as "wealth privilege," "income disparity," and "economic justice" into discourse, ostensibly to spotlight resource inequalities and advocate for fairness and social responsibility. However, this linguistic smokescreen masks a more insidious agenda – one that seeks not to rectify imbalances but to sow discord, division, and discontent.

Their language manipulation is a calculated strategy to corrode societal norms, creating a culture of perpetual grievance and perpetual division. By redefining words and concepts, they stoke resentment and foster an environment where any dissent is branded regressive or harmful, quashing legitimate debate and free exchange of ideas.

In essence, the linguistic manipulation orchestrated by Cultural Marxists serves as a Trojan horse, camouflaging their true intent of societal upheaval and control under the guise of virtuous language reform.

President Trump's establishment of the 1776 Commission was seen by many as a direct response to the encroaching influence of CRT in federal institutions and education. The commission aimed to reinforce America's foundational ideals and cultural heritage, positioning itself against the rise of CRT.

In response to growing apprehensions about the ascendancy of CRT, roughly 25 U.S. states have actively taken steps to limit or entirely prohibit the incorporation of CRT-related materials in schools. For instance, Florida enacted a ban specifically targeting CRT content in public school classrooms. These measures intend to curb the dissemination of a distorted historical narrative that casts America's foundational principles and history in a negative light.

These reactions underscore a prevailing concern among conservative circles regarding the infiltration of Marxist ideologies, notably CRT, into educational systems. The actions taken by the 1776 Commission and multiple states signify a pushback against a deliberate effort to undermine America's heritage and founding values. CRT's emphasis on systemic racism and oppression aligns with

Marxist agendas, portraying the nation's history in an unfavorable manner. The intent behind countering CRT's influence is to safeguard a more optimistic and traditional understanding of America's founding principles, thwarting a Marxist strategy aimed at discrediting the nation's cultural bedrock to advance socialist ideologies.

Joe Biden's swift action to revoke Trump's executive orders associated with the 1776 Commission signifies a notable shift in addressing racial justice and historical narratives. His consistent attention to systemic racism and the implementation of policies aimed at addressing disparities in law enforcement, healthcare, and education hint at a shift toward ideals often associated with socialism in his administration.

Biden's emphasis on racial issues carries the risk of oversimplifying complex societal challenges, potentially worsening divisions rather than nurturing unity. There is concern that this approach might widen existing divides and exploit racial tensions for political gain instead of earnestly pursuing effective solutions. Critics contend that this strategy capitalizes on racial divisions for political advantage, manipulating them to secure support or divert attention from broader societal concerns. This tactic holds the potential to deepen societal fault lines, amplifying divisions within the community.

Marxism's methodology heavily relies on dividing society along numerous fault lines. It strategically promotes narratives that breed resentment and exploit existing discontent to advance its ideological agenda. This calculated exploitation of societal divisions frequently exacerbates polarization and social conflict, eroding the essential unity and stability within communities. The result is a fractured social landscape where trust and cooperation are undermined, ultimately hindering collective progress and fostering a climate of perpetual discord.

Marxism actively tries to challenge and dismantle established cultural norms, viewing these institutions and values as fundamental pillars that sustain societal disparities. Central to Marxist ideology is the belief that before communism can be implemented, society's existing structure must be deconstructed entirely. To achieve this, Marxism employs a deliberate strategy, advocating narratives that systematically question and erode traditional beliefs. This concerted effort aims to sow seeds of doubt and discontent, contributing to the fracturing of societal unity.

This Marxist approach involves methodically deconstructing prevailing cultural values and norms. By fostering skepticism and dissent toward deeply rooted beliefs, Socialists seeks to cultivate widespread disillusionment. The calculated intent is to weaken the cohesion fostered by cultural values within communities, gradually eroding the foundations of societal coherence.

Systematically chipping away at the bedrock of shared cultural values engenders an environment conducive to discord and division. Purposeful erosion of these values creates rifts that undermine social cohesion, rendering communities vulnerable to fragmentation and internal conflicts.

This deliberate dismantling of cultural norms forms an active campaign aimed at destabilizing the societal fabric. Communists' ultimate goal is to induce a sense of disarray by eroding the common ground provided by cultural values, fostering an atmosphere where discord supersedes unity and cooperation.

Cultural Marxists have strategically utilized various cultural mediums—media, music, and art—as channels to disseminate their ideologies and significantly impact public perception. The influential power of media in shaping societal attitudes has been pivotal, exploited by subversive communist elements.

These infiltrators have placed sympathetic individuals within media organizations, effectively controlling narratives and disseminating biased material to sway public opinion. The "45 Goals of Communism," disclosed in 1963, explicitly called for infiltration of diverse media spheres, aiming to gain control over influential platforms such as radio, television, films, and even student newspapers. Their ideological influence within significant media roles actively shapes public discourse, molding opinions over time.

Communists have extended their reach to publishing houses, film studios, and broadcast networks, using radio, television, and motion pictures to propagate narratives aligned with their agendas. Their influence extends to student newspapers, manipulating content to shape the minds of younger generations towards their long-term objectives.

Marxists employ a strategic manipulation of media narratives, deliberately disseminating information that amplifies existing societal divisions. By emphasizing grievances and highlighting disparities, they instigate discontent, fostering a craving for radical societal change. This approach deliberately exploits instances of societal injustice or discord as triggers to foster dissatisfaction with established systems, aiming to sow widespread disillusionment and an appetite for upheaval.

This method of narrative manipulation often involves cherry-picking events and framing them in a way that evokes emotions and heightens tensions. By spotlighting disparities and injustices while sidelining counter-narratives or positive developments, these tactics aim to cultivate a pervasive sense of dissatisfaction, cultivating the belief that radical change is the sole viable solution.

The intention is to foster a pervasive atmosphere of distrust and discontent, creating divisions between societal factions and undermining confidence in existing institutions. By fueling discontent through carefully crafted narratives,

Marxists seek to rally support for their ideologies and agendas, capitalizing on resulting social unrest to advocate for sweeping systemic changes.

The infiltration of mainstream media by leftists raises concerns due to its potential impact on public opinion. Biased reporting, selective coverage, and narrative manipulation within these outlets have contributed to distorted perceptions and skewed understanding of economic and political systems. Often, these media sources portray capitalism negatively while subtly promoting socialist ideals, influencing the populace's perception and belief systems.

Hollywood, a colossal force in the media realm, wields significant influence in shaping public opinion and cultural norms through its compelling content. However, a critical analysis of Hollywood's historical instances reveals its role in endorsing and disseminating socialist and communist ideals. One prominent case of Hollywood engaging with socialist concepts unfolds in Warren Beatty's 1981 film *Reds*, narrating the involvement of American journalist John Reed in the Russian Revolution. The movie depicts Reed and his cohorts as impassioned revolutionaries championing the cause of the working class and propagating socialist notions. Its accolades and recognition brought forth substantial conversations regarding the portrayal of communism in media, spurring ongoing discussions about the sway of socialist and communist ideologies within the entertainment industry.

Media bias and manipulation are evident through practices such as selective reporting, skewed information presentation, and narrative manipulation, shaping distorted perspectives on various ideologies. Some media outlets exhibit a concerning favoritism towards communism, distorting events or policies to impede the formation of comprehensive viewpoints.

Selective reporting becomes apparent when outlets prioritize stories aligning with a specific narrative while sidelining opposing views, especially when examining historical communist regimes. It tends to downplay atrocities and human rights abuses, distorting reality by presenting a one-sided interpretation of events, undermining journalistic objectivity.

Examining Cuba as an example reveals a concerning trend in media portrayal. While certain outlets highlight perceived achievements in Cuban healthcare and education under communism, they often downplay or omit reports of severe human rights abuses and political repression. This selective approach nurtures misconceptions about such regimes, creating an incomplete narrative that overlooks the harsh reality of political oppression, lack of democratic freedoms, and economic hardships faced by many within these societies.

The manipulation of information serves as a powerful tool that reinforces leaders' authority, promotes ideological agendas, and cultivates personality cults. Certain U.S. media outlets, leaning toward leftist ideologies, tend to magnify perceived achievements during leaders' tenures, such as the case of Venezuela's Hugo Chávez. They emphasize poverty reduction and advancements in healthcare while sidelining or downplaying severe economic crises and human rights violations. This biased portrayal tends to paint socialism in a positive light while largely ignoring or minimizing its significant downsides and the suffering of affected populations.

By selectively presenting achievements without providing the broader context of systemic issues, these outlets contribute to a skewed and incomplete understanding of the consequences of socialist governance. This one-sided portrayal obscures the reality faced by citizens living under these regimes, often overshadowing their struggles and the detrimental impacts of authoritarian governance and economic mismanagement.

The techniques used in framing news stories contribute significantly to the promotion of leftist perspectives, often portraying communist ideas in a favorable light while discrediting opposing viewpoints. For instance, when reporting on socialist protests, media outlets might focus heavily on the demonstrators' social justice goals while overlooking instances of violence or looting. This selective coverage not only presents a biased narrative but also shapes public opinion by favoring socialism, prompting concerns about the manipulation of ideologies through media channels.

The combination of framing techniques and selective reporting serves as a powerful tool to sway public opinion toward Marxist ideas. By selectively highlighting aspects that align with socialist ideologies while downplaying or omitting inconvenient realities, media coverage creates an illusion of feasibility surrounding these ideologies. This biased portrayal often steers away from critical examinations of the associated challenges and complexities, hindering comprehensive analysis and healthy debate on these ideologies.

This manipulation of information through framing and selective reporting fosters a skewed understanding of socialist ideologies. By presenting a one-sided narrative that emphasizes the perceived benefits without addressing the inherent complexities or potential drawbacks, media coverage limits the public's ability to engage in informed discussions and critical evaluations of these ideologies. This imbalance in coverage not only influences public opinion but also impedes a more nuanced understanding of the broader implications and challenges posed by socialist ideas.

Recent revelations, as seen in a Project Veritas video capturing CNN's Charlie Chester discussing information manipulation, have intensified concerns about media integrity. The footage reveals CNN Director Charlie Chester openly discussing the use of propaganda tactics to bolster Joe Biden's image and undermine Donald Trump during the 2020 election. This unfiltered admission has sparked widespread debates surrounding the ethical standards upheld within media operations and solidified CNN's perceived role in influencing election outcomes through heavily biased reporting.

Charlie Chester's revelations provide a rare glimpse into the inner workings of media, exposing deliberate efforts to manipulate information and mold public opinion in favor of a specific political candidate. This disclosure has not only dealt a significant blow to CNN's credibility but has also heightened skepticism about the news network's commitment to unbiased reporting and journalistic integrity.

The blunt and candid nature of Chester's statements has ignited discussions regarding the ethical boundaries that media organizations should uphold. It has prompted critical reflections on the depth of media influence on public perception and its potential impact on democratic processes, raising questions about the extent to which media bias can sway elections and shape the political landscape.

Furthermore, the release of this video has reignited broader debates about the role of the media in shaping public discourse and its susceptibility to biases and manipulations.

The Hunter Biden laptop saga epitomizes a concerning trend of selective reporting and information omission within certain media circles. In October 2020, the New York Post released a controversial story based on emails and files purportedly sourced from Hunter Biden's laptop. These materials raised questions about potential unethical business dealings and connections to his father, Joe Biden, who was a presidential candidate at the time. Several mainstream media outlets either downplayed or completely ignored the story, failing to provide impartial coverage or conduct a thorough investigation into the significant allegations. Many suspect that this omission could have been motivated by political considerations, perhaps intended to shield Joe Biden's reputation, particularly during a crucial phase of the presidential campaign.

The deliberate choice of some media platforms to sideline this story sparked widespread concern about media bias and the suppression of information that might have impacted the public's perception of a presidential candidate. The lack of comprehensive coverage and investigation into the claims surrounding Hunter Biden's laptop raised questions about journalistic integrity and the responsibility of the media to objectively report significant news, regardless of its potential impact on political figures.

The characterization of the 2020 riots as "peaceful protests" by certain mainstream media outlets sparked debates centered on whether this portrayal was influenced by socialist sympathies, potentially leading to a distortion of the true nature of the events. These debates brought media bias into question, prompting discussions about its potential alignment with socialist agendas.

Amidst the backdrop of 2020, a wave of protests swept through various U.S. cities in response to alleged incidents of police brutality. While the majority of these protests remained peaceful, a subset spiraled into chaos, marked by violence, looting, arson, and widespread property damage. Certain media outlets chose to emphasize the peaceful aspects of these demonstrations, often downplaying or neglecting coverage of the violent incidents that occurred concurrently.

Sympathetic alignment with socialist ideologies may have influenced certain media platforms to manipulate the narrative surrounding the riots. By framing these tumultuous events as peaceful protests, these outlets obscured the destructive elements and underlying lawlessness, potentially aligning with the socialist cause championed by some protesters. This skewed representation of the riots could have influenced public opinion by downplaying the severity of the situation and its broader implications.

This biased reporting raised legitimate concerns about media manipulation in service of leftist ideologies, possibly overlooking the destructive impact of violent behavior. The disproportionate emphasis on portraying the protests as peaceful rather than providing a comprehensive depiction of the events highlighted worries about media impartiality. Such concerns raised questions about whether certain media outlets prioritize serving ideological agendas over the fundamental tenets of objective reporting and truthfulness.

In the broader political landscape, particularly evident during the 2020 election, numerous left-leaning media outlets notably exhibited a distinct preference for Biden over Trump. This inclination was observed through several channels: biased coverage that consistently favored Biden, editorial endorsements in support of his candidacy, narratives crafted to align with Biden's promises, and selective reporting that accentuated Biden's strengths while undermining or downplaying Trump's achievements.

The media bias towards Biden was conspicuous across multiple fronts. Left-leaning outlets consistently provided coverage that often cast Biden in a favorable light, presenting his policies, speeches, and actions in a more positive manner compared to Trump. Editorial endorsements and opinion pieces frequently supported Biden's candidacy, echoing his proposed agendas and visions while less favorably portraying Trump's policies and actions.

Moreover, narratives promoted by these outlets were strategically aligned with Biden's promises and campaign themes, crafting stories that underscored his proposed solutions and downplayed or omitted criticisms. This included selective reporting that emphasized Biden's strengths, accomplishments, and proposals while sidelining or minimizing Trump's achievements or positive developments during his administration.

The bias exhibited by these media outlets during the 2020 election highlighted a clear preference for Biden, shaping public discourse and influencing voter perceptions. This orchestrated portrayal contributed to a narrative that bolstered Biden's candidacy, aligning with his campaign strategies and, in some instances, overshadowing an objective and balanced presentation of contrasting perspectives between the candidates.

Throughout history, communist regimes have demonstrated adeptness in utilizing propaganda and disinformation to manipulate public opinion and further their revolutionary objectives. These strategic tactics aim to undermine democratic institutions, create societal division, and destabilize established systems. With the rise of social media, these tactics have gained new, influential avenues for dissemination.

Propaganda, a cornerstone of communist regimes, involves the intentional and biased spread of information designed to shape public perception. It often portrays democratic systems as oppressive tools serving capitalist interests. Propaganda messages advocate for the elimination of private property, highlight class struggle, and seek to stoke discontent among citizens. By presenting their revolutionary ideologies as solutions to societal issues, propagandists aim to erode trust in established institutions and foster disillusionment among the populace.

In contrast, disinformation entails the deliberate dissemination of false or misleading information. This tactic capitalizes on emotional triggers, exploits existing grievances, and leverages contentious issues to attract attention and provoke reactions. Its goal is to blur the lines between fact and fiction, creating doubt, confusion, and a pervasive sense of distrust within society, making it challenging for the public to discern truth from falsehood.

The use of disinformation as a tool for manipulating public opinion and serving specific agendas involves purposefully spreading false or misleading information. It exploits emotions and societal tensions, aiming to create doubt and confusion while undermining public trust and the ability to distinguish factual information from misinformation.

Moreover, in today's landscape, certain nations orchestrate state-sponsored disinformation campaigns to sow discord within democratic societies. These campaigns exploit divisive societal topics, disseminate false narratives about political figures or events, and spread misleading information to influence public opinion, ultimately polarizing societies and fostering distrust among citizens.

Social media has emerged as a potent tool for communist subversive elements to orchestrate disinformation campaigns. These online platforms provide swift access to vast audiences. The viral nature of content on social media significantly amplifies the impact of such campaigns, increasing the likelihood of exposure and the dissemination of misleading information.

Extremist groups and ideologically driven entities also exploit online platforms to disseminate biased or misleading narratives. They capitalize on the inherent ambiguity in disinformation to advance their agendas. These groups actively exploit online spaces to radicalize individuals, shape public opinions, and recruit supporters, leveraging online anonymity and the broad reach of social media to propagate their skewed narratives.

This trend has led to a concerning evolution in propaganda methods. As these groups adapt to the digital landscape, their manipulation of online platforms facilitates the rapid dissemination of biased or misleading information. Through these platforms, they aim not only to radicalize and recruit but also to sow discord, polarize societies, and corrode trust in established institutions.

Subversive entities often leverage fake accounts and bot networks to intensify divisive narratives, spreading fabricated information and manipulating visual content. These tactics involve creating false profiles and deploying automated bot networks to artificially amplify certain storylines, exacerbating societal divisions and exploiting existing fault lines in public sentiment.

The digital era presents unique challenges, especially regarding visual content. Images and videos can be easily altered or taken out of context, making it increasingly difficult for the public to verify their authenticity. This widespread dissemination of altered or misleading visual content not only contributes to public skepticism but also fuels uncertainty about the credibility of information sources. It leads to a breakdown in trust, hindering the public's ability to discern genuine news from manipulated content and ultimately undermining the integrity of the democratic system.

One concerning trend revolves around the strategic use of the term "disinformation" by certain groups, particularly those aligned with Marxist ideologies. This calculated deployment of the term serves a specific purpose: to discredit alternative narratives or information, effectively stifling dissent and delegitimizing any information that challenges their ideological stance. By categorizing opposing viewpoints as disinformation, these groups seek to monopolize the narrative, silencing diverse perspectives and undermining critical discourse.

This tactic of labeling dissenting opinions as "disinformation" poses a significant threat to open discourse and the free exchange of ideas within democratic societies. It obstructs the pursuit of truth, stifles the inclusion of varied perspectives, and contributes to the erosion of trust in information sources. By weaponizing the term in this manner, these groups aim to seize control of the narrative, curtail debate, and erode the credibility of any opposition, thereby undermining the very pillars of healthy and robust democratic dialogue.

Moreover, this selective use of the term "disinformation" to suppress dissent is particularly insidious. It not only obstructs the flow of diverse viewpoints but also manipulates public perception, creating an environment where certain ideas or opinions are automatically dismissed as false or misleading. This deliberate manipulation impedes genuine discourse and fosters an atmosphere where differing perspectives are delegitimized, corroding the foundational values of democratic exchange and hindering the pursuit of truth and understanding.

Communists strategically rewrite history and exploit media, particularly social platforms, to disseminate distorted narratives. These tactics fuel conflict and splinter communities, undermining societal unity. Propaganda and disinformation, wielded in such ways, exacerbate divisions, impede constructive dialogue, and corrode trust in democratic systems and institutions.

Marxists are motivated by an unyielding zeal to reshape society, their ultimate aim fixated on the demolition of established power structures. At the crux of their mission lies a relentless assault on the concept of cultural hegemony, which they indict for perpetuating a set of ideas and values that cater to and perpetuate the dominance of a specific societal class. To further their agendas, communists deftly harness the realms of music, art, and culture as potent tools in their ideological arsenal.

A study of historical archives unveils deliberate and calculated efforts by Marxist movements to instrumentalize artistic and cultural expressions for ideological ends. These endeavors often manifest in the portrayal of socialist principles, glorification of heroism, and narratives of resistance against the prevailing cultural hegemony. Communists champion art that serves as a bastion exclusively resonating with the struggles and aspirations of the working class, lambasting classical art forms as detached and alienated from the mundane realities of ordinary people.

This strategic deployment of culture as a revolutionary apparatus is a calculated maneuver aimed at subverting the societal norms and values entrenched in the dominant culture. By co-opting music, literature, visual arts, and other cultural forms, socialists seek to propagate their revolutionary ideals and challenge the prevailing narrative perpetuated by the dominant societal class.

Their vehement critique of classical art as elitist and disconnected stems from their conviction that it serves as a tool of the bourgeoisie, perpetuating an exclusionary cultural realm that sidelines the experiences and struggles of the proletariat. Communists advocate for a cultural renaissance that not only reflects but actively champions the daily realities, aspirations, and strife of the working class, striving to create a cultural landscape that aligns with their vision of an egalitarian society.

However, this weaponization of culture often veers into propaganda and censorship under socialist regimes. Artistic expressions that deviate from the prescribed narrative or fail to align with the party's ideological ethos are censored or suppressed, stifling creative freedom and fostering a narrow, ideologically driven cultural landscape.

In their zealous pursuit of societal restructuring, communists often utilize culture as a tool for societal change and coercively impose a homogenized cultural narrative that stifles diversity of thought and expression. The struggle for cultural supremacy becomes a battleground where communist revolutionary ideals clash with existing cultural norms, often at the expense of artistic autonomy and pluralistic cultural expressions.

Communists perceive classical art as a symbol of entrenched cultural elitism, representing the very societal hierarchies they endeavor to dismantle. Their criticism of classical art is not merely an aesthetic divergence but a strategic assault on the cultural edifices that bolster the existing power structures. Their goal is to recalibrate, or rather revolutionize, the artistic landscape, envisaging a reevaluation and reconstruction that aligns with their political and social ideologies.

At the core of their artistic agenda lies a fervent advocacy for collective art creation superseding individual expression. They champion a paradigm where the artistic endeavors reflect communal values and serve as a vessel for propagating the collective consciousness of the masses. This entails a systematic reshaping of aesthetic values, steering them away from the perceived opulence and exclusivity associated with classical art toward a portrayal of the struggles, aspirations, and collective identity of the proletariat.

Socialists embark on an audacious mission to distort classical art forms, employing alternative interpretations and manipulating historical contexts to spotlight what they deem as societal injustices or remnants of colonial legacies. This revisionist approach seeks to deconstruct classical masterpieces, stripping them of their perceived aristocratic or imperialistic connotations, and refashioning them as vessels of revolutionary fervor or vehicles for highlighting the plight of the oppressed.

In their fervor to dismantle symbols associated with aristocratic rule or imperialistic legacies, communist iconoclasts target specific classical art and symbols. Monuments, statues, or artistic expressions tied to the glorification of aristocracy or colonial conquests become focal points of their cultural revolution. Through acts of defacement, removal, or reinterpretation, these symbols are challenged, often with a fervor bordering on iconoclasm, aiming to obliterate the perceived vestiges of societal hierarchy and domination.

However, this communist approach to art and cultural revisionism is not without controversy. Critics argue that while it aims to dismantle existing power structures, it risks replacing them with another form of ideological hegemony. The forced reinterpretation of classical art and symbols, coupled with the obliteration of historical contexts, may pave the way for the imposition of a singular, propagandistic narrative, stifling diverse interpretations and eroding artistic autonomy.

The calculated use of modern art as a tool to subvert classical art aligns seamlessly with communism's overarching agenda of societal reconstruction and the redefinition of cultural norms. This strategic maneuver finds its roots in several concerning facets ingrained within communist ideologies, echoing their fundamental objective of upending established hierarchies and challenging the status quo.

Modern art's divergence from traditional techniques and styles constitutes a deliberate challenge to the timeless aesthetic standards cherished by classical art. It stands as a symbolic rejection of cultural heritage and a deliberate departure from the values entrenched within traditions of artistic excellence. This departure signifies not just a break from the past but also resonates with the communists' ambition to disrupt societal hierarchies, often at the expense of damaging and undermining long-standing artistic traditions.

The inherent dissonance within modern art, arising from its departure from realism and the abandonment of traditional techniques, serves as another facet cynically exploited by socialists in their endeavor to undermine classical art. This dissonance intentionally disrupts the established norms of appreciation and veneration often associated with classical art forms. By eliciting a sense of discordance and challenging viewers' preconceived notions, modern art becomes a tool for instigating skepticism and introspection regarding established norms and power structures.

Communists leverage this dissonance in modern art as a means to erode the perceived reverence and respect accorded to classical art. They strategically manipulate this artistic departure from tradition to sow seeds of doubt in the minds of the audience, encouraging a reevaluation of established artistic canons and societal norms.

However, this calculated manipulation of modern art often courts controversy, eliciting criticism for its perceived disregard for artistic heritage and the intentional disruption of aesthetic traditions. While the disruption might serve the Marxist agenda of societal upheaval, it risks sacrificing the richness and historical depth intrinsic to classical art forms, substituting them with an aesthetic landscape devoid of cultural continuity and depth.

The communist strategy of exploiting modern art's dissonance to challenge established norms is emblematic of their relentless pursuit of societal transformation. Yet, in their quest to dismantle established hierarchies, they confront a paradox – the potential sacrifice of artistic heritage and continuity in favor of a revolutionary, albeit discordant, cultural landscape.

The calculated subversion of classical art serves as a tactical weapon in the broader arsenal deployed by communists aiming to incite societal upheaval. It stands as a strategic maneuver to erode the narrative control wielded by those in positions of authority, fundamentally challenging the status quo.

Marxists argue that by subverting classical art, they can forcibly elevate the experiences of the masses, wielding art as a manipulative instrument to amplify the voices of marginalized communities. In their view, this manipulation of artistic expression becomes a means to spotlight social injustices that they attribute solely to the prevailing status quo. These acts of artistic subversion serve as bold visual allegories, portraying a deliberate rupture from historical oppressions and symbolizing their fervent intent to sever ties with a perceived oppressive past.

Socialists perceive classical art as an embodiment of the elite's cultural dominance, entrenched in the historical narratives crafted and perpetuated by the ruling classes. By subverting these artistic conventions and overturning established norms, they aim to disrupt the narrative hegemony maintained by the ruling class, forcibly thrusting to the forefront the narratives and experiences of the marginalized and oppressed.

This deliberate subversion of classical art becomes a potent tool for communists to wield against the established order, sparking a cultural insurgency aimed at challenging entrenched power structures. It becomes a means of visual dissent, challenging the hegemonic control of historical narratives and aiming to rewrite the cultural script, portraying the struggles and aspirations of the masses that have long been suppressed.

However, this weaponization of art often invites criticism for its inherent manipulation and oversimplification of historical complexities. Critics argue that while the subversion might aim to amplify marginalized voices, it risks oversimplifying nuanced historical narratives, potentially distorting the richness and depth intrinsic to classical art forms.

The "45 Goals of Communism" purportedly aimed at manipulating American culture by controlling artistic expression served as a strategic blueprint. Through calculated observations of cultural changes and shrewd ideological maneuvers, they stealthily permeated the art world, subtly shaping artistic norms and institutions to align with their agenda. The influence of Marxist ideals, a complex interplay of factors, has shaped American artistic expressions, engendering a transformative shift in cultural dynamics.

Marxists championed unconventional art forms that challenged established aesthetics and norms. They fervently advocated for abstract, enigmatic creations intentionally designed to confound the public, undermining appreciation for well-established artistic traditions and casting doubt on the intrinsic value of art itself.

Cultural exchange between American artists and their communist counterparts facilitated the infiltration of socialist ideals, subtly molding US artistic perspectives. The social upheaval of the 1960s and 1970s, influenced by socialist and communist ideologies, catalyzed a transformation in cultural narratives. Concepts such as workers' rights, manipulated by communist ideologies, permeated the American labor movement, spawning art, music, and culture that distorted notions of equality and social justice.

Under the sway of communism, artists wielded their platforms to critique capitalism or advocate for more equitable systems, promoting divisive ideologies antithetical to the foundational principles of the United States. Independent collectives emerged, embracing radical ideologies that not only challenged established norms but also eroded fundamental American values.

The deliberate objective of replacing "good sculpture" with "shapeless, awkward, and meaningless forms" manifested in the observable shift in artistic representation. Marxists aimed to challenge public aesthetic sensibilities by endorsing deliberately unorthodox and abstract art forms, fostering discord and chaos within cultural values, engendering a sense of disorientation and unease.

The manipulation of art critics and museum directors was pivotal in advancing Marxist cultural aspirations. By exerting control over these figures, leftists could influence art discussions, promoting art that aligned with their ideological agenda.

Endorsing perplexing and meaningless art aligns with broader ideological strategies. Marxists sought to challenge cultural norms by elevating art that systematically undermined conventional notions of beauty and meaning. This strategy aimed to detach artistic expression from traditional values, casting doubt on the very essence of art itself.

By challenging established norms and values through cultural symbols, socialists aimed to foster widespread discontent and disillusionment, aligning with their revolutionary agenda. Their ultimate goal was to eradicate narratives that did not conform to their radical ideologies, provoking individuals to question the bedrock of their society. This calculated manipulation of cultural symbols aimed to sow seeds of doubt and discord, fueling a societal shift toward a narrative that aligns solely with their revolutionary zeal.

Leftist ideologies such as Marxism and communism harbor a fervent ambition to deconstruct entrenched societal hierarchies and foster a sense of social equity. In their pursuit of these grand objectives, communist regimes ingeniously manipulate and regiment music, strategically deploying it as a potent propaganda tool to sculpt a society that aligns with the regime's ideological blueprint.

This orchestrated manipulation of music involves a calculated effort to propagate compositions that exalt the proletariat, extoll the virtues of revolution, and amplify the tenets advocated by the ruling party. Music becomes a carefully crafted vehicle to perpetuate the narratives and principles deemed indispensable by the regime. Compositions glorify the toils and struggles of the working class, serving as anthems that lionize their perseverance and resilience in the face of societal injustices.

Communist regimes skillfully engineer music and anthems designed to inflame revolutionary fervor and kindle a sense of solidarity among the working class. These musical creations are meticulously crafted tools wielded to instigate collective action and fervent loyalty to the party's cause. They stir emotions, evoke a sense of camaraderie, and galvanize the masses toward the singular goal of advancing the regime's agenda.

Moreover, music becomes a vehicle for fostering a sense of unity and loyalty to the party and its objectives. Anthems and compositions, carefully composed and disseminated by the regime, serve as rallying cries, unifying the populace under the ideological banner of the ruling party. These musical creations seep into the fabric of daily life, permeating gatherings, celebrations, and public events, ingraining the party's doctrines into the collective consciousness of the populace.

Amidst this orchestrated musical propaganda, dissenting voices and alternative expressions are systematically suppressed. Artists deviating from the prescribed narrative face censorship, exile, or worse, as the regime vehemently guards against any musical expressions that deviate from the sanctioned ideological discourse.

This calculated manipulation of music by communist regimes reflects a profound understanding of its emotive power and its capacity to shape beliefs and perceptions. By meticulously engineering musical compositions, anthems, and cultural expressions, these regimes wield music as a formidable weapon to indoctrinate, unify, and perpetuate their ideological hegemony, effectively orchestrating societal conformity in accordance with their revolutionary vision.

Communists perceive classical music, deeply interwoven with Western cultural heritage, as emblematic of a cultural paradigm they vehemently oppose. To them, classical music embodies elitism, opulence, and privilege—qualities antithetical to their commitment to egalitarianism and collective principles. Their overarching goal is not merely the devaluation of classical music but to reshape societal norms and dismantle what they perceive as class distinctions entrenched within Western cultural narratives.

Their concerted effort to devalue classical music is part of a broader strategy aimed at restructuring cultural norms in alignment with their collectivist ideals. By undermining the perceived elitism and privilege associated with classical music, communists strive to impose a homogenized cultural landscape that echoes their ideological principles. This calculated erosion of classical music from the cultural fabric serves as a means to destabilize Western cultural heritage, symbolizing a deliberate effort to redefine societal values.

To subvert Western culture, Marxists frequently critique revered classical composers who represent the zenith of Western cultural achievements. Figures such as Beethoven, revered for their prominence and cultural significance, come under fire as their legacy contradicts the collectivist principles central to communism, perpetuating notions of elitism and individual brilliance. This perspective intertwines with discussions on representation and inclusivity, with critics highlighting the historical lack of diversity among classical music composers and performers.

Communists leverage the perceived lack of diversity within the classical music sphere to advance their agenda of undermining Western culture. They criticize the historical dominance of a select few composers, advocating for the "cancellation" of these figures as a means to challenge the established cultural canon. By critiquing the lack of representation and diversity, communists weaponize these discussions, using them to delegitimize classical music's significance within the broader cultural discourse.

This calculated strategy is not merely an attack on classical music but a concerted effort to dismantle the pillars of Western cultural heritage, reshaping the narrative to align with their vision of a more inclusive and egalitarian society. However, critics argue that the strategy of devaluing classical music risks eroding the rich tapestry of cultural heritage, potentially substituting it with an ideological landscape that oversimplifies and diminishes the nuanced contributions of classical music to the cultural mosaic.

Popular music has long served as a catalyst for subversive expression, providing a potent platform to challenge authority and societal norms. Communists have recognized and harnessed this influential power ingrained within popular music, strategically leveraging it as a means to subvert dominant culture and disrupt established norms, thereby shaping and distorting societal perceptions.

The influence of Marxism on popular music becomes particularly evident in genres such as protest songs, where musicians employ their artistry to voice dissent and rally against perceived injustices. These songs serve as anthems of resistance, wielding lyrics and melodies as weapons to galvanize movements, provoke societal introspection, and instigate change. They articulate the discontent of marginalized voices, amplifying their grievances and challenging the status quo, effectively becoming a soundtrack for dissent and social upheaval.

Moreover, the nihilistic ethos inherent in punk rock, in particular, stands as a testament to the subversive tendencies exploited by communist ideologies. Punk rock, characterized by its raw and rebellious nature, becomes a canvas for challenging societal structures and rebelling against the establishment. Its confrontational lyrics and aggressive sound challenge authority, question societal norms, and embrace an anti-establishment sentiment, aligning closely with the revolutionary fervor espoused by communism.

Socialists recognize the inherent potential of popular music to stir emotions, provoke thought, and shape perceptions. By infiltrating these musical spheres, they strategically propagate ideologies that challenge the established order and fuel societal dissent. This calculated manipulation of popular music becomes a vehicle for disseminating revolutionary ideas, sowing seeds of discontent, and fostering a sense of disillusionment with the existing societal framework.

However, this strategic leveraging of popular music by communists also sparks controversy. While music serves as a conduit for expressing grievances and advocating for change, the intentional distortion and manipulation of societal perceptions through music risk fostering a culture of discord and disarray. The glorification of rebellion and nihilism, while an effective tool for challenging authority, also poses the risk of eroding societal values and moral fabric.

In essence, popular music, through its subversive potential, becomes a battleground where communist ideologies exploit the inherent power of melodies and lyrics to challenge established norms, provoke societal upheaval, and advance their revolutionary agendas. In their quest for societal change, communists advocating for reform and foster an environment of societal decay and discord.

Jazz and rock and roll, two pivotal musical genres with profound cultural impacts, possess an allure that resonates particularly well with Marxists aiming to harness societal discontent. These genres, celebrated for their widespread appeal and influence cutting across diverse demographics, serve as effective conduits for the dissemination of leftist ideologies. Leveraging the magnetic pull of jazz and rock, communists strategically co-opt these musical forms to advance their agenda, wielding them as weapons to subvert target cultures and erode cherished traditions.

Jazz, with its improvisational and often discordant nature, reflects the spirit of anarchy and rebellion against established structures championed by communism. Its syncopated rhythms and improvisational style symbolize a departure from traditional musical norms, mirroring the communist fervor for challenging societal order and stability.

These genres facilitate the transmission of subversive ideas through their lyrics and themes, boldly challenging conservative norms regarding morality and sexuality. Rock and roll, in particular, thrives on provocative, controversial subject matters, frequently delving into themes of rebellion, recklessness, materialism, and social chaos. Lyrics often touch upon contentious topics such as sexuality, drug use, and societal rebellion, evoking conflicts over acceptable behavior within families and wider societal spheres.

Marxists adeptly incorporate their propaganda into these themes, seamlessly weaving their ideologies into the fabric of jazz and rock and roll. By infusing their narratives into the lyrics of these genres, they cultivate disdain for established norms, promoting a culture that discourages critical thinking among listeners. The strategic insertion of socialist propaganda within these musical realms seeks to erode societal values, glorify rebellion against authority, and ultimately undermine the foundations of traditional cultural norms.

In essence, jazz and rock and roll, celebrated for their revolutionary spirit and cultural impacts, become battlegrounds where communists strategically infiltrate to disseminate their ideologies. In their calculated efforts to exploit these musical forms, communists use music as more than a means of artistic expression; they also weaponize it to erode societal values and traditions.

Communists employ a strategic tactic by associating popular music with their ideologies, using it as a vehicle to infiltrate and manipulate cultural narratives. By intertwining their destructive ideologies with popular music, they aim to insidiously plant their principles into the societal consciousness, gradually fostering division and disunity among those who uphold traditional values.

The calculated association of socialist ideas with popular music serves as a potent tool for infiltrating the collective psyche. Through the infectious melodies and captivating rhythms of popular songs, communists clandestinely embed their ideologies, weaving them into the very fabric of societal norms and cultural narratives. This subtle but pervasive infiltration of socialist ideas within the realm of popular music allows for a gradual erosion of traditional values and perspectives over time.

By strategically intertwining their ideologies with popular music, Marxists exploit the influential power of melodies and lyrics to subliminally disseminate their ideas. Through catchy tunes and relatable lyrics, they embed narratives that subtly challenge established values and beliefs. This calculated manipulation of popular music allows for the insidious dissemination of leftist ideals, gradually corroding societal values and perspectives without overt confrontation.

The long-term consequence of this manipulation is the gradual fracturing of societal unity. By exploiting the universal appeal of popular music, communists sow seeds of discord and division among different segments of society. This intentional infusion of divisive ideologies into the melodies and lyrics creates rifts among individuals who hold contrasting beliefs, eroding the common ground that fosters unity and shared societal values.

In essence, the calculated association of communist ideas with popular music becomes a subtle but powerful tool for infiltrating and manipulating cultural narratives. In their efforts to exploit music as a conduit for disseminating their ideologies, communists undermine societal unity, fracturing the very fabric that binds diverse communities together.

The 1960s witnessed a seismic cultural shift propelled by the forceful impact of rock and roll music, a movement that stood as a catalyst in reshaping societal norms during a time of profound turbulence. This genre actively rebelled against established norms, boldly challenged authority and institutionalized values, and fervently rejected the traditional ethos upheld by the older generation.

Influenced by left-leaning ideologies and a fervent desire for societal change, the countercultural movement of the 1960s provided an exceptionally fertile ground for the fusion of communist ideals with popular music. This era witnessed deliberate and concerted efforts aimed at challenging deeply entrenched societal norms and institutions that had long dictated prevailing values. The countercultural movements of the time harbored a spirit of dissent and revolt against established conventions, creating an ideal environment for Marxists to intertwine their messages within a generation already questioning and challenging prevailing societal norms.

The countercultural movements of the 1960s propelled an ethos that questioned the status quo, challenging conventional norms of morality, social structure, and governance. It was within this fervent atmosphere of dissent and rebellion that communists found an opportune moment to infuse their messages into the ethos of the counterculture. Themes of anti-establishment sentiments, critiques of capitalist structures, and calls for societal revolution were seamlessly interwoven into the lyrical and thematic fabric of popular music, especially within the rock and roll genre.

Marxists adeptly utilized the countercultural movement's penchant for challenging authority and societal norms to subtly propagate their ideologies through popular music. The rebellious spirit inherent in rock and roll and the countercultural movements offered an avenue for communists to disseminate their messages of social change, class struggle, and anti-establishment sentiments to a generation receptive to questioning the norms and values of the time.

In effect, the confluence of left-leaning ideologies and the countercultural movement of the 1960s provided fertile ground for socialists to intertwine their messages with popular music, harnessing the rebellious spirit of the era to propagate their ideologies to a generation already at odds with established societal norms. In their pursuit of leveraging music as a conduit for societal change, communists weaponized music for ideological purposes.

The Frankfurt School emerged as a formidable intellectual force that significantly shaped the countercultural movements of the mid-20th century. Their critical examination of capitalist society and mass culture resonated deeply with the counterculture's fervent rejection of conventional norms, fueling a paradigm shift in societal perspectives. The School's research into conformity, alienation, and the pervasive influence of mass culture left an indelible imprint on the counterculture, steering its focus toward themes of personal liberation, self-discovery, and societal transformation.

The Frankfurt School's academic work laid the groundwork for the counterculture's defiance against established societal norms. By focusing on analyzing the inner workings of capitalist society, highlighting its control mechanisms, and portraying mass culture as dehumanizing, the School's ideas found resonance among those seeking change. This intellectual foundation fueled a movement that aimed to dismantle existing structures but often veered into advocating for a haphazard, subjective notion of freedom and authenticity.

Notably, Herbert Marcuse, a prominent Jewish figure within the Frankfurt School, played a pivotal role in linking the School's ideas with the ethos of the counterculture. As a key intellectual figure, Marcuse acted as a bridge between the theoretical framework of the Frankfurt School and the burgeoning countercultural movements. His concepts, such as "repressive tolerance" and "liberating tolerance," struck a resonant chord within the counterculture's demands for freedom of expression and social transformation.

Marcuse's notion of "repressive tolerance" suggested that the idea of tolerance in society could be a façade, concealing and perpetuating systems of control and oppression. This concept resonated strongly with the counterculture, fueling their challenge against what they viewed as the two-faced nature of seemingly tolerant societal frameworks. Moreover, "liberating tolerance" urged the active opposition and restructuring of oppressive systems to achieve what was perceived as real freedom and societal advancement, closely aligning with the counterculture's quest for what they deemed genuine and authentic living.

Marcuse's intellectual offerings acted as a driving force, pushing the counterculture to scrutinize established societal norms. They prompted a quest for what was deemed genuine personal and societal change, yet they often leaned towards subjective interpretations of freedom and expression that lacked a coherent foundation.

The cultural revolution of the 1960s marked a significant period in the propagation of communist ideologies, utilizing countercultural movements as platforms to challenge deeply rooted societal norms and structures. This era witnessed a strong emphasis on a deliberate departure from traditional norms. As a consequence, there was a fundamental reassessment of established authority figures and societal frameworks, with the younger generation often viewing traditional family values as constraints that belonged to an outdated era.

These countercultural movements were not only platforms for challenging established norms but also active agents in advancing a communist agenda. They set out to contest prevailing norms and institutions, aiming to dismantle entrenched hierarchies and foster what a more equitable society. Embracing alternative lifestyles, cooperation, and shared ownership, these movements championed concepts such as communal living and collective ownership, principles that strongly echoed the foundational tenets of communism.

The rebellion against societal norms extended beyond the institutional level to challenge familial authority figures. Young people questioned the values upheld by their parents and the broader society. This rupture in generational ideologies highlighted a significant generational divide, as younger individuals sought to redefine societal norms in alignment with their own interpretations of freedom, self-expression, and societal equality.

Communist ideologies have historically aimed to subvert traditional family roles and erode the sanctity of the family institution, a notion evident in the "45 Goals of Communism." These goals sought to discredit and diminish the significance of the family unit while promoting values such as promiscuity and easy divorce. This approach aligned with the broader Marxist perspective that sought to redefine societal structures and values.

The Frankfurt School, associated with cultural Marxism, undertook a critical analysis of traditional family structures. From their standpoint, these structures reinforced capitalist principles and perpetuated social disparities. They claimed that families played a pivotal role in upholding prevailing ideologies, acting as vehicles for perpetuating social inequalities rather than being centers of stability and support.

From a Marxist perspective, traditional family values endorsed by religious institutions were considered contributors to societal inequality. They contended that these values diverted attention away from systemic concerns, effectively weakening collective action among the working class. The church's endorsement of customary family roles and gender norms was seen as reinforcing hierarchical systems that communists sought to dismantle in their pursuit of societal equality.

The undermining of family values often led to societal instability and the erosion of core familial support systems. This dissolution of family values contributed to social fragmentation and an absence of cohesive support structures for individuals within society.

Proponents of traditional families underscore the substantial benefits these structures offer for children's well-being and overall societal cohesion. Comprising dedicated partnerships between mothers and fathers, these familial setups establish a bedrock of stability that significantly nurtures a child's emotional, psychological, and social development. Children raised within these families gain from consistent role models of both genders, fostering a well-rounded understanding of masculinity and femininity. This exposure to diverse gender roles contributes to the cultivation of strong social skills and a healthy self-concept. The emotional security provided by traditional families is fundamental, as the unwavering commitment between two caregivers creates a reliable support system that fortifies stability, bolsters self-esteem, enhances emotional resilience, and promotes overall mental well-being.

Moreover, intact traditional families offer a continuum of familial heritage and ancestral connection. Growing up within a family that upholds time-honored traditions, values, and cultural customs instills a deep sense of belonging and attachment to one's roots. This upbringing imparts a sense of legacy and connection, strengthening their identity and grounding them in a rich cultural heritage.

Traditional families also represent a vital bulwark of resistance against state overreach. Communists aim to dismantle these familial foundations, which serve as centers of identity and opposition against government control. By disrupting these familial bonds, socialist regimes intend to weaken potential centers of opposition or dissent. Severing these connections leaves individuals more susceptible to state manipulation and control, as these ruptured familial ties diminish alternative sources of allegiance. The deliberate destabilization of families aims to isolate individuals, cultivating a dependence on the state and increasing vulnerability to manipulation. Prioritizing loyalty to the state over familial ties serves to bolster state control while eroding the significance of personal values and relationships tied to the traditional family structure, ultimately promoting a societal reliance on state authority.

Communist regimes methodically employ a range of strategic measures aimed at dismantling and corroding traditional family structures, ultimately seeking to isolate individuals and solidify their control. This orchestrated endeavor serves several calculated purposes, all geared toward undermining familial units.

Firstly, communists aggressively challenge conventional gender roles within families, striving to provoke discussions around equality and societal change. Their goal is to disrupt established gender norms, advocating for a restructuring of family dynamics to align with a more equitable framework.

Secondly, they implement a multitude of strategies to undermine traditional family values. This encompasses advocating for collective ownership, diminishing the significance of nuclear families, and endorsing communal child-rearing. These measures purposefully disrupt the conventional roles of parents and the transmission of time-honored values, deliberately weakening familial bonds and fostering allegiance to the state over family loyalty.

Moreover, socialists actively promote alternative moral values within family units. They critique established values associated with family, religion, and societal norms, intending to erode their influence. Their methods encompass highlighting individualism over collective responsibilities and advocating for unconventional relationships within the family structure.

The concept that communists leverage pornography to undermine traditional family values arises from their ideologies seeking to dismantle societal structures, including traditional families, in order to advocate for socialist ideals. Within this narrative, the deliberate promotion and accessibility of pornography are viewed as strategies used by communist elements to corrode the moral fabric linked to family and societal values.

Legally, the landscape surrounding pornography in the United States has been shaped by diverse court rulings interpreting the First Amendment's protection of free speech. Federal law neither explicitly legalizes nor criminalizes pornography. Court cases, such as *Roth v. United States*, 354 U.S. 476 (1957), clarified that obscenity is not shielded by the First Amendment. However, the definition of obscenity remains fluid and varies across communities. Consequently, the legality of pornographic material is mainly regulated by local and state laws, with some states imposing restrictions on its production, distribution, or sale, while others consider it within the domain of protected speech.

The widespread availability and consumption of pornography have sparked concerns regarding their impact on traditional family values, intimacy, relationships, and familial dynamics. Exposure to explicit content can distort perceptions of intimacy and relationships by portraying unrealistic scenarios, potentially influencing personal relationship expectations and straining familial bonds. Persistent exposure distorts perceptions of healthy sexuality, promoting objectification and unrealistic body standards while prioritizing physical attributes over emotional connections, indirectly affecting family bonds and intimate relationships.

Furthermore, research indicates a correlation between excessive pornography consumption and mental health issues such as addiction, desensitization, and increased vulnerability to conditions such as depression or anxiety. These challenges may strain relationships and lead to breakdowns in communication within the family structure.

Moreover, the easy accessibility of pornographic material raises concerns about inadvertent exposure to children, potentially shaping their understanding of relationships and sexuality in ways conflicting with parents' attempts to instill traditional family values. This accessibility poses challenges for parents in monitoring and guiding their children's exposure to explicit content, impacting the family environment and moral values within the household.

Ultimately, the consumption of pornography may conflict with ethical and moral considerations integral to traditional family values, such as respect, commitment, and moral standards. When consumption contradicts these values within a family, it can lead to ethical conflicts, disagreements, and tensions among family members.

By destabilizing or degrading moral standards, leftists aim to weaken the foundation of traditional families and societal norms, potentially fostering an environment more conducive to revolutionary change.

The tactics used in these concerted efforts can vary but consistently aim at subverting traditional family structures. This includes promoting the concept of collective ownership to replace private property, downplaying the importance of the nuclear family, and even exploring communal child-rearing. These methods are systematically employed to challenge entrenched family norms and instill alternative moral values aligned with communist objectives, ultimately aiming to weaken the foundational principles of traditional families.

Communist regimes execute calculated strategies targeting religious and cultural traditions closely tied to family values, purposefully driving a wedge between the state and the foundational family unit. Their approach involves challenging religious teachings within families, actively fostering skepticism toward values that uphold familial unity and moral integrity. This calculated approach stems from the fear that a strong family structure might challenge the authority of the state, thus posing a threat to the allegiance towards communist ideology.

The resolute drive of communists to reshape society and uproot established power structures clashes fundamentally with religious institutions. This conflict arises from a stark divergence in their visions for society. Communism champions just systems and collective resource ownership, a stark contrast to religious institutions staunchly aligned with traditional family values entrenched in age-old doctrines, accentuating rigid gender roles and marital conventions.

The adherence of religious institutions to these traditional family values poses a significant challenge for socialists aiming for broader societal transformations. By reinforcing these conventional values, religious entities solidify gender roles and perpetuate marital norms deeply ingrained in religious doctrine. This entrenched emphasis on traditional structures and roles raises considerable concerns for Marxists, who fear these norms could act as formidable barriers impeding the monumental societal changes they hope to achieve.

Marxism's critique of religious institutions stems from its aspiration for a classless and equitable society. The alignment of churches with conservative ideals and the perpetuation of hierarchical gender roles starkly contradict Marxism's overarching goal of establishing a society devoid of class distinctions, founded on universal equality. The perpetuation of these conservative values by religious entities directly challenges the communists' vision of societal restructuring and significantly hampers their efforts to dismantle hierarchical structures.

The conflict escalates between communism and religious institutions due to their starkly divergent visions. While socialists advocate for dismantling established power structures and envision an egalitarian society, they accuse religious institutions of stubbornly clinging to traditional values that, in their perspective, perpetuate inequality and uphold divisions based on class.

This critique underscores the ideological clash stemming from deeply entrenched religious doctrines confronting the communists' zealous pursuit of societal transformation. It illuminates the core disparity in their approaches toward societal organization, with communism striving for radical societal reconfiguration while religious institutions tenaciously cling to deeply rooted values and hierarchical structures.

In the mid-20th century, individuals and groups influenced by socialist ideologies strategically infiltrated American churches, seeking to manipulate and subvert traditional Christian teachings to align with their agendas. These infiltrators interpreted religious doctrines through a Marxist lens, cunningly employing concepts such as social justice and communal ownership to gain traction within the church community.

A notable instance was the Christian Communist movement of the 1920s and 1930s, attempting to reconcile Christian principles with Communist ideologies. Similarly, in the 1970s, the amalgamation of Marxist ideals with religious beliefs created tensions within church circles as conflicting ideologies clashed over concepts such as collective ownership and personal salvation.

These instances highlight calculated efforts to align church narratives with Marxist interpretations, aiming to sway not only theological discussions but also influence the dynamics of church leadership. The infiltration was a deliberate maneuver to manipulate religious doctrines and narratives, potentially causing significant shifts in the ethos and functioning of churches, all to fit within the contours of socialist thought.

Marxist feminists undermine traditional family structures by challenging deeply ingrained gender roles, asserting that these roles perpetuate inequality while upholding capitalist ideals. Their primary goal is not merely gender equality but a complete overhaul of marriage's structure, advocating a reevaluation of the family institution itself. This endeavor seeks to question and redefine the family's role, strategically aiming to disrupt established hierarchies and power dynamics within families.

Their pursuit goes beyond challenging gender norms within families. They push for collective child-rearing and shared responsibilities, promoting the idea of a broader community or state involvement in child-rearing, reminiscent of the proverbial "It takes a village." This narrative actively encourages women's participation in the workforce and advocates for shared domestic responsibilities, promoting financial self-reliance to shake up traditional family norms and diminish reliance on male breadwinners.

Feminist groups associated with this ideology assert women's autonomy in reproductive choices, advocating for unrestricted access to contraception and abortion. These advocacies challenge the traditional societal expectations of women solely as mothers, seeking to break free from these constraints.

Betty Friedan, a prominent Jewish figure in shaping the second-wave feminism of the 1960s, sparked conversations about gender roles. Her advocacy aimed to eliminate societal limitations on women's roles, particularly within homemaking, initiating changes in workplace dynamics and advancements in reproductive rights.

The approach adopted by Marxist feminists has sparked criticism for its radical intentions to deconstruct the family. By promoting a collective approach to child-rearing and advocating for reduced dependence on traditional family structures, they undermine the foundational fabric of the family unit. Their relentless push for gender equality within the family disregards the significance of traditional family dynamics and values, leading to societal fragmentation and diminishing the importance of parental roles in nurturing and raising children.

The countercultural movements of the 1960s and 1970s emerged as a significant force that redefined societal norms, including those surrounding family life. These movements challenged and disrupted conventional perceptions of family structures and values. This disruption resonated with certain elements of Marxist thought, particularly in their inclination towards alternative lifestyles and communal living as acts of resistance against established power structures.

These countercultural ideals fostered a broader societal shift, sparking profound reflections and reevaluations about the fundamental roles of institutions, including the family, in shaping individuals' lives. This cultural transformation both mirrored the changing attitudes of the era and acted as a catalyst, actively challenging and reshaping conventional norms that had been deeply ingrained in society for generations.

The countercultural movements encouraged a rethinking of the family's role, questioning its traditional dynamics and hierarchical structures. Embracing notions of communal living and alternative family models, they advocated for non-conventional ways of cohabitation and child-rearing. This stance critiqued the nuclear family model, viewing it as a product of capitalist structures and advocating for its transformation into a more collective and equitable arrangement.

Furthermore, these countercultural movements called into question societal norms, seeking to break away from traditional patterns of behavior and hierarchical systems. Their emphasis on personal freedom, individual autonomy, and rejection of established authority profoundly influenced discussions about familial relationships, contributing to a wider discourse on family values and dynamics.

The societal shifts in the United States since the 1960s have significantly altered the traditional family unit, largely influenced by the sexual revolution of that era. This period introduced heightened sexual freedom and experimentation, challenging established family values and norms. Unfortunately, this challenge has manifested in a marked increase in divorce rates and a rise in single-parent and blended families, which have contributed to the destabilization of the once-stable family structure.

These shifts in family dynamics are often attributed to deliberate societal promotion of promiscuity and the facilitation of easy divorces, creating an environment that prioritizes short-term gratification over long-term commitments. These trends are viewed through a lens critical of certain communist principles that emphasize individual liberation and the dismantling of traditional societal norms. The ease of divorce and encouragement of non-committal relationships are calculated strategies aimed at deliberately disrupting the enduring structures and values of the institution of marriage. This calculated approach is aimed at diminishing the influence of the family unit on individuals, fostering a culture where long-term commitments are undervalued and personal connections are transient.

The deliberate disintegration of traditional family structures is a strategic maneuver aligned with the objectives of Marxist ideology. This calculated disassembly serves as a systematic challenge to deeply embedded societal norms and power dynamics. Its purpose extends beyond mere familial restructuring; it potentially redirects individuals' loyalty away from established institutions, fostering a shift towards increased dependency on governmental entities. This disruption in familial bonds and values coincides with the Frankfurt School's critique of families as instruments that propagate capitalist ideals and reinforce societal inequalities.

Throughout history, Marxists have strategically targeted traditional gender roles as part of their broader endeavor to disrupt entrenched societal structures and hierarchical systems. These efforts are not confined to family dynamics but encompass religious practices and cultural norms as well. Their advocacy for the eradication of these deeply ingrained gender roles and norms is rooted in the belief that they constitute fundamental components of the societal framework they want to deconstruct.

Communists perceive the traditional family structure as a formidable obstacle to their societal goals. They advocate for communal living arrangements that harmonize with Marxist ideologies emphasizing collective ownership, shared responsibilities, and the dissolution of class-based hierarchies. To them, the specific gender roles and ownership of property within the traditional family reinforce societal inequalities and perpetuate capitalist values.

Their vision of communal living aims to dismantle the nuclear family model, wherein private property and inheritance are passed down through generations. Instead, they propose a communal system where resources, responsibilities, and child-rearing are shared among the community. By eradicating the concept of private property and individual family units, their objective is to eliminate perceived societal disparities and foster a sense of equality and unity among individuals.

Within this communal framework, individual families are deemed divisive, perpetuating class distinctions. Communists advocate for shared ownership of property and resources, including childcare and household responsibilities, to achieve what they perceive as a more equitable distribution of labor and resources within the community. Their aim is to deconstruct traditional family structures they believe reinforce inequality and favor capitalist ideals.

Ultimately, their goal is to shape a society wherein the community collectively tends to its members, erasing the necessity for individual family units. This communal approach endeavors to reshape societal values and redefine the fundamental unit of society, challenging the influence and role of the traditional family within the larger community.

The Frankfurt School employs a critical theoretical lens to dismantle traditional boundaries and question established societal norms, particularly in areas concerning sexuality and gender. Their approach seeks to challenge and critique prevailing paradigms. In contemporary gender discussions, particularly within the United States, cultural Marxists have introduced a lexicon including terms such as "cisgender," "genderqueer," "non-binary," and "genderfluid." These linguistic inventions aim to disrupt traditional binary gender constructs and reconstruct perceptions of gender, reflecting their broader progressive agenda centered on advocating for social change and confronting established power structures.

This manipulation of language is a strategic tactic within a broader movement that intends to distort and convolute our understanding of gender, stretching it beyond recognizable limits. These terms, introduced to encompass a wide spectrum of gender identities, are part of a cultural Marxist agenda aimed at dismantling longstanding, binary perceptions of gender. The goal behind this linguistic alteration is to subvert the traditional understanding of gender, eroding societal norms by disrupting established perceptions. It is a deliberate attempt to dismantle the fundamental principles of binary gender identities, unsettling the very foundations of our cultural values and norms. Many critics draw parallels between such terms and George Orwell's "Newspeak" from *1984*.

The term "toxic masculinit" has become a powerful tool frequently used in association with Marxist ideologies aimed at dismantling the traditional family structure. It frames male behaviors aligned with traditional gender roles in a negative light. It also oversimplifies multifaceted male behavior and stifles discussions on gender roles.

By reducing masculinity to a singular negative stereotype, "toxic masculinity" overlooks the rich diversity of male behaviors, emotions, and attitudes. This narrow depiction unfairly brands all aspects of masculinity as harmful, stifling open dialogue on gender roles and alienating men who feel unfairly judged.

Furthermore, the pervasive use of this term risks creating an environment where men hesitate to embrace positive aspects of traditional masculinity, fearing the "toxic" label. Ideologies influenced by socialism tend to associate fundamental masculine attributes with notions of oppression and dominance. This unwarranted stigma categorizes all traditional expressions of masculinity as inherently detrimental, aligning with their broader objective of dismantling cultural norms that support societal structures.

The idea of "toxic masculinity" presents not only individual challenges but also deeply impacts family dynamics and traditional roles within households. When men hesitate to embrace their roles as protectors and primary providers due to the fear of being branded "toxic," it significantly affects family units.

The deliberate promotion of negative perceptions associated with traditional masculinity, leading men to hesitate in fulfilling their traditional roles within families, creates a sense of uncertainty and instability. As men face discouragement from embodying their expected protective roles, defending families and communities becomes an area of contention. This hesitance, whether due to fear of being labeled as "toxic" or reluctant to exhibit traditional masculine traits, contributes to a weakened defensive posture within the traditional family structure.

This erosion of the family's protective framework opens a vulnerability exploited by Marxist ideologies seeking societal restructuring. By subtly influencing perceptions and norms within families, communism finds a pathway to reshape societal foundations. The reluctance of men to assume their protective roles is a strategic ploy aimed at weakening the traditional family unit, making it more receptive to the adoption of Marxist ideologies. As families face uncertainty and instability due to disrupted gender roles, communist influences find fertile ground to introduce their narrative, altering societal norms and reshaping ideologies with minimal opposition.

The influence of Cultural Marxists in driving progressive social changes, particularly in advocating for gender equality and LGBTQ+ rights, has been significant. Their efforts aim to challenge conservative societal norms by normalizing diverse sexual expressions, including homosexuality and non-binary identities, within the broader framework of human experience. This aligns with the objectives outlined in the "45 Goals of Communism," strategically presenting diverse sexual expressions as "normal, natural, and healthy."

The emergence and growing visibility of same-sex relationships and non-binary identities have disrupted traditional gender and family norms, profoundly transforming societal values. The LGBTQ+ movement addresses and reshapes established elements of traditional families, encompassing aspects such as marriage, parenthood, and ingrained gender roles.

Central to this transformation is the Frankfurt School's deliberate focus on influencing culture, media, and education. This emphasis has shifted societal norms by portraying diverse sexual expressions in a positive light. Over time, this advocacy has led to a more tolerant and accepting society, influenced by evolving generational perspectives. The increasing visibility of LGBTQ+ movements remains closely interlinked with these cultural shifts.

The LGBTQ+ community challenges traditional family structures by advocating for recognition and acceptance of diverse sexual orientations and gender identities. They reimagine family structures, creating diverse family models such as same-sex parenting and chosen families. Additionally, their advocacy challenges rigid gender roles within families, encouraging inclusivity of various gender identities. This movement questions established norms about marriage, parenthood, and gender roles, sparking conversations about family definitions and dynamics.

Legally, these advocacy efforts have led to alterations such as the legalization of same-sex marriage and anti-discrimination protections, recognizing non-traditional families. The educational and cultural portrayal of diverse family structures and gender identities has reshaped societal perceptions beyond traditional norms, contributing to a broader acceptance of diverse family units and gender expressions.

Critics aligned with conservative ideologies express concerns that the LGBTQ+ movement's advocacy for diverse sexual orientations and non-binary identities challenges traditional family values, leading to the erosion of established norms. This shift may render the family unit more vulnerable to broader societal restructuring, including the acceptance of ideologies such as communism.

Their argument rests on the belief that traditional heterosexual family models act as pillars upholding societal stability. They suggest that any deviation from these established models could weaken the foundational structures of society, making it more amenable to profound societal changes. By challenging conventional family norms, the LGBTQ+ movement could set the stage for a larger-scale societal shift, creating an environment conducive to Marxist ideologies.

This perspective suggests a correlation between the breakdown of traditional family values and the potential destabilization of societal structures. Critics fear that if the traditional family model loses its centrality and acceptance, it might signify a departure from longstanding societal norms.

This destabilization could create fertile ground for radical leftist ideologies to gain more traction by taking advantage of the weakened societal foundations.

Communists harbor a deep-seated opposition to churches, rooted in their staunch support for traditional family values. They view these values as upholders of inequality, stiflers of progress, and contradictory to socialist doctrines. This fundamental clash arises from the communists' apprehension that churches' reinforcement of traditional family values could pose significant obstacles to the widespread societal transformations they desire. Essentially, the discord centers around the churches endorsing what communists perceive as potential impediments to their overarching agenda of societal overhaul.

For Marxists, traditional family values, often rooted in religious teachings, represent a set of social norms and beliefs that cement hierarchical structures and preserve societal divisions. The churches' emphasis on preserving these values stands in direct opposition to the communists' quest for radical societal change, which involves dismantling established hierarchies and eliminating perceived inequalities.

This clash with churches is not merely about ideological differences; it is a struggle for influence over societal narratives and norms. Marxists perceive churches as wielding significant influence in shaping societal beliefs and behaviors, particularly in upholding traditional family structures. Therefore, the communists' opposition to churches is deeply intertwined with their ambition to overhaul societal norms and values, seeing the churches as guardians of values that contradict their vision for a transformed society.

Communist regimes use a heavy-handed approach toward shutting down churches, seeing them as potential threats to their authoritarian rule. For these regimes, closing churches serves as a means to assert control, ensuring ideological conformity and eradicating potential opposition. This deliberate action aims to undermine the influence of religious institutions and consolidate centralized power within the state's grasp.

Promoting atheism or secularism is often a cornerstone of these regimes, actively discouraging religious practices and suppressing religious fervor. During cultural revolutions, religious institutions become prime targets for systematic reshaping of societal norms, emphasizing socialist ideals over religious teachings.

The closure of churches serves a dual purpose: It curtails the flow of information that might challenge the state's narrative while reinforcing the government's control over societal ideologies. In instances where religious entities resist communist rule, shutting down churches becomes a strategic maneuver to suppress dissent and maintain social order.

The closure of religious institutions, notably churches, during the global COVID-19 outbreak of 2020 was purportedly a response by governments to mitigate the spread of the virus. However, this move prompted discussions about the balance between protecting public health and safeguarding individual freedoms, particularly the rights associated with religious practices.

One of the central points of contention emerged from the apparent disparity in treatment between religious gatherings and the operation of large retail stores during the pandemic. This contrast triggered debates focusing on ethical and legal grounds, with critics questioning the fairness of allowing secular businesses to remain open while imposing restrictions or outright bans on religious congregations. This selective treatment raised concerns about favoring secular activities over spiritual gatherings, prompting debates about constitutional protections of religious freedom.

Those supporting the government's stance emphasized the urgency of curbing the spread of the virus as a primary motivation behind restrictions on religious gatherings. They argued that certain commercial establishments providing essential goods—such as groceries and pharmacies—played a pivotal role in daily life, justifying their continued operation. These businesses were seen as better equipped to enforce safety protocols due to their resources and space, allowing more effective adherence to distancing measures.

Advocates highlighting discrimination point to instances where restrictions on religious gatherings seemed more stringent compared to those on secular activities. This discrepancy is indicative of bias against religious practices, sparking concerns about the fair and equitable application of regulations.

Instances where government actions potentially infringed upon religious freedoms have been cited as evidence of hostility. These incidents, interpreted as neglecting or undermining religious rights, have fueled concerns about governmental overreach and potential violations of First Amendment rights protecting freedom of religion. The differential treatment between religious and secular entities during pandemic-related closures has been portrayed as a deliberate effort to impede religious practices, sparking tensions between implementing public health measures and preserving constitutionally guaranteed religious liberties.

The issue of whether governments possess the authority to shutter churches, especially in times such as the COVID-19 pandemic, is brimming with profound legal questions. The closure of churches in 2020 fueled discussions revolving around the essence of religious freedom, fundamentally enshrined in the First Amendment of the U.S. Constitution.

Embedded within this constitutional cornerstone lies the "Free Exercise Clause," ensuring both individuals and religious institutions the unimpeded right to practice their faith. This extends to various aspects of religious engagement, encompassing worship, congregation, and the expression of beliefs. This constitutional protection is not just for individuals; it embraces religious entities such as churches, synagogues, mosques, and temples, reflecting the Founding Fathers' commitment to safeguarding individual liberties, especially the freedom to engage in religious practices.

Amid these closures, numerous religious groups and individuals sought legal recourse, arguing that they were unfairly targeted or that their constitutional rights were trampled upon. The crux of these legal battles rested on the belief that the government overstepped its boundaries by singling out religious institutions for closure while permitting other sectors to function.

During the COVID-19 pandemic, courts grappled with the task of balancing government-mandated restrictions on religious gatherings against public health considerations. This complex scenario triggered a reevaluation of the "strict scrutiny" standard, demanding that restrictions serve a compelling government interest, have precise limitations, and employ the least intrusive methods. Some courts justified curbs on religious assemblies due to the pandemic's severity, while others contested broad or discriminatory limits disproportionately impacting religious practices.

During the height of stringent lockdowns and widespread closures brought on by the pandemic, churches and religious institutions showed remarkable adaptability. Swiftly pivoting their operations, these institutions ensured that spiritual services remained accessible to their congregants despite the challenging circumstances.

A pivotal aspect of this adaptation was the emergence of online platforms as a central pillar of continuity. Churches transitioned their traditional gatherings to virtual settings, harnessing the power of live-streaming and online platforms for ceremonies, prayer meetings, and community interactions. Livestreamed religious ceremonies became widespread, serving as a conduit for delivering spiritual guidance and sermons directly to congregants' homes. Religious leaders connected intimately with their followers through these virtual services, providing comfort and fostering a sense of community in the midst of physical isolation. These technological transitions allowed for remote participation while adhering to health guidelines, ensuring both safety and spiritual nourishment.

Online forums and interactive sessions became essential tools, enabling congregants to uphold fellowship, engage in religious discussions, and extend support to one another amidst the challenges posed by the pandemic.

This embrace of technology not only showcased the agility and innovation of churches but also served as a bulwark against government attempts to close down physical places of worship. The swift adoption of virtual platforms circumvented the need for physical closures, enabling the continuation of spiritual services even during challenging times.

This adaptability underscored these institutions' resilience in safeguarding the spiritual well-being of their communities. By maintaining a strong sense of community through online services, churches upheld religious practices while complying with governmental mandates, striking a delicate balance between faith and safety.

Overall, the successful transition to virtual services not only preserved unity and faith among congregants but also spotlighted the role of technology in upholding religious freedoms and nurturing community bonds during times of adversity.

As the pandemic's landscape shifted, various regions adopted phased reopening plans tailored to places of worship. These strategies were meticulously designed, incorporating limited capacities, stringent social distancing norms, mask mandates, and adaptable safety protocols. This approach aimed not only to safeguard public health but also to navigate potential conflicts concerning constitutional rights, offering a delicate balance in a rapidly evolving situation.

The government's imposition of restrictions on religious gatherings stirred concerns regarding potential church closures in the future. These actions triggered widespread worries about a growing trend encroaching upon religious practices and limiting fundamental freedoms, evoking deep-seated concerns about governmental overreach into these critical rights.

The limitations imposed on religious gatherings became a focal point for debates centered on the intricate balance between implementing public safety measures and preserving religious liberties. Many perceived these measures as a troubling precursor, raising fears that continued government intervention might impede the free exercise of religious beliefs.

There was a fear that these restrictions could establish precedents that would encroach upon the autonomy of religious institutions, hindering the free expression of faith. This landscape painted a concerning picture where governmental actions threatened cherished and constitutionally protected rights.

The concerns voiced about this period underscore the need to protect the rights of religious expression and assembly. Safeguarding religious liberties remains an indispensable cornerstone of a society that values freedom and democracy.

Marxists criticize liberal democratic systems such as the United States' constitutional framework, viewing them as symbols of capitalist exploitation and social inequality. This aligns with the "45 Goals of Communism," which sought to undermine American culture and discourage the teaching of its history. Socialists aim to diminish the significance of traditional American history by framing it as a minor component within a broader global context, intending to steer societal values away from established norms. They scrutinize historical figures such as the Founding Fathers, portraying them as self-serving aristocrats and racists, aiming to challenge entrenched narratives and reshape public perceptions.

Their emphasis on some of the Founding Fathers' ownership of slaves is meant to highlight the supposed dissonance between their championed ideals of liberty and their personal actions. Portraying them as indifferent elites serves to underscore criticisms of capitalist systems, accentuating class divisions and the neglect of the working class. These portrayals seek to dismantle their glorification and challenge the principles they embodied.

Recent educational and public discussions echo these critiques, spotlighting flaws in the lives of the Founding Fathers. These contemporary efforts align with communist strategies to contest prevailing narratives, endeavoring to reshape perspectives on historical figures and societal values.

The U.S. political left's efforts to reshape historical narratives have sparked concerns about the nation's commitment to preserving its historical legacy. The deliberate destruction of statues, particularly those of historical and cultural significance, can be strategically employed by communist movements to subvert dominant cultural narratives and challenge the established order. This tactic seeks to weaken the cultural foundations upholding societal structures, thereby creating space for new ideologies and power dynamics to emerge. By erasing historical symbols, Marxists aim to undermine the legitimacy of the dominant culture, paving the way for their own ideas and values to take root.

Within the context of a socialist revolution, the toppling of statues assumes a multifaceted role. It transcends mere physical removal, symbolizing a profound shift in historical narratives and a challenge to existing power structures, reflecting a broader sentiment of societal transformation. Communists frequently target statues, especially those depicting historical figures they associate with authority, colonialism, and inequality, as a means to symbolize the overthrow of oppressive systems and the establishment of a new order. The destruction of statues and cultural heritage sites has ignited contentious debates regarding whether the removal of specific statues amounts to erasing history and disrespecting historical figures, such as the Founding Fathers, including George Washington, Thomas Jefferson, Ben Franklin, James Madison, et al.

Communists have harbored long-standing animosity towards America's Founding Fathers due to fundamental ideological differences between communism and the principles upon which the United States was founded. Central to Marxism is the concept of class struggle, in which the working class seeks to challenge the dominance of the capitalist class. Given that many of the Founding Fathers were affluent landowners, many communists view them as representatives of the ruling class and contributors to the marginalization of the working class.

One significant point of contention revolves around the emphasis on private property and capitalism that characterized the ideas of many American Founding Fathers. Communists perceive these concepts as perpetuating inequality and enabling the exploitation of marginalized groups, in stark contrast to communist principles of collective ownership and economic equality.

Furthermore, the prominence given to individual rights and freedoms in documents such as the Bill of Rights clashes with communism's emphasis on collective interests over individual autonomy. Marxists argue that these individualistic values uphold capitalism and the status quo, obstructing the pursuit of a more equitable society. The framework of representative democracy established by the Founding Fathers is met with skepticism by communists, who claim that this system protects the interests of the ruling class while preserving societal inequalities.

Even Robert E. Lee, celebrated for his strategic victories during the Civil War, found himself ill-equipped to contend with the formidable challenge presented by the American progressive movement. In August 2017, Charlottesville, Virginia, became the epicenter of a fierce clash between "white nationalist" groups and Antifa over the city council's decision to remove the statue of Confederate general, Robert E. Lee. This decision stemmed from concerns that the monument was perceived as a sign of disrespect towards certain segments of the city's community.

This challenge finds its quintessential expression in the "Swords into Plowshares" initiative, which involves disassembling the monument of the Southern leader, reducing it to pieces, and planning to repurpose the fragments for new public works projects in alignment with contemporary sensibilities.

The 2023 destruction of the Robert E. Lee statue in Charlottesville, regarded by some as an act aimed at erasing history, is a calculated provocation targeting the American right. Despite appeals for "healing" and redressing historical injustices, the orchestrated destruction and its timing imply a political motive.

The act of toppling statues is not merely a physical removal but also a strategic means of challenging prevailing historical narratives and reshaping history to align with revolutionary ideals. It symbolizes the removal of figures who epitomize the previous ruling class and its injustices. This act has profound psychological impacts, demoralizing those associated with the old regime while emboldening the revolutionary movement and its supporters. It serves as a potent symbol of reclaiming public spaces, signifying the reshaping of the urban environment in alignment with their values and aspirations. It represents a tangible manifestation of the revolution's progress and a rejection of symbols tied to the past regime.

The U.S. Constitution serves as a bedrock for safeguarding individual freedoms and rights, putting it at odds with the collective ideology and centralized control intrinsic to Marxism. It stands as the cornerstone of the nation's governance, securing fundamental rights and establishing a system of checks and balances among the government's branches. The Second Amendment, guaranteeing the right to bear arms, underscores a core facet of individual liberty. Meanwhile, the separation of powers among branches remains a vital mechanism, preventing any single branch from wielding excessive authority and upholding the democratic ideals on which the nation was founded.

This principle of the Constitution, separating powers among the executive, legislative, and judicial branches, presents a formidable challenge to communists seeking to consolidate power. This deliberate system of checks and balances impedes the concentration of authority, a crucial aspect of Marxist ideologies.

By dividing power among independent branches, the Constitution prevents any singular branch or individual from amassing unchecked control—a cornerstone in communist systems. Moreover, the system ensures that no branch dominates or manipulates others. For instance, Congress checks the President's authority by legislating and allocating funds, while the judiciary reviews the legality of legislative and executive actions. This setup prevents the absolute authority sought in communist regimes.

Additionally, the Constitution establishes the framework for free and fair elections, a fundamental democratic practice conflicting with the centralized control advocated in socialist systems. Elections facilitate the peaceful transfer of power, making it arduous for a single party or leader to perpetuate indefinite control, a common feature in communist regimes.

In essence, the Constitution's separation of powers acts as a safeguard against the consolidation of unchecked authority, contrary to the core principles of communism that advocate centralized and all-encompassing control. This structure ensures that no single entity exerts unchallenged power, presenting inherent challenges for communists to consolidate and maintain the level of authority outlined in their ideologies.

Communist agendas consistently target the Constitution, perceiving it as a barrier hindering the establishment of a socialist society. Marxist theory condemns the Constitution, asserting that it serves the capitalist class, perpetuates class-based disparities, and obstructs the attainment of social justice. Marxists critique its principles, such as individual rights and private property, deeming them impediments to collectivism, arguing that it prioritizes individual freedoms over the collective and favors private property at the expense of societal welfare.

In this critical perspective, the Constitution is depicted as a tool wielded by the ruling class to uphold their power. According to this narrative, economic dominance in capitalist democracies translates into substantial political influence, allowing the elite to shape policies that favor their interests while disregarding the needs of the less privileged. Critics argue that the Constitution, which lies at the heart of the nation's governance, inherently caters to the interests of the capitalist elite.

Certain radical factions have fervently pursued strategies aimed at subverting the Constitution. These groups employ tactics intended to dismantle the foundational principles and institutions outlined in this revered document. They view the Constitution as a hindrance to societal progress and seek to undermine its fundamental tenets through disruptive measures and ideological resistance.

The National Archives' assertion in 2020 that the U.S. Constitution harbors "harmful content" linked to "racist, sexist, misogynistic, and xenophobic opinions" stirred significant controversy. This characterization of the Constitution as structurally racist faced a strong backlash, with many arguing that it oversimplifies intricate historical contexts and dismisses the diverse contributions of numerous individuals.

Advocates seeking to undermine the Constitution often argue for its reassessment, suggesting that certain aspects need updating to ensure relevance and inclusivity in an ever-evolving society. They contend that adjusting language or interpretations could bridge societal gaps and rectify historical injustices.

An opinion piece published in The Hill in 2020 proposed modifying the language of the Constitution in response to allegations of racism and sexism, sparking calls from activists for amendments or reinterpretations of specific constitutional elements. The prospect of altering the Constitution's language to align with contemporary values has prompted contemplation about the underlying motives driving such proposals.

Critics of these endeavors to alter or reinterpret the Constitution raise significant concerns, cautioning against hastily making revisions that could undermine the document's foundational principles. They warn against compromising the historical integrity of the Constitution, stressing the importance of preserving its essence while acknowledging and learning from past imperfections.

This document encapsulates the essence of the rights and freedoms of the American people, meticulously crafted to maintain a delicate balance of power, protect individual liberties, and provide the framework for governance. Any attempt to amend or reinterpret its fundamental elements poses a threat to this finely tuned equilibrium.

Although the idea of adjusting constitutional language to suit modern values may seem enticing in a rapidly evolving society, it is a treacherous path to tread. Such alterations might inadvertently weaken the document's protections, shaking the very foundation upon which the nation's laws and governance rest. Changes made in response to transient societal shifts risk unforeseen consequences, potentially altering the core principles that have safeguarded citizens' rights for generations.

Altering the Constitution could establish a precedent inviting future modifications not driven by the collective will of the people but by passing societal pressures or political agendas. This jeopardizes transforming a foundational document into a malleable tool, susceptible to interpretations based on fleeting whims, thus undermining its integrity.

The Constitution's resilience and adaptability have been maintained through a rigorous amendment process designed to demand extensive deliberation and consensus. This process ensures that any changes genuinely reflect the will of the people, grounded in enduring values rather than fleeting trends.

Leftist groups have strategically employed legal tactics to challenge fundamental aspects of American society. Aligned with objectives outlined in the "45 Goals of Communism," they have exploited court decisions and alleged civil rights violations, aiming to destabilize various American institutions. This calculated strategy, drawing from historical precedents and contemporary observations, seeks to erode the American system's integrity and weaken its democratic pillars.

This use of legal maneuvers is aimed at systematically undermining the Constitution, chipping away at its foundations. The ultimate goal is to exploit legal intricacies, identify vulnerabilities, and ultimately dismantle the nation's constitutional framework. This erosion of foundational principles poses a significant challenge to the stability of the American system.

An example can be found in terms of religious practices in education. Marxists strategically interpret the "separation of church and state" principle to exclude religious practices from public education. Aligned with the "45 Goals of Communism," their calculated efforts aim to eradicate religious expression in educational systems. This has resulted in the elimination of prayer and religious expressions from schools through legal interpretations and advocacy for secularism. This strategic manipulation has significantly restricted religious practices within educational contexts, reshaping the landscape of religious freedom in American education.

During the Cold War, communist movements used civil rights arguments to challenge institutions, creating divisions and undermining public trust. Today, factions aligned with leftist ideologies continue using lawsuits and legal challenges to push agendas aligned with communist principles. Critics worry about judges interpreting the Constitution liberally, potentially resulting in policy changes reflecting personal beliefs rather than the Framers' original intent.

There are growing concerns about attempts by Democrats to influence the Court and reshape fundamental principles. Fears exist about judicial decisions exceeding constitutional interpretation and advocating for policy changes from the bench, potentially undermining the Constitution's core protections. Proposals to expand the Supreme Court with more justices raise worries about the judiciary's integrity and the consequences of altering the Court's composition.

Communists execute a multifaceted strategy to assert their influence over societal structures and advance their agenda. Their tactics begin with infiltrating pivotal institutions such as educational systems, media platforms, and religious entities. This calculated effort aims to challenge moral values, disrupt education systems, destabilize social frameworks, diminish religious involvement, and reshape traditional family dynamics. Leveraging democratic principles such as freedom of speech, expression, and association, they propagate their doctrines across various sectors, particularly within movements advocating for social justice, equity, and labor rights. Marxists strategically exploit issues related to social justice, class conflict, and equality to create moral urgency and forge alliances among like-minded supporters, gradually altering societal norms.

A crucial element of this strategy involves dismantling aspects of Western culture perceived as contributing to inequality and exploitation. Leftists employ various tactics, including propaganda, media manipulation, and cultural influence, often targeting youth through educational systems and youth groups to shape perceptions. They adeptly manipulate media and propaganda to depict Western culture as morally decadent and corrupt while promoting their own ideological framework. Educational systems and curricula are focal points, with historical narratives revised to emphasize class struggles and portray Western achievements as products of exploitation. Even religious institutions face scrutiny as communism seeks to promote atheism and secularism, framing religion as a tool of oppression.

Marxists have pursued an agenda to supplant established revealed religions with ideologies revolving around social and political principles. Their efforts to penetrate churches and propagate a "social" variant of religion echo their strategic endeavors. By engaging religious institutions and advocating interpretations aligned with their ideologies, their aim has been to shift religious attention toward societal issues, veering away from traditional spiritual aspects.

Moreover, their campaign to undermine the credibility of the Bible and promote intellectual maturity as an alternative corresponds with their overarching ideological strategy. Marxists have targeted established religious beliefs, promoting secular and rational viewpoints. Their goal involves dismantling the authority of religious texts while highlighting the significance of intellectual independence, steering the societal narrative away from conventional religious values.

Cultural production becomes a conduit for disseminating Marxist ideologies through a range of artistic mediums such as literature, films, music, and creative works. These media serve as potent vehicles for normalizing leftist viewpoints and advancing Marxist agendas. By tapping into existing societal grievances such as wealth inequality, corruption, or perceived flaws, these strategies create a narrative that deeply resonates with a segment of the population. This narrative fuels a pressing call for radical change, effectively fragmenting public unity and eroding the stability of democratic institutions.

Through artistic and literary movements, communists adeptly disrupt prevailing societal values, advocating for revolutionary ideals. They strategically infuse these forms of expression with messages that challenge established norms and promote alternative social orders. By presenting compelling narratives in artistic and cultural forms, Marxists hope to provoke reflection, sow dissent, and foster a climate receptive to revolutionary change. This approach extends beyond mere entertainment or artistic expression; it serves as a subtle yet powerful tool to shape perceptions, mold ideologies, and ultimately reshape the fabric of society in alignment with Marxist principles.

Think tanks, research centers, and intellectual circles are crucial platforms utilized by Marxist intellectuals to propagate their viewpoints. These spaces serve as hubs for shaping public discourse, influencing policy discussions, and guiding academic inquiries in alignment with Marxist ideologies.

Within these intellectual circles, Marxist thinkers enjoy the liberty to explore, collaborate, and disseminate their perspectives freely. They leverage academic freedom to contribute to the dissemination and advocacy of Marxist ideologies. Through research, publications, conferences, and seminars, these institutions foster an environment conducive to advancing socialist principles.

Marxist intellectuals engage in critical analysis and scholarly debates within these forums, offering alternative perspectives on socio-economic systems, governance structures, and cultural paradigms. They contribute to shaping academic discourse by presenting arguments that challenge conventional narratives, advocating for societal transformation based on Marxist principles.

These intellectual spaces are hotbeds for fostering and nurturing progressive thought leadership. Through their influence on academic research, policy discussions, and public debates, Marxist intellectuals wield significant power in reshaping the ideological landscape. They foster a deeper understanding of Marxist theories, ultimately steering the socio-political thought towards a direction that aligns with their radical ideologies.

In recent years, Marxist doctrines have gained ground within the American ideological spectrum. This rise has been fueled by issues such as economic inequality, the concentration of wealth, and amplified concerns for social justice. These ideologies have infiltrated academic circles, shaping critical perspectives on capitalism. This growing influence presents a concerning challenge for the United States.

Maximo Alvarez, a Cuban defector, who fled the island in 1961 draws from his harrowing firsthand encounters with communist regimes in his home country to issue a stark warning about the significant threat of communism to America.

He pointed out the empty promises "under any communist regime [are]: 'Free education, free healthcare, defund the police, trust a socialist state more than your family and community…'"[14] "I can never forget all those who grew up around me,…who suffered and starved and died because

---

[14] Smith, Justin O. "Willing to Risk Everything for Freedom: All Eyes Are On Cuba and America." *The Blue State Conservative*, 15 Jul. 2021, thebluestateconservative.com/2021/07/15/willing-to-risk-everything-for-freedom-all-eyes-are-on-cuba-and-america/.

they believed those empty promises. They swallowed the communist poison pill."[15]

Alvarez's deep-seated concerns stem from his observations of the infiltration of communist ideologies within American culture and institutions. In his cautionary statements, he vividly portrays communism as a "poison pill," a metaphor that highlights both the allure these ideologies might hold for certain individuals and the perilous consequences they could unleash. His analogy serves as a stark reminder of the potential risks inherent in embracing communist ideals, forewarning about the perilous erosion of personal freedoms, individual rights, and the very foundation of the capitalist system that defines America.

Marxists actively work towards fostering an environment that primes society for revolutionary shifts, incrementally molding it to align with communist ideologies. Yet, underlying this transformation is a growing apprehension about its trajectory. The pursuit of an idealistic notion of justice, a hallmark of these changes, can often veer towards imposing stringent controls and forfeiting personal freedoms. The annals of history bear witness to the aftermath of communist regimes, unveiling a troubling pattern: The ascent of totalitarianism and the erosion of individual liberties. This historical backdrop stands as a stark reminder of the peril inherent in the establishment of such systems.

The upcoming chapter delves into how leftist radicals seek to infiltrate political parties and reshape the American

---

[15] Brown, Jon. "Cuban Refugee Warns Americans Have Already 'Swallowed' Communism's 'Poison Pill'." *DailyWire.com*, 28 Apr. 2021, www.dailywire.com/news/cuban-refugee-warns-americans-have-already-swallowed-communisms-poison-pill? utm_source=facebook&utm_medium=social&utm_campaign=ben shapiro&fbclid=IwAR3kjrRljG_8OHDL9eWaAWcdsA_5BXCjE_ gv7gOiAphiv9VXzJhBx0mAruI.

system, aiming for a more authoritarian governance model. It details how communist groups strategically position members within government institutions and the Democratic Party to influence legislative agendas and reshape the political landscape. This investigation sheds light on the infiltration of communist ideologies into American politics.

Chapter 4

Covert Comrades

Leftist radicals harbor ambitions to fundamentally transform the American system, a shift that could usher in a centralized and authoritarian form of governance. The "45 Goals of Communism," strategically aimed at seizing control of one or both of the US political parties, illustrating a concerted effort to infiltrate and influence the core of the political structure. Communist groups employ calculated strategies to permeate government institutions, strategically placing their members or sympathizers within advisory roles, agencies, and political offices. This positioning within the corridors of power grants them significant leverage to mold legislative agendas, steer executive actions, and craft administrative strategies, thereby challenging the established democratic frameworks.

Their agenda is not solely about policy advocacy. It extends to reshaping the entire political landscape by championing policies that align with their revolutionary narrative and collectivist ideology. This influence seeps into public discourse, altering the narratives and ideals that govern the nation's political dialogue. Their overarching goal is to ultimately reshape the foundation of the political structure itself.

Gerald Flurry, a prominent conservative Christian author, vocalized deep-seated concerns about the threat posed by the radical Left to the fundamental fabric of the United States. Flurry, alongside other like-minded individuals, has raised alarm bells regarding the potential implications of actions such as the deconstruction of constitutional norms and the consolidation of national control.

In expressing these apprehensions, Flurry has gone so far as to suggest a dire scenario: The possible transformation of the United States into a communist state, envisaging a radical overhaul that would supplant the current democratic government with an oppressive regime. This alarming assertion reflects a deep-seated fear within certain circles about the direction the nation is heading, emphasizing fears of a systemic shift that could significantly undermine the nation's established values and governance structures.

General Douglas MacArthur and Senator George W. Malone (R-NV), both esteemed figures in American history, echoed profound concerns about the nation's security, albeit from different vantage points. MacArthur, a highly respected military leader, expressed trepidation about covert forces eroding the country's core values from within. His concerns revolved around the potential infiltration of these forces, which could undermine the foundational principles upon which the nation was built.

Similarly, Senator George W. Malone warned about the actions of a well-organized political-action group. He cautioned against their aims of establishing a one-party state that could pose a significant threat to the nation's economic and social autonomy. Malone's fears centered on the potential erosion of democratic checks and balances, emphasizing the dangers of a concerted effort to disrupt the established governance systems, potentially leading to a scenario where the fabric of democracy itself could be shredded.

"Flag Officers 4 America," a coalition comprising more than 120 retired military officers, articulated their apprehensions in an open letter, emphasizing the mounting dangers posed by the ascendancy of Marxist ideologies within the United States under Democratic leadership. They underscored the threat to the constitutional republic and fundamental freedoms, drawing attention to what they deemed as an alarming trend jeopardizing the nation's democratic foundations and core liberties.

This chapter explores the clandestine influences and subversive strategies employed by individuals associated with socialist ideologies and sympathies embedded within the Democratic Party. It dissects the party's marked shift toward the left, notably contrasting this shift with the historical moderate and centrist origins characterizing the era of John F. Kennedy. The primary objective is to illuminate the dynamics shaping the contemporary political landscape, with a focus on unraveling the potential implications of these influences on the democratic process and the foundational principles of the party. By delving into historical context, ideological underpinnings, and the gradual seepage of left-leaning ideologies into the party's framework, it exposes the disconcerting reality of communist infiltration and its potential ramifications within one of America's pivotal political entities.

Henry Wallace's Progressive Party, also known as the Progressive Party of 1948, emerged under the leadership of Henry A. Wallace, who had previously served as Vice President during Franklin D. Roosevelt's presidency. This progressive political faction emphasized civil rights, labor rights, and advocated for a diplomatic approach toward the

Soviet Union during the early stages of the Cold War. However, the party disbanded in 1955, prompting a significant migration of its members to the Democratic Party. This influx of former Progressive Party members played a substantial role in reshaping the ideological direction of the Democratic Party, contributing significantly to its shift towards more progressive positions.

Subsequent to the Progressive Party's dissolution, individuals associated with communist circles in Hawaii redirected their efforts toward clandestinely infiltrating the Democratic Party. They strategically targeted labor unions, placing sympathetic leaders in key positions to sway endorsements and gather campaign support for Democratic candidates. This methodical approach led to the displacement of moderate and conservative figures within the Democratic Party, making way for advocates of pro-union and communist ideologies. Consequently, this shift inclined the party toward a more progressive, left-leaning stance, aligning its policies more closely with those espoused by Marxist principles.

Over time, those aligned with socialist ideologies assumed influential roles within the Democratic Party, leaving a marked impact on its policy direction and ideological framework. While the extent of communist influence varied across regions and levels of government, the overarching trend leaned toward a more progressive and pro-union orientation within the party. This shift was corroborated by historical trends, shifts in ideological perspectives, and tangible alterations in policy, solidifying a perceptible left-leaning stance within the Democratic Party.

There are emerging signs pointing towards a calculated effort by Democratic strategists to infiltrate the

Republican Party by promoting progressive candidates who feign support for conservative values. This tactical maneuver aims to implant progressive agendas within the Republican Party's landscape, intending to mold its trajectory. A noteworthy example unfolded during a runoff for a Democratic U.S. Senate candidate in South Carolina, where Krystle Matthews introduced the notion of "secret sleepers." These individuals would outwardly present themselves as conservatives but covertly uphold progressive principles. This strategy essentially aims to influence the direction of the Republican Party by introducing ostensibly conservative figures who align more with leftist values.

While there have been strategic efforts by Democratic operatives to influence the Republican Party by backing progressive candidates, the overall shift within the GOP does not appear as prominent or as directly linked to progressive infiltration as seen in the Democratic Party. While there might be individual instances of Marxist influences or attempts at infiltration, the core conservative base of the Republican Party has remained relatively intact.

In contrast, the Democratic Party has undergone a notable ideological transformation, marked by the ascendance of self-identified democratic socialists and influential left-leaning figures championing socialist ideals and policies. This shift reflects a broader trend within the Democratic Party towards a more progressive orientation, challenging traditional party stances.

This evolution is underscored by the growing prominence of voices advocating for expansive policies such as universal healthcare, exemplified by discussions surrounding initiatives such as Healthcare for All. The Green New Deal, another focal point, encapsulates the party's intensified focus on environmental policies and socioeconomic reforms.

The Democratic Party's ideological shift is not solely propelled by these new policy proposals but also by a shift in rhetoric and priorities. This shift can be linked to the rise of progressive grassroots movements within the party, which have successfully pushed the agenda towards more left-leaning policies and challenged established norms.

As a result, the Democratic Party's ideological landscape has noticeably shifted, accommodating more progressive voices and fostering discussions on socio-economic policies that were once considered fringe within the party. This shift has led to internal debates on the party's direction and represents a pivotal moment in its history as it navigates between its traditional roots and a more progressive future.

The rise of influential figures such as Alexandria Ocasio-Cortez (AOC), Senator Elizabeth Warren (D-MA), and Andrew Gillum illuminates a pronounced tilt toward progressive ideologies within the Democratic Party. AOC, a prominent voice representing New York's 14th congressional district, has taken a leading role in advocating for democratic socialist principles, challenging the core tenets of the capitalist economic system. Her advocacy spans a spectrum of policies addressing income inequality, corporate influence, and ambitious initiatives such as Medicare for All, the Green New Deal, and a higher minimum wage.

Similarly, Senator Elizabeth Warren has emerged as a forceful advocate for progressive policies, centering her platform on remedying economic disparities, holding corporations accountable, and broadening access to vital services such as healthcare and education. Warren's emphasis on restructuring the capitalist system to foster greater equity resonates strongly within the leftist faction of the Democratic Party.

Andrew Gillum, the former Democratic Mayor of Tallahassee, Florida, left a significant impact during his 2018 gubernatorial campaign by highlighting progressive principles such as expanded healthcare access, educational investments, and climate action. Though Gillum may not explicitly align with socialism, his policy positions often mirror many progressive ideals. However, critics argue that these policies might lead to increased government dependency and potentially undermine individual freedoms.

The rising influence of figures such as Ocasio-Cortez, Warren, and Gillum within the Democratic Party signals a concerning shift. While they advocate for progressive policies tackling income inequality, social justice, and access to services, their ascent highlights a growing faction within the party pushing toward more interventionist measures. This surge raises fears about an increasing embrace of socialist-leaning ideologies within the Democratic ranks. Some critics worry that these policies, veering toward socialism, may significantly expand government control, undermine individual freedoms, and lead to economic dependencies that erode personal initiative and innovation.

The growing prominence of politicians advocating for these ideologies reflects a societal shift where a considerable segment of the population seeks solutions aligned with Marxist ideals. Yet, within the Democratic Party, this shift raises concerns about the potential repercussions of adopting more socialist-leaning policies. Such measures could tip the balance toward larger government intervention, potentially stifling free-market dynamics and individual liberties.

Former Democratic presidential contender, Pete Buttigieg, took a stand in line with his party by advocating for the elimination of the Electoral College, aiming to transition to a popular vote system. He joined the ranks of many Democrats who criticize the Electoral College for occasionally granting victory to candidates despite losing the popular vote. However, the Electoral College was designed to ensure that the interests of smaller states are protected within the presidential election process.

The Electoral College stands as a crucial safeguard for the United States' republican form of government, providing a structural balance between the interests of populous states and smaller states. Rather than a direct popular vote, which would emphasize sheer majority rule, the Electoral College embodies the nation's republican ideals by incorporating a system that promotes the representation of all states.

This system was intentionally crafted by the Founding Fathers to prevent the dominance of highly populated states over less populated ones. It grants smaller states a more proportionate say in the presidential election process, ensuring that their interests are not overshadowed by larger, more populous states. Without this safeguard, candidates might focus solely on campaigning in densely populated areas, neglecting the concerns and needs of less populous regions.

The Electoral College reflects the Founders' vision of a federal republic, where each state, irrespective of size, has a voice in the selection of the nation's leader. It upholds the federalist principles embedded in the Constitution, maintaining a balance between state sovereignty and centralized authority. In essence, it fortifies the nation's republican framework by safeguarding against the tyranny of the majority, ensuring that the interests of all states are considered and represented in the presidential election.

In alignment with the Democratic Party, Buttigieg supports comprehensive immigration reform, echoing the party's approach to address immigration issues comprehensively. Democrats advocate for a pathway to citizenship for undocumented individuals already residing in the country, considering it a pivotal element of reform. This pathway is seen as a means to integrate these individuals into the legal framework, granting them the ability to contribute actively to society and partake in civic activities, notably including voting.

Progressives within the Democratic Party frequently champion more liberal immigration policies. They see immigration as vital for societal enrichment, fostering diversity, and adding to cultural vibrancy. Additionally, progressives strongly believe that an inclusive immigration policy aligns with their vision of social justice. They criticize stringent immigration laws as exclusionary and discriminatory, advocating for fair and humane treatment for all individuals, regardless of their nationality or immigration status.

Some observers speculate that Buttigieg's views might have been influenced by his father, Joseph Buttigieg, a former professor with ties to Marxist ideologies and a prominent figure in the International Gramsci Society. This connection raises questions about potential ideological influences shaping Buttigieg's policy positions, particularly regarding governance structures and immigration policies.

Representative Ilhan Omar (D-MN) has been a prominent advocate for socialist policies and extensive reforms within America's economic and political systems, frequently targeting capitalism. Detractors argue that her propositions pose a serious risk of destabilizing the economy, potentially undermining the bedrock principles of free-market capitalism.

Omar's proposals may incite economic turmoil, seen as deliberate steps toward pushing socialist ideologies. Disrupting established capitalist structures could introduce market uncertainty, stifle business innovation and investment, and trigger economic downturns, leading to widespread instability.

Moreover, these critics stress the vital historical role of free-market capitalism in driving economic growth and prosperity. Any deliberate upturning of these principles might result in economic inefficiencies, curbing individual freedoms in economic decision-making. Omar's initiatives could potentially threaten the stability and prosperity of the American economy. Such intentional destabilization might serve as a strategic move to pave the way for more socialist measures.

Isra Hirsi, Omar's daughter, has expressed support for radical ideologies that challenge capitalism, notably favoring a more Marxist approach. Her stance has drawn criticism from those who believe that such ideologies could erode individual freedoms, stifle innovation, and negatively impact the country's economic framework.

Senator Richard Blumenthal (D-CT), who has Jewish heritage, actually endorsed the Communist Party. This endorsement occurred during a speech at an awards ceremony organized by the Connecticut People's World Committee, which has affiliations with the Communist Party USA and the Marxist People's World news site. During the event, Lisa Bergmann, a member and organizer of the Young Communist League USA, openly advocated for joining the Communist Party and expressed her belief in socialism as the solution to what she perceives as capitalism's failures.

Furthermore, co-emcee Ben McManus urged attendees to join the Communist Party and advocated for a socialist system. McManus invited attendees "to join the Communist Party in this epic time as we make good trouble to uproot systemic racism, retool the war economy, tax the rich,...and create a new socialist system..."[16] Their objectives encompassed dismantling alleged systemic racism, overhauling the economy, instituting higher taxes on the wealthy, and fostering a socialist society. Bergmann's remarks echo a rising tide of support for socialism in the nation and underscore the eagerness of certain individuals to align with the Communist Party.

McManus's remarks shed light on a disturbing trend toward embracing socialist ideals, indicating a worrisome inclination among certain factions to align with the Communist Party to advance these principles. The objectives outlined—wiping out systemic racism, restructuring the war economy, imposing heavier taxes on the wealthy, and striving for a socialist society—propose extensive transformations. These objectives underscore a dedication to reshaping economic structures and advocating for a more equitable distribution of wealth and resources. This surge in enthusiasm mirrors a concerning societal shift, as some segments flirt with perilous alternatives while attempting to address systemic issues.

The fervor surrounding these socialist aspirations raises red flags regarding the erosion of fundamental democratic values and the potential disregard for individual liberties. Embracing these sweeping changes risks undermining the principles of free-market capitalism and veering toward a system that historically stifles innovation, limits personal freedoms, and impedes economic growth.

---

[16] Ross, Chuck. "Blumenthal Speaks at Communist Party Awards Ceremony." *The Washington Free Beacon*, 14 Dec. 2021, freebeacon.com/democrats/blumenthal-speaks-at-communist-party-awards-ceremony/.

Moreover, the romanticized portrayal of socialist ideals often downplays the inherent risks and failures associated with such systems. History has demonstrated the inherent inefficiencies and hardships of communist regimes, which have often led to economic stagnation, restricted freedoms, and overall societal decline.

These individuals not only champion socialist policies but also employ rhetoric steeped in left-leaning ideologies, pushing for measures such as income redistribution, universal healthcare, and climate change action. The party's platform has shifted alarmingly over time, bolstered by the ascent of progressive candidates and the dangerous resonance of socialist ideas among specific segments of the party's base, fueling this unsettling transformation.

Gerald Flurry, editor-in-chief of "The Trumpet," espoused the belief that Barack Obama had led an anti-American movement, aiming to transform the United States into a socialist state. Flurry based this position on Obama's presidential actions, notably policies that indicated a shift towards radicalism after his 2008 election. For instance, the Affordable Care Act (Obamacare) was seen as a substantial stride towards government-controlled healthcare and increased economic intervention, aligning closely with socialist ideals. Flurry also highlighted Obama's use of executive orders as an example of excessive presidential power, sidestepping the legislative process and evading the Constitution's checks and balances.

Obama's academic background in political science at Columbia University exposed him to the Frankfurt School and Cultural Marxism. The theories stemming from this school prioritize cultural and ideological factors to steer social change and challenge established power structures.

This exposure may have influenced Obama's perspectives on societal issues and politics.

Throughout his presidency, Obama championed policies embracing principles of multiculturalism and political correctness. His approach to diversity, inclusion, and social justice reflected the impact of Cultural Marxist ideas encountered during his education and interactions within intellectual circles. These changes encompassed specific domains such as healthcare, immigration, and environmental considerations, advocating for increased government involvement in the economy and a more equitable distribution of wealth.

During Obama's tenure, strategic personnel and policy changes were made in alignment with socialist principles, sometimes replacing individuals holding strong patriotic convictions with proponents of Marxist ideologies. This calculated strategy allowed Obama to build a network of political allies across various institutions. Furthermore, his choices for judges often leaned towards a willingness to challenge constitutional provisions, potentially undermining constraints on government authority and paving the way for more radical agendas in policymaking.

Dr. Scott Lively, an author and pastor, has suggested that Biden might be covertly influenced by Obama. This speculation about Obama's sway within the Biden administration prompts inquiries into the complex power dynamics of Washington, D.C. Lively suggests that Obama exerts significant behind-the-scenes influence, using Joe Biden as a means to advance his own radical agenda.

This viewpoint insinuates a clandestine level of control, portraying Obama as the mastermind orchestrating Biden's decisions from the shadows. It paints a picture of

Obama leveraging Biden's presidency to take calculated risks and execute strategic maneuvers while evading direct accountability for the outcomes.

Tulsi Gabbard, a former Democratic congresswoman from Hawaii and presidential candidate, tweeted that "Biden is just a front man."[17] The tweet from Tulsi Gabbard raises suspicions about the extent of former President Obama's influence and control within the current Biden administration. Gabbard's assertion that Biden is merely a "front man" implies that there may be someone else, such as Obama, exerting significant influence and control over the president's decision-making process.

Maria Bartiromo, a prominent journalist, has pointed out that Biden frequently communicates with former President Obama, leading to suggestions that Obama is exerting significant influence over the current administration. She reported, "I know Biden's on the phone all the time with Obama and I'm hearing he's running things from behind the scenes."[18]

Conservative commentator Bill O'Reilly asserts that former President Obama is playing a significant role in shaping President Biden's policies and decision-making. He

---

[17] "Biden is Obama's 'front man' – Tulsi Gabbard." *RT*, 3 May 2022, www.rt.com/news/554883-tulsi-gabbard-ministry-truth/.

[18] Hoft, Jim. "Maria Bartiromo: 'I Know Biden's on the Phone All the Time with Obama and I'm Hearing He's Running Things from Behind the Scenes' (VIDEO)." *Gateway Pundit*, 28 Mar. 2021, www.thegatewaypundit.com/2021/03/maria-bartiromo-know-bidens-phone-time-obama-hearing-running-things-behind-scenes-video/.

maintained: "It is him [Obama]…who is calling a lot of the shots for Joe Biden."[19]

The similarity between the policies of the Biden administration and those championed during the Obama era suggests a notable influence behind the scenes. Former President Obama's acknowledgment of common policy domains, such as the Affordable Care Act, climate action, and efforts to enhance opportunities through community colleges, highlights a significant continuity between the two administrations. His expressed satisfaction with the Biden administration's alignment with his agenda intensifies speculation about his role in shaping its trajectory.

This alignment underscores a potential correlation between the policy decisions made by the Biden administration and the legacy of the Obama presidency. It leads to pondering whether Obama's voice and counsel carry weight in molding the current administration's direction and agenda. This connection between their policies raises pertinent questions about the extent of Obama's influence and the nature of his involvement in shaping the Biden administration's strategies and objectives.

House Speaker Nancy Pelosi's characterization of the "Build Back Better" initiative as an extension of Obama's policies reinforces this narrative. It not only signals the resonance of Obama's legacy but also suggests a deliberate effort to continue and expand upon his initiatives. Such

---

[19] Chang, Samantha. "Bill O'Reilly: No Question Obama Is 'Calling a Lot of the Shots for Joe Biden.'" *The Western Journal*, 8 Jun. 2021, www.westernjournal.com/bill-oreilly-no-question-obama-calling-lot-shots-joe-biden/? utm_source=mewe&utm_medium=westernjournalism&utm_conte nt=2021-06-08&utm_campaign=manualpost.

acknowledgments from key political figures indicate a parallelism that hints at a more profound influence exerted by Obama on the Biden administration's policy trajectory.

Moreover, critics have pointed to specific appointments within the Biden administration as tangible evidence supporting the alignment with progressive ideologies. Republican Sen. John Thune of South Dakota has observed President Biden's interactions since taking office and suggested that he detects the influence of Biden's staff pushing the administration towards more left-leaning policies. The presence of advisors and cabinet members with past affiliations to Obama's administration, known for advocating left-leaning policies, accentuates the continuity of his influence. Their roles within the current administration signify a deliberate choice to retain individuals intimately familiar with Obama's policies, suggesting an ongoing guidance and influence in shaping the Biden administration's agenda.

The suggestion that Biden might lack independent decision-making has stirred discussions on the intricate power dynamics guiding his administration's policies, prompting questions about who truly shapes its trajectory behind closed doors. The persistence of Obama-era policies and the presence of key figures from his administration within Biden's team suggest an influential force beyond mere ideological alignment. This hints at a more nuanced involvement in shaping policy direction behind the scenes. Such suspicions raise concerns about unelected figures, particularly Obama, possibly wielding influence over decisions and potentially challenging democratic principles. If proven true, this could fundamentally challenge democratic values, raising doubts about decision-making transparency and policy legitimacy, thus undercutting the mandate granted to an elected president by the American people.

President Nayib Bukele's accusations against the Biden administration, alleging financial support for left-wing communist groups, raise questions about the administration's ideological orientation. This could potentially reinforce the perception that Biden's team leans toward leftist ideologies. Biden's consistent advocacy for progressive values—such as labor rights, healthcare reforms, and social safety nets— reflects a dedication to left-leaning policies that involve government intervention, aligning with principles seen in socialist systems.

The alleged support for these groups could indicate sympathies toward socialist ideologies, raising concerns about endorsing economic redistribution and social programs —key aspects of socialist ideologies. The backing might be seen as promoting socio-economic equality through policies in line with leftist principles, especially in foreign aid and development contexts.

Considering these allegations alongside Biden's historical advocacy for progressive policies prompts scrutiny into his administration's ideological stance. If substantiated, these claims could reinforce the perception that Biden's team leans left, potentially influencing its domestic and foreign policy approaches in ways consistent with Marxist ideologies.

The Democratic Party's pivot towards socialist inclinations represents a stark deviation from its historical stance, aligning with ideologies akin to Marxism, notably supported by figures such as Nancy Pelosi and Barack Obama. This ideological shift mirrors the growing influence of progressive and leftist ideologies within the party. Observable policy trends echo historical communist goals, characterized by expanded government control in economic sectors, the enlargement of welfare programs, and a commitment to advancing workers' rights. The party's advocacy for wealth redistribution, increased government involvement, the pursuit of universal healthcare, and a gamut of progressive policies underscores a definitive transformation in its ideology. This embrace of socialist principles occurs despite historical evidence revealing the shortcomings and failures of societies governed by similar ideologies, signifying a significant departure from traditional party values.

Critics' concerns about Marxist ideologies' influence on Biden's administration span various policy fronts, including constitutional rights, governance, and economics. Some retired generals and admirals express concern over the administration's frequent use of executive orders, viewing the issuance of over 50 orders in a short span as a threat to the constitutional checks and balances system. This rapid issuance consolidates power within the executive branch, potentially challenging the constitutional framework designed for a balanced distribution of power among government branches.

Moreover, critics question the administration's resolve in safeguarding the nation's interests and core values, particularly highlighting weaknesses in national security and border control. The porous southern border has become a focal point of contention, with critics linking it to increased crime stemming from illegal immigration. They point to urban violence and a breakdown of law and order as indicators of inadequacies in Democratic governance, questioning the administration's ability and desire to address these pressing issues.

Critics highlight proposed measures such as higher taxes on the wealthy and expanded government roles in social programs as straying from foundational American principles. They argue that these initiatives prioritize wealth redistribution and increased government intervention, diverging from the country's historical emphasis on individual liberties and free-market principles. Economic worries, including escalating inflation and surging gas prices, are attributed by critics to Democratic policies such as the Green New Deal, which have contributed to a loss of energy independence and economic instability.

Universal Basic Income (UBI) has gained traction within certain Democratic circles as a potential solution to economic inequality and poverty. While not universally embraced by all Democrats, some prominent figures within the party have advocated for UBI as part of their policy platforms.

One of the notable proponents of UBI within the Democratic Party is Andrew Yang, who ran for president in the 2020 election. Yang's presidential campaign prominently featured UBI as a key policy proposal, advocating for a "Freedom Dividend" that would provide $1,000 per month to every American adult. His rationale centered on addressing the challenges posed by automation and technological advancements, which he believed would lead to widespread job displacement.

Yang's advocacy for UBI resonated with many Democrats and garnered attention for the concept on a national stage. His focus on the economic impacts of automation and the potential displacement of jobs due to technological advancements struck a chord with those concerned about the future of work and income inequality.

Additionally, amidst the economic turmoil caused by the COVID-19 pandemic, some Democratic lawmakers proposed temporary forms of direct cash payments to Americans as part of relief efforts. Stimulus payments and expanded child tax credits were introduced as measures to provide immediate financial assistance to individuals and families affected by the pandemic. Although these measures were temporary and differed in scope from a comprehensive UBI, they reflected a willingness within the party to explore direct cash transfers as a means of economic relief.

The Democratic Party's interest in Universal Basic Income (UBI) aligns with its broader goals of addressing income inequality and creating a social safety net for low-income individuals and families. While UBI remains a subject of debate within the party, its promotion by certain Democratic figures underscores its shift towards socialism.

UBI, although not inherently Marxist, shares resemblances with Marxist principles. Marxism advocates for a classless society with collective ownership of wealth and resources, mirroring UBI's call for wealth redistribution. By promising regular cash payments to everyone, irrespective of employment or income status, UBI echoes Marxist ideals of wealth sharing within society, criticized by some as fostering dependency on state aid rather than individual effort.

Challenging the traditional capitalist model, UBI provides income regardless of employment status, leading critics to argue that it undermines the ethos of earning a living through work. Detractors fear it might reduce incentives to contribute to the workforce, potentially hindering productivity and perpetuating reliance on state aid. While proponents suggest UBI could lessen reliance on traditional wage labor, critics worry it might diminish motivation for seeking better opportunities or contributing to the economy through work.

Universal Basic Income (UBI) bears similarities to the "Iron Bowl" policy implemented during Mao Zedong's era in China. The "Iron Bowl" initiative aimed to ensure job stability and provide social welfare benefits to urban workers, predominantly within state-owned enterprises (SOEs). Similarly, UBI proposes regular cash payments to individuals, reminiscent of the comprehensive provisions offered by the "Iron Bowl."

The "Iron Bowl" policy guaranteed job security and an array of benefits, including healthcare, housing, subsidized food, and pensions. Likewise, UBI intends to offer a safety net in the form of financial assistance to all, irrespective of employment status, resembling the comprehensive welfare provisions under the "Iron Bowl."

Both policies aimed to instill a sense of security among individuals, fostering loyalty and allegiance to the governing body. The "Iron Bowl" sought to solidify the commitment of workers to the Communist Party by meeting their fundamental needs, just as UBI proponents argue for providing financial security to all citizens, ensuring their welfare and potentially fostering allegiance to the Democrat Party.

However, both systems are flawed. The "Iron Bowl" system, lacking ties between job security and individual performance, led to inefficiencies within state-run industries. Similarly, critics of UBI express concerns about potential drawbacks, such as fostering dependence on state aid, diminishing work ethic, and disrupting the traditional capitalist system. Critics argue that UBI, like the "Iron Bowl," might lack accountability, potentially leading to economic inefficiencies and hindering innovation.

Universal Basic Income (UBI) has drawn criticism due to its conflicts with fundamental capitalist principles. One key contention against UBI revolves around the notion that it might diminish the incentive to work. In capitalist economies, the work-reward relationship drives productivity and innovation. UBI's provision of a guaranteed income regardless of employment status might disincentivize some individuals from actively seeking work or contributing productively to the economy.

Moreover, critics argue that UBI could disrupt market dynamics by injecting additional income into the population. This influx of funds might lead to increased consumer spending, potentially driving up demand for goods and services. This surge in demand could trigger price inflation, disrupting the natural equilibrium of supply and demand, which is integral to free-market economies.

Financing UBI involves significant wealth redistribution through taxation or other means. Detractors see this redistribution of wealth as conflicting with the core principles of capitalism, specifically the notion of individual property rights and the free exchange of goods and services in the market. Taxing income or wealth to fund UBI might encroach upon the profits earned through individual entrepreneurship and effort.

Critics also raise concerns about the potential for UBI to foster a culture of dependence on government support. They argue that providing a universal stipend might erode the drive for individual initiative and self-reliance, values that underpin the capitalist ethos. This reliance on a government stipend could potentially dampen the entrepreneurial spirit and dilute the sense of personal responsibility within society.

Furthermore, UBI's impact on labor markets is questioned. Critics suggest that by providing a guaranteed income, individuals might become more selective in their employment choices or demand higher wages. This shift could disrupt the natural negotiation process between labor and capital, altering the dynamics of the labor market as defined by capitalist economies.

UBI initiatives have spurred debates regarding their constitutionality within the United States. Critics often argue that implementing UBI could conflict with various constitutional principles.

One argument revolves around the federal government's authority to enact such programs. The US Constitution outlines the government's limited powers, primarily through the Commerce Clause and the General Welfare Clause. UBI might exceed these enumerated powers, as it is not explicitly defined as a federal responsibility, and the Constitution reserves powers not delegated to the federal government to the states or the people.

Another aspect pertains to the Tenth Amendment, emphasizing states' rights. Critics argue that implementing a nationwide UBI might overstep states' authority to regulate their internal affairs and social welfare programs. It could infringe upon states' abilities to craft their own policies tailored to their unique economic and social circumstances.

Additionally, opponents often highlight potential violations of the Due Process Clause of the Fifth Amendment. They argue that UBI might interfere with the fundamental concept of property rights and individual liberty, as it involves redistributing wealth through mandatory taxation to provide a universal income. Critics contend that forcing citizens to contribute to a UBI program against their will might infringe upon their rights to their own property and earnings.

Moreover, the establishment of a UBI program could be seen as a form of wealth redistribution, raising questions about equal protection under the law as guaranteed by the Fourteenth Amendment. Such programs might create disparities between individuals who contribute to the system and those who receive benefits, potentially leading to unequal treatment and constitutional challenges based on discriminatory grounds.

The federal government's handling of the COVID-19 pandemic, marked by strategies such as lockdowns and business closures, ignited debates about individual liberties and economic rights. While ostensibly aimed at quelling the virus's spread, these measures had profound economic and societal repercussions. To counter these effects, the government introduced financial aid and stimulus packages. However, this extensive intervention in the economy prompted comparisons to socialist practices.

The mandated closure of small businesses amid the 2020 pandemic emerged as a focal point for critics. They contend that these shutdowns precipitated economic hardships, job losses, and business closures. This outcome appears aligned with objectives reminiscent of communist ideologies: dismantling small-scale private enterprises and consolidating economic control among a privileged few. These closures disproportionately affected smaller businesses, eroding economic diversity and favoring larger corporations—an outcome echoing Marxist notions of centralized economic control.

The pandemic expedited existing trends toward augmented government intervention and the implementation of social welfare policies, capitalizing on the crisis to propel these movements forward. Government aid and relief initiatives proved pivotal for the survival of small businesses, fostering an environment where industry control and government intervention garnered increased acceptance.

These shutdowns amplified reliance on government assistance programs, prompting individuals and businesses to rely on state support for survival. The economic fallout weakened conventional capitalist structures, fostering a societal inclination toward alternative ideologies such as socialism. This escalating dependency signals a shift toward collectivist values often associated with communism, raising worries about their enduring influence on societal beliefs and economic systems.

Biden's "equity" agenda has also drawn criticism for its emphasis on racial-based wealth redistribution, departing from America's core value of impartial treatment. This shift, moving away from equal opportunity towards mandated redistributive measures based on demographic factors, challenges the fundamental principles of limited government and individual liberties, eroding the traditional American ethos.

The debates within the Democratic Party regarding reparations for historical slavery encompass a wide spectrum of opinions. While some Democrats champion reparations as a means to rectify historical injustices and systemic racism, critics harbor deep reservations about the practicality and equity of such measures. They question the feasibility of identifying eligible recipients and determining fair compensation, citing logistical challenges in tracing lineage for a just program. Critics fear that singling out a specific group for reparations might sow divisions among racial or ethnic communities, potentially undermining the principle of equal treatment under the law.

Financial implications weigh heavily in the concerns of reparations' detractors, who caution against the substantial costs to the government. This raises worries about funding sources and the strain on public resources. Critics worry that implementing reparations might redirect funds from crucial social programs or essential government priorities, adversely impacting taxpayers and the broader economy.

Another significant challenge highlighted by critics revolves around the historical complexities associated with assigning responsibility and accountability for reparations. The aftermath of slavery poses intricate challenges in attributing responsibility and determining suitable compensation. Concerns about unintended consequences, such as deepening divisions among racial or ethnic groups, compound critics' arguments against reparations.

Moreover, critics labeling reparations as Marxist point out the parallels between reparations and Marxist principles of wealth redistribution. Reparations could be construed as aiming to equalize economic disparities between different social groups. This mirrors Marxist ideologies focusing on rectifying historical inequalities by restructuring societal and economic systems, advocating for wealth and resource redistribution to create a more equitable society.

The critique against reparations extends to their conflict with the 14th Amendment, which mandates equal protection under the law for all citizens. Tying reparations to racial criteria for compensation might be viewed as discriminatory. This selective treatment based on race challenges the Amendment's essence of fairness and impartiality for all citizens, irrespective of their background. Race-based reparations might face legal challenges due to disparities in treatment based solely on racial classification, potentially violating the 14th Amendment's equal protection clause. Overall, programs favoring or discriminating by race contradict the foundational guarantee of equal treatment outlined in the 14th Amendment.

Several initiatives within the Democratic Party have concerned advocates of limited government and individual liberties due to perceived influences of Communist ideologies. The proposals to defund the police and enforce stricter gun control are viewed as expanding government control, potentially diminishing citizens' rights to self-governance and protection. These measures have sparked unease among proponents of limited government. For individuals valuing smaller government and maximal personal autonomy, these policies signal a troubling trend toward an enlarged state apparatus. This shift diverges from their principles of smaller government and individual autonomy, raising concerns about threatened personal liberties. This expansion of government authority prompts criticism from advocates of limited government and individual rights, fearing the erosion of freedoms and the concentration of state power.

Charles Lipson, a political science professor at the University of Chicago, contends that the Democratic Party's recent endeavors to expand the social-welfare system significantly deviate from its foundational principles. This shift poses the risk of fundamentally transforming the essence of American society and potentially steering it towards a less free environment. Lipson is concerned about the broader implications of this shift in policies. He warns that such changes could pave the way for a system that gravitates toward one-party rule, eroding the principles of a multi-party democratic setup that the United States has historically embraced. Lipson is wary of these alterations as they might lead to a consolidation of power within a single political entity, thereby limiting the diversity of viewpoints and policies crucial for a robust and balanced democratic society.

Victor Davis Hanson, a prominent conservative figure, has voiced deep-seated apprehensions about the Democratic Party's intentions, pointing to a series of objectives that could significantly reshape core components of the American democratic system. Among these concerns, Hanson highlights the Democrats' ambitions to overhaul or eliminate institutions integral to the nation's democratic framework. Central to his critique are the proposed changes to the Electoral College, seen as a potential target for reform or removal by the Democratic Party. He also underscores concerns about potential changes to the Second Amendment, signaling a desire for stricter gun control laws that could redefine Americans' constitutional rights. Additionally, Hanson points to worrisome signs regarding freedom of speech, citing potential restrictions through hate speech legislation that could curtail the protections enshrined in the First Amendment. Moreover, he emphasizes the party's ambitions to reshape the Supreme Court, potentially altering its balance and direction, which could significantly impact the nation's judiciary. There are also concerns raised about rethinking the concept of states' representation and advocating for a national voting law that might not mandate identification, potentially compromising the integrity of the electoral process.

Hanson explained Democrat goals: "We don't like the rules we play by, so we want to do the following. We want to get rid of the Electoral College that's in the Constitution. We want to get rid of the Second Amendment that's in the Constitution. We want to restrict the First Amendment with something we call hate speech and suppress free expression. We want to get rid of the nine-person Supreme Court that's been here for 160 years. We want to get rid of the idea of 50 states that's been here for 60 years. We want to get rid of the Constitutional idea that the state sets balloting laws and has a national voting law that says you have to…you cannot ask a person to have an ID. And so we want to get rid of the 180-year filibuster. So this party has attacked every element of the democratic experience. They felt that it wasn't viable or useful for their own agenda, so this is a kind of projection they're in."[20]

Hanson's observations underscore a broader concern: a potential clash between the Democratic Party's policy goals and the established democratic norms and values that have long defined the American political landscape.

Within the Democratic Party, there is a push for stricter gun control measures, aligning with policy proposals aimed at regulating firearms. However, these efforts often clash with the protections guaranteed by the Second Amendment. The Second Amendment, a fundamental

---

[20] Dowling, M. "Lincoln Project: 'We Want to Burn the Republican Party to the Ground'." *Independent Sentinel*, 15 Nov. 2022, www.independentsentinel.com/lincoln-project-we-want-to-burn-the-republican-party-to-the-ground/.

constitutional right, safeguards the right to bear arms and serves as a defense against government overreach, allowing individuals to protect themselves, their families, and their property.

The Democratic Party's advocacy for enhanced background checks, firearm limitations, and magazine restrictions sparks debates regarding potential infringements on Second Amendment rights. Some argue that these measures might limit law-abiding citizens' access to firearms without effectively addressing the root causes of gun violence. Advocates of gun rights contend that any legislative action intending to restrict access to firearms undermines this constitutional right, potentially upsetting the intended balance of power between citizens and the state, and posing a threat to the foundational freedoms ensured by the Constitution.

Communist regimes have historically pursued policies to disarm citizens, and several reasons support this strategy. First, disarming citizens consolidates power within the government. In totalitarian regimes, such as those under Communist rule, the central authority aims to maintain absolute control over the population. By disarming citizens, governments limit their ability to resist or challenge the state's authority, ensuring the dominance of the regime.

Secondly, disarming the population is an effort to prevent dissent and uprisings against the government. Communists, seeking to maintain their unchallenged authority, consider an armed populace as a potential threat to the stability of their regime. Disarming citizens helps suppress any resistance or opposition, curbing the possibility of armed rebellions or organized resistance movements.

Moreover, disarming citizens serves the purpose of enforcing ideological control. Marxist regimes aim to uphold strict ideological conformity among the population. Limiting access to firearms aligns with this goal by restricting opportunities for alternative ideologies or armed groups that might challenge the ruling doctrine.

Another factor is the elimination of potential opposition. Communist governments often view armed individuals or groups, especially those not aligned with the state's ideology, as threats to their control. Disarmament measures are used to neutralize these opposition forces, ensuring a more compliant and submissive population.

Lastly, disarming citizens allows socialist governments to maintain a monopoly on the use of force. By restricting access to firearms, the state can dictate the terms of conflict and control the extent of violence. This effectively establishes the government as the sole authority on the use of force within society.

In countries under Communist rule throughout history, policies aimed at restricting access to firearms were common. These measures, often justified as promoting public safety or preventing crime, primarily serve to consolidate power, minimize challenges to authority, and solidify the control of the ruling regime. Ultimately, disarming citizens becomes a tool for Communist governments to secure their authority and limit potential resistance.

The Democratic Party strongly pushes for gun control under the banner of public safety, proposing measures such as enhanced background checks and firearm restrictions to create safer communities. Yet, amidst this emphasis on reducing firearm-related tragedies, doubts linger among some individuals about whether these actions genuinely represent the party's true intentions concerning broader disarmament objectives.

Biden's remarks hinting at his ability to interpret the Second Amendment as he sees fit have sparked considerable concern, particularly regarding his executive authority on gun rights. These statements have sparked concerns as they surpass the defined limits of executive power in the U.S. governmental system. The interpretation of the Constitution, including the Second Amendment, is not within the President's purview; instead, this role is expressly designated to the judiciary, specifically the Supreme Court.

In the United States, the Supreme Court plays a crucial role in interpreting the Constitution. This authority, as granted by the Constitution itself, establishes the judiciary as an independent branch tasked with interpreting laws, including the Constitution. The doctrine of judicial review, established by precedent in *Marbury v. Madison*, 5 U.S. (1 Cranch) 137 (1803), confirms the Supreme Court's responsibility in assessing the constitutionality of laws and executive actions, ensuring alignment with constitutional principles.

The President's primary role centers on executing laws and shaping policies, separate from the judiciary's duty to interpret the Constitution. While presidents nominate justices and judges, their function does not encompass constitutional interpretation. Presidential opinions on constitutional matters hold weight but do not supersede the Supreme Court's authority. Ultimately, the Court's decisions establish legal precedents, guiding the nation's interpretation of the Constitution and safeguarding individual rights, including those protected by the Second Amendment.

Thus, Biden's assertion of interpretive authority over the Second Amendment contradicts the established U.S. governance system, where the judiciary, particularly the Supreme Court, holds the ultimate responsibility for constitutional interpretation. Such claims by the executive branch encroach upon the separation of powers in the U.S. government, unsettling those who prioritize the core values of the country's governance.

Throughout Biden's tenure, the administration delved into extensive discussions regarding executive orders aimed at gun control. These measures sought to enact stricter regulations on gun sales, reinforce background checks, and address the rising concerns surrounding "ghost guns," which lack serial numbers. One primary goal was to close the so-called "gun show loophole" by mandating comprehensive background checks for all sales, extending scrutiny to prevent ineligible individuals from obtaining firearms through private transactions. Additionally, there were talks about potential executive orders concerning firearm accessories, such as stabilizing braces modifying pistols, and considerations about imposing serialization and background checks for parts used in "ghost guns."

However, these proposed executive orders encountered opposition. Critics cited concerns about potential overreach beyond the boundaries enshrined in the Second Amendment. They argued that implementing such measures might require a constitutional amendment, positing that neither legislative nor executive action could infringe upon this constitutional right.

In the United States, executive orders must adhere to the Constitution. While the President possesses the authority to issue such orders under Article II, this power is not limitless. Executive orders are expected to operate within constitutional boundaries and refrain from overriding existing laws. While they guide federal agencies in administrative tasks and law enforcement, they cannot create new laws or infringe upon the authority of other branches of government.

The constitutionality of executive orders is subject to scrutiny, with courts, including the Supreme Court, empowered to assess their adherence to the Constitution. If an order is found to conflict with constitutional principles, it can be legally contested and invalidated through judicial proceedings.

The U.S. Constitution stands as the paramount law, requiring all legislation, whether from Congress or states, to align with its mandates. Laws conflicting with the Constitution are deemed unconstitutional and voided. The concept of judicial review, established in *Marbury v. Madison*, grants courts the authority to evaluate the constitutionality of laws, ensuring adherence to fundamental constitutional principles.

When a court deems a law or an executive order unconstitutional, it loses legal standing. This principle, derived from the Supremacy Clause, establishes the Constitution, federal laws, and treaties as supreme, prevailing over conflicting state laws or governmental actions. Such rulings establish benchmarks for future cases, mandating adherence to constitutional principles for legitimacy and enforcement.

The Democratic Party's push for gun control, framed as a means to ensure public safety, regularly slams into a significant roadblock—the Second Amendment's constitutional protections. This hurdle obstructs the party's pursuit of comprehensive gun control reforms. The Second Amendment's roots lie in the Founding Fathers' multifaceted intentions, with a crucial element being the shield against tyranny.

During the drafting of the Constitution and the Bill of Rights, the Founding Fathers harbored deep concerns about concentrated power and the potential for governmental tyranny. They championed the notion that an armed populace served as a barricade against potential governmental overreach. To them, the populace's right to bear arms was a tool to resist any governmental deviation from democratic ideals, guarding against infringements on citizens' freedoms.

The phrasing of the Second Amendment, highlighting the necessity of "a well-regulated Militia" for the security of a free state, underscores this anxiety. It was intricately linked to the concept of an armed and organized citizenry poised to counter external threats and, critically, any authoritarian leanings within the government.

Drawing from historical sources such as the English Bill of Rights and their experiences during the colonial era, the Founders highlighted the significance of an armed population as a counterweight to potential governmental oppression. They viewed citizens' ability to possess firearms as a fundamental right vital for preserving individual liberties and maintaining a balance of power between the government and the people.

Communists, proponents of collective ownership and resource control, confront a theoretical clash with the ideals enshrined in the Second Amendment. This amendment was instituted to safeguard individual freedoms, particularly the right to bear arms, as a defense against government encroachment.

From a Marxist standpoint, the abolition of the Second Amendment aligns with their objectives for several reasons. Firstly, communists often pursue centralized control to redistribute resources and realize their envisioned Marxist utopia. The presence of an armed populace poses a substantial obstacle to centralized control. Removing this right could potentially pave the way for a more centralized power structure, aligning with their objectives.

Secondly, socialist ideologies historically prioritize the elimination of potential opposition to revolutionary changes. The right to bear arms empowers citizens to resist such revolutionary alterations or authoritarian actions, presenting a challenge to the establishment of a communist regime.

Moreover, communist ideologies advocate for an overhaul of societal structures encompassing economic, political, and social systems. The Second Amendment, preserving individual rights to arms, might be perceived as an impediment to enacting such societal reforms by proponents of communism.

In essence, the rationale guiding a communist agenda to dismantle the Second Amendment stems from the belief that centralized control and transformative societal changes could encounter obstacles posed by an armed populace exercising its constitutional rights.

The Biden administration's enforcement of a vaccine mandate for businesses with 100 or more employees sparked nationwide controversy. This mandate, presented as a strategy to combat COVID-19, required full vaccination or regular testing for employees.

Detractors strongly criticized the mandate, condemning it as an egregious government overreach and an assault on personal freedoms. They argued that such mandates coerced individuals into vaccination against their will and disregarded their autonomy in making health decisions.

Debates intensified regarding the federal government's authority to enforce these mandates. Many voiced concerns that these broad mandates encroached upon state rights and excessively interfered with private businesses, potentially causing economic disruptions and imposing heavy administrative burdens on employers.

Supporters of limited government involvement condemned the mandates, emphasizing the importance of preserving individual medical choices and granting businesses autonomy in setting their vaccination policies. They criticized the administration for exceeding its authority, asserting that the mandates contradicted fundamental principles of personal choice.

Opposition to vaccine mandates often centered on the violation of personal freedoms and autonomy, drawing parallels between aspects of the mandate and authoritarian control. These mandates signaled governmental intrusion into personal healthcare decisions, essentially enforcing compliance through institutional requirements or penalties.

Viewed through an authoritarian lens, the mandates were a method for the state to dictate personal health choices and restrict individual liberties. This perspective reflected concerns about excessive governmental control over various aspects of citizens' lives.

Utah's attorney general, Sean Reyes, criticized the Biden administration's COVID-19 vaccination mandates, describing them as "autocratic." He objected to the federal government's claimed authority to dictate medical decisions for individuals and employers, regardless of their vaccination stance. Reyes considered Biden's directive as an unprecedented intrusion into the realm of private businesses, echoing the ongoing debate over balancing public health measures with individual liberties.

Senator Mike Lee, a Utah Republican, similarly lambasted Biden for pressuring private citizens into medical procedures, particularly COVID-19 vaccinations. He argued that vaccine mandates infringe upon personal freedoms. He strongly criticized Biden, accusing him of disregarding constitutional principles, which he sees as a threat to the fabric of the nation. Lee said, "From ignoring property rights, to shirking his duty at the border, and now, coercing private citizens to undergo a medical procedure, Joe Biden has shown a wanton disregard for the U.S. Constitution. As a would-be autocrat, Biden endangers the very fibers of this great nation. Freedom and agency are the hallmarks of the American experiment."[21] Lee underscored that American freedom and individual agency are fundamental aspects of the nation's identity, expressing skepticism regarding Biden's commitment to the Constitution and the potential erosion of American values.

The Biden administration's vaccine mandate has sparked a barrage of legal challenges from various states and organizations. It is crucial to distinguish between a mandate and a law: Laws undergo a legislative process, while mandates often stem from executive actions targeting

---

[21] Droney, Pat. "Rep. Mast urges Americans 'do not comply!', says 'ignore Biden's illegal mandates like he ignores our immigration laws,'" *Law Enforcement Today*, 15 Sept, 2021, www.lawenforcementtoday.com/rep-mast-urges-americans-do-not-comply-says-ignore-bidens-illegal-mandates-like-he-ignores-our-immigration-laws/.

specific policy goals or urgent situations. This difference leaves mandates open to legal challenges and constitutional scrutiny, separate from the usual legislative route. These challenges have become the focal point of prolonged legal battles, rigorously scrutinizing the federal government's authority and the constitutionality of enforcing such measures.

The legal challenges revolve around several crucial points. Firstly, opponents argue that the mandate infringes upon states' sovereignty by imposing federal requirements on businesses and employees within their jurisdictions. This argument centers on disrupting the balance of power between the federal government and individual states, encroaching on the latter's rights to self-governance.

Secondly, legal challenges scrutinize the constitutional basis for the federal government's mandate on vaccinations or testing for private businesses. Critics assert that the mandate surpasses federal authority and lacks a clear foundation in constitutional law, particularly concerning public health and labor regulations.

Economic implications are another focal point in these legal battles. Opponents highlight the potential administrative burdens and operational disruptions that this mandate inflicts on businesses, leading to adverse effects on productivity, employment, and overall economic stability.

Moreover, these legal challenges dive into fundamental questions regarding individual liberties, medical autonomy, and the government's role in public health. Critics argue that mandates infringe upon personal freedoms and medical choices, essentially coercing individuals to comply with medical interventions against their will.

These mandates have stirred debates about their alignment with the US Constitution and the protection of individual liberties. Critics highlight potential infringements on constitutional principles, such as encroachments on the right to liberty and privacy. They argue that these mandates breach the Tenth Amendment by overshadowing states' rights to manage public health within their jurisdictions.

Concerns also arise regarding potential violations of the First Amendment's freedom of religion, as mandates could clash with individuals' religious beliefs. Compelling vaccinations may contradict religious convictions, potentially infringing on the right to practice one's faith freely.

Additionally, these mandates might contravene the Fourteenth Amendment's guarantee of equal protection under the law. Mandates create disparities, burdening individuals who choose not to get vaccinated and potentially leading to discrimination.

While acknowledging the importance of public health measures, critics stress the need for a delicate balance between public health concerns and individual rights. The constitutionality of these mandates remains hotly contested, leading to ongoing legal challenges aimed at determining their alignment with the fundamental principles enshrined in the US Constitution.

The argument connecting mandated vaccines to Marxist principles often centers on the ideology's emphasis on communal welfare and collective responsibility. Within Marxist perspectives, the paramount focus revolves around advancing the collective welfare of the working class and society as a whole.

Advocates of mandated vaccines might draw parallels between these mandates and Marxist ideals of communal welfare. They emphasize the Marxist principle of addressing societal issues collectively, prioritizing the common good over individual concerns. From this viewpoint, vaccination mandates are presented as a means to safeguard the health of the community, portraying them as a reflection of a commitment to the greater good in line with Marxist ideologies.

However, such an alignment provokes valid concerns regarding the extent of governmental control over personal health decisions and individual freedoms. Mandated vaccines raise critical debates about the balance between communal well-being and individual autonomy. This discussion intersects with broader societal debates about the role of government and the boundaries of individual rights within the framework of societal governance. The tension between collective health interests and personal liberties becomes a crucial point of contention, sparking ongoing dialogues about the extent of governmental intervention in private spheres, particularly regarding health-related choices.

The escalating legal feud between the Federal Trade Commission (FTC) and Amazon regarding alleged monopolistic practices reflects a burgeoning anti-capitalist sentiment within government agencies under the Biden administration. This clash exposes the fundamental discord between Amazon's market-oriented strategies and the rising influence of communist ideologies within bureaucratic spheres, indicating a widening ideological gap and potential conflict between capitalist-driven entities and the growing sway of anti-capitalist ideologies in governmental bodies.

The legal feud between the FTC and Amazon, kicking off in September 2023, has stirred heated discussions regarding alleged monopolistic practices in e-commerce. While the FTC, alongside 17 state attorneys, accuses Amazon of stifling innovation and distorting fair competition through anti-competitive strategies, Amazon touts the benefits to consumers from its strategies. Amazon denies engaging in monopolistic behavior, pointing to fierce competition from industry giants such as Walmart and Target.

Marxism champions communal resource management, diametrically opposed to Amazon's pursuit of profit maximization and market supremacy. This capitalist drive undermines equitable resource distribution and fortifies social hierarchies, starkly challenging the purported egalitarian base of Marxist beliefs. Amazon diverges from the notions of collective resource ownership and fair distribution. Communism seeks to abolish private ownership and market competition, preferring shared resources and communal administration. Amazon, entrenched in a profit-focused capitalist paradigm, fundamentally clashes with these communist principles, centered on market dominance and wealth accumulation. Furthermore, Amazon's concentration of wealth and power conflicts with the communist goal of fair resource distribution and communal ownership.

Additionally, Amazon's competitive strategies, centered around maximizing profits and wielding substantial influence across sectors, could be interpreted as exploitative within a communist ideology aiming to eliminate hierarchical structures and labor exploitation.

Overall, Amazon's embodiment of capitalist principles, its pursuit of profit, and its reinforcement of hierarchical structures face opposition from adherents of socialism. Amazon's success within the capitalist framework triggered heightened scrutiny from the FTC, inciting regulatory attention from those aligned with Marxist viewpoints. This perspective paints a picture of Amazon being targeted for takedown due to its capitalist stance by those who secretly favor communist ideologies.

The Democratic Party's pivot toward more statist and Marxist-leaning policies presents a shift within American politics, indicating inclinations toward authoritarianism. This transition is evident through proposals advocating heightened government intervention in healthcare and industry, coupled with a focus on wealth redistribution to address income inequality, all hallmarks of a statist and socialist economic framework. The Biden administration's approval ratings have steeply declined, reaching a record low of 36%, indicating a growing dissatisfaction among the American populace with the administration's trajectory and its embrace of Marxist-influenced ideologies.

Many who supported Joe Biden's candidacy expected a moderate leader fostering unity in a polarized political climate. However, his administration has shifted leftward, notably in policies such as relaxed immigration approaches and calls for stricter gun control and increased social media censorship. These actions have sparked debates regarding their implications for national security, societal harmony, and justice. Moreover, concerns about soaring government spending, proposed tax hikes, and expanded government intervention in the economy have fueled worries about the potential long-term consequences, particularly burdening future generations. The focus on wealth redistribution and income equality has amplified fears of a move toward communist ideologies.

Furthermore, growing unease arises from the administration's frequent use of executive orders and unilateral actions bypassing the legislative process. This trend raises alarms about the concentration of excessive power within the executive branch, potentially undermining the critical checks and balances vital for a healthy democracy.

The following chapter delves into how endeavors linked to communism have worsened societal divisions, heightened political polarization, and ignited civil unrest. By looking into the penetration of these ideologies into the nation's framework, the chapter scrutinizes how Marxist doctrines foster social discord and corrode established societal structures, ultimately destabilizing the bedrock of democracy.

Chapter 5

Destabilization to Crisis

The United States, renowned for its democratic and republican traditions, faces a series of unprecedented challenges and internal tensions. Over recent decades, Marxist ideologies have gained traction within American society, notably in academia, media, and certain political movements. This ascent of Marxist thought has coincided with heightened societal disruptions and exacerbated political divisions. Debates revolving around economic inequality, identity politics, and social justice have further deepened the existing schisms, prompting concerns about the potential for destabilization leading to a state of crisis within the nation.

At the heart of America's identity lie democratic values, individual liberties, and a capitalist economic system. Its founding principles are rooted in concepts of self-governance, personal freedoms, and limited government interference. Capitalism, integral to the American ethos, champions private ownership, economic competition, and individual prosperity via market-driven mechanisms.

However, Marxist ideologies directly challenge established institutions and social norms, posing a stark contrast to American principles. Communism seeks a classless, stateless society with collective resource ownership and equitable wealth distribution, advocating the elimination of social hierarchies through shared ownership and fair wealth allotment. In direct opposition, America's foundation rests on democratic principles, individual freedoms, and a capitalist economic structure, emphasizing private ownership and market-driven competition.

Proponents of communism advocate for the dismantling of America's very core – its ideals, national identity, and political framework. They view the destruction of existing power structures, supported by capitalist economies, as essential. This process involves overthrowing established social, economic, and political systems, challenging and discrediting fundamental values and institutions integral to the nation's identity.

This chapter explores the profound impact of Marxist ideologies on the social and political fabric of the United States. It seeks to unravel the multifaceted repercussions of communism-associated efforts that have significantly deepened societal rifts, escalated political polarization, and sparked civil unrest. By examining the infiltration of leftist ideologies within the historical context of the country, the chapter sheds light on the disruptive implications of communism. Moreover, it scrutinizes the ways in which socialist doctrines fuel social discord and sow the seeds of dissent, ultimately destabilizing traditional societal structures. Understanding this progression is essential to grasp the broader influence of communism on the stability and foundational principles of democracy within America.

A communist revolution is a complex process that unfolds across ideologies, society, and politics. The initial phase, known as ideological subversion, involves deliberately demoralizing the targeted society by exploiting vulnerabilities and sowing discord. Agents of change strategically disrupt institutions and exploit social, political, and economic vulnerabilities, aiming to weaken established structures and institutions.

In pursuit of societal transformation, certain communist proponents use rhetoric that emphasizes disparities between the affluent elite and the economically disadvantaged. They highlight the alleged injustices and exploitation within the capitalist framework, aiming to foster divisions and unite the working class against what they perceive as oppressors.

Through impassioned speeches, printed materials, and online platforms, these proponents disseminate their ideology. They emphasize the stark differences in living standards, shedding light on the struggles endured by the working class—meager wages, job insecurity, and limited access to essentials. Their aim is to stoke resentment and indignation within the working class toward the capitalist class. As tensions rise, some leftist factions may organize protests and labor strikes, demanding better working conditions, fair wages, and wealth redistribution.

Some of these groups may advocate for revolutionary action to dismantle the capitalist government and establish a Marxist regime. They passionately argue that the capitalist system perpetuates structural inequality and exploitation. By using provocative rhetoric and highlighting the struggles of the working class, they hope to spark collective action and rally individuals around radical change. Their messaging often revolves around exposing elite excesses while amplifying the plight of the marginalized, creating a sense of urgency for drastic societal transformation.

In the United States, the aversion to communism finds its roots in the enduring influence and success of capitalism, which has been a cornerstone of the nation's economic landscape. Throughout history, capitalism has been a driving force behind remarkable economic growth, prosperity, and the elevation of living standards. Its core tenets—such as private ownership, competitive markets, and entrepreneurial spirit—have been instrumental in fostering innovation, driving technological advancements, and generating wealth.

During periods of economic abundance characterized by thriving businesses, increased job opportunities, and an elevated standard of living, the allure of radical ideologies such as communism tends to wane. Capitalism's ability to create prosperity fosters a sense of stability and financial security among individuals, diminishing their inclination toward embracing radical ideological shifts. The economic triumphs brought forth by capitalism often lead to a prevailing preference for maintaining the existing system, underpinned by values of individualism, personal liberties, and the pursuit of personal success and affluence.

Additionally, one of capitalism's achievements is the cultivation of a robust middle class. The opportunities it offers enable many to climb the socioeconomic ladder, granting access to a comfortable lifestyle and avenues for upward mobility. This sense of upward progress and economic stability acts as a bulwark against the appeal of radical socialist ideologies. Individuals, benefiting from financial security and opportunities for advancement, are less inclined to entertain ideologies that could disrupt their financial stability and personal freedoms.

The accomplishments of capitalism in fostering economic prosperity and individual advancement lay a strong foundation for societal resilience against ideologies advocating drastic systemic changes, particularly during phases of economic stability and progress.

Moreover, economic stability, consistent employment, and the potential for upward mobility naturally mitigate the appeal of radical economic transformations. Those benefiting from financial stability tend to safeguard their gains, creating a prevailing sentiment in favor of preserving the status quo. This success promotes values that prioritize individualism, personal freedoms, and the flourishing of the capitalist system.

During economic downturns, however, Marxist ideologies tend to gain ground, exploiting the vulnerabilities exposed by challenging economic periods. The allure of socialism, promising economic security and fair wealth distribution, becomes enticing amidst income disparities and a lack of access to vital resources. Dissatisfaction with the government's economic handling peaks, and socialist policies appear as a seemingly viable solution to financial difficulties.

To sway Americans towards embracing communism, advocates may resort to what they call political warfare—a strategy aimed at dismantling the established capitalist system. This method involves disseminating information, mobilizing movements, and employing psychological tactics to make socialism appear acceptable and relatable. The goal is to disrupt societal complacency and gradually convince people of Marxism's supposed virtues.

Yuri Bezmenov's insights into ideological subversion unveiled a four-stage strategy used by the Soviet Union to undermine Western societies. Central to his theory, the destabilization phase stands as the third step, succeeding the demoralization stages and heralding a crisis aimed at normalizing an alien Marxist ideology within a targeted society.

During the destabilization phase, the primary objective is to magnify existing societal divisions and exploit vulnerabilities, deliberately sowing widespread turmoil. This strategic phase employs multifaceted tactics involving the amplification of social, political, and economic issues within the target society. The intent is to foster pervasive distrust in institutions, corrode social unity, and foment chaos and instability.

Bezmenov highlighted a spectrum of methods instrumental in achieving destabilization. These tactics encompass the deliberate promotion of social unrest by exacerbating divisions rooted in race, class, ideology, or other societal fault lines. Further strategies involve the deliberate targeting of pivotal institutions—government, media, education, and religion—to corrode public trust. Economic manipulation serves as another facet, creating discontent and social upheaval, while cultural subversion seeks to dismantle traditional values, weakening the societal fabric.

The ultimate goal within this phase is the perpetuation of a continuous state of crisis, rendering society increasingly vulnerable and ripe for substantial transformation. By exploiting inherent societal fractures and amplifying discontent, the destabilization phase sets the stage for a potential collapse or a dramatic reconfiguration of the targeted society's structure.

Bezmenov's framework provides a lens through which to understand how ideological subversion aims to corrode a society's foundations, paving the way for the acceptance of an alternative ideology. Although his observations were primarily rooted in Soviet tactics during the Cold War, the principles he espoused hold relevance across various contexts of ideological manipulation and subversion.

Political warfare, intricately woven into this process, functions as a duality employing both violent and non-violent avenues. While overt violence aims to challenge authority directly, the subtlety of non-violent tactics rests in their capacity to manipulate public sentiment and mobilize masses. The manipulation of information, often wielded through propaganda, emerges as a pivotal tool, cunningly exploiting societal grievances to intensify existing polarization.

In today's globally connected world, the rapid dissemination of information facilitates the unchecked proliferation of propaganda and divisive narratives. This unfiltered deluge has the potential to deepen societal chasms as individuals, under the sway of extreme ideologies, further distance themselves from opposing viewpoints.

The ramifications of this form of political warfare on societal stability loom ominously. The propagation of divisive ideologies and the calculated exploitation of grievances possess the dangerous potential to ignite social unrest, erode trust in institutions, and sow seeds of skepticism and discord. Ultimately, this Machiavellian approach significantly contributes to the destabilization of society, corroding trust and exacerbating societal rifts.

Within the Maoist Insurgency model, the insidious use of political warfare aligns itself ominously with Marxist ideologies, intending to advance their objectives. Derived from the tactics of Chinese Communist leader Mao Zedong, this concept amalgamates both violent and non-violent methods to rally support toward a unified cause.

This framework of political warfare extends beyond mere military conquest, delving into the manipulation of minds, the control of public sentiment, and the orchestrated consolidation of backing for a specific ideological agenda. Echoing Marxist principles, Maoist insurgents prioritize garnering public allegiance, acknowledging that real power resides within the people.

The array of tactics employed in Maoist political warfare spans a spectrum of manipulative strategies. From the pervasive dissemination of propaganda and the insidious spread of deceptive misinformation to the strategic agitation and exploitation of sympathetic factions, these calculated efforts aim to exploit societal grievances, ferment a sense of injustice, and discredit established authorities. The approach shrewdly blends direct confrontations through armed actions with the subtler cultivation of non-violent movements, drawing sympathizers and expanding their support base.

This elaborate scheme involves manipulation of public sentiment and the methodical gathering of backing while systematically undermining credibility of the dominant system through the widespread dissemination of propaganda, false narratives, and infiltration into influential institutions such as universities and labor unions. The ultimate goal remains the subversion of existing power structures while rallying support behind the Marxist insurgency.

Moreover, the Maoist model of political warfare consciously harnesses psychological tactics, using narratives and rhetoric designed to exploit societal grievances and nurture collective disillusionment. By capitalizing on discontent and nurturing a shared sense of resentment, insurgents seek to unify their followers while sowing seeds of doubt in established systems.

This calculated blend of violent and non-violent methodologies, bolstered by deceptive propaganda and manipulative psychological tactics, starkly highlights the coercive and manipulative essence of Marxist ideologies. It illuminates the exploitation of public sentiment and collective support as fundamental instruments to propagate an ideology that ultimately threatens the very fabric of societal stability.

G. Edward Griffin, renowned for his writings on diverse political and economic themes, delves into a two-pronged strategy proposed for a potential Communist revolution in America—one that unfolds in stages of violence and subsequent non-violence. The violent phase is a calculated endeavor aiming to plunge society into chaos, anarchy, and widespread confusion, strategically orchestrated to incite a crisis within the government.

This calculated upheaval seeks to create a strategic opening for Communist-led guerrilla forces to rapidly seize power amidst the turmoil. The strategy involves a deliberate campaign of orchestrated destruction, including the intentional setting of fires in urban centers, rural villages, forests, fields, and barns. This deliberate chaos is engineered to cause significant damage, strategically necessitating the widespread deployment of defense and rescue units across vast areas. This dispersion aims to create vulnerabilities, facilitating the ambush and neutralization of law enforcement and National Guard units.

The use of large-scale fires in this context extends beyond physical damage; it aims to deliver a psychological blow to the American populace. The deliberate spread of fires is intended to instill fear, panic, and a sense of helplessness among ordinary citizens. This calculated fearmongering is designed to compel individuals to seek refuge and avoid interference with the guerrilla factions targeting crucial community power hubs.

Griffin's portrayal of this violent phase within the proposed Communist revolution is alarming and deeply concerning. The outlined strategy is crafted to sow discord, undermine societal stability, and orchestrate deliberate acts of destruction. This calculated chaos, aimed at weakening governmental structures, paints a distressing picture of a planned upheaval designed to induce widespread fear and confusion among American citizens.

Communists have historically utilized periods of societal upheaval and chaos as opportunities to advance their ideologies and ascend to power. During times of economic turmoil, social unrest, or political instability, they strategically capitalize on discontent within society. By positioning themselves as the solution to prevailing chaos, Marxists offer their ideology as an alternative to the existing systems, gaining support among disillusioned segments of the population.

One of their key tactics involves exploiting and exacerbating existing social divisions. Communists fuel discontent among different societal groups, intensifying divisions to weaken established systems. By widening these divides, they undermine the cohesion of existing structures, presenting socialism as the remedy for societal strife and offering a vision of unity under their system.

Chaos also provides communists with an opportune moment to agitate for change. They mobilize supporters, utilize propaganda, and provoke protests or demonstrations to challenge the status quo. Through these actions, they project communism as the answer to societal problems, promising radical transformations in governance and societal structures.

Furthermore, communists seek to undermine the credibility of existing institutions during times of chaos. They exploit the instability to discredit governmental, economic, and social structures, labeling them as ineffective or corrupt. By eroding public trust in these institutions, Marxists lay the groundwork for their system's perceived superiority and necessity.

In moments of leadership crises or societal turmoil, communists position themselves as strong leaders capable of restoring order and stability. They exploit the vacuum created by weak leadership, presenting their ideologies as the solution. This allows them to gain control and establish their systems under the guise of stability and progress.

There are growing fears surrounding individuals advocating for a sweeping transformation of the United States, often at the expense of the existing republican system. Influential figures such as Bernie Sanders and Alexandria Ocasio-Cortez contribute to a shifting U.S. political landscape that mirrors stages associated with a transformative communist revolution. Their ideologies and proposed policies align with radical shifts that disrupt established norms and institutions.

Simultaneously, grassroots movements within the country, spewing leftist ideologies, champion causes such as workers' rights, racial justice, environmental conservation, and wealth redistribution. While these causes may appear noble on the surface, their underlying motives often challenge traditional cultural norms and aim to overhaul societal structures, signaling profound shifts in societal values.

Moreover, factions embedded within these movements harbor inclinations toward radical tactics, advocating for direct action and civil disobedience as tools to challenge and disrupt democratic institutions. Their agenda propels them to organize protests, strikes, and various forms of civil unrest with the explicit goal of sowing chaos and pressuring the government into adopting more radical policies. This approach is grounded in the belief that conventional democratic mechanisms are inadequate in addressing perceived systemic injustices, therefore necessitating immediate and forceful methods to enact transformative change.

This alignment with disruptive tactics, which often affect societal stability, raises serious concerns. The endorsement of civil disobedience and organized chaos to impose ideological agendas reflects a dismissive attitude towards democratic norms and institutions. It also highlights a dangerous precedent of disregarding established democratic processes in favor of coercive and disruptive methods to force ideological changes upon the nation.

Established in 2016 and led by Bob Avakian, a lifelong communist and a prominent figure in the Marxist-Leninist Revolutionary Communist Party of the United States (RCP-USA), Refuse Fascism has risen as a force driving nationwide demonstrations. Avakian's resolute statement of the organization's objectives underscores a call for nothing short of revolution, dismissing any notion of reform as inconsequential. His bold statement, "We need a revolution. Anything else…is just bulls**t,"[22] serves as a stark testament to their commitment to radical transformation.

At its core, Refuse Fascism wants to dismantle the existing capitalist and republican government system, starkly deviating from the democratic principles that have historically shaped governance in the United States. Under the guidance of Bob Avakian's party, they have presented a proposed constitution for the envisioned New Socialist Republic in North America. This proposed system advocates for a "dictatorship of the proletariat" as the governing structure, firmly rooted in the tenets of Marxist ideology. This envisaged framework positions the Revolutionary Communist Party as the supreme authority, exerting significant control over governance and decision-making processes.

The proposed system underscores a centralized leadership approach, with the Party assuming a pivotal role in shaping the envisioned socialist republic and wielding substantial authority over security and governance matters. While an Executive Council would enforce laws and defend the new constitution, ultimate leadership would rest with the Revolutionary Communist Party. The armed forces, militias, and security entities would operate within a hierarchical leadership framework, bridging the central Executive Council and the Revolutionary Communist Party.

---

[22] Heyes, JD. "Retired CIA Officer Sends Dire Warning to America: The Left's Marxist Revolution Isn't Concerned about Who Wins the November Election." *Civil War News*, 16 Sep. 2020, www.civilwar.news/2020-09-16-retired-cia-officer-sends-dire-warning-marxist-revolution.html.

The concept of a "dictatorship of the proletariat" aligns with Marxist ideology, aspiring to guide society towards a stateless and classless communist order. Refuse Fascism's ambition is to supplant the existing democratic framework with a model akin to countries such as Cuba and China, both of which have faced criticism for curtailing individual freedoms and human rights.

Growing concerns have emerged regarding the potential consequences of Refuse Fascism's objectives and the ideological orientation of its leadership. History has shown the risks tied to concentrated power in centralized leadership structures, potentially undermining checks and balances in decision-making. The Party's predominant role raises concerns about political diversity, the safeguarding of dissenting opinions, and the protection of minority rights.

Understanding the breadth of their agenda is crucial as their ultimate goal is a complete reshaping of the country. Their intent is nothing short of toppling the constitutional republic, aiming to replace it with an entirely different system. These individuals are essentially revolutionaries, and their envisioned revolution signifies a complete overhaul of the existing constitutional republic.

Radical communists view the existing legal system as an instrument of capitalist dominance, effectively upholding and perpetuating societal inequalities. Their strategy involves actively participating in civil disobedience and organized protests aimed at confronting established laws and authorities, all in the pursuit of their revolutionary vision. This deliberate disobedience to the law seeks to carve out room for alternative narratives and revolutionary ideals, often willing to bear the consequences of heightened tensions, potential violence, or property damage in the process.

The phenomenon of radical communist actions challenging the legal framework is epitomized by anti-capitalist protests and movements, notably the 2011 Occupy Wall Street movement. In this grassroots uprising, activists in the United States intentionally disrupted and confronted the established capitalist system.

During Occupy Wall Street, protesters congregated in public spaces, most notably Zuccotti Park in New York City, to voice their grievances against perceived injustices embedded within capitalism. Their focus centered on issues such as corporate influence in politics, income inequality, and the unequal distribution of resources. Through sustained protests and the occupation of public spaces, their intent was to draw attention to the systemic disparities inherent within the system.

A significant element was their deliberate defiance of authority and established legal norms. Occupying public spaces without official permission and resisting orders to disperse directly challenged the legitimacy of the existing order. These actions were aimed at shedding light on the systemic issues perpetuated by the legal and economic frameworks.

The primary goal was to elicit responses from authorities and the broader public, instigating discussions about the boundaries of dissent, freedom of expression, and the government's role in upholding capitalism. This form of civil disobedience aimed to create a collision between the values upheld by the legal system and those advocated by the movement.

For certain left-leaning groups, the pursuit of their ideological objectives takes precedence over upholding democratic principles. This outlook leads them to advocate for any means necessary to undermine their political adversaries. They downplay the importance of the democratic system in favor of advancing their radical agenda, fostering a climate where the ends justify the means, even if it means ignoring legal boundaries or societal norms.

Their prioritization of revolutionary goals above the democratic process often places them in direct conflict with established legal frameworks and societal norms. This stance fosters an environment where dissent and opposition are not just tolerated but actively encouraged, often at the expense of social stability and the rule of law. The readiness to adopt confrontational tactics and challenge established laws reflects a fundamental belief in the necessity of radical change, which entails subverting the systems they seek to replace.

Marxism operates as the moral compass that rationalizes these radical strategies. The "45 Goals of Communism" were strategically crafted to legitimize violence and insurrection as intrinsic elements within the American tradition. Consequently, Marxist influences have significantly molded the perception that violence and insurrection can serve as legitimate tools for protest and resistance.

At the core of this Marxist approach lies the concept of class struggle. Communists strategically engineer conflict between the working class and capitalist factions by exploiting existing social disparities and grievances. They depict prevailing economic and social systems as oppressive, aiming to stoke dissatisfaction and unrest. The ultimate aim is to usher in a society devoid of class distinctions and to mitigate economic inequalities. However, this goal often justifies actions typically deemed undemocratic or ethically questionable, including resorting to violent protest tactics, disrupting political processes, and tolerating censorship to silence dissenting voices.

The propagation of the notion of a "united force" as a solution to societal problems finds its roots in the influence of Marxist ideologies across various groups. Encouraging students and specialized interest groups to collectively unite in response to societal issues has been observed as a method to foster a sense of solidarity among those who share grievances against the existing system. This aligns with the broader agenda of challenging entrenched power structures and advocating for transformative change. This calculated approach aims to unify individuals and evoke powerful revolutionary sentiments, all with the overarching objective of dismantling established societal frameworks, including deeply entrenched power structures within the United States.

Historical examples illustrate the deliberate pursuit of revolutionary ambitions by Marxist movements, underscoring communism's adeptness at disrupting established political and national identities while advancing their mission to destabilize entrenched structures and espouse revolutionary principles. These instances serve as stark reminders of communism's disruptive potential and its determined drive to challenge and reshape established societal norms and structures.

In recent years, a surge of protests and demonstrations has erupted, purportedly addressing issues such as racial inequality, economic disparities, and environmental challenges. These public displays of discontent have significantly contributed to heightened tensions and escalated divisions across the nation. Instances of riots, looting, assaults on law enforcement, and widespread violence in various cities have injected chaos into the situation. The proliferation of mass protests and grassroots movements, advocating for sweeping societal changes, stems from deep-seated grievances surrounding alleged income inequality, racial injustice, and supposed systemic oppression. These events evoke troubling memories of historical revolutionary upheavals, raising concerns about the potential emergence of a societal crisis. This surge in social unrest signals a worrisome prospect of radical shifts, including the looming threat of a communist revolution.

Furthermore, the concerning link between student riots and broader public protests is often construed as a calculated tactic aimed at inciting larger social disturbances. Communists have adeptly utilized student unrest to ignite broader public protests against programs or organizations perceived as targets of socialist opposition. By channeling the energy of student activists into larger demonstrations, their aim is to sow seeds of dissent, challenging established norms and societal structures.

The orchestrated actions of violent mobs in urban centers stem from methodical planning and coordination, tracing back to various groups harboring deep animosity towards the United States. The nation faces a deliberate onslaught, with urban unrest being orchestrated by well-organized and interconnected antagonistic networks. Entities such as Antifa and Black Lives Matter exemplify this strategy through their orchestration of protests and demonstrations, often escalating into violent clashes that exacerbate social turmoil and deepen societal rifts.

Antifa's historical ties to communism, originating from its roots in the anti-fascist movement of the Weimar Republic in the 1930s and affiliations with the German Communist Party (KPD), are particularly worrisome. The group's use of direct action and confrontational tactics raises significant concerns about the potential for violence and encroachments on individual freedoms. Furthermore, the chaos caused by disruptions to public order, economic activities, and public safety endangers communities.

The engagement of certain individuals in protest movements has sparked suspicions of a deliberate agenda aimed at reshaping societal and political landscapes in accordance with socialist ideals. Post-presidency, Barack Obama established a Tactical Operations Center (TOC) near the White House, featuring secure office spaces and a staff residence, reportedly intended for use by Michelle Obama and the Obama Foundation. Obama's approach involved leveraging progressive nonprofit organizations, notably Organizing for Action (OFA), an evolution of his initial campaign entity, Obama for America.

These entities, in partnership with the Obama Foundation and the National Democratic Redistricting Committee, established a conspicuous presence near Pennsylvania Avenue, seemingly positioned to counter the actions of the Trump administration. Obama openly expressed support for anti-Trump protests, leading some to interpret his stance as tacit backing for an ongoing "army of agitators" challenging his Republican successor throughout his term.

Speculation has emerged regarding Obama's potential utilization of this center to coordinate efforts with various groups, including Black Lives Matter (BLM) and Antifa, potentially aligning with sympathetic factions within the government. These speculations raise concerns about potential collaborations aiming to undermine the democratic process and incite unrest.

Some assert that within the US, socialists strategically employ immigration as a tool to intentionally destabilize society. This viewpoint contends that by advocating for more lenient immigration policies, leftists aim to incite social, economic, and political disruption. An influx of immigrants, coming with diverse cultural backgrounds and varied economic needs, could intensify competition for resources, strain social services, and foster societal tensions. The motive is to sow discord, challenge established power structures, and lay the groundwork for transformative socialist agendas.

Critics of liberal immigration policies voice concerns about the potential over-saturation of the job market, leading to heightened competition for employment. This increased competition might result in diminished wages and fewer job prospects for citizens, particularly those in low-skilled or entry-level positions. Detractors also express apprehensions about the strain on social welfare programs, suggesting that a larger population could burden public services such as education, healthcare, and social assistance.

Moreover, the swift influx of immigrants from varied cultural backgrounds could potentially lead to social tensions and difficulties in assimilation. Worries often arise regarding the formation of ethnic enclaves, which might hinder social cohesion and contribute to a sense of division among communities. Critics caution that a failure to assimilate could foster isolated cultural pockets, potentially undermining the broader national identity.

Detractors suggest that a significant population surge resulting from liberal immigration policies might strain the nation's infrastructure. Cities and communities could struggle to accommodate the influx of residents, leading to issues such as overcrowded schools, inadequate housing, heightened traffic congestion, and other challenges that could impact the overall quality of life.

Furthermore, liberal immigration policies can be a contributing factor to political polarization. Differing viewpoints on immigration might exacerbate existing ideological divides, as segments of the population express frustration over what they perceive as a lack of control in immigration processes. This frustration could fuel the rise of political movements and figures advocating for stricter immigration policies, potentially widening societal rifts.

The Democratic stance on immigration encompasses several facets, notably endorsing comprehensive immigration reform that emphasizes a pathway to citizenship for illegal aliens already residing in the country. Among their supported initiatives is Deferred Action for Childhood Arrivals (DACA), providing protection and work permits to undocumented individuals brought to the USA as children.

During Barack Obama's presidency (2009-2017), U.S. immigration policies underwent significant changes through legislative adjustments, executive actions, and global influences. These shifts, heavily tilted toward leniency, led to criticism, seen by some as disregarding proper immigration controls and the rule of law.

The establishment of the DACA program in 2012 was particularly contentious. This initiative drew severe criticism for offering temporary relief from deportation and work authorization to specific illegal immigrants brought to the U.S. as children, sidestepping citizenship status without resolving underlying issues.

President Obama advocated for comprehensive reform, supporting initiatives such as the DREAM Act and broader citizenship paths for illegal aliens. However, these efforts faced congressional obstacles, failing to gain traction for enactment.

To address concerns about deportations, the Obama administration adjusted enforcement priorities in 2014, aiming to focus on individuals with criminal records or identified security threats. Critics viewed this as insufficient control over an out-of-control system.

Moreover, Democrats endorse policies creating legal avenues for skilled workers and temporary laborers to enter the USA. Detractors argue this overlooks impacts on local job markets and fails to prioritize American citizens' employment needs.

On a global scale, Democrats support inclusive refugee and asylum policies, positioning the USA as a refuge for those fleeing violence or persecution. Critics argue these policies lack thorough screening mechanisms, potentially compromising national security.

The Democratic Party's rallying cry of "diversity is our strength" has drawn parallels to George Orwell's concept of "newspeak" from his dystopian novel, *1984*. In Orwell's world, newspeak was a tool to manipulate thoughts, and critics argue that slogans such as "diversity is our strength" oversimplify the intricacies of diversity. This simplification fails to address the complexities of integration, social harmony, and cultural clashes. Such oversimplification contributes to societal rifts by portraying diversity as an unqualified boon while disregarding potential challenges.

This portrayal makes proponents of the slogan seem indifferent to genuine concerns about multiculturalism.

Lenient immigration policies strategically serve Democrats by seeking favor among immigrant communities. Advocacy for initiatives such as DACA or citizenship pathways positions Democrats as allies to these groups, aiming to secure support and potentially sway immigrant voters. This calculated approach also targets newly naturalized citizens and those gaining legal status, intending to shift their political allegiance toward the Democratic Party based on immigration stances. The party's narrative of compassion and inclusivity through lenient immigration policies is a tactical move to attract voters prioritizing humanitarian values. Democrats anticipate demographic shifts in areas with growing immigrant populations, foreseeing increased support for the party due to shared immigration viewpoints. Additionally, these policies aim to engage and mobilize immigrant communities strategically, seeking to heighten political involvement and secure votes based on these specific approaches.

The Democratic Party's stance on immigration exacerbates internal instability. These policies create social, economic, and political turbulence, raising concerns about border management, national security, economic impacts, and cultural assimilation. Detractors point to lax enforcement of immigration laws and a lenient approach to border control, exposing vulnerabilities exploited by criminal syndicates and individuals with malicious intentions.

Criticism extends to Democratic policies that gives benefits to undocumented aliens. These measures are viewed as incentives for illegal immigration, straining public resources and exacerbating economic disparities. The resulting surge in population places immense pressure on resources, overwhelming communities already grappling with economic disparities.

Moreover, critics emphasize the national security risks associated with liberal immigration policies. An open system hampers the identification and monitoring of security threats, potentially enabling individuals with malicious intent to exploit lenient immigration policies. The absence of comprehensive vetting processes raises concerns about national security, with skeptics warning that these gaps could be exploited, posing significant risks to public safety.

Senator Lindsey Graham (R-S.C.) voiced concerns about individuals from terrorist watch list countries and ISIS suspects crossing the porous U.S. southwestern border. Despite inquiries, DOJ officials could not (or would not) provide answers. Graham urged allocating more resources, believing the broken southern border could serve as an entry point for international terrorists unless policies change.

The influx of migrants presents a myriad of complex challenges that extend well beyond sheer numbers, encompassing economic, social, and cultural realms. Concerns persist about the process of assimilation, potential clashes among cultures, and the strain on social unity, all of which contribute to deepening societal divisions. The collision of diverse backgrounds within a society often sparks conflicts, heightens social tensions, and disrupts the established social order.

Open immigration policies serve as gateways for individuals aligned with leftist ideologies. Detractors express grave concerns about these ideologies infiltrating critical sectors such as education, media, and politics, where they can manipulate societal narratives, influence policies, and sow discord within society.

Of particular concern is the dissemination of destabilizing ideas and ideologies. Open immigration could enable communists to manipulate political processes, backing candidates and policies aligned with their agenda, potentially inciting polarizing debates and undermining overall political stability.

Economic disparities often associated with immigration are seen as fertile ground for communists to garner support for socialist policies and workers' movements. By exploiting these disparities, Marxist factions may advocate for policies that escalate social unrest and economic instability, ultimately jeopardizing the country's economic bedrock.

Significant concerns surround the potential impact on cultural integration. Inadequate efforts to ensure successful assimilation could result in the formation of isolated communities, detached from the broader American fabric. Within these isolated enclaves, individuals with radical ideologies might exploit open immigration policies to carve out like-minded communities, posing threats to both social cohesion and national security. These enclaves could serve as breeding grounds for the propagation of extremist ideologies, posing a dual threat by potentially fostering divisions and impeding overall social cohesion.

Moreover, the landscape of extensive immigration, particularly without comprehensive integration measures, creates a backdrop ripe for manipulation by Marxists to amplify narratives centered around class struggle. By capitalizing on existing grievances, they might intensify societal fractures and erode the sense of national solidarity.

Furthermore, there are valid concerns that a substantial influx of immigrants from diverse backgrounds might dilute the established sense of national identity and shared values in the United States. Critics worry about potential clashes between the values and traditions of immigrant communities and the established American norms, which could lead to tensions that impact societal unity and erode historical traditions integral to the nation's identity.

Critics also emphasize worries about certain newcomers aiming to reshape the country to align with their preferences instead of assimilating into American society, drawing parallels with historical examples where socio-economic challenges prompted immigrants to embrace socialist ideologies in response to their circumstances.

Within the Eastern European Jewish communities of the late 19th and early 20th centuries, marked by poverty and discrimination, many with Jewish heritage found solace in Marxist ideologies, including communism. These ideologies promised equity, social justice, and economic advancement. As a result, numerous individuals from this background became key figures in early communist movements.

A notable figure among them is Leon Trotsky, originally known as Lev Davidovich Bronstein, who held a pivotal position during the formative years of the Bolshevik Revolution in Russia, contributing significantly to the establishment of the Soviet Union.

Born into a Jewish family in Ukraine, Trotsky was exposed to socialist and revolutionary concepts from a young age. Throughout the early 20th century, he resided in various cities, including London, Vienna, and New York City. During his time in New York, he participated in political activities and made contributions to socialist publications, further shaping his involvement in leftist ideologies.

Trotsky became an active member of the Russian Social Democratic Labor Party and later aligned himself with the Bolshevik faction led by Vladimir Lenin. He emerged as a key figure within the Bolshevik movement. He assumed leadership of the Red Army during the Russian Civil War and held a prominent position within the Soviet government.

The rapid influx of migrants under liberal immigration policies fuels a whirlwind of societal and cultural shifts, opening the floodgates to divergent ideologies. This surge poses a dire threat to the existing balance of power within society, paving the way for the rise of polarizing ideals that corrode the very fabric of social harmony and cohesion. This disintegration directly imperils national unity and stability.

The Democratic Party's embrace of such liberal immigration policies, tied closely to their progressive agenda, raises alarm bells regarding vulnerabilities ripe for exploitation, especially in times of political tumult. These policies sow seeds of disruption within established societal structures, further deepening existing divides. Opportunistic groups could strategically maneuver in these volatile conditions, aiming to wrest control away from the established order.

The fallout from these policies threatens substantial demographic shifts that could aggravate societal fractures. Individuals with clandestine agendas may exploit these divisions, stoking discord to erode national identity and unity, ultimately seeding internal conflict.

The Communist Party relentlessly pursues its agenda of dismantling established societal norms and structures, perpetually seeking methods to disrupt and undermine the existing order. At its core, their pursuit of a violent revolution aims to upend the prevailing social and economic framework, advocating for the establishment of a socialist state—an ideology inherently flawed and historically proven to be catastrophic.

This ideology rationalizes the use of violence as an essential means to challenge and dismantle what they perceive as oppressive structures within society. Communism justifies violent upheaval on the premise that those in power within the current system will not relinquish power willingly. This rationale serves as a dangerous justification for resorting to violent means in pursuit of their objectives, all under the guise of achieving so-called social justice and equality.

Advocates of violent revolution assert that radical societal transformation is indispensable to forge a classless, stateless society, an ideology derived from the flawed premises of Marxist theory. They adamantly propagate the notion that genuine societal progress arises solely from incessant class struggle. According to this perspective, prevailing oppressive systems—particularly capitalism—are portrayed as the perpetual engines behind societal inequality and exploitation, disproportionately affecting the working class. Proponents of violent revolution advocate for the working class to seize control of production and governance, purportedly paving the way for a more equitable society.

The rationalization of violence within revolutionary movements is justified through philosophical, ethical, and political viewpoints. From the communist standpoint, violent action during a revolution is depicted as a justifiable response to perceived violence and exploitation by the ruling class and imperial powers. Marxists justify revolutionary violence as a means of liberation from oppression, painting the populace of the targeted nation as victims of imperialistic foreign dominance, resulting in colonization and exploitation.

This viewpoint perceives the existing system as inherently unjust, using this rationale to justify violent action aimed at its dismantlement in favor of establishing a more equitable society. Socialists argue that prevailing systems such as capitalism economically exploit the working class, denying them their fair share of resources and opportunities. Violence, within this context, is deemed necessary to break free from subjugation and create a more equitable society where authority supposedly rests with the masses.

The rationale behind using violence to shape public opinion is rooted in the belief that the magnitude of violence and its consequences can coerce individuals into embracing socialist or communist ideologies.

In the United States, communist ideologies have faced significant obstacles in rallying support around class struggles. Consequently, they have strategically pivoted towards emphasizing racial arguments to advance their agenda. While discussions centered on class might resonate with specific demographics, they fail to gain traction across broader American society. This limitation has prompted Marxist movements to leverage racial arguments as a tactical tool for mobilization and coalition-building.

America's socio-economic landscape, shaped by race, ethnicity, and cultural diversity, has compelled these socialist-leaning movements to accentuate racial divides. Slavery, segregation, and racial disparities have left enduring divisions along racial lines. By exploiting these divisions, these movements tap into shared outrage surrounding issues such as "systemic racism" and inequality, aiming to sow discontent across diverse demographic groups. Their primary objective is to exploit perceived systemic inequities as a springboard for revolutionary societal changes.

This strategic maneuver facilitates the forging of cross-racial alliances and broader coalitions to propel their objectives forward. Furthermore, it allows them to frame their struggle as a battle against deeply ingrained historical injustices, infusing their movement with a moral imperative that transcends traditional class-based narratives. This calculated shift in focus seeks to mobilize a diverse population towards their radical aspirations.

Moreover, in today's globally interconnected landscape, these movements acknowledge the potential to emulate successful strategies employed in other nations. Racial arguments have played pivotal roles in movements such as the anti-apartheid struggle in South Africa, serving as a blueprint for similar approaches in the United States.

Author Manning Johnson highlighted the Communist Party's calculated focus on the African American population, acknowledging their potential for significant revolutionary impact compared to other groups. Moscow aimed to incite a spirit of rebellion among Black individuals, fostering violent racial conflict, all with the ultimate goal of sowing division within America.

The Communist Party actively disseminated the notion that African Americans constituted a distinct nation within the United States, enduring oppression and exploitation by a colonialist, imperialist, and racially biased America. Throughout the early to mid-20th century, select members of the Communist Party actively sought to recruit African Americans as potential allies in their fight against racial oppression and economic disparity. They emphasized the purported deeply entrenched racism and exploitation faced by African Americans, advocating for the recognition of this community as a distinct group entitled to both liberation and self-determination.

Aligned with their strategic approach, the Communist Party championed the liberation and self-determination of this perceived nation, advocating for its secession from the United States and the establishment of an autonomous entity within predominantly Black regions in the South. The envisioned framework for this nation closely mirrored the

Soviet system, aligning with the Communist Party's ideological principles.

This calculated approach formed a pivotal aspect of the broader vision held by the Communist Party, notably during the 1930s and 1940s when they sought to establish a popular front to disseminate socialist principles. Engaging with marginalized communities, including African Americans, was considered a tactical maneuver to broaden the party's support base and amplify the potential for revolutionary change within the nation.

The 14th Amendment, a cornerstone of American constitutional law, presents a formidable barrier against attempts by Marxists aiming to exploit racial tensions for their political gains. Enshrined within its framework is the fundamental principle of providing equal protection under the law for all citizens, regardless of their racial background. This constitutional safeguard effectively counters efforts to manipulate racial divisions for political purposes and reinforces the nation's commitment to inclusivity while rejecting discrimination.

Ratified in 1868, the 14th Amendment emerged as a pivotal instrument in confronting systemic racism and inequality. Its primary objective was to lay a sturdy foundation for addressing racial discrimination following the Civil War and the abolition of slavery. The profound impact of this amendment is evident in its provisions, granting citizenship to all individuals born or naturalized in the US, irrespective of their racial heritage. Landmark civil rights cases such as *Brown v. Board of Education*, 347 U.S. 483 (1954) and legal battles combating discriminatory practices in voting and housing underscore the enduring historical significance of this constitutional amendment.

The 14th Amendment's constitutional mandate of equality stands as a powerful barrier against divisive tactics, notably countering communist efforts to divide Americans along racial lines. Emphasizing equal protection, this amendment establishes a strong legal and moral framework that actively combats societal fragmentation based on race. It fosters a unified American identity, transcending racial divisions and serving as a defense against narratives propagated by communists seeking to exploit racial polarization. Consequently, attempts to exploit racial divisions to sow discord among Americans have faced resistance.

The Communist Party's influence within the African American community has triggered a range of responses. While some found allure in the party's promises of equality and justice, others approached cautiously, apprehensive about embracing what they saw as a foreign ideology.

Manning Johnson, an African American figure prominent within the Communist Party USA during the 1930s, initially found himself drawn to the party's commitments to racial equality and social justice. Yet, Johnson's involvement uncovered a starkly different reality. His disillusionment stemmed from witnessing the party's manipulative and exploitative tactics, particularly concerning African Americans. Observing the deliberate exploitation of Black communities for the party's revolutionary aims, Johnson discerned their ulterior motives and divisive strategies. His rejection of communism evolved as he became increasingly aware of the party's deceptive methods and their insincere stance on racial equality.

As Johnson delved more deeply into the workings of the Communist Party, he became an outspoken critic, eventually distancing himself from the party. Through his book, *Color, Communism, and Common Sense*, Johnson aimed to expose the party's deceitful practices and their harmful impact on racial unity and social cohesion in America. His journey, from initial engagement to staunch opposition, illuminated the exploitation of racial issues by political entities, offering invaluable insights into their manipulative agendas.

Unfortunately, other individuals have embraced the communist narrative on race. At the National Black Power Convention in Tulsa, Oklahoma, held in 1968, several speakers passionately voiced their views on race, oppression, and societal transformation. One speaker vehemently denounced "White supremacy," capitalism, imperialism, and fascism, advocating for their dismantling. Another urged a united front of Black revolutionary progressives to confront their adversaries.

The discourse took a disconcerting turn when a speaker endorsed a retaliatory approach, even suggesting the training of gang members for revolution and targeting White individuals. Another speaker envisioned a future where Black people would eliminate all associations with Whiteness, advocating racial determinism and propagating the belief that the emergence of a Black nation would lead to the decline of the White race. Such rhetoric perpetuates dangerous and divisive ideologies, fueling racial animosity.

These speakers bought into the communist narrative on race, casting capitalism as a breeding ground for racial prejudices. They propagated the idea that capitalism inherently fostered racism and disregarded the potential for peaceful trade and interactions to ease biases in diverse communities. Their failure to acknowledge the potential for collaborative engagement across racial lines hindered the exploration of peaceful paths to address societal issues, perpetuating divisions and nurturing antagonism.

Capitalism, regardless of race, provides economic opportunities and encourages businesses to welcome diverse talent, driving innovation. Responsive to varied consumer needs, capitalism prompts companies to cater to different racial groups, expanding economic avenues. It also promotes interactions among diverse communities, fostering mutual understanding. Merit-based recruitment fosters diverse workplaces, challenging stereotypes. Capitalism's adaptation to diversity influences inclusivity in products and services, while commercial exchanges build networks transcending racial boundaries, emphasizing common interests.

Their embrace of the communist narrative on race deepened their belief in the inherent link between racial struggles and economic systems. While acknowledging historical exploitation and systemic injustices faced by African Americans, this narrative oversimplified the complexities of race and capitalism. By framing capitalism as the root cause of racial tensions, they discounted the potential for constructive dialogue and cooperation among diverse racial groups within a capitalist framework. This stance contributed to perpetuating divisive ideologies and impeded the pursuit of peaceful solutions to societal challenges.

The convergence of these elements creates an unstable environment ripe for unrest, increasing the likelihood of imminent events that could profoundly strain the nation's stability. Movements advocating for radical shifts in politics significantly contribute to growing protests and unrest, fundamentally reshaping the social and political landscape. Experts predict sporadic, highly charged uprisings that could culminate in significant events across the United States. These movements gain momentum under specific conditions, acting as catalysts for prolonged conflict and exposing vulnerabilities within a relatively short period.

In this context, the surge in movements advocating for systemic change worsens the fragility of social cohesion and governmental stability. Rooted deeply in socialist ideologies, these movements opportunistically exploit economic distress, political discord, and instances of social injustice to mobilize widespread discontent. Their fervent calls for radical transformation, sometimes pushing for a complete societal overhaul, foster an environment steeped in suspicion, disenchantment, and turmoil within American society.

Strategically maneuvering amidst societal instability, these movements capitalize on upheavals as pivotal gateways to promote socialist ideologies. They leverage heightened discontent during periods of turmoil, exploiting societal fault lines to sow the seeds of radical transformation.

These movements advocating for societal change employ a calculated strategy, tactically advancing radical ideologies. Their multifaceted approach revolves around exploiting societal discontent and upheaval, positioning socialism as a viable solution to prevailing societal problems. Through these deliberate actions, they strategically embed socialist ideals within the fabric of societal discourse and discontent.

Activists keenly point out perceived failures and injustices within existing social, economic, and political structures. Whenever societal unrest arises or vulnerabilities within these systems become apparent, they seize these moments as opportunities. By highlighting systemic flaws, inequalities, and injustices, they craft a narrative that resonates with disenchanted segments of society.

This narrative serves a dual purpose: eroding confidence in established structures while presenting socialism as an alternative—a remedy to the alleged deficiencies of current systems. They construct a compelling argument linking grievances to socialist principles, advocating for a progressive shift toward socialism.

Employing persuasive tactics, adherents of Marxist ideologies leverage emotional appeals and utopian promises, emphasizing socialism's inherent egalitarian ideals. Their advocacy for a fairer, more equitable society, especially in times of turmoil or disenchantment, strikes a chord.

These movements manipulate the narrative surrounding societal problems, portraying socialism as both morally superior and a practical solution. During periods of societal fragility, they steer discourse toward advocating for a systemic overhaul—replacing existing structures with socialist principles is pitched as a solution to societal woes. This calculated approach aims not only to spur change but to fundamentally alter society's ideological underpinnings toward socialism.

Rooted in Marxist ideals, their narratives seek to systematically disrupt established social orders and governance structures. Seizing upon societal instability and discontent, they opportunistically leverage these moments to advance their communist agenda. They spotlight system deficiencies during upheaval, seeking to erode trust in established structures while promoting socialism as a comprehensive solution.

In times of unrest, they exploit vulnerabilities, presenting socialist ideologies as a remedy for societal ills. Their persuasive tactics highlight socialism's egalitarian aspects, promising a fairer society. By capitalizing on societal discontent, they position socialism as a principled response to perceived shortcomings in the current order, manipulating moments of upheaval to champion socialist principles in restructuring existing systems.

Growing fear envelops the United States, fueled by concerns of heightened instability and the looming specter of a potential communist revolution. This unease arises from a convergence of various factors—escalating social tensions, shifting ideological landscapes, and the intricate interplay of political dynamics. Collectively, these elements paint a worrying picture, suggesting an imminent upheaval that could profoundly impact multiple aspects of society.

Democrats aligning with the Black Lives Matter (BLM) movement have faced criticism for their support of disruptive actions that have caused considerable nationwide disruption. During the George Floyd trial (2021), Maxine Waters (D-CA) made contentious statements encouraging persistent street protests and explicitly advocating for escalated conflict, even calling for the public confrontation of officials from the Trump administration. These statements raised concerns about fostering hostility, incivility, and potential violence. Her remarks seemingly endorsed tactics involving the harassment of politicians with differing opinions, contributing to the creation of intimidating crowds.

While the First Amendment protects the right to freedom of speech, it is not absolute, especially concerning speech that incites violence. The Supreme Court's decision in *Brandenburg v. Ohio*, 395 U.S. 444 (1969) established criteria for determining when speech transitions into incitement. Waters' call for confrontation could be interpreted as meeting these criteria due to her deliberate intent to promote confrontational actions that might lead to violence, raising arguments that her speech goes beyond the protective boundaries of the First Amendment.

The surge in social unrest across the nation serves as a critical warning sign, signaling a crisis on the horizon capable of sparking transformative and potentially revolutionary change. Large-scale protests, grassroots movements, and fervent rallies advocating for sweeping societal reforms highlight deep-rooted grievances concerning wealth inequality, racial injustices, and systemic oppression. These events echo historical periods marked by revolutionary fervor, pointing to an increasingly volatile situation demanding attention and caution.

Following Donald Trump's victory in the 2016 election, a consortium of leftist groups, such as the Socialist ANSWER Coalition, Code Pink, and Disrupt J20, made public declarations of their intentions to orchestrate protests during Trump's inauguration in Washington, D.C. Their primary objective was to disrupt the peaceful transition of power while voicing their opposition to Trump's presidency. Further amplifying this agitation were organizations such as OFA (Organizing for Action) and Moveon.org, reportedly bolstered by funding from George Soros, a figure known for his leftist beliefs and Jewish heritage.

George Soros, a proponent of left-leaning causes and progressive policies, notably advocates for wealth redistribution and increased government intervention, especially considering Soros's Open Society Foundations' support for policies such as universal healthcare. His funding of left-leaning political campaigns, critiques of unregulated capitalism, and advocacy for global governance further fuel these assertions. However, Soros himself defines his political stance as open society liberalism, representing a purported middle ground between unregulated capitalism and authoritarian socialism.

The 2016 inauguration protests were part of a broader wave of demonstrations that unfolded on and around inauguration day. Activists in numerous cities, spanning from New York and Los Angeles to Chicago and Oakland, voiced their dissent through anti-Trump marches. These gatherings aimed to express dissatisfaction with the incoming administration.

Regrettably, several of these demonstrations escalated into riots characterized by disruptive behavior and instances of violence. Across various cities such as Los Angeles, Oakland, and Seattle, the shift from peaceful protests to destructive actions, including vandalism and confrontations, unfolded. In some cases, protests turned tragically violent, as seen in Seattle where a shooting left five people injured. Similarly, incidents in Minneapolis during 2019 depicted left-wing rioters targeting supporters of President Trump, engaging in group assaults and acts of arson.

The tumultuous protests of 2020 marked a series of destructive behaviors, including rioting, looting, and arson, significantly damaging buildings and compromising the safety of law enforcement officers and the public. These events were ignited by the tragic death of George Floyd, a Black man who died while in police custody, illuminating sustained civil unrest characterized by violence and property damage.

Groups such as Antifa and BLM, categorized as domestic terrorist organizations by some, espouse an agenda that involves a comprehensive overhaul of fundamental aspects of the nation, encompassing governmental, economic, and social structures. This ambitious agenda mirrors the core tenets of Marxist ideology, advocating for sweeping societal change through revolutionary methods to address deep-seated inequalities.

In 2020, the Black Lives Matter (BLM) movement surged to prominence, gaining widespread attention across the United States. Notably, in Minneapolis, individuals linked with BLM engaged in the targeted vandalism of over 1,500 businesses and buildings, resulting in substantial financial losses for many.

In Minneapolis, a notable incident occurred involving Minneapolis City Council member Andrea Jenkins and individuals associated with the BLM movement. During this event, there was a confrontation where individuals identifying with BLM essentially barricaded a public figure and presented demands, raising concerns about the intentions behind these actions and their potential consequences for the political process and public discourse. Under duress, Andrea Jenkins was compelled to endorse a statement ensuring non-prosecution for those implicated in the incident. This concession sparked concern about the implications of acquiescing to demands under coercive circumstances.

During 2020, the BLM movement accumulated a substantial $90 million in donations, indicating broad-based support for its mission. This considerable financial influx came from diverse sources, spanning Democratic supporters, corporate entities, and even high-profile figures such as Mitt Romney (R-UT). However, the financial decisions of BLM co-founder Patrisse Cullors, particularly her substantial investment of $3.2 million in real estate, have ignited controversy regarding the potential misappropriation of movement funds.

The messaging strategies employed by the BLM movement played a crucial role in manipulating public perception. Despite its name ostensibly highlighting concerns about racial justice, the movement's true motives have been subject to wide-ranging interpretations. Statements from the movement's co-founders, Patrisse Cullors and Alicia Garza, openly identifying as "trained Marxists," shed light on a more sweeping revolutionary agenda. This agenda extends beyond addressing racial disparities and police misconduct, signaling a penchant for resorting to disruptive or violent tactics to accomplish their objectives. The movement's ideological underpinning, deeply rooted in Marxism, steers BLM's aims, emphasizing a focus on addressing socioeconomic disparities, promoting wealth redistribution, and advocating for the restructuring of societal institutions. These objectives align all too well with the principles espoused by communism, painting a concerning picture of the movement's true agenda and its alignment with a historically failed ideology.

Furthermore, the comparison drawn by Cullors between her book and Mao Zedong's "Little Red Book" has sparked widespread fear about the potential radical agenda underlying the BLM movement. This parallel has invoked deep concerns regarding the misalignment of the movement with traditional American values, such as individual liberty and a free-market economy. Such comparisons raise legitimate questions about the trajectory of the movement and the values it promotes, stirring unease about its ideological direction and implications.

The use of the raised fist symbol by the BLM movement has sparked controversy due to its historical associations with communist movements and its representation of radical ideologies. Originating during the Bolshevik Revolution in Russia, the raised fist symbol became a defining emblem for communist parties globally, signifying their resistance against capitalism and established societal norms. This symbol has resonated with various countercultural and radical movements advocating for left-wing ideologies, some of which have historically advocated for violent methods to achieve their revolutionary objectives.

The raised fist symbol is steeped in oppression and authoritarianism. Regimes founded on Marxist principles led to totalitarian systems, systematically violating human rights, suppressing dissent, and enforcing strict societal controls. These regimes caused widespread suffering and resulted in enormous loss of life. The association of the raised fist symbol with such regimes raises concerns about its potential to glorify ideologies that have a track record of leading to systemic abuse and widespread misery.

Critics have raised concerns about the BLM movement's association with riots and the consequential destruction, highlighting the adverse effects on marginalized communities and the broader struggle against racial inequality. The use of violence and property damage during protests exacerbates societal divisions and hinders progress toward achieving racial justice. Moreover, these actions have resulted in significant harm to already marginalized communities, raising questions about the movement's strategies and their impact on those it claims to represent. Some critics suggest that the BLM movement's ultimate objective might extend beyond addressing racial injustices and could involve the establishment of a socialist society.

Antifa, an abbreviation for "anti-fascist," has gained significant attention through multiple waves of social and political activism. The movement operates with a decentralized structure, comprising individuals who align themselves with leftist and communist ideologies. Ostensibly, Antifa's goal is to counter far-right ideologies and combat racism. Its roots can be traced back to Germany, where it served as the militant arm of the German Communist Party (KPD).

Employing direct action techniques, Antifa often resorts to violence during protests and demonstrations. This strategy involves using force, fear, and aggressive methods to advance their objectives and stifle dissenting voices. Acts include assault, battery, wielding deadly weapons, arson, and vandalism, leading to property damage, confrontations with adversaries, and clashes with law enforcement. Such actions have raised concerns about the use of violence under the pretext of "anti-fascism," fueling worries that it may serve as a catalyst for a communist revolution.

A notable incident connected to Antifa was the tragic shooting of Tusitala "Tiny" Toese, an unarmed member of the Proud Boys, during a medical freedom rally in Olympia, Washington. The shooter, Benjamin Anthony Varela, had affiliations with both Antifa and the Democratic Socialists of America (DSA). Additionally, individuals associated with Antifa were captured on video by Elijah Schaffer, a correspondent for The Blaze, engaging in destructive behavior. These individuals were observed dragging steel fences from the Target Center, creating disorder and contributing to the overall damage during the protests. Schaffer himself became a target of violence as Antifa members sprayed him with mace in a separate incident.

Another distressing event involved an Antifa-affiliated group incorrectly identifying several minors as participants in a Patriot March. Unfortunately, these innocent minors were surrounded by the group, sprayed with to mace, and chased along the boardwalk. One of the minors suffered violent shoving to the ground and a brutal assault, resulting in severe injuries, including a concussion. These injuries necessitated immediate medical attention at a hospital, highlighting the troubling and harmful consequences of violent actions perpetrated by Antifa-affiliated individuals.

In June of 2020, a faction of Antifa protesters in Seattle took a concerning and unprecedented step by cordoning off a six-block area downtown and openly declaring their intention to overthrow the U.S. government. This self-proclaimed territory became known as the Capitol Hill Autonomous Zone (CHAZ), where they asserted that the United States no longer held authority.

Within the confines of the CHAZ, protesters created distinct borders using barricades, effectively preventing law enforcement access. Within this self-declared autonomous zone, the CHAZ established its own regulations and structure, with a private militia taking on security responsibilities. The presence of an armed militia and the exclusion of law enforcement contributed to an atmosphere of uncertainty and potential danger, leading to questions about who was responsible for maintaining public safety and order within the CHAZ.

The inception of the CHAZ bore semblance to an action tantamount to waging war against the U.S. government. This perception stems from various facets: Primarily, the establishment of the CHAZ posed a direct challenge to the sovereignty of the U.S. government by carving out an autonomous enclave with its governance structure within American territory. Furthermore, the physical occupation and control of territory within the

CHAZ could be construed as a confrontational maneuver seeking to assert dominion over U.S. soil.

Moreover, declarations asserting independence from U.S. rule within the CHAZ appeared as a calculated effort to undermine the established government's authority while endeavoring to instate an alternative order. The resistance against law enforcement, fortified by erected barriers to impede their entry into the CHAZ, may be perceived as a deliberate defiance against government authority and an attempt to establish an independent jurisdiction.

The presence of an armed militia within the CHAZ and their attempt to project power in the declared autonomous zone suggests a deliberate armed resistance, challenging the U.S. government's authority and jurisdiction. Additionally, the establishment of a separate governing structure within the CHAZ, complete with its regulations and governance, appeared to be a calculated effort aimed at replacing the authority of the U.S. government with an autonomous ruling body.

Observations of the CHAZ revealed a governing structure that mirrored certain characteristics associated with communist ideologies. The zone's approach to decision-making, where participants aimed for consensus or majority rule in general assemblies or community meetings, resembled patterns found in communist ideologies, emphasizing collective decision-making.

Reports suggesting efforts within CHAZ to share resources and communalize facilities aligned with communist ideals of collective ownership, blurring individual ownership lines.

The attempt to establish an autonomous governance structure independent of the American governmental system, asserting independence and creating an alternative governing body, resembled aspects seen in revolutionary communist movements.

Furthermore, the emphasis on equality and community engagement in CHAZ echoed principles often associated with Marxist ideologies, emphasizing communal well-being and egalitarianism.

Indications of makeshift justice systems or alternative conflict resolution methods within CHAZ mirrored aspirations found in communist systems, but these efforts were part of a broader context that signaled a challenge to established governmental authority and an attempt to establish an independent ruling body within the zone.

The CHAZ endured for over two weeks, a period marked by the tragic loss of five lives in separate incidents. Eventually, Seattle's police intervened, dismantling the CHAZ by apprehending a small group of protesters who resisted dispersal. These distressing events highlighted the absence of formal law enforcement within the zone and the potential repercussions of allowing an unregulated and autonomous area to persist without intervention.

Criticism has been directed towards the city's leadership regarding their handling of the CHAZ's formation, specifically the decision to vacate the East Precinct without maintaining a nearby law enforcement presence. This delay in intervention during the initial stages might be seen as enabling the establishment of the CHAZ, prompting further debate on the appropriateness of such responses to civil unrest.

Mayor Durkan's reaction to the CHAZ's emergence in Seattle has provoked significant discussions about potential legal and ethical implications. With reference to the legal definition of treason in the U.S. Constitution (Article III, Section 3), there has been scrutiny over Mayor Durkan's decision to provide assistance, such as portable toilets, to the CHAZ. Some view this action as aiding groups whose goals contradict those of the United States. Although the intent might have been driven by humanitarian concerns, the provision indirectly supported the logistical operations within the autonomous zone, leading to questions about the alignment of her actions with the best interests of the city and country.

Seattle's city officials, led by Mayor Jenny Durkan, actively supported progressive policies and ideologies, emphasizing social justice, income equality, and addressing systemic issues within law enforcement. Their engagement in various progressive movements, including advocacy for LGBTQ+ rights and workers' rights, showcases their alignment with leftist ideologies.

The officials' support for the CHAZ can be seen as linked to their sympathy towards socialist causes and ideologies. Mayor Jenny Durkan and her team consistently promoted policies resonating with socialist principles, advocating for income equality and systemic reforms within law enforcement.

Their involvement in championing workers' and LGBTQ+ rights further highlights their alignment with leftist and socialist-leaning ideologies. This inclination towards socialist causes likely influenced their approach to the emergence of the CHAZ, as it reflected certain aspects of communal living, shared resources, and community-based governance reminiscent of socialist ideals centered around collective decision-making and resource distribution.

The aftermath of the violent riots in 2020 had a profound impact on the nation, exacting a somber toll. Regrettably, 47 lives were lost amid the widespread destruction, marking this period as the most destructive sequence of riots in U.S. history in terms of insurance claims. The extent of the damage became apparent as over 700 police officers were injured, and property damage estimates ranged from $1 billion to $2 billion. Notably, the city of Portland, Oregon, bore a heavy burden, grappling with around $2.3 million in damages, including the deliberate fire set at a federal courthouse, underscoring the severity of the impact on public safety and infrastructure.

The recent escalation in violent protests has triggered mounting apprehension regarding the underlying motives and methods of these movements. A striking incident unfolded in Portland, Oregon, on May 28, 2021, when around 75 protesters linked to Antifa and Black Lives Matter turned to violence, targeting journalists. One of the victims was the well-known conservative writer, Andy Ngo. He was pursued through the streets, tackled, and subjected to physical assault.

Upon closer scrutiny, distinct parallels become evident between certain protest actions and the characteristic elements associated with revolutions. These actions seem to echo the historical movements of Marxist insurgencies aimed at destabilizing and overthrowing established regimes. The deliberate use of force against individuals with dissenting opinions mirrors tactics historically employed during revolutionary upheavals to suppress dissent and control the narrative.

This incident reflects a disconcerting trend within certain protest movements, mirroring characteristics reminiscent of historical Marxist revolutionary tactics. The deliberate targeting of individuals with different viewpoints, employing intimidation tactics against the press, and resorting to physical violence to suppress dissent bear striking resemblance to strategies historically employed during communist revolutionary movements.

Incidents in cities such as Portland, Seattle, and elsewhere underscore this troubling pattern. The adoption of violent measures, stifling of dissent, and attacks on free speech resonate with historical revolutionary strategies. These actions prompt significant inquiries about the true intentions behind these ostensibly "peaceful protests."

According to intelligence agencies such as Forward Observer, there has been a notable rise in left-wing mobilization and grassroots movements advocating for progressive socio-political reforms. The nation's deep polarization and internal divisions have cultivated an environment conducive to embracing revolutionary tactics. These strategies historically aimed to widen societal divides and disrupt established norms, challenging the prevailing order.

Drawing from his extensive experience in the Middle East and South Asia, retired CIA officer Sam Faddis has drawn attention to striking parallels between ongoing events in the United States and historical strategies employed by Marxist, Leninist, and communist movements to seize power. He underscores resemblances with past revolutions, particularly the violent establishment of the Soviet Union. The observed tactics of disruption and instability mirror patterns witnessed during the tumultuous inception of the Soviet Union, suggesting a recurring tactic of exploiting chaos to create a power vacuum.

Moreover, the strategic exploitation of incidents involving police violence as a pretext for insurrection underscores a deliberate manipulation of public perception. This approach seeks to garner support for radical change and mirrors historical revolutionary strategies. Faddis argues that these instances of police violence are opportunistically utilized as a pretext for insurrection, with the ultimate goal of dismantling the existing social, economic, and political framework—a strategy reminiscent of historical approaches by groups seeking radical change.

Throughout history, revolutionary movements have capitalized on moments of social unrest, often ignited by instances of police violence and racial injustice, to advance broader societal changes. This reflects historical methods of mobilizing supporters towards the overarching goal of overhauling prevailing social, economic, and political structures. Calls to defund the police or restructure economic systems echo past revolutionary agendas and indicate a desire for radical systemic transformation.

Within the leftist movement, certain factions have embraced anti-government rhetoric as a means to voice their discontent with established institutions and governmental structures. A notable incident took place during a protest in Seattle, where Antifa members were recorded chanting "death to America" and burning U.S. flags. These actions transcend mere acts of defiance; they carry profound significance by symbolizing a rejection of the nation's core values and principles. Such expressions go beyond typical protests and align more closely with the aspirations of a movement aiming for radical change.

The Democrats' alignment with disruptive actions and their support for the radical left has sparked significant criticism and divided opinions. A recent example of this alignment was the decision to prominently display the Black Lives Matter (BLM) banner at U.S. facilities on the anniversary of George Floyd's death, triggering mixed reactions. For some observers, the Biden administration's endorsement of the BLM banner could be perceived as an implicit backing of a movement they believe glorifies a controversial figure. This perception is exacerbated by BLM's vocal advocacy for societal restructuring and its association with leaders who openly identify as Marxists or support socialist principles, fueling concerns that the movement promotes a radical communist agenda.

Furthermore, the allocation of taxpayer funds by the local government in Washington, D.C., to paint the phrase "BLACK LIVES MATTER" on a prominent street has amplified debates about the responsible use of public resources. There is a segment of the population that views this action as an indirect endorsement of a movement they deem to have been involved in terroristic activities. The decision to allocate public funds to the promotion of a contentious movement has prompted questioning about the government's prioritization of such initiatives amid a landscape of diverse societal needs and challenges.

This perspective is exemplified by the outspoken sentiments of Nicole Thomas-Kennedy, a former candidate for the Seattle City Attorney role, with affiliations to Antifa, and her campaign manager, Tye Reed. Thomas-Kennedy's explicit agenda to dismantle capitalism and advocate for communism, coupled with her vocal criticism of the United States, underscores a radical political stance that challenges the fundamental economic and political structures of the country. Her pledged intention to selectively abstain from prosecuting certain offenses has sparked concerns regarding the equitable application of the law and the impartial administration of justice. Such a stance harbors the potential to erode the foundational principles of fairness and impartiality integral to the legal framework. Thomas-Kennedy's expressed views closely mirror those of radical Antifa factions, raising legitimate concerns about their potential impacts on the legal system and the broader societal ethos.

Moreover, lawyers, upon becoming officers of the court, swear an oath to uphold the constitution and abide by the rule of law. This oath obligates them to prioritize justice, fairness, and adherence to the constitutional principles that underpin the legal system. Any indication of departing from this commitment, such as advocating for selective enforcement or undermining established legal norms, could compromise the integrity of the legal profession and the justice system as a whole. Thomas-Kennedy's stated positions, especially concerning the deliberate non-prosecution of certain offenses, challenge this oath and cast doubts on her fidelity to upholding the constitutional tenets that form the bedrock of the legal profession.

The responsibility of an attorney, especially one seeking a position within the legal system, extends beyond personal beliefs and political ideologies. It encompasses a duty to uphold the law without bias, ensuring that justice is served impartially. Any deviation from this principle raises ethical and legal concerns, as it threatens the very essence of a fair and just legal system. Thomas-Kennedy's alignment with positions that potentially compromise the foundational principles of legal equity and impartiality necessitates a careful consideration of the implications of such perspectives within the legal sphere.

Similarly, Tye Reed's vocal endorsement of communism, coupled with his advocacy for violence and alarming suggestions of employing lethal measures against departing police officers, evoke significant concern. Reed's decision to wear a t-shirt depicting a burning Seattle Police Department SUV with the phrase, "This is a policy proposal," further intensifies worries regarding the endorsement of violent actions against law enforcement. Such actions raise alarms about the potential escalation of tensions between protesters and the police, suggesting a confrontational and aggressive approach to addressing grievances. Reed's outspoken advocacy for communism and the implicit approval of violent tactics against law enforcement authorities underscore a radical stance that can fuel further discord and volatility within the community. Such attitudes pose risks to public safety and the stability of law enforcement-community relations, potentially exacerbating existing tensions and eroding trust between law enforcement and the public.

Certain factions within the Left actively pursue the dismantling of the police force, perceiving it as a significant obstacle against the advancement of radical ideologies.

Marxists recognize the potential for chaos in the absence of law enforcement, which they view as a crucial element for destabilizing the prevailing capitalist system. This destabilization is a prerequisite for ushering in a Marxist government. The removal of the police—often perceived as aligned with the current system—is deemed an essential step for the Left to seize governmental control and implement its envisioned societal framework.

The response of local officials to the leftist civil unrest suggests an inclination towards sympathy for the cause, as they have not taken steps to suppress it. Throughout the period of social upheaval characterized by protests and riots, a number of local authorities failed to uphold law and order. Critics argue that governments turned a blind eye to widespread riots, permitting violence against American citizens as a strategy to advance political goals. Critics also contend that state officials granted unexplained privileges that facilitated the riots and even commended and supported these disruptions as "peaceful protests."

In November 2018, a distressing incident marred the streets of Philadelphia as a conservative "We the People" rally on Independence Mall was met with a counter-action that turned violent. Among the protesters, two Marine Corps Reservists bore the brunt of aggression from Antifa members. The Marines endured a barrage of verbal abuse coupled with physical assaults. The attackers hurled derogatory terms such as "Nazis" and "White Supremacists" while subjecting the Marines to punches, kicks, and pepper spray, culminating in the theft of one Marine's cellphone.

In the aftermath, legal proceedings were initiated against the responsible individuals. Joseph Alcoff, a prominent figure within DC Antifa, along with Thomas Massey and Tom Keenan, faced serious felony charges for their roles in the assault. Alcoff, specifically, faced charges including aggravated assault, ethnic intimidation, and conspiracy.

However, despite their active involvement in assaulting the Latino Marines, none of the three Antifa members were sentenced to jail time. This outcome sparked suspicions of political partiality within the judicial system. Philadelphia District Attorney Larry Krasner, who is Jewish and has connections to George Soros, found himself at the center of allegations suggesting influence over case outcomes. These allegations have cast doubt over the impartiality and fairness of the legal proceedings, particularly in cases with political undertones.

Such suspicions of political bias within the judicial system further exacerbate concerns about the equitable and unbiased application of the law. They raise fundamental questions about the extent to which external influences, whether political or otherwise, may sway the course of justice.

In Oregon, an extensive number of deferred adjudication agreements were approved by prosecutors in relation to federal felony cases stemming from the 2020 protests. Out of the 96 individuals initially charged in connection with the violent riots, a striking 47 saw their charges ultimately dropped. This significant dismissal rate has raised eyebrows regarding the impartiality and alignment of prosecutors with leftist causes in handling cases linked to civil unrest.

The exceptionally high number of dropped charges points to leniency in the approach of prosecutors towards individuals involved in the violent riots. Critics argue that such a lenient disposition indicates a sympathetic stance or alignment with the ideological motives behind the protests.

The decisions made by prosecutors to drop charges in numerous cases related to the riots of 2020 have raised concerns about the selective enforcement of the law and the consistent application of justice. Such actions not only have implications for law and order but also perpetuate a narrative suggesting preferential treatment or reluctance to hold individuals accountable for their actions during certain instances of civil unrest. This approach might be interpreted as a form of tacit endorsement or sympathy towards the leftist ideologies behind the protests.

On August 18, 2020, during a riot in Portland, Oregon, Antifa members engaged in violent actions, including throwing Molotov cocktails at the County Sheriff's Department Headquarters. Responding to the chaos and disorder, Officer Corey Budworth, a member of the Portland Police Department's "Rapid Response Team," used a baton to strike one of the rioters, Teri Jacobs. Following an internal assessment, Budworth's superiors concluded that his actions were warranted considering the circumstances surrounding the riot.

Multnomah District Attorney Mike Schmidt, recognized for his progressive leanings, indicted Budworth on a fourth-degree misdemeanor assault charge. This action elicited strong reactions, with some suggesting that the indictment appeared to be shaped more by political factors than by an unbiased assessment of the incident. Schmidt has consistently embraced left-leaning viewpoints, championing progressive criminal justice reform, promoting police accountability, and aligning his policy priorities and affiliations with progressive goals.

The decision to indict Officer Corey Budworth amid heightened societal tensions against law enforcement raises suspicions of potential political motivations at play. Bringing charges during a period marked by public dissatisfaction with law enforcement prompts inquiries into whether the indictment aimed to appease protesters, potentially undermining an impartial assessment. This situation suggests a possible rush to judgment influenced by external pressures, prioritizing immediate responses over the careful application of due process.

District Attorney Mike Schmidt's alignment with a region recognized for its progressive stance and his vocal advocacy for reform and police accountability may have influenced the decision to pursue charges. Given the ongoing debates surrounding police reform and calls for reduced police presence, the indictment might be perceived as a calculated move to exhibit a commitment to reform efforts and address demands for substantial changes within law enforcement.

Following the indictment, the entire Rapid Response Team resigned. The police union expressed disappointment and voiced apprehensions, suggesting that the highly regarded public servant, Budworth, had become collateral damage due to city officials pursuing their own agendas. The disbandment of the Rapid Response Team has sparked concerns among law-abiding Portland residents. This specialized unit played a crucial role in managing civil unrest and upholding public safety during riots and large-scale demonstrations. The dissolution of the team may lead to a gap in the city's capacity to handle such situations, potentially leaving them less secure in times of turmoil.

Eva Warner, a transgender Antifa member involved in the Portland riots, was caught attempting to blind the police using a laser. Surprisingly, U.S. Attorney for the District of Oregon, Scott Erik Asphaug, dismissed Warner's federal charges in September 2020, accompanied by a mere 20 hours of community service. This lenient resolution conveys a troubling message about the consequences of engaging in violent conduct during protests. The handling of Warner's case suggests sympathy for left-leaning causes, as Asphaug's leniency might be viewed as favoring those tied to Antifa and aligned with the left, raising concerns about bias influencing the legal proceedings.

Indiana Attorney General Todd Rokita and attorneys general from 16 other states have voiced significant concerns and directed pointed criticism at the Department of Justice (DOJ) and Federal Bureau of Investigation (FBI). Their collective discontent stems from a palpable lack of action to hold accountable those responsible for the series of violent and criminal activities that unfolded throughout the summer of 2020.

Their criticisms spotlight a prevailing frustration over the perceived inaction or inadequate efforts to address the incidents of violence, unrest, and criminal behavior that marked numerous protests and civil disturbances committed by leftists during that period. Despite widespread occurrences of violence, property damage, and other illegal actions witnessed across various states, there appears to be a noticeable absence of comprehensive investigations and subsequent measures of accountability undertaken by federal law enforcement agencies.

The leniency shown toward agitators charged with rioting and engaging in violent activities has sparked considerable concerns regarding accountability and public safety. The minimal repercussions faced by BLM and Antifa rioters, even those involved in damaging federal buildings, through brief stints of community service, do not serve as an adequate deterrent against future violence.

This lenient approach in prosecuting rioters has raised scrutiny regarding a potential sympathetic disposition towards socialist causes or leftist ideologies within the judicial system. The leniency displayed by authorities might reflect a form of tacit support for the ideological motivations that fueled the protests, rather than a neutral pursuit of justice.

Attorney General Rokita's and other state attorneys general's dissatisfaction underscores a broader concern: that the leniency exhibited in handling individuals involved in violent activities might signal an alignment with the ideological underpinnings of certain movements rather than a steadfast commitment to impartial justice.

The dissemination of Marxist ideologies by extremist factions has significantly fueled the unrest gripping American cities, aiming not just to protest but to fundamentally overturn democratic principles and instigate chaos. Groups such as Black Lives Matter and Antifa, deeply entrenched in far-left ideologies, advocate not for a nationwide revolution, seeking to entirely overhaul societal structures. Some within these factions openly embrace communist ideals, envisioning a future where the means of production are under state control.

The proliferation of these radical ideologies poses a dire threat by fostering deep-seated discord and ideological strife, fundamentally challenging the bedrock of democratic principles and societal stability. The propagation of Marxist ideals is a challenge to the established order, a force that threatens to reshape the socio-political landscape in ways that sow division and conflict.

These movements strategically deploy various elements to drive revolutionary change: organized protests, the dissemination of their ideologies through multiple channels, and disruptive actions aimed at unsettling the status quo. Tactics such as protests and strikes echo historical Marxist insurgents, reflecting a calculated approach to incite upheaval and confront the prevailing norms. While peaceful protests, protected by the First Amendment, embody democratic forms of expression, these protests often hover on the edge of escalation, risking a descent into violence or the propagation of incendiary rhetoric.

The deliberate destabilization of the United States is part of a meticulously crafted strategy aiming to steer the nation towards a communist revolution. Historical records and recent events highlight various groups intentionally disrupting societal norms. Using tactics such as information warfare, polarization, and leveraging digital platforms such as social media, these coordinated efforts often originate from foundations and front organizations openly hostile to the country, reflecting historical patterns of undermining national stability. Exploiting genuine grievances becomes a tool to incite upheaval, fracturing social unity, eroding institutional trust, and widening divisions—a deliberate strategy fostering discontent with the existing societal structure.

As a result, concerns have escalated about the potential emergence of a communist revolution reshaping American institutions into a totalitarian regime, potentially eroding national sovereignty. Communism, both a socio-economic and political ideology, aims for a classless society with collective ownership of the means of production by the working class. Some within this movement advocate for class struggle and revolutionary methods, asserting that the current capitalist system perpetuates exploitation, inequality, and oppression, necessitating a radical transformation towards a fairer society.

At its core, communism seeks to erase traditional class divisions inherent in private ownership, advocating for collective ownership of resources, industries, and wealth redistribution to address wealth and power disparities characteristic of capitalist societies.

This destabilization campaign employs various strategies manipulating the economy, influencing political dynamics, and amplifying social conflicts to heighten tensions and destabilize the situation. Tactics include economic disruptions, strategic political maneuvers, and the amplification of social discord through covert operations, information manipulation, and propaganda dissemination. This ongoing disruptive pattern intensifies disorder, erodes social cohesion, undermines institutional trust, and deepens societal divisions. The consequence of this orchestrated chaos could set the stage for a communist revolution.

A violent revolution often serves as a prelude to a subsequent, nonviolent socialist revolution, a concept deeply embedded in Marxist theory known as the Proletarian Revolution. Here, the strategy envisages a violent upheaval to enable the working class (proletariat) to topple the ruling capitalist class (bourgeoisie) and establish a society founded on socialist or communist principles. Advocates of this method seek to galvanize public support by leveraging the fear of further violence and suffering.

History offers a wealth of evidence detailing the severe repercussions of violent revolutions. They tend to disrupt economies, dismantle social structures, and destabilize governance systems, leading to profound uncertainty and chaos. Moreover, such movements often attract extremists pursuing personal agendas, resulting in human rights abuses and the ascent of authoritarian regimes. The persistence of violence and instability frequently creates an environment where the public reluctantly accedes to gradual socialist reforms pursued through peaceful means, effectively enabling the transition to a socialist society. However, this method relies more on coercion and manipulation than the genuine acceptance of these ideological principles.

Forecasts concerning potential future conflicts suggest meticulously orchestrated clashes, acts of sabotage, and large-scale incidents reminiscent of historical revolutions. These predictions draw from historical patterns, strategic calculations, and the deliberate fomenting of societal unrest and governmental upheaval. Over time, clandestine agitators have been strategically deployed to gain an upper hand over adversaries. By capitalizing on heightened emotions during periods of turmoil, covert forces aim to amass greater support for their cause. They await opportune moments to minimize the likelihood of robust counter-responses, taking advantage of a distracted general population engrossed in their own challenges.

This strategic maneuver raises significant concerns regarding the potential for a dramatic escalation into a tumultuous revolution. The calculated timing of disruptive activities, coupled with the exploitation of societal grievances, presents a substantial risk of destabilization, potentially paving the way for significant societal transformations or, in the worst-case scenario, a full-fledged communist revolution.

Lenin and Trotsky's ascent to power during the October Revolution of 1917 marked a pivotal historical moment. Under the guidance of the Bolshevik Party, they used force to overthrow the Provisional Government and establish a socialist regime. Following their seizure of power, they adopted a strategy known as revolutionary parliamentarianism to consolidate their authority and implement their socialist agenda.

Revolutionary parliamentarianism involves a two-pronged approach, known as the "pincers movement," skillfully harnessing political influence from both upper echelons and grassroots levels. This approach played a crucial role in the early years of the Bolshevik government under Lenin and Trotsky, allowing them to advance their socialist agenda during a critical period in Russian history.

The Bolsheviks used their control of state institutions to enact socialist policies and reforms, such as industry nationalization and land redistribution. This top-down approach allowed them to swiftly execute these policies, establishing legitimacy and firmly solidifying their governance.

Simultaneously, the Bolsheviks embraced grassroots activism and organization to mobilize the masses and gain widespread support. They encouraged active participation from workers, peasants, and soldiers in decision-making, fostering a sense of ownership and pride in the revolution. Grassroots initiatives aimed to legitimize the Bolshevik government among the general population and secure popular endorsement. The broad-based support generated through these grassroots efforts not only conferred legitimacy on the Bolshevik government but also bolstered its stability.

The convergence of state institutions and grassroots activism played a pivotal role in consolidating Bolshevik authority and securing popular support. Lenin and Trotsky's ultimate goal was to establish a government representing the interests of the working class and the broader proletariat, aiming to construct a socialist state that would eventually lead to a classless, communist society.

Critics of revolutionary parliamentarianism expressed profound apprehensions about its inherent authoritarian tendencies, particularly when observing its implementation during the Russian Civil War. The Bolsheviks, while advocating for a parliamentary system, encountered significant challenges in consolidating their authority and suppressing opposition. In their pursuit of establishing a proletarian government, they resorted to using military force and imposing stringent measures, thus compromising the initial democratic ideals and fostering an emergent authoritarianism.

The case of revolutionary parliamentarianism in Czechoslovakia between 1946 and 1948 stands as a compelling historical example of a seemingly nonviolent political strategy that ultimately led to the demise of freedom and democracy within the nation.

Under the guidance of Jan Kozak, a Czech communist strategist, this method involved a dual strategy: Advancing communist objectives while subtly paving the way for totalitarian rule. It employed organized grassroots mobilization and orchestrated street demonstrations, supported by funding from higher echelons. This combination of bottom-up activism and top-down coordination exerted substantial pressure on the established government and institutions.

The demonstrations initially sprang from specific grievances, leading to legislative changes that broadened governmental authority in response to highlighted issues. One of the pivotal grievances fueling protests in Czechoslovakia during this period was the fervent demand for land reform. These demonstrations primarily advocated for agricultural restructuring, pushing for the redistribution of land from large landowners to peasants and smaller farmers. The protesters aimed to instigate legislative changes that would address the inequality in land ownership, seeking to provide land to those who worked it and were often marginalized or landless. The resulting legislation was manipulated to serve the broader objectives of the communist movement, ultimately consolidating power and control.

A critical aspect of this strategy involved immense pressure from below, compelling even anti-communist legislators to acquiesce to opposition objectives in the pursuit of restoring order. This maneuver enabled the communist movement to advance its agenda, often overpowering opposition due to the urgency of the situation.

This method culminated in the legal takeover of the military and police, laying the groundwork for the realization of radical objectives. Czechoslovakia transformed into a Moscow satellite state without resorting to armed conflict. This success of revolutionary parliamentarianism effectively signaled the end of freedom and democracy within the nation.

The Czechoslovakian case showcases how revolutionary parliamentarianism capitalized on democratic processes to amass power, employing political maneuvers, alliances, and subtle coercion that undermined the true spirit of democracy. Despite the absence of overt violence, implicit threats or even the suggestion of potential chaos served as coercive tactics.

Revolutionary parliamentarianism undermines democratic legitimacy by exploiting the potential for violence. This approach manipulates democratic systems to consolidate power, using calculated political maneuvers and alliances to subtly coerce, eroding the core principles of democracy. Even without overt violence, the implicit threats and the looming specter of chaos coerce officials into accepting a leftward shift.

Throughout history, movements have drawn inspiration from Marxist ideologies as catalysts for societal transformation. The Moscow faction proposed a unique method to steer America toward a communist system, advocating a nonviolent strategy rooted in peaceful and lawful means. Unlike endorsing violence or armed uprisings, this faction championed reforms and incremental shifts toward socialist principles, aiming for a gradual, widely accepted path to their communist objectives.

The proponents of this nonviolent strategy believed in a peaceful transition to socialism to facilitate smoother societal evolution, minimizing widespread resistance. They aimed to gain broader public support and create a less tumultuous path toward transforming the existing socio-political structure. Their strategy relied on the assumption that a peaceful transition could bring about lasting change without the upheaval often linked to revolutionary movements.

This approach targeted key societal structures, advocating for policy changes, social reforms, and grassroots activism to gradually shift public opinion toward socialist ideals. The aim was to shape public perception and support for Marxist ideologies, steering the nation's governance and socio-economic frameworks closer to their envisioned communist utopia.

This nonviolent strategy presented itself as a more acceptable and practical method for transforming the United States, rooted in the belief that gradual, non-disruptive changes could reshape societal values and systems. By leveraging peaceful means, they sought to create a platform appealing to a wider audience, enabling a transition they deemed more sustainable and inclusive. Ultimately, their goal was for the nation to embrace socialist tenets without the upheaval associated with violent revolutions.

Throughout history, nonviolent movements have effectively mobilized various groups using civil disobedience, protests, and strikes to push for social and political change. They attract support from different backgrounds, highlighting moral superiority to gain sympathy and international backing. This method, while avoiding violence, is strategic in positioning itself as a powerful force for reforms, garnering widespread acceptance and credibility.

Revolutionary parliamentarianism in the USA spotlights the calculated use of legal and political strategies to further ideological agendas while operating within the democratic system. Within this landscape, leftist movements in the U.S. are strategically employing this approach, capitalizing on the potential for heightened unrest to advance socialist policies. This calculated maneuvering maintains a veneer of tranquility as long as the overall trajectory aligns with a shift towards the left.

The crux of concern lies in the gradual transformation of the intricate fabric of political and societal structures through the utilization of democratic mechanisms. This method of reshaping these structures raises alarms about the potential compromise of pluralistic governance and the foundational integrity of democratic principles.

What underscores this unease is the looming possibility of undermining the fundamental tenets upon which authentic democracy thrives: inclusivity, fairness, and the equitable representation of diverse viewpoints. As these tactics unfold, the fear is not just about the current state of affairs but the long-term ramifications that could erode the essence of a genuinely democratic society.

Some proponents of communism advocate for two distinct approaches in their pursuit of societal change. One faction endorses revolutionary parliamentarianism, aiming to harness democratic systems for radical transformations within society. However, when these methods fail to yield desired outcomes, another faction of radical communists advocates for a more direct approach, emphasizing the significance of class struggle and the complete overthrow of existing societal structures.

Advocates of revolutionary communism perceive inherent injustices within society that demand urgent and transformative change. They claim that the core foundations of capitalism sustain an unequal distribution of resources, concentrating power and wealth among a select privileged class while exploiting the working class solely for profit, neglecting their well-being and dignity. They contend that incremental reforms within a capitalist system are insufficient to rectify persistent imbalances, firmly asserting that revolutionary tactics are necessary to dismantle structures perpetuating economic disparity and social injustice.

At the heart of the revolutionary communist perspective lies a core belief: the capitalist framework inherently perpetuates cycles of exploitation and systemic inequalities. Advocates contend that achieving fundamental societal change demands revolutionary upheaval. They envision a reshaped economic landscape characterized by collective ownership and decision-making that empowers the working class, liberating them from the pitfalls embedded within the structures of capitalism. This vision entails a paradigm shift away from individualized ownership and profit-driven motives towards a communal approach to resource allocation and governance.

After a communist revolution, the period of normalization instigates significant changes within a society's socio-economic framework. The core objective behind the revolution is the dismantling of existing political hierarchies and structures, aiming for collective ownership and governance of resources. Normalization becomes pivotal for restoring order after the disruptive events of a revolution.

The aftermath of violent upheavals often brings about suffering, instability, and tragic loss of life. The ideals of a classless society and equality, purportedly championed by communist movements, can be deeply compromised amidst the chaos caused by violent upheavals.

The normalization process involves influential institutions, particularly the media, working to establish a sense of routine and widespread acceptance regarding the post-revolution aftermath. The media plays a crucial role in reinforcing the narrative of consensus and normalcy regarding the outcome. The ultimate aim is to shape the perception that the new regime is legitimate, solidifying the newly installed government's position as the recognized authority.

Industries and economic activities undergo extensive restructuring to align with the new ideological paradigm. A central focus of this phase is the establishment of institutions in line with Marxist principles, often involving the introduction of social welfare initiatives to ensure equitable resource distribution. Additionally, there is a strong emphasis on achieving economic stabilization and reconstruction to counter potential disruptions caused by the revolution. This results in substantial investments in infrastructure and industries that conform to socialist ideals.

The working class unites in a bid to seize control over the means of production, aiming to dismantle established power structures perceived to sustain wealth and privilege for a select few. Proponents champion this movement as a grand redistribution of resources and opportunities, pledging universal access to societal benefits. They paint a picture where hierarchical systems and oppressive frameworks dissolve, with the people collectively managing governance. This narrative presents socialism as a means to erase social, economic, and political divisions by diffusing power widely among the populace.

Yet, historical evidence reveals a stark contrast between this idealistic depiction and the reality. Socialist systems have consistently struggled to fulfill their promises. Instead of widespread prosperity, they often lead to economic stagnation, suffocating innovation and hampering growth. Rather than dismantling hierarchies, they often breed bureaucratic mazes where power consolidates within a new ruling elite, perpetuating the very inequalities they vowed to eradicate.

Far from fostering equality, socialism tends to stifle individual ambition and initiative. State-controlled economies and excessive regulations create barriers to entrepreneurship, obstructing personal growth and advancement. This system ends up rewarding political connections and favoritism over merit or effort, sowing disillusionment and impeding societal progress.

Moreover, the pledge of universal access to advantages frequently falls short. Socialist systems do not offer equal opportunities; instead, they entrench disparities, granting privileges to the ruling class while imposing scarcity and limitations on the rest under centralized authority.

The idea of collective governance often becomes a façade, concealing the emergence of authoritarian regimes claiming to serve the collective interest. Concentration of power in the hands of the state leads to oppression, censorship, and the silencing of dissent, undermining the very democratic ideals socialism purports to champion.

Murray Bessette, a former professor of government at Morehead State University and now with the Victims of Communism Memorial Foundation, highlighted the recurring historical pattern where regimes rooted in Marxist principles have consistently led to oppressive governance. These societies bear the hallmarks of control through propaganda, widespread information censorship, the stifling of free thought, the erasure of individuality, and the enforcement of rigid conformity. He explained, "[The raised fist] is a symbol used by movements that establish oppressive systems, as every system established along Marxist lines has been. The common thread is [an] understanding of all social, economic and political relations as a contestation for power between a class of oppressors (i.a., rich, White, heterosexual, male) and a class of oppressed."[23]

The uncertainties surrounding the normalization phase post-communist revolution stem from historical precedents wherein such movements culminated in dire consequences, including the emergence of authoritarian regimes and egregious human rights violations. Critics raise valid concerns about the potential for centralized power to be exploited, leading to the rise of totalitarian tendencies. They

---

[23] Lott, Maxim. "BLM Clenched-Fist Symbol Has Little-Known Communist History, Critics Say." *Fox News*, 15 Apr. 2021, www.foxnews.com/politics/black-lives-matter-antifa-clenched-fist-symbol-communist-history.

fear that individual liberties might be compromised in the pursuit of the state's perception of the collective good. An excessively powerful state, despite its goals for a fairer society, could undermine the very principles it claims to champion.

In its most extreme case, a totalitarian regime could enforce an iron-fisted version of egalitarianism by suppressing individual abilities, accomplishments, and competence under the guise of eradicating inequality. The promise of socialism to disperse power and foster societal unity often masks a darker reality. Instead of delivering equality and empowerment, it tends to stifle progress, breed inequality, and concentrate power among a select few, ultimately hindering societal advancement and curtailing individual freedoms.

The next chapter delves into the constraints imposed on freedom of speech, particularly the challenges faced by dissenting perspectives. This issue gains significant prominence in the contemporary landscape, notably with the advent of cancel culture and widespread media bias. These developments have sparked valid concerns about the deliberate silencing of dissenting voices and the erosion of open discourse and diverse opinions.

Chapter 6

Weaponized Censorship

While the United States has historically championed free speech, recent times have witnessed a growing concern over the surge in censorship. The modern era, defined by remarkable technological advancements and the rapid expansion of social media, has reshaped the landscape of public discourse. Yet, this transformation has also seen the rise of a phenomenon influenced by cultural Marxism that poses a threat to freedom of expression and individual liberties.

In the pursuit of ideological conformity, widespread censorship and information control have curbed dissenting viewpoints, discouraging independent thought that deviates from the established narrative. Tactics such as censorship and cancelling are wielded to regulate information flow, manipulate perceptions, and reinforce the desired narrative. The leftists' command over both foreign and domestic media outlets has restricted diverse viewpoints, creating a substantial barrier to well-rounded perspectives and impeding critical reporting. This suppression not only stifles the development of comprehensive viewpoints but also bolsters the dominance of the prevailing ideology.

This chapter explores the formidable impact of censorship, a powerful tool that reshapes the landscape of political discourse, social interactions, and the exchange of ideas. Within this transformation, social media platforms emerge as crucial players, sparking an inquiry into their role in defining the limits of public discourse and their impact on American democracy. We navigate the intricate interplay among technology, politics, and the preservation of free speech, shedding light on the multifaceted challenges and implications arising from the growing potency of censorship within the United States.

In democratic societies, the bedrock of freedom of speech stands firm, safeguarding citizens' liberty to articulate ideas, beliefs, and critiques without the specter of censorship or reprisals. This unrestricted freedom serves as the catalyst for vibrant debates, a spectrum of perspectives, and an open exchange of ideas that are pivotal in elevating public discourse.

Yet, the advent of the digital age, characterized by the dominance of online platforms, has brought forth not only revolutionary communication possibilities but also concerning trends in censorship. Internet censorship has transformed into a tool utilized to restrict access to websites and content that challenge governing authorities or diverge from prevailing socialist narratives. Some platforms have adopted censorship tactics that stifle the dissemination of specific viewpoints, notably conservative ones, across social media and digital channels, effectively stifling their expression. The rise of cancel culture, where online communities collectively shun individuals for expressing contentious ideas, compounds concerns about suffocating dissenting voices and constraining the free exchange of diverse perspectives.

Throughout history, communist regimes have systematically suppressed free speech using various methods to maintain control over public discourse. State control and censorship were cornerstones of this suppression, where governments imposed strict laws to regulate media, tightly controlled newspapers, broadcasting, and access to information contradicting the official party line. Any dissent or criticism faced swift and severe consequences, often resulting in imprisonment, censorship, or intimidation. This control extended beyond traditional media, encompassing literature, arts, and any form of expression challenging the ruling ideology.

Marxist regimes engaged in political repression and persecution, targeting intellectuals, dissenters, writers, and artists who expressed views contrary to the established narrative. Opposition parties and individuals questioning the government faced persecution, creating an atmosphere of fear that discouraged open discussion or critique. Those voicing dissent were subjected to imprisonment, exile, or, in extreme cases, execution, contributing to a climate of suppression and self-censorship.

Propaganda played a pivotal role in communist regimes, shaping public opinion and controlling societal beliefs. State-controlled media disseminated propaganda glorifying the ruling party while demonizing dissenters or ideological opponents. Educational systems were harnessed to indoctrinate citizens, promoting the party's ideologies and suppressing alternative viewpoints. Cultural movements like China's Cultural Revolution aimed to eradicate 'counter-revolutionary' thoughts, purging intellectuals, stifling artistic expression, and enforcing strict adherence to the prevailing ideology. This eradication severely limited artistic freedom and academic inquiry.

Furthermore, dissent within the communist parties themselves was met with suppression. Internal purges and ideological campaigns targeted dissenting voices, fostering a culture of conformity and discouraging internal criticism or debate. This consolidation of power within the party reinforced the suppression of diverse opinions and reinforced strict adherence to the party's dogma, effectively limiting intellectual freedom and stifling open dialogue. The suppression of free speech within communist regimes not only controlled the narrative but also created an environment where dissent was silenced, diverse viewpoints were absent, and intellectual freedom was severely curtailed.

Cancel culture, fueled by a fervent pursuit of social accountability, frequently adopts punitive measures against individuals or groups expressing dissenting or controversial views. This rapid and pervasive public condemnation, amplified through the omnipresence of social media, creates an atmosphere where individuals hesitate to articulate opinions that deviate from prevailing narratives. Consequently, it engenders self-censorship, constraining the breadth of perspectives vital for nurturing robust and meaningful dialogue within a democratic society.

Historical communist regimes employed an array of strategies to effectively "cancel" dissenters, aiming to quash opposition and enforce ideological uniformity. This cancel culture, echoing these historical precedents, manifests through an impassioned quest for social accountability often resorting to punitive actions against those expressing dissent or contentious opinions.

Similar to the tactics employed in Marxist regimes, contemporary cancel culture thrives on swift and public condemnation, capitalizing on the extensive influence of social media. Individuals challenging established ideologies or diverging from prevailing narratives encounter swift and widespread censure, paralleling the treatment of dissenters in historical communist societies. This intensified scrutiny and social ostracization effectively silence those expressing unconventional or dissenting viewpoints.

The fear instilled by cancel culture echoes the climate of fear pervasive in historical communist regimes, where voicing dissent incurred severe repercussions. In today's context, individuals fear repercussions such as public shaming, jeopardizing livelihoods, or facing social exclusion, fostering self-censorship and reluctance to express opinions diverging from mainstream narratives. This self-censorship stifles the array of perspectives crucial for fostering a vibrant and meaningful discourse within a democratic framework.

In both historical communist regimes and contemporary cancel culture, the practice of silencing dissent aims to mold opinions and enforce conformity to prevailing ideologies. This trend undermines the core principles of free speech and open discourse in democratic societies, threatening the essential diversity of viewpoints crucial for healthy dialogue.

The evolution of political correctness, associated with Cultural Marxism, has become associated with stifling dissent—a concern raised by critics worried about its impact on free speech. This evolution aligns with the rise of cancel culture, which shuts down differing voices through "canceling," fostering an environment that discourages diverse perspectives. This fusion of political correctness and cancel culture creates an atmosphere where certain expressions are deemed unacceptable, hindering progress and challenging the essence of free expression in democracy.

Driven by a pursuit of social accountability, cancel culture penalizes controversial views, leading individuals to hesitate in expressing divergent opinions. This self-censorship limits the crucial range of perspectives necessary for robust democratic discussions. The rapid condemnation of dissent by cancel culture, resembling communist tactics, leverages social media to suppress challenging viewpoints, instilling a fear that stifles free speech. Both historical regimes and contemporary cancel culture seek to impose conformity, eroding the indispensable diversity of thought vital for dynamic democratic discourse.

The far-reaching implications of these trends resonate beyond mere individual freedom of expression; they strike at the core of democratic discourse itself. The free flow of ideas and the respectful exchange of divergent opinions form the bedrock of a vibrant and healthy democracy. Yet, the imposition of constraints on dissenting viewpoints poses a significant risk of stifling intellectual diversity and obstructing societal advancement.

Safeguarding the freedom to express dissenting opinions is about preserving the very essence of critical thinking and fostering an environment conducive to innovation and progress. In a society where diverse perspectives are celebrated and dissent is encouraged, it sparks the kind of intellectual ferment necessary for addressing complex challenges. It is within this space of differing viewpoints that innovation thrives, solutions emerge, and societal evolution takes place.

When dissent is stifled or suppressed, it truncates the spectrum of ideas available for consideration, limiting the pool from which creative solutions may arise. Societal progress often emerges from the clash and reconciliation of opposing viewpoints, allowing for a synthesis of ideas that can lead to more comprehensive and nuanced approaches to societal issues. Without the freedom to dissent, this process of intellectual exploration and growth is curtailed, posing a threat to the dynamic fabric of a democratic society.

Moreover, the suppression of dissenting opinions not only stifles innovation but can also engender a climate of conformity, where individuals feel compelled to adhere to prevailing narratives rather than express genuine beliefs or concerns. This conformity, in turn, hampers the authenticity of public discourse and may prevent the identification of crucial issues that require attention or alternative solutions that need investigation.

Hence, safeguarding the freedom to express dissenting opinions is not merely about protecting individual liberties but is fundamental to nurturing an environment that values critical thinking, encourages intellectual diversity, and propels societal advancement. It is about embracing dissent as a catalyst for growth, innovation, and the continual evolution of a democratic society.

Marxists often adopt a seemingly contradictory stance regarding free speech, leveraging it strategically to suit their objectives and amplifying their message when it aligns with their narrative. However, their commitment to this principle appears conditional, subject to change when it clashes with their ideological agenda or challenges their narrative.

During times when Marxists find themselves in the minority or aim to contest prevailing power structures, they passionately advocate for free speech as a means to voice dissent and challenge established ideologies. Yet, once they attain influence or ascend to positions of authority, their fervor for free speech often diminishes, giving way to a more selective approach.

Leftists frequently perceive free speech as a pragmatic tool, readily endorsing it when it bolsters their cause and provides a platform for their viewpoints. However, when confronted with ideas that contradict their ideology or threaten their agenda, their stance tends to shift towards endorsing censorship or advocating for restrictions on speech. This shift is often rationalized under the guise of protecting vulnerable groups or maintaining societal harmony.

Marxists' selective embrace of free speech appears more strategic than principled, serving as a means to advance their goals rather than embodying an unwavering commitment to the principle itself. Their readiness to curtail speech that opposes their ideology contradicts the foundational tenets of free expression and undermines the diversity of opinions essential for a vibrant and open society.

"The 45 Goals of Communism" illuminates strategies aimed at undermining the bedrock of free speech in a society that holds it dear, ultimately paving the way for a culture of suppression. This approach revolves around individuals embracing leftist ideologies strategically assuming influential positions within major corporations. Leveraging their authority, they promote Marxist beliefs, gradually shaping public opinion, molding media narratives, and steering legislative agendas to align with their ideological stance.

This method involves infiltrating influential sectors, particularly corporate entities, where individuals sympathetic to leftist ideologies incrementally exert their influence. Leveraging their positions, they guide discussions and decisions, subtly advocating for ideologies resonating with socialist beliefs. As they ascend to influential positions, they wield their power to mold public sentiment through media channels and sway legislative directions.

The entrenched propagation of specific ideologies within influential spheres restrains the free flow of diverse ideas. By sculpting narratives and influencing pivotal decisions, these individuals stifle viewpoints that challenge their ideological alignment. This gradual molding of public opinion and control over media content threatens to sideline alternative perspectives, diminishing the breadth and diversity of viewpoints vital for a robust democratic society that upholds free speech.

Essentially, the infiltration of influential sectors by those aligned with leftist ideologies embodies a subtle form of subversion, restricting the open exchange of ideas and eroding the cornerstone of free speech in American society.

In the realm of social media, there is a noticeable surge in the application of content control measures and censorship tactics, often reflecting a selective approach to free speech, particularly among certain left-leaning groups. These tactics encompass a spectrum, ranging from account suspensions and demonetization to categorizing content as "disinformation," alongside using algorithms to suppress the visibility of specific posts.

The influence of leftist ideologies within social media platforms is evident through the deployment of these content control mechanisms. Instances abound where users expressing dissenting or conservative viewpoints face punitive actions, such as suspension or shadow banning, ostensibly for violating community guidelines or supposedly spreading misinformation. These moderation tactics often echo the ideological inclinations of those in control of these platforms.

The interpretation of terms such as "hate speech," "misinformation," or "disinformation" within social media platforms often aligns with subjective inclinations, frequently leaning toward leftist ideologies. Consequently, content that challenges prevailing leftist ideologies or veers from mainstream narratives faces the threat of being flagged as offensive or misleading, often resulting in diminished visibility or outright removal.

Individuals aligned with leftist ideologies frequently use the term "disinformation" as a pretext to censor contentious information that contradicts their beliefs or preferred narratives. This subjective application provides those in power with the means to restrict or eliminate opposing information across platforms, stifling dissenting opinions and shaping public opinion in line with their narratives.

Tagging dissenting information as "disinformation" lays the groundwork for censorship, fostering an environment that suppresses diverse viewpoints. This tactic is aimed at muting dissent, diminishing the visibility, accessibility, and credibility of these perspectives, thereby hindering informed debates and undermining dissenters' ability to sway public opinion.

Similarly, the broad categorization of certain speech as "hate speech" by leftists frames speech itself as a form of violence, justifying censorship practices such as deplatforming and shadow-banning. This expansive definition risks misuse, leading to the suppression of opposing views, curtailing free expression, and impeding the vital diversity of perspectives crucial for a vibrant public discourse.

The ambiguous nature of "hate speech" and "disinformation," lacking clear legal definitions in the United States, raises concerns about the erosion of individual liberties. This trend restricts free speech by classifying viewpoints as "offensive" or "politically incorrect," ultimately stifling the range of perspectives in public discourse.

Furthermore, framing "speech as violence" poses a significant threat to free speech, stifling opposing viewpoints essential in a democratic society. Encouraging open dialogue counters objectionable speech by fostering understanding and addressing prejudices. Allowing contentious speech to be openly discussed offers an opportunity to confront and refute harmful ideas instead of resorting to marginalization.

Excessive censorship grounded in the belief of "speech as violence" risks inciting resistance, deepening societal divisions, and cultivating "echo chambers," limiting exposure to diverse perspectives. Encouraging open debate is crucial for nurturing critical thinking and challenging incorrect beliefs, providing a more effective means to counter harmful ideologies than simply silencing them.

The manipulation of content visibility through algorithms further showcases the influence of Marxist perspectives in social media. While these algorithms are ostensibly designed to refine user experience, they can intentionally prioritize content that aligns with specific ideological viewpoints, while curtailing the exposure of dissenting opinions.

This infiltration of leftist ideologies within social media platforms has fostered an environment where dissenting or unconventional opinions encounter hurdles in reaching broader audiences. This suppresses the diversity of opinions and obstructs open dialogue, contradicting the principles of free speech and stifling the richness of discussions vital for a thriving democratic discourse.

In essence, the incursion of leftist ideologies into social media platforms is evident through content control measures and censorship tactics that often favor socialist narratives while marginalizing dissenting viewpoints. This trend raises significant concerns about the impact of ideological biases on the open exchange of ideas, potentially undermining the fundamental principles of open discourse within these digital spheres. Social media platforms have employed various content control methods and censorship targeting certain users, including account suspensions, demonetization, labeling content as "disinformation," and using algorithms to limit post visibility.

Following the 2020 presidential election, an unprecedented wave of doubt emerged regarding the election's legitimacy. This surge of skepticism created a tumultuous period marked by far-reaching repercussions, particularly evident in the domain of social media. Individuals daring to question the election outcome faced substantial consequences, with many experiencing swift de-platforming as a result of expressing their concerns.

The aftermath of the election witnessed an explosive surge in allegations of election fraud, fueled by a fervent belief among a significant segment of the population that the election results were marred by irregularities and inconsistencies. This wave of doubt rapidly gained momentum, sweeping through various sections of the populace and triggering widespread questioning of the election's legitimacy.

Former Republican Michigan State senator Patrick Colbeck's insights into election integrity bear significant weight. As the former vice-chair of elections and government reform in the Michigan State Senate, Colbeck provided a firsthand account of the 2020 election as a certified poll challenger in Detroit. His observations revealed irregularities, including late-night ballot drops, poll challengers obstructed from observing counts hidden behind taped pizza boxes, and dubious media narratives circulating around these events. These sworn testimonies, presented under oath, add a critical layer of legitimacy to election fraud claims.

The controversy surrounding former CIA officer John Sipher's revelations implies potential intelligence agency interference in the 2020 election outcome. Sipher's bold claims, particularly on platforms such as Twitter, where he openly credited himself with discrediting the Hunter Biden "laptop from hell" story and boasted about steering the election away from Donald Trump, has sparked widespread debate and scrutiny.

Sipher's assertion that the Hunter Biden laptop story was part of a carefully orchestrated Russian disinformation campaign has faced significant challenge and debunking, raising substantial concerns about potential intelligence agency involvement in manipulating public opinion and shaping election outcomes.

His affirmation of influencing the election away from Trump has heightened discussions and debates about the role intelligence officers may have played in influencing the democratic process. This revelation reinforces suspicions that the election was not free and fair.

The aftermath of the election sparked a pervasive distrust in its outcome, particularly evident among supporters of President Trump. Surveys and polls unveiled a staggering level of skepticism, with a mere 39 percent of registered voters expressing confidence in the election's fairness. Within the Republican Party, a prevailing sentiment emerged, challenging the legitimacy of Biden's victory, a belief held by a significant majority.

This widespread distrust significantly influenced the dynamics within the Republican Party. A substantial faction questioned the lawfulness of Biden's ascent to office, with an overwhelming majority of Republicans rejecting the notion of his legitimate presidency.

Senator Rand Paul (R-KY) has consistently voiced his belief that the 2020 election experienced irregularities leading to its theft. His public statements and appearances have reiterated his view that the election lacked the necessary transparency and confidence in its outcomes. In response to Chris Krebs, the former United States Director of CISA, who claimed the election was the most secure ever, Sen. Paul strongly disagreed. He argued that Krebs' assertion of security due to the absence of issues such as deceased individuals voting, non-citizens participating, or violations of absentee voting rules was erroneous. Sen. Paul expressed concern that some interpreted Krebs' statement as an indication of a problem-free election, insisting that Krebs had not thoroughly investigated the issues.

A considerable number of individuals staunchly maintain that President Trump was the rightful winner. Surveys indicate a resounding 63 percent of Republicans hold the view that Donald Trump should have been acknowledged as the legitimate president. Moreover, a striking 41 percent of the American populace does not recognize Joe Biden's presidency as legitimate.

Representative Burgess Owens (R-Utah) shares his viewpoint, firmly supporting the belief that Trump was the rightful winner. Owens stated, "There's no question in my mind that I think he won."[24]

Data from the Morning Consult-Politico polling revealed a diverse array of sentiments regarding the election's overturn. An astounding 35 percent of registered voters, spanning various political affiliations, support the idea of overturning the election results.

The founder and CEO of MyPillow, Mike Lindell, stated that Trump won by more than 10 million votes.[25]

General McInerny estimated that "President Trump got 78 million votes. Biden may have been lucky to get 70..."[26]

Financial and geopolitical analyst, Martin Armstrong, professional historian with degrees from Berkeley and

---

[24] Davidson, Lee. "Burgess Owens Explains Why He'll Challenge Trump's Loss on the House Floor." *The Salt Lake Tribune*, 31 Dec. 2020, www.sltrib.com/news/politics/2020/12/31/burgess-owens-explains/.

[25] Sharp, Keely. "WATCH: Mike Lindell Declares Trump Will be Reinstated on August 13." *Think Americana*, 6 July 2021, thinkamericana.com/watch-mike-lindell-declares-trump-will-be-reinstated-on-august-13/.

[26] Carr, Julie. "General Thomas McInerney Outlines New Evidence Alleging Nationwide Ballot Tampering to Prevent Trump Landslide." *The Tennessee Star*, 18 November 2020, tennesseestar.com/2020/11/18/general-thomas-mcinerney-outlines-new-evidence-alleging-nationwide-ballot-tampering-to-prevent-trump-landslide/?fbclid=IwAR3FkjHvT5qvm8kgC-FR4mjQ_H99H7teqopuVhgo-jBDcCFGKoFZV_0uKN8.

Harvard, suggested that up to 38 million votes were illegally changed from Trump to Biden.[27]

Republican Rep. Matt Gaetz of Florida said, "Donald Trump won a landslide election among people who actually showed up and voted...The farther you got away from the validation of the voter and their identity, the more Joe Biden's margins went up. I mean, with the people whose votes weren't validated who came in by the mail, Joe Biden was getting vote totals that would have made Bashar al-Assad blush."[28]

Rep. Mo Brooks (R-AL) stated, "I'm quite confident that if we only counted lawful votes cast by eligible American citizens, Donald Trump won the Electoral College,

---

[27] Herman, Carl. "Q's 'Nothing can stop what is coming' = NCSWIC sting of Dominion 'voting' machine election fraud + treason? Game-ender if true!" *Carlherman.blogspot.com*, 15 Nov. 2020, carlbherman.blogspot.com/2020/11/qs-nothing-can-stop-w h a t - i s - c o m i n g . h t m l ? fbclid=IwAR2pCryCJMaCNNz0C9dzozaOlu0Tt0vfktfISx9BTjNl M3jN58jenCz_N4Q.

[28] Davis, Jack. "Matt Gaetz Makes Stunning Election Promise for January 6th." *The Western Journal*, 20 Dec. 2020, www.westernjournal.com/matt-gaetz-makes-stunning-election-p r o m i s e - j a n u a r y - 6 t h / ? utm_source=facebook&utm_medium=westernjournalism&utm_co ntent=2020-12-20&utm_campaign=manualpost&fbclid=IwAR35 MvHa5ldGD4BoZZoUr2vLH8Jg4sRt3RAIZPtLQeD9AmOduqvn ZlANuW0.

and we should not be counting illegal votes and putting in an illegitimate President of the United States."[29]

Fox Business Host Maria Bartiromo stated that an intel source informed her that President Trump won the election. There are claims that suggest Trump would have secured 305 electoral votes if election fraud had not occurred. However, without any alleged fraud, he might have reached 318 electoral votes, surpassing the 270 needed to win the presidency.

"Dick Morris, along with Lee Atwater, Jim Carville, and Karl Rove...has come to the same conclusion...: This election was unfairly stolen from the president and the American people and the Democrats are going to get away with it."[30]

Actor Jon Voight conveyed his solidarity with a group of Americans who share his skepticism about the legitimacy of Joe Biden's presidency. Voight stressed that it's apparent to many that the notion of Biden's rightful election is unfounded. He joined those who echoed his sentiments,

[29] Brooks, Mo. "'Trump Won the Electoral College' — I Can Be a Part of the 'Surrender Caucus' or I Can Fight for Our Country." *Breitbart*, 15 Dec. 2020, www.breitbart.com/clips/2020/12/15/mo-brooks-trump-won-the-electoral-college-i-can-be-a-part-of-the-surrender-caucus-or-i-can-fight-for-our-country/?fbclid=IwAR1qhUA16w72042k9vZrsaGPcAMIgQk0O8I_pxjLpnx94TXK9rY4jw0mtRo.

[30] "Newsmax: Confident the Election Was Stolen from President Donald Trump, Former Democrat Strategist and White House Adviser-Turned-Author Dick Morris...Is Not Confident It Can Be Fixed." *DrewBerquist.com*, 17 Nov. 2020, www.drewberquist.com/2020/11/dick-morris-says-election-stolen-and-little-chance-of-changing-it/?fbclid=IwAR14EkX2E9PTUGBklxFAI8gPrYGt_QrknrN45VaV7n16GYxR29d-JaCpt4c.

expressing profound dismay at the assertion that Biden was legitimately elected as President.

The skeptical sentiment was unmistakably evident during Kamala Harris' motorcade in Guatemala City, marked by a gathering prominently displaying a "Trump Won" banner, emblematic of their stance on the election's outcome. These events underscore the pervasive disbelief in Biden's legitimate victory in the 2020 election, highlighting the widespread lack of trust in its authenticity.

At the Texas Republican Party's in-person convention, the party took a definitive stance by adopting a platform that declared the 2020 election and subsequently Biden's presidency as illegitimate. This stance reflected the party's shift towards more conservative ideologies, explicitly rejecting the certified election results and citing various claims, including constitutional violations and election fraud in key states favoring Biden.

Numerous courageous individuals stepped forward, offering sworn statements and diverse evidence to support their claims of witnessing election irregularities. Their evidence spanned affidavits, videos, data analyses, and anecdotal reports, detailing altered ballots, the removal of Trump ballots, and allegations of software manipulation affecting votes. Their readiness to blow the whistle often came at a considerable personal cost, with many facing security threats and requiring federal protection for their willingness to testify.

However, these individuals encountered significant resistance and consequences when attempting to voice their concerns about the electoral process, especially on social media platforms. Many were de-platformed or marginalized merely for expressing doubts about the election's integrity. This crackdown on dissenting viewpoints created a chilling effect on investigating potential irregularities, heightening the obstacles faced by those striving for transparency in the electoral process.

Despite risking personal safety to highlight electoral discrepancies, these whistleblowers faced staunch resistance and punitive actions. Social media platforms became battlegrounds where individuals questioning the election's integrity faced severe repercussions, including de-platforming or shadow-banning. This environment stifled dissent and discouraged open inquiry into the election's legitimacy.

Rudy Giuliani, as President Trump's attorney, played a vocal role post-election, alleging voter fraud and irregularities, especially in key swing states. His prominent stance significantly fueled widespread skepticism regarding the integrity of the election. Giuliani's public addresses, press conferences, and legal involvement amplified claims that raised doubts about the legitimacy of the electoral process in multiple states.

However, Giuliani's narrative faced staunch opposition from various social media platforms and websites. These platforms employed diverse tactics to address what they deemed as unfounded allegations. Labeling or restricting content associated with Giuliani became a common response to curb the spread of what they claimed was misinformation. Some platforms implemented fact-check labels or restricted the visibility of Giuliani's posts, echoing strategies reminiscent of authoritarian regimes that control information dissemination to stifle dissent.

Comparisons between these measures and historical instances of information control by authoritarian regimes could shed light on the severity of these actions. For example, drawing parallels to censorship tactics utilized in past regimes—such as restricting access to dissident voices or discrediting oppositional narratives—can illustrate the gravity of limiting Giuliani's platform and diminishing his ability to challenge the election results.

These actions taken by social media platforms hindered Giuliani's capacity to counter the mainstream narrative and present his side of the argument effectively. The restrictions placed on his content curtailed its reach and impact, hampering his efforts to offer alternative perspectives or contest the prevailing narrative about the election's validity. Ultimately, this curtailment of his digital presence significantly impeded his ability to challenge the election results and effectively communicate his viewpoint to the public.

Sidney Powell, a member of President Donald Trump's legal team, championed claims of extensive election fraud and irregularities following the 2020 election, particularly emphasizing the contention that Dominion Voting Systems, a voting technology company, conspired to manipulate the election outcome in favor of Joe Biden.

Sidney Powell asserted, "President Trump won by a landslide," estimating by "probably somewhere between 350 and 400 electoral college votes."[31] Powell said that there is

---

[31] Adams, Mike. "Full transcript of bombshell interview: Gen. Michael Flynn, Gen. Thomas McInerney with Brannon Howse – Identity of KRAKEN revealed." *Natural News*, 29 Nov. 2020, www.naturalnews.com/2020-11-29-full-transcript-interview-gen-michael-flynn-gen-thomas-mcinerney.html; HealthRanger. "Sydney Powell: 'Staggering' Evidence of Vote Fraud, Dominion Machines Engineered by China, Venezuela, Cuba and DESIGNED to Steal Elections Worldwide... Release the Kraken!" *Distributed News*, 14 Nov. 2020, www.distributednews.com/474618.html.

"more than enough evidence in the public now to more than reverse the election in at least five states."[32]

"Sidney Powell…said that she has documented proof that Donald Trump won the election, not by thousands of votes, but by millions of votes that were shifted by the Smartmatic software, which was designed explicitly for that purpose…"[33] She reported, "President Trump actually received 7 million more votes than he was given…"[34] She estimated that President Trump received "at least 80 million votes."[35]

Powell and her legal team launched a series of lawsuits aimed at contesting the election results across several states. Despite the claims' substantive content, many of these legal endeavors were dismissed primarily on procedural grounds rather than on the merits of the allegations.

The aftermath of Powell's involvement wielded a double-edged impact on her reputation. Among her supporters, she was lauded as a staunch defender of electoral integrity, someone courageous enough to confront

---

[32] "Sidney Powell: America is now a 'Communist regime.'" *Natural News*, 7 May 2021, www.naturalnews.com/2021-05-07-sidney-powell-america-now-a-communist-regime.html#.

[33] "Sidney Powell: Smartmatic, Dominion Stole Millions of Votes from Trump - Smartmatic is a Crown Jewel of the British Empire." *LaRouchePac*, 16 Nov. 2020, larouchepac.com/20201116/sidney-powell-smartmatic-dominion-stole-millions-votes-trump.

[34] Rugg, Colin. "May Have to Get Witness Protection": Sidney Powell Gives Big Update On Election Investigations." *Trending Politics*, 21 Nov. 2020, archive.is/wip/qXV9k.

[35] Rugg, Colin. "80 Million Votes": Sidney Powell Drops Bombshell Prediction About the Finalized 2020 Election." *Trending Politics*, 18 Nov. 2020, archive.is/wip/UhmAb.

irregularities in the democratic process. However, critics viewed Powell's actions with skepticism, expressing concern that her dissemination of contentious and potentially damaging information could erode public confidence in the electoral system.

This contentious scenario amplified itself in the realm of social media and online platforms. Efforts to limit the spread of what was deemed contentious or unverified information led various social media platforms and websites to take measures such as labeling or restricting the dissemination of content associated with Powell's claims. This censorship raised questions about the balance between regulating potentially misleading information and stifling public discourse and information flow. It accentuated the conflict between controlling information and allowing diverse viewpoints to circulate freely.

The landscape post-2020 election has unveiled a disconcerting trend reminiscent of historical maneuvers employed by authoritarian regimes to control information and quell opposing perspectives. Lawyers and individuals questioning the election's legitimacy faced unprecedented pushback and punitive actions, echoing tactics historically seen in repressive regimes. These dissenters encountered a barrage of consequences ranging from content removal on social media platforms to outright bans from online forums, all under the guise of categorizing their views as "disinformation" or unacceptable "Wrongthink."

One of the most alarming repercussions emerged in the professional realm. Professionals, including doctors and lawyers, found their licenses revoked for daring to voice opinions deemed politically incorrect or challenging the mainstream narrative. These instances underscore a worrying erosion of freedom of expression, where dissenting views face severe penalties, raising profound concerns about the constraints on individual liberties.

While acknowledging the importance of rigorous investigation into claims of election fraud, delving into the specifics of proving or debunking these allegations is beyond the scope of this book. The purpose here is to highlight the broader issue: the censorship and suppression of dissenting voices. Election fraud claims serve as a notable example of this broader narrative—where individuals expressing skepticism or questioning prevailing viewpoints face severe consequences, often being labeled or silenced, regardless of the veracity of their claims. The focus remains on the overarching theme of stifled discourse and the ramifications faced by those who diverge from the accepted narrative, irrespective of the specific topic under discussion.

The practice of labeling dissenters as "conspiracy theorists" or bearers of "misinformation" is reminiscent of tactics historically employed to discredit critics in repressive regimes. It is a tactic that not only dismisses alternative viewpoints but aims to silence opposition by undermining their credibility, mirroring oppressive measures in authoritarian settings. What is concerning is the highly polarized political climate, where questioning the election process is met with extreme characterization, tagged as "quasi-fascist, anti-democratic, and insurrectionist." This labeling reflects the divisive nature of political discourse, discouraging critical thinking and open debate.

In one public address, Biden labeled 300 Republican candidates on the ballot as "election deniers" due to their steadfast refusal to accept the legitimacy of the 2020 election results. White House Chief of Staff Ron Klain confirmed that the Biden's remarks were specifically directed at Republicans who support the implementation of stricter voting laws and who cast doubt on the authenticity of his victory in the 2020 election.

Branding individuals as "election deniers" and labeling them as enemies of the state may be viewed as a calculated move by the establishment to delegitimize opposition challenging existing power structures. This tactic aims to undermine the credibility of dissenting voices by linking them with a term that implies opposition not just to a specific election result but to the very foundation of the state. Seen in this context, such labeling tactics align, at least partially, with Marxist principles by reinforcing and safeguarding the dominant narrative upheld by those in authority.

From a Marxist perspective, which closely examines power dynamics and class conflicts, this labeling strategy appears as a tool to uphold the legitimacy of the current system. Marxism emphasizes the role of ideological control in maintaining the status quo. By branding dissenters as enemies of the state, this approach aims to suppress alternative viewpoints and sustain the dominant ideological control. This concept of hegemony reflects the normalization of values and beliefs of the ruling class as societal norms, effectively sidelining dissenting perspectives challenging this hegemonic control.

Furthermore, this tactic of categorization might function to consolidate the ruling class's authority by discrediting dissenters as adversaries of the state. By linking questioning election outcomes with opposition to the state itself, there is an insinuation that those challenging the established narrative pose a threat to the stability and legitimacy of the entire system. Consequently, this could foster an environment where diverse voices are marginalized, allowing the preservation of existing power structures without encountering substantial challenge.

Following the 2020 election, the political rift widened when certain Democrats labeled American citizens protesting election fraud as "seditionists." This intensified an already contentious issue. Moreover, the government's pursuit of legal action and imprisonment against those challenging the official election narrative is seen as an attempt to suppress opposition.

Senator Jeanne Shaheen's (D-N.H.) characterization of Republicans who refused to acknowledge Joe Biden's electoral victory as bordering on sedition and treason has triggered significant reactions across the political spectrum. Her comments have sparked in-depth discussions on the limits of political dissent, the repercussions of contesting election outcomes, and the legal definitions of sedition and treason.

Shaheen perceives contesting election results as a breach of lawmakers' constitutional oaths and damaging to public trust. Reactions to this stance differ: Some emphasize the importance of respecting results for the effective functioning of government, while others view rejection as a threat to the foundations of democracy.

It is crucial to understand the legal definitions of treason and sedition under U.S. federal law. Treason involves either waging war against the United States or providing aid and comfort to its adversaries, carrying the weight of the death penalty. On the other hand, seditious conspiracy involves conspiring to overthrow the government or obstruct its laws through the use of force. These definitions, embedded in the U.S. criminal code, establish a high threshold for identifying instances of treason or seditious behavior.

Critics opposing Shaheen's stance emphasize that in a healthy democracy, political dissent and questioning election legitimacy are essential. They stress that freedoms such as speech and open discourse are vital for holding government officials accountable and ensuring transparency in the electoral process. These critics caution that labeling political disagreements as sedition or treason go too far, potentially silencing legitimate concerns about the electoral system and hindering free expression and open debate.

In a democratic system, scrutinizing and debating election processes is not inherently treasonous or seditious. These discussions play a fundamental role in ensuring electoral integrity, holding officials accountable, and maintaining transparency. When these debates are restricted under charges of treason or sedition, there is a risk of suppressing valid concerns and stifling democratic discourse. The ability to question, investigate, and address election irregularities is crucial for upholding democratic principles of accountability and transparency.

In Antrim County, Michigan, attorney Matt DePerno found himself at the center of the 2020 election results controversy due to discrepancies uncovered within the county's electoral process. His involvement stemmed from representing individuals and groups concerned about specific election outcomes in Antrim County. Central to this dispute were allegations of irregularities within the vote tabulation systems, particularly pointing to the Dominion Voting Systems software used in the county. These allegations suggested potential errors in the tabulation process that could have impacted the accuracy of reported election results.

To address these concerns, DePerno initiated legal actions to challenge the functionality and reliability of the voting machines and software in Antrim County. His aim was to investigate potential vulnerabilities or flaws within the software that might have influenced vote counts' accuracy. The goal was to bring transparency to the electoral process and ensure the integrity of the election machinery.

During DePerno's pursuit to obtain authorization for a forensic auditors' report, Michigan Attorney General Dana Nessel, who is of Jewish descent, directed a tweet at "Lawyers who practice in Michigan." The tweet highlighted the professional responsibility of lawyers to avoid filing baseless lawsuits and misleading the court.

The timing and focus of Nessel's tweet suggested an implicit threat to legal practitioners involved in cases challenging the election results. Its arrival during an ongoing hearing added complexity, raising questions about potential interference, biases, or attempts to influence the court's decision-making process. These warnings, alongside the potential for government intervention, imply an over-reach of authority, sparking concerns about potential constraints on free speech and creating a chilling effect on those expressing doubts about election outcomes.

The alignment of Michigan Attorney General Dana Nessel's tweet with Matt DePerno's hearing raised concerns about potentially suppressing dissenting voices challenging the election narrative. This timing and tone ignited debates about governmental efforts to stifle dissent and control narratives, contradicting principles of free speech. It fostered an environment where expressing dissent might involve legal risks or scrutiny, posing a threat to free speech. If official actions curtail dissent, it undermines constitutional freedoms and diminishes trust in the legal system, disrupting the essence of democracy.

Preserving the integrity of the electoral process means allowing citizens to engage freely in open discourse, examine election procedures, and express concerns without fear of punitive actions or suppression. Successfully managing these complexities requires that governmental actions, especially investigations, respect and safeguard citizens' fundamental rights. Such measures are critical for upholding democracy's foundational principles amid the contentious debates that often follow elections.

Evan McMullin, known for his roles as a CIA operative, policy director for the House Republican Conference, and his independent presidential candidacy in 2016, suggested publicly identifying and shaming individuals who support Trump's election fraud claims. This proposal sparked heated debates and ethical concerns within political circles, prompting significant fears about the potential misuse of such information.

Critics rightly express concerns about the grave implications of this proposal. There is a fear that such a list could become a tool for targeted harassment or contribute significantly to a culture of "canceling" individuals included on it. Those listed might face severe personal or professional repercussions solely based on their beliefs, regardless of the accuracy or legitimacy of their claims.

The public distribution of lists based on political beliefs carries the risk of igniting public shaming and targeted discrimination, fostering an atmosphere of intimidation and apprehension. Such a list could be used as a weapon against political adversaries, potentially demonizing or isolating certain individuals, stifling oppositional voices, or coercing those with differing political viewpoints. These tactics fundamentally undermine democratic principles such as free speech.

McMullin's proposed list draws alarming parallels to historical tactics employed by communist regimes to silence dissent and consolidate power. Compiling lists of perceived adversaries was a common method in such regimes to control individuals with opposing political views, instilling fear among the populace.

This proposal echoes strategies used by authoritarian regimes by suggesting the marginalization of dissenters based solely on political beliefs, fostering an environment of fear and exclusion. Such actions align with historical communist approaches aimed at suppressing opposition, limiting free expression, and eliminating dissenting voices. They pose a clear threat to democratic principles such as free speech, open discourse, and the right to hold differing political views without fear of reprisal.

Employing such lists to marginalize political opponents and enforce conformity with a specific political narrative mirrors totalitarian methods that undermine the foundations of democratic societies. These actions risk further dividing communities, breeding distrust, and jeopardizing the principles of pluralism and tolerance, which are essential for a healthy democratic society.

The freedom of citizens to question elections and scrutinize their outcomes is pivotal for a robust democracy. This allowance serves as a critical check on election conduct, ensuring fairness, transparency, and adherence to established rules. Civil discourse, where individuals freely express viewpoints and engage in meaningful dialogue, nurtures an informed and engaged citizenry, fostering a more vibrant and inclusive society.

Scrutiny surrounding elections often triggers investigations and audits that significantly contribute to transparency and accountability within the electoral system. Safeguarding the right to question elections is imperative, serving as a bulwark for election integrity, reinforcing governmental accountability, and fostering civic engagement — integral facets for a resilient democratic society.

Efforts to stifle discussions or disagreements about election matters risk dissuading individuals from raising legitimate concerns, posing a significant threat to democratic values. Additionally, these actions might compromise transparency and accountability within the democratic framework. Imposing control or limitations on narratives in public forums risks withholding vital information necessary for citizens to make informed decisions, hindering the democratic process by limiting access to diverse perspectives and impeding the public's ability to form comprehensive judgments based on various viewpoints

Growing apprehensions have surfaced concerning the potential abuse of social media platforms for censorship.

These digital spaces wield immense influence, shaping the flow of information and exerting substantial impact on the dynamics of elections. Leaked communications have shed light on instances where tech giants such as Facebook purportedly faced political pressure to limit the visibility of specific individuals or groups. These revelations suggest calculated efforts to suppress voices espousing diverse political viewpoints. Moreover, allegations have surfaced suggesting operatives linked to the Biden campaign sought to influence Facebook to restrict the reach of then-President Trump, their political adversary.

Persistent accusations of political bias and content suppression have plagued major tech entities such as Google, Facebook, and YouTube. Claims of preferential treatment toward Democrats have surfaced, leading to prominent conservative figures encountering bans or restrictions on major platforms. Many contend that these measures were orchestrated to diminish their political influence. Whether it was Twitter suspending accounts, Facebook implementing fact-checks, or YouTube restricting monetization on specific channels, these actions have ignited significant concerns about potential biases and the stifling of conservative perspectives.

Critics argue that these tech giants have collaborated with Democrats to silence dissenting voices, citing algorithmic manipulation as a tool to censor conservative content. These concerns have sown deep-seated doubts regarding the impartiality and neutrality of these platforms as arenas for political discourse. The fear of manipulation or selective treatment in content moderation has raised questions about the platforms' commitment to fostering an open exchange of diverse political opinions without favoritism or suppression.

Devin Nunes, a former California Republican lawmaker and ex-chairman of the House Permanent Select

Committee on Intelligence, has alleged the presence of informants or agents from government agencies such as the FBI, Justice Department, and potentially the Department of Homeland Security within certain platforms. Nunes has further implied that major tech companies such as Apple, Google, Facebook, and Twitter engage in surveillance practices to monitor the American population and establish content management guidelines. He expresses apprehension about granting censorship powers to left-leaning tech platforms, viewing it as a potential violation of the First Amendment.

The First Amendment stands as the bedrock of American democracy, anchoring fundamental rights such as freedom of speech. It serves as a shield, encompassing a wide spectrum of expressions, even misinformation or disinformation, asserting that speech should not be solely judged on its accuracy. Consistently, the U.S. Supreme Court has held that the government cannot censor or restrict speech merely because it contains false information.

At its core, the First Amendment unequivocally decrees, "Congress shall make no law... abridging the freedom of speech, or of the press..." This amendment constructs a framework shielding diverse expressions, ensuring non-interference by the government with these essential rights. Explicitly prohibiting the government from curbing speech based on content or viewpoint, it grants individuals the inalienable right to express their beliefs, regardless of their popularity, controversy, or criticism of the government. This liberty cultivates an environment where diverse perspectives thrive, nurturing an open exchange crucial for a vibrant democracy.

Preserving freedoms of speech, expression, and the press is a linchpin in democracy. Corporate entities influenced by the government censoring political speech pose a substantial risk to democratic values. Transparent governance and public oversight become crucial to prevent abuses of power and unwarranted restrictions on political discourse.

Furthermore, Title 42, Section 1983 of the United States Code serves as a legal recourse, granting individuals the right to seek legal action against government officials or entities if they believe their constitutional rights were violated under the "color of law." Originating as part of the Civil Rights Act of 1871, this statute serves as a crucial avenue for individuals seeking redress for violations of their civil rights.

The collaboration between various U.S. federal agencies and social media platforms in combating "disinformation" has raised significant concerns about potential encroachments on free speech protected by the First Amendment. Leaked documents disclosed by investigative journalists Ken Klippenstein and Lee Fang have illuminated efforts by the U.S. Department of Homeland Security (DHS) to censor information that, while factually accurate, might contradict certain narratives, particularly in the online realm.

The Election Integrity Partnership (EIP) faced allegations of contributing to censorship initiatives leading up to the 2020 election. Accusations suggest that EIP provided tools to federal government entities and Democratic Party groups to counter "disinformation." This system purportedly enabled entities such as the Department of Homeland Security and the State Department to flag content for potential suppression or warning labels on major tech platforms.

The establishment of the Disinformation Governance Board (DGB), spearheaded by Nina Jankowicz, has sparked comparisons to Orwell's "Ministry of Truth,"a raising concerns about controlled information distribution. While disclaiming operational authority, the Department of Homeland Security's perceived influence over the DGB, later transferring its responsibilities to the Cybersecurity and Infrastructure Security Agency (CISA), has prompted worries about government oversight in managing online content and the potential imposition of regulations.

Disinformation, as defined by the Department of Homeland Security (DHS), constitutes the intentional dissemination of false information. However, it is essential to note that the government lacks the authority to censor disinformation due to the First Amendment.

Legal precedents, notably cases such as *United States v. Alvarez*, 567 U.S. 709 (2012), underscore the protection afforded by the First Amendment even to false statements, barring specific exceptions such as defamation or incitement to violence. Permitting authorities to label information as false could potentially hinder legitimate discussions and viewpoints, potentially empowering the government to suppress disagreeable ideas, ultimately eroding the open discourse vital to a democratic society. Safeguarding even false speech remains crucial for fostering a marketplace of ideas and robust debate. Upholding this protection ensures that even contentious or erroneous speech can be expressed without fear of government reprisal.

The Biden administration's collaboration with Silicon Valley to counter perceived "disinformation" has stirred concerns regarding privacy, civil liberties, and its profound influence on online discourse. There is widespread apprehension that subjective interpretations of "disinformation" might lead to biased or excessive content moderation, raising questions about the fair and impartial treatment of diverse viewpoints in online spaces. This partnership has triggered debates surrounding the potential consequences for free speech and the risks of overreach in regulating online content. The subjective nature of defining and addressing disinformation has sparked fears of censorship and the curtailing of legitimate expression and debate.

After the 2020 election, social media platforms responded to election fraud allegations by implementing measures to shape the election narrative and restrict the spread of certain perspectives.

Twitter faced a barrage of allegations regarding censorship and manipulation in the wake of the 2020 election, such as restricting the sharing of posts about Trump's victory. The social media giant was accused of censoring pro-Trump accounts, manipulating follower counts, removing groups such as Stop the Steal, and temporarily locking The New York Post's account. Twitter faced allegations related to the use of tools such as "shadow banning" to reduce the visibility of certain tweets or user accounts. The banning of individuals associated with Gateway Pundit, discussing election irregularities in Detroit, further fueled debates about regulating online speech and content moderation.

Amid these controversies, revelations surfaced about the FBI's role in pinpointing specific tweets and pressuring Twitter to censor a former Republican official based solely on a Politifact article. This involvement accentuated concerns about the government's active intervention in shaping online discussions on social media platforms.

Reports emerged detailing regular meetings between Twitter executives and law enforcement and intelligence entities, including Yoel Roth, Twitter's former head of Trust and Safety. These meetings indicated significant involvement in discussions regarding content moderation, election security, and strategies to counter foreign influence. Leaked data suggested the involvement of Twitter's Vijaya Gadde in shaping CISA's anti-disinformation strategies and discussions about countering internet information operations, potentially including the creation of a government portal to flag content for removal on platforms such as Facebook and Instagram. To facilitate this collaboration, a dedicated channel named "us2020_xfn_enforcement" was set up, exclusively serving senior Twitter executives and federal enforcement and intelligence agencies to make decisions linked to the 2020 election. This close interaction between tech platforms and government entities raised concerns about violating First Amendment rights and the potential for government influence over free speech online.

Reports indicated Twitter maintained specialized teams compiling blacklists targeting prominent conservative users, aiming to decrease the visibility of conservative tweets through methods such as "shadow banning," discreetly curbing the reach and visibility of certain users or content. Moderators were able to categorize users into lists such as "Trends Blacklist," "Search Blacklist," and "Do Not Amplify," effectively restricting the reach and discoverability of their content without their knowledge.

One significant instance was Twitter's ban on The New York Post's contentious story about Hunter Biden's foreign ties and Biden family corruption. Mainstream outlets downplayed the story, labeling it as "Russian disinformation," and refused to acknowledge its authenticity. Twitter's restrictions on sharing related articles were an attempt to censor controversial information and shield Joe Biden from scrutiny, raising concerns about its impact on the election outcome.

During Dr. Shiva Ayyadurai's campaign as a Massachusetts Republican Senate candidate, Twitter removed his allegations of voter fraud. He filed a federal lawsuit, alleging a breach of his civil rights when the government hindered his political speech to influence an election. His lawsuit exposed collaboration between election officials and social media platforms aimed at suppressing speech.

Subsequent investigations revealed the involvement of employees from the Massachusetts Secretary of State's office in directing these deletions. Reports indicated the establishment of a specialized channel for senior executives to coordinate election enforcement. Dr. Ayyadurai exposed both Twitter's "Trusted Twitter Partnership" between the government and the platform and the "partner support portal," exclusively accessible to select governmental entities. This portal granted officials the authority to flag and delete content using their "Twitter Partner Status," showcasing close collaboration between Twitter and federal enforcement and intelligence agencies regarding moderation of election-related content.

On Twitter, President Trump's criticism of mass mail-in voting faced visibility restrictions through filtering mechanisms imposed by platform executives. During the January 6, 2021 Capitol protest, Twitter temporarily suspended Trump's account and imposed limitations on official presidency-associated accounts until the transition to the new Biden administration.

On January 20, 2021, Twitter permanently banned President Trump from their platform following his tweet, "I will not be going to the Inauguration." Twitter claimed concerns about potential incitement to violence or harm as reasons for his removal. This marked the first instance of Twitter deleting a sitting head of state's account, signaling a broader trend where major tech companies suppress conservative voices. The banning of a sitting U.S. president from significant social networks underscored these platforms' influence in managing information and shaping public discourse. In response to his ban, Trump used another account to criticize Twitter for stifling free speech, alleging collusion between Twitter employees and Democrats to silence him and his supporters. Twitter promptly removed this tweet and suspended the Trump campaign's "Team Trump" page.

Twitter's action in removing Donald Trump's personal account while he was still in office raised concerns about the immense power of social media platforms in regulating public discourse, fueling debates about Big Tech's role in controlling political speech. Critics highlighted inconsistencies in Twitter's policy enforcement, pointing out that while the sitting president faced a permanent ban, tweets from known terrorists and the Chinese communist regime were tolerated on the platform. This discrepancy amplified opinions that the platform unfairly targeted conservative viewpoints while sheltering left-leaning perspectives.

In subsequent developments, Elon Musk assumed the role of Twitter's CEO in October 2022, heralding significant changes within the platform. These changes included the removal of key executives such as Vijaya Gadde and Yoel Roth. Additionally, Musk reversed the permanent ban on former President Trump's account, marking a significant shift in Twitter's approach under new leadership.

Despite Facebook's claims of championing "free speech," it became entangled in censorship and content control during the 2020 US election. Allegations surfaced regarding Facebook's surveillance of users and disclosure of private conversations to federal officials. These accusations primarily targeted individuals expressing skepticism about the 2020 election or airing anti-government sentiments.

A concerning revelation, brought to light by investigative journalists Lee Fang and Ken Klippenstein, exposes a troubling collaboration involving government agencies, Democratic operatives, and influential figures within Facebook's sphere of influence. This collective effort aimed to silence dissenting voices, sparking significant concerns about freedom of speech and the extent of government sway over content decisions on the platform. Reports revealed a systematic procedure employing a specialized Facebook portal designed for government officials to flag content requiring regulation or suppression across platforms such as Facebook and Instagram.

In response to the 2016 election, the company developed an algorithm called Crosscheck or "XCheck" to combat "hate speech" and doubts about election integrity. Whistleblower Ryan Hartwig, a bilingual content moderator at Cognizant working for Facebook, revealed biased censorship practices. Hartwig encountered instances where viral videos depicting events, even those complying with policies, were removed. Expressions of skepticism about the election's legitimacy prompted bans and content restrictions by left-wing groups. Facebook enforced a prohibition on the use of the phrase, "Stop the steal."

Leading up to the 2020 election, Facebook introduced significant policy changes. It banned new political ads and restricted content to sharing primarily mainstream media sources, often favoring a pro-Biden stance. These measures negatively impacted President Trump and other Republicans, hindering their ability to purchase ads and circulate campaign messages.

Claims attributed to undisclosed sources within the US Department of Justice suggest close monitoring of messages and public posts by American users on Facebook.

Content expressing anti-government sentiments or questioning the 2020 presidential election's legitimacy reportedly was flagged and reported to the FBI. Allegedly, a collaboration between a Facebook employee and the FBI, spanning nearly 19 months, involved identifying and labeling content as "subversive" and promptly sharing it with the Bureau's domestic terrorism operational unit. This process purportedly occurred without subpoenas, raising legal questions about their data acquisition practices. Facebook supposedly complied with these requests, providing substantial amounts of data and images to the FBI.

Notably, the platform implemented a system granting exemptions to specific users, including politicians and incumbent government officials, essentially creating a "privileged class of speakers."

Florida Governor Ron DeSantis voiced serious reservations about Facebook's "Crosscheck" or "XCheck" whitelisting system, prompting an investigation into potential breaches of state election laws. Governor DeSantis emphasized the necessity for transparency regarding Facebook's impact on elections, particularly at local and state levels. Governor DeSantis criticized Facebook for clandestinely manipulating elections, stressing that such actions undermine the fundamental principles of democracy and people's rights to choose their representatives without interference from Silicon Valley. He directed Florida's Secretary of State, Laurel Lee, to explore all legal means to uncover any violations within the state.

Accusations have surfaced, alleging a concerning collaboration between major tech corporations and Democratic officials in California. Reports post-election suggest that California authorities pressured prominent social media platforms—Twitter, Facebook, Google, and YouTube—to censor posts questioning the legitimacy of the 2020 election. The Office of Election Cybersecurity within the

California Secretary of State's office actively monitored social media content and urged the removal of specific posts, resulting in their deletion. These actions have ignited alarm over infringements on Americans' First Amendment rights due to the suppression of speech regarding election-related controversies.

In the aftermath of the 2020 election, a notable shift occurred within the digital sphere, giving rise to alternative social media platforms such as Gab, Gettr, Minds, and Mewe specifically designed to cater to conservative voices. These platforms were established to offer spaces where conservative viewpoints could flourish, fostering open and uncensored conversations. Concurrently, initiatives geared toward creating conservative-focused online infrastructure aimed to provide unencumbered outlets for expression, introducing diversity into the digital realm. Users gravitated toward these alternatives as they sought platforms with looser content moderation policies and forums that championed free speech, deviating from the more regulated environments of mainstream platforms.

However, this pivot towards alternative platforms might face significant challenges due to Biden's advocacy for increased social media censorship. For instance, Gab, a platform known for its more permissive content policies, might encounter hurdles in maintaining its open dialogue environment if subjected to heightened regulations proposed by the Biden administration. The platform's commitment to free speech, which attracted users seeking unrestricted expression, might clash with potential mandates for stricter content moderation. Consequently, such platforms may find it challenging to maintain their original appeal if pressured to adopt more stringent censorship measures in line with Biden's proposed policies.

The broader implication is that the trend of migrating towards platforms promoting free speech and accommodating diverse viewpoints might encounter obstacles in the face of increased censorship efforts. As users seek spaces where they can express themselves freely, potential government interventions for more stringent content regulation could restrict the availability of such platforms. This conflict between user preference for free expression and governmental calls for increased censorship poses a significant challenge to the sustainability of alternative platforms catering to diverse ideological viewpoints.

Biden's advocacy for heightened social media censorship has sparked profound worries about safeguarding freedom of speech. This rapid escalation in online restrictions mirrors authoritarian tactics, raising concerns about stifling valid discussions and potentially targeting certain groups, thereby threatening the core principles of free speech. The risk lies in constraining acceptable discourse, curtailing diverse viewpoints, and eroding the democratic essence of free speech within digital realms.

The trajectory toward increased censorship, reminiscent of totalitarian regimes, presents troubling implications. It is not solely about limiting expression but also the potential repercussions: stifling open exchange and muting dissenting voices or marginalized perspectives, jeopardizing the vibrant nature of public debate essential for a thriving democratic society.

The parallels observed with authoritarian tactics stand as a stark warning, extending beyond just silencing individual opinions to the potential erosion of the democratic ideal itself. This trend could grant disproportionate control to those in power, allowing them to shape narratives and shield certain viewpoints from scrutiny or critique.

The alarming collusion between government and corporate entities in suppressing political speech exacerbates these concerns. Revelations about government involvement in social media censorship heighten worries about violations of free speech and overreach. Collaborations to monitor, flag, and censor content mirror authoritarian practices, challenging the core principles of free speech and individual liberties. Concerns about data exchanges between tech firms and law enforcement agencies lacking proper legal authorization spark accusations of abuse of power and intrusions on free speech and privacy rights, in stark contrast to the protections outlined in the First Amendment.

The alliance between Big Tech and government entities raises concerns about power concentration and its potential implications for fundamental constitutional principles. Government involvement in content moderation risks stifling certain viewpoints, restricting the diversity of opinions, and influencing broader conversations about elections and politics, which could significantly impact democratic processes.

Government interventions in content moderation within digital spaces may create apprehension and constraints. The fear of repercussions or having views suppressed might discourage people from voicing dissent or participating in discussions, particularly those related to elections. This erosion of open information exchange can profoundly influence public perceptions, leading to biased or incomplete understandings of critical issues, including electoral processes.

Amid persistent challenges to Western culture, the defense of free speech becomes paramount. History serves as a cautionary tale, highlighting the dangers associated with silencing speech, often laying the groundwork for totalitarianism.

At the heart of a vibrant democracy lies open dialogue and mutual respect for divergent opinions. Democracy thrives by upholding free speech, ensuring a proliferation of diverse ideas, and fostering an environment where peaceful dissent nurtures adaptable and responsive democratic traditions. Suppressing opposing viewpoints fundamentally undermines the essence of democracy, stifling the exchange of ideas vital for the thriving and evolving fabric of society.

President George Washington's wise words emphasize the pivotal role of free speech in nurturing critical thinking and active citizen engagement. He warned, "If men are to be precluded from offering their sentiments on a matter, which may involve the most serious and alarming consequences that can invite the consideration of mankind, reason is of no use to us; the freedom of speech may be taken away, and dumb and silent we may be led, like sheep, to the slaughter." This quote highlights the risks of curbing speech within a democracy. Restricting speech not only curtails individual rights but also imperils the resilience of a democratic society.

The upcoming chapter delves into how communist regimes manipulated courts for control in the past. In the US today, concerns linger about biased justice and political cases, especially after high-profile instances involving figures such as former President Trump. These worries center around the use of legal tactics to silence dissent, potentially stifling opposition and diverse viewpoints. The chapter also explores the challenges faced by traditional conservatives, particularly following events such as the Capitol protests, shedding light on ideological conflicts within American politics and law.

Chapter 7

Political Purges

Throughout history, communist regimes notoriously exploited the justice system, utilizing politicized trials and fabricated charges to maintain control. Recently, concerns have surfaced in the United States regarding potential political manipulation of the justice system. Incidents involving prominent figures such as former President Donald Trump have sparked suspicions of selective prosecution driven by partisan motives. This has cast doubt on the fairness of the system, raising concerns that legal tactics may be employed to silence opposition and suppress differing opinions. These worrisome developments suggest a potential curtailment of dissent through legal means, hindering the free expression of opposing voices.

Moreover, the chapter explores the hurdles encountered by traditional conservatives in the U.S., shedding light on contemporary political purges. Though not as extreme as historical purges, concerns persist, particularly regarding individuals such as the January 6 Capitol protestors, perceived by some as political prisoners. There is a growing apprehension that Americans adhering to traditional values might be deliberately sidelined, potentially paving the way for a substantial ideological shift. These concerns illuminate an ideological conflict brewing within the nation's political and legal domains, indicating deep-seated challenges to traditional viewpoints and democratic principles.

During the 20th century, especially within authoritarian regimes embracing communist ideologies, the landscape was marred by political purges—a deliberate and systematic elimination of individuals considered undesirable within a specific political or organizational sphere. Among the alarming features of this era were the emergence of show trials, meticulously choreographed legal dramas that bore little resemblance to genuine judicial processes. These trials, bereft of judicial integrity, primarily functioned to fulfill political agendas, particularly the elimination of perceived internal adversaries or voices of dissent within the ruling regime.

The accused individuals were an eclectic mix, including political rivals, intellectuals, and those deemed threats to the established ideology or leadership. They became pawns in a larger game, where the objective was not justice but the removal of perceived obstacles to the regime's authority and ideology. These trials underscored a troubling reality—a grotesque misuse of legal frameworks to consolidate power and eliminate opposition within these totalitarian structures.

These orchestrated trials were more than mere legal proceedings—they were grand spectacles meticulously designed to capture widespread media attention. They were carefully constructed to weave a narrative that not only solidified the regime's authority but also validated its actions. They aimed to sow seeds of fear, not just within domestic borders but also among international audiences.

What made these trials particularly egregious was their predetermined nature. Verdicts seemed to be decided well before the legal process had begun, often through coercion leading to false confessions from the defendants. In essence, the trials operated as a farce, a mere show that provided a thin veil of legitimacy to justify the persecution and targeted removal of individuals deemed threatening to the regime.

During the Stalinist era in the Soviet Union, the infamous Moscow Trials of the 1930s stand as a harrowing example of show trials. These judicial charades accused prominent Bolsheviks and military figures of concocted conspiracies against the state. The chilling reality behind these trials was the extraction of coerced confessions, leading inexorably to executions. These trials were not about justice but rather a grotesque theater aimed at eliminating perceived threats to Stalin's power.

Similarly, China's Cultural Revolution plunged the nation into a chaotic period marked by numerous show trials. Chairman Mao Zedong wielded these trials as a weapon to preserve what he considered ideological purity. The targets were diverse, encompassing intellectuals, party officials, and anyone perceived as a potential counter-revolutionary force. The trials, steeped in manipulation and devoid of fairness, symbolized a calculated effort to suppress dissent and solidify Mao's authority over the country's ideological landscape. The repercussions were devastating, leaving an indelible scar on China's history.

These show trials, staged deliberately in the public eye, operated as a chilling cautionary tale, vividly showcasing the dire repercussions awaiting dissenters while bolstering unwavering allegiance to the ruling regime. Their public nature was not incidental; it was a strategic display of power meant to instill fear and enforce conformity within society. The psychological aftermath was staggering, leaving an indelible mark on the collective psyche—sparking an atmosphere rife with apprehension and self-censorship, where individuals feared expressing any notion contrary to the established narrative.

On the international stage, these trials were met with condemnation. They stood as stark examples of gross human rights violations and a mockery of due process. The global community recoiled at these blatant abuses of justice, viewing them as egregious affronts to fundamental rights and principles. Such condemnation underscored the trials' notoriety, tarnishing the reputation of the regimes that orchestrated them while drawing attention to the need for safeguarding the integrity of justice and human rights on a global scale.

The enduring legacy of these highly publicized show trials reverberates through the collective memory of societies that bore witness to such travesties. They stand not just as historical events but as haunting reminders of the horrendous abuse of power, the systematic erosion of justice, and the alarming lengths to which authoritarian regimes would go to assert and maintain control.

These trials etch a cautionary tale into the consciousness of nations, serving as poignant markers of a dark chapter in their history. They symbolize the manipulation of justice for political ends, highlighting the vulnerability of legal systems when subjected to the whims of tyrannical rule.

Drawing parallels between the ongoing legal proceedings involving former President Donald Trump and historical show trials uncovers compelling similarities, particularly regarding political motivations, the spectacle of public theater, and potential implications for justice and public perception.

President Trump's presidency revolved around a steadfast commitment not only to fortifying the American economy but also to safeguarding the nation and its individual liberties against looming threats from radical socialist ideologies. This dedication was not just a policy stance; it was the very cornerstone of his vision for America —an aspiration to preserve the nation as a bastion of freedom.

His dedication to fortifying the American economy extended beyond fiscal policies; it encompassed safeguarding the nation's core values and sovereignty. Trump envisaged a robust and thriving economy as the bedrock of American prosperity and global competitiveness. This economic vision interwove with a broader aspiration: securing individual liberties against ideological threats, aiming to preserve the essence of American identity and freedom.

Throughout his tenure, Trump prioritized economic stability as the linchpin for national prosperity. His emphasis on a thriving economy was not just rhetoric; it was a guiding principle shaping his policy initiatives and governance.

Central to his economic vision was the pursuit of a thriving job market. He enacted policies aimed at catalyzing job growth by alleviating regulatory burdens on businesses. This strategy aimed to fortify American enterprises, affording them the freedom to expand, innovate, and generate more employment opportunities. Trimming regulations, Trump aimed to cultivate a more conducive environment for businesses to flourish, nurturing an ecosystem ripe for sustainable economic growth.

Trump's push for reduced government regulations and a streamlined bureaucracy stemmed from a desire to cultivate a business-friendly environment, aiming to spark economic expansion and innovation by removing barriers that stifled entrepreneurial endeavors. His goal was to foster an atmosphere conducive to business growth, empowering industries to thrive and fostering a cycle of sustainable economic progress.

The administration's economic policies aimed at revitalizing various sectors of the economy, stimulating job growth, and reducing regulatory burdens on businesses. By implementing tax cuts and rolling out regulatory reforms, Trump sought to create an environment conducive to business growth and innovation, fostering a climate primed for economic prosperity.

Trump's commitment to economic strength was evident in his trade policies, notably his emphasis on reconfiguring trade agreements to prioritize American interests and bolster domestic manufacturing. This deliberate shift aimed to level the global trade field for American industries, fostering competitiveness and rejuvenating key sectors of the economy. His strategies sharply deviated from Marxist principles, focusing on domestic manufacturing and restructuring trade deals to fortify industries, a direct contrast to Marxist ideologies aiming to dismantle capitalist systems.

Furthermore, Trump's approach to international trade negotiations was a strategic move to protect national interests, diverging from Marxist ideals centered on global unity and the dissolution of national boundaries. His focus was on reshaping trade relationships to benefit American industries and workers, safeguarding national economic interests.

By championing domestic manufacturing and advocating revamped trade agreements, Trump sought to amplify the nation's economic prowess globally, challenging the Marxist vision that prioritizes global unity over national interests. Essentially, his trade policies went beyond safeguarding national interests; they directly contradicted fundamental Marxist principles, highlighting a broader ideological clash between capitalist and Marxist ideologies in international trade and economic governance.

Trump's economic strategies went beyond numerical metrics; they represented a deliberate endeavor to empower American businesses, reinforce the job market, and fortify the nation's economic bedrock. His vision aimed to establish an ecosystem where businesses could flourish, innovation could thrive, and the American economy could stand robust against global challenges.

Throughout his presidency, Trump prioritized economic stability as a crucial component of national prosperity, pursuing policies aimed at job growth, reduced regulations, and support for American businesses—directly challenging Marxist principles that advocate for a radical restructuring of economic systems, including the elimination of private ownership.

The Trump administration's tenure saw remarkable economic achievements, marked by record-low unemployment rates and pre-pandemic stock market highs. These indicators, coupled with regulatory reforms and tax cuts, played a pivotal role in bolstering the nation's economic expansion. Trump's overarching pledge to fortify the economy and safeguard individual liberties epitomized his vision for an America characterized by resilience and freedom. This commitment translated into a series of policies strategically designed to foster economic robustness, enhance national security measures, and uphold the sanctity of individual freedoms.

Furthermore, his emphasis on minimal government interference struck a chord with a significant segment of the populace. It mirrored a belief in empowering individuals to make their own choices free from bureaucratic constraints. Trump's vision embraced the concept that a smaller, less intrusive government could cultivate an environment conducive to personal freedom and economic growth, empowering citizens to pursue their aspirations without unnecessary limitations.

At the core of Trump's presidency lay a resolute commitment to safeguarding individual liberties, distinctly at odds with the core tenets of Marxist ideologies. His governance championed minimal government intervention and the preservation of fundamental freedoms, such as free speech and the right to bear arms. These principles formed the bedrock of a broader narrative intricately woven around defending and preserving core American values.

Trump's dedication to individual liberty encapsulated a belief in empowering citizens to exercise their rights and make independent choices, free from excessive government intrusion. He emphasized that a smaller, less obtrusive government fosters an environment where personal freedoms can flourish, driving innovation, creativity, and economic prosperity.

In Trump's governance, the pillars of national security and sovereignty emerged as central themes, embodying pivotal aspects of his agenda. At the core of Trump's governance lay a commitment to safeguarding American citizens, evident through his staunch advocacy for strict border security measures and a robust military. He ardently championed border security as a cornerstone in preserving the nation's safety and sovereignty, extending beyond mere physical demarcation to encapsulate a comprehensive vision aimed at fortifying the country's integrity against external threats. His policies addressed concerns about unauthorized immigration, recognizing strengthened border security as crucial in protecting against potential security risks while asserting the nation's authority over its borders.

Trump's emphasis on a robust military was integral to safeguarding national security, prioritizing readiness to defend the nation's interests and uphold sovereignty in a complex global landscape. Complementing his focus on border security, he positioned a strong military as a cornerstone of national defense, stressing the significance of maintaining military supremacy. His policies aimed to fortify defense capabilities, modernize military infrastructure, and secure resources to protect American interests domestically and globally.

His overarching emphasis on national security and sovereignty reflected a vision of safeguarding American interests across multiple fronts. Trump's policies reflected a proactive stance aimed at protecting the nation's borders, bolstering defense capabilities, and recalibrating international engagements to serve the best interests of the United States. These efforts were framed within a broader narrative of safeguarding the nation's autonomy and security in an ever-evolving global landscape.

Trump's governance stood as a firm barrier against the Marxist vision, which often promotes a borderless world and the gradual dissolution of individual nation-states. His policies and rhetoric actively opposed the ideas of borderless globalism and the dissolution of national identities inherent in Marxist ideology. Central to Trump's stance was the staunch defense of national sovereignty, emphasizing the importance of distinct borders and a strong, autonomous nation. His approach strategically aimed at resisting the encroachment of socialist ideologies seeking to diminish the significance of individual nations and their self-governance.

Through his governance, Trump consistently championed the reinforcement of borders, emphasizing national autonomy and protecting American interests against socialist influences. His policies were crafted with the intent of fortifying the United States against ideological infiltration, promoting the idea that a nation's strength lies in its ability to preserve its identity, sovereignty, and self-determination.

During his tenure, President Trump actively combated encroaching Marxist influences across various fronts. His administration executed policies bolstering free-market principles, advocating for reduced regulations, lower taxes, and fostering business growth. These strategies directly countered the inclination toward expansive government control often associated with Marxist ideologies. Additionally, his leadership accentuated traditional American values, emphasizing patriotism, celebrating national heritage, and highlighting individual success stories. These actions served to counter narratives that align with Marxist criticisms of capitalist structures.

Trump's firm focus on fortifying national sovereignty, advocating stringent border security, and prioritizing American workers in trade negotiations starkly opposed globalist tendencies linked with Marxist internationalism. His presidency championed American exceptionalism, free enterprise, and the idea of national self-determination as a direct counterbalance to communist influences.

One of Trump's central tenets was the staunch defense of core freedoms such as free speech and the right to bear arms. These positions directly challenged Marxist principles that historically favor centralized control over such liberties. His strong stance underscored these rights as vital components of a free society, standing against ideologies favoring state dominance over individual expression and self-protection.

In juxtaposition to collectivist ideals associated with Marxism, Trump's advocacy championed individual autonomy and minimized government interference in personal matters. This stark contrast delineated opposing governance philosophies: one valuing individual freedoms encapsulated in Trump's vision and another promoting a more interventionist state, often aligned with socialist leanings. Trump's emphasis on individual liberty served as a defining pillar of his presidency, encapsulating a vision of America deeply rooted in personal freedom and limited government intervention.

Trump's policies sought to fortify the nation's core interests, which fundamentally challenged the collective, state-centric vision associated with Marxist ideologies. His proactive stance against globalism, communism, and a corrupt political establishment not only showcased his opposition to key Marxist principles but also mobilized a significant segment of the population against these ideologies. This positioned him as a formidable obstacle to the socialist agenda's further penetration into American politics and policies.

Trump's rejection of political correctness resonated with a substantial segment of the population concerned about the encroachment of such ideologies into societal institutions. His stance directly opposed the prevailing cultural Marxist narrative, which had gained traction in broader society. This cultural Marxist framework often pushes for the deconstruction of traditional values and societal norms, seeking to critique established cultural and social structures deemed oppressive. Trump's vocal dedication to traditional American values, including patriotism, individualism, and national pride, struck a chord with many. His messaging aimed at preserving these values resonated with those who felt a sense of erosion amid societal changes and cultural shifts.

Many viewed Trump's refusal to adhere to political correctness as a bold departure from societal norms dictating language and behavior. For those feeling stifled by what they saw as an overly restrictive culture, his willingness to speak bluntly about contentious issues was a breath of fresh air. His approach resonated with those who felt silenced or marginalized by the constraints of political correctness.

In essence, President Trump's policies served as a defense against the encroachment of Marxist influences on national autonomy. His staunch opposition to globalism, communism, and a corrupt political establishment positioned him as a direct adversary of the socialist agenda. Trump's commitment to safeguarding the American economy, national sovereignty, and individual liberties starkly contrasted with the core principles of Marxism.

Unlike Marxist ideologies advocating collective ownership of production and extensive government control, Trump prioritized individual freedoms, limited government intervention, and a market-oriented economy. This ideological divergence became a defining aspect of his presidency, setting the stage for a deeper clash with the socialist narrative.

This clash between Trump's beliefs and Marxism extended beyond ideology into a societal debate on cultural values. While Trump emphasized preserving traditional values such as national sovereignty and individual freedoms, Marxism aimed to dismantle established cultural norms and structures.

The conflict primarily stemmed from economic differences. Communism advocates for a classless society and collective ownership of production, in contrast to Trump's capitalist approach focused on individual liberties and limited government intervention. His anti-globalism stance, promoting protectionist trade policies and national interests, directly contradicted communist ideals of international solidarity and cooperation.

Beyond economics, Trump's opposition to socialist and communist ideologies encompassed stringent immigration policies and a rejection of political correctness. These stances highlighted profound ideological divides, making Trump's political stance incompatible with the aspirations of those adhering to Marxist ideologies. The conflict represents not just a political disagreement but also a fundamental clash in values and visions for society.

Marxist groups, propelled by ambitions of global expansion and the promotion of open borders, persistently pursue extending their influence over America. They view Trump's America-First policies as significant barriers hindering their objectives. The strained relationship between Democrats and Trump's presidency, primarily centered on his

"America First" agenda, starkly contradicts their overarching goals.

The conflict between Trump's policies and Marxist ideals epitomizes an extensive ideological battle. His emphasis on prioritizing American interests and sovereignty firmly positions him against the Marxist agenda, which aims to erode national boundaries and accelerate worldwide integration. Trump's "America First" stance starkly contrasts the aspirations of global expansion and open borders advocated by Marxist factions.

This ideological clash exposes a fundamental difference in worldviews. Trump's staunch support for national sovereignty and the significance of individualism directly contradicts the Marxist perspective, which champions international integration and collective governance. This divide fueled persistent efforts by leftists to remove Trump from the political landscape, given his strong opposition to socialist ideologies.

Trump's enduring popularity within the Republican Party solidifies his status as a formidable figure, reflecting robust support among conservatives for his resolute stand against globalism, communism, and political corruption. This steadfast alignment of political power with Trump's anti-Marxist stance holds the potential to profoundly shape the GOP's trajectory. It establishes a firm resistance against Marxist ideologies and policies within the party's framework. Moreover, Trump's continued sway within the GOP suggests a deeply rooted anti-communist sentiment in conservative politics, presenting substantial hurdles for socialist ideas to gain traction in the party.

This enduring support for Trump underscores the significance of his anti-Marxist stance within the Republican

Party. His opposition to globalism, communism, and political corruption has solidified his position as a leading voice against leftist ideologies. The resonance among conservative voters signals a rejection of Marxist principles and aligns with broader sentiments against ideologies leaning towards collective governance, extensive state control, and the erosion of national identity. Consequently, Trump's ongoing influence within the GOP is poised to continue shaping the party's course, establishing a platform resistant to Marxist ideas and policies, thereby significantly influencing conservative politics in the future.

Trump's staunch opposition to these ideologies and initiatives has positioned him as a prominent adversary to socialist and globalist agendas. His focus on preserving national sovereignty directly opposes the aims of groups seeking expansive global integration. This profound clash of perspectives has positioned Trump as a significant barrier to the implementation of these agendas, eliciting both criticism and staunch support from contrasting segments of society.

The intersection of these divergent interests sets the stage for an intense political battleground, marked by a series of strategies designed to undermine Trump. A myriad of tactics, including the manipulation of narratives, identity politics, and orchestrated media campaigns, have been weaponized against Trump and his administration. This concerted effort involves a complex web of actors, from the "deep state" and globalists to influential figures in banking sectors and even some establishment Republicans. What unified these disparate groups was their alarm at Trump's confrontational stance against Marxist ideologies. It prompted them to rally together, leveraging political maneuvers grounded in these narratives, all aimed at ousting Trump from power and neutralizing him as a political force.

The array of legal actions taken against Donald Trump bears striking resemblances to historical show trials, suggesting deeply rooted political motivations. Historical show trials under communist regimes were notorious for weaponizing the legal system to eliminate adversaries and stifle any form of dissent. Similarly, the myriad of legal cases against Trump harbor distinct political motives, primarily aiming to discredit and marginalize him from the political landscape. This comparison highlights a troubling pattern, indicating that legal proceedings against Trump might be serving as a political tool rather than as a pursuit of justice.

These legal proceedings have evolved into public spectacles that draw intense media scrutiny. Just as historical show trials were meticulously staged for widespread media coverage, the legal actions against Trump have been highly publicized, significantly shaping public opinion and discourse. This mirrors historical show trials' strategies, potentially swaying public opinion, shaping narratives, and influencing perceptions of justice.

The media frenzy surrounding Trump's legal battles mirrors the dramatic spectacle of historical show trials, where events were sensationalized for public consumption. How these legal proceedings are portrayed in the media goes beyond mere legal arguments, potentially shaping public opinion and altering perceptions of the accused. These battles, akin to historical theatrics, draw fervent attention and polarization from both the public and media, often diverging from factual legal discussions. Instead, they become sensationalized spectacles driven by political agendas, risking the compromise of impartial justice amidst the pursuit of attention and support.

These parallels underscore the significant impact on public sentiment. Similar to historical show trials' aims of manipulating public opinion, ongoing legal actions involving Trump have the potential to polarize public sentiment. The narratives formed around these cases wield substantial power in swaying public perceptions, shaping notions of justice, and deepening existing political divides.

The resemblance between historical show trials and the legal actions against Trump extends to the concerning issue of predetermined outcomes. In many historical show trials orchestrated by communist regimes, verdicts were coerced or predetermined, lacking genuine due process. This historical context raises serious doubts about the fairness and impartiality of the legal actions against Trump. Concerns loom over potential political biases exerting undue influence within the legal process, casting shadows on the integrity and objectivity of these proceedings. Many fear that political agendas might overshadow an earnest pursuit of justice, raising the specter of predetermined outcomes seen in historical show trials.

Moreover, the multifaceted legal battles waged against Donald Trump are a deliberate effort within the Democratic party to effectively sideline him from the political sphere. These proceedings are seen as strategic maneuvers not solely aimed at addressing legal concerns but as systematic attempts to discredit and marginalize Trump as a viable political opponent. Assertions suggest that these legal battles are orchestrated to tarnish Trump's credibility and construct a narrative that undermines his political influence.

Furthermore, the timing and proliferation of legal actions against Trump have sparked suspicions regarding their partisan nature. The surge in legal challenges following his presidency goes beyond genuine legal concerns, but rather are a strategic endeavor to tarnish Trump's reputation, diminish his political standing, and consequently, eliminate him as a viable political contender.

The historical context of politically motivated legal actions, reminiscent of show trials used by socialist regimes to silence dissenters or political adversaries, intensifies these concerns. This comparison underscores the notion that certain legal actions against Trump might not prioritize justice but could be part of a broader strategy to sideline him from political relevance. The perception of targeting through legal battles, particularly amid contentious political climates, raises crucial questions about the genuine pursuit of justice versus the manipulation of legal mechanisms for political expediency.

The Democratic opposition against former President Trump transcended mere ideological differences, revealing a strategic agenda aimed at obstructing his governance. Instances such as impeachment proceedings and legal challenges to Trump's policies were strategic tactics designed to derail his administration's objectives. These actions were calculated maneuvers driven by political motivations rather than solely rooted in ideological discrepancies.

The relentless barrage of legal challenges, investigations, and impeachment proceedings constituted a concerted effort to impede and disrupt Trump's presidency, intentionally aiming to undermine its effectiveness. This sustained opposition had multifaceted goals: weakening the administration, causing disruptions in policy implementation, and tarnishing Trump's public image.

These efforts formed part of a broader political resistance, stretching beyond policy disagreements. They significantly influenced the trajectory and effectiveness of the presidency, creating a landscape where governance was consistently under siege. The orchestrated onslaught of legal and procedural challenges worked in tandem to curtail the administration's capacity to govern and execute policies effectively. This strategy aimed not only to challenge Trump's actions but to fundamentally undermine the very functionality of his presidency.

The FBI's Mueller inquiry, headed by Special Counsel Robert Mueller, delved into allegations of collusion between the Trump campaign and Russia during the 2016 election. The investigation did not uncover evidence of conspiracy, and many viewed it as part of a broader effort to cast doubt on Trump's presidency, reflecting political motivations.

Critics point to the issuance of surveillance warrants against Trump campaign advisor Carter Page, which relied on information from the discredited Steele Dossier, funded by the Democratic National Committee and the Clinton campaign. This reliance raises significant concerns about the investigation's impartiality and credibility, pointing to political bias influencing the process.

Adding fuel to the skepticism were text messages exchanged between high-ranking FBI officials such as Peter Strzok and Lisa Page, containing disparaging remarks about Donald Trump. These messages, unveiled during an inquiry into the handling of the Russia investigation, raised serious doubts about the FBI's objectivity and fairness, intensifying concerns about bias within the Bureau.

The FBI's conduct during the investigation lacked transparency, as crucial information was withheld from both the public and Congress. Additionally, allegations emerged suggesting selective leaks of information by certain FBI personnel to the media, aimed at tarnishing Trump's reputation and undermining his presidency. Instances where sensitive details from the investigation surfaced in the public domain validate these claims, amplifying concerns about the impartiality of the FBI's actions and its role in the broader political landscape.

The impeachment trials against Trump became focal points of contention, with critics alleging that these proceedings mirrored tactics reminiscent of authoritarian regimes, specifically in their politically motivated nature. The first trial, originating from a phone call with Ukrainian President Zelensky in December 2019, charged Trump with abuse of power and obstruction of Congress. However, Trump was acquitted by the Senate in February 2020 due to a lack of compelling evidence.

The second impeachment in January 2021, following the Capitol protest, accused Trump of inciting insurrection. Despite the House impeaching him for a second time, the Senate trial, conducted after Trump had left office, ended in acquittal, exposing deep partisan divides within the political landscape.

Critics, notably Senator Marsha Blackburn (R-TN) among others, contended that both impeachment proceedings lacked substantial evidence of criminal wrongdoing. Instead, they saw these trials as politically motivated endeavors aimed at tarnishing Trump's public image and destabilizing his political influence.

The use of impeachment trials, especially the second one held after Trump's presidency had ended, reflects a concerning tactic associated with totalitarian regimes. In such regimes, legal proceedings are often leveraged as tools to eliminate opposition and damage political adversaries' reputations. By pursuing impeachment with inadequate evidence, the Democrats employed tactics reminiscent of communist regimes to stifle opposition and weaken Trump's influence.

The focus on impeaching Trump without compelling evidence of criminal acts raised concerns about the manipulation of legal processes for political ends, a tactic historically employed by socialist regimes. These actions aligned with strategies aimed at suppressing political opponents, resembling the practices seen in regimes where legal mechanisms are exploited to eliminate dissent and solidify power.

Providing context, on January 6, 2021, approximately one million Trump supporters gathered in Washington, DC, exercising their right to free speech and assembly to express their frustration over the 2020 election and show support for their candidate.

During the Stop the Steal rally, Trump addressed his supporters, urging them to "peacefully and patriotically" protest at the Capitol while the electors were casting their votes. A whistleblower confirmed that those involved were passionate Americans expressing grievances via peaceful protests, with no intention to commit criminal activity, violence, or harm.

However, the initially peaceful Stop the Steal rally took a drastic turn as a riot involving a few hundred individuals erupted at the Capitol. The situation escalated as the crowd moved towards the Capitol's West Side, leading to clashes with law enforcement, deployment of tear gas, and the use of rubber bullets.

The ensuing riot disrupted the certification of Joe Biden's election victory and tragically resulted in the death of Ashli Babbitt, a Trump supporter fatally shot by a police officer while attempting to enter a secured area. Subsequent to these events, claims emerged that individuals associated with the FBI acted as agents provocateur among the mob, actively encouraging unlawful behavior. Unfortunately, former Senate Sergeant at Arms Michael Stenger, responsible for security, passed away before he could present evidence regarding "professional agitators" fueling the riot.

The aftermath of the Capitol riot sparked considerable concerns regarding the treatment of individuals, especially Trump supporters who were present during the protest. Observers noted a stark resemblance between the response to these events and historical tactics often used by communist regimes to suppress political opposition. Central to these concerns was the protection of First Amendment rights, particularly the rights to assemble and petition for grievances, which became a critical focal point in evaluating the aftermath.

Many protesters firmly believed they were exercising their constitutional rights by assembling and demonstrating, actions they perceived as safeguarded by the First Amendment. However, the response they encountered, marked by arrests, detentions, and legal actions, appeared indiscriminate in its reach and application.

Many participants in the Capitol riot believed that they had tacit or implicit permission to enter the Capitol, viewing their involvement as a legitimate exercise of their constitutional rights. However, the reality of their subsequent treatment starkly contrasted with their initial expectations.

Instead of encountering swift and fair legal proceedings, individuals involved found themselves in situations where their right to a speedy trial appeared to be denied.

Moreover, individuals present solely to document the event or express their political viewpoints found themselves unexpectedly targeted, facing legal consequences that seemed disproportionate to their actions or intentions. Such responses infringed upon fundamental First Amendment rights. This concern extended beyond those directly involved in the riot to encompass individuals who were simply present or engaged in the peaceful expression of their political beliefs.

The stark disparity between what many protestors anticipated and the stark reality they faced stands as a glaring contrast. They were firmly convinced that their participation aligned with a lawful demonstration, exercising their rights within what they believed to be constitutional bounds. However, the aftermath posed unforeseen challenges. Countless individuals found themselves thrust into a web of intricate legal procedures, enduring prolonged detentions and delayed trials that seemed at odds with the constitutional tenet of fair and expeditious justice, a cornerstone of the Sixth Amendment.

The rapid and sweeping legal actions, lacking discernment among participants, have provoked apprehensions about the fairness of the response. The absence of due process and the widespread detentions have ignited concerns about the preservation of constitutional rights.

The subsequent legal response has created a situation where individuals find themselves detained without the promised recourse afforded by the Constitution. Many participants faced detention for lengthy periods, directly contradicting the Sixth Amendment's guarantee of a speedy and public trial. Additionally, a significant number were denied bail altogether.

The measures implemented after the protests have sparked legitimate concerns regarding the potential consequences for free speech and the fundamental right to peaceful assembly. These actions have drawn disquieting parallels to historical suppression tactics employed by regimes against dissent, especially political opposition. Such comparisons have instilled fears of potential stifling of dissent and curtailment of freedom of expression, raising serious alarms about upholding democratic principles in the aftermath of these events.

The treatment of those involved in the January 6 protests revealed disconcerting resemblances to oppressive tactics using by authoritarian regimes seeking to silence political opposition. Firstly, the swift and extensive punitive actions, often lacking nuanced distinctions among participants, mirrored the tactics employed to suppress dissent in communist regimes. Many people faced mass detentions and legal repercussions without clear differentiation between those peacefully assembling and those involved in violent acts.

Moreover, a glaring denial of due process, a cornerstone of fair judicial systems, was evident. Numerous Trump supporters endured prolonged detentions without bail or the prospect of speedy trials. This dismissal of swift and equitable legal proceedings starkly contradicted the principles enshrined in constitutional rights, particularly the Sixth Amendment's assurance of the right to a speedy and public trial.

The actions taken against these individuals, seemingly based on their political affiliations or beliefs, echoed the purges witnessed in communist regimes. The punitive measures seemed to target a broad array of participants, blurring distinctions between those engaged in violent acts and those peacefully expressing their political views. This indiscriminate approach to punishment bore striking similarities to the purges carried out in oppressive regimes where political affiliation or opposition played a significant role in determining punishment.

Overall, the treatment of the January 6 protestors, characterized by mass detentions and disproportionate legal actions, evoked troubling parallels to the tactics employed by historically repressive regimes known for suppressing political opposition. These distressing similarities have raised profound concerns about the equitable treatment and safeguarding of constitutional rights for anyone on the "wrong" political side.

The aftermath of the protests has amplified apprehensions about the erosion of fundamental rights. The widespread detentions and legal actions seemed to target participants without adequately differentiating between those engaged in violent actions and those peacefully expressing their political views. This failure to make nuanced distinctions in assigning accountability jeopardizes the core tenets of a just and equitable legal system, compromising the very essence of fairness and due process.

In the wake of the Capitol protest, Democrats accused Trump of inciting a riot, branding it an "insurrection" to try to block his future tenure in office. This accusation set the stage for investigations, with claims it aimed to overturn the 2020 election results.

The US House Select Committee, mostly comprised of Democrats, initiated an inquiry to explore whether Trump's actions and rhetoric contributed to the violence. Opinions diverged: Democrats asserted Trump's election fraud claims heightened tensions, while others argued his remarks were protected by the First Amendment.

In a consequential ruling, US District Judge Amit Mehta suggested a connection between Trump and rioters, indicating Trump sought to disrupt the 2020 election certification.

The committee's final report, predominantly drafted by Democrats, accused Trump of orchestrating a "multi-part conspiracy" to overturn the 2020 election, positioning him as the primary cause of the Capitol riot. Echoing Judge Mehta's view, the report implied that Trump's intentions did not need to explicitly incite insurrection, opening a potential legal debate on public figures' accountability for their supporters' actions.

Endorsed unanimously, the report recommended charges such as defrauding the United States, making false statements, obstruction, and inciting an insurrection. The decision on pursuing criminal charges rested with federal prosecutors, and the committee advocated for Trump's future disqualification from holding office.

Trump vehemently defended himself against the scrutiny of the January 6 Committee, denouncing it as a farcical "Witch Hunt" and a rigged "Kangaroo Court" orchestrated by the "Democrat Congress." With his characteristic boldness, he staunchly maintained his innocence, attributing the committee's actions to his leading position in the polls, which transcended party lines.

Firmly viewing the congressional committee's maneuvers as an egregious abuse of power, Trump saw them as a calculated effort to persecute him politically and derail his ambitions for the presidency in 2024. He perceived the investigative machinery as a tool wielded by his adversaries, aiming to thwart his return to the White House.

In Trump's eyes, the investigation was just one piece of a broader series of politically motivated actions, seemingly connected to his 2024 presidential run. He asserted that this was a retaliatory move, a sort of payback for Republican-led inquiries into Joe Biden and his son, Hunter.

Standing by his side, Trump's attorney, Harmeet Dhillon, lambasted the investigation as an extravagant political witch-hunt. Dhillon did not mince words, accusing committee members of brazenly abusing their power, lacking any genuine legislative purpose behind their actions.

Trump expressed a sense of vindication when the "Unselect Committee" seemingly backed down, choosing to withdraw their subpoena related to the January 6 protest and the 2020 election. He interpreted this either as a tacit acknowledgment of his innocence or as a prelude to an impending legal defeat for the committee.

Representative Scott Perry's (R-PA) comparison of the committee's televised hearings to a "Soviet-style show trial" vividly encapsulates the concerns and skepticism surrounding the committee's motives and methods. This analogy draws attention to the political agenda driving the proceedings, implying that justice might be compromised in favor of partisan interests.

The reference to "Soviet-style show trials" invokes a dark historical context, highlighting the authoritarian nature of those proceedings. In Soviet-era show trials, the façade of justice was upheld while the trials were inherently politicized, predetermined, and orchestrated to serve the political aims of the ruling regime. Often, the trials served as a means to eliminate political opponents or dissidents, where the accused were used as pawns in a spectacle meant to justify preconceived outcomes.

Perry's comparison suggests a parallel between these notorious show trials and the hearings conducted by the committee, hinting at concerns that the proceedings might prioritize political expediency over impartial inquiry and fairness. It underscores apprehensions that the committee's motives might not really be about seeking truth and accountability, but rather about political posturing or seeking to discredit and sideline political opponents.

Representative Matt Gaetz (R-FL) has expressed reservations about the committee's intentions, suggesting political motivations. He implies that the investigation might be aimed at hindering Trump's candidacy in the 2024 elections, raising concerns about strategic efforts to tarnish Trump's reputation, deter his political ambitions, or even disqualify him from future office.

Gaetz's skepticism aligns with broader apprehensions that the committee's focus on Trump's role and future political implications may overshadow a thorough examination of the incident. This skepticism reflects the current politically charged climate, characterized by noticeable party divisions. The committee's predominantly Democratic composition raises doubts about its impartiality and underlying motives. Gaetz, echoing sentiments shared by many, poses essential questions about whether the committee's efforts genuinely prioritize objective fact-finding or if they are being utilized for political reprisal or disqualification purposes.

His argument encapsulates broader concerns about the potential misuse of investigative powers for partisan gains, emphasizing the crucial need for transparency and fairness in such pivotal inquiries, especially when intertwined with the intricate political landscape.

Former Representative Tulsi Gabbard (D-HI) emerged as a prominent critic of the legitimacy of the January 6 investigation, challenging its dependence on "idle gossip and rumors" in the prosecution of pro-Trump officials. Her focus on the principles of due process and evidence-based inquiries reveals profound concerns about the investigation's methodology and the potential divergence from fair and factual examinations.

In Gabbard's perspective, the reliance on "idle gossip and rumors" raises legitimate questions about the accuracy and credibility of the information underpinning the inquiry.

Her critique addresses the need for a thorough and credible investigative process that adheres to the principles of justice.

Furthermore, Gabbard's stance contributes to the debate surrounding the January 6 investigation, shedding light on the intricacies and sensitivities inherent in such high-profile inquiries.

These critiques collectively underscore concerns about the committee's approach, alleging that it may be more focused on political outcomes than objective fact-finding. Comparisons to Soviet-style trials, objections about the reliance on rumors rather than evidence, and accusations of political motivations all contribute to the argument that the committee's actions resemble tactics used in show trials to sideline political opposition.

Attorney and author, Norm Eisen, who is of Jewish descent, and his associates have become synonymous with deploying lawfare strategies to hinder Trump and his supporters. Their track record is marked by repeated attempts at impeachment against Trump, initially aimed at invalidating the 2016 election results. Subsequently, they shifted their focus towards influencing the 2024 election. Eisen's lawfare ally, Joseph Sellers, notably represented Bennie Thompson in a lawsuit against Trump, which set the groundwork for the ostensibly bipartisan January 6 Select Committee chaired by Thompson. After his tenure at Citizens for Responsibility and Ethics in Washington (CREW), Eisen established a fresh lawfare entity, the States United Democracy Center, specifically targeting "election deniers" seeking public office. This organization has actively engaged in anti-Trump lawfare, particularly concerning the events of January 6. Through these strategic legal maneuvers, Eisen and his cohort aim to sideline those aligned with Trump while shaping the political landscape ahead of the 2024 elections.

Attorney Marc Elias's proposition to use the 14th Amendment to limit Republican participation in the 2022 and future elections has sparked debate. Originating from the post-Civil War era, this constitutional provision aimed to prevent former Confederate officials from holding public office without a congressional pardon. However, the contemplation of extending its use to disqualify figures such as Donald Trump, who contested the 2020 election, has stirred both constitutional and political controversies.

The prospect of wielding the 14th Amendment in this manner has drawn sharp criticism, primarily due to fears of potential misuse. Critics express deep concerns that present-day Republican lawmakers might unfairly be labeled as insurrectionists for political gain.

Furthermore, the proposed use of the 14th Amendment in this capacity could establish a dangerous precedent for future politicians. The apprehension is that this maneuver could create a troubling trend where disqualification from public office might stem from unproven allegations of incitement, further deepening political divides and undermining due process.

Consider Representative Madison Cawthorn (R-NC), who faced allegations of inciting an insurrection, shedding light on the dangers of the potential misuse of applying the 14th Amendment. Accused for his pre-January 6, 2021, statements that some critics claimed fueled the Capitol riot, these accusations against Cawthorn lacked substantial evidence or a formal legal process to substantiate them. This scenario underscores the risk of subjecting influential figures to allegations of incitement without due process or a fair trial. It underscores the hazards of using such allegations as grounds for disqualification from public office without a comprehensive investigation or legal proceedings to establish guilt.

The concern here is the establishment of a precedent where accusations, unsupported by concrete evidence or proper legal scrutiny, become a basis for disqualifying candidates from participating in the democratic process. This scenario raises alarm about the potential for sidelining political adversaries or dissenting voices from political engagement based solely on unproven allegations or political expediency.

Elias's suggestion ominously echoes the tactics historically employed by communist regimes to silence political adversaries. The contemplation of leveraging the 14th Amendment in this manner raises profound concerns about the potential abuse of legal mechanisms to suppress political adversaries, drawing unsettling parallels with strategies historically utilized in communist regimes to quash political opposition. The idea of categorizing individuals as insurrectionists without affording them due process or presenting clear evidence of wrongdoing mirrors the tactics employed to sideline dissenting voices.

This approach seeks to exclude political opponents from the democratic process, posing a direct challenge to the principles of fair representation and constitutional rights. By labeling individuals without a fair and transparent legal process, it not only risks infringing on their rights but also undermines the fundamental tenets of justice. This strategy not only has immediate consequences for the individuals involved but also carries broader implications for the health of democratic institutions, fostering an environment where political adversaries can be marginalized without proper legal scrutiny.

In the aftermath of the Capitol riot, the narrative casting Donald Trump as the instigator of an insurrection was tactically deployed to thwart his resurgence in the 2024 political landscape. This accusation, strategically maneuvered within the realms of both legality and public opinion, emerged as a potent tool aimed at eroding Trump's credibility and casting a pervasive shadow over any potential future political aspirations.

Critics delving into Trump's speech leading up to January 6 argue that, despite its fervor and contentious nature, his words fell short of a direct call for violence or insurrection. They highlight Trump's explicit directive for his supporters to engage in peaceful and patriotic protests, suggesting that his language contradicts the notion of incitement.

Moreover, a heated debate surrounds the characterization of the events on January 6 as a full-fledged insurrection. Opponents of this classification contend that a true insurrection involves an organized attempt to seize control of institutions or overthrow a government, motives absent from the Capitol protest. They underscore the overwhelming majority of peaceful protesters, distancing the incident from a coordinated overthrow effort.

The insistence on linking Trump to an insurrection transcended mere accountability; it constituted a strategic maneuver to dismantle his political standing and potentially bar him from future elections. By framing him as the mastermind behind the chaos, this narrative sought to depict Trump's return to office as a perilous threat to democracy, thereby justifying actions to disqualify him from future ballots.

The allegation that Trump's rhetoric fueled the Capitol riot became a divisive line between political factions. Democrats pointed to his claims of election fraud as contributing to heightened tensions, indirectly holding him responsible for the Capitol incident. In contrast, others shielded Trump under the umbrella of the First Amendment, arguing that his speech did not explicitly incite violence.

The Colorado Supreme Court's groundbreaking decision in December 2023 to disqualify Donald Trump from the presidential race, citing the 14th Amendment's Section 3 and his alleged involvement in the Capitol attack, has launched a legal battle. Trump's swift appeal to the U.S. Supreme Court extends this high-stakes confrontation, potentially affecting far more than just Colorado.

The interpretation of Trump's rhetoric amid the Capitol riot remains contentious. While legal standards for incitement necessitate explicit calls for immediate unlawful action, Trump's passionate speech, albeit controversial, lacked explicit calls for violence. Common political phrases such as "fight" and "never give up" were employed more metaphorically than as direct incitements.

Section 3 of the 14th Amendment sets a rigorous bar for disqualification from public office, reserved for individuals engaged in insurrection against the Constitution, demanding a formal finding of guilt through proper legal processes.

The application of the 14th Amendment should involve meticulous examination and due process to ensure fairness, avoiding the restriction of political participation based on subjective speech interpretations. Levying accusations of incitement without substantial legal grounds could establish a worrisome precedent.

The portrayal of Trump as the instigator was crafted to strategically curb his political return. It aims to tarnish his image as a guardian of law and order, effectively sidelining him from any future political ambitions. Ultimately, it was a calculated move to diminish Trump's chances in the 2024 presidential race.

The November 2022 raid on Trump's Mar-a-Lago residence has been perceived by many as yet another attempt to sideline a political opponent. Trump's departure from the White House was swiftly followed by claims suggesting the mishandling and removal of classified documents. While some files were reportedly surrendered by Trump's team, suspicions arose regarding the potential withholding of additional materials, including government documents earmarked for the National Archives.

Attorney Marc Elias and US Attorney General Merrick Garland's subsequent actions in appointing a special counsel to investigate potential violations of the Espionage Act have drawn considerable scrutiny. Elias suggested the application of a legal statute, 18 US Code § 2071, against Trump. This heightened legal scrutiny has led to speculations about the potential implications for Trump, including fines, imprisonment, and the potential bar from holding public office.

The context of a president's authority to declassify documents within their executive powers is crucial. The declassification process involves a series of steps, ensuring careful consideration of national security implications and potential risks. While presidents have the authority to declassify documents, this power is not absolute, and exceptions exist to maintain classification in specific circumstances such as protecting ongoing intelligence operations.

Moreover, it is important to note that while a criminal indictment might not automatically disqualify Trump from seeking the presidency in 2024, it could substantially impair his chances. The Constitution establishes fundamental criteria for presidential candidacy, and the legislative branch cannot alter these requirements. Nevertheless, a criminal indictment could significantly undermine Trump's candidacy.

The raid itself, involving a substantial number of FBI agents and the seizure of materials, has faced criticism for its unnecessary nature. Representative Mike Turner (R-OH) and others have questioned the need for such a high-profile and intrusive operation, suggesting that less aggressive measures could have been explored.

Trump's response to the raid was laced with indignation, alleging political bias and the exploitation of the justice system for partisan ends. He framed the FBI's actions as part of a series of political witch hunts orchestrated by Democrats to hinder his political future and suppress voices within the MAGA movement. Trump's rhetoric painted the raid as politically motivated, equating it to oppressive tactics employed by totalitarian regimes to stifle political opponents.

In essence, the controversy surrounding the raid on Mar-a-Lago and the subsequent legal actions against Trump underscore deep-seated concerns about the potential misuse of law enforcement and legal mechanisms to target political adversaries and influence electoral outcomes. These actions risk politicizing law enforcement and justice systems, potentially undermining the democratic process and fair participation in elections.

There is broad concern among conservatives about perceived bias within the federal law enforcement apparatus and the use of investigations to target political opponents. Prominent Republicans, including Kevin McCarthy (R-CA), Republican National Committee (RNC) Chairwoman Ronna Romney McDaniel, and Representative Marjorie Taylor Greene (R-GA), criticized the raid on Trump's residence. Senator Rick Scott (R-FL) and Congresswoman Maria Salazar (R-FL) also condemned the raid, expressing worries about democratic values. They voiced concerns about the politicization and weaponization of law enforcement agencies, especially within the Department of Justice (DOJ). Additionally, they expressed fears about political motivations behind Trump's prosecution, suggesting it aims to obstruct his return to politics. They feared a predetermined outcome, drawing parallels with communist show trials.

Senator Marsha Blackburn's (R-TN) characterized the situation as a politically motivated witch hunt reflecting the concerns of many conservatives about bias and partisanship within investigations and legal actions targeting Donald Trump.

Kevin McCarthy expressed frustration with what he perceived as the excessive politicization and weaponization of the Department of Justice (DOJ) in response to the raid. McCarthy denounced the agency for unacceptable behavior. He criticized US Attorney General Merrick Garland, who is of Jewish descent, alleging that the Department of Justice has become excessively politicized. McCarthy promised thorough oversight and extensive investigations once Republicans regain control of the House.

Representative Jim Jordan (R-OH) voiced concerns about what he sees as a pattern of Democrats using intelligence and law enforcement agencies to target their political adversaries.

Governor Ron DeSantis of Florida accused federal agencies of weaponizing themselves against political opponents. He highlighted a double standard in the treatment of individuals, such as Hunter Biden.

Senator Marco Rubio (R-FL) sees a pattern of persecution against Trump and his supporters, likening it to tactics in some Latin American countries. He specifically criticized the FBI raid as a weaponization of justice by leftist Democrats.

Representative Troy Nehls (R-TX) criticized the FBI's actions, interpreting them as part of a continuous effort to attack and discredit Trump. He viewed these actions as an extension of previous challenges Trump has faced over the years. Nehls commended Trump as an honorable patriot who remains steadfast, emphasizing that no wrongdoing has been proven against him and that the allegations have not tarnished his reputation.

Congresswoman Lauren Boebert (R-CO) criticized the raid and urged a GOP Select Committee to investigate. She emphasized her worry about the country's trajectory and expressed concerns about potential future targets if a stand is not taken.

Dr. Ben Carson, former Secretary of the U.S. Department of Housing and Urban Development (HUD), expressed alarm at the politicization and weaponization of the FBI, comparing it to authoritarian regimes such as those of Mao and Castro.

Indiana Representative Victoria Spartz, who grew up in the Soviet Union, likened the raid to tactics employed by the KGB. She expressed deep concerns about the potential chilling effect on political opposition.

Joe Kent, a former Republican candidate for the U.S. House of Representatives, has underscored the notable coordination between the left and the administrative state, citing the FBI raid on Donald Trump's Florida residence as a prime example. This collaboration represents a concerted effort by the left to challenge the fundamental values of America, with the intention of gaining control at various levels and leveraging it against the interests of the people. Emphasizing the urgency of a unified response, Kent has called for a cohesive force to safeguard the republic. He has stressed the critical importance of rallying together in opposition to these threats to the foundational principles of the nation.

In an interview with Univision, Donald Trump claimed that the legal challenges he faces, including charges related to his prior administration, hush money payments, subversion of the 2020 election, and civil fraud allegations, are politically motivated and represent a weaponization of the U.S. justice system. Trump expressed, "They've made indictments in order to win an election. They call it weaponization..."[36]

---

[36] "Trump hints at using FBI to prosecute opponents." *RT*, 11 Nov. 2023, www.rt.com/news/587056-us-trump-prosecute-opponents/.

New York Attorney General Letitia James, a Democrat, made a bold declaration of her intent to prosecute Donald Trump during her 2018 campaign, a move that preceded any revelations about alleged fraud by the Trump Organization. Prior to any emerging details, James openly expressed her commitment to challenging what she deemed an illegitimate presidency and went on to characterize Trump as "incompetent" and "ill-equipped" for the highest office in the country.

This overt expression of prosecutorial intent raises legitimate concerns about the potential interplay of political motivations and the impartiality of the legal process. By publicly announcing a determination to prosecute a specific individual before the initiation of any formal investigation or presentation of evidence, there arises a risk of undermining the fundamental principle of the presumption of innocence. Such a public stance can be perceived as politically motivated, casting doubt on the fairness and objectivity of the legal proceedings.

Notably, Donald Trump Jr. has been vocal in accusing New York Democrats, including Attorney General Letitia James, of engaging in political persecution against his father. This accusation adds to the contentious nature of the situation, suggesting that the legal actions against Donald Trump may be influenced by political considerations rather than a strict commitment to the pursuit of justice.

The public declaration of intent by New York Attorney General Letitia James to prosecute Donald Trump, even before specific details of alleged misconduct had surfaced, bears a striking resemblance to Lavrentiy Beria's infamous principle: "Show me the man, and I'll find you the crime." Beria, the head of Joseph Stalin's secret police, epitomized a style of justice characterized by political persecution and manipulation of legal processes to target individuals based on political motivations rather than concrete evidence of wrongdoing.

In a parallel fashion, James' pre-emptive announcement of her desire to prosecute Trump introduces an unsettling echo of Beria's approach. By openly expressing an intent to target a specific individual before the commencement of a thorough investigation or presentation of evidence, there is a risk of aligning with Beria's principle of finding a crime to fit the person. This tactic not only challenges the presumption of innocence, a cornerstone of a fair legal system, but also introduces concerns about the potential for politically motivated legal actions.

While the context and scale of the situations differ, the parallel lies in the potential abuse of legal processes for political ends. Beria's approach was infamous for its disregard for justice in favor of political expediency, and any perception that legal proceedings are initiated with a predetermined agenda rather than an impartial pursuit of the truth can erode public trust in the justice system. The onus is on legal authorities to ensure that investigations are conducted diligently, fairly, and without preconceived notions, avoiding the pitfalls of Beria's manipulative maxim.

In Trump's perspective, the ongoing investigations represent a continuation of past efforts to undermine his presidency. He vehemently characterizes these probes as a politically motivated "witch hunt," framing them as a concerted effort by his opponents to discredit him, silence his supporters, and hinder his future political aspirations. Trump's criticism extends to the Democratic prosecutors involved, whom he accuses of engaging in misconduct, harassment, and the selective leaking of information to tarnish his reputation and undercut his presidency. According to Trump, their actions are lacking legal objectivity, driven instead by political motives that he contends compromise the fairness of the investigative process.

In asserting that he was unfairly targeted within a corrupt political system, Trump contends that investigators pursued relentless yet ultimately fruitless inquiries. Despite extensive efforts, involving numerous subpoenas, exhaustive document reviews, and prolonged interviews, no evidence of wrongdoing was uncovered. This narrative underscores his perspective that the investigations, rather than revealing substantive misconduct, were emblematic of a political agenda aimed at besmirching his legacy.

Additionally, he raises a broader concern about the potential precedent set by politically motivated actions from prosecutors. Trump cautions that subjecting a former president to such scrutiny could establish a perilous precedent for the country, suggesting that if they could target him in this manner, they could do the same to any individual in the future. This warning reflects his broader apprehension about the potential misuse of legal processes for political ends and the impact it may have on the democratic fabric of the nation.

Beyond the specific case involving Trump, there is a growing chorus of critics voicing concerns about politically motivated investigations within the U.S. justice system. Allegations are emerging that suggest the Biden administration may have inappropriately leveraged law enforcement authority to quell political dissent. This development has set off alarm bells among civil liberty advocates, prompting apprehensions about potential encroachments on constitutional rights and freedoms. Critics argue that these investigations unfairly target political opponents, raising troubling questions about selective prosecution and the introduction of bias into legal actions. The overarching fear lies in the concentration of legal charges against individuals holding opposing political views, leading to broader doubts about the fairness and neutrality of the legal system.

These concerns extend beyond individual cases and extend to the federal law enforcement structure itself. Critics emphasize the susceptibility of the system to manipulation for political purposes, pointing to a worrisome trend where partisan interests could influence investigations and legal proceedings, especially when directed against political adversaries.

The prosecution and legal actions taken against those who question the official narrative of the 2020 election have ignited widespread concerns about the state of free speech. A significant segment of the population harbors deep doubts about the legitimacy of Joe Biden's presidency, grounded in a belief that the election was tainted by fraudulent practices. This skepticism has placed politicians, activists, and ordinary individuals in the crosshairs of legal repercussions merely for expressing doubts or raising questions about voter fraud and irregularities during the election. The consequence is a chilling effect on free expression, as individuals find themselves navigating legal consequences simply for engaging in discourse that challenges the prevailing narrative. The broader implications of these actions raise profound questions about the health of democratic values, the protection of civil liberties, and the potential erosion of trust in the legal and electoral systems.

Preserving the integrity of a fair and transparent electoral system necessitates an open dialogue where citizens can express their concerns without fear of reprisal. Allegations of election irregularities should be subject to impartial scrutiny and legal proceedings to ascertain their validity. Suppressing discussion on such critical issues hampers the democratic process and undermines public trust in the electoral system. Upholding the principles of a fair democratic society involves fostering an environment where citizens can engage in constructive discourse about the electoral process without facing punitive actions for their views.

Concerns about voter irregularities gained significant traction nationwide, causing widespread worry among citizens. However, these concerns encountered substantial resistance from various authorities. The government's responses to allegations of voter fraud and irregularities following the 2020 election were aimed at stifling dissent and downplaying skepticism toward the electoral process, thereby limiting the fundamental right to express concerns.

In an effort to bolster Joe Biden's presidency and maintain the perception of a fair election, Democrats vehemently opposed any assertions of election irregularities, dismissing them as unfounded conspiracy theories. This opposition extended to discrediting such claims as misinformation, resulting in active censorship on social media platforms. Attempts at audits or legal challenges were swiftly rejected, reinforcing the narrative of election integrity and silencing dissenting voices.

The Democrats' active suppression of inquiries into the 2020 election stems from various concerns, primarily rooted in the fear that acknowledging doubts about the election's integrity might directly challenge the legitimacy of Joe Biden's presidency. Widespread skepticism could erode public trust in the electoral process, posing a potential threat to the government's authority and stability, thereby impacting the nation's political landscape. Democrats are hesitant to allow persistent doubts about the 2020 election to persist, as continuous uncertainty may trigger demands for further investigations.

The concerted efforts by Democrats to suppress claims about the 2020 election are strategically aligned with their overarching interests. The primary objective is to uphold and maintain the legitimacy of the Biden administration, protect public trust in the electoral system, and prevent the exacerbation of existing political divisions. Initiatives calling for audits or investigations have faced staunch resistance from Democrats, who categorically labeled these efforts as partisan attacks or threats to democracy. This resistance, coupled with the rush to conclude the election without a thorough examination, has contributed to the emergence of allegations of suppression.

Essentially, the environment shaped by the Democrats' actions has resulted in genuine concerns being dismissed rather than addressed, contributing to a deepening overall distrust in the electoral system. A more transparent and thorough approach to handling claims of irregularities would better serve the overarching goal of fostering trust and confidence in the democratic process.

Courts played a crucial role in examining these allegations. Yet, they often declined to hear the evidence presented. Many cases related to election irregularities were swiftly dismissed, citing procedural issues or lack of standing, without delving into the substantive claims brought forth. This approach left many claims unaddressed and contributed to public skepticism.

Furthermore, the media's response to election fraud allegations contributed to a sense of betrayal. Instead of engaging in in-depth investigations into the claims of voter fraud, many media outlets swiftly dismissed these assertions. They often labeled such claims as baseless or lacking evidence without conducting thorough inquiries. This rapid dismissal in the public sphere further heightened concerns about the credibility of the electoral process.

The emergence of alternative groups of Trump electors following the 2020 Presidential election triggered a significant response from Democrats. These alternative electors presented their slate before the official certification of the Electoral College results during a joint session of Congress on January 6, 2021, particularly in crucial battleground states such as Pennsylvania, Michigan, Wisconsin, and Georgia.

Constitutional mandates dictated that these proposed electors needed to convene and be certified at the state Capitol by a specific deadline. However, during the official certification process, these alternative slates were not recognized, and the electoral votes from these states were ultimately allocated to Joe Biden, solidifying his victory in the 2020 election.

Following the aftermath of the election, Trump electors faced legal entanglements, notably subpoenas issued by the FBI. These subpoenas, viewed by many as part of an anti-Trump agenda advanced by the January 6th Committee, raised accusations of harassment against the electors. Kathy Berden, one of the electors, chose not to respond to the subpoena, navigating the contentious legal situation without direct engagement. A similar situation unfolded with another elector, Amy Facchinello, who was also served a subpoena, sparking concerns about the coercive nature of the legal proceedings.

These actions targeting the Trump electors were seen by many as attempts to suppress concerns about the 2020 election. The involvement of federal agencies and the January 6th Committee in subpoenaing and potentially harassing these electors implied a concerted effort to deter any alternative narrative or challenges to the official election outcome. This move was a means to reinforce the legitimacy of Joe Biden's victory and discourage any dissent or exploration of electoral irregularities, suppressing any debate about the integrity of the election results.

The situation in Michigan added a layer of partisan conflict and legal implications to the already polarized aftermath of the 2020 election. Attorney General Dana Nessel, known for her leftist ideologies, openly expressed intentions to pursue legal action against the Trump-aligned electors.

In Pennsylvania, the FBI's issuance of subpoenas aimed at multiple Republican legislators, including U.S. Representative Scott Perry, stirred significant controversy over the alleged involvement of these officials in the appointment of alternate electors during the tumultuous 2020 election. Representative Perry, a retired Army brigadier general and a staunch supporter of former President Donald Trump, found himself at the center of the FBI's scrutiny, a circumstance that some believe could be influenced by his alignment with Trump and his outspoken conservative stance.

The FBI's actions took a contentious turn when Perry's phone was confiscated without prior communication with his legal counsel. The phone's contents encompassed a wide spectrum, ranging from Perry's legislative and political endeavors to personal conversations with family, constituents, and acquaintances. Perry strongly denounced this intrusive act, condemning the FBI's actions as excessive and aggressive, likening them to "banana republic tactics" that overstepped the bounds of government authority.

The timing of the phone seizure, occurring shortly after the House committee's subpoenas targeting Perry and other Republican legislators who had declined voluntary cooperation in the investigation of the January 6th Capitol riot, adds layers of complexity to the situation. Perry had previously labeled the committee's probe as a "witch hunt," casting doubts on its impartiality.

The FBI's series of visits and subpoenas directed at Representative Scott Perry have sparked questions about the underlying motivations driving these investigations. Concerns regarding due process and the potential influence of political motives have been raised, with critics voicing suspicions that these inquiries might carry a partisan agenda, potentially aimed at members of the opposition party.

The federal raid on Jeffrey Clark's residence in Lorton, Virginia, on June 22, 2022, conducted by a team of over a dozen DOJ law enforcement officials in the early morning, has sparked significant controversy. Clark, who served under former President Donald Trump from 2018 to 2021 as the Assistant Attorney General for the DOJ's Environment and Natural Resources Division, was aligned with Trump's claims of voter fraud following the 2020 presidential elections. The operation raises concerns about its timing, scale, and potential political implications.

This event has ignited discussions about the potential weaponization of law enforcement agencies for political purposes. Russ Vought, President of the Center for Renewing America, has expressed deep concerns about the growing trend of politicizing law enforcement actions in the United States. He condemned the search of Clark's house, asserting that it was directly linked to Clark's involvement in investigating voter fraud allegations. Tom Fitton, President of Judicial Watch, went a step further, characterizing the raid as a political assault. He criticized the Biden administration for targeting and mistreating political adversaries who have dared to challenge the legitimacy of the election. Mollie Hemmingway, Editor-in-Chief for the Federalist, expressed dismay, likening the raid to tactics reminiscent of the Soviet era and highlighting the discomfort in witnessing such occurrences within the United States. The allegations and criticisms underscore a broader fear of a government using its enforcement arm to suppress dissent or investigations into matters that could challenge its legitimacy.

The comparison drawn by Hemingway to Soviet-era tactics resonates with concerns about authoritarian regimes' historical use of law enforcement to target political opponents. In communist regimes such as the Soviet Union, the state often exploited law enforcement agencies to silence dissent and intimidate opposition voices. Critics argue that actions such as the raid on Clark's residence could symbolize a concerning shift towards similar tactics, where dissenting voices or those investigating election irregularities face intimidation or scrutiny.

The fear of mirroring such tactics also reflects worries about the erosion of democratic principles. In a democratic society, the independence and impartiality of law enforcement agencies are paramount to upholding the rule of law and protecting citizens' rights, regardless of their political affiliations or beliefs. When law enforcement actions become entangled with partisan interests, it raises fundamental questions about the integrity of the justice system and the protection of individual freedoms.

Overall, the comparison to Soviet-era tactics serves as a stark warning about the potential consequences of using law enforcement as a tool to target political opponents, emphasizing the importance of preserving the rule of law and safeguarding democratic values.

The concerns surrounding due process and legal procedures have become woven into broader apprehensions regarding political bias and the overall credibility of American institutions, particularly in the aftermath of the 2020 election. Within this complex landscape, the notion of a two-tiered justice system has gained prominence, driven by noticeable disparities in treatment across select high-profile cases, giving rise to a narrative of unequal justice influenced by political leanings.

At the core of this perception is the apparent bias within law enforcement agencies, prominently exemplified by the FBI. When investigations or actions appear to target specific political ideologies, a growing belief emerges that these agencies may function as instruments to suppress dissent rather than impartially uphold justice. This sentiment intensifies when the outcomes of investigations seem to favor one political narrative over another.

The selective application of justice in high-profile cases further fuels concerns about the erosion of due process and the integrity of legal procedures. Instances where individuals associated with particular political affiliations face disproportionate consequences or, conversely, enjoy lenient treatment contribute to the perception of a justice system influenced by political considerations.

Moreover, the public's confidence in the fairness and impartiality of American institutions is eroded when legal actions appear to align with political motivations. The perceived politicization of law enforcement agencies not only undermines the credibility of investigations but also diminishes public trust in the fundamental principles of justice.

This troubling trend intersects with the broader context of post-2020 election narratives, where suspicions of political interference in legal processes have become intertwined with concerns about the democratic fabric of the nation. The perception of a two-tiered justice system, shaped by political biases, contributes to a climate of skepticism regarding the equal application of the law.

These concerns extend beyond the electoral process and encompass the government's stance toward activists and dissenters challenging its authority. Allegations range from deliberately targeting political adversaries to employing tactics such as censorship or stifling opposing viewpoints. Furthermore, there are claims hinting at the misuse of federal agencies to investigate or intimidate political opponents.

Threatening legal action against individuals expressing legitimate concerns about the election outcome draws disconcerting parallels with historical tactics associated with oppressive regimes, notably those rooted in communist ideologies. The deployment of legal measures to silence dissent, rather than fostering open dialogue or transparent investigation, mirrors strategies employed by authoritarian regimes to quell opposition and impose a singular narrative.

Initiating legal action against those questioning or challenging election results raises profound concerns about the potential abuse of power and the infringement upon free speech and democratic processes. This approach implies an effort to intimidate or coerce individuals into silence, discouraging opposition to the accepted narrative. Such tactics undermine the principles of open discourse, transparency, and the right to question and challenge established narratives—integral components of democratic societies.

In democratic societies, the inherent right to question, scrutinize, and engage in open discourse about elections is fundamental to ensuring transparency, accountability, and the overall integrity of the electoral process. Curtailing or actively suppressing this right raises concerns reminiscent of tactics seen in regimes with centralized control over information.

Communist regimes historically controlled information flows tightly, shaping narratives to align with their preferred ideologies. Similarly, when claims or questions regarding election integrity are censored, it mirrors the information control tactics observed in authoritarian regimes. This restriction on the public's access to diverse perspectives impedes a thorough examination of electoral processes, hindering democratic principles of transparency and informed public discourse.

Moreover, a common tactic of socialist regimes is to label dissent as subversion or a threat to the state. When questions about election integrity are suppressed by branding them as baseless conspiracy theories or partisan attacks, it mirrors the authoritarian strategy of discrediting dissenting voices rather than engaging in open and constructive dialogue.

Additionally, communist regimes have a historical track record of resisting external scrutiny or independent investigations. Similarly, efforts to dismiss calls for audits or investigations into election processes, under the guise of threats to democracy, can be interpreted as avoiding transparency and hindering efforts to address legitimate concerns.

Totalitarian regimes often prioritize maintaining political power, often at the expense of democratic principles. Suppressing discussions about election integrity in a democracy, particularly when allegations arise, may be perceived as an attempt to preserve political power by avoiding a thorough examination that could challenge the perceived legitimacy of those in office.

One significant consequence of suppressing the right to question elections is the potential deepening of public distrust. Communist regimes have faced widespread distrust due to a lack of transparency and accountability. Similarly, suppressing legitimate questions about elections may contribute to a broader erosion of trust in democratic institutions—a key pillar of any functioning democracy.

The cumulative effect of these responses, from courts dismissing cases to media outlets swiftly rejecting claims, has been to suppress the discussion and investigation of irregularities. While intended to maintain stability and confidence in the electoral system, this reaction has raised questions about the democratic process itself. Many citizens feel unheard, contributing to an ongoing atmosphere of distrust surrounding the 2020 election and its aftermath.

This multifaceted set of concerns underscores broader apprehensions about fair treatment for those expressing dissent or challenging established authority. The allegations span various issues, including potential violations of freedom of expression, limitations on open discourse, and even the alleged manipulation of governmental bodies to suppress opposing political perspectives. Such concerns prompt essential inquiries about the boundaries of governmental power, the preservation of civil liberties, and ensuring individuals' rights to dissent without fear of reprisal.

Whistleblowers within the FBI have shed light on allegations of politicization and misconduct, unveiling a landscape marked by improper actions and the infusion of political agendas into the bureau's operations. These insiders have revealed concerning tactics such as pervasive surveillance, harassment, and intimidation, which seem calculated to quell opposition to the Biden administration and deter dissent by instilling an atmosphere of fear and distrust. There is a concern that these measures could herald an era of widespread surveillance, potentially constituting a grave infringement upon the constitutional rights guaranteed to citizens.

The tactics unveiled by these whistleblowers bear eerie resemblance to methods employed during past eras, particularly by regimes employing authoritarian or communist strategies. The deliberate use of surveillance and intimidation tactics to stifle dissent echoes historical precedents where dissenting voices were silenced through coercive means, reflecting a disconcerting parallel with strategies used by authoritarian regimes to maintain control and quash opposition. The alleged infiltration of political motivations into the workings of the FBI raises fundamental questions about the sanctity of democratic principles, the protection of civil liberties, and the impartiality of law enforcement agencies.

In June 2022, Congressman Jim Jordan raised concerns about the involvement of former FBI officials in purging employees with conservative viewpoints. These allegations draw disquieting parallels to historical episodes, such as Stalinist purges, where political adversaries were systematically removed from positions of influence.

The accusations surrounding the removal of individuals based on their conservative perspectives raise valid questions about potential biases and encroachments on individuals' rights to hold dissenting political beliefs. In a democratic framework, the ability to express diverse viewpoints without facing punitive actions due to political affiliations is a cornerstone of civil liberties.

The actions of the FBI in recent years have raised concerns about the neutrality and fairness of law enforcement, particularly in cases involving political figures. Critics have pointed to instances where Democrats are alleged to have utilized the federal law enforcement apparatus to target former President Trump and those associated with him during his tenure. They argue that these investigations, extending beyond typical civil matters, were driven by political motivations rather than solely upholding the law.

This use of federal law enforcement agencies for politically motivated investigations raises questions about potential abuses of power within the system. These investigations exceeded the ordinary scope of legal scrutiny and were emblematic of an effort to undermine or discredit political adversaries.

The concerns are not solely about the scrutiny of Trump but extend to broader implications for the impartiality of the justice system. They underscore the need for law enforcement agencies to operate independently, without succumbing to political pressures or agendas, to ensure fair and unbiased investigations.

The controversy surrounding the probe into alleged Russian interference in the 2016 election, coupled with subsequent investigations into members of the Trump administration, suggests a politically motivated approach aimed at undermining the legitimacy of the Trump presidency. This perception gains strength when one observes a notable absence of comparable levels of investigations concerning individuals or incidents linked to the opposing political faction, further solidifying the perception of a two-tiered justice system.

The concept of a two-tiered justice system underscores a disparity in the treatment of individuals based on their political affiliations. Those aligned with the ruling party often enjoy preferential treatment, benefiting from legal leniency, while dissenters face selective prosecution and severe penalties. This imbalance compromises the independence and impartiality of the judiciary, pressuring judges to prioritize the government's interests.

Individuals such as Susan Rosenberg, a Jewish communist associated with bombings and violent acts, received preferential treatment. Rosenberg's history involves her association with the far-left revolutionary organization Weather Underground during the late 1960s and 1970s. This radical group sought to overthrow the U.S. government and employed militant tactics, including bombings targeting government buildings. Rosenberg was also involved with the May 19th Communist Organization (M19CO), engaging in violent acts to foment a communist revolution within the United States.

Rosenberg's arrest in 1984 and subsequent conviction on charges related to weapons and explosives possession resulted in a 58-year prison sentence. In 2001, during the final days of President Bill Clinton's tenure, her sentence was commuted, leading to her release. As of 2021, Rosenberg served on the board of directors for the nonprofit organization "Thousand Currents," which supported social and environmental justice initiatives, including fiscal sponsorship for the Black Lives Matter Global Network Foundation.

In 2020, civil unrest and riots led by Antifa and BLM resulted in violent acts, property damage, and clashes with law enforcement. Many protestors involved received lenient sentences, raising concerns about disparities in the criminal justice system's responses to different offenses. Some attribute perceived leniency during those riots to prosecutorial discretion influenced by sympathies toward a leftist political agenda, suggesting the criminal justice system might have been used to shield leftists advancing a socialist agenda on the streets.

In June 2021, Senator Ron Johnson and several Republican lawmakers expressed concerns about the differential treatment of Capitol protestors compared to rioters in Portland and other locations. They highlighted extensive property destruction during the 2020 social justice protests and pointed to DOJ statistics revealing deaths and injuries to federal and local officers during the 2020 riots.

The senators raised concerns about potential bias, suggesting that the DOJ's handling of cases showed favorable treatment towards Portland rioters compared to Capitol protestors. This sparked a debate on unequal treatment based on political ideologies, fueling fears that such differential treatment might erode public trust in the criminal justice system.

The difference in responses to the 2020 rioters, Susan Rosenberg's case, and the participants in the January 6th Capitol protest spotlights profound inconsistencies within the justice system. Those aligned with a favored leftist ideology receive more leniency, while conservatives face harsher consequences, revealing that political biases influence justice and contribute to unequal treatment within the system.

Comparing the treatment of the 2020 rioters and Capitol protestors exposes a marked disparity in responses, possibly rooted in the narratives each group represented. The 2020 rioters, linked with the Marxist narrative of social justice and equality, were afforded more leniency as compared to the Capitol protestors.

Those involved in the 2020 riots often rallied around causes endorsed by the left-leaning spectrum, advocating for social and racial justice. This alignment with the preferred narrative influenced the leniency observed in their cases, perceived by some left-leaning prosecutors as justified expressions of frustration against systemic problems.

In contrast, the Capitol protestors were predominantly seen as proponents of conservative ideology, perceived as a challenge to the desired socialist norms and governance. This perception contributed to a harsher response, viewing their actions as an assault on the Democrats' vision of a socialist America.

This stark contrast in treatment based on political alignment mirrors a troubling trend reminiscent of tactics seen in communist regimes. In such systems, political loyalty often dictated legal treatment. Those in line with the ruling ideology enjoyed leniency, while dissenters faced severe repercussions.

The same pattern appears evident in the lenient treatment of individuals supporting the favored leftist narrative—such as the 2020 rioters—contrasted with the unforgiving treatment of Capitol protestors, aligned with conservative ideals. This trend reflects the manipulation of justice for political gains, akin to oppressive practices seen in Marxist regimes.

When justice hinges on political affiliation, it undermines the foundational principle of equal justice under the law. Such practices not only damage the credibility of the legal system but also perpetuate a climate of fear and injustice, akin to tactics used by communist regimes to suppress opposition and consolidate power.

The intertwining of doubts about the electoral process with perceptions of biased law enforcement actions has given rise to a broader narrative of distrust among certain factions within the Republican base. These concerns about due process and the handling of legal procedures are integral components of a larger pattern that erodes faith in the fairness and impartiality of the American justice system.

Former House Republican leader Kevin McCarthy's critique of U.S. Attorney General Merrick Garland has thrust a longstanding and contentious issue within American politics into the spotlight: The politicization of the Department of Justice (DOJ). In a pointed Twitter statement, McCarthy accused Garland's department of reaching "an intolerable state of weaponized politicization."

McCarthy's public stance resonates with the concerns voiced by several Republicans who are apprehensive that the actions of the DOJ might be swayed by political motivations rather than a steadfast dedication to upholding the rule of law.

The Department of Justice, functioning as the country's foremost law enforcement agency, carries the weighty responsibility of operating independently and without political influence. This autonomy is essential to preserve the integrity and credibility of the justice system. McCarthy's reservations underline a growing worry among some that the DOJ's decisions and practices might be influenced by political considerations, potentially compromising its commitment to impartiality and the fair application of the law. The critique from McCarthy and other Republicans points to a broader concern about the neutrality of the DOJ and the impact of partisan inclinations on its functioning.

The Biden administration has faced criticism for targeting dissenting voices. Under Biden's leadership, various groups, including MAGA Republicans, Trump supporters, conservatives, and even moderates, have been labeled as "threat actors," raising concerns about the handling of political discourse and potential bias within federal assessments. White House Press Secretary Karine Jean-Pierre's statements, suggesting that MAGA supporters pose a threat to American democracy, have drawn significant attention.

The introduction of the "National Strategy for Countering Domestic Terrorism" by the Biden administration has sparked concerns. While aimed at addressing perceived drivers behind domestic terrorism, such as racism and bigotry, this initiative has led to increased surveillance by agencies such as the FBI and the Department of Homeland Security (DHS). These measures raise troubling parallels with historical communist regimes' tactics, prompting apprehensions about their impact on civil liberties.

A significant concern is the potential targeting of political adversaries, where certain right-leaning principles, once considered legitimate discourse, now risk being labeled as "extremist narratives." Advocating for limited government intervention, particularly in areas such as healthcare or economic policies, was traditionally part of conservative discourse and recognized as a legitimate perspective in political discussions.

However, this stance has faced increasing labeling as an "extremist narrative" or portrayed as opposition to collective welfare. Such characterization potentially frames it as a threat to national security or stability. Consequently, these labels impact discussions concerning policies related to government control, creating limitations for dissenting viewpoints and stifling debates on the essential balance between individual liberties and governmental authority. This classification is viewed as a direct challenge to the fundamental tenets of free speech, restraining debates on critical topics such as election integrity and democratic values.

Moreover, the Department of Homeland Security's classification of individuals questioning the legitimacy of the 2020 election as potential national security threats has triggered widespread unease. Questioning the election's legitimacy is a fundamental expression of free speech and should not be stigmatized as a security concern.

This labeling of groups has been detailed in a bulletin released by the DHS's National Terrorism Advisory System, in response to federal guidelines on terrorism. The bulletin flags individuals who allegedly spread what the administration deems "false" narratives and "misinformation" aimed at undermining trust in U.S. government institutions. It identifies various symbols, including those linked to movements such as "Boogaloo," anarcho-capitalism, and warrior culture representations, offering visual cues for law enforcement to spot "extremist and disaffected individuals," including specific political group symbols and generic patriotic symbols.

Controversies have arisen regarding the bulletin's association of symbols from the American Revolution, such as the Gadsden flag and generic Revolutionary War imagery, with "Militia Violent Extremism." Critics question the FBI's categorization of symbols related to "Anti-Government or Anti-Authority Violent Extremists." The inclusion of symbols associated with American Revolution-themed T-shirts has sparked doubts about the accuracy of the assessment, prompting queries about the FBI's stance on fundamental liberties and the Bill of Rights.

The classification of American Contingency as a "mainstream militia," primarily involved in online activities with a limited history of violence, has sparked concerns about the FBI's emphasis on monitoring internet-based discussion groups. This aligns with historical practices of the agency, which have sometimes raised questions about targeting government critics solely for expressing their opinions.

The government's current tactics of targeted scrutiny and the labeling of specific political beliefs draw alarming parallels with historical methods employed by communist regimes. These regimes, recognized for suppressing dissent and consolidating authority, historically controlled the narrative by stifling opposition voices and categorizing dissenting ideologies as threats to national security. In the present context, labeling dissenting viewpoints as "extremist narratives" mirrors historical methods of demonizing differing ideologies, marginalizing dissent, and restricting free expression, echoing the practices of authoritarian regimes.

The heightened surveillance of dissenting individuals today mirrors the control tactics used by authoritarian regimes to foster fear and inhibit free expression. There is a potential for the weaponization of laws or security measures to target political adversaries, reflecting historical methods used to silence dissenting voices by framing them as enemies of the state. The consequences of stigmatizing dissent as a threat to national security also mirror historical tactics that led to the persecution of individuals holding differing views, risking social exclusion or punitive actions, akin to historical instances in totalitarian regimes.

Communist regimes have historically employed a strategic approach of demonizing their opponents as a prelude to purges and crackdowns on dissent. This tactic seeks to consolidate power, suppress opposition, and control the narrative to maintain authority. Demonizing opponents serves the crucial purpose of consolidating power within the ruling elite by framing dissenting voices as enemies of the state, justifying drastic actions to eliminate threats and garnering support among the population and within the party for purges and repressive measures.

Control of information is another key aspect, as communist regimes aim to control the narrative and discredit alternative perspectives. Demonizing opponents is a tactic to discredit differing viewpoints, portraying them as false ideologies spread by enemies, thereby establishing a pretext for suppressing dissent. Demonization also functions as a preemptive defense against potential counter-revolution, characterizing dissent and opposition as potential seeds of counter-revolution, justifying preemptive actions and legitimizing purges as necessary measures to protect the socialist state from internal threats.

Within communist parties, demonization is used to stifle internal criticism, branding internal critics as traitors or enemies and justifying purges to remove perceived threats to party unity. Finally, the strategy creates an atmosphere of fear, discouraging dissent and promoting self-censorship among the population. The fear instilled by demonization facilitates the implementation of purges without widespread resistance. In essence, demonization of opponents serves as a strategic precursor to purges, establishing a narrative that justifies the elimination of perceived threats to the ideology, consolidates power, controls information, and creates an environment of fear and compliance essential for the regime's survival.

The Biden administration's focus on racism linked to white Americans raises apprehensions about the possible criminalization of a substantial segment of the population. Former FBI and CIA agent, Tracy Walder, claimed, "Being a white supremacist is not a mental illness, it's a crime."[37] This statement has sparked debate due to its conflict with constitutional principles, particularly those surrounding freedom of speech and expression.

The proposal to categorize Americans based on their political beliefs, particularly in connection to perceived white supremacy, and the potential consideration of legislation resembling the Patriot Act targeting white males have generated considerable concern. The resonance with the Patriot Act is particularly troubling, suggesting the

---

[37] NewsNation Prime. "'Being a White Supremacist Is Not a Mental Illness, It's a Crime': Former FBI." *YouTube*, uploaded by NewsNation Prime, 28 Aug. 2023, www.youtube.com/watch?v=-IZ8MD9k_78 at 1:30.

possibility of implementing surveillance measures or legal actions that target individuals specifically due to their racial or gender identity. Such proposals provoke fears of systemic discrimination and encroachments on the civil rights of a particular demographic, evoking concerns about fair treatment, equal protection under the law, and the right to privacy.

Critics express apprehension regarding the Biden administration's emphasis on addressing a specific form of racism and bigotry associated with white Americans. This emphasis, when compared to the extensive surveillance and legislation under the Patriot Act, amplifies broader concerns about the potential impact on civil liberties and individual freedoms. The overarching worry is that broad categorizations and targeted actions might suppress free speech and hinder the expression of dissenting viewpoints, raising questions about the balance between combating discrimination and preserving fundamental rights in a democratic society.

In response to these developments, various political figures have raised significant concerns. Senator Ted Cruz directly confronted FBI Director Christopher Wray during a Senate hearing, drawing attention to a training document that labeled patriotic symbols as extremist. Cruz accused the FBI of political bias and criticized what he perceived as an oversight of other groups, such as Antifa or Black Lives Matter. Representative Jim Jordan further expressed these concerns by penning a letter that delved into the FBI's handling of cases related to "domestic violence extremism." In the letter, Jordan alleged potential corruption and ideological bias within the bureau, intensifying the scrutiny surrounding these issues.

At the heart of this discussion lies the safeguarding of free speech, a principle enshrined in the First Amendment.

Preserving the right to express even contentious viewpoints, such as advocating for ideologies such as white supremacy, sparks concerns about potential violations of individuals' rights. Criminalizing an ideology risks penalizing beliefs over actions, potentially eroding the bedrock of democratic values.

Laws that specifically target a particular demographic can face challenges regarding their constitutionality due to violations of the Equal Protection Clause in the Fourteenth Amendment. When legislation singles out people based on race, gender, or other protected characteristics, it inherently creates unequal treatment under the law, contradicting the principle of equal protection. Such laws risk perpetuating discrimination, disadvantaging individuals within that group, and encroaching on individual rights guaranteed by the Constitution. Permitting these laws sets a troubling precedent, undermining foundational principles and potentially eroding social unity.

The foundations of the United States rest significantly on European heritage, largely influenced by White settlers, shaping its identity and institutions. Acknowledging this underscores the enduring impact of European heritage on American society, deeply rooted in its history.

Examining historical strategies used by communist regimes reveals parallels with ongoing shifts in the USA. Efforts challenging entrenched cultural norms linked to dominant groups aim to reshape societal frameworks, reminiscent of strategies used to transform prevailing norms. This context is vital in discussions about the targeting of the dominant white European culture.

Advocates of socialism in the USA often emphasize policies challenging economic hegemony, seeking wealth redistribution and improved social welfare. In history, communist regimes strategically confronted and reshaped dominant cultures, aiming to deconstruct structures sustaining societal norms for an envisioned egalitarian society.

Actions in the US challenging elements of traditional cultural frameworks tied to dominant groups attempt to modify entrenched norms, echoing historical Marxist strategies to replace prevailing norms with new ideological paradigms.

In pursuing socialism, the focus often centers on reshaping economic structures for equality. Within the US, where the dominant culture intertwines closely with economic power, socialist proponents advocate policies challenging this hegemony, aiming for wealth redistribution and expanded social welfare. These policies might be seen as reducing the economic influence of the dominant culture.

Marxists often target the dominant culture as it reflects and reinforces existing power structures and inequalities. They view it as aligned with the interests of the ruling class, perpetuating societal hierarchies that oppress the working class. By challenging and replacing these cultural narratives, socialists aim to create an egalitarian society that prioritizes the interests of the working class, aligning with Marxist ideals of equality.

Within the historical context of communism, dissidents were systematically classified not just as enemies of the state but also as adversaries opposing the dominant cultural and ideological fabric. Communist regimes wove a narrative designating anyone diverging from the prevailing ideology or impeding the communist revolution as a threat to their order.

Dissent—whether political, cultural, or ideological—was routinely perceived as a challenge to the state's ideology or an obstacle to the revolutionary metamorphosis. Those contesting the socialist culture or the march of the communist revolution were framed as counter-revolutionaries or impediments to societal advancement. This characterization served as the rationale for severe punitive actions, ranging from isolation and social marginalization to imprisonment, forced labor, and execution.

The eras of Lenin and Stalin during the Bolshevik Revolution and the subsequent rule in Soviet Russia actively deployed this tactic. Individuals or groups opposing the Communist Party's ideology were labeled as "counter-revolutionaries" or tagged as "enemies of the people." The consequence was widespread purges, imprisonment in labor camps (gulags), and executions, tactics wielded to fortify authority and eliminate opposition. Parallel strategies were adopted in Maoist China, where dissenters were construed as threats to the revolutionary framework, facing dire consequences such as public humiliation, incarceration, or even capital punishment.

The objective aimed to stifle any contestation against the Marxist cultural and ideological norms. Communist regimes wanted to sow an atmosphere of fear, prompting individuals to abstain from expressing dissenting views for fear of severe reprisals. Framing dissent as a menace to revolutionary ideals or state security was a strategic move by these regimes to perpetuate control, obliterate opposition, and shape the societal narrative.

In essence, dissenters—whether challenging the ideology or impeding the revolutionary narrative—were systematically categorized as enemies of the state. This historical context underscores how dissent, whether against the ideological framework or cultural norms, was systematically suppressed and eradicated, facilitating the consolidation of power and control by communist regimes.

In the United States, conservatives are viewed as adversaries by socialists due to deep-seated differences in ideology and policy objectives. Socialists advocate for a more even-handed allocation of wealth and resources, advocating for a larger government role in ensuring social welfare and addressing economic disparities. Conversely, conservatives lean towards minimal government intervention, prioritizing individual freedoms and free-market principles.

The ideological divergence between conservatism and socialism spans economic policies, social welfare, and the scope of government intervention. Conservative values center on fewer regulations, smaller government, and lower taxes—directly conflicting with Marxist proposals that call for significant government involvement in the economy and expanded social programs.

Beyond economic differences, conservatives often champion traditional values and established societal norms, while socialists seek progressive societal changes. This cultural contrast amplifies ideological disparities, particularly on issues such as LGBTQ+ rights, racial justice, and gender equality.

From a Marxist perspective, conservative policies hinder strides towards economic equality and social justice. The resistance of conservatives to embrace policies supporting wealth redistribution, social safety nets, and progressive societal reforms impede communist agendas aimed at forging a more equitable society.

Ultimately, the perceived threat of conservatives to socialists in the U.S. hinges on their divergent visions for government roles, economic policies, and societal values, potentially obstructing the advancement of socialist principles and reforms.

The categorization of conservatism as domestic terrorism echoes the historical tactics of authoritarian regimes, including communist regimes, which aimed to suppress opposition. Dissenters were often labeled as enemies of the state or national security threats, justifying severe measures such as social exclusion, imprisonment, and even execution.

The uptick in surveillance over conservative viewpoints bears a troubling resemblance to tactics used by communist regimes, fostering an atmosphere where expressing dissent becomes increasingly risky.

This scenario suggests a government inclination to monitor and cast suspicion on dissenting views, potentially infringing upon civil liberties and suppressing opposing opinions under the guise of national security. Unfairly associating conservative beliefs with terrorism poses a significant risk, possibly justifying stringent measures and restricting their freedom to express divergent viewpoints.

The path toward ideological confrontation hints at a potential domestic conflict targeting dissenters, especially those critical of Marxist ideals or differing from the desired narrative. If left unchecked, this trajectory may justify treating conservatives unfairly as societal threats, leading to the suppression of their voices and curtailing their rights.

This labeling and targeting under the guise of national security could establish a dangerous precedent, potentially marginalizing conservative voices from public discourse and civic engagement.

The mounting perception that federal agencies are targeting political adversaries raises deep concerns regarding potential abuses of power. When law enforcement actions are seemingly driven by political beliefs, it undermines the fundamental fairness within society. This is especially evident in cases such as the aftermath of the January 6, 2021 Capitol protest, where there are troubling indications that political motivations influenced prosecutorial actions, directly threatening the foundation of a fair and just society.

Legal actions taken against former President Trump and his supporters have intensified concerns about the politicization of justice. The emphasis on prosecuting cases linked to contesting election results sparks skepticism regarding the preservation of First Amendment rights. These legal pursuits prioritize partisan interests over impartial justice, eroding the credibility of legal processes and undermining the bedrock of fairness and equality in the law.

Former President Trump stood as a symbol for capitalist, conservative America, championing values that sharply contrasted with the ideologies of socialism. His administration advocated for policies rooted in free-market capitalism, championing reduced regulation and prioritizing economic growth—stances fundamentally divergent from the principles advocated by Marxism, which emphasize collective ownership, wealth redistribution, and extensive government involvement in socio-economic spheres.

Under Trump's leadership, America embodied the spirit of individual enterprise, highlighting the centrality of free-market mechanisms in shaping the economy. His agenda was focused on slashing taxes, nurturing business expansion, and cutting down on regulations—a blueprint that resonated deeply with capitalist principles, underscoring the importance of private enterprise and minimal government intervention in economic domains.

In stark contrast, socialists endeavor to reshape this capitalist framework, advocating for increased government intervention in economic affairs to achieve greater income equality and uplift marginalized communities through social welfare programs. From their standpoint, Trump's America epitomized a capitalist society marked by concentrated wealth, glaring disparities in opportunity, and inadequate systemic support for the most vulnerable.

For socialists, Trump's tenure represented a force counter to their vision of a fairer society. They perceived his policies as emblematic of a system that prioritized corporate interests over societal welfare, exacerbating wealth disparities and consolidating the power of the affluent. Consequently, Trump became a symbol of capitalist America built on conservative ideals—a system vehemently opposed by socialists seeking to challenge and transform it through their ideological lens.

The opposition from socialist factions against Trump evolved into a broader ideological conflict—an ongoing clash between Trump's embodiment of capitalist conservatism and the socialist vision for a society characterized by equity and collective consciousness. His presidency became a focal point for socialists, symbolizing a system they aimed to fundamentally reshape to align with their vision of a more just and inclusive society.

Achieving a socialist state in the USA demands a seismic shift away from the entrenched beliefs and structures championed by Trump and his supporters. Marxists argue that this transformation requires dismantling the capitalist values and systems these followers endorse, considering them as formidable barriers thwarting the path toward a Marxist utopia.

Trump's supporters have consistently aligned themselves with constitutionalist values, advocating for limited government intervention, free-market capitalism, and individualism—beliefs that sharply clash with the core tenets of Marxist socialism, which champion collective ownership and socio-economic equality.

Constitutionalists uphold the principles enshrined in the U.S. Constitution. They prioritize limited government interference, defend individual freedoms, advocate for states' rights, and adhere closely to the original interpretation of the Constitution as intended by the Founding Fathers. However, these principles collide with the ideologies of those leaning toward socialist beliefs.

The core beliefs of constitutionalists center on safeguarding personal liberties and property rights—principles fundamentally at odds with Marxist ideologies that emphasize collective ownership and centralized control. Constitutionalists also advocate for minimal government interference in citizens' lives, a position that directly challenges the expansive government control supported by communist systems.

Furthermore, constitutionalists' backing of free-market capitalism, where private enterprise and competition drive the economy with minimal government intervention, sharply contrasts with communist ideals advocating for centralized planning and state ownership of industries.

Another crucial aspect of constitutionalist ideology is the defense of states' rights within the federal system—a stance that diverges from the preference for a more centralized government structure seen in leftist leanings.

Moreover, constitutionalists aim to preserve the original interpretation of the Constitution and resist efforts to reinterpret it to align with collectivist ideologies. This stance challenges attempts by those with communist inclinations to modify the Constitution's meaning to suit their ideologies.

These supporters are often criticized by socialists, who depict them as guardians of a capitalist mindset perpetuating significant wealth gaps and reinforcing existing power structures, hindering societal reform. In essence, the diverging ideologies between constitutionalists and proponents of Marxist ideologies fundamentally conflict on the role of government, individual freedoms, economic systems, and the interpretation of the Constitution. These differences give rise to ideological tensions and conflict between these groups.

From a Marxist perspective, Trump's base assumes the role of gatekeepers protecting a system that consolidates wealth among a select few, perpetuating societal inequities and impeding progress toward a socialist state. Their commitment to conservative values and resistance to expanded government intervention in socio-economic affairs directly contradicts the principles of Marxist doctrine, which advocate for collective resource ownership, equitable wealth distribution, and extensive governmental involvement in ensuring citizens' welfare.

Communists perceive Trump's followers as formidable barriers—a blockade hindering the necessary social and economic transformations required to pave the way for a socialist state. Their support for policies promoting individualism, deregulation, and unrestricted capitalism directly challenges socialism's core objectives: dismantling class hierarchies, redistributing wealth equitably, and striving for a more egalitarian society.

Communist regimes often silenced opposition through legal and extrajudicial means, drawing parallels to current legal actions against Trump and his supporters, particularly in election disputes. This targeted approach raises concerns of selective prosecution, echoing historical tactics used by totalitarian regimes to eliminate political adversaries. Identifying and pursuing individuals based on their political allegiance mirrors authoritarian strategies employed by communist regimes, casting doubt on justice and potentially suppressing political opposition. The potential misuse of legal measures raises grave concerns about fairness, paralleling historical regimes' manipulation of the legal system to silence dissent.

The handling of people connected to the January 6th Capitol protest has ignited a contentious debate, raising concerns about fairness and the potential for selective prosecution based on political views. While acknowledging the necessity to condemn violence and illegal conduct, a compelling argument has emerged, underscoring what many see as a disproportionate response, particularly towards individuals with certain political affiliations.

A significant number of those facing charges were not directly implicated in violent acts but were primarily accused of trespassing or other minor offenses. The perceived excessiveness of charges against these non-violent participants becomes apparent when compared to the penalties often observed for similar actions in other protest scenarios. The swift and forceful legal reaction following the events of January 6th has given rise to suspicions of bias or political motivations guiding the prosecutions. Critics have pointed to disparities in the handling of analogous protests or civil unrest incidents, notably the violent 2020 riots, raising serious concerns about inconsistent approaches to charging individuals involved.

There is a troubling perception that individuals associated with specific political ideologies or figures faced harsher treatment. This disparity in legal actions suggests a targeted approach towards those aligning with particular political viewpoints, potentially overshadowing the primary objective of addressing any criminal behavior during the event.

Furthermore, the apprehension of potential political repercussions may have influenced the severity of charges against those perceived to support specific political figures or movements, such as Trump or the MAGA movement. This fear could act as a deterrent for others expressing dissent or participating in lawful protests, apprehensive of facing similar legal consequences.

Attendees of the Stop the Steal Capitol protest, many of whom were staunch Trump supporters, were deeply concerned about election integrity in 2020, with the aim of backing Trump and addressing irregularities. The protest symbolized their dedication to a conservative, capitalist America, focusing on expressing dissent over election concerns. Their emphasis was on unity with Trump and the defense of conservative values in politics.

The characterization of the January 6th Capitol protest as an "insurrection" has sparked debates about its portrayal, with some suggesting it is a strategic maneuver employed by certain Democrats to justify severe actions against Trump supporters. Labeling the protest as an "insurrection" framed the incident as a coordinated attack on democracy, casting Trump supporters as a collective threat to the nation's stability and justifying more stringent measures against them.

The use of such a powerful term created a narrative that conflated the actions of a minority with the broader base of Trump supporters, legitimizing rigorous legal actions, investigations, and limitations on their political engagement. This tactic draws parallels with strategies observed in communist regimes, where dissent was labeled as threats to the state to suppress opposition and consolidate power.

In communist governments, dissenters were often categorized as enemies of the government or the people, using strong terms to portray them as threats. Similarly, characterizing the protest as an "insurrection" could be seen as an attempt to demonize Trump supporters and justify harsh measures against them, mirroring the tactics of suppressing dissent in communist regimes.

Moreover, socialist regimes depict dissenters as a collective threat, using sweeping terms to portray dissidents as dangers to the established order. Similarly, painting Trump supporters as a monolithic threat to democracy echoes this tactic and may serve to rally public sentiment against them.

The strategic manipulation of language and narratives to justify actions against political adversaries bears resemblance to strategies observed in communist regimes, where labeling dissent as a threat is a common tool for suppressing opposition.

Labeling the January 6 protest as an "insurrection" served as a basis to invoke the 14th Amendment of the U.S. Constitution, which prohibits individuals engaged in insurrection or rebellion against the Constitution from holding public office. By characterizing the events of January 6 in this manner, certain individuals and lawmakers suggested that it could be used to prevent Donald Trump from seeking public office again.

Section 3 of the 14th Amendment explicitly addresses individuals involved in insurrection or rebellion against the United States, barring them from holding public office unless Congress grants an exemption through a two-thirds vote.

The argument posited that by inciting or encouraging the events on January 6, Trump may have met the criteria for engaging in or supporting an insurrection against the United States. Consequently, some lawmakers viewed this as grounds to disqualify him from holding public office in the future.

In summary, the characterization of the protest as an "insurrection" was strategically used as a foundation to explore legal and constitutional avenues, specifically invoking the 14th Amendment, with the intention of preventing Donald Trump from running for or holding public office again.

The emergence of the "Trump Accountability Project," notably acknowledged by Michael Simon, a former Obama campaign staffer, raises alarms reminiscent of tactics historically associated with communist regimes. The roster, previously accessible on the project's website, categorizes individuals as "known collaborators," encompassing prominent figures from the Trump administration, including political appointees such as Mike Pompeo, Betsy DeVos, Mike Meadows, Kayleigh McEnany, Kellyanne Conway, Steve Bannon, and federal judges nominated by President Trump, such as Brett Kavanaugh and Amy Coney Barrett. The reported involvement of former staffers associated with Democrats Barack Obama and Pete Buttigieg in compiling a list of individuals linked to President Donald Trump and his administration has sparked significant concern and drawn parallels to historical practices of targeting political enemies.

The project's explicit objective to document and monitor individuals associated with the Trump administration, including supporters, government staff, donors, legal professionals, and endorsers, for the purpose of holding them accountable for their roles, echoes historical practices of creating lists to target perceived adversaries. Moreover, public figures such as Jake Tapper of CNN and Jennifer Rubin of the Washington Post, who is of Jewish descent, have proposed measures to hold Trump supporters accountable. Rubin's suggestion to disqualify individuals who questioned the election results or alleged voter fraud from holding public office, corporate board positions, faculty roles, or gaining acceptance into what she termed as "polite society" raises concerns about the potential repercussions and ostracization of individuals based on their political beliefs.

The endorsement of this initiative by Rep. Alexandria Ocasio-Cortez further accentuates concerns regarding the potential use of such lists to limit opportunities or stigmatize individuals based on their political associations. Her emphasis on the importance of future accountability for Trump supporters contributes to the narrative of identifying and potentially penalizing individuals based on their past affiliations or support for a particular political figure.

The similarities drawn between this initiative and historical practices of creating lists to target political enemies or dissenters underscore worries about the erosion of democratic norms. Such actions, reminiscent of past opprssive regimes' practices, raise fundamental questions about freedom of association, expression, and the potential for retribution based on political beliefs.

The "65 Project," reportedly led by prominent figures such as leftist author, David Brock, and former Democratic Senate Majority leader Tom Daschle, has generated significant unease by specifically targeting attorneys who supported former President Donald Trump, particularly those involved in challenging the 2020 election results. This agenda, seeking to single out lawyers based on their political affiliations, evokes disturbing echoes of historical tactics employed to suppress dissent. The strategy, centered on attorneys' political leanings, directly challenges the principles of fairness and impartiality integral to the legal profession. Lawyers have an ethical duty to represent clients regardless of their political beliefs, and any attempts to intimidate or penalize them for taking on politically sensitive cases strike at the core of the right to legal representation and the sanctity of the rule of law.

David Brock's involvement in "The 65 Project," known for his targeting of conservatives, adds a layer of complexity. His filing of bar complaints against figures such as Senator Ted Cruz (R-TX), Jenna Ellis (a Trump attorney), and Joe DiGenova (another Trump attorney) raises concerns about the potential misuse of legal mechanisms for political retribution. Targeting attorneys based on their clients and political affiliations undermines the legal profession's foundational principles, which prioritize the right to legal representation and lawyers' advocacy for their clients without fear of reprisal.

Entities such as Media Matters, linked to David Brock, are actively focusing attention on attorneys associated with Trump, indicating a concerted effort to retaliate against those holding differing political views. Legal professionals such as Jenna Ellis, Cleta Mitchell, Joe DiGenova, and Boris Epshteyn have faced alleged orchestrated legal attacks, with reports suggesting that an undisclosed dark money group affiliated with prominent Democratic figures plans to file complaints and air advertisements targeting over 100 attorneys involved in Trump's post-election lawsuits. This tactic appears aimed at dissuading legal professionals from future election result challenges, potentially impacting the democratic process itself.

Furthermore, the targeting of attorneys, including Arizona Attorney General Mark Brnovich and Texas Attorney General Ken Paxton, through bar complaints and legal actions, reflects a troubling trend of weaponizing legal processes against political adversaries. The misuse of bar complaints to silence opposition undermines the integrity of the legal system and instills fear among attorneys handling politically sensitive cases.

The case involving Jonathan Mosely, an attorney representing January 6 protesters, whose license was revoked by the Virginia State Bar, heightens concerns about attorneys being singled out based on their clients and political affiliations. Mosely's involvement in cases linked to the events of January 6 made him a focal point for scrutiny.

While bar complaints play a crucial role in upholding ethical standards within the legal sphere and are designed to address genuine breaches of professional conduct, when these complaints focus on an attorney's clients or political connections rather than legitimate ethical concerns, they become tools wielded to suppress political opposition or divergent viewpoints. The revocation of Mosely's license by the Virginia State Bar raises concerns that his involvement in cases related to a contentious event became grounds for disciplinary action, rather than stemming from any concrete evidence of ethical misconduct.

The California State Bar's investigation into John Eastman stemmed from his involvement in legal activities following the 2020 presidential election. Eastman, a prominent conservative lawyer and former legal advisor to President Trump, became a focal point due to his role in advocating for legal challenges to the election results. Specifically, his legal opinions and representation of President Trump's claims regarding election irregularities drew substantial attention.

The aftermath of the investigation led to substantial consequences for Eastman's career, culminating in his resignation from Chapman University's law school. This step underscored the significant impact legal inquiries can have on an individual's professional standing and livelihood.

The investigation into Eastman's conduct sparks concerns about the complex relationship between legal inquiries and potential political motivations. Such investigations might be used to target individuals holding dissenting political opinions or affiliations. This dynamic poses a looming threat, deterring individuals from engaging in open discourse, advocacy, or even legitimate legal representation due to fears of career and reputational damage.

Furthermore, Eastman's case initiates broader discussions about fundamental principles such as free speech, academic autonomy, and the right to legal representation. This investigation transcends individual circumstances, delving into deeper debates concerning the safeguarding of individual rights within academic and legal spheres.

The targeting of Eastman based on his political associations raises considerable concerns about the potential politicization of legal processes, which undermines the core tenets of impartiality and fairness within the legal profession. This situation prompts a critical examination of the extent to which political considerations might influence legal inquiries, potentially jeopardizing the principles of due process, equitable treatment, and the right to legal representation regardless of political beliefs.

Sidney Powell's immersion in the post-2020 election fallout thrust her into a tumultuous landscape where legal practitioners navigated treacherous waters amid intense political polarization.

Her zealous pursuit of legal challenges in the wake of the election, notably tied to claims of election irregularities and fraud, drew substantial attention. Powell became a focal point of controversy, facing not just scrutiny but also a barrage of multiple civil lawsuits and even recommendations for sanctions from the State Bar of Texas. These repercussions were largely perceived as consequences for her alignment with President Trump and her efforts to contest the election results.

The indispensable role of lawyers in upholding democratic processes is evident in cases challenging election results. Attorneys play a pivotal role in representing clients and addressing electoral concerns within the legal framework. However, targeting legal professionals involved in election-related cases poses a grave threat to the democratic process itself.

Preserving the ethical integrity of the legal realm is paramount, ensuring that disciplinary actions or license revocations are not used as tools to suppress legal representation in politically sensitive cases. Upholding the legal system's integrity implies safeguarding attorneys' rights to represent clients without facing retribution solely based on the nature of their cases or their political alignments.

Targeting lawyers engaged in cases challenging election results poses a significant threat to the democratic process. It stifles legitimate legal avenues for addressing electoral concerns, ultimately undermining the system's ability to ensure free and fair elections—a cornerstone of any healthy democracy.

Aggressive tactics aimed at silencing dissent, particularly within the legal sphere, extend beyond inhibiting free expression—they threaten democratic engagement. Manipulating legal mechanisms to target political adversaries mirrors strategies employed by communist regimes, eroding the fairness and impartiality vital for a democratic society. Such actions not only undermine the legal profession's credibility but also pose a risk of diminishing civic participation and public trust in the system.

Intimidating legal professionals engaged in election fraud cases undermines their ability to ensure electoral fairness and address potential irregularities. The repression of attorneys sends a dangerous message, potentially deterring future legal challenges and undermining the system's ability to ensure free and fair elections. Such actions erode public trust in the legal system, impacting future participation in legal challenges and democratic checks and balances.

Today's socio-political landscape exhibits a troubling trend: The systematic marginalization of conservative voices, often disguised under the semblance of countering extremism or protecting national security. This trend involves labeling certain right-leaning principles or expressions as "extremist" or "dangerous narratives." Such categorization mirrors historical communist tactics used to vilify dissent, leading to potential social ostracization or punitive actions against those with differing opinions.

A chorus of voices, including former Representative Tulsi Gabbard, Representative Chip Roy (R-TX), Representative Claudia Tenney (R-NY), and conservative podcast host, Liz Wheeler, have raised alarm about concerning trends in the U.S. political landscape. These figures have articulated significant apprehensions about the manipulation of governmental power, concerns over the weaponization of federal agencies, and the politicization of law enforcement and investigative bodies. Their collective unease paints a troubling picture, underscoring fears of suppression of dissent, manipulation of public opinion, and the consequences for those challenging established political narratives.

Former Representative Tulsi Gabbard argued that the biggest threat to democracy is not Trump supporters but entrenched elites in Washington who have manipulated the government. Gabbard suggested that these elites, in collaboration with corporate media, aim to suppress dissent, manipulate public opinion, and hinder Donald Trump's 2024 presidential bid.

Representative Chip Roy (R-TX) has voiced concerns about the Biden administration's use of governmental power to suppress citizens, asserting that it has transformed the US government into an oppressive force, employing its police power for such purposes.

Representative Tenney has expressed worries about federal agencies being "weaponized," sparking ongoing debates about the potential politicization of law enforcement and investigative bodies. These actions, along with IRS investigations, raise concerns among the public, even among those who might not support Trump but value freedom.

Liz Wheeler, a conservative podcast host, has criticized the White House for the politicization of the

Department of Homeland Security (DHS). In a tweet, she raised concerns about what she perceived as the politicization of the DHS, highlighting potential consequences for dissenting voices. She tweeted, "Welcome to your communist future. You may not criticize the government or you will be imprisoned."[38] This paints a worrying picture of potential repercussions for those challenging the prevailing political narrative.

Representative Marjorie Taylor Greene (R-GA) has been a vocal advocate for the removal of key government officials, pointing fingers at figures such as Attorney General Merrick Garland, FBI Director Christopher Wray, and US Attorney Matthew Graves. Greene accuses these officials of not only neglecting their duties but also of wielding their positions as political tools, targeting those seen as adversaries to Joe Biden's administration.

Greene's allegations are rooted in specific actions taken by these officials. For instance, she claims that Christopher Wray led a "war" against Biden's opponents, suggesting an abuse of power and partisanship within the FBI. Furthermore, she accuses US Attorney Matthew Graves of unfairly targeting Capitol protestors, raising concerns about the infringement of their rights under his watch.

She has particularly singled out Attorney General Merrick Garland, accusing him of using the FBI as a tool to serve Biden's personal agenda. One of her main points of contention involves the authorization of a search at Trump's home, which Greene claims was an attempt to derail any

---

[38] Moore, Mark. "DHS warns against mistrust of US government in latest terror bulletin." *New York Post*, 9 Feb. 2022, nypost.com/ 2022/02/09/homeland-security-labels-conspiracy-theories-a-terror-threat/.

potential return to public office, casting doubts on the impartiality and motives behind the action.

By initiating articles of impeachment against Garland, Greene took a firm stance against partisan bias and actions undermining public trust. These officials have overstepped their bounds, manipulating their positions to influence political landscapes and stifle opposition. The push for their removal reflects Greene's concern for the abuse of power within high-ranking government offices and its potential impact on the democratic process.

In the current socio-political landscape, there is an unmistakable tension brewing between the rise of Marxist ideologies and those supporting traditional capitalist values. The next chapter delves into the seismic shifts in societal paradigms, where Marxist principles, advocating for collective ownership and socio-economic equality, are gaining prominence. Simultaneously, staunch defenders of the established constitutional republic are pushing back against the threat to individual freedoms, free-market capitalism, and limited government intervention.

Chapter 8

The Gathering Storm

Over the past few years, the socio-political landscape of the United States has undergone a significant change, departing notably from its longstanding adherence to constitutional principles and capitalist traditions. This shift in the national ethos has seen a notable rise in the prevalence and advocacy of socialist ideals, setting off intense debates that reverberate across the entire political spectrum. The emergence of these Marxist principles has fundamentally altered the dialogue around governance, economics, and societal values, introducing a new paradigm that challenges the established norms and structures of American society. This transformation has become a focal point, sparking deep-seated concern about the country's identity, its future trajectory, and the essential values upon which its systems are built.

The burgeoning influence of communism represents an alarming challenge to the fundamental principles of the constitutional republic. These ideologies advocate for sweeping changes in property rights and economic structures, mirroring disturbing echoes of the authoritarian practices found in historical Marxist regimes. The looming specter of a potential communist ascendancy foretells a cataclysmic political and economic upheaval. This grim prospect entails the drastic elimination of private property rights and the imposition of state ownership over critical economic assets, resulting in a radical restructuring of the economic landscape. Such a seismic shift would reverberate across industries, triggering chaotic disruptions in trade dynamics, fundamental changes in labor policies, and significant realignments in investment patterns. The ripple effects would inundate businesses and the job market, unleashing a wave of uncertainty and instability.

A government under such a regime would likely heavily prioritize control and surveillance, resonating with characteristics reminiscent of past communist regimes. Similar to historical instances, this could involve pervasive control, censorship, and restrictions on freedom of speech and media. The rise in surveillance to monitor dissent could become a prevalent and alarming facet of this system.

The erosion of property rights and the move toward communal ownership and wealth redistribution, echoing communist ideologies, raises substantial concerns. Departing from the traditional American emphasis on individualism, this shift, encapsulated by Klaus Schwab's notion of "You will own nothing and be happy," sparks concerns about potential losses in individual rights and economic transformations. This alteration may undermine capitalism and individualism, potentially sacrificing them in the pursuit of collective "happiness."

This sentiment of "You will own nothing and be happy" is increasingly visible through platforms such as Uber, Airbnb, and co-working spaces in the USA. While some hail this as a positive shift toward shared ownership and resource efficiency, others argue that it chips away at values of personal responsibility and ownership, making individuals reliant on external entities, even for basic needs. The emphasis on environmental sustainability is viewed by some as a disguise for curtailing personal freedoms and fostering dependency. Critics are deeply concerned about the implications of a future where individual ownership diminishes in favor of collective happiness.

The concerns raised here shed light on the looming risk of power being centralized among entities that govern access to resources. Traditional ownership has empowered people to control their possessions and determine their use. However, a shift toward an access-oriented model may strip away individual autonomy and decision-making, fostering reliance on intermediaries who could infringe upon personal freedoms and deepen societal divides. This transition could leave people vulnerable to manipulation by those who control resource access, jeopardizing independent decision-making. Moreover, this change might unsettle long-term stability, as ownership offers a sense of security, while reliance on access introduces uncertainties about resource availability, potentially causing anxiety and demanding constant adaptation. Shared ownership models might not consistently align with sustainability aims, potentially encouraging overconsumption and wastefulness. Furthermore, embracing an access-based model could lead to heightened data collection and surveillance, igniting concerns regarding privacy infringements and the potential misuse of personal information.

Communist societies historically favor collective objectives over individual freedoms, where the government's central authority often restricts personal autonomy. Drawing parallels to certain occurrences in the USA, the imposition of travel restrictions amid the COVID-19 pandemic sparked worries about encroaching upon personal liberties. The acceptance of these measures might normalize extensive government control over citizens' movements, creating a precedent for ongoing interventions that gradually erode individual freedoms. This normalization could set a troubling precedent, potentially laying the groundwork for further encroachments on personal liberties in the future, fundamentally altering the landscape of individual freedoms within the country.

During the Soviet era, the ideological rigidity of the communist regime in the USSR stifled diverse perspectives, effectively limiting intellectual discourse to a narrow range of acceptable ideologies. The government wielded immense control over individual liberties and movement, imposing mechanisms such as internal passports and residence permits to surveil and regulate both local and international travel. These measures significantly restricted citizens' mobility, curtailing not only international travel, but also impeding their movements within their own country. These stringent controls were justified as essential for maintaining social stability and reinforcing the government's grip on the populace, serving as a tool to enforce conformity to state ideologies.

Possession of internal passports was obligatory for every citizen in the Soviet Union, tightly governing and restricting movement within the country's borders. Individuals found lacking valid internal passports faced severe repercussions. Those caught without proper documentation risked arrest, detention, or legal penalties. In some cases, being without an internal passport could lead to imprisonment or deportation to the Gulags—forced labor camps notorious for their brutal conditions. The Gulags housed political dissidents and various offenders, subjecting them to grueling labor under harsh circumstances. The absence of the required internal passport was not a minor infraction but could result in severe legal consequences, including imprisonment in these oppressive labor camps.

The concept of the "15-minute city" in the United States is provoking discussions regarding its potential impact on fundamental rights, particularly the freedom of movement and the liberty to travel. At its core, the right to travel encompasses the autonomy to decide where one resides and works. While the 15-minute city model aims to reduce commute times, the extensive regulations endorsing this concept could limit the flexibility individuals have in choosing their place of residence. The stringent zoning laws promoting life within these compact urban zones might confine inhabitants to activities solely within their immediate surroundings. This narrowing of movement could curtail the freedom to participate in a diverse array of activities beyond the designated vicinity, potentially constraining personal choices and limiting opportunities for broader exploration outside the confined area.

The growing traction of the 15-minute city concept sparks apprehensions regarding potential shifts toward rigid regulations on movement, reminiscent of historical regimes imposing strict limitations on citizens' mobility. This localized living approach, if stringent zoning regulations were imposed within the model, might confine movement beyond designated zones. Such regulations could impinge on the freedom to select one's residence and limit exploration or engagement in activities outside of specified areas, echoing historical internal passport systems' limitations.

Simultaneously, the introduction of a national digital ID system raises valid concerns about privacy infringement and potential government overreach. While the system initially aims to streamline identification processes and bolster security, its evolution could facilitate extensive surveillance and control over citizens' movements. Centralized databases containing comprehensive personal data might lead to heightened monitoring of individuals' daily activities, transactions, and online behavior. This intensified data collection could erode privacy rights, granting governments unprecedented insight into citizens' lives. Such a national digital ID could become a prelude to an internal passport system, where government scrutiny and regulation of individuals' movements and activities could increase significantly. This system might limit mobility, bar access to services or locations, and potentially subject non-compliers to discrimination or penalties.

United States' citizens have a fundamental right to travel within the country, upheld by the Supreme Court as an essential facet of individual freedom. Landmark cases such as *Shapiro v. Thompson*, 394 U.S. 618 (1969) underscore the unconditioned and personal nature of this right. It prohibits penalties imposed by one state on citizens from another and protects against unjust hindrances from being placed on individuals seeking to establish themselves in new locales. While emergency situations might warrant temporary movement restrictions, it is crucial to ensure that they remain proportional and temporary, avoiding lasting patterns of constraint. Any policies that substantially infringe upon the right to travel would face legal challenges, and courts would evaluate the balance between governmental interests and individual rights.

As previously discussed, some Marxist governments have implemented policies that restrict travel for various reasons. These limitations on citizens' mobility were often imposed through measures such as exit visas, border controls, or travel restrictions. The rationale behind such constraints has varied, encompassing motives such as maintaining state control, preventing dissent, or safeguarding against brain drain—where skilled individuals leaving the country might adversely affect the economy or national interests.

Contemporary debates surrounding environmental concerns intersect with discussions about limiting carbon emissions, particularly in the realm of transportation, especially automobiles. The desire to reduce carbon emissions, primarily attributed to vehicles, is rooted in their claimed contribution to greenhouse gas emissions and subsequent climate change.

Policies aimed at reducing emissions, such as enforcing fuel efficiency standards, implementing carbon taxes, or incentivizing the adoption of electric vehicles, primarily aim to curb environmental damage. However, a contrasting viewpoint suggests that these measures might also serve as veiled attempts to limit personal vehicle usage, potentially encroaching upon people's freedom to travel by car.

Stringent regulations on emissions could be construed as efforts to discourage personal car ownership and usage. Such measures might steer individuals toward alternative transportation modes or even diminish their overall travel. If these environmental policies become overly aggressive or restrictive, they could curtail personal mobility and infringe upon people's autonomy in choosing their preferred mode of transportation, and thereby impinging upon their right to travel.

Marxist ideas, infiltrating American society and policy, deeply unsettle proponents of individual liberty.

Socialists herald these policies as remedies for social disparities and essential service provision. Yet, looming are concerns about dire consequences and the erosion of personal freedoms.

The ascendance of far-left ideologies, tethered to Marxist principles, alarms a significant populace. This Marxist takeover agitates the fabric of American democracy, casting doubt on elections and democratic institutions. These ideologies wield palpable influence, challenging traditional American values through policy and cultural shifts.

While socialist notions aim to remedy social gaps and fortify services, critics fear their encroachment on personal liberties. The specter of heightened governmental control, synonymous with progressive ideologies, threatens individual freedoms and augments the state's authority in disquieting ways.

The debate concerning Marxist ideals transcends economics, probing broader societal anxieties. Some dread the prospect of adopting these ideologies, fearing that it will disrupt societal norms and governance, potentially undermining the bedrock principles of the American republic.

Author Mike Adams issued a stark warning, highlighting an imminent shift from the American Republic towards a communist United Socialist States of America (USSA). In his vision, this transition poses a dire threat to personal freedoms, painting a haunting picture of an impending reality marked by oppressive collectivism and individual subjugation under a totalitarian regime. Adams foresees a trajectory leading to the complete annihilation of cherished liberties.

His portrayal of this grim future encompasses a landscape rife with enforced vaccinations, draconian lockdowns curtailing movement, stifling of free speech, and compromised electoral processes. The specter of authoritarian control looms large, promising a reality where individual autonomy and fundamental rights wither away in the face of an encroaching, suffocating system.

Whole Foods CEO, John Mackey, has expressed concerns about the growing influence of socialists and their potential threat to personal liberties. He believes that socialists are gaining power, and this has raised worries about the liberties he has taken for granted throughout his life being under threat. He warned that "a lot of the liberties that I've taken for granted most of my life, I think, are under threat…I feel like socialists are taking over."[39]

Under socialist systems, an escalation in government intervention and control often paves the way for the erosion of individual liberties. Advocates of socialism frequently push for expanded government oversight across various societal domains. While their purported aim is to foster a fairer and more equitable system, the actual execution of these policies frequently backfires, resulting in suppression of personal freedoms.

As the government assumes an augmented role in supervising economic activities, social welfare, and resource allocation, power becomes increasingly centralized within

---

[39] Smith, E.J. "WHOLE FOODS CEO: 'Socialists Are Taking Over'." *Your Survival Guy*, 11 Aug. 2022, www.yoursurvivalguy.com/personal-security/the-great-reset/whole-foods-ceo-socialists-are-taking-over/?utm_source=MeWe&utm_medium=Social&utm_campaign=8-11-22&utm_id=Social.

the state apparatus. This consolidation of authority tends to encroach upon the freedoms individuals hold dear. For instance, extensive governmental control over industries or private enterprises hampers entrepreneurial freedom and stifles innovation. Decision-making transitions from individuals and businesses to centralized authorities, stifling creativity and initiative in the process.

Moreover, in the pursuit of equality and social justice, Marxist regimes often impose stringent regulations that curtail personal freedoms. These restrictions might manifest as limitations on freedom of speech or expression, enforced to maintain ideological conformity and suppress dissent or alternate perspectives that challenge the dominant narrative.

Additionally, heightened government control over vital services such as healthcare or education, while intended to ensure universal access, severely restricts personal choices. People may find their autonomy diminished in selecting preferred services or providers, as options become standardized or dictated by state mandates.

Furthermore, socialist systems frequently entail substantial redistribution of wealth through taxation and extensive social programs. While ostensibly aimed at addressing socioeconomic disparities, this approach can severely disincentivize individual effort and hard work. Excessive taxation diminishes the rewards of personal success, potentially leading to a dearth of incentives for innovation and productivity. In extreme cases, this hampers overall societal progress, stagnating growth and development.

Roger Daltrey, the lead singer of the British rock band, The Who, has expressed criticism towards the woke generation and warned about the failures of communism in the Soviet Union and other countries. He lamented. "[I]t's terrifying, the miserable world [the woke generation] is going to create for themselves."[40]

Daltrey's comments underscore grave apprehensions regarding the current societal landscape and the potential fallout from the ascent of cultural Marxism. He expresses deep concerns about the zealous pursuit of social justice and activism by the woke generation, warning of potential unforeseen repercussions that could significantly impact individual freedoms and the global order.

Drawing parallels to the failures of communism, Daltrey delivers a cautionary message about the dangers inherent in Marxist ideologies. He emphasizes the historical track record of such extremist beliefs, highlighting the myriad risks they pose. These include the rise of authoritarian regimes, economic inefficiencies, and widespread human rights abuses, serving as poignant reminders of the pitfalls of misguided idealism.

Daltrey's position accentuates the urgent need to learn from history's lessons, advocating for caution in embracing ideologies that might curtail individual freedoms and sow discord. His remarks serve as a stark warning against the consequences of unchecked ideological fervor, stressing the vital importance of safeguarding individual liberties.

---

[40] Mastrangel, Alana. "The Who's Roger Daltrey Slams 'The Woke Generation': They're Creating a 'Miserable World for Themselves,' 'We've Seen the Communist System Fail.'" *Breitbart*, 7 May 2021, www.breitbart.com/entertainment/2021/05/07/the-whos-roger-daltrey-slams-the-woke-generation-theyre-creating-a-miserable-world-for-themselves-weve-seen-the-communist-system-fail/.

Seeking to dismantle the core concept of America, be it through revolutionary or subversive methods, would undoubtedly encounter formidable resistance, fostering deep societal divisions. The American identity is intricately woven into the historical, cultural, and social tapestry of the nation. It is a fabric held together by principles that generations have embraced, revered, and defended.

A significant number of citizens hold steadfast to these principles, recognizing their pivotal role in shaping the nation's trajectory. There is a collective acknowledgment that preserving democratic ideals and upholding capitalist values stands as a linchpin for safeguarding individual freedoms, propelling innovation, and sustaining economic prosperity. These principles are fundamental pillars upon which the American identity stands.

Embedded within the American ethos lies a profound commitment to individual autonomy and the pursuit of happiness through the avenue of free enterprise and personal initiative. It is this ethos that has fueled generations of entrepreneurial spirit, fostering a climate where innovation thrives, and dreams are pursued.

The American identity is an amalgamation of shared beliefs that have propelled the nation forward. It embodies a reverence for freedom and a commitment to individual agency. Attempts to dismantle or undermine these foundational aspects risk igniting profound societal ruptures, as they strike at the very heart of what defines the American essence. It is this collective ethos that unites Americans across diverse backgrounds, underscoring a shared commitment to the principles that have woven the nation's intricate fabric for over two centuries.

Amidst a mounting Marxist influence, various groups and individuals have mobilized. Heightened concerns revolve around a surge in government influence, encroachments on personal liberties, and an escalating divergence in fundamental ideologies. A palpable unease is brewing among many individuals who perceive deliberate government actions as contributing to the country's decline. This surge of activism has catalyzed the emergence of conservative media outlets, grassroots movements, and political campaigns, all banding together to reclaim and fortify traditional American values.

This resurgence of activism marks a pivotal moment in American society, coinciding with a surge in polarization that threatens national unity. This widening division has manifested through intense debates and emerging rifts within communities, hinting at a fragile cohesion within the nation.

An alarming aspect of this increasing discord is the rise in violence targeting conservatives and Republicans. Aggressive acts have garnered attention in public demonstrations and across social media platforms, amplifying the widening political gap. This escalation of hostility from certain factions in the left-wing community towards conservatives exacerbates existing tensions, fostering an atmosphere of heightened distrust and unease.

The events surrounding Kyle Rittenhouse during the Kenosha riots in August 2020 were fraught with a series of escalating encounters, shaped by numerous contributing factors. Rittenhouse, a 17-year-old from Illinois, ventured into Kenosha amidst the turmoil following Jacob Blake's police shooting. Armed with a rifle, his aim was to protect property and provide medical aid, but the night unfolded into a string of clashes between him and protesters, characterized by several physical altercations.

Amidst the chaos, Rittenhouse asserted self-defense when confronted by violent rioters in the midst of the turmoil. Accounts suggested attempts to disarm Rittenhouse and threats against his life by left-wing agitators. In these intense moments, Rittenhouse discharged his weapon, resulting in harm to purported Antifa members who were attacking him.

The shootings during the Kenosha riots resulted in injuries and fatalities, involving Joseph Rosenbaum, Anthony Huber, and Gaige Grosskreutz. Joseph Rosenbaum, 36 at the time, was fatally shot during the unrest. Anthony Huber, 26, was shot and killed under circumstances suggesting an attempt to disarm Rittenhouse. Gaige Grosskreutz, also 26, sustained injuries but survived the incident.

Subsequently, Rittenhouse faced charges, including homicide and reckless endangerment, with his defense centered around claims of acting in self-defense. His trial became a focal point for debates on self-defense laws, Second Amendment rights, and the broader socio-political context of protests and civil unrest in the United States, culminating in his acquittal.

While Rittenhouse underwent legal scrutiny, others involved in the altercations were not charged or prosecuted, sparking criticism and debate. The disparate legal outcomes prompted concerns about unequal justice, advocating for legal repercussions against those engaging with Rittenhouse that night.

The aftermath of Rittenhouse's trial highlighted deep-seated tensions and the potential for similar confrontations in the future. Ongoing societal divisions, exacerbated by political and ideological rifts, continue to incubate conflicts, erupting during periods of unrest. The prevalence of protests over contentious issues amplifies the likelihood of clashes between opposing groups or individuals, potentially resulting in similar confrontations in the future.

America stands at a pivotal moment, teetering on the edge of ideological divergence between conservatives steadfast in preserving the Constitutional Republic and progressives advocating for an increased socialist agenda, hurtling toward an inevitable collision.

Conservatives firmly stand for preserving the Constitutional Republic, prioritizing individual freedoms, limited government intervention, and upholding the rule of law. They champion the Constitution's values, emphasizing individual liberties, free markets, and the separation of powers crucial to American governance. Concerned about socialist policies, conservatives fear they might erode freedoms, stifle markets, and undermine the nation's traditional values. They see increased government intervention as potentially limiting personal liberties and hindering economic growth.

In contrast, progressives advocate for a socialist approach, advocating expanded government involvement across societal realms. They aim to tackle socioeconomic disparities through policies promoting income equality, strengthening social welfare programs, and increasing government intervention in sectors such as healthcare and education. Their vision leans towards a more significant state role to secure social justice and redistribute wealth, intending to address perceived inequalities. Leftists argue that the current system sustains inequalities and social injustices, supporting a more inclusive society through socialist-inspired policies.

While political disparities have long been woven into the nation's history, recent decades have witnessed an alarming surge in partisanship. This surge widened ideological gaps, distinctly dividing progressives and conservatives. These divisions are widely recognized as a potential crisis fueled by several catalysts, notably the rise of identity politics, increasing economic disparities, and the profound impact of social justice movements. Together, these elements pose a grave threat to national unity and stability, heightening concerns about the country's trajectory.

The rise of identity politics in public discourse emphasizes group identities over shared national values, amplifying societal fractures and entrenching ideological differences. This focus erodes the middle ground of bipartisan cooperation, overshadowing broader principles and leading to a fragmented societal landscape. This intensification of identity-based politics exacerbates rifts between opposing ideologies, hindering efforts to find common ground and fostering a polarized landscape lacking in dialogue and understanding.

Economic disparities have played a pivotal role, fostering feelings of disenfranchisement and deepening divisions among various socioeconomic strata. The perceived inequality in wealth distribution and opportunities has fueled discontent, driving ideological divisions and further fracturing the nation.

Furthermore, while social justice movements ostensibly advocate for inclusivity and equality, their aim to champion societal changes has sown seeds of controversy. This impact on social norms and values has sparked ideological tensions, exacerbating discord within various societal spheres.

This ideological conflict spans various arenas, from congressional policy debates to societal discussions on critical issues such as healthcare, taxation, and social justice. The widening divide between these ideological factions has heightened tensions, with each side perceiving the other's vision as a looming threat to the nation's future.

This clash between conservatives upholding the Constitutional Republic and progressives advocating for more socialist measures represents a profound ideological divide—a struggle over the soul of the nation. It encompasses contrasting visions for the role of government, individual freedoms, and the trajectory of American society. This impending clash epitomizes these competing visions, positioned to shape the country's path in the years ahead.

Amidst mounting tension, a prevailing sentiment resonates among many Americans—an unwavering determination to safeguard their freedoms. This shared resolve echoes across diverse segments of the population, signifying a collective commitment to defend enduring values integral to the American identity. Many stand prepared to fiercely defend these cherished principles against foreign or domestic threats. This resilience and determination epitomize the enduring spirit of Americans—a steadfast commitment to safeguard the foundational freedoms upon which the nation was built.

Mark Brnovich, Attorney General of Arizona, staunchly opposes communism in the USA, and he is determined to take immediate action to guide the nation's future in a direction that safeguards its fundamental values and principles. He declared, "If we don't have this fight now, I don't want to look back 25 or 50 years from now and have people ask, 'What did you do when the United States was becoming a socialist or Marxist country?' I want to be able to say, 'I stopped it.'"[41]

The intensifying conflict between staunch capitalists and fervent communists has become a pressing challenge to national unity, fueling deep-seated resentment and creating what many term a "perfect storm." Although political divisions have long been ingrained in the United States, the looming specter of communism has amplified apprehensions about the prospect of a future civil conflict.

This escalating ideological clash between advocates of capitalism and proponents of socialism has led to a profound polarization across societal and political landscapes. The fundamental differences in economic and social ideologies have exacerbated existing divisions, stirring heated debates, and fostering a climate of growing animosity.

The concern stems from the historical context, where the ideological chasm between capitalism and communism has led to conflicts and upheavals in various parts of the world. The fear of a similar division taking root within the United States, undermining its unity and stability, is a cause for significant worry among many.

Moreover, the fervor surrounding these opposing ideologies has reached a point where the collision threatens not just political discourse but the very fabric of societal cohesion. The entrenchment of these conflicting viewpoints risks further alienating factions, potentially leading to heightened tensions and, in extreme cases, social discord and unrest. Finding common ground amidst such ideological disparity becomes increasingly challenging, raising concerns

---

[41] "Diamond and Silk." "Letter From 41 Legislators from Multiple States Call for Nationwide Audit & Decertification." 7 Oct. 2021, www.diamondandsilkinc.com/tabletalknews/tlk4gz3whncfhj4-seman-hgadt-s4pbz-wapxk-ng7sx-a4lsn.

about the ability to navigate this turbulent terrain without fracturing the nation's unity.

Over half of Trump voters and 41 percent of Biden voters indicate support for the notion of blue or red states seceding from the Union. Notably, this sentiment intensifies within the Southern Republican demographic, where a striking 66 percent express favor towards Southern states exiting the United States. These statistics illuminate a pervasive discontent with the current state of national governance, transcending party lines and underscoring the depth of political fractures within the electorate.

These figures paint a vivid picture of dissatisfaction cutting across partisan affiliations, emphasizing the profound disillusionment prevailing among voters from both political camps. The considerable support for the idea of states breaking away from the Union signifies a troubling lack of confidence in the efficacy of the current governance structure and a profound yearning for change.

The noteworthy endorsement of secessionist ideas among a significant portion of voters—be it Trump or Biden supporters—serves as a stark reminder of the pronounced divisions within the nation. It reflects the prevailing frustration with national governance, pointing towards a growing sentiment that the current political establishment is unable to effectively address the concerns of a substantial segment of the population.

These statistics spotlight the urgent need for a comprehensive reassessment of the nation's governance and political landscape. They underscore a critical juncture where the nation grapples not only with political polarization but also with a collective desire for a governance paradigm that addresses the diverse needs and perspectives of its citizens.

An illustrative case of this discontent is Texas state lawmaker Representative Kyle Biedermann, who aims to propose a secession referendum. He argues that the federal government no longer reflects the values held by Texans. Biedermann's initiative to introduce legislation for a referendum, giving Texans the opportunity to vote on reinstating Texas as an autonomous republic, showcases the transformation of political discontent into tangible steps.

His proposed action signifies a tangible manifestation of the deepening rift between state and federal ideologies. By advocating for the possibility of Texas becoming an independent country once more, Biedermann underscores the growing sentiment of disillusionment with the current federal governance structure among certain politicians.

Moreover, Biedermann's endeavor represents a broader trend wherein political dissatisfaction is evolving beyond mere rhetoric. It is a move towards taking concrete measures to address grievances and assert state autonomy. This initiative, although currently symbolic, signifies a significant shift in the political landscape, signifying the potential trajectory of discontented states seeking greater autonomy.

English broadcaster and reporter, Piers Morgan, expressed his concerns about the United States' divisive state and the erosion of unity. He lamented, "RIP, the United States of America. The country's name must go, right? I mean, there comes a point where America is so patently DIS-united that it's no longer appropriate to call itself 'United…' If Americans can't even come together on July 4 to celebrate the day the nation was formed, and many choose to denigrate the US anthem and flag, how can the nation still call itself the United States? I don't want the USA to die. I want it to live up to the spirit of its name. So, stop p*ssin' on the red, white and blue. Or call it the Disunited States of America and be done with it."[42]

Morgan highlighted the glaring absence of unity, notably palpable during significant events such as July 4th celebrations, where stark disagreements and disrespect toward national symbols emerged. He stressed that these divisions have penetrated to such an extent that even symbolic occasions meant to honor the nation's birth are tainted by discord.

The prevailing political landscape is marked by fervent ideological clashes that prioritize group identities, fostering a sense of tribalism and at times eclipsing individual rights while reinforcing allegiance to bureaucratic structures. This climate has engendered heightened social turbulence within the United States, stemming from mounting political polarization. The widening chasms and ideological disparities among contrasting factions have exacerbated tensions, intensifying the divide. Firmly entrenched convictions and an enduring "us versus them" mindset perpetuate this polarization.

This approach centered on identity holds the inherent risk of fracturing societal cohesion, paving the way for potential destabilization. The escalating emphasis on group identities over shared values and unity bears semblance to broader strategies often associated with communism. The elevation of group identity above national unity aligns with ideologies that historically promote division and societal fragmentation, posing a risk to the fabric of the nation.

---

[42] Jones, Kipp. "As Left Attacks July Fourth, Piers Morgan Issues Fiery Warning from Great Britain." *The Western Journal*, 7 July 2021, www.westernjournal.com/left-attacks-july-fourth-piers-morgan-issues-fiery-warning-great-britain/?utm_source=mewe&utm_medium=westernjournalism&utm_content=2021-07-07&utm_campaign=manualpost.

The expanding chasm of discord within the United States has become an intricate web of deeply entrenched beliefs and perceptions, making the quest for common ground a daunting task. The complexity of this challenge arises from multifaceted ideological disparities that have evolved and solidified over time.

The very nature of these divisions—rooted in fundamental beliefs, societal values, and interpretations of core principles—contributes to the intricate fabric of discord. They are deeply ingrained convictions that have shaped individuals' identities and ideologies over generations. This profound attachment to differing viewpoints and the emotional investment behind these perspectives significantly complicates the process of finding common ground.

Additionally, the proliferation of echo chambers, reinforced by social media algorithms and selective exposure to information, has fortified ideological bubbles. These insular spaces intensify polarization, fostering a sense of detachment from opposing viewpoints and, in turn, impeding efforts to bridge these divides. Furthermore, past attempts at reconciliation have often faced hurdles due to systemic issues, deep-seated distrust, and the entrenchment of ideological stances.

In the wake of escalating tensions and fears surrounding the potential for widespread civil unrest, a growing contingent has called for stringent gun control measures. These voices often surface amid concerns that the country may be hurtling toward a significant internal conflict. One suggested tactic to address this is disarmament —a move aimed at tightening regulations on public access to firearms. This could involve implementing stricter gun control laws, mandating buyback programs, or enforcing tighter oversight on firearm sales. The goal is to mitigate perceived risks associated with an extensively armed populace during periods of heightened volatility and potential conflict.

However, this push for disarmament has been met with robust resistance. Opponents argue that such measures encroach upon the fundamental rights outlined in the Second Amendment, potentially eroding the rights of individuals to bear arms.

The proposed strategies have sparked intense debates regarding personal freedoms and the extent of governmental intervention. Detractors of stringent gun control policies caution that restricting access to firearms could deprive citizens of their ability to defend themselves, especially during unstable periods.

The contention around disarmament revolves around the idea that, while it is purportedly aimed at ensuring public safety and curbing violence, it could concurrently grant the government increased control over law enforcement and security measures, without the risk of citizens using firearms for self-defense. Proponents argue that reducing the prevalence of firearms in society will, in turn, reduce violent crimes or tragic incidents involving guns. They advocate for limiting access to firearms to decrease violence and criminal behavior.

However, one of the contentious aspects of disarmament is the potential power shift between citizens and the state. Critics argue that citizens, stripped of their means for self-defense, might increasingly rely on law enforcement for protection, relinquishing personal autonomy and agency for their own safety. The implicit assumption that individuals cannot be trusted with firearms for self-defense stirs skepticism regarding how disarmament might compromise citizens' ability to defend themselves and their families during dangerous situations.

Throughout history, the insidious strategy of disarming citizens has been inexorably linked to broader efforts aimed at imposing Marxist ideologies upon societies. It is a maneuver consistently adopted by communist regimes to consolidate power, suppress dissent, and eviscerate any form of resistance after seizing control. It is a systematic effort to align citizens with the state's agenda, nullifying any hint of defiance.

Communist regimes, once they have usurped power, meticulously strip civilians of their means to resist. Their goal is to render any organized opposition feeble by depriving them of access to arms. This manipulation creates a population less capable of mounting any challenge, further cementing the government's unassailable dominance.

Moreover, this disarmament tactic serves as a preemptive strike, aiming to stifle potential uprisings against the new regime. It ensures that any hint of dissent does not culminate in armed resistance, reinforcing the government's efforts to squash opposition and retain absolute control.

This tactic functions as a psychological maneuver, dissuading citizens from even considering resistance or dissent. It fosters dependence on the government for security while systematically eradicating any semblance of citizen empowerment.

This recurring pattern, witnessed in numerous communist regimes, underscores how disarmament plays a pivotal role in consolidating control. It is not just about seizing weapons; it is about incapacitating any opposition,

512 ★ CODE RED

extinguishing their means and resolve to resist, and ensuring compliance with the state's mandates.

Marxist ideologies perceive armed conservative groups as an imminent threat. In the context of the United States, armed conservatives are viewed as a formidable obstacle to ideologies antithetical to traditional American values. These values, deeply rooted in individual freedoms, limited government intervention, and the upholding of constitutional principles, stand in stark opposition to the collectivist ideals promoted by communism.

Conservative groups, closely aligned with core American values, regard the right to bear arms as a safeguard for these principles. The presence of armed conservatives, staunch defenders of traditional American values, poses a significant challenge to leftist ideologies aiming to centralize power and reshape societal norms.

Historically wary of armed opposition, communist movements view armed conservative factions as major obstacles to implementing their ideological agenda. The armed defense of traditional American values by conservative groups stands as a robust barrier against collectivist beliefs that could dismantle the established societal order.

For socialists striving to enforce their ideologies, the presence of armed conservative factions signifies a fierce resistance to radical change and an unwavering defense of the status quo. This perceived threat significantly obstructs the imposition of Marxist ideals, as armed conservatives stand resolutely against collectivist principles that fundamentally oppose cherished American values.

Tucker Carlson, a prominent American conservative political commentator, alleges that Democrats advocate for more stringent gun control measures due to their apprehensions about potential uprisings from the public. These propositions for gun restrictions are a pretext to assert control over the populace, rather than a sincere endeavor to preserve lives. Disarming the public would eradicate resistance to the Democrats' policies. He cites historical cases where gun control was used to institute authoritarian regimes in nations such as China and Cuba. Proponents of stricter gun laws are predominantly driven by a quest to retain their grip on authority, rather than a true commitment to ensuring public safety.

Representative Lauren Boebert (R-CO) has strongly rebuked Biden for classifying ordinary firearms as "weapons of war." She has taken direct aim at the President's remarks, notably his reference to extreme military capabilities such as F-15 jets, which could be construed as a tactic to intimidate dissenters. Boebert has identified a contradiction within the administration's stance. Her critique centers on the sharp contrast between the government's backing of civil unrest on the part of leftists, calls to defund law enforcement, and efforts to curtail citizens' rights to self-defense. According to Boebert, "Biden will call widely-purchased firearms 'weapons of war,' but then he'll tell you that you need an F-15 or a nuke to keep the federal government in check. This regime will encourage riots, defund the police and try to take away Americans' right to self-defense. Madame Speaker, the American people are not on board with the Biden regime's hypocritical gun-grabbing. Instead, they are buying guns at a record rate."[43]   Boebert's position mirrors a larger concern amongst conservatives about the implicit threat to employ military assets in domestic contexts.

The Democrats' drive for gun control measures, alongside their pursuit of political consolidation, has sparked significant concern among a considerable portion of society. These individuals emphasize the necessity of upholding Second Amendment rights. Their stance revolves around the belief that preserving these rights is vital to safeguarding individual freedoms and acting as a check against government overreach. The right to own firearms, entrenched in the Second Amendment, is considered a fundamental principle in maintaining liberty and bolstering defenses against tyranny.

Efforts to disarm citizens routinely face staunch resistance, primarily stemming from apprehensions about human rights violations, intrusions into personal liberties, and the potential loss of a defense mechanism against government actions. The notion of disarmament tends to reinforce the perception that authorities are impinging upon individual freedoms, intensifying existing divides, and provoking considerable opposition. Those steadfast in their defense of liberty vehemently oppose relinquishing firearms, citing historical instances where disarmament precipitated oppression and, in dire cases, genocide.

Supporters of the Second Amendment emphasize the profound cultural, historical, and legal linkages of the United States to gun ownership. Owning firearms is a bulwark for

---

[43] Walsh, Martin. "Boebert Unleashes on Biden: 'Rules For Thee But Not For My Crackhead Parmesan-Smoking Gun Criminal Son'." *Conservative Brief,* 7 July 2021, conservativebrief.com/ boebert-unleashes-44507/?utm_source=CB&utm_medium=ABC.

self-protection, the upholding of freedom, and resistance against tyranny. Gun control measures risk eroding the protections enshrined in the Second Amendment. They highlight the severe implications of limiting civilian access to firearms in the ongoing tussle between governmental authority and individual rights, warning of a slippery slope toward heightened restrictions.

The emergence of grassroots movements advocating for the preservation of Second Amendment rights underscores a deep commitment to upholding the United States Constitution. These movements operate at the local level, passionately championing constitutional principles and citizens' rights to bear arms. Their focus on well-organized militias for self-defense harkens back to a time when the Founding Fathers envisioned a nation where individuals played a crucial role in the collective defense of the republic.

The Second Amendment has been a focal point of contention, rooted in the historical context of the Founders' vision for a nation reliant on a well-regulated militia. The Founding Fathers recognized that an organized militia, composed of everyday citizens, was pivotal for safeguarding the fledgling republic. Hence, the Second Amendment was crafted with the aim of allowing citizens to actively participate in defending the nation, arming them as integral members of the militia.

Beyond merely acknowledging the right to own firearms, the Second Amendment sought to empower citizens to contribute to the defense of the nation. This foundational principle was essential for upholding the republic against external threats or serving as a defense in the absence of a standing army.

The language of the amendment itself—"A well regulated Militia, being necessary to the security of a free State, the right of the people to keep and bear Arms, shall not be infringed"—underscores this critical interplay between citizens' right to bear arms and their role in maintaining a well-regulated militia for the security of the state.

The essence of the Second Amendment was about recognizing the people's duty as defenders of the republic. This duty necessitated the freedom to bear arms for collective defense and the preservation of liberty.

The Second Amendment explicitly protects citizens' right to bear arms, not only as a matter of individual defense but as a fundamental protection against government overreach. It serves as a crucial check on government authority, ensuring that citizens have the means to safeguard themselves, their families, and their liberties from potential threats, even from within their own government.

This Amendment does not grant rights; it acknowledges and safeguards a pre-existing right of the people that predates the nation's founding. It was intended to restrain the government from infringing upon this natural right. According to the Second Amendment, the government lacks legitimate authority to infringe upon or restrict the people's right to keep and bear arms.

Any attempt to regulate or disarm law-abiding citizens runs counter to the core principles enshrined in the Constitution. The Second Amendment was established to ensure that citizens maintain the means to defend themselves, their families, and their freedoms from any potential threat, including a tyrannical government.

The principle of unconstitutional laws being void is firmly embedded in the foundation of the American legal system. As established in the landmark case of *Marbury v. Madison*, 5 U.S. (1 Cranch) 137 (1803), the Supreme Court declared its authority to review and nullify laws that contravene the Constitution, setting the precedent of judicial review.

Marbury v. Madison solidified the principle that the Constitution stands as the supreme law of the land. Any legislation or government action that violates its provisions is deemed unconstitutional and therefore null and void. Chief Justice John Marshall, in delivering the opinion of the Court, asserted that it is the duty of the judiciary to interpret the Constitution and ensure that laws align with its provisions. Should any law conflict with the Constitution, the judiciary has the authority to declare it invalid.

This principle fundamentally establishes that laws inconsistent with the Constitution have no legal force or effect. It underscores the supremacy of the Constitution over any legislative enactment, rendering unconstitutional laws null and unenforceable.

The concept of judicial review, as articulated in *Marbury v. Madison*, forms the cornerstone of the separation of powers and checks and balances within the U.S. government. It ensures that the judiciary acts as a guardian of the Constitution, ensuring that the laws passed by the legislature and actions taken by the executive branch adhere to the Constitution's provisions.

In essence, *Marbury v. Madison* established the bedrock principle that any law that runs counter to the Constitution is void ab initio, or void from the beginning. This ruling underscores the vital role of the judiciary in upholding the supremacy of the Constitution and ensuring that the rule of law prevails, even over legislative enactments.

Within the United States, a considerable number of law enforcement officers, including police officers and sheriffs, identify with conservative values. This trend is mirrored in the U.S. military, where a substantial portion leans toward conservative ideologies. Statistics show that approximately 30% of military members identify as Republicans, while about 40% align as Independents, which often includes adherents of Libertarian and constitutional beliefs.

Regardless of their political affiliations, each American soldier pledges an oath to uphold and defend the Constitution of the United States. This commitment transcends personal political leanings and remains a fundamental principle ingrained in the military culture.

Additionally, many veterans, particularly those with extensive combat experience, tend to embrace conservative viewpoints. These veterans are committed to combating oppression and addressing internal threats, drawing from their experiences to safeguard the values enshrined in the Constitution.

This convergence of conservative values among law enforcement, military personnel, and veterans underscores a broader commitment to upholding constitutional principles. It reflects a dedication to protecting the nation's foundational values, emphasizing the significance of these values in maintaining the integrity of the country's institutions.

The commitment and deep-rooted principles of conservative law enforcement and military personnel, shaped by their rigorous training and allegiance to the Constitution, present a formidable challenge to Marxist objectives. Their steadfast dedication to core American values, such as individual freedoms, constitutional defense, and resistance to government encroachment, establishes a robust barrier against ideologies that seek to undermine these foundational principles.

In situations where Marxist ideologies pose a threat to these cherished beliefs, military members leaning towards conservatism may staunchly resist any departure from constitutional governance. Their unwavering commitment to upholding quintessential American values—such as advocating for free-market economics and safeguarding personal liberties—might clash with the aims of Marxist agendas, which typically pursue centralized control and the redistribution of resources.

These individuals, steeped in principles honed through their training, stand as a bulwark against ideologies that challenge the essence of the Constitution. Their commitment to safeguarding the fundamental tenets of the nation underscores their pivotal role as guardians of America's foundational values and constitutional integrity. Their allegiance to these principles positions them as stalwart defenders against any ideologies that may threaten the core essence of the nation's democratic ideals.

Within specific segments of the military, there are concerns regarding the prospect of domestic unrest or conflicts. These concerns stem from multifaceted sources, including social and political tensions, polarization, and a perception of diminishing societal stability.

Importantly, this perspective does not connote an eagerness for conflict or a desire to incite one. Instead, it underscores a sense of responsibility and readiness among certain military personnel to comprehend various potential scenarios impacting national security and stability.

The overwhelming majority of military members are committed to upholding the Constitution, ensuring national security, and preserving peace. Their training emphasizes respect for civilian authority and adherence to the rule of law.

In conservative circles, diverging opinions have emerged regarding the reliance on the military during hypothetical scenarios such as a communist revolution. Doug Casey, writer, speculator, and libertarian philosopher, has sounded a cautionary note, advising against counting on the military for aid in such circumstances. He highlights the Department of Defense's efforts to stifle conservative viewpoints within the ranks of soldiers as a cause for concern.

Casey draws attention to the manipulation of military institutions by authoritarian figures. History illustrates how leaders with totalitarian tendencies or dictatorial inclinations recognize the critical importance of neutralizing potential sources of opposition within the military and police forces. Their strategies often involve reshaping these institutions, steering them away from dissent or resistance and aligning them to serve their agendas without questioning their authority.

This pattern echoes a deliberate and calculated effort by such leaders to mold the security apparatus into a loyal tool of their governance, ensuring it upholds their interests without challenging their power. By suppressing dissent or ideological diversity within these vital institutions, these leaders aim to consolidate control and eliminate potential resistance from within the very structures designed to protect the nation.

The susceptibility of these institutions to political sway highlights the potential hazards of a compromised military. Such a military might deviate from safeguarding the interests of the populace and the constitutional framework, instead aligning with the mandates of a governing authority. This alignment poses a significant threat, potentially undermining the fundamental pillars of the republic.

The U.S. military's commitment to non-partisanship stands firm as a pillar of its effectiveness in safeguarding national interests amidst political ebbs and flows. However, mounting concerns regarding potential departures from this cherished non-partisan stance, particularly the infiltration of Marxist ideologies within military ranks, raise alarms about core values and operational effectiveness.

Throughout history, the military's neutrality, transcending political affiliations, has been pivotal in executing missions impartially, prioritizing the nation's security above political agendas. Yet, recent events shed light on encroaching ideologies that deviate from the institution's fundamental principles.

The infiltration of Marxist ideologies signals potential erosion of unity and foundational principles steering the military's ethos and operations. This concern surpasses accommodating viewpoints; it strikes at the very essence of the military's identity and its ability to function effectively.

These concerns stem from the realization that divergent beliefs could fracture the cohesive bond among military units, risking the erosion of trust and unity crucial for their collective strength. Unity is not merely soldiers working together; it is a shared commitment, trust, and adherence to principles that transcend personal convictions.

The military's strength lies not just in weaponry or strategy but in its unity of purpose and steadfast adherence to shared principles—elements susceptible to compromise with the infiltration of divisive ideologies. Any compromise in unity or trust could directly impede operational effectiveness, jeopardizing the military's role in safeguarding national interests.

The coexistence of capitalist and Marxist ideologies within the military presents significant challenges due to their inherent contradictions and foundational differences. Capitalism, centered on private ownership and a market-driven economy, clashes fundamentally with communism, which advocates for collective ownership, planned economies, and aims to eliminate class distinctions. In a military environment where unity and a shared purpose are paramount, such ideological clashes can create rifts that hinder operational effectiveness.

Moreover, the military's role in safeguarding national interests contrasts with communism's aspirations to dismantle national boundaries, potentially creating discord in objectives.

Throughout history, communist regimes have systematically weakened their military forces as part of a deliberate strategy to eliminate potential opposition and solidify their rule. These regimes perceive independent institutions, particularly the military, as threats to their authority. As a result, they strategically undermine the military's strength to consolidate their power and remove obstacles to absolute control.

A robust military acts as a shield, deterring potential adversaries and bolstering national security. Its role in civil conflicts is pivotal, maintaining law and order, ensuring stability, and upholding constitutional values.

A weakened military, facing critical challenges such as personnel shortages and reduced readiness, significantly undermines its capacity to effectively address both domestic and foreign threats. These vulnerabilities create substantial risks, potentially empowering foreign entities to probe the nation's defenses, instigate international conflicts, and pose a direct threat to the nation's sovereignty and interests.

Moreover, in a state where the military lacks strength, strategic planning, mobilization, and the execution of intricate operations—essential for both national defense and managing internal conflicts—encounter substantial impediments. These limitations elevate the probability of operational failures and escalate casualties, jeopardizing not only the military's effectiveness but also the safety of its personnel.

This weakened state of military readiness becomes a prime target for exploitation by communist agents seeking to undermine stability and consolidate power. They could exploit these vulnerabilities by instigating or exacerbating internal conflicts, sowing discord among groups, and infiltrating systems weakened due to military inadequacies. Communist ideologies often thrive in environments of chaos and instability, and a compromised military serves as a fertile ground for them to manipulate situations to their advantage.

Furthermore, a compromised military struggles to uphold fundamental values and support patriots or groups that champion these principles. This struggle perpetuates internal strife, allowing communists to extend their influence, exacerbate social discord, and potentially plunge the nation into widespread devastation. The absence of a strong military not only endangers national security but also weakens the nation's ability to safeguard its core values against subversive ideologies.

One of the common tactics used by socialist regimes is purging or marginalizing military leadership and personnel who exhibit loyalty to nationalistic or non-party affiliations. They replace these individuals with loyalists who pledge allegiance solely to the ruling party. This process reshapes the military hierarchy to align with the regime's ideological agenda, eliminating potential dissenters.

Additionally, these regimes intentionally implement policies to degrade military capabilities, such as insufficient funding, neglecting modernization efforts, or sidelining crucial training programs. These deliberate acts aim to erode the military's ability to resist or counter the regime's authority.

By subverting the military, these regimes transform the armed forces into tools for enforcing their will rather than safeguarding national interests. This weakens the military's role as a defender of the nation, ensuring compliance with the regime's dictates.

Ultimately, the deliberate weakening of the military under such regimes serves as a strategy to eliminate potential challenges to the ruling party's supremacy. It dismantles the military's allegiance to national values, ensuring the regime's control without internal opposition or threats from within military ranks.

Furthermore, a compliant yet uninspired military and police force can pave the way for aspiring dictators seeking power consolidation. These dictators align these institutions with their ideologies, removing officers or personnel who do not conform to their goals, thus shaping forces more likely to unquestioningly follow orders without resistance. This manipulation undermines the institutions' loyalty to the nation's values, placing them at the disposal of authoritarian regimes.

Historical examples vividly demonstrate the dangers of reshaping military institutions to strictly adhere to a particular ideology. In the lead-up to the 1917 Russian revolution, the Bolsheviks resorted to cunning strategies to undermine the military, effectively weakening the nation's defenses to facilitate their rise to power.

Exploiting the soldiers' fatigue and disillusionment from World War I, the Bolsheviks embarked on insidious propaganda campaigns. They exploited grievances, promising peace, land, and bread to manipulate soldiers into supporting their cause while purposefully sowing discord within military ranks.

Bolshevik agents infiltrated the armed forces, planting sympathizers and propagandists who actively disrupted military discipline and spread subversive ideas. Their tactics included encouraging disobedience, mutinies, and desertions, aiming to fracture the military's loyalty and unity.

These manipulative tactics deliberately disrupted the chain of command, undermining military leadership and urging soldiers to question orders and rebel against their officers. The Bolsheviks sought to dismantle the military's ability to function cohesively and effectively, exploiting existing discontent to render the armed forces impotent.

Josef Stalin's era provides a striking example of this manipulation. His purge of competent officers from the

Soviet military due to suspicions about their alignment with his ideals led to severe consequences. The politically aligned Soviet Army, lacking experienced leadership, suffered a significant defeat against a smaller, more innovative Finnish force during the 1939 invasion. This episode illustrates how tailoring the military to a specific ideology can impair its operational capabilities. Stalin's zeal to align the military with his beliefs resulted in the removal of capable leaders, leaving a weakened force ill-equipped to face tactical challenges. The purge deprived the military of invaluable expertise, wisdom, and strategic insight, severely compromising its ability to adapt and innovate on the battlefield.

The trajectory of the US military and its re-alignment with leftist ideologies has drawn parallels to Bolshevik tactics, triggering concerns about a departure from its foundational principle of non-partisanship. This shift, reminiscent of historical instances where political ideologies infiltrated military structures, has sparked intense debates about the institution's integrity and its susceptibility to specific ideological influences.

Evidence indicates a discernible tilt towards leftist ideologies within the military landscape, drawing comparisons to historical movements that emphasized ideological conformity over operational readiness. Instances of incorporating critical race theory, gender-related training, and a heightened emphasis on social justice issues within military policies have intensified discussions about whether the military is embracing a more progressive stance at the expense of its primary mission: ensuring national security.

These recent developments reflect a departure from the military's core duties. While recognizing the importance of diversity and inclusivity, concerns arise when these initiatives overshadow or distract from the critical task of maintaining combat readiness. The integration of ideological narratives within the military hierarchy, notably public endorsements of specific leftist viewpoints by influential leaders, has heightened apprehensions about the institution's growing alignment with progressive ideologies.

Moreover, the infusion of leftist ideologies into military educational curricula and training programs has sparked controversy. An excessive emphasis on these perspectives risks undermining the military's preparedness by diverting attention away from essential training and operational requirements. This trend has also raised concerns about potential divisions within the ranks, as contrasting viewpoints on social and political issues threaten to erode cohesion and disrupt the unity necessary for effective military operations.

The question of balance between accommodating diverse viewpoints and preserving the military's focus on its core mission remains contentious. An excessive embrace of leftist ideologies may compromise the military's effectiveness, potentially undermining its ability to respond to emerging threats and safeguard national interests.

Lt. Col. Matthew Lohmeier, a former instructor and distinguished fighter pilot, penned the book, *Irresistible Revolution: Marxism's Goal of Conquest & the Unmaking of the American Military*. His deep-seated concerns revolve around what he perceives as the encroachment of a "neo-Marxist agenda" within the military framework.

At the core of Colonel Lohmeier's critique lies the dissemination of materials at his base that portray the United States as a "White supremacist nation." Such characterization contradicts the foundational principles and patriotic values, raising concerns about the ideological direction these materials might steer the military toward.

The portrayal of the United States as a White supremacist nation oversimplifies its complex identity. While acknowledging past challenges, the nation's foundations emphasize equality, individual rights, and justice for all. Significant strides in civil rights, diverse political leadership, and the nation's multicultural makeup contradict a singularly White supremacist label. Branding the entire nation disregards ongoing efforts for racial equality and ignores the nation's commitment to inclusivity and progress.

General Mark Milley's advocacy for diversity and anti-extremism measures, including the incorporation of Critical Race Theory (CRT) into military education, has ignited a contentious debate. Advocates view these steps as pivotal in addressing racial injustices, fostering inclusivity, and reflecting the diverse fabric of America within the armed forces. However, concerns arise about Milley's emphasis on political matters, potentially stifling open discussions, disrupting unity, and even impacting military preparedness. There is apprehension that these policies might create divisions among service members along racial and gender lines, eroding the foundational principle of unity in the military.

The integration of social and political concepts, particularly those associated with CRT, has spurred heated discussions regarding their suitability in a military context. This debate, exemplified by Lohmeier's reservations, delves into whether these ideologies align with the military's core mission, which is primarily focused on national defense.

Including CRT in military training prompts concerns regarding its alignment with the paramount objective of national defense. CRT's focus on societal power dynamics rooted in race could potentially divert attention from crucial combat readiness training. There is concern that its introduction might sow ideological divisions and impede the necessary unity for effective military operations. While acknowledging the importance of understanding social dynamics, the inclusion of CRT might detract from the military's primary duty of defending the nation, potentially disrupting readiness and unity within the forces. Prioritizing aspects directly contributing to combat readiness and unit cohesion remains crucial to uphold the military's fundamental role in national defense.

The introduction of CRT in military education might exacerbate division, divert focus from unity, and compromise national defense efforts. While addressing social issues is important, integrating CRT could risk diluting attention from critical tasks vital for national defense, ultimately compromising readiness and the cohesive spirit fundamental to the military's ethos of collective purpose.

There is considerable concern over training materials that categorize specific beliefs or viewpoints, such as opposition to abortion, skepticism toward LGBTQ agendas, or adherence to traditional Catholic views on gender and feminism, as potential indicators of extremism. This categorization overlooks the fact that these beliefs are often personal or religious in nature, not advocating violence or the overthrow of established order. Such labelling poses a risk of stifling diverse perspectives and healthy discourse within the military, contradicting the principles of inclusivity and tolerance that it aims to uphold.

Lohmeier raises alarm about the increasing presence of neo-Marxist ideologies in military education, citing instances such as labeling the US as a "White supremacist nation." This is part of a broader shift in training that aligns with a neo-Marxist analysis focusing on societal power structures rooted in race. His concerns extend to the integration of CRT-related concepts, which he believes reflect a neo-Marxist interpretation emphasizing power struggles and systemic oppression in society. Additionally, labeling certain conservative viewpoints as "extremist" mirrors a push within the military to challenge established norms, mirroring a neo-Marxist objective of altering traditional societal structures.

Efforts within the military to address perceived white extremism involve extensive monitoring of social media activities to identify individuals deemed to have extremist backgrounds. This includes specific attention to countering perceived negative influences associated with the Trump movement within the military community. These initiatives claim to protect military cohesion, unity, and operational efficiency by guarding against threats posed by extremist ideologies.

Because of their broad application to all service members and collaboration with national security and federal law enforcement agencies, these measures have sparked contentious debates regarding infringements on individual rights, particularly freedom of speech and association. Critics express skepticism about categorizing individuals based solely on ideological beliefs, questioning the criteria used to label someone as an extremist and expressing concerns about subjective interpretations accompanying such classifications. They caution against initiatives that might result in targeting individuals solely because of their political beliefs, lacking substantial evidence tying them to extremist activities.

The term "White supremacists" introduces complexity, encompassing a wide range of beliefs and affiliations, leading to worries about potential mischaracterizations or misidentifications. There is skepticism regarding the possibility of unjust actions against service members who might hold conservative or constitutionalist viewpoints but are not involved in any extremist activities.

The absence of a universally accepted Pentagon definition for "extremism" has led to the Counter-Extremism Working Group (CEWG) taking on the significant task of formulating a comprehensive definition that delineates extremist behaviors or beliefs. This initiative aims to establish a clear framework that ensures uniformity in identifying actions or ideologies that could potentially undermine military cohesion and its overarching mission.

At the helm of the "Countering Extremism" initiative is Bishop Garrison, tasked with a substantial responsibility in tackling extremism within the military ranks. However, his remarks regarding the classification of ordinary political opinions and personal beliefs as national security risks have triggered concerns about the scope and implications of this initiative. Garrison's considerable authority in making such classifications brings to the forefront the intricate balance between shielding the military from extremist influences and safeguarding individuals' rights to hold diverse political opinions and personal beliefs. This has raised pertinent questions about the criteria and processes employed in making such classifications and their potential impact on the freedom of thought and expression within the military.

Mike Berry, the general counsel for First Liberty Institute, a Marine Corps reservist, and an advisor to the Counter-Extremism Working Group (CEWG), raises pivotal points surrounding the composition and objectives of the CEWG. His critical observation revolves around the CEWG's makeup, expressing concern over the majority of appointed experts exhibiting partisan affiliations, some of whom endorsed Biden. This inclination sparks inquiries about the initiative's objectivity and impartiality. Berry underscores the absence of conservative representation and significant military experience within the CEWG, emphasizing the necessity of diverse perspectives in advisory groups, especially when tackling issues such as extremism.

Berry challenges the notion of widespread extremism within the military, citing only 21 service members separated for extremist activities over the past five years. This stance prompts queries regarding whether an extensive focus on identifying and removing individuals labeled as extremists might divert attention and resources from other critical concerns, such as addressing external threats posed by major geopolitical players.

Highlighting the challenge of prioritizing security considerations, Berry advocates for directing resources toward addressing substantial external threats such as China, Russia, Iran, and North Korea.

Moreover, Berry raises alarms about potential infringements on individuals' First Amendment rights amid Biden's efforts to purge the military of "extremists." He expresses concerns about the CEWG's plan to redefine extremism, potentially encompassing constitutionally-protected speech. His apprehensions center on the proposed monitoring of service members' social media accounts, perceiving it as encroaching on thoughts and beliefs rather than solely focusing on actions.

In response to the mounting apprehension, Garrison offered clarifications, pivoting the emphasis from ideologies to "behavior." This shift signals an attempt to address actions that might pose a risk to national security rather than targeting beliefs per se. By acknowledging the complexity inherent in identifying and addressing extremism while preserving individuals' rights to their beliefs, this correction seeks a more nuanced approach that navigates the intricate balance between security concerns and personal freedoms.

Concerns regarding the redefinition of extremism by progressive voices intersect with a larger debate on the role of language in shaping political ideologies. The individuals defining extremism could tailor this concept to align with specific political leanings, influencing the thoughts and beliefs held within the military. This potential alteration raises significant concerns about its impact on the military's cultural fabric, the promotion of diverse perspectives, and the preservation of free expression within its ranks.

Furthermore, the endeavor to redefine extremism could result in the identification and subsequent removal of individuals deemed "extremist" due to their adherence to patriotic or conservative values. Such categorization risks stigmatizing certain ideologies, potentially excluding viewpoints closely aligned with traditional American values, thereby creating a climate of exclusion.

The anxiety around the targeting of conservatives within the "extremism" framework arises from several observations. The lack of a universally accepted definition leaves room for subjective interpretations, potentially branding conservative viewpoints as extremist. Additionally, groups responsible for addressing extremism, especially those dominated by progressive members, might introduce biases against traditional beliefs, nurturing an environment that suppresses these ideologies within the military.

The ambiguous definition of extremism raises the risk of marginalizing individuals with conservative perspectives. Policies limiting expressions of conservative ideologies heighten fears that the label of "extremism" is being used to push conservatives out of the military. This combination of factors fuels growing worries that "extremism" could become a justification for singling out and removing individuals with conservative beliefs from the military, casting doubt on the fairness and impartiality of these measures.

The military landscape has undergone notable transformations, prompting discussions regarding its alignment with the Biden administration's left-leaning policies. These shifts have sparked concerns over the diminishing political diversity within the armed forces, especially evident in the Department of Defense's removal of conservative viewpoints from its ranks.

The removal of Lt. Col. Lohmeier from his command has set off a firestorm of debate, revealing the challenging balance between freedom of expression and the expected behavior of military leaders. Some perceive his ousting as a consequence of his principled stand against a surge of leftist ideologies infiltrating the military's ethos. Lohmeier's outspokenness highlights legitimate worries about leftist influences impacting military practices and potentially undermining its core values.

Lohmeier's removal was a consequence of his conservative stance and criticism of the military's leftist policies. His vocal opposition to encroaching progressive ideologies resulted in his removal. This situation sheds light on a broader concern about whether dissenting conservative voices encounter repercussions for challenging dominant leftist trends within military culture. The incident prompts significant contemplation regarding the military's approach to dissenting viewpoints, raising inquiries about the inclusivity of conservative perspectives within the armed forces and the potential consequences for those critical of leftist policies.

Army Major Samuel Sigoloff's observations shed light on a troubling aspect within the military: The potential purge of individuals who refuse orders that they consider unlawful or unethical.

The military holds a fundamental principle that personnel are obligated to refuse unlawful orders. This principle is grounded in both military regulations and international laws of armed conflict. Soldiers are expected to refuse to obey orders they perceive as illegal, immoral, or contrary to the laws of war, and they are encouraged to report such orders through proper channels.

However, a purge against those who exercise this right presents a worrisome scenario. If dissent and refusal to carry out unlawful orders result in punitive actions or separation from service, it could deter individuals from upholding their ethical obligations. This could lead to a chilling effect on the ethical discourse necessary for a morally conscious military.

The recent cases and discussions around the dismissal of military personnel, including Lt. Col. Lohmeier, have raised concerns about whether voicing dissent or ethical concerns could lead to professional repercussions. The balance between maintaining discipline and allowing for ethical discussions and the refusal of potentially unlawful orders remains a delicate one. It is crucial for the military to foster an environment where ethical concerns are addressed without fear of retribution, ensuring the adherence to lawful and moral directives while maintaining discipline and operational readiness.

Beyond these concerns, there are worries about the potential weakening of the military's capabilities. Critics have raised questions about policies such as sex reassignment procedures in the ranks and extremism stand-downs, suggesting that these initiatives might divert resources and attention from essential military operations. Some critics are also concerned about how these internal debates might be perceived by foreign adversaries, such as China and Russia. These debates over ideological pursuits within the military could create perceptions of weakness, potentially compromising the U.S. military's ability to project strength and maintain deterrence.

Lt. Col. Paul Douglas Hague's resignation after devoting nearly two decades to the U.S. Army exemplifies the impact of ideological shifts within the military. His departure stood as a principled opposition to what he perceived as an "ideologically Marxist takeover" entrenched within both the military hierarchy and the U.S. government.

Hague's resignation marked a profound protest, reflecting his conviction that leftist ideological currents were reshaping the military and governmental structures. He believed this transformation contradicted the foundational principles and values that had initially spurred his enlistment. His departure served as a stark testament that this issue extended far beyond rhetoric, affecting concrete personnel decisions and leadership paradigms.

The weighty choice to resign after such dedicated service underscores the depth of Hague's conviction that the very ideals he had vowed to defend were under threat.

The aftermath of "woke" cultural Marxist policies on military recruitment strategies reveals unintended consequences that contribute to a decline in enlistments. These policies, aimed at fostering diversity and inclusivity, have introduced hurdles in attracting suitable candidates to join the armed forces.

Concerns have arisen regarding the potential divergence from the primary purpose of recruitment: identifying highly qualified individuals for military service. A singular focus on meeting diversity quotas might impede enlistments, potentially undermining the readiness and effectiveness of the armed forces.

This debate centers on how flawed "woke" policies impact recruitment strategies. The strong emphasis on diversity could dissuade potential enlistments by deviating from prioritizing qualifications and capabilities in candidates.

Furthermore, when recruitment strategies solely prioritize diversity goals, there is a risk of undervaluing the importance of selecting the most qualified candidates, potentially affecting the readiness and effectiveness of the armed forces.

Examining the influence of these policies on potential recruits, particularly those leaning conservative, becomes crucial. The infiltration of cultural Marxism through "woke" policies might alienate individuals who uphold traditional

American values. This perceived clash of ideologies could deter these recruits from considering military enlistment.

Recognizing these facets highlights the unintended consequences of "woke" policies on enlistment figures and emphasizes the potential compromise they pose to the armed forces' readiness.

The deliberate weakening of the US military has become evident with the infiltration of Marxist influences into its policies and practices. Ideologies such as CRT and identity politics have made their way into military training and educational materials, drawing attention away from core training, readiness, and operational effectiveness. This shift compromises the military's strength, prioritizing ideological conformity over its primary mission of safeguarding national defense.

At the core of these Marxist-influenced ideologies lies an intent to erode traditional American values. Figures such as Lt. Col. Matthew Lohmeier express concerns about characterizations labeling the United States as a "white supremacist nation," seeing it as a calculated attempt to undermine patriotic values within military ranks. Critics also highlight the categorization of certain beliefs—such as opposition to abortion, skepticism toward LGBTQ agendas, or adherence to traditional religious beliefs—as indicators of extremism. This erosion could sow discord and diminish morale among service members, challenging unity within the armed forces.

A pivotal aspect of this issue is the shift in the military's focus. Prioritizing social justice issues and identity-based training overshadows the primary mandate of national defense. This emphasis on ideological aspects dilutes the military's readiness and operational effectiveness, jeopardizing its ability to address evolving threats.

Moreover, concerns arise regarding the perception of political activism among high-ranking military officials aligned with leftist ideologies. This alignment blurs the line between military duties and political advocacy, undermining the military's impartiality and commitment to serving the nation above partisan interests. This politicization compromises the institution's credibility and its effectiveness in fulfilling its core duties.

Marxist-influenced ideologies intentionally redirect the focus of the US military away from its core mission of national defense. The erosion of traditional values, internal divisions, compromised operational readiness, and concerns about political activism collectively contribute to the assertion of a deliberate effort to weaken the military from within through ideological subversion.

For the reasons outlined above, counting solely on military intervention to counter a communist takeover is unrealistic. It is crucial to explore alternative approaches to address this threat. Unfortunately, efforts to challenge and dismantle communist regimes through peaceful means have historically encountered significant obstacles due to the oppressive nature of these systems.

The methods used to suppress dissent within these regimes—such as censorship, imprisonment, and violence against political dissidents—create an atmosphere of fear and intimidation. These tactics serve to obstruct the organization and progress of non-violent movements, severely undermining their potential to effect change through peaceful measures.

The foundational principle of class struggle within communism often involves coercive tactics by the ruling class to maintain their grip on power. This complicates peaceful transitions, while the dominance of state-controlled media and the suppression of independent institutions further restrict the dissemination of alternative perspectives, impeding efforts for non-violent engagement.

Any deviation from the prescribed Marxist doctrine typically results in severe punishment, amplifying the difficulties of organizing peaceful dissent. Despite these significant challenges, peaceful resistance emerges as the most effective and ethically sound strategy to counter the influence of communism.

Unlike military intervention, which often brings extensive human suffering and perpetuates conflict, non-violent resistance aligns with ethical principles by advocating for justice without resorting to violence. This approach garners broader international support, standing on the moral high ground and drawing attention to the plight of those oppressed by socialist regimes.

Moreover, peaceful resistance lays the groundwork for sustainable change. History has shown that violent revolutions tend to perpetuate cycles of oppression and instability. In contrast, non-violent movements foster long-term stability by prioritizing reconciliation, inclusivity, and democratic values, creating a space for dialogue, understanding, and cooperation.

One of the strengths of peaceful resistance lies in its ability to unify diverse groups within society. By transcending differences and emphasizing shared values and aspirations, non-violent movements build a stronger, more inclusive front against communism, bolstering resilience and broadening appeal.

Additionally, non-violent resistance carries significant weight on the global stage, attracting attention, support, and solidarity from other nations. This creates diplomatic pressure on Marxist regimes and encourages internal reforms. The peaceful nature of the resistance starkly contrasts with the repressive tactics of ruling regimes, often leading to internal questioning within the ruling class.

Certain individuals have shown remarkable ingenuity in devising non-violent strategies aimed at achieving peaceful change in such restrictive environments. Their efforts highlight the potential for peaceful resistance to effect significant and lasting positive change, paving the way for a more inclusive, just, and stable society without perpetuating cycles of violence and suffering.

Mahatma Gandhi, a central figure in India's struggle for independence from British colonial rule, is renowned for his adept use of nonviolent resistance, known as "satyagraha" or "truth force." Gandhi's approach played a pivotal role in India's eventual attainment of independence in 1947.

He championed acts of civil disobedience, where individuals deliberately violated unjust laws to demonstrate the moral righteousness of their cause and expose the injustices of British colonial rule, forming a fundamental element of his nonviolent approach. Non-cooperation with British authorities was a fundamental pillar of Gandhi's strategy, encompassing boycotting British-made goods, refusing to pay taxes, and resigning from government positions. The overarching objective was to undermine British control and underscore India's self-sufficiency, ultimately weakening the British administration through noncompliance.

Gandhi had a remarkable talent for mobilizing large numbers of people, organizing peaceful protests, marches, and strikes that drew participants from diverse backgrounds and regions of India. The unity he fostered among the Indian population was a critical element of his strategy, recognizing the strength that arose from mass participation.

A key aspect of Gandhi's philosophy was the power of suffering, as he, along with his followers, willingly endured physical and emotional hardships, including violence from British authorities, without retaliation. This self-restraint aimed to showcase their unwavering commitment to nonviolence and garner international sympathy for their cause.

Gandhi's steadfast commitment to nonviolence played an instrumental role in India's journey to independence, inspiring numerous civil rights movements and leaders worldwide, including figures such as Dr. Martin Luther King, Jr.

Dr. Martin Luther King, Jr. is celebrated for his adept use of nonviolent methods, such as protests, strikes, boycotts, sit-ins, and civil disobedience, to advance the civil rights movement in the United States. He confronted systemic racism and segregation, leading to significant advancements in civil rights for African Americans.

Gene Sharp, a distinguished political scientist and activist, carved out a unique space in the realm of nonviolent resistance by methodically outlining the fundamental principles behind successful nonviolent campaigns. His work stands apart from the personal narratives and philosophies left by eminent figures such as Gandhi and Dr. Martin Luther King, Jr., offering a comprehensive analysis rather than individual perspectives.

In his seminal work, *The Politics of Nonviolent Action*, Sharp scrutinized the methods and techniques employed in numerous nonviolent struggles across history. He identified common patterns and principles that have consistently proven effective in achieving political and social change through nonviolent means. This exhaustive analysis serves as both a theoretical framework and a practical guide for activists and organizers on a global scale, providing invaluable insights into the strategies of nonviolent resistance.

During the 1960s, Sharp introduced the groundbreaking "theory of nonviolent action," a strategic approach to conflict resolution that unequivocally rejects violence. His approach encompasses social, psychological, and economic dimensions, offering a strategic framework for challenging oppressive regimes without resorting to conventional military methods. Interestingly, his strategies were even noted in a 2015 paper by the Russian Institute of Strategic Studies and Predictions, suggesting an association with the United States' Hybrid War field manual.

Central to Sharp's concept is the use of strategic nonviolent action to undermine collective government support, potentially leading to the collapse of states. This involves capturing public attention, disrupting the status quo, and fostering discontent and dissent among the population. At its essence lies the mobilization of large segments of society through nonviolent means such as protests, strikes, boycotts, and civil disobedience. The ultimate goal is to weaken the legitimacy and authority of the government by eroding its support pillars, potentially culminating in the nonviolent collapse of the state.

Sharp's influential book, *From Dictatorship to Democracy*, and his strategic framework for nonviolent revolution have wielded substantial influence on political movements worldwide, particularly in Eastern Europe. His ideas, often translated into peaceful protests and strategic actions, have been utilized to challenge or overthrow targeted governments in various countries, demonstrating the tangible impact and applicability of his theories in real-world scenarios.

Sharp's work has perturbed the Kremlin due to its linkage with the "color revolutions" in Georgia, Kyrgyzstan, and Ukraine. In these instances, leaders were seen displaying copies of *From Dictatorship to Democracy*. Vladislav

Surkov, an adviser to Vladimir Putin, attributed the tactics employed during the 2011 anti-government protests in Moscow to Sharp's book. This recognition resulted in Sharp being viewed as one of the most dangerous threats to the Russian state.

History has demonstrated that peaceful change is attainable, as seen through multiple instances showcasing the efficacy of nonviolent approaches in confronting and ultimately dismantling socialist regimes. The collapse of communism in Eastern Europe and the dissolution of the Soviet Union serve as compelling examples, highlighting that popular movements, nonviolent protests, and international pressure can precipitate profound political transformations.

In 1980, Poland grappled with communist rule, causing widespread hardship. The Solidarity movement emerged when shipyard workers demanded improved working conditions and political freedoms. Despite government crackdowns and the imposition of martial law in 1981, Solidarity persisted in its non-violent resistance through strikes, protests, and disseminating information. Over time, resilience, changing geopolitics, and economic challenges led to negotiations. The Round Table Talks in 1989 resulted in an agreement for partially free elections and a peaceful transition to democracy. Semi-free elections in 1989 marked the beginning of the end for communist rule in Poland.

Under the Communist Party's repressive regime, Czechoslovakia experienced the Velvet Revolution in 1989. It was a largely non-violent uprising driven by students, intellectuals, and civic activists. A peaceful student protest met with police brutality sparked public outrage, leading to widespread protests demanding democratic reforms and an end to communism. Protests, strikes, and public demonstrations gained momentum, characterized by a commitment to non-violence, civil disobedience, and peaceful negotiations. As the protests persisted, the communist government engaged in negotiations, eventually leading to the resignation of the government and the formation of a transitional government. The first free elections in 1990 marked a decisive shift away from communism.

Hungary played a pivotal role in the peaceful and nonviolent dismantling of communism in Eastern Europe during the late 1980s. The country's shift from communism to democracy was defined by a series of crucial events and factors.

A watershed moment unfolded on May 2, 1989 when Hungary, led by Prime Minister Miklós Németh, partially opened its border with Austria. This decision allowed citizens from East Germany and other Eastern Bloc nations to travel westward through Hungary. Tens of thousands seized this opportunity to flee to the West, placing immense pressure on the East German government and ultimately contributing to the events that led to the fall of the Berlin Wall.

Internally, Hungary underwent a transformation propelled by peaceful protests led by various factions, including civil society organizations, opposition political parties, and students. The Hungarian Democratic Forum (MDF), a prominent opposition party, played a key role in mobilizing resistance against the ruling Hungarian Socialist Workers' Party (Communist Party).

The Round Table Talks were instrumental in the country's transition. These negotiations involved discussions between the ruling Communist Party and diverse opposition groups. Through these talks, Hungary adopted a new democratic constitution, setting the stage for free and fair elections and facilitating a peaceful transfer of power.

On March 25, 1989, Hungary conducted its first free elections, leading to the peaceful transition of power from the Communist Party to the opposition. The ruling Hungarian Socialist Workers' Party evolved into the Hungarian Socialist Party (MSZP) and engaged in the democratic electoral process.

Furthermore, Hungary enacted laws in 1990 that marked the end of one-party rule, embraced political pluralism, and established a democratic framework. The country embraced economic reforms, transitioning from a centrally planned economy to a market-oriented system, aligning with the broader changes occurring in the region.

Hungary's peaceful and constitutional shift from communism to democracy served as a model for neighboring Eastern European nations. The events in Hungary significantly contributed to the collapse of the Eastern Bloc and the conclusion of the Cold War. This transition in Hungary stands as a pivotal milestone in the demise of communism in Eastern Europe, highlighting the country's dedication to nonviolence and dialogue, which played a critical role in the wider movement toward democratic change.

The collapse of the communist German Democratic Republic (GDR) was primarily fueled by nonviolent protests, culminating in the fall of the Berlin Wall in 1989. These peaceful demonstrations played a crucial role in the GDR's downfall, contributing to a broader wave of change that ultimately led to the country's reunification in 1990. This historic event stands as a powerful testament to the transformative potential of nonviolent movements in challenging oppressive regimes.

During the 1980s, the GDR grappled with severe economic challenges, a stagnant political system, and the suppression of civil liberties. Dissatisfaction with the regime had been brewing for years, but the catalyst for widespread nonviolent protests was the populace's yearning for greater freedoms, democratic reforms, and economic change.

Peaceful protests, spearheaded by church-led movements and opposition groups, began sprouting up across East Germany. Pastor Christian Führer, a key figure in these early protests at the St. Nicholas Church in Leipzig, organized regular "Monday Demonstrations." While these protests started modestly, they gained momentum as word spread, drawing individuals from diverse backgrounds.

The nonviolent nature of these demonstrations played a pivotal role in garnering both domestic and international support. Images of East German citizens holding candles and singing songs of peace starkly contrasted with the oppressive regime they sought to change. This moral high ground helped sway public opinion and encouraged more people to join the protests.

The pivotal moment arrived on November 9, 1989, when the East German government announced the opening of the Berlin Wall. This decision was a response to the escalating peaceful protests and the growing demand for freedom and democracy.

With the fall of the Berlin Wall, a significant period of change commenced. East Germans crossed into West

Berlin, and in the ensuing months, more peaceful demonstrations, negotiations, and discussions ensued. The authoritarian government of East Germany, under Erich Honecker's leadership, was compelled to step down, making way for a more reform-oriented leadership.

The call for reunification with West Germany gained momentum. Through peaceful protests, dialogues, and negotiations between East and West German leaders, Germany was reunified on October 3, 1990. The GDR ceased to exist, and Germany emerged as a unified, democratic nation.

The peaceful collapse of the GDR stands as a triumph of nonviolent resistance, grassroots movements, and the inherent human quest for freedom and democracy. It vividly illustrates the potency of nonviolence in effecting political change, even in the face of oppressive regimes. The fall of the Berlin Wall remains an enduring symbol of hope, unity, and the remarkable power of peaceful protest in surmounting division and oppression.

Under Nicolae Ceaușescu's communist regime in Romania, citizens endured severe repression, censorship, and egregious human rights abuses. In December 1989, anti-government protests erupted in Timișoara, swiftly spreading across various cities. The government's efforts to quell the protests led to violent clashes, intensifying public outrage. Notably, segments of the Romanian military defected, siding with the protesters. Mass demonstrations in Bucharest ultimately culminated in Ceaușescu's capture, subsequent trial, and execution. While not signifying a complete overthrow of communism, these events marked the demise of a particularly oppressive regime.

The collapse of the USSR emerged from a complex interplay of multiple factors, with peaceful protests playing a significant role in this historical transformation.

Mikhail Gorbachev's policies in the 1980s—perestroika (economic restructuring) and glasnost (openness)—created an environment conducive to peaceful protests. Glasnost, specifically, fostered greater political discourse and allowed dissent to surface.

The Baltic states, notably Lithuania, Latvia, and Estonia, voiced their desire for independence through peaceful means. The Singing Revolution featured massive nonviolent protests—singing national songs and forming human chains—that challenged Soviet rule, ultimately leading to their restored independence in 1991.

Moscow became a focal point for peaceful protests. The August 1991 coup attempt by hardline Communists sparked widespread opposition. Civilians, led by Russian President Boris Yeltsin, congregated around key government sites, effectively thwarting the coup. This failure weakened the centralized authority of the USSR.

National movements in Ukraine and the Caucasus sought independence peacefully. The Ukrainian independence movement, led by figures such as Vyacheslav Chornovil and Leonid Kravchuk, culminated in Ukraine's declaration of independence in 1991.

Western nations' advocacy for human rights and democratic reforms exerted international pressure on the Soviet Union, supporting domestic opposition movements.

Worker strikes and civil disobedience were widespread across the Soviet Union, highlighting economic hardships and discontent with the Soviet system, notably in the late 1980s and early 1990s. Economic instability severely undermined the Soviet Union. Economic decline coupled with diminishing faith in the Soviet system eroded the government's control.

In December 1991, the Soviet republic leaders, in the Belavezha Accords, declared the peaceful dissolution of the USSR, marking its end.

While the fall of the USSR resulted from a multifaceted mix of political, economic, and international pressures, peaceful protests and nonviolent resistance played pivotal roles. They significantly altered power dynamics, fostering political pluralism, and paving the way for democracy in the region.

These historical examples illustrate the power of nonviolent resistance in challenging and dismantling communist regimes. They highlight the role of mass mobilization, persistence, international support, and strategic non-violent tactics in bringing about positive political change.

While peaceful protests can be effective, it is important to acknowledge that pushback from the regime is a common occurrence. In countries under communist rule, political repression emerges as a recurring feature. These regimes often prioritize the supremacy of the state over individual rights and liberties. Dissent and opposition are typically suppressed through various means, including censorship, restrictions on freedom of speech, and limitations on political participation. Citizens often find themselves under surveillance, facing arbitrary detentions, and experiencing restricted mobility.

An anti-communist refugee provided insight into life behind the Iron Curtain, where some apparent liberties existed, but the Communist Party's economic control discouraged people from exercising their theoretical rights: "You Americans have funny ideas about the life under communism. Apparently, you think there's a communist soldier standing on every street corner with a rifle and bayonet to keep the people in line but this isn't so. Oh sure, in the beginning there were plenty of soldiers, and executions, and deportation to slave labor camps but we don't see much of that anymore. The open violence lasted only for about a year or year and a half and then the anti-communist leadership was liquidated, and now to the casual observers, there's a great deal of apparent calm and freedom. For instance, I lived in the largest city in the country. We had a large park directly across the street from a beautiful church. They left one church open, one in the entire country primarily for guided tours of visiting Americans who had come to see if religion was being persecuted. Anytime I wanted to, I could have gone into that park, stood on a bench and spoken out against communism. Then I could have walked across the street into that church and knelt down in prayer and I wouldn't have been arrested or bothered in any way but you can be sure I did not do these things because if I had, the very next day the wheels of the bureaucracy would have begun to turn and I would have been informed that my quota food stamps have been cut, my allotment for clothing and shoes had been reduced, my allocation for living quarters had been downgraded, and finally my job assignment had been changed from the kind of work for which I'd been trained to menial labor at lower pay. So, none of us did any of those things that we were theoretically entitled to do because of the tremendous power the Communist Party had over our economic existence..."[44]

The emergence of Central Bank Digital Currencies (CBDCs) has ignited debates about their impact on financial control, privacy, and personal liberties. While they are praised for their efficiency and potential to address inequalities, a closer examination reveals troubling implications.

CBDCs, often highlighted for their efficiency, come with a significant trade-off: they compromise financial privacy and individual autonomy due to their centralized control by authorities. Integrating CBDCs into e-government services, despite promising efficiency, raises red flags concerning privacy and autonomy. Their digital nature allows government surveillance, posing risks to privacy rights, freedom of association, and civil liberties. This pervasive monitoring could stifle dissenting voices and foster self-censorship, while exposing transactions could make individuals vulnerable to public scrutiny, especially when linked to digital identities.

The introduction of CBDCs intensifies control, granting unprecedented oversight into financial transactions and economic policies. This elevated control opens pathways for financial discrimination, centralized monetary control, wealth redistribution, and stifling dissent. It empowers governments to manipulate financial behavior to silence opposition, potentially denying crucial services to non-conformists.

---

[44] Griffin, G. Edward. "Here's the Democrat-run Communist Game Plan to Take Over the USA (Video + Transcript) More Deadly Than War (1969)." *State of the Nation*, 30 Oct. 2020, stateofthenation.co/?p=33996.

CBDCs also raise concerns about suppressing resistance and subjecting citizens to perpetual surveillance. Transactions conducted through CBDCs erode financial anonymity, deterring legitimate financial activities and potentially fostering discriminatory practices. There is apprehension that measures executed through CBDCs, such as negative interest rates or capital controls, might discourage saving, encourage excessive spending, and restrict fund movement, amplifying financial instability during crises.

The implementation of CBDCs, despite central banks operating independently from governments, raises concerns about potential governmental overreach and control reminiscent of past communist systems. Their digital capabilities for surveillance might enable identification and stifling of dissenting voices, coercing conformity by controlling financial transactions.

The concern over CBDCs reflects a historical pattern where economic control deterred individuals from exercising their rights. In a similar vein, CBDCs might dissuade dissent due to potential economic repercussions, thus potentially limiting individual autonomy under the guise of financial control.

In summary, CBDCs extend beyond simple financial tools and could evolve into instruments that consolidate government control, erode personal freedoms, and undermine individual autonomy, echoing historical instances of governmental overreach and control.

The implementation of a comprehensive social credit system within communist regimes serves as a powerful tool to suppress dissent. This system, designed to perpetually monitor citizens' actions and viewpoints, erodes personal privacy and civil liberties. It is exploited by governments to silence opposition, discriminate against those with differing beliefs, and limit the freedom of expression and association. The lack of transparency in the scoring process leaves citizens without recourse to challenge biased decisions, further undermining accountability.

Despite the intended aim of encouraging positive behavior, when wielded by oppressive governments, social credit systems can be manipulated to suppress dissent and exert control over citizens. Extensive surveillance, punitive measures for dissent, manipulation of public opinion, exacerbation of social divisions, and lack of transparency contribute to the erosion of civil liberties and freedom.

Social credit systems, such as China's Social Credit System (SCS), evaluate individuals based on social, financial, and behavioral conduct. The system's daily scoring impacts personal lives, social interactions, and financial stability, significantly affecting individuals' overall well-being.

For individuals holding low social credit scores, daily life is fraught with challenges. They encounter obstacles when traveling, accessing education, healthcare, housing, and employment. Social stigma and exclusion due to perceived untrustworthiness result in public shaming, social isolation, and strained relationships, impacting personal and domestic life. The fear of repercussions leads to self-censorship, eroding freedom of speech and expression.

In essence, the social credit system can transform into a contentious tool of control within oppressive regimes. Prioritizing scores over personal beliefs undermines privacy, freedom, and the ability to express dissent, ultimately corroding fundamental rights and liberties.

In oppressive regimes, dissenters often encounter rejection and isolation. The ruler may not enforces conformity through direct threats of death; instead, dissent is seemingly tolerated, yet those who oppose are pushed to the fringes. Despite the existence of civil rights on paper, their practical value diminishes in an environment that marginalizes and neglects those who hold contrasting views.

This context gives rise to a subtler form of tyranny, where dissent is allowed but met with exclusion and isolation. Individuals expressing differing opinions might not face immediate physical harm or death, but they experience marginalization and a loss of social standing. While technically retaining their rights, these rights lose their effectiveness in an environment that sidelines and abandons dissenters.

This type of tyranny operates insidiously, relying on social pressure and psychological tactics to stifle disagreement and suppress opposition. It serves as a potent tool for those in power to retain control and enforce compliance without resorting to overt violence. This profoundly impacts free speech, interpersonal relations, and societal harmony, exerting a significant influence on both individuals and the broader society.

Exploring strategies to counter government suppression and navigate the impact of CBDCs involves diversifying assets, using encrypted tools, and fostering alternative financial systems.

Diversifying assets by investing in tangible forms such as gold, silver, real estate, or commodities serves as a vital shield against vulnerabilities inherent in digital currencies such as CBDCs. These tangible assets offer a buffer against cyber risks, shielding against potential currency devaluation, and enhancing overall financial security. Gold and silver, considered traditional safe-haven investments, particularly shine in uncertain economic climates. Including these precious metals in financial plans not only ensures digital privacy but also acts as a guard against currency devaluation and mitigates risks associated with CBDCs.

Additionally, employing encrypted messaging services and Virtual Private Networks (VPNs) bolsters online privacy, shielding personal information from surveillance and adding an extra layer of security against government scrutiny.

Moreover, recognizing concerns over CBDCs and biases in mainstream platforms, the creation of alternative payment systems aims to provide neutral spaces where diverse viewpoints can interact without censorship or favoritism. These initiatives counter concentrated power dynamics and offer an open platform for financial transactions and discussions.

Navigating government surveillance requires practical tactics. Prioritizing offline transactions and cash usage in daily activities helps reduce digital footprints and minimizes surveillance in oppressive environments. Utilizing encrypted communication tools such as secure messaging apps and VPNs protects personal information from surveillance, adding a layer of privacy and security. Engaging in local community networks or informal economies offers alternative resources outside centralized systems, fostering resilience in the face of government control.

Additionally, educating oneself and others about surveillance risks empowers individuals to make informed choices and take necessary precautions when dealing with extensive government surveillance and control. By diversifying assets, employing encrypted tools, integrating safe-haven assets, fostering neutral financial platforms, and adopting strategies to navigate oppressive regimes, individuals can counter the effects of government surveillance and control.

Presently, America grapples with challenges reminiscent of the upheaval during the Civil War era. The radical Left, deeply entrenched in Marxist doctrines, remains steadfast in its mission to subvert the foundational principles of the United States in their pursuit of a socialist utopia.

The divisions between constitutional conservatives and socialist radicals create significant barriers to national unity. These rifts echo the fractures observed during the onset of the Civil War in 1860, representing an unprecedented polarization. The surge of "woke Marxism" amplifies the pursuit of power through ideals rooted in social justice, identity politics, and cultural transformation. While advocates champion diversity and justice, there is a risk of heightening societal divides along racial and gender lines. Policies under the Biden administration have notably widened these gaps, fostering internal discord within communities and eroding established traditional values and norms. The prospects for finding common ground and seeking compromises are increasingly remote.

The potential for armed conflict stands as a final recourse to protect the constitutional republic, should peaceful alternatives fail to stop the Marxist clampdown on our cherished rights and liberties. President Thomas Jefferson's evocative words, "The tree of liberty must be refreshed from time to time with the blood of patriots and tyrants," highlight the potential sacrifices that may be necessary to save America from a complete communist takeover.

CONCLUSION

The covert infiltration of communist ideals within the United States is a deeply concerning trend, constituting what can be described as a 5th column. This clandestine network strategically embedded itself within pivotal sectors, exercising substantial influence over the nation's ideological landscape.

Their sphere of influence permeates crucial cultural, educational, and media domains, where their impact shapes societal norms and molds public discourse.

Within the media landscape, this group adeptly manipulates narratives and controls information flow to align with their Marxist ideology. Positioned strategically in influential roles, they steer news coverage and editorial policies, skillfully guiding public opinion toward socialist beliefs. Their mastery over information dissemination holds immense sway, fundamentally shaping societal perceptions and fostering inclinations toward progressive ideologies.

Their reach also extends into education, where they seek to instill socialist ideals in impressionable young minds. Manipulating curricula, textbooks, and academic discourse within educational institutions, they prioritize collectivism over individualism and advocate socialism over capitalism. This deliberate emphasis on communist ideologies within educational materials aims to reshape the beliefs of future generations, potentially redirecting the nation's core values and trajectory.

In cultural spheres, certain narratives, artistic expressions, and intellectual circles echo Marxist ideologies. These cultural movements advocating for societal change often reflect elements of Marxist thought, contributing to the normalization and dissemination of communist ideals.

Community organizations, advocacy groups, and grassroots movements serve as platforms to advance socialist principles. Through these bodies, they push for policies and societal changes aligned with leftist ideals, fostering widespread acceptance of socialist ideologies.

Their impact also resonates within political circles, where they wield substantial influence by funding sympathetic candidates or advocating for progressive policies. This strategic maneuvering enables them to shape agendas and steer policies toward their communist utopia.

A notable aspect is the expansion of bureaucracy and increased government intervention, mirroring core tenets of Marxist ideology advocating for an expanded state role in social and economic spheres. These developments align with Marxist principles favoring centralized authority and extensive state involvement in economic matters.

Collaborations between bureaucratic factions and leftist political groups further these agendas, promoting policies inclined toward wealth redistribution, heightened governmental oversight, and regulatory structures akin to socialist ideologies. These policy pursuits align with fundamental communist notions, emphasizing collective welfare over individual freedoms. This network's pervasive influence poses a significant challenge to the traditional values and structures of America.

The pervasive infiltration of Marxist ideologies in various segments of American society significantly shapes perceptions and molds public discourse. This steady normalization of socialist ideologies across critical sectors raises profound concerns, casting a shadow over societal operations and highlighting the potential repercussions of embracing socialist policies. This infiltration directly threatens democratic principles, freedom of speech, and individual liberties, imperiling the bedrock of the nation's traditional values and economic systems.

While communism often promises immediate equality and wealth redistribution, the focus on short-term gains poses significant risks that undermine the core tenets of liberal democracy and erode fundamental aspects of society.

At the heart of liberal democracy lies the protection of individual rights and freedoms. However, Marxist ideologies, in their pursuit of collective equality, frequently encroach upon individual liberties. Prioritizing the collective good over individual autonomy leads to constraints on personal freedoms in the name of equality. This erosion weakens the foundation upon which liberal democracies are built, curtailing citizens' autonomy and agency.

Moreover, these ideologies challenge the sanctity of private property ownership, a cornerstone of free-market capitalism. Communism advocates for abolishing private property to redistribute wealth and resources among the populace. These policies undermine incentives for innovation, entrepreneurship, and investment—critical drivers of economic growth in free-market economies. The erosion of property rights disrupts market mechanisms essential for economic prosperity, stifling innovation and hindering sustainable long-term growth.

Additionally, these leftist ideologies often entail centralized control over resources and the means of production, leading to inefficiencies and stagnation. Concentrating power in the hands of the state restricts competition and innovation, hindering economic dynamism and progress. This centralized control hampers adaptation to evolving market demands and technological advancements, impeding the ability to evolve and excel in a rapidly changing global landscape.

Ultimately, prioritizing short-term equality over long-term sustainability poses a significant risk to the foundational principles of liberal democracy. The erosion of individual rights, disregard for private property ownership, and limitations on economic freedom inherent in these leftist ideologies hinder societies' ability to flourish and adapt in the long run. This jeopardizes the prosperity and vitality of nations in the ever-evolving socio-economic landscape.

Historical experience vividly portrays the detrimental effects of nations embracing communism, unveiling a grim narrative of oppressive governance, central planning, and the perilous trade-off between collective aspirations and individual freedoms.

A deep examination of these nations' histories unravels a recurring pattern—a gradual swelling of governmental authority and its devastating aftermath. As government authority expands, it intrudes into nearly every facet of citizens' lives. Policies molded to enforce collective ideals systematically erode personal freedoms, suffocating autonomy under oppressive regulations that smother individual expression and innovation. These constraints strangle creativity, discourage risk-taking, and obliterate the emergence of diverse ideas necessary for societal progress.

Simultaneously, the burgeoning government erects a labyrinthine bureaucratic edifice. The proliferation of administrative structures fosters inefficiencies and bureaucratic entanglements. Decision-making processes grow convoluted, sabotaging adaptability and responsiveness to societal and economic shifts. This bureaucratic quagmire sabotages flexibility, rendering rapid and effective responses to emerging challenges increasingly difficult.

Economically, the suffocating grip of centralized control disrupts established market mechanisms. State intervention replaces market-driven dynamics, resulting in skewed resource allocation and inefficiencies. The stifling of private enterprise and innovation saps economic dynamism, stunting growth. The dearth of incentives for entrepreneurship stifles initiative, contributing to a void of innovation crucial for sustained economic progress.

This collective impact paints a bleak portrait of a society ensnared in bureaucratic hurdles, straitjacketed individual freedoms, and asphyxiated innovation. The initial pursuit of collective progress through centralized control births unintended consequences—societal stagnation, economic inefficiency, and an inability to adapt in an ever-changing world.

Ultimately, this cyclical narrative underscores the precarious balance between state authority and individual liberties. Overbearing governmental control, purportedly intended to foster collective progress, invariably transforms into a formidable obstacle, thwarting innovation, constraining progress, and smothering the vibrancy of a society ignited by diverse perspectives and individual contributions.

The United States faces a complex array of challenges—from economic downturns and inflationary pressures to soaring gas prices, supply chain disruptions, and shortages of essential goods. Many attribute these issues to the Biden administration's increasing embrace of socialist policies and the nation's significant shift towards the left.

Certain Biden policies, notably in border control and increased regulations, bear troubling resemblances to Marxist ideals. These actions signal a shift toward collectivist ideologies, sparking deep concerns about the country's socio-economic trajectory.

Moreover, the proliferation of regulatory measures across diverse economic sectors intensifies fears of an expanding government reach. These regulations harken back to socialist-rooted policies, heightening worries about governmental interference in areas traditionally governed by free market dynamics.

Policies regarding border controls and regulations prompt worries about the nation's inclination toward collectivist trends. The surge in regulatory actions across economic sectors exacerbates concerns about an expanding government role, disrupting the delicate balance between market forces and the cherished individual liberties ingrained in the nation's history.

The shift toward policies echoing socialist principles poses a significant threat to the cherished American values grounded in free-market capitalism and limited government involvement. The encroachment of these socialist ideas challenges the core principles of American governance, established to safeguard against concentrated power and uphold democratic equilibrium.

The predominant influence of leftist ideologies across critical information platforms—news outlets, educational institutions, and social media—raises concerns about biased information dissemination. This situation sparks worries about deliberate manipulation to conform to narrow ideological agendas, intensifying the nation's polarization. This ideological division carries significant implications for America's future, affecting not only ideological unity but also the fundamental values of our democratic system.

Fundamentally, the challenges faced by the United States stem from an increasing acceptance of socialist principles. The shift away from traditional American values rooted in free-market capitalism and minimal government intervention contributes significantly to the socio-economic obstacles confronting the country today.

These trends highlight a discernible departure from cherished American ideals centered on free-market capitalism and limited government intervention. The expanding government role in both the economy and society signifies a shift away from these foundational values, prompting discussions about preserving the essence of American democracy. This noticeable trend towards socialist policies poses a substantial threat to the bedrock of American values. The encroachment of these ideals challenges the essence of American governance, established to prevent centralized power and maintain a balance of power among the various institutions.

The ideological divergence fundamentally challenges the foundations of the country's governance. Resolving these conflicts will shape our governance structures, societal norms, and the core identity of the nation.

The attempt to transition the United States into a communist state faces staunch opposition due to a complex interweaving of factors deeply ingrained in the American system. Advocates striving for such a vast societal transformation encounter formidable obstacles stemming from a multitude of sources. These span cultural and historical disparities, ideological clashes, legal intricacies, and economic complexities deeply interwoven into the nation's fabric.

Culturally, the United States encompasses a diverse tapestry of beliefs, values, and traditions that starkly contrast with the communal ideals championed by communist ideologies. This cultural diversity fosters a strong sense of individualism and a dedication to personal freedoms, inherently at odds with the collective principles envisioned by Marxist doctrines.

Furthermore, the nation's historical narrative, rooted in the ideals of liberty, democracy, and free-market capitalism, acts as a foundational barrier against radical ideological shifts. The American identity, shaped by a legacy of advocating for individual liberties and economic freedom, fundamentally opposes the centralized control advocated by communism.

Ideologically, a profound clash exists between the principles of an open, free society and the tenets of a centrally planned, collectivist state. The deeply ingrained belief in the sanctity of individual rights and limited government contradicts the expansive governmental control inherent in Marxist ideologies.

Legally, the United States boasts robust institutions fortified by checks and balances, serving as bulwarks against radical shifts in governance. Supported by the Constitution and a robust legal framework, these institutions act as safeguards against activities challenging the nation's democratic foundation.

Economically, the nation's commitment to free-market capitalism and entrepreneurial innovation starkly contrasts with the collectivization and state-controlled economies advocated by communist doctrines. The resilience of the American economic system, renowned for nurturing innovation and prosperity, presents a significant obstacle to the wholesale adoption of Marxist ideals.

The resilience of these multifaceted factors entrenched within the American system collectively constructs a formidable defense against the ambitious push toward socialism.

Cultural Marxism has emerged as a powerful force subtly reshaping American institutions by repurposing Marxist ideologies to challenge traditional cultural norms and values. A cohort of intellectuals and activists, drawing from Marxist theories, strategically penetrated influential spheres such as academia, media, and the arts. Their objective was to cultivate a new cultural dominance, disrupting the established order and promoting their radical ideological agendas.

There are concerns regarding the education system potentially instilling Marxist ideologies in young minds under the guise of progressive education. These teachings might initiate a shift in generational values, potentially steering society towards communism. This narrative highlights the cultural impact, suggesting a deliberate manipulation of societal values and norms to align with their ideological principles.

The nation's institutions, deeply rooted in democratic principles and fortified by cultural, historical, legal, and economic foundations, have the potential to counteract such subversive activities.

The consequences of America succumbing to communism would echo across every aspect of its existence, fundamentally altering the core of individual liberties and societal progress.

Communism inherently tightens its grip on economic dynamism and innovation. Its centralized control stifles entrepreneurial ventures and drains the source of creativity and advancement. Striving for equality through redistribution often leads to resource misallocation and persistent shortages in vital goods and services.

This shift in America's socio-economic structure would bring profound implications for its growth trajectory. The very backbone of the nation's prosperity—the free-market system—would face significant challenges. The quintessential American strengths of innovation and competitiveness might diminish, limiting opportunities for personal and professional growth. Such limitations could constrain the potential of citizens, narrowing career options and hindering avenues for progress.

Moreover, embracing communist ideologies could sculpt a societal landscape where individual advancement takes a backseat. Prioritizing collective welfare might suppress personal aspirations, curtailing opportunities for individual evolution and fulfillment.

Adopting socialism might confine citizens within national borders, curtailing their freedom to explore opportunities overseas. Historical patterns demonstrate that communist ideologies impose strict limitations on emigration, diminishing individuals' autonomy and their freedom to travel.

In essence, a shift towards socialism in America would stifle citizens' economic, personal, and professional freedoms, blocking paths to growth and progress. These constraints risk eroding the nation's economic vigor, undermining the diverse opportunities that have historically embodied the American dream.

The establishment of communist regimes has consistently entailed the suppression of fundamental freedoms and the stifling of dissent to assert control. Throughout history, dissent within such regimes has been systematically suppressed using tools such as censorship, state-controlled media, and harsh measures that restrict free speech. If these principles were to infiltrate American governance, there is a risk of undermining freedom of expression—a cornerstone of democratic societies.

In a socialist framework, civil liberties such as privacy and due process face compromises. These regimes often prioritize state interests over individual rights, leading to invasive surveillance and unfair judicial processes. Such erosions of civil liberties could fundamentally reshape the landscape of American society.

Additionally, communist regimes are notorious for stifling cultural diversity and independent thinking, enforcing conformity to state-endorsed ideologies. This imposition threatens to suffocate diverse opinions, creativity, and critical thinking—essential elements for societal progress and development.

Marxist ideologies often nurture centralized authority, resulting in an expansion of government control and the enforcement of stringent regulations. This intrusion into personal spheres could significantly curtail individual freedoms and agency, imposing restrictions on everyday life.

The imposition of communism in America could significantly impede freedom of expression and impose stringent regulations, encroaching upon the autonomy and liberties of American citizens. Such a transformation would directly challenge the foundational democratic values of the nation, fundamentally reshaping American society.

Another concern lies in the potential loss of the option for individuals to seek refuge elsewhere if America falls to socialism. Historically, people from countries under communist rule have sought sanctuary in more democratic nations for better opportunities and greater freedoms. Yet, if America were to adopt communism, this escape route would vanish.

Countering Marxist subversion and safeguarding the foundational principles of the United States hinge on strengthening education and fortifying democratic institutions against ideological conformity.

Education is the bedrock of safeguarding republican values, shaping the perspectives of future generations. It's essential to equip the youth with a deep understanding of civic duties, critical thinking skills, and a comprehensive grasp of the Constitution and historical perspectives. Creating an educational environment that embraces diverse viewpoints and rigorous analysis empowers students to discern and counter attempts at ideological manipulation.

Encouraging critical thinking stands as an essential cornerstone. It empowers individuals to challenge ideologies and cultivate intellectual independence. By nurturing this skill, people can scrutinize information critically, shielding themselves from simplistic narratives or rigid beliefs. This capability allows them to form opinions grounded in evidence and rational analysis, rather than succumbing to manipulative tactics.

Civic education serves as a linchpin in shaping a populace well-versed in democratic values and governance structures. Instilling civic responsibility and a deep appreciation for democratic principles fosters an active and engaged citizenry, a robust defense against attempts to undermine republican institutions.

Through education, individuals gain an understanding of American history and principles, empowering them to identify and resist ideological influences. This foundational knowledge enables critical engagement with information, nurturing a society adept at upholding democratic values.

Educational endeavors that impart knowledge about American history and principles instill an appreciation for the nation's democratic heritage. This cultivates a sense of civic duty and a firm commitment to upholding democratic values, nurturing an informed, engaged citizenry capable of safeguarding the nation's identity.

Furthermore, education serves as a barrier against ideological manipulation by imparting knowledge of American history and principles, instilling civic responsibility, and fostering a profound appreciation for republican ideals. It nurtures intellectual independence, enabling individuals to resist coercion or indoctrination.

Integral to civic education is equipping citizens with the knowledge and critical thinking skills to discern genuine activism from actions that undermine democratic values. Emphasizing the bedrock of democracy, citizens' rights, and responsibilities prepares individuals to recognize and assess actions aligned with democratic principles.

Highlighting the benefits of American principles and values is crucial in countering the allure of alternative ideologies. Demonstrating the successes inherent in individual freedoms, democratic governance, and the rule of law presents a compelling narrative that contrasts with the empty promises of communism.

Celebrating individual freedoms, inherent in American society, highlights the value of autonomy and personal agency. Showcasing stories of individuals achieving success, innovation, and self-fulfillment through these liberties underscores their profound impact on societal progress. It illustrates how the freedom to pursue aspirations and express oneself fosters a dynamic society, promoting innovation, creativity, and diverse perspectives.

Likewise, extolling the virtues of democracy—where every voice counts—emphasizes its inclusivity and responsiveness. Contrasting this with the centralized authority and lack of pluralism in Marxist ideologies underscores the significance of democratic governance, representation, and the protection of minority rights.

Highlighting the successes and merits of American principles paints a vivid picture of the concrete advantages derived from a society rooted in individual freedoms, democratic governance, and the rule of law. The steadfast emphasis on the rule of law, ensuring impartial justice and protection through a transparent legal system, stands in stark contrast to the arbitrary and often inadequate legal safeguards witnessed in communist regimes. This narrative emerges as a guiding light, countering the deceptive allure of promises by ideologies such as communism and revealing the tangible, enduring benefits of a society founded on liberty, democracy, and justice.

Advocating for free-market capitalism and entrepreneurship highlights the benefits of economic freedom: innovation, creativity, and the transformative impact of private enterprise. It champions individual initiative, fostering innovation and creativity. Celebrating entrepreneurship showcases its role in driving economic growth, job creation, and technological advancement, benefiting society as a whole. Emphasizing the efficiency of market-driven economies contrasts them with bureaucratic, state-controlled systems, promoting fairness and meritocracy. This advocacy underscores how economic freedom nurtures prosperity, innovation, and inclusivity, offering a strong response to collectivist ideologies that stifle economies.

Efforts aimed at fostering an informed citizenry through media literacy and civic education play a crucial role in fortifying defenses against subversion. Media literacy programs empower individuals to distinguish credible sources, thus strengthening their immunity against manipulation. Equipping people with critical thinking skills enables them to navigate the vast sea of information, effectively discerning truth from misinformation. These initiatives not only bolster defenses but also safeguard democratic institutions, upholding fundamental democratic values.

It is essential to educate individuals on the methodologies employed by radical groups in infiltrating institutions. This education provides people with the awareness and tools necessary to identify signs of influence and manipulation. By taking a proactive approach, individuals are empowered to recognize subversive activities that threaten the integrity and values of institutions.

Comprehending these strategies involves exploring tactics such as propagating dissemination, coercion, and systematic infiltration into key positions within institutions. Shedding light on these methods enables individuals to discern subtle signs of ideological influence or attempts to undermine an institution's mission and values.

Raising awareness about these strategies allows institutions to implement effective countermeasures. Education about infiltration strategies aids in devising proactive measures. Institutions can establish comprehensive protocols and mechanisms to address and mitigate attempted or actual infiltration by radical groups. This proactive stance ensures institutions are better equipped to safeguard their integrity and values against external threats.

Community engagement and cooperation serve as crucial pillars in safeguarding democratic values and fortifying resilience against subversion. Encouraging local participation and collaborative problem-solving not only nurtures unity and shared responsibility but also bolsters resilience. Empowering communities in governance and civic activities cultivates a sense of ownership, enhances social cohesion, and acts as a barrier against manipulation.

The promotion of collaborative solutions not only fosters dialogue but also values diverse perspectives, erecting a formidable defense against external attempts to exploit divisions or sow discord.

Active community engagement becomes a bastion of trust, fortifying defenses against misinformation and threats to democratic principles. Open dialogue facilitates understanding and respect for differing viewpoints, reinforcing institutional integrity and proactively defending against external influences. Cultivating civil discourse and embracing respectful disagreement reinforces democratic resilience, ensuring a cohesive and inclusive society that welcomes dissent while upholding democratic ideals.

A comprehensive approach involving education, media literacy, and open dialogue acts as a stronghold against threats to democratic values. Equipping citizens with knowledge, critical thinking skills, and the ability to engage in informed discussions fortifies the foundation of democracy, ensuring its endurance in an ever-evolving society. Upholding individual liberties through open discourse and defending freedom of expression creates an environment where diverse viewpoints thrive, honoring dissent as a barrier against attempts to enforce ideological uniformity.

Strengthening the bedrock of American democratic institutions stands as our foremost duty in safeguarding the nation's core democratic principles. These institutions serve as vital guardians, shielding against potential threats to the republic, ensuring that authority remains accountable to the people. Reinforcing these structures is indispensable in upholding the nation's pledge to democratic governance and preventing any concentration of power that might erode fundamental democratic ideals.

Empowering the legislative, executive, and judicial branches is imperative, securing their autonomy and efficacy. Safeguarding their independence and functionality from undue influence entails enhancing their capacity to fulfill roles without external pressures.

Preserving the integrity of electoral processes is pivotal, ensuring fairness and transparency while warding off interference. This secures the populace's voice as the cornerstone of democracy.

Fostering civic engagement and participation reinforces the bond between citizens and their government. Active involvement in governance and community initiatives holds officials accountable, strengthening the democratic process and the connection between the government and its people.

Transparency and accountability within governmental bodies play a pivotal role. Establishing robust transparency mechanisms bolsters public trust and reinforces democratic values.

Collaboration among diverse stakeholders — governments, civil society organizations, and educational institutions—is essential in erecting a robust defense against threats to democratic integrity. This coalition aligns efforts to counter challenges, creating a unified front against attempts to undermine democratic principles, thereby fortifying the nation's resilience.

Each entity within this coalition holds a crucial role in countering subversion. Civil society organizations rally public awareness and resilience against subversion. Educational institutions equip individuals with critical thinking and understanding of democratic principles, fortifying societal resilience.

Collaboration among stakeholders ensures a comprehensive defense against subversion by maximizing the effectiveness of strategies deployed against such tactics, reinforcing democratic values, and safeguarding the nation's institutions.

The United States faces a critical moment, contending with persistent subversive efforts from the radical left, aiming to embed Marxist ideologies into our national identity. This demands resolute opposition to their advancement and the encroachment of communism. Protecting American principles, reinforcing institutional foundations, and upholding the republic's legacy require a unified dedication to preserving democratic values, staunchly defending individual freedoms, and safeguarding institutional integrity against this looming threat. A steadfast commitment to democratic ideals forms the foundation of a governance framework rooted in accountability, representation, and the defense of individual rights. These principles are crucial in fostering a thriving society that prioritizes economic growth, values civil liberties, and upholds democratic principles.

The preservation of a free-market economy, marked by competition, innovation, and entrepreneurial vigor, remains pivotal in driving economic growth and prosperity.

This economic ethos creates an environment conducive to investment, job creation, and technological advancements, offering avenues for individual and collective progress.

Safeguarding individual liberties remains integral in preserving the essence of a free society. Protecting rights such as freedom of speech, assembly, and religion fosters an environment where diverse perspectives thrive, promoting societal progress and innovation.

Promoting a culture that values diversity of thought, intellectual curiosity, and the protection of individual liberties not only solidifies our societal resilience but also amplifies our capacity to navigate the complexities posed by ideological challenges.

By safeguarding these ideals—democratic values, a free-market economy, and individual liberties—America can remain a beacon of hope, providing refuge for those fleeing oppressive regimes. This commitment fortifies the nation's role as a sanctuary embodying freedom, equality, and opportunity.

Furthermore, fortifying our institutions—whether in education, media, or governance—against ideological subversion becomes crucial. Ensuring that these pillars of our society remain bastions of impartiality, free thought, and democratic principles serves as a bulwark against the erosion of our core values.

Remaining vigilant against radical ideologies that threaten the fabric of our democratic society is imperative. Through fostering a collective commitment to our foundational principles, engaging actively in informed discourse, and fortifying our institutions against ideological infiltration, we can uphold the legacy of freedom, democracy, and individual autonomy that defines our nation.

This endeavor necessitates unity in purpose and an unwavering dedication to preserving the fundamental principles that define us. By steadfastly adhering to the core tenets of democracy, our nation bolsters its resilience against ideologies challenging our traditional values. This resolute stance not only safeguards the essence of democracy but also serves as a guiding beacon, ensuring a vibrant spirit of liberty and prosperity for our citizens.

United in purpose, there exists a collective determination to shape a future where liberty flourishes, prosperity thrives, and the timeless values ingrained in the American identity endure. Upholding these values necessitates safeguarding our nation's republican heritage through active engagement and participation.

Together, let us endeavor for a future where liberty thrives, prosperity prevails, and the enduring values of America remain steadfast. Safeguarding our nation's republican heritage through active participation is essential in upholding trust, unity, and democratic principles— aligning closely with governance by, of, and for the people. This collective commitment is pivotal in preserving the essence of our national identity and securing a future that upholds the cherished ideals we hold dear.

REFERENCES

"'#Texit': A Texas State Lawmaker Says He Will Propose a Referendum on Seceding from the US Because the 'Federal Government Is Out of Control'." *Business Insider*, www.businessinsider.com/ texit-texas-state-lawmaker-suggests-referendum-to-secede-from-us-2020-12.

"300,000 Undelivered Ballots In Michigan And Other States Now A Judge Gets Involved." *Newstalk WBCK 95.3*, 4 Nov. 2020, wbckfm.com/300000-undelivered-ballots-in-michigan-and-other-states-now-a-judge-gets-involved/?trackback=fbshare_mobile&fbclid=IwAR2QDy_h2yAGRNn1f o9JTkk4_0waohbf-cejvGD2CmqqjwefG132UTc2aRE.

Adams, Mike. "A 'day of reckoning' is coming – Lin Wood reveals, 'the evidence I have is stunning!'" *Natural News*, 2 Dec. 2020, www.naturalnews.com/2020-12-02-lin-wood-day-of-reckoning-is-coming-evidence.html.

Adams, Mike. "CAUGHT! Election data analyzed, producing detailed list of over 500,000 votes SWITCHED from Trump to Biden via voting machine software theft, with heavy fraud focused on swing states." *Natural News*, 11 Nov. 2021, www.naturalnews.com/2020-11-11-election-data-analyzed-votes-switched-biden-software.html#.

Adams, Mike. "Communist Subversion of America Is Nearly Complete: Left-Wing Media 'Soviet-Style Overthrow' In Progress." *Natural News*, 9 January 2017, www.naturalnews.com/ 2017-01-09-communist-subversion-of-america-is-nearly-complete-left-wing-media-soviet-style-overthrow-yuri-bezmenov.html.

Adams, Mike. "Full transcript of bombshell interview: Gen. Michael Flynn, Gen. Thomas McInerney with Brannon Howse – Identity of KRAKEN revealed." *Natural News*, 29 Nov. 2020, www.naturalnews.com/2020-11-29-full-transcript-interview-gen-michael-flynn-gen-thomas-mcinerney.html.

Adams, Mike. "Intelligence Update: The Great Reset vs. the Great Awakening – the Grand Battle Taking Place Right Now for the

Future of America and the Free World." *NewsTarget*, 19 Nov. 2020, www.newstarget.com/2020-11-19-election-intelligence-update-great-reset-great-awakening.html.

Adams, Mike. "Red Resurgence: Dems collude with CIA to launch intelligence operation that ALTERS voting machine results in Pennsylvania and other swing states." *Natural News*, 1 Nov. 2020, www.naturalnews.com/2020-11-01-dems-collude-with-cia-operation-scorecard-alters-votes.html#.

Adams, Mike. "Sidney Powell has 'smoking gun evidence' to PROVE massive election fraud in the next two weeks." *Natural News*, 21 Nov. 2020, www.naturalnews.com/2020-11-21-sidney-powell-has-smoking-gun-evidence-to-prove-massive-election-fraud.html.

Adams, Mike. "Situation Update – Nov. 26th – Flynn in place, DoD aligned, rendition flights ACTIVE." *Natural News*, 26 Nov. 2020, www.naturalnews.com/2020-11-26-situation-update-nov-26th-flynn-in-place-dod-rendition-flights.html.

Adams, Mike. "Situation Update, Dec. 14th – Calls grow for Insurrection Act, window of opportunity Dec. 18th – 24th." *Natural News*, 14 Dec. 2020, www.naturalnews.com/2020-12-14-situation-update-dec-14th-insurrection-act-opportunity.html.

Adams, Mike. "Situation Update, Dec. 16th – Epic counterattack readied against 'Cyber Pearl Harbor.'" *Natural News*, 16 Dec. 2020, www.naturalnews.com/2020-12-16-situation-update-dec-16th-epic-counterattack-readied-against-cyber-pearl-harbor.html.

Adams, Mike. "The communist subversion of America is nearly complete: Left-wing media has already achieved 3 out of 4 steps for Soviet-style overthrow of American society and government." *Natural News*, 9 Jan. 2017, www.naturalnews.com/2017-01-09-communist-subversion-of-america-is-nearly-complete-left-wing-media-soviet-style-overthrow-yuri-bezmenov.html#.

Aitken, Peter. "Recent Cuban immigrant and college student shocked by peers' perception of socialism, seeks to dismantle it." *Fox News*, 19 Jan. 2022, www.foxnews.com/us/recent-cuban-immigrant-college-student-shocked-perceptions-socialism.

Alexander, Harriet. " 'The population will rise up': Tucker Carlson says Democrats 'know they rule illegitimately' and want to enact tougher gun laws to maintain their own power," *DailyMail.com*, 2 June 2022, www.dailymail.co.uk/news/article-10877445/ Carlson-Democrats-know-rule-illegitimately-trying-disarm-people-rise-up.html.

Alexander, Rachel. "The Left Dominates the Legal System, and They're Taking Down GOP Election Attorneys en Masse." *Townhall*, May 30, 2022, townhall.com/columnists/rachelalexander/ 2022/05/30/the-left-dominates-the-legal-system-and-theyre-taking-down-gop-election-attorneys-en-masse-n2607956.

"Alexis de Tocqueville > Quotes > Quotable Quote." *Goodreads*, www.goodreads.com/quotes/6708861-it-s-not-an-endlessly-expanding-list-of-rights-the.

"Alexis de Tocqueville > Quotes." *Goodreads*, www.goodreads.com/ author/quotes/465.Alexis_de_Tocqueville.

Allen, Virginia. "Trump Announces Members of Commission Focused on Teaching Youth About America's Founding." *The Daily Signal*, 18 Dec. 2020, www.dailysignal.com/2020/12/18/trump-announces-members-of-commission-focused-on-teaching-youth-about-americas-founding/? utm_source=rss&utm_medium=rss&utm_campaign=trump-announces-members-of-commission-focused-on-teaching-youth-about-americas-founding&fbclid=IwAR0Sw29HzF9vpjmK2TeZV8cW-2kIoK9 EHFgdtfVKwIMd_V4wR9Ob5JgKPBY.

American Mercury magazine, December 1957, pg. 92. "Quotes On The New World Order." *Jesus-Is-Savior.com*, www.jesus-is-savior.com/False%20Religions/Illuminati/ quotes_on_the_new_world_order.htm.

"Americans' trust in media hits record low – poll." *RT*, 18 Jul, 2022, www.rt.com/news/559201-gallup-us-confidence-poll/.

"Amistad Lawyer: FBI Collecting Data on Vote Fraud." *Newsmax*, 30 Nov. 2020, www.newsmax.com/politics/FBI-voter-fraud/ 2 0 2 0 / 1 1 / 3 0 / i d / 9 9 9 3 6 9 / ?

fbclid=IwAR1R9mWiKSTiKTZZaakZz6MkzTgzXsPQdiXyaR
GY04TybdW8rH44dzqxTn0.

Anderson, Bob. "Courts Repeatedly Refused To Consider Trump's
Election Claims On The Merits." *The Federalist*, 11 March
2021, thefederalist.com/2021/03/11/courts-repeatedly-refused-
to-consider-trumps-election-claims-on-the-merits/?
fbclid=IwAR2lNz5H7cqvlXzA6sWt6Os-EkmLubxZ-
XmGOObqWF5WZ4bNGk0maS9sVHY.

Anderson, William L. "The Attempt to Prosecute Donald Trump Is
Unleashing More Than Our Political System Can Handle."
Mises Institute, 10 Aug. 2022, mises.org/wire/attempt-
prosecute-donald-trump-unleashing-more-our-political-system-
can-handle.

Andrews, Douglas. "Out-of-Control FBI Seizes a Congressman's
Cellphone." *The Patriot Post,* 10 Aug. 2022, patriotpost.us/
a r t i c l e s / 9 0 4 4 8 ?
mailing_id=6877&utm_medium=email&utm_source=pp.email.
6877&utm_campaign=snapshot&utm_content=body.

"Anomalies in Vote Counts and Their Effects on Election 2020." *Vote
Integrity*, 24 Nov. 2020, votepatternanalysis.substack.com/p/
voting-anomalies-2020.

"Antifa supporter calls for the systematic killing of white people." *OAN*,
14 May 2021, www.oann.com/antifa-supporter-calls-for-the-
systematic-killing-of-white-people/.

Arcand, Cameron. "Barack Obama: Joe Biden Is 'Finishing the Job'
Using People from 'My Administration.'" *The Western Journal*,
1 June 2021, www.westernjournal.com/barack-obama-joe-
biden-finishing-job-using-people-administration/?
utm_source=facebook&utm_medium=huckabee.

Arcand, Cameron. "Poll: 57% of Texas Voters Disapprove of Biden's
Handling of Immigration and Border Security." *The Western
Journal*, 28 June 2021, www.westernjournal.com/poll-57-texas-
voters-disapprove-bidens-handling-immigration-border-
s e c u r i t y / ?
utm_source=mewe&utm_medium=westernjournalism&utm_co
ntent=2021-06-28&utm_campaign=manualpost.

Armstrong, Martin. "Democrats Hate Small Business – the Bourgeoisie." *Armstrong Economics*, 28 Sept. 2021, www.armstrongeconomics.com/world-news/taxes/democrats-hate-small-business-the-bourgeoisie/.

Arrow, Ruaridh. "Gene Sharp: The Academic Who Wrote the Playbook for Nonviolent Revolution." *Politico*, 30 Dec. 2018, www.politico.com/magazine/story/2018/12/30/gene-sharp-obituary-academic-nonviolent-revolution-223555/.

Arter, Melanie. "Barrasso: 'It Is Fraud to Have People Move to Georgia, Register to Vote, Vote, Then Leave'." *CNS News*, 12 Nov. 2020, cnsnews.com/article/washington/melanie-arter/barrasso-it-fraud-have-people-move-georgia-register-vote-vote-then?utm_source=facebook&utm_medium=cns&utm_campaign=n-Georgia-fraud&fbclid=IwAR20JoOoiLSie-VPnRRy6-VkYW4OOmHOtkL2z_993QpWDK6bsh_LrRxnqn4.

Arter, Melanie. "Sidney Powell: 'This Is Stunning, Heartbreaking, Infuriating, and the Most Unpatriotic Acts I Can Even Imagine.'" *CNS News,* 19 Nov. 2020, cnsnews.com/article/washington/melanie-arter/sidney-powell-stunning-heartbreaking-infuriating-and-most?utm_source=facebook&utm_medium=cns&utm_campaign=n-powell-infuriating&fbclid=IwAR0wnpj3wsRbBkgLnTjyJ9Y20VOvS1f1BBhNbX5k-0U1GxMgy_ekhZcIG2E.

Assistant Editor. "Missouri Attorney General Files Landmark Lawsuit Against Biden for Colluding with Big Tech — Evidence from The Gateway Pundit Plays Major Role in Case." *Gateway Pundit*, 22 June 2022, www.thegatewaypundit.com/2022/06/missouri-attorney-general-files-landmark-lawsuit-biden-colluding-big-tech-evidence-gateway-pundit-plays-major-role-case/?utm_source=Gab&utm_campaign=websitesharingbuttons.

Assistant Editor. "WAYNE ROOT: It's Time for Civil Disobedience: Here is How We Stop Biden Vaccine Mandates." *Gateway Pundit*, 3 Oct. 2021, www.thegatewaypundit.com/2021/10/wayne-root-time-civil-disobedience-stop-biden-vaccine-mandates/?fbclid=IwAR19PizbYCDAnXFC6VATTin-y1fk_oWdJkzuxfJIJkNslcu84dVOYdvMTk8.

Atkinson, Grant. "Nick Searcy Tells Sean Hannity the Sinister Plan Behind All the Media's Jan 6 Lies." *The Western Journal*, 18 Dec. 2021, www.westernjournal.com/nick-searcy-tells-sean-hannity-sinister-plan-behind-medias-jan-6-lies/?utm_source=mewe&utm_medium=westernjournalism&utm_content=2022-01-06&utm_campaign=manualpost.

Atkinson, Grant. "Trump Warns of CRT and Leftist Gender Theory in Schools: 'Our Biggest Danger Is from Within'." *The Western Journal*, 12 April 2022, www.westernjournal.com/trump-warns-crt-leftist-gender-theory-schools-biggest-danger-within/?utm_source=mewe&utm_medium=westernjournalism&utm_content=2022-04-12&utm_campaign=manualpost.

Atkinson, Grant. "Trump's Best Speech Ever? 90-Second Clip from Friday May Be the Best Trump Footage We've Ever Seen - We Worship God, Not Gov't." *The Western Journal*, 19 June 2022, www.westernjournal.com/trumps-best-speech-ever-90-second-clip-friday-may-best-trump-footage-ever-seen-worship-god-not-govt/.

Austin, Michael. "2022 Candidate Condemns Black Lives Matter as 'Terrorist Organization.'" *The Western Journal*, 23 July 2021, www.westernjournal.com/2022-candidate-condemns-black-lives-matter-terrorist-organization/?utm_source=facebook&utm_medium=teaparty&utm_content=2021-07-23&utm_campaign=manualpost.

Austin, Michael. "Alert: DHS Targets Joe Rogan, Trump Supporters - 'Terrorism Threat to US Homeland.'" *The Western Journal*, 9 Feb. 2022, www.westernjournal.com/alert-dhs-targets-joe-rogan-trump-supporters-terrorism-threat-us-homeland/?utm_source=mewe&utm_medium=westernjournalism&utm_content=2022-02-09&utm_campaign=manualpost.

Austin, Michael. "Poll: The Majority of Likely Voters Now Believe Cheating Impacted the Results of the 2020 Election." *The Western Journal*, 11 Jun. 2021, www.westernjournal.com/poll-majority-likely-voters-now-believe-cheating-impacted-results-2020-election/?utm_source=mewe&utm_medium=westernjournalism&utm_content=2021-06-11&utm_campaign=manualpost.

Austin, Michael. "The Second Civil War: Special Forces Vet Issues a 'Call to Arms' Against the Left's Takeover in Latest Book." *The Western Journal*, 2 July 2021, www.westernjournal.com/second-civil-war-special-forces-vet-issues-call-arms-lefts-takeover-latest-book/?utm_source=mewe&utm_medium=westernjournalism&utm_content=2021-07-02&utm_campaign=manualpost.

Bai, Gary. "'Such Courage': Trump Praises Texas GOP for Disavowing Result of 2020 Presidential Election." *The Epoch Times*, 21 June 2022, www.theepochtimes.com/such-courage-trump-praises-texas-gop-for-disavowing-result-of-2020-presidential-election_4548837.html?slsuccess=1.

Ball, Molly. "The Secret History of the Shadow Campaign That Saved the 2020 Election." *TIME*, 4 Feb. 2021, time.com/5936036/secret-2020-election-campaign/.

Bart, Sheldon. "Shaking Off the Leftist Philosophy." *American Thinker*, 26 Oct. 2021, www.americanthinker.com/articles/2021/10/shaking_off_the_leftist_philosophy.html.

Barton, Nolan. "Whistleblower Zach Vorhies warns public of Google's push to 'destabilize US and make it fall' – Brighteon.TV." *Natural News*, 10 September 2021, www.naturalnews.com/2021-09-10-whistleblower-warns-google-out-to-destabilize-us.html.

Basham, Patrick. "Reasons why the 2020 presidential election is deeply puzzling." *Spectator*, 27 Nov. 2020, spectator.us/topic/reasons-why-the-2020-presidential-election-is-deeply-puzzling/.

Basham, Patrick. "STALIN said it's not important who votes but how they are counted writes." *Democracy Institute*, 7 Nov. 2020, democracyinstitute.org/patrick-bashams-sunday-express-article-assesses-us-election-pollingtemp/.

Becker, Kyle. "Articles of Impeachment Accusing President Biden of 'Treason' Have Been Introduced in the House of Representatives." *Trending Politics*, 22 Oct. 2022, trendingpolitics.com/articles-of-impeachment-accusing-president-biden-of-treason-have-been-introduced-in-the-house-of-representatives-knab/?utm_source=Prather.

Becker, Kyle. "Mark Zuckerberg has been issued a Congressional letter demanding evidence on FBI's 2020 election interference." *El American*, 1 Sep. 2022, www.sott.net/article/471679-Mark-Zuckerberg-issued-Congressional-letter-demanding-evidence-on-FBIs-2020-election-interference.

Becker, Kyle. "President Trump Reacts to 'Bombshell' Election Fraud Evidence Uncovered in Fulton County Audit." *Becker News*, 14 July 2021, beckernews.com/president-trump-reacts-to-bombshell-election-fraud-evidence-uncovered-in-fulton-county-audit-40278/.

Becker, Kyle. "Rasmussen poll: More Americans Than Ever Believe It is 'Likely' Cheating Took Place in 2020 Election." *Trending Politics*, 11 Oct. 2021, trendingpolitics.com/more-americans-than-ever-believe-it-is-likely-cheating-took-place-in-2020-election-knab/?utm_source=DS21.

Bedard, Paul. "Exclusive: Report confirms 2020 abuses and RNC deploys 'year-round' election integrity unit." *Washington Examiner*, 19 Aug. 2021, www.washingtonexaminer.com/washington-secrets/exclusive-report-confirms-2020-cheating-rnc-deploys-year-round-election-integrity-unit.

Bedard, Paul. "Stuck: Most still say Biden 'cheating' beat Trump." *Washington Examiner*, 13 Apr. 2021, www.washingtonexaminer.com/washington-secrets/stuck-most-still-say-biden-cheating-beat-trump?fbclid=IwAR1HBk3SJsvGwtOeEL0ElFevIUVWGJ8OVSWuRaq_rkOAh_TkQmg5FQtiXIw.

Behrends, Rebecca. "GOP Poll Worker in 2020 Detroit: 'They Treated Me Like a Criminal!'" *American Thinker*, 6 Nov. 2021, www.americanthinker.com/articles/2021/11/gop_poll_worker_in_detroit_they_treated_me_like_a_criminal_.html.

Benno, Ameer. "Former FBI Assistant Director: Arrests Aren't Enough, We Have to Take Down People Close to Trump, Sitting Congressmen to Stop 'Domestic Terrorism.'" *The Western Journal*, 17 Jun. 2021, www.westernjournal.com/former-fbi-assistant-director-arrests-arent-enough-take-people-close-trump-sitting-congressmen-stop-domestic-terrorism/?

utm_source=mewe&utm_medium=westernjournalism&utm_co
ntent=2021-06-18&utm_campaign=topdaily.

Benton, Carina. "Totalitarian Left Promises Purges And Punishment For
All Trump Voters." *The Federalist*, 10 Nov. 2020,
thefederalist.com/2020/11/10/totalitarian-left-promises-purges-
a n d - p u n i s h m e n t - f o r - a l l - t r u m p - v o t e r s / ?
fbclid=IwAR1BaOAVt0hVKGNdjk_GFM1VSYdWIYJHs9qL6
SA7SJVng0TtepJGN3-Np0M.

Besner, Caren. "Politics and the Politicization of the US Military."
American Thinker, 21 Sept. 2021, www.americanthinker.com/
a r t i c l e s / 2 0 2 1 / 0 9 /
politics_and_the_politicization_of_the_us_military_.html.

"BEWARE: The *Purple Revolution* Comes To America..." *State of the
Nation*, 13 Nov. 2016, stateofthenation2012.com/?p=56307.

"Biden aide speaks of 'one final warning.'" *RT*, 3 Nov. 2022,
www.rt.com/news/565918-biden-final-warning-election/.

"Biden is Obama's 'front man' – Tulsi Gabbard." *RT*, 3 May 2022,
www.rt.com/news/554883-tulsi-gabbard-ministry-truth/.

"Biden Weaponizing Government against Americans - Congressman."
RT, 19 Nov. 2022, www.rt.com/news/566811-biden-
weaponized-government-against-americans-congressman/.

Blair, Douglas. "I'm a Former Teacher. Here's How Your Children Are
Getting Indoctrinated by Leftist Ideology." *The Daily Signal*, 16
Aug. 2020, www.dailysignal.com/2020/08/16/im-a-former-
teacher-heres-how-your-children-are-getting-indoctrinated-by-
l e f t i s t - i d e o l o g y / ?
fbclid=IwAR20WZxAK9hT33K0GQXG0JjBR2ZMSW02k_z4
9KGIAzZB1Eh7Y2khPkjlqd8.

"BLM City Leader Quits After Discovering 1 Shocking Fact." *GOP
World. n.d.* gopworld.com/blm-city-leader-quits-after-
discovering-1-shocking-fact/.

"'Blown Communist Plot' — Whistleblower Reveals the Plan." *The
Millennium Report*, 11 Aug. 2020, themillenniumreport.com/

2020/08/its-a-full-blown-communist-plot-whistleblower-reveals-the-plan/.

Bokhari, Allum. "Report: Twitter and Facebook Had Regular Meetings with DHS on Censoring Americans." *Breitbart*, 31 Oct 2022, www.breitbart.com/tech/2022/10/31/report-twitter-and-facebook-had-regular-meetings-with-dhs-on-censoring-americans/.

Bokhari, Allum. "Ron DeSantis Orders Investigation of Facebook's Alleged Election Law Violations." *Breitbart*, 27 Sep. 2021, www.breitbart.com/tech/2021/09/27/ron-desantis-orders-investigation-of-facebooks-alleged-election-law-violations/.

"Bombshell: CIA Officer Openly Confesses To Rigging 2020 Election For Joe Biden And Says They Would Do It Again." 28 Mar. 2022, en-volve.com/2022/03/28/bombshell-cia-officer-openly-confesses-to-rigging-2020-election-for-joe-biden-and-says-they-would-do-it-again/.

Bonchie. "After the FBI's Trump Raid, Don't Take the Bait." *RedState*, 8 Aug. 2022, redstate.com/bonchie/2022/08/08/after-the-fbis-trump-raid-dont-take-the-bait-n609212?utm_source=rsmorningbriefing&utm_medium=email&utm_campaign=nl&bcid=c60ab093f53f74e11bdf28039caf21066e3dd4ea153ff877c6f9c0d45d1b39fe.

Bonchie. "HUGE: Mark Milley Pledged to the Chinese to Commit Treason in Order to Undermine Donald Trump." *RedState*, 14 Sept. 2021, redstate.com/bonchie/2021/09/14/huge-mark-milley-pledged-to-the-chinese-to-commit-treason-in-order-to-undermine-donald-trump-n442812.

Boose, Matthew. "In Joe Biden's America, Whites Are the Enemy." *American Greatness*, 27 Jun. 2021, amgreatness.com/2021/06/27/in-joe-bidens-america-whites-are-the-enemy/.

"Boris Johnson claims 'deep state' plot against Brexit." *RT*, 19 Jul. 2022, www.rt.com/news/559259-booris-johnson-deep-state/.

Boyd, Barbara. "Biden's Fools and Incompetents Are Fully Exposed: Will You Stand and Fight Now?" *LaRouchePac*, 19 July 2021, w w w . l a r o u c h e p a c . c o m /

biden_s_fools_and_incompetents_are_fully_exposed_will_you
_ s t a n d _ a n d _ f i g h t _ n o w ?
utm_campaign=20210719_zoom_bmb&utm_medium=email&u
tm_source=larouchepac.

Boyd, Barbara. "Surrender Is Not an Option; Anything Less Than Pure
Fighting Optimism Now Will Lose the War." *LaRouchePac*, 15
Dec. 2020, larouchepac.com/20201215/surrender-not-option-
anything-less-pure-fighting-optimism-now-will-lose-war.

Boyd, M. E. "Has America Become 'A Realm Beyond Words?'"
American Thinker, 1 Nov. 2021, www.americanthinker.com/
a r t i c l e s / 2 0 2 1 / 1 1 /
has_american_become_a_realm_beyond_words.html.

Bridge, Robert. "America, Your History Is Being Erased: Why
Destroying the Robert E. Lee Statue Is an Insult to the Nation."
RT, 1 Nov. 2023, https://www.rt.com/news/586353-robert-lee-
statue-us/.

Brooks, Emily and Joseph Simonson. "Pete Buttigieg's father was a
Marxist professor who lauded the Communist Manifesto." *The
W a s h i n g t o n E x a m i n e r* , 2 A p r . 2 0 1 9 ,
www.washingtonexaminer.com/news/pete-buttigiegs-father-
was-a-marxist-professor-who-lauded-the-communist-manifesto.

Brooks, Liam. "As Fear of COVID Wanes, a Hard Leftist Pivot Back to
Climate Change." *American Thinker*, 6 Nov. 2021,
w w w . a m e r i c a n t h i n k e r . c o m / a r t i c l e s / 2 0 2 1 / 1 1 /
as_fear_of_covid_wanes_a_hard_leftist_pivot_back_to_climate
_change.html.

Brooks, Mo. "'Trump Won the Electoral College' — I Can Be a Part of
the 'Surrender Caucus' or I Can Fight for Our Country."
Breitbart, 15 Dec. 2020, www.breitbart.com/clips/2020/12/15/
mo-brooks-trump-won-the-electoral-college-i-can-be-a-part-of-
the-surrender-caucus-or-i-can-fight-for-our-country/?
fbclid=IwAR1qhUA16w72042k9vZrsaGPcAMIgQk0O8I_pxjL
pnx94TXK9rY4jw0mtRo.

Brown, Jon. "Cuban Refugee Warns Americans Have Already
'Swallowed' Communism's 'Poison Pill.'" *DailyWire.com*, 28
Apr. 2021, www.dailywire.com/news/cuban-refugee-warns-

americans-have-already-swallowed-communisms-poison-pill?
utm_source=facebook&utm_medium=social&utm_campaign=b
enshapiro&fbclid=IwAR3kjrRljG_8OHDL9eWaAWcdsA_5BX
CjE_gv7gOiAphiv9VXzJhBx0mAruI.

Brown, Spencer. "Chairman of the Joint Chiefs Mark Milley Compared
Trump to Hitler, His Supporters to Brownshirts: New Book."
Townhall, 15 Jul. 2021, townhall.com/tipsheet/spencerbrown/
2021/07/15/chairman-of-the-joint-chiefs-mark-milley-
compared-trump-to-hitler-his-supporters-to-brownshirts-
n2592613.

Burroughs, Dillon. "Fox News Cuts Trump Border Visit Feed After He
Starts Talking About Election." *The Western Journal*, 30 Jun.
2021, www.westernjournal.com/fox-news-cuts-trump-border-
visit-feed-starts-talking-election/?
utm_source=mewe&utm_medium=westernjournalism&utm_co
ntent=2021-06-30&utm_campaign=topdaily.

Burroughs, Dillon. "Trump Comments on Big News Emerging from
Election Audit: 'The Crime of the Century!'" *The Western
Journal*, 25 May 2021, www.westernjournal.com/trump-
comments-big-news-emerging-election-audit-crime-century/?
utm_source=facebook&utm_medium=huckabee.

Byrne, Patrick. "How DJT Lost the White House, Chapter 4: The
Christmas Doldrums (December 23- noon January 6)."
Deepcapture.com, 4 Feb. 2021, www.deepcapture.com/
2021/02/how-djt-lost-the-white-house-chapter-4-the-christmas-
doldrums-december-23-noon-january-6/.

Calvin, Donna. "The 45 Communist Goals as Read into the
Congressional Record, 1963." *Watchwoman on the Wall*, 2011,
www.beliefnet.com/columnists/watchwomanonthewall/
2011/04/the-45-communist-goals-as-read-into-the-
congressional-record-1963.html.

"Capitol riot committee to seek charges against Trump – reports." *RT*, 17
Dec, 2022, www.rt.com/news/568421-trump-criminal-charges-
january-6/.

Carlson, Tucker. "Tucker Carlson: Yes, dead people voted in this election
and Democrats helped make it happen." *Fox News*, 11 Nov.

2020, www.foxnews.com/opinion/tucker-carlson-2020-presidential-election-voter-fraud-dead-voters? fbclid=IwAR3b7CTYSArWle0VrPQwnyT4CTVs4APsBYFbuh MalsJk_nFDvNInTb-x2b8.

Carr, Julie. "General Thomas McInerney Outlines New Evidence Alleging Nationwide Ballot Tampering to Prevent Trump Landslide." *The Tennessee Star*, 18 November 2020, tennesseestar.com/2020/11/18/general-thomas-mcinerney-outlines-new-evidence-alleging-nationwide-ballot-tampering-to-prevent-trump-landslide/?fbclid=IwAR3FkjHvT5qvm8kgC-FR4mjQ_H99H7teqopuVhgo-jBDcCFGKoFZV_0uKN8.

Carr, Julie. "Steve Bannon Explains the Biden Business Model of the Political Class, China's Threat, and Information Warfare." *The Tennessee Star*, 29 Oct. 2020, tennesseestar.com/2020/10/29/steve-bannon-explains-the-biden-business-model-of-the-political-class-chinas-threat-and-information-warfare/?fbclid=IwAR3GaOEap7lehQ8RgMpVUgGFuOghkiIeqWwK6 H432flJCGDmZGPYGT9eap0.

Carter, Belle. "Prophecy and Politics: Dr. Scott Lively says Obama is using Biden as avatar in fight against Putin – Brighteon.TV." *Natural News*, September 28, 2022, www.naturalnews.com/2022-09-28-obama-using-biden-as-avatar-fighting-putin.html.

Catenacci, Thomas. "Michigan, Wisconsin Elections Officials Refuse to Explain Sudden Biden Vote Influx." *Daily Caller*, 4 Nov. 2020, dailycaller.com/2020/11/04/michigan-wisconsin-elections-officials-refuse-explain-sudden-joe-biden-vote-influx/.

Cathell, Mia. "EXPOSED: PBS chief counsel advocates for 're-education camps' for children of Trump supporters." *The Post Millennial*, 12 Jan. 2021, thepostmillennial.com/exposed-pbs-chief-counsel-re-education-camps.

Cathell, Mia. "New Senate findings 'confirm the connections' between Biden family and Chinese, Russian governments" *PM*, 23 Nov. 2020, thepostmillennial.com/new-senate-findings-confirm-the-connections-between-biden-family-and-chinese-russian-governments/.

CD Media Staff. "BREAKING: Merrick Garland's Wife 'Advises' On Election Audits, Like The Maricopa Audit DOJ Threatened In Arizona." October 11, 2021, creativedestructionmedia.com/investigations/2021/10/11/breaking-merrick-garlands-wife-advises-on-election-audits-like-the-maricopa-audit-doj-threatened-in-arizona/.

"Census reveals weird anomaly: Shows millions less voted in 2020 election than official tally." *The Election Wizard*, 4 May 2021, electionwiz.com/2021/05/04/census-reveals-weird-anomaly-shows-millions-less-voted-in-2020-election-than-official-tally/?fbclid=IwAR2xYrMNTiwveBvx2eJC7IvKJaxV9mUWY79mj5d_cFVHzTssjP3MBrxVlyQ.

Chaitin, Daniel. "Jim Jordan says 14 FBI whistleblowers have come forward." *Washington Examiner*, 15 Aug. 2022, www.washingtonexaminer.com/news/justice/jim-jordan-14-fbi-whistleblowers.

Chang, Samantha. "Amid troubling audits, poll reveals good chunk of DEMOCRATS now doubt Biden won election fairly." *The Western Journal*, 26 Jul. 2021, www.wnd.com/2021/07/amid-troubling-audits-poll-reveals-10-democrats-now-doubt-biden-won-election-fairly/?ff_source=Email&ff_medium=wnd-breaking&ff_campaign=breaking&ff_content=breaking.

Chang, Samantha. "Bill O'Reilly: No Question Obama Is 'Calling a Lot of the Shots for Joe Biden.'" *The Western Journal*, 8 Jun. 2021, www.westernjournal.com/bill-oreilly-no-question-obama-calling-lot-shots-joe-biden/?utm_source=mewe&utm_medium=westernjournalism&utm_content=2021-06-08&utm_campaign=manualpost.

Chang, Samantha. "Watch: 1st-Generation American Pays for 3-Minute Ad Warning About AOC, Democratic Socialism." *The Western Journal*, 11 Jun. 2021, www.westernjournal.com/watch-1st-generation-american-pays-3-minute-ad-warning-aoc-democratic-socialism/?utm_source=mewe&utm_medium=westernjournalism&utm_content=2021-06-11&utm_campaign=manualpost.

Chapman, Michael W. "Poll: 66% of Republican Voters Say Presidential Race Was 'Not' Free and Fair Election." *CNS News*, 18 Nov. 2020, cnsnews.com/article/national/michael-w-chapman/

poll-66-republican-voters-say-presidential-race-was-not-free-
a n d ?
utm_source=facebook&utm_medium=cns&utm_campaign=n-
poll-election&fbclid=IwAR2ykStM2IzJljGjncisRIC0l2zCkXA-
W0bpVM1F6z3d1Hr2c325iH9Vw-s.

"Chinese Professor Reveals Plot in Shock Video: US Elites and China
Have Teamed Up to Take Control Of America." *Revolver*,
December 9, 2020, www.revolver.news/2020/12/chinese-
professor-reveals-plot-in-shock-video-us-elites-and-china-have-
teamed-up-to-take-control-of-america/.

Cicero, Linda A. "Robert Conquest: Revealing the horror of Stalin."
BBC, 6 Aug. 2015, www.bbc.com/news/magazine-33788518.

Clarfield, Geoffrey. "The Ten Commandments of Critical Race Theory."
The American Thinker, 29 Aug. 2021,
www.americanthinker.com/articles/2021/08/
the_ten_commandments_of_critical_race_theory.html.

Clark, Joseph. "Pentagon gets 'woke': Whistleblowers reveal segregation
for 'privilege walks,' critical race theory." *The Washington
Times*, 11 June 2021, www.washingtontimes.com/news/2021/
jun/11/pentagon-whistleblowers-troops-segregated-privileg/.

Clemons, Jay. "Pentagon Sued Over Complaints of Teaching Critical
Race Theory at Military Academies." *Newsmax*, 26 July 2022,
www.newsmax.com/newsfront/pentagon-army-navy/
2022/07/26/id/1080414/.

Coates, Erin. "Rep Demands Removal of CRT-Teaching Military
Academy Prof, Warns if We Let It Continue 'We Will Be
Responsible for This Nation's Demise'." *The Western Journal*, 8
July 2021, www.westernjournal.com/rep-demands-removal-crt-
teaching-military-academy-prof-warns-let-continue-will-
responsible-nations-demise/?
utm_source=mewe&utm_medium=westernjournalism&utm_co
ntent=2021-07-08&utm_campaign=manualpost.

"Communist China Running 'Slow Coup' to Defeat America From
Within: Patrick Byrne." *Vision Times*, 1 Jan. 2021,
www.visiontimes.com/2021/01/01/communist-china-running-
slow-coup-to-defeat-america-from-within-patrick-byrne.html.

Conradson, Jordan. "Arizona Attorney General Mark Brnovich Responds to Biden Admin's Threats: 'My Office Is NOT AMUSED With DOJ's POSTURING'." *Gateway Pundit*, 14 June 2021, www.thegatewaypundit.com/2021/06/arizona-attorney-general-mark-brnovich-responds-biden-admins-threats-office-not-amused-dojs-posturing/.

Conradson, Jordan. "Arizona Election Fraud: 2 Months After They Were Identified Illegally Deleting 2020 Election Records, Three Individuals Remain Unpunished, Unidentified and Uncharged by AG Mark Brnovich." *Gateway Pundit*, 27 Nov. 2021, www.thegatewaypundit.com/2021/11/arizona-election-fraud-two-months-since-identified-illegally-deleting-2020-election-records-three-individuals-remain-unpunished-attorney-general-mark-brnovich/.

Conradson, Jordan. "Arizona State Senator Wendy Rogers: DOJ 'Will Be LEGALLY DEALT WITH – The Nation Is Looking To Arizona' (Video)." *Gateway Pundit*, 14 June 2021, www.thegatewaypundit.com/2021/06/arizona-state-senator-wendy-rogers-doj-will-legally-dealt-nation-looking-arizona-video/.

Conradson, Jordan. "Kamala Harris Poses In Front Of Communist Ho Chi Minh Bust – 'The WORST Photo Op For An American In That Country Since Jane Fonda Donned A Helmet There In 1972.'" *Gateway Pundit*, 28 Aug. 2021, www.thegatewaypundit.com/2021/08/kamala-harris-poses-front-communist-ho-chi-minh-bust-worst-photo-op-american-country-since-jane-fonda-donned-helmet-1972/?utm_source=add2any&utm_medium=PostBottomSharingButtons&utm_campaign=websitesharingbuttons.

Conradson, Jordan. "PRESIDENT TRUMP on the Biden Admin's Attempts To Shut Down Arizona Audit: 'They Want It Over With Because They Seem to Know What Will Be Found.'" *Gateway Pundit*, 13 Jun. 2021, www.thegatewaypundit.com/2021/06/president-trump-biden-doj-attempts-stop-audit-want-seem-know-will-found/.

Conradson, Jordan. "WATCH: AZ State Rep. Mark Finchem Expects Arrests in Arizona: "Maricopa County Isn't The Only County – We Are Waiting for Indictments" *Gateway Pundit*, 28 Nov. 2021, www.thegatewaypundit.com/2021/11/watch-az-state-rep-mark-finchem-expects-arrests-arizona-maricopa-county-isnt-county-audit-pima-county/.

Conradson, Julian. "Thousands of Patriots Attend Trump Speech in Phoenix – Crowd Circles the Arena – 'Trump Won' Banner Dropped from Balcony (Video)." *Gateway Pundit*, 25 Jul. 2021, www.thegatewaypundit.com/2021/07/thousands-patriots-attend-trump-speech-phoenix-crowd-goes-wild-trump-won-banner-dropped/.

Cooter. "Why Didn't the Georgia Senate Decertify the 2020 Election Results? Now We Know…" *Steadfast Clash*, 20 Dec. 2021, steadfastclash.com/the-latest/why-didnt-the-georgia-senate-decertify-the-2020-election-results-now-we-know/.

Cordle, Vaughn. "How to get from here to serfdom quick." *American Thinker*, 11 Jan. 2022, www.americanthinker.com/blog/2022/01/how_to_get_from_here_to_serfdom_quick.html#ixzz7HheRudqK.

Cortes, Steve. "CORTES – Even CNN's Polling Shows Energized 2022 Voters Are Split on Whether 2020 Was Stolen." *The National Pulse*, 14 Dec. 2021, thenationalpulse.com/analysis/cortes-even-cnns-polling-shows-energized-2022-voters-are-split-on-whether-2020-was-stolen/.

Couch, Matt. "How RINO's Cotton and McConnell Secretly Plotted Against Trump to Undermine His Election-Fraud Claims, New Book Says it All." *The DC Patriot*, 15 October 2021, thedcpatriot.com/how-rinos-cotton-and-mcconnell-secretly-plotted-against-trump-to-undermine-his-election-fraud-claims-new-book-says-it-all/.

Cox, Hannah D. "Weren't We Always Extremists?" *Hannahdcox.com*, 3 Jul. 2021, hannahdcox.com/1452/2021/07/03/werent-we-always-extremists/.

Cox, Isa. "AZ Lawmaker to Biden's AG: Don't Touch AZ Ballots or Machines or You'll Spend Time in AZ Prison." *The Western Journal*, 14 June 2021, www.westernjournal.com/az-lawmaker-bidens-ag-dont-touch-az-ballots-machines-spend-time-az-prison/?

ff_source=mewe&ff_medium=westernjournalism&ff_campaign
=topdaily&ff_content=2021-06-23.

Coy, Andrew W. "1776 or 1619: Why it Really, Really Matters." *American Thinker*, 26 Sept. 2021, www.americanthinker.com/ a r t i c l e s / 2021/09/1776_or_1619_why_it_really_really_matters.html.

Coy, Andrew W. "The Silent Coup." *American Thinker*, 15 Feb. 2022, w w w . a m e r i c a n t h i n k e r . c o m / a r t i c l e s / 2 0 2 2 / 0 2 / the_silent_coup.html.

Coyner, Vince. "There Was No Insurrection But There Was A Coup." *American Thinker*, 6 Jan. 2022, www.americanthinker.com/ a r t i c l e s / 2 0 2 2 / 0 1 / there_was_no_insurrection_but_there_was_a_coup.html.

"Critical Race Theory may violate Civil Rights Act, the Constitution: Dr. Carol Swain." *Natural News*, 23 June 2021, www.naturalnews.com/2021-06-23-critical-race-theory-may-violate-civil-rights.html.

Cruz, Ted. "Ted Cruz Grills FBI Director over Document Claiming 'Patriotic Symbols Are Extremist'." *The Daily Fetched*, 5 Aug. 2022, www.dailyfetched.com/ted-cruz-grills-fbi-director-over-document-claiming-patriotic-symbols-are-extremist/.

Daily Wire News. "Nearly 90 Retired Generals, Admirals Demand Milley, Austin Resign: Focused On 'Wokeness' Vs. Winning Wars." *DailyWire.com*, 30 Aug. 2021, www.dailywire.com/ news/nearly-90-retired-generals-admirals-demand-milley-austin-resign-focused-on-wokeness-vs-winning-wars? i t m _ s o u r c e = p a r s e l y - a p i ? utm_source=cnemail&utm_medium=email&utm_content=0831 21-news&utm_campaign=position2.

Davidson, John Daniel. "At NATO And G7, Biden Advances An 'America Last' Foreign Policy." *The Federalist*, 16 June 2021, thefederalist.com/2021/06/16/at-nato-and-g7-biden-advances-an-america-last-foreign-policy/.

Davidson, Jordan. "Democrats Compile List Of Names Targeting White House Staff, Trump Campaign, Judges, And Donors." *The*

Federalist, 7 Nov. 2020, thefederalist.com/2020/11/07/
democrats-compile-list-of-names-targeting-white-house-staff-
trump-campaign-judges-and-donors/.

Davidson, Lee. "Burgess Owens Explains Why He'll Challenge Trump's
Loss on the House Floor." *The Salt Lake Tribune*, 31 Dec. 2020,
www.sltrib.com/news/politics/2020/12/31/burgess-owens-
explains/.

Davis, Jack. "Arizona Commits to Full Hand Recount, 'Broad and
Detailed' Audit of Machines." *The Western Journal*, 21 Mar.
2021, www.westernjournal.com/arizona-commits-full-hand-
recount-broad-detailed-audit-machines/?
utm_source=facebook&utm_medium=empowerconservatives&
fbclid=IwAR0mm8UQJ_IWyaYOBaDeE5sKAdJar9VVkhZN
MEHefn7j-eHEi-rwxtA-lMA.

Davis, Jack. "Black Lives Matter Backs Cuba's Communist Regime,
Blames US Government in New Statement." *The Western
Journal*, 15 July 2021, www.westernjournal.com/black-lives-
matter-backs-cubas-communist-regime-blames-us-government-
new-statement/?
utm_source=mewe&utm_medium=westernjournalism&utm_co
ntent=2021-07-15&utm_campaign=manualpost.

Davis, Jack. "Matt Gaetz Makes Stunning Election Promise for January
6th." *The Western Journal*, 20 Dec. 2020,
www.westernjournal.com/matt-gaetz-makes-stunning-election-
promise-january-6th/?
utm_source=facebook&utm_medium=westernjournalism&utm
_content=2020-12-20&utm_campaign=manualpost&fbclid=Iw
AR35MvHa5ldGD4BoZZoUr2vLH8Jg4sRt3RAIZPtLQeD9A
mOduqvnZlANuW0.

Davis, Jack. "State Police Assisting in Hunt for Individuals Making
'False Claims' About 2020 Election." *The Western Journal*, 9
July 2021, www.westernjournal.com/state-police-assisting-
hunt-individuals-making-false-claims-2020-election/?
utm_source=mewe&utm_medium=westernjournalism&utm_co
ntent=2021-07-09&utm_campaign=manualpost.

Davis, Jack. "Trump Calls for the 'Immediate' Release of Mar-a-Lago
Documents: 'The World Is Watching'." *The Western Journal*, 12
Aug. 2022, www.westernjournal.com/trump-calls-immediate-

release-mar-lago-documents-world-watching/?
utm_source=mewe&utm_medium=westernjournalism&utm_co
ntent=2022-08-12&utm_campaign=manualpost.

Davis, Jack. "What We've Been Waiting For: Judge May Release
Bombshell Report on Dominion Voting Machines in Georgia."
The Western Journal, 1 Feb. 2022, www.westernjournal.com/
waiting-judge-may-release-bombshell-report-dominion-voting-
m a c h i n e s - g e o r g i a / ?
utm_source=mewe&utm_medium=westernjournalism&utm_co
ntent=2022-02-01&utm_campaign=manualpost.

Davis. Jonathan. "Former Special Forces Operator: 'Color Revolution'
Tactics Were Employed Against Trump." *Trending Politics*, Jan.
2021, trendingpolitics.com/former-special-forces-operator-
color-revolution-tactics-were-employed-against-trump/?
utm_source=collin&utm_medium=instagram&fbclid=IwAR33
R W C 1 Y e b H o L - a 4 R Z 2 H 4 t 3 4 z X -
u8uq5K4f_8BkDWTlApmfz11nc9jUMXk.

Davis, Jonathan. "Justice Dept. Set to Form New Special 'Domestic
Terrorism' Unit." *Conservative Brief*, 11 January 2022,
conservativebrief.com/justice-set-57813/.

Davis, Sean and Mollie Hemingway "'Don't Mention Joe Being
Involved': Bombshell Texts Show Effort To Hide Joe Biden's
Involvement In Hunter's Business Deals." *The Federalist*, 23
Oct. 2020, thefederalist.com/2020/10/23/dont-mention-joe-
being-involved-bombshell-texts-show-effort-to-hide-joe-
bidens-involvement-in-hunters-business-deals/.

DeBlasi, Anthony J. "The Mindless Attempt to Remake America."
American Thinker, 12 Nov. 2021, www.americanthinker.com/
a r t i c l e s / 2 0 2 1 / 1 1 /
the_mindless_attempt_to_remake_america.html.

"Deep Insider Explains How Trump's Closest Advisors
DELIBERATELY 'Ran Out The Clock' To Cover Up Election
Theft!" *State of the Nation*, 30 Jan. 2021,
stateofthenation2012.com/?p=133059.

"Deep State's Obamanation Desperately Resists Trump's Wrecking Ball." *State of the Nation*, 9 Mar. 2017, stateofthenation2012.com/?p=66949.

DeLong, James V. "Standing with John Eastman." *American Thinker*, 12 Oct. 2021, www.americanthinker.com/blog/2021/10/standing_with_john_eastman.html.

De Luce, Dan and Mosheh Gains. "Believing in white supremacy, for example, is 'extremism.' Pentagon orders new steps to tackle extremism in the ranks." *NBC News*, 9 Apr. 2021, www.nbcnews.com/news/military/pentagon-orders-new-steps-tackle-extremism-ranks-n1263658.

DeSoto, Randy. "AZ AG Tells Garland: We Will Not Tolerate DOJ Trying to Interfere with Arizona Audit." *The Western Journal*, 15 June 2021, www.westernjournal.com/az-ag-tells-garland-will-not-tolerate-doj-trying-interfere-arizona-audit/?utm_source=mewe&utm_medium=westernjournalism&utm_content=2021-06-15&utm_campaign=manualpost.

DeSoto, Randy. "Inexhaustible Trump Launches 'Completely Different Strategy' To 'Stop the Steal.'" *The Western Journal*, 21 Dec. 2020, www.westernjournal.com/inexhaustible-trump-launches-completely-different-strategy-stop-steal/.

DeSoto, Randy. "It's OK When Dems Do It: Feds Dropped Charges Against Rioters from Trump's Inauguration." *The Western Journal*, 7 Jan. 2022, www.westernjournal.com/ok-dems-feds-dropped-charges-rioters-trumps-inauguration/?utm_source=mewe&utm_medium=westernjournalism&utm_content=2022-01-07&utm_campaign=manualpost.

DeSoto, Randy. "The Bible's Teachings Provide a Bulwark Against Marxism and Socialism Rising in the US." *The Western Journal*, 1 Jun. 2021, www.patriotproject.com/bibles-teachings-provide-bulwark-marxism-socialism-rising-us/.

"DHS Has Secured the Nation's Election Systems, but Work Remains to Protect the Infrastructure." *Homeland Security*, 22 Oct. 2020, supremelaw.org/authors/DHS/DHS.watermark.pdf.

"Diamond and Silk." "Letter From 41 Legislators from Multiple States Call for Nationwide Audit & Decertification." 7 Oct. 2021, www.diamondandsilkinc.com/tabletalknews/tlk4gz3whncfhj4-seman-hgadt-s4pbz-wapxk-ng7sx-a4lsn.

Díaz, Itxu. "Itxu Díaz: The Left Is Running Out of Scare Tactics, And That Might Be the Scariest Thing of All." *The Western Journal*, 7 Jul. 2021, www.westernjournal.com/itxu-diaz-left-running-scare-tactics-might-scariest-thing/?utm_source=mewe&utm_medium=westernjournalism&utm_content=2021-07-07&utm_campaign=manualpost.

Diserio, Rebecca. "Computer Analyst: Trump Won MI & WI, Locates 'Electronic Ballot Dump For Biden.'" *Mad World News*, 18 Nov. 2020, madworldnews.com/computer-analyst-trump-won/.

Diserio, Rebecca. "Pollsters Who Got It Right In 2016: Trump Won In A Landslide & We Can Prove It." *Mad World News*, 16 Nov. 2020, madworldnews.com/pollsters-right-2016-trump-won/.

Dougherty, Michael Brendan. "The Coming Color Revolution." *National Review*, 11 Aug. 2020, www.nationalreview.com/2020/08/the-coming-color-revolution/?fbclid=IwAR3SVf67MwiEH_4Z9woFOsTSyr3-nW2rQQfqtRYC47b89lEBjEyv_U9moSc.

Dowling, M. "Buffalo, NY Is Turning Communist." *Independent Sentinel*, 23 Oct. 2021, www.independentsentinel.com/buffalo-ny-is-turning-communist/.

Dowling, M. "Lincoln Project: 'We Want to Burn the Republican Party to the Ground'." *Independent Sentinel*, 15 Nov. 2022, www.independentsentinel.com/lincoln-project-we-want-to-burn-the-republican-party-to-the-ground/.

Dowling, Paul. "Did President Trump Spring a Trap on Treasonous Democrats on Election Night?" *Conservative News Daily*, 29 Nov. 2020, www.conservativenewsdaily.net/breaking-news/did-president-trump-spring-a-trap-on-treasonous-democrats-on-election-night/?fbclid=IwAR28K49BCXYD-Za8UykaIZVxvXOKOsQ7PVOizObIyy1OAPZUSGcGgTixXKg.

Droney, Pat. "Rep. Mast urges Americans 'do not comply!', says 'ignore Biden's illegal mandates like he ignores our immigration laws,'" *Law Enforcement Today*, 15 Sept, 2021, www.lawenforcementtoday.com/rep-mast-urges-americans-do-not-comply-says-ignore-bidens-illegal-mandates-like-he-ignores-our-immigration-laws/.

Duclos, Susan. "The New World Order We Were Warned Was Coming Is Now Here And America Will Never Be The Same - Medical Martial Law, Empty Shelves, Radical Socialism And More, All In The Name Of Control." *All News PipeLine*, 23 Oct. 2021, allnewspipeline.com/New_World_Order_We_Were_Warned_Is_Coming.php.

Duffy, Daniel. "Genocidal Regimes and Leftist Apologists." *American Thinker*, 16 Dec. 2021, https://www.americanthinker.com/articles/2021/12/genocidal_regimes_and_leftist_apologists.html.

Dunetz, Jeff. "WATCH: Speaker At National Black Power Rally Says 'Kill Everything White In Sight.'" *Flag and Cross*, 2 June 2021, flagandcross.com/watch-speaker-at-national-black-power-rally-says-kill-everything-white-in-sight/.

Dunleavy, Jerry. "Senate investigators: New records 'confirm' troubling Biden family links to China and Russia." *Washington Examiner*, 18 Nov. 2020, www.washingtonexaminer.com/news/senate-investigators-new-records-confirm-troubling-biden-family-links-to-china-and-russia.

Dunn, J.R. "No, the U.S. is Not on its Knees." *American Thinker*, 14 Oct. 2021, www.americanthinker.com/articles/2021/10/no_the_us_is_not_on_its_knees.html.

Dunn, Morgan. "The Story of The Guangxi Massacre, When Mao Zedong's Red Guard 'Banqueted' on Human Meat." *ATI*, 16 Sept. 2021, allthatsinteresting.com/guangxi-massacre.

Durden, Tyler. "Tulsi Gabbard: Washington Elite Pose 'Greatest Threat' To Democracy." *ZeroHedge*, 18 Aug. 2022, www.zerohedge.com/political/tulsi-gabbard-washington-elite-pose-greatest-threat-democracy.

Dwyer, Mark Andrew. "What Denying Election Fraud Accomplishes." *American Thinker*, 28 Dec. 2020, www.americanthinker.com/articles/2020/12/what_denying_election_fraud_accomplishes.html?fbclid=IwAR0iv3uAR33mkD4ptaJi_L1-RA_e6_askiS7D8yjheYje8I6ll6i_qUMi9M.

Dyers, J.E. "Election 2020: This IS the fight you were appointed for." *Liberty Unyielding*, 6 Nov. 2020, libertyunyielding.com/2020/11/06/election-2020-this-is-the-fight-you-were-appointed-for/.

Eastman, John C. "Trying to Prevent Illegal Conduct From Deciding an Election Is Not Endorsing a 'Coup.'" *American Greatness*, 30 Sept. 2021, amgreatness.com/2021/09/30/trying-to-prevent-illegal-conduct-from-deciding-an-election-is-not-endorsing-a-coup/.

Editorial Staff. "What is Cultural Marxism?" *Nordic Resistance Movement*, 10 Feb. 2019, nordicresistancemovement.org/what-is-cultural-marxism/.

Eidson, John. "Report: All Hell Is About To Break Loose In Georgia." *The Blue State Conservative*, 6 Sept. 2021, thebluestateconservative.com/2021/09/06/report-all-hell-is-about-to-break-loose-in-georgia/.

"Election Integrity: 62% Don't Think Voter ID Laws Discriminate." *Rasmussen Reports,* 13 Apr. 2021, www.rasmussenreports.com/public_content/politics/general_politics/april_2021/election_integrity_62_don_t_think_voter_id_laws_discriminate.

Emmons, Libby. "BREAKING: President Trump announces FBI has RAIDED Mar-a-Lago." *PM*, 8 Aug. 2022, thepostmillennial.com/breaking-president-trump-announces-fbi-has-raided-mar-a-lago.

Emmons, Libby. "Ilhan Omar's daughter comes out as a communist after supporting riots, calling for insurrection." *PM*, 20 May 2021, thepostmillennial.com/ilhan-omars-daughter-comes-out-as-a-communist-after-calls-for-violent-insurrection.

Enloe, Chris. "Dem senator says Republicans who challenge election are 'bordering on' treason a crime punishable by death." *Blaze Media*, 19 Dec. 2020, www.theblaze.com/news/shaheen-republicans-bordering-on-treason-election-challenge?fbclid=IwAR3brJa_K3dYxFsE892qUovGGsfdh5I8Q57W0Hee6MxPi0wsc7GIxngZ8i0.

Enloe, Chris. "Sources, Trump lawyer make eyebrow-raising accusations against FBI agents who conducted Mar-a-Lago raid: 'Trying to shield what they're doing'." *The Blaze*, 10 Aug. 2022, www.theblaze.com/news/sources-trump-attorney-accusations-fbi-mar-a-lago-raid.

Ertelt, Steven. "Dozens of House Republicans will Challenge Electoral College Vote January 6." *LifeNews.com*, 28 Dec. 2020, www.lifenews.com/2020/12/28/dozens-of-house-republicans-will-challenge-electoral-college-vote-january-6/?fbclid=IwAR1J_vdI_DkIkqGOHSBzucs1IlfEIT0Ug4QRs21xAuFZWWBR2jxMXJmWHo0.

Faddis, Sam. "Guest Post: A Retired CIA Ops Officer Warns; The Left's Communist Revolution Doesn't Care About Elections." *Revolver*, 10 Sep. 2020, www.revolver.news/2020/09/cia-officer-warns-left-wing-revolution-does-not-care-about-elections/.

Fairbanks, Cassandra. "Aggressive BLM Activists Block Minneapolis City Council Member's Car, Force Her to Sign Statement Saying Rioter's Charges Will Be Dropped (VIDEO)." *Gateway Pundit*, 30 June 2021, www.thegatewaypundit.com/2021/06/aggressive-blm-activists-block-minneapolis-city-council-members-car-force-sign-statement-saying-rioters-charges-will-dropped-video/.

Farah, Joseph. "The night of long knives – tech-style." *WND*, 10 Jan. 2021, www.wnd.com/2021/01/night-long-knives-tech-style/?ff_source=facebook&ff_medium=wnd&ff_campaign=dlvrit&ff_content=2021-01-11.

Favocci, Christine. "Watch: Did She Say the Quiet Part Out Loud? Pelosi Calls Biden's 'Build Back Better' Agenda Obama's." *The Western Journal*, 28 Sept. 2021, hwww.westernjournal.com/watch-say-quiet-part-loud-pelosi-calls-bidens-build-back-

b e t t e r - a g e n d a - o b a m a s / ?
utm_source=facebook&utm_medium=huckabee.

"FBI accuses 'conspiracy theorists' of weaponizing Twitter Files." *RT*, 22
    Dec. 2022, www.rt.com/news/568706-fbi-defends-meddling-
    conspiracy-twitter/.

"FBI Agents Are Privately Targeting Michigan Trump Electors." *Trump
    Nation News*, 4 July 2022, trumpnationnews.org/2022/07/04/
    fbi-agents-are-privately-targeting-michigan-trump-electors/.

"FBI must be abolished – former US presidential candidate." *RT*, 19 Dec.
    2022, www.rt.com/news/568546-ron-paul-disband-fbi-twitter/.

Ferrechio, Susan. "Google Spam Filter Cost Republicans $2 Billion In
    Lost Donors." *Technocracy News & Trends*, 5 July 2022,
    www.technocracy.news/google-spam-filter-cost-republicans-2-
    billion-in-lost-donors/.

Fetzer, James. "The Gauntlet is Thrown Down. Oath Keepers to
    President: "Invoke the Insurrection Act or We Will Fight a
    Bloody and Desperate Revolution to Throw-off Biden / Chi-
    Com Puppet Regime." *Jamesfetzer.org*, 24 Dec. 2020,
    jamesfetzer.org/2020/12/the-gauntlet-is-thrown-down-
    oathkeepers-to-president-invoke-the-insurrection-act-or-we-
    will-fight-a-bloody-and-desperate-revolution-to-throw-off-
    biden-chi-com-puppet-regime/.

Fidler, Virginia. "Socialism always ends in destruction." *Natural News*, 3
    Dec. 2018, www.naturalnews.com/2018-12-03-socialism-
    always-ends-in-destruction.html.

Fleetwood, Shawn. "NYT Pretends To Debunk Poll Worker 'Conspiracy.'
    One Day Later, The 'Election Deniers' Were Vindicated." *The
    Federalist*, 5 Oct. 2022, thefederalist.com/2022/10/05/nyt-
    pretends-to-debunk-poll-worker-conspiracy-one-day-later-the-
    election-deniers-were-vindicated/.

Flurry, Gerald. "The Roots of America's Dangerous Turn Left." *The
    Trumpet*. Jan. 2016, www.thetrumpet.com/13314-the-roots-of-
    americas-dangerous-turn-left.

Flynn, Michael. "Gen. Flynn Exclusive: 10 INDISPUTABLE FACTS on the 2020 Election That Argue for Audits." *The Western Journal*, 30 Jul. 2021, www.westernjournal.com/gen-flynn-exclusive-10-indisputable-facts-2020-election-argue-audits/.

Foelker, Rebecca Sunny. "A movie about the Holodomor has eerie similarities to today's America." *American Thinker*, 10 Sept. 2021, www.americanthinker.com/blog/2021/09/a_movie_about_the_holodomor_has_eerie_similarities_to_todays_america.html.

Foer, Franklin. "The Trump Regime Is Beginning to Topple." *The Atlantic*, 6 June 2020, www.theatlantic.com/ideas/archive/2020/06/how-regime-change-happens/612739/.

Folks, Jeffrey. "Communist Elitism." *American Thinker*, 8 Oct. 2021, www.americanthinker.com/articles/2021/10/communist_elitism.html.

"Food as a Weapon of War." *Encyclopedia.com*, www.encyclopedia.com/food/encyclopedias-almanacs-transcripts-and-maps/food-weapon-war#:~:text=Providing%20or%20withholding%20food%20during,and%20explosives%20of%20opposing%20armies.&text=A%20major%20focus%20of%20the,had%20followed%20World%20War%20I.

Fomenko, Timur. "Why Joe Biden is more dangerous than Donald Trump." *RT*, 8 Feb. 2023, www.rt.com/news/571182-biden-trump-us-sotu/.

Foster, Michael. "Exclusive — Joe Kent After Primary Victory: 'We Must Unify' to Fight the Left, Administrative State." *Breitbart*, 10 Aug. 2022, www.breitbart.com/politics/2022/08/10/exclusive-joe-kent-after-primary-victory-we-must-unify-to-fight-the-left-administrative-state/.

Freiburger, Calvin. "Wisconsin audit finds state election commission ignored law in 2020 presidential race." *LifeSite*, 28 Oct. 2021, www.lifesitenews.com/news/wisconsin-audit-finds-state-election-commission-ignored-law-in-2020-presidential-race/.

"FTC Sues Amazon for Illegally Maintaining Monopoly Power." *Federal Trade Commission (ftc.gov)*, 26 Sept. 2023, www.ftc.gov/news-events/news/press-releases/2023/09/ftc-sues-amazon-illegally-maintaining-monopoly-power.

Fu, Eva. "EXCLUSIVE: 'I Didn't See Donald Trump Sweating at All': GOP Lawmakers Who Met Trump Say He's Not Perturbed by FBI Raid." *The Epoch Times*, 11 Aug. 2022, www.theepochtimes.com/i-didnt-see-donald-trump-sweating-at-all-gop-lawmakers-who-met-trump-say-hes-not-perturbed-by-f b i - r a i d _ 4 6 5 8 6 2 1 . h t m l ? utm_source=partner&utm_campaign=ZeroHedge.

Fuentes, Martine. "Build back Bolshevik." *American Thinker*, 1 Nov. 2021, www.americanthinker.com/blog/2021/11/build_back_bolshevik.html.

Gant, James. "Judge who signed off the FBI raid on Donald Trump's Mar-a-Lago mansion donated $2,000 to Barack Obama's campaign and represented Jeffrey Epstein's Lolita Express pilots, his scheduler and 'Yugoslavian sex slave'." *Dailymail.Com*, 9 Aug. 2022, www.dailymail.co.uk/news/article-11095583/Judge-signed-FBI-raid-Mar-Lago-represented-Jeffrey-Epsteins-workers.html.

Geller, Pamela. "Pelosi Says Capitalism Has Not Helped US Economy, Argues 'We Have To Correct That.'" *Geller Report*, 18 Sept. 2021, gellerreport.com/2021/09/pelosi-says-capitalism-has-not-h e l p e d - u s - e c o n o m y . h t m l / ? utm_source=dlvr.it&utm_medium=facebook.

George, Liz. "120+ retired military flag officers warn US 'under assault' by socialists, Marxists, urges Americans to fight back." *American Military News*, 11 May 2021, americanmilitarynews.com/2021/05/120-retired-military-flag-officers-warn-us-under-assault-by-socialists-marxists-urges-a m e r i c a n s - t o - f i g h t - b a c k / ? utm_source=quayle&utm_campaign=alt&utm_medium=facebook.

"Global Defense Contractor IT Expert Testifies in Italian Court He and Others Switched Votes in the U.S. Presidential Race." *NOQ Report*, Jan. 6, 2021, noqreport.com/2021/01/06/global-defense-contractor-it-expert-testifies-in-italian-court-he-and-

others-switched-votes-in-the-u-s-presidential-race/?
fbclid=IwAR1U2VegMFLXX5s1Xicvmb_2eulf2A5By2Zaxgs
NgnkpI8cym6sSTaP1sG0.

"Globalists Threatened Trump With War If He Did Not Leave The White House." *War Room With Owen Shroyer*, 22 July 2021, banned.video/watch?id=60fa243240edd2093577e9b7.

Golden, C. Douglas. "Democrats Explore Using Obscure Section of Constitution to Ban Trump from Office." *The Western Journal*, 7 Jan. 2022, www.westernjournal.com/democrats-explore-using-obscure-section-constitution-ban-trump-office/?utm_source=mewe&utm_medium=westernjournalism&utm_content=2022-01-07&utm_campaign=manualpost.

Golden, C. Douglas. "Election Manipulation Nightmare: DeSantis Opens Investigation Into Facebook." *The Western Journal*, 28 Sep. 2021, www.westernjournal.com/election-manipulation-nightmare-desantis-opens-investigation-facebook/?utm_source=mewe&utm_medium=westernjournalism&utm_content=2021-09-28&utm_campaign=manualpost.

Golden, C. Douglas. "It's Spreading: MI County Calls Out Dominion, Demands Audit and Answers About Election Manipulation." *The Western Journal*, 23 June 2021, www.westernjournal.com/spreading-mi-county-calls-dominion-demands-audit-answers-election-manipulation/?utm_source=mewe&utm_medium=westernjournalism&utm_content=2021-06-23&utm_campaign=topdaily.

Golden, C. Douglas. "Report: Prosecutors Are Trying to Break Up a Network of US Antifa Cells for the First Time." *The Western Journal*, 11 Dec. 2021, www.westernjournal.com/report-prosecutors-trying-break-network-us-antifa-cells-first-time/?utm_source=telegram&utm_medium=westernjournalism&utm_campaign=telegramfeed&utm_content=2021-12-11.

Golden, C. Douglas. "Watch: Tucker Carlson Guest Paints Grim Picture of Military 'Anti-Extremist' Witch-Hunt." *The Western Journal*, 13 June 2021, www.westernjournal.com/watch-tucker-carlson-guest-paints-grim-picture-military-anti-extremist-witch-hunt/?utm_source=mewe&utm_medium=westernjournalism&utm_content=2021-06-13&utm_campaign=manualpost.

Goldstein, Lorrie. "GOLDSTEIN: Freeland questions whether 'capitalist democracy' still works." *Toronto Sun*, 19 Aug. 2023, torontosun.com/opinion/columnists/goldstein-freeland-questions-whether-capitalist-democracy-still-works.

Gomez, Christian. "EU Globalists and Chinese Communists Team Up To Protect NWO." *The New American*, 25 Jun. 2018, www.thenewamerican.com/world-news/europe/item/29379-eu-globalists-and-chinese-communists-team-up-to-protect-nwo#disqus_thread.

Gonzalez, Pedro. "The Hunt for Dissidents." *The American Mind*, 1 July 2021, americanmind.org/features/whos-next/the-hunt-for-dissidents/.

Goodin, Emily. "FBI raids Mar-a-Lago: Trump said his home was 'under siege by large group of agents who even broke into my safe'." *Daily Mail*, 8 Aug. 2022, www.dailymail.co.uk/news/article-11093449/FBI-agents-raid-Mar-Lago-Trump-says-home-siege-agents.html.

GOP World. "BLM City Leader Quits After Discovering 1 Shocking Fact." *GOP World*, web.archive.org/web/20210621230208/https://gopworld.com/blm-city-leader-quits-after-discovering-1-shocking-fact//

Gray, Tony. "Trump Supporters Will Be Targeted After Mar-a-Lago Raid, Part of Leftist 'Playbook' as Seen in Latin America: Sen. Rubio." *Resist the Mainstream*, 12 Aug. 2022, resistthemainstream.org/sen-rubio-issues-warning-to-trump-supporters-following-mar-a-lago-raid/?utm_source=telegram.

Gray, Tony. "Watch: Michael Flynn Says 'We Have Two Separate Governments': 'One That Actually Gets Elected' & One 'That Operates Under No Rules.'" *Resist the Mainstream*, 8 Oct. 2021, resistthemainstream.org/watch-michael-flynn-explains-the-two-separate-governments-the-u-s-has/?utm_source=telegram.

Green, John. "School's Out – For the Marxists." *American Thinker*, 9 Oct. 2021, www.americanthinker.com/articles/2021/10/schools_out__for_the_marxists.html.

Green, Ryan. "Biden Says the Quiet Part Out Loud: "It's About Who Gets to Count the Vote" (VIDEO)." *Simply Patriot*, 15 Dec. 2021, simplypatriot.com/politics/biden-says-the-quiet-part-out-loud-its-about-who-gets-to-count-the-vote-video/.

Green, Ryan. "NEVER FORGET: Dems Rioted, Attacked, Beat Trump Supporters During Their Insurrection." *Mad Patriot News*, 20 Dec. 2021, www.madpatriotnews.com/never-forget-dems-rioted-attacked-beat-trump-supporters-during-their-insurrection/?utm_source=google&utm_medium=sm&utm_campaign=tlg_wac.

Greenberg, Jay. "Putin: 'Wokeness Is Evil and It's Destroying the West' Russian president warns same thing 'happened In Russia' - 'It destroys values.'" *Neon Nettle*, 22 Oct. 2021, neonnettle.com/news/17128-putin-wokeness-is-evil-and-it-s-destroying-the-west-.

Greenfield, Daniel. "What a Stalin Quote about Rigging Elections Reveals about the 2020 Election." *Frontpagemag*, 30 Dec. 2020, www.frontpagemag.com/fpm/2020/12/what-stalin-quote-about-rigging-elections-reveals-daniel-greenfield/?fbclid=IwAR27OQmtJZ0w6LsZyTam07HIngF0UpB1q9xVtffYZAoMNJX4T1CLVF-HSog#.X-w2WDkjd3Q.facebook.

Greenley, Larry. "Next Step to World Government: Atlantic Union." *The New American*, 9 Mar. 2020, www.thenewamerican.com/print-magazine/item/34944-next-step-to-world-government-atlantic-union?fbclid=IwAR2u5WqOk-netjF2WHw3U0kIuZBLFk8jXgW_6eUrs2lUdyJ0olEVD0rMi0A

Griffin, G. Edward. "Here's the Democrat-run Communist Game Plan to Take Over the USA (Video + Transcript) More Deadly Than War (1969)." *State of the Nation*, 30 Oct. 2020, stateofthenation.co/?p=33996.

Grossman, Hannah. "North Korean Defector: I Am Terrified of the 'Massive Indoctrination Coming from the Left' in Public Schools." *Fox News*, 15 June 2022, www.foxnews.com/media/north-korean-defector-i-am-terrified-of-the-massive-indoctrination-coming-from-the-left-in-public-schools.

Hagopian, Joachim. "One World Governance and the Council on Foreign Relations. 'We Shall Have World Government…by Conquest or Consent.'" *Global Research*, 24 Jan. 2021, www.globalresearch.ca/one-world-governance-and-the-council-on-foreign-relations-we-shall-have-world-government-by-conquest-or-consent/5541363.

Hale, Mark. "Lawyer Drops Election BOMBSHELL: Vote-Tabulator Machine Totals Can Be Changed." *Patriot Truth News,* 18 May 2021, patriottruthnews.com/latest-news/lawyer-drops-election-bombshell-vote-tabulator-machine-totals-can-be-changed/?utm_source=google&utm_medium=sm&utm_campaign=mewe_ptn.

Hall, Jon N. "How Mike Pence Fell Short on January 6." *American Thinker*, 15 Feb. 2022, www.americanthinker.com/articles/2022/02/how_mike_pence_fell_short_on_january_6.html.

Hannity Staff. "HANNITY: The Left Wants All Americans to 'Submit to Their Will' or Be Labeled 'Dumb Racists'." *Hannity.com*, 9 June 2021, hannity.com/media-room/hannity-the-left-wants-all-americans-to-submit-to-their-will-or-be-labeled-dumb-racists/.

Hannity Staff. "THIS IS REAL: Biden State Dept Unfurls 'Black Lives Matter' Flags at Some Embassies." *Hannity*, 26 May 2021, hannity.com/media-room/this-is-real-biden-state-dept-unfurls-black-lives-matter-flags-at-some-embassies/.

Hanson, Jason. "Decorated CIA Officer Warns: 'They're Coming For You.'" *cf.spybriefing.com*, cf.spybriefing.com/save-america?ld-trk=1_14421954182435612&utm_campaign=USB&utm_content=Lockerdome&utm_medium=Display&utm_source=Lockerdome.

Hanson, Victor Davis. "How Constitutional Systems and Citizenship Perish." *The Daily Signal*, 7 Oct. 2021, www.dailysignal.com/2021/10/07/how-constitutional-systems-and-citizenship-perish/?utm_source=TDS_Email&utm_medium=email&utm_campaign=MorningBell&mkt_tok=ODI0LU1IVC0zMDQAAAGAF_sk OUYSLaRZj03TJ-QtnklFqdgUm3hRl3w1g4wrzTm4vds_rfIPSQuxRh3yK_EVck bV-oZmd3ZEh9oyAPGWQLPOn07YQWVCj5IMKPIvVx3zsXJs.

Hanson, Victor Davis. "The US Military Isn't a Revolutionary People's Army Yet, But It's Getting There Under Woke Officers." *The Western Journal*, 30 June 2021, www.westernjournal.com/ victor-davis-hanson-us-military-isnt-revolutionary-peoples- a r m y - y e t - g e t t i n g - w o k e - o f f i c e r s / ? utm_source=mewe&utm_medium=westernjournalism&utm_co ntent=2021-07-01&utm_campaign=manualpost.

Harris, Niamh. "'Evil, Corrupt Leftists Want To Tear Down This Nation' Says Jon Voight." *NewsPunch*, 11 Nov. 2020, newspunch.com/ evil-corrupt-leftists-want-to-tear-down-this-nation-says-jon- v o i g h t / ? fbclid=IwAR0PN7_Q5M57yVNZP3BCLXc8pLe6krB_2WAW IDnh_HWptH5393G6nk2e-BI.

Harris, Niamh. "IT'S HAPPENING: Rep. Matt Gaetz to Formally Challenge Electoral College Votes." *Newspunch*, 21 Dec. 2020, newspunch.com/its-happening-rep-matt-gaetz-to-formally- c h a l l e n g e - e l e c t o r a l - c o l l e g e - v o t e s / ? fbclid=IwAR3CFTi9bwTAmCeJzl9Jr_zY26rGKvKX_nk- nkgIVvUjUBkE2yqupX7wMXE.

Haskins, Justin. "Introducing the 'Great Reset,' World Leaders' Radical Plan to Transform the Economy." *MSN*, MSN, 25 June 2020, www.msn.com/en-us/news/politics/introducing-the-great-reset- world-leaders-radical-plan-to-transform-the-economy/ar- B B l 5 X G s U ? fbclid=IwAR0nHYaWwbRdVMkSXaHZtrRXG7XbRMRBS55 XWIzGCMR6InTtHuuQAn8iiu0.

Hawkins, Justin. "Al Gore, UN Secretary-General, others now demanding 'Great Reset"of global capitalism." *Fox Business,* 24 Jun. 2020, www.foxbusiness.com/markets/al-gore-un- s e c r e t a r y - g e n e r a l - g r e a t - r e s e t - g l o b a l - c a p i t a l i s m ? f b c l i d = I w A R 1 8 g s 7 1 d B f q N O 0 d q M K p i 0 u M - pRdMlU8yL2qaF_F_n5n2Xo6usxpzcuo37Q.

HealthRanger. "Sydney Powell: 'Staggering' Evidence of Vote Fraud, Dominion Machines Engineered by China, Venezuela, Cuba and DESIGNED to Steal Elections Worldwide... Release the K r a k e n ! " *D i s t r i b u t e d N e w s*, 1 4 N o v. 2 0 2 0, www.distributednews.com/474618.html.

Henry, Michael. "Show me the man and I'll show you the crime." *The Oxford Eagle*, 9 May, 2018, www.oxfordeagle.com/2018/05/09/show-me-the-man-and-ill-show-you-the-crime/.

"Henry A. Kissinger Quotes." *AZ Quotes*, www.azquotes.com/author/8103-Henry_A_Kissinger.

Herlihy, Brianna. "Arizona AG asks FBI, IRS to investigate election integrity watchdog True the Vote." *Fox News*, 14 Oct. 2022, ttps://www.foxnews.com/politics/arizona-ag-asks-fbi-irs-investigate-election-integrity-watchdog-true-vote.

Herman, Carl. "Q's 'Nothing can stop what is coming' = NCSWIC sting of Dominion 'voting' machine election fraud + treason? Game-ender if true!" *Carlherman.blogspot.com*, 15 Nov. 2020, carlbherman.blogspot.com/2020/11/qs-nothing-can-stop-what-i s - c o m i n g . h t m l ? fbclid=IwAR2pCryCJMaCNNz0C9dzozaOlu0Tt0vfktfISx9BTj NlM3jN58jenCz_N4Q.

Heyes, JD. "Biden betrayal of America continues as he orders DHS to cancel remaining border wall contracts as $100 million in materials lay dormant." *Natural News*, 14 Oct. 2021, www.naturalnews.com/2021-10-14-biden-cancels-remaining-border-wall-contracts.html.

Heyes, JD. "Biden Pentagon's 'Extremism' Czar Seeks to Purge All MAGA Personnel in Bid to Purge Patriots from Last Viable American Institution: The Military." *Natural News*, 17 May 2021, www.naturalnews.com/2021-05-17-biden-pentagon-purging-all-patriots-from-military.html#.

Heyes, JD. "Detroit whistleblower comes forward, describes massive voter fraud for Biden with repeat ballot counting." *Natural News*, 19 Nov. 2020, naturalnews.com/2020-11-19-detroit-whistleblower-massive-voter-fraud-biden-repeat-counting.html.

Heyes, JD. "Devin Nunes believes FBI, DOJ running assets on Twitter." *Natural News*, 19 Dec. 2022, www.naturalnews.com/2022-12-19-devin-nunes-believes-fbi-doj-running-assets-on-twitter.html.

Heyes, JD. "Even The NY Times now exposing the ACLU as being run by lunatic Leftists more interested in virtue signaling than defending civil liberties." *Natural News*, 11 June 2021, www.naturalnews.com/2021-06-11-ny-times-exposing-aclu-leftists-virtue-signaling.html.

Heyes, JD. "Judicial Watch finds documents indicating California Democrats coordinated with Big Tech to censor election posts from American users." *Natural News,* 17 May 2021, www.naturalnews.com/2021-05-17-california-democrats-big-tech-censor-election-posts.html#.

Heyes, JD. "Obama, Clinton, Dems finding ways around presidential records law while Trump's house gets raided by FBI." *Natural News*, 14 Aug. 2022, www.naturalnews.com/2022-08-14-obama-clinton-dems-get-around-presidential-records-law-trumps-house-gets-raided-fbi.html.

Heyes, JD. "Only Democrats favor election fraud: Nearly every European country requires government-issued ID to cast ballots." *Natural News*, 13 Jun. 2021, www.naturalnews.com/2021-06-13-every-european-country-voter-id-election-fraud.html#.

Heyes, JD. "Retired CIA officer sends dire warning to America: The Left's Marxist revolution isn't concerned about who wins the November election." *Civil War News*, 16 Sept. 2020, www.civilwar.news/2020-09-16-retired-cia-officer-sends-dire-warning-marxist-revolution.html.

Heyes, JD. "Revealed: Facebook illegally SPIES on private messages of users who question 2020 election or express anti-government sentiment, REPORTS them to Feds." *Natural News*, 16 Sept. 2022, www.naturalnews.com/2022-09-16-facebook-spied-users-question-2020-election-reported-them-to-feds.html.

Heyes, JD. "ROGUE FBI was spying on 'far-right extremists' months before false-flag Capitol demonstration." *Natural News*, 21 June 2021, www.naturalnews.com/2021-06-21-fbi-was-spying-on-extremists-before-capitol-riot.html.

Heyes, JD. "So fake: Joe Biden is so mind-addled his handlers built a phony 'Oval Office' for him across from the White House so he can read his answers from a teleprompter." *Natural News*, 16 Oct. 2021, www.naturalnews.com/2021-10-16-joe-biden-handlers-built-a-phony-oval-office-for-him.html.

Heyes, JD. "The Biden regime has officially become a terrorist organization, throws in with BLM that terrorizes America and targets White people with race-based hatred and violence." *Natural News*, 27 May 2021, www.naturalnews.com/2021-05-27-biden-regime-officially-terrorist-org-throws-in-with-blm.html#.

Heyes, JD. "The Left called Trump a fascist but Biden actually is one: MAGA protesters being treated worse than prisoners in third-world dictatorships." *Natural News*, 18 June 2021, www.naturalnews.com/2021-06-18-maga-protesters-being-treated-worse-third-world-prisoners.html.

Heyes, J.D. "The Marxist left is pushing for a full breakup of America so the tyrants can rule over the ashes unchallenged by patriots: And they're using race to do it." *Natural News*, 18 Jun. 2021, www.naturalnews.com/2021-06-18-marxist-left-full-breakup-america-tyrants-rule-over-ashes.html.

Heyes, JD. "The White House won't admit Cubans oppose communism because the Biden regime LOVES Communism." *Natural News*, 19 July 2021, www.naturalnews.com/2021-07-19-white-house-wont-admit-cubans-oppose-communism.html.

Heyes, JD. "Whistleblowers Reveal 'Anti-American Indoctrination' in the Military as Woke Left Seeks Takeover." *Natural News*, 17 June 2021. www.naturalnews.com/2021-06-17-woke-left-trying-to-take-over-the-military.html#.

Heyes, JD. "World Economic Forum seeks to enslave Americans by replacing free-market capitalism with 'Great Reset' to roll out global socialism." *Newstarget*, 22. Oct. 2020, www.newstarget.com/2020-10-22-world-economic-forum-enslave-americans-replacing-capitalism-great-reset.html.

Himalaya New Zealand. "Tug of War Within the National Intelligence Agency: DNI Ratcliffe's Election Meddling Report has been postponed." *GNews*, 17 Dec. 2020, gnews.org/660000/.

Hoffman, Ari. "Leaders of the Democratic Socialists of America travel to Venezuela to meet with dictator Nicolas Maduro." *PM*, 5 Jul. 2021, thepostmillennial.com/leaders-of-the-democratic-socialists-of-america-travel-to-venezuela-to-meet-with-dictator-nicolas-maduro.

Hoft, Jim. "53% of Republicans think Trump is the true president. Rasmussen: Majority of American Voters Support Full Forensic Audits of Election Results." *Gateway Pundit*, 23 June 2021, www.thegatewaypundit.com/2021/06/rasmussen-majority-american-voters-support-full-forensic-audits-election-results/.

Hoft, Jim. "Another 375,000 watched Trump's live speech on RSBN Rumble. MUST SEE... COMPARE AND CONTRAST: Which Candidate Won the 2020 Election? – Independence Day Edition." *Gateway Pundit*, 3 Jul. 2021, www.thegatewaypundit.com/2021/07/must-see-compare-contrast-candidate-won-2020-election-independence-day-edition/.

Hoft, Jim. "Arizona Lawmaker Responds to AG Garland: 'You Will Not Touch Arizona Ballots or Machines Unless You Want to Spend Time in Arizona Prison.'" *Gateway Pundit*, 11 Jun. 2021, www.thegatewaypundit.com/2021/06/arizona-lawmaker-responds-ag-garland-will-not-touch-arizona-ballots-machines-unless-want-spend-time-arizona-prison/.

Hoft, Jim. "Beattie on The War Room: January 6th Committee a Pretext To Justify Labeling Trump Supporters As Domestic Terrorists." *Gateway Pundit*, 3 July 2022, www.thegatewaypundit.com/2022/07/beattie-war-room-january-6th-committee-pretext-justify-labeling-trump-supporters-domestic-terrorists/.

Hoft, Jim. "Breaking: Another Hit by Dirty Marc Elias — Democrats File Lawsuit to Block 3 Republicans from Wisconsin Ballot for Challenging Fraud in 2020 Election." *Gateway Pundit*, 10 Mar. 2022, www.thegatewaypundit.com/2022/03/breaking-another-hit-dirty-marc-elias-democrats-file-lawsuit-block-3-republicans-wisconsin-ballot-challenging-fraud-2020-election/?utm_source=Gab&utm_medium=PostTopSharingButtons&utm_campaign=websitesharingbuttons.

Hoft, Jim. "BREAKING: Biden DOJ Steps In - Issues Guidelines Cautioning States Performing Audits of Election Results."

Gateway Pundit, 28 July 2021, www.thegatewaypundit.com/2021/07/breaking-biden-doj-steps-issues-guidelines-cautioning-states-performing-audits-election-results/.

Hoft, Jim. "BRUTAL! Matt Gaetz NAILS Sec. of Defense Lloyd Austin on His Racist Trainings and Crazed Advisors — Secretary Austin Spins BS (VIDEO)." *Gateway Pundit*, 23 June 2021. www.thegatewaypundit.com/2021/06/brutal-matt-gaetz-nails-sec-defense-lloyd-austin-racist-trainings-crazed-advisors-secretary-austin-spins-bs-video/.

Hoft, Jim. "Developing: Milwaukee Elections Chief Lost Elections Flash Drive in Morning Hours of November 4th When Democrats Miraculously Found 120,000 Votes for Joe Biden." *The Gateway Pundit*, 13 Nov. 2020, www.thegatewaypundit.com/2020/11/developing-milwaukee-elections-chief-lost-elections-flash-drive-morning-hours-november-4th-democrats-miraculously-found-120000-votes-joe-biden/.

Hoft, Jim. "DISCOVERED: Facebook and Twitter Private Portals Where Democrats, Government Officials and Corporate Elites Meet to Ban Unwanted Conservative Content." *Gateway Pundit*, 31 Oct. 2022, www.thegatewaypundit.com/2022/10/discovered-facebook-twitter-private-portals-democrats-government-officials-corporate-elites-meet-ban-unwanted-conservative-content/.

Hoft, Jim. "DOJ's Two-Tiered Justice System at Work: Violent Trans Antifa Activist Has Federal Charges Dropped for Assaulting Portland Police and Trying to Blind Them." *Gateway Pundit*, 30 Dec. 2021, www.thegatewaypundit.com/2021/12/dojs-two-tiered-justice-system-work-violent-trans-antifa-activist-federal-charges-dropped-assaulting-portland-police-trying-blind/.

Hoft, Jim. "Elections Expert Seth Keshel Releases National Fraud Numbers: Finds 8.1 Million Excess Votes in US Election, Affirms Trump Won PA, MI, WI, NV, AZ, GA and MN." *Gateway Pundit*, 2 Aug. 2021, www.thegatewaypundit.com/2021/08/elections-expert-seth-keshel-releases-national-fraud-numbers-finds-8-1-million-excess-votes-us-election-affirms-trump-won-pa-mi-wi-nv-az-ga-mn/.

Hoft, Jim. "Elections Expert: 'We Now Have 4 Million Ineligible and Dead Voters on American Voter Rolls' (VIDEO)." *Gateway*

Pundit, 18 Oct. 2016, www.thegatewaypundit.com/2016/10/elections-expert-now-4-million-ineligible-dead-voters-american-voter-rolls-video/.

Hoft, Jim. "EXCLUSIVE: Oath Keepers Stewart Rhodes Releases First Statement from Alexandria Prison to The Gateway Pundit - Feds Are Threatening Life in Prison (AUDIO)." *Gateway Pundit*, 12 May 2022, www.thegatewaypundit.com/2022/05/exclusive-oath-keepers-stewart-rhodes-releases-first-statement-alexandria-prison-gateway-pundit-feds-threatening-life-prison-audio/.

Hoft, Jim. "EXCLUSIVE: Top Trump Campaign Insider Speaks Out – 'RNC Did Not Want Us to Fight for the President – They Collected $220 Million for Legal Fees – Where Did It Go?'" *Gateway Pundit*, 12 July 2021, www.thegatewaypundit.com/2021/07/exclusive-top-trump-campaign-insider-speaks-rnc-not-want-us-fight-trump-collected-220-million-legal-fees-go/.

Hoft, Jim. "Facebook Was Spying on Personal Messages of Americans Who Questioned the 2020 Election – Turned Them Over to the FBI." *Gateway Pundit*, 15 September 2022, www.thegatewaypundit.com/2022/09/facebook-spying-personal-messages-americans-questioned-2020-election-turned-fbi/.

Hoft, Jim. "Former CIA Senior Operations Officer John Sipher Openly Brags About Swinging Election for Biden with Disinformation Campaign on Hunter Biden's Laptop." *Gateway Pundit*, 30 March 2022, www.thegatewaypundit.com/2022/03/former-cia-senior-operations-officer-john-sipher-openly-brags-swinging-election-biden-disinformation-campaign-hunter-bidens-laptop/?utm_source=Gab&utm_campaign=websitesharingbuttons.

Hoft, Jim. "Fun Fraud Fact: Wisconsin Added 29% of Their ENTIRE VOTING POPULATION to Voter Rolls in 10 Months Prior to 2020 Election — 957,977 New Names!" *Gateway Pundit*, 11 Apr. 2022, www.thegatewaypundit.com/2022/04/fun-fraud-fact-wisconsin-added-29-entire-voting-population-voter-rolls-10-months-prior-2020-election-957077-new-names/.

Hoft, Jim. "HERE THEY ARE: The Five Most Obvious Acts of Fraud in the 2020 Election that You Are No Longer Allowed to Discuss." *The Gateway Pundit*, 17 Jan. 2021,

www.thegatewaypundit.com/2021/01/five-obvious-acts-
fraud-2020-election/?fbclid=IwAR3zlGqlw8zh-
BoFpdYRdu9slpXK5ICarYY8xHMscyZTAnHnvNbr-zNaTes.

Hoft, Jim. "History Repeats Itself: Democrats Are Using Tactics of the
Marxists of 1917 in Russia – Their Final Assault on America
Begins... Tonight." *Gateway Pundit*, 8 Aug. 2022,
www.thegatewaypundit.com/2022/08/history-repeats-
democrats-using-tactics-marxists-1917-russia-final-assault-
america-begins-tonight/.

Hoft, Jim. "HUGE! Revolver News Breaks Report on Likely Deep State
Plants Inside Jan. 6 Uprising — WAS IT ALL PLANNED?"
Gateway Pundit, 15 June 2021, www.thegatewaypundit.com/
2021/06/huge-revolver-news-breaks-report-likely-deep-state-
plants-inside-jan-6-uprising-planned/.

Hoft, Jim. "It's Kind of Boring Out Here" – Arizona Reporter
STUNNED After NO ONE Shows Up at Campaign Event with
Joe Biden AND Kamala Harris (VIDEO)." *Gateway Pundit*, 11
Oct. 2020, www.thegatewaypundit.com/2020/10/kind-boring-
arizona-reporter-stunned-no-one-shows-campaign-event-joe-
biden-kamala-harris-video/.

Hoft, Jim. "Maria Bartiromo: 'I Know Biden's on the Phone All the Time
with Obama and I'm Hearing He's Running Things from Behind
the Scenes' (VIDEO)." *Gateway Pundit*, 28 Mar. 2021,
www.thegatewaypundit.com/2021/03/maria-bartiromo-know-
bidens-phone-time-obama-hearing-running-things-behind-
scenes-video/.

Hoft, Jim. "Mayorkas Releases New Rules on Extremism – DHS Will
Target Anyone Who Believes Election Was Stolen or Who
Challenged Fauci's Everchanging COVID Narrative." *Gateway
Pundit*, 13 Mar. 2022, www.thegatewaypundit.com/2022/03/
mayorkas-releases-new-rules-extremism-dhs-will-target-
anyone-believes-election-stolen-challenged-faucis-
everchanging-covid-rules/.

Hoft, Jim. "MUST READ: Democrats Were ONLY Able to 'Win' in 2020
By Breaking Chain of Custody Laws in EVERY SWING
STATE." *Gateway Pundit*, 10 Feb. 2021,
www.thegatewaypundit.com/2021/02/must-read-democrats-

able-win-2020-breaking-chain-custody-laws-every-swing-state/.

Hoft, Jim. "NOTE TO STACEY ABRAMS – FIND A GOOD LAWYER: True the Vote Announces They Are Releasing Addresses of ALL Ballot Trafficking Stash Houses." *Gateway Pundit*, May 8, 2022, www.thegatewaypundit.com/2022/05/note-stacey-abrams-find-good-lawyer-true-vote-announces-releasing-addresses-ballot-trafficking-stash-houses/.

Hoft, Jim. "UPDATE: Explosive Whistleblower Documents Support Missouri AG and Gateway Pundit's Lawsuit Against Biden Regime's Conspiring with Big Tech to Censor Free Speech." The *Gateway Pundit*, 29 June 2022, www.thegatewaypundit.com/2022/06/update-explosive-whistleblower-documents-support-missouri-ag-gateway-pundits-lawsuit-biden-regimes-conspiring-big-tech-censor-free-speech/.

Hoft, Jim. "Voter Fraud in Michigan – Massive Dump of Over 200,000 Ballots for Biden All the Sudden Appear Overnight...Update: Officials Call It a 'Typo.'" *Gateway Pundit*, 4 Nov. 2020, www.thegatewaypundit.com/2020/11/voter-fraud-michigan-massive-dump-200000-ballots-biden-sudden-show-overnight/.

Hoft, Jim. "We All Know It's True: 58% of Voters Now Believe Cheating was Likely in 2020 Election — Up from 54%." *Gateway Pundit*, 18 Jan. 2022, www.thegatewaypundit.com/2022/01/know-true-58-voters-now-believe-cheating-likely-2020-election-54/.

Hoft, Jim. "We Were Threatened - Exclusive Interview with Doug Logan from Cyber Ninjas on the Arizona Senate Forensic Audit - Updated." *Gateway Pundit*, 28 Sept. 2021, www.thegatewaypundit.com/2021/09/threatened-exclusive-interview-doug-logan-cyber-ninjas-arizona-senate-forensic-audit/.

Hoft, Joe. "Alabama AG Steve Marshall Makes Democrat Senator Sheldon Whitehouse Look Like a Fool When Asked Whether Biden Was President." *Gateway Pundit*, 25 Mar. 2022, www.thegatewaypundit.com/2022/03/alabama-ag-steve-marshall-makes-democrat-senator-sheldon-whitehouse-look-like-fool-asked-whether-biden-president/.

Hoft, Joe. 'BIG TECH COLLUSION: Facebook, Twitter and Google Announce Measures to Censor Pro-Trump Information Before the Election.' *Gateway Pundit*, 11 Sept. 2020, www.thegatewaypundit.com/2020/09/big-tech-collusion-facebook-twitter-google-announce-actions-prevent-trump-win/.

Hoft, Joe. "BREAKING: AG Merrick Garland Announces that His DOJ Will Scrutinize Any Post-Election Audits for Evidence of Voting Law Violations!" *Gateway Pundit*, 11 June 2021, www.thegatewaypundit.com/2021/06/breaking-ag-merrick-garland-announces-doj-will-scrutinize-post-election-audits-evidence-voting-law-violations/.

Hoft, Joe. "BREAKING EXCLUSIVE: Evidence China Was Colluding with the Bidens and Providing Information on How to Defeat President Trump in the 2020 Election." *Gateway Pundit*, 5 Jan. 2021, www.thegatewaypundit.com/2021/01/breaking-exclusive-evidence-china-colluding-bidens-providing-information-defeat-president-trump-2020-election/.

Hoft, Joe. "BREAKING EXCLUSIVE – HUGE: Ballot Printing Companies Better Lawyer Up – 2020 Ballots Were Modified in Multiple Republican Areas Forcing Adjudication and Potential Fraudulent Vote Switching." *Gateway Pundit*, 11 June 2021, www.thegatewaypundit.com/2021/06/breaking-exclusive-huge-printers-ballots-better-lawyer-2020-ballots-modified-multiple-republican-areas-forcing-adjudication-potential-fraudulent-vote-switching/.

Hoft, Joe. "BREAKING EXCLUSIVE: System 'Glitch' Also Uncovered In Wisconsin – Reversal of Swapped Votes Removes Lead from Joe Biden." *Gateway Pundit*, 9 Nov. 2020, www.thegatewaypundit.com/2020/11/breaking-exclusive-system-glitch-also-uncovered-wisconsin-reversal-19032-votes-removes-lead-joe-biden/.

Hoft, Joe. "BREAKING EXCLUSIVE: UN, US, Facebook and Smartmatic Executives Conspired Together Before the 2020 Election and Many of Same Officials Now Trying to Stop or Derail 2020 Election Audits Taking Place." *Gateway Pundit*, 5 Jun. 2021, www.thegatewaypundit.com/2021/06/breaking-exclusive-un-us-facebook-smartmatic-executives-connived-together-2020-election-now-trying-stop-derail-2020-election-audits-taking-place/.

Hoft, Joe. "BREAKING HUGE – President Trump: 'They Are Going to Decertify This Election!'" *The Gateway Pundit*, 11 Sept. 2021, www.thegatewaypundit.com/2021/09/breaking-huge-president-trump-going-decertify-election/?utm_source=Gab&utm_campaign=websitesharingbuttons.

Hoft, Joe. "BREAKING: Michigan 'Computer Glitch' Fixed, Had Switched 6,000 Votes from President Trump to Biden – GOP Demands 47 More Counties Corrected." *Gateway Pundit*, 6 Nov. 2020, www.thegatewaypundit.com/2020/11/breaking-michigan-computer-glitch-fixed-giving-president-trump-2500-votes-gop-demands-47-counties-corrected/.

Hoft, Joe. "CHEATERS: President Trump Warns Against 4am Ballot Drops and an Hour Later Wisconsin and Michigan Drop 300,000 Ballots For Democrats and ZERO for Trump." *Gateway Pundit*, 4 Nov. 2020, www.thegatewaypundit.com/2020/11/cheaters-president-trump-warns-4am-ballot-drops-hour-later-wisconsin-michigan-drop-300000-ballots-democrats-zero-trump/.

Hoft, Joe. "Corrupt DOJ and FBI Attempt Coup d'état of Trump Presidency and Get Away With It." *Gateway Pundit*, 18 Oct. 2022, www.thegatewaypundit.com/2022/10/corrupt-doj-fbi-attempt-coup-detat-trump-presidency-get-away/.

Hoft, Joe. "Currently Over 5 Million Questionable, Unlawful or Spurious Ballots Identified in 2020 Election in PA, GA and AZ — Will Republican Party Do Anything or Will They Allow this to Continue?" *Gateway Pundit*, 10 Feb. 2022, www.thegatewaypundit.com/2022/02/exclusive-currently-5-million-invalid-ballots-identified-2020-election-pennsylvania-georgia-arizona-validating-trump-won/.

Hoft, Joe. "Dominion is Panicking in Pennsylvania Because Their Machines Likely Weren't Properly 'Hardened' and Shouldn't Have Ever Been Put in Use." *Gateway Pundit*, 5 Jan. 2022, www.thegatewaypundit.com/2022/01/dominion-panicking-pennsylvania-machines-likely-werent-properly-hardened-shouldnt-ever-put-use/.

Hoft, Joe. "EXCLUSIVE: Radical Far-Left Group (EIP) Created Partnership with Government and Social Media to Censor and Ban Any 2020 Election Reporting – The Gateway Pundit Was

Top Target." *The Gateway Pundit*, 21 July 2022, www.thegatewaypundit.com/2022/07/exclusive-radical-far-left-group-eip-created-partnership-government-social-media-crush-2020-election-reporting-gateway-pundit-top-target/.

Hoft, Joe. "FINAL 2020 RALLY TALLY: President Trump Had Largest Crowds at His Rallies in US History – Biden Had Some of the Smallest." *Gateway Pundit*, 3 Nov. 2020, www.thegatewaypundit.com/2020/11/final-2020-rally-tally-president-trump-largest-crowds-rallies-us-history-biden-smallest/.

Hoft, Joe. "HUGE: Defend Florida Releases Interim Report – 800,000 Inactive Voters in 2020 Election, A Third of Those Canvassed Didn't Live at Registered Address." *Gateway Pundit*, February 3, 2022, www.thegatewaypundit.com/2022/02/huge-defend-florida-releases-interim-report-800000-inactive-voters-2020-election-third-canvassed-didnt-live-address-registered/?utm_source=Email&utm_medium=the-gateway-pundit&utm_campaign=dailyam&utm_content=daily.

Hoft, Joe. "'I'm Really Disgusted with Republicans Who Are Telling Us to Move On...The Base Feels as Though a Massive Civil Injustice Was Done to Them' – Charlie Kirk from Turning Point USA on 2020 Election Fraud." *Gateway Pundit*, 4 Apr. 2022, www.thegatewaypundit.com/2022/04/really-disgusted-republicans-telling-us-move-base-feel-though-massive-civilization-injustice-done-charlie-kirk-turning-point-usa-2020-elect/.

Hoft, Joe. "Lawrence Sellin:.The Second American Civil War is Underway." *Gateway Pundit*, 9 Apr. 2022, www.thegatewaypundit.com/2022/04/lawrence-sellin-second-american-civil-war-underway/.

Hoft, Joe. "More Than Half of Americans Believe Cheating Tainted the 2020 Presidential Election and the Number of Americans Who Believe This Is Increasing." *Gateway Pundit*, 11 Oct. 2021, www.thegatewaypundit.com/2021/10/half-americans-believe-cheating-tainted-2020-presidential-election-number-americans-believe-going/?fbclid=IwAR0_GHe-cOiaONURDypig7iULq2mo_PM0PhJ5NOPhbgi203EGURyu-hY7n4.

Hoft, Joe. "MUST READ: This Is Why the Democrats are So Afraid of a Valid Audit in Maricopa County – the Results Are Insane." *Gateway Pundit*, 26 Apr. 2021, www.thegatewaypundit.com/2021/04/democrats-afraid-valid-audit-maricopa-county-results-insane/.

Hoft, Joe. "New Fascist Group Led by Media Matters Founder David Brock and former Democrat Majority Leader Tom Daschle is Targeting Attorneys Who Supported President Trump Following 2020 Election Steal." *Gateway Pundit*, 8 Mar. 2022, www.thegatewaypundit.com/2022/03/media-matters-marxists-now-advising-group-target-attorneys-represented-president-trump-stolen-2020-election/.

Hoft, Joe. "Poll Shows That Only 6% of Republicans Believe that Joe Biden's 2020 Election Win Was "Definitely Legitimate." *Gateway Pundit*, 30 Dec. 2021, www.thegatewaypundit.com/2021/12/poll-shows-6-republicans-believe-joe-bidens-2020-election-win-definitely-legitimate/.

Hoft, Joe. "REMINDER: Georgia's Raffensperger, Sterling and Fuchs All Connected to Firm that Helps Georgia Democrats Run as Republicans." *Gateway Pundit*, 9 Dec. 2021, www.thegatewaypundit.com/2021/12/reminder-georgias-raffensperger-sterling-fuchs-connected-firm-helps-georgia-democrats-run-republicans/.

Hoft, Joe. "Testimony – Blames 'White Rage' for Jan. 6 Attacks – Brags About Reading Marx and Lenin (VIDEO)." *Gateway Pundit*, 23 June 2021, www.thegatewaypundit.com/2021/06/read-mao-tse-tung-read-karl-marx-read-lenin-chairman-us-joint-chiefs-staff-mark-milley/.

Hoft, Joe. "The Award for Worst Political Strategy in History Goes to Republicans Who Sided with Communist-Democrats in Stealing 2020 Election." *Gateway Pundit*, 1 Jun. 2021, www.thegatewaypundit.com/2021/06/award-worst-political-strategy-history-goes-republicans-sided-communist-democrats-stealing-2020-election/?utm_source=Gab&utm_campaign=websitesharingbuttons.

Hoft, Joe. "The Biden Administration's Top Priority Is to Arrest and Punish Anyone Who Objects to Their Un-American and Unconstitutional Agenda." *Gateway Pundit*, 11 July 2021, www.thegatewaypundit.com/2021/07/biden-administrations-top-priority-arrest-punish-anyone-objects-un-american-unconstitutional-agenda/.

Hoft, Joe. "The Fix Is In – Democrats Start to Prep America for Their Mid-Term Steal." *Gateway Pundit*, 20 June 2022. www.thegatewaypundit.com/2022/06/fix-democrats-start-prep-america-mid-term-steal/

Hoft, Joe. "UPDATE: Swing State Ballots Were Missing Legally Required Chain of Custody Documentation Giving Democrats Impossible and Likely Fraudulent Wins in Battleground States." *Gateway Pundit*, 14 Jun. 2021, www.thegatewaypundit.com/2021/06/accounting-bogus-ballots-missing-legally-required-chain-custody-documentation-president-trump-likely-won-2020-election-landslide/.

Hoft, Joe. "Video Uncovered of China Professor Claiming US Elites Teamed Up with China to Take Control of America." *Gateway Pundit*, 7 Jul. 2021, www.thegatewaypundit.com/2021/07/video-uncovered-china-professor-claiming-us-elites-teamed-china-take-control-america/.

Hoft, Joe. "We're Going to Take Back Our Country from These Lunatics: Massive Crowd in Georgia Greets President Trump." *Gateway Pundit*, 25 Sept. 2021, www.thegatewaypundit.com/2021/09/going-take-back-country-lunatics-massive-crowd-georgia-greets-president-trump/.

Hoft, Joe. "Who Is Really Running the Biden Gang? It's Not Joe Biden, So Who Could It Be?" *Gateway Pundit*, 9 Jan. 2021, www.thegatewaypundit.com/2021/01/really-running-biden-gang-not-joe-biden/.

Hoft, Joe. "Why Has Wisconsin Done Nothing With the 200,000 Ballots Its Supreme Court Claimed Were Likely Invalid In the 2020 Election?" *Gateway Pundit*, 2 Feb. 2021, www.thegatewaypundit.com/2021/02/wisconsin-not-done-anything-200000-ballots-supreme-court-claimed-likely-invalid-2020-election/.

Hohmann, Leo. "2nd retired general calls on Trump to crush coup plotters: 'This is more dangerous than the civil war'."

LeoHohmann.com, 13 Dec. 2020, leohohmann.com/ 2020/12/13/2nd-retired-general-calls-on-trump-to-crush-coup-plotters-this-is-more-dangerous-than-the-civil-war/? fbclid=IwAR3OZeUpT1gaxpDv1Ggkz3guw3I0BWQ4WEI8fS 37MYVByd7NkSuVRNcyi-M.

Horton, Adrian. "Colbert on Biden's 6 January address: 'Hell yes! That is the Joe Biden we stole this election for!'" *The Guardian*, 7 Jan. 2022, www.newsbreak.com/news/2479641567959/colbert-on-biden-s-6-january-address-hell-yes-that-is-the-joe-biden-we-stole-this-election-for? _f=app_share&s=a99&share_destination_id=MTI5MTA4NjQ1 LTE2NDE1OTQ5Njg1MjU=&pd=08jj3VQL&hl=en_US.

Howley, Patrick. "Massive 'Fraudulent' Votes And Apparent Nursing Home Vote Fraud Found in Delaware In 2020 Election." *National File*, 30 Sept. 2021, nationalfile.com/massive-fraudulent-votes-and-apparent-nursing-home-vote-fraud-found-in-delaware-in-2020-election/.

Howley, Patrick. "WATCH: Black Democrat Operative Blows The Lid off Democrat Voter Fraud in Texas." *National File*, 4 Aug. 2021, nationalfile.com/watch-black-democrat-operative-blows-the-lid-off-democrat-voter-fraud-in-texas/.

Howse, Brannon and Leo Hohmann. "Sidney Powell Reveals U.S. Government Patents Enabling Election Fraud: 'Your Votes Have Been Stolen With Computer Algorithms Since 2000.'" *Worldview Weekend Broadcast Network*, 14 Oct. 2021, www.worldviewweekend.com/news/article/sidney-powell-reveals-us-government-patents-enabling-election-fraud-your-votes-have.

Hryce, Graham. "Donald Trump remains a potent political force despite the US midterm election results." *RT*, 19 Nov. 2022, www.rt.com/news/566759-trump-midterm-us-results/.

Huckabee, Mike. "A Majority believe there was cheating at the ballot box." *MikeHuckabee.com*, 18 Apr. 2021, www.mikehuckabee.com/latest-news?id=AA0FDD28-C2A0-4DA9-BA6F-A27610071C6F.

Huckabee, Mike. "Buyer's Remorse Showing Up in Polls." 2 June 2021, www.mikehuckabee.com/latest-news?id=63FCB913-F72B-4D75-A34D-03C67FC214FF.

Huckabee, Mike. "Communism is a Vicious, Inhuman System." *Mikehuckabee.com*, 16 Jul. 2021, www.mikehuckabee.com/latest-news?id=422138CF-5BC4-475A-B0C2-8B429CBFB11F.

Huckabee, Mike. "Extremists." *Mike Huckabee*, 11 July 2021, www.mikehuckabee.com/latest-news?id=BD1130A2-75BB-4378-A588-C2C8CCBD20A1.

Huckabee, Mike. "Here it is: Update on challenges to Maricopa audit." 19 May 2021, www.mikehuckabee.com/latest-news?id=163BD982-7B42-4EA6-AB04-FC0F673A4352.

Huckabee, Mike. "In Democrats' playbook, the 'Russia Hoax' refuses to die." *MikeHuckabee.com*, 21 May 2021, www.mikehuckabee.com/latest-news?id=8EB57E85-2B3E-428C-8AE5-E50E0372F940.

Huckabee, Mike. "Proof 'Progressives' Want to Bring Back Last Century's Failed Ideas." *Mikehuckabee.com*, 24 May 2021, www.mikehuckabee.com/latest-news?id=BBCF92C9-73EB-43E0-A5C5-44D441B94A9A.

Huckabee, Mike. "True The Vote leaders jailed for not revealing source." 1 Nov. 2022, www.mikehuckabee.com/latest-news?id=E76463BA-AC11-40AD-B151-939C1CD4DC3E.

Huckabee, Mike. "Trump to America: 'DO YOU MISS ME YET?'" *MikeHuckabee.com*, 15 Oct. 2021, www.mikehuckabee.com/latest-news?id=E1F7313D-3810-48B6-9A55-297E14EE9438.

Huff, Ethan. "Biden Campaign Bragged about Rigging Brazilian Election against Bolsonaro." *Natural News*, 3 Nov. 2022, www.naturalnews.com/2022-11-03-biden-campaign-bragged-rigging-brazilian-election-bolsonaro.html.

Huff, Ethan. "Entire Portland Police Rapid Response Team resigns after city indicts one of its members for engaging violent left-wing rioters." *Natural News*, 18 June 2021, www.naturalnews.com/

2021-06-18-entire-portland-police-rapid-response-team-resigns.html.

Hunter, Greg. "2020 Election Biggest Crime & Cover-Up Ever – Mike Lindell." *USAWatchdog*, 7 Aug. 2021, usawatchdog.com/2020-election-biggest-crime-cover-up-ever-mike-lindell/.

Hurt, Charles. "Charles Hurt: Trump Is Back, And He Ain't Backing Down." *Breitbart*, 14 Jul 2021, www.breitbart.com/politics/2021/07/14/charles-hurt-trump-is-back-and-he-aint-backing-down/.

"ICYMI: Newsmax: 'Study: 2020 Election Polls Underestimated Support for Republicans, Trump.'" *Save America*, 19 Jul. 2021, www.donaldjtrump.com/news/news-xrzswykq3z.

"INTEL: US Military Raided Scytl Servers In Germany For Evidence After Vote Switching Scandal." *Great Game India*, 14 Nov. 2020, greatgameindia.com/us-military-raided-scytl-germany/?fbclid=IwAR1qqOoJM7IZScaZNMRxAqcjOtC1JItUvTHsBSV0Bw6u-tVFM1cgGZiixc8.

Jacobs, Emily. "Top Chinese professor boasts of operatives in top of US 'core inner circle.'" *New York Post*, 8 Dec. 2020, nypost.com/2020/12/08/professor-claims-china-has-people-in-americas-core-inner-circle/?fbclid=IwAR2suGIa3lv62CqczywnaWCRn8CJnUyzUmGSi3Xku-Oj8ViDSVt5hlRdwjg.

"Jan 6 committee withdraws Trump subpoena." *RT*, 29 Dec. 2022, www.rt.com/news/569142-trump-subpoena-january6-committee-withdrawn/.

"January 6 committee recommends charges for Trump." *RT*, 19 Dec. 2022, www.rt.com/news/568545-jan6-panel-criminal-trump/.

Jean, Divine. "Judge Jeanine Sheds Light on Presidential Election's Discrepancies." *Fortitude News*, 28 Nov. 2020, fortitudenews.com/news/judge-jeanine-sheds-light-on-presidential-elections-discrepancies/?fbclid=IwAR28l1SKckdR1SRIgZgzcZyUL4n4unrdXhBaN4cPcMI-v4-Isjjyvcw910.

Jenkins, Laura Elizabeth. "Street Party Footage Shows Intensely Peaceful Crowd- You Decide if This Fits the DOJ and Mainstream Media's Narrative." *American Gulag*, 30 Aug. 2022, americangulag.org/street-party-footage-shows-intensely-peaceful-crowd-you-decide-if-this-fits-the-doj-and-mainstream-medias-narrative/.

"Joe Biden is 'Stalinist' – Trump." *RT*, 11 Jun. 2023, www.rt.com/news/577864-us-biden-stalinist-trump/.

Johnson, Ron, et al. "Letter to Attorney General Merrick Garland Regarding Differential Treatment of Capitol Rioters and Portland Protesters." June 2021.

Jones, Kipp. "ABC News Calls for 'Cleansing' of Trump Supporters in Wake of Capitol Incursion." *The Western Journal*, 8 Jan. 2021, www.westernjournal.com/abc-news-calls-cleansing-trump-supporters-wake-capitol-incursion/?utm_source=facebook&utm_medium=huckabee&fbclid=IwAR3SoWc93Mc9D18H9JBKMU7D61_1JuzntvdypLIUDpWJVgrnSpPETvwYWKo.

Jones, Kipp. "As Left Attacks July Fourth, Piers Morgan Issues Fiery Warning from Great Britain." *The Western Journal*, 7 July 2021, www.westernjournal.com/left-attacks-july-fourth-piers-morgan-issues-fiery-warning-great-britain/?utm_source=mewe&utm_medium=westernjournalism&utm_content=2021-07-07&utm_campaign=manualpost.

Jones, Kipp. "Biden's CNN Town Hall Total Failure as It Draws Smaller Audience Than Normal Night at Fox News." *The Western Journal*, 22 Jul. 2021, www.westernjournal.com/bidens-cnn-town-hall-total-failure-draws-smaller-audience-normal-night-fox-news/?utm_source=mewe&utm_medium=westernjournalism&utm_content=2021-07-23&utm_campaign=topdaily.

Jones, Kipp. "Defense Officials Confirm Trump Is Still Commander in Chief, Refuse to Participate in Military Coup to Oust Him." *The Western Journal*, 9 Jan. 2021, www.westernjournal.com/defense-officials-confirm-trump-still-commander-chief-refuse-participate-military-coup-oust/?utm_source=facebook&utm_medium=westernjournalism&utm_content=2021-01-09&utm_campaign=manualpost&fbclid=Iw

A R l X t Z 4 -
OeqxoGIFvWWo9f5hl__dgZ_chvB4sh3vi6C2uZVDBKSDFbh
wq_w.

Jones, Kipp. "Portland Now at Antifa's Mercy as Entire Riot Control
Squad Resigns in Disgust." *The Western Journal*, 17 June 2021,
www.westernjournal.com/portland-now-antifas-mercy-entire-
riot-control-squad-resigns-disgust/?
utm_source=mewe&utm_medium=westernjournalism&utm_co
ntent=2021-06-27&utm_campaign=topweekly.

Jones, Kipp. "Social Worker Charged with 134 Felony Counts of
Election Fraud." *The Western Journal*, 9 Nov. 2020,
www.westernjournal.com/social-worker-charged-134-felony-
counts-election-fraud/?
ff_source=facebook&ff_medium=westernjournalism&ff_campa
ign=manualpost&ff_content=2020-11-29.

Jones, Kipp. "Twitter's Ban of Trump Just Opened an Entire New Line of
Criticism." *The Western Journal*, 9 Jan. 2021,
www.westernjournal.com/twitters-ban-trump-just-opened-
entire-new-line-criticism/?
utm_source=facebook&utm_medium=huckabee&fbclid=IwAR
2oR1ShpfePJjy2sMVNV3lQzcyXp0qGAmdQSypkSOT_HR47
cvv4VQb_aN4.

Jones, Kipp. "We Feel Like We're on a Terror Watch List: FBI Won't Stop
Harassing Couple Who Never Entered Capitol on Jan. 6." *The
Western Journal*, 7 July 2021, www.westernjournal.com/feel-
like-terror-watch-list-fbi-wont-stop-harassing-couple-never-
entered-capitol-jan-6/?
utm_source=mewe&utm_medium=westernjournalism&utm_co
ntent=2021-07-07&utm_campaign=manualpost.

Jose, Andrew. "Federal Agents Raid Home of Trump-Era DOJ Official in
Move Decried as 'Soviet-Style Approach.'" *The Western
Journal*, 23 June 2022, www.westernjournal.com/federal-
agents-raid-home-trump-era-doj-official-move-decried-soviet-
style-approach/.

Justice, Tristan. "Biden Family Whistleblower: Joe Biden Is
'Compromised' By Communist China." *The Federalist*, 27 Oct.
2020, thefederalist.com/2020/10/27/biden-family-
whistleblower-joe-biden-is-compromised-by-communist-

china/?fbclid=IwAR0Iinxhok-0YMiqQ3l3qVK3-
t9fedalqNlDuUNn9Ite-J3_RuzzvG1X8aU#.X-
KHK7K9eGU.facebook.

Kachelman, John L. "History is Unerring, Redundant and Unforgiving:
The Shocking Parallels of the 1917 Russian Bolshevik
Revolution to 2020 US Leftist Rebellion." *The Gateway Pundit*,
27 Oct. 2020, www.thegatewaypundit.com/2020/10/history-
unerring-redundant-unforgiving-shocking-parallels-1917-
russian-bolshevik-revolution-2020-us-leftist-rebellion/.

Kaminsky, Gabe. "Trump Slams Democrats For Crime Surge: They 'Hate
Our Country'." *The Federalist*, 7 June 2021, thefederalist.com/
2021/06/07/trump-slams-democrats-for-crime-surge-they-hate-
our-country/?utm_campaign=ACTENGAGE

Kamioner, David. "Dick Morris Says Election Stolen and Little Chance
of Changing It." *DrewBerquist.com*, 17 Nov. 2020,
www.drewberquist.com/2020/11/dick-morris-says-election-
stolen-and-little-chance-of-changing-it/?
fbclid=IwAR14EkX2E9PTUGBklxFAI8gPrYGt_QrknrN45Va
V7n16GYxR29d-JaCpt4c.

Kelly, Julie. "Why Is the Government Hiding January 6 Video Footage?"
American Greatness, 10 May 2021, amgreatness.com/
2021/05/10/why-is-the-government-hiding-january-6-video-
footage/.

Kent, Simon. "U.N.'s Guterres Warns a 'New Model for Global
Governance' Is Coming." *Breitbart*, 21 Jul. 2020,
www.breitbart.com/politics/2020/07/21/u-n-s-guterres-warns-
new-model-for-global-governance-is-coming-to-redistribute-
power-and-wealth/?
fbclid=IwAR3iWpHvEbWjTz0adZkF0QBtiAnj8AmI-
k0GD2bYlQaDLFVVF7B8z7edC6A.

Kershaw, Brett. "Flashback: Gerald Ford's Eerie Prediction Could Soon
Come True for Kamala Harris." *The Western Journal*, 9 Jun.
2021, www.westernjournal.com/flashback-gerald-fords-eerie-
prediction-soon-come-true-kamala-harris/?
utm_source=mewe&utm_medium=westernjournalism&utm_co
ntent=2021-06-09&utm_campaign=topdaily.

Kirgis, Frederic L. "International Agreements and U.S. Law." *Insights, American Society of International Law*, 27 May 1997, www.asil.org/insights/volume/2/issue/5/international-agreements-and-us-law.

Klatzkin, Shmuel. "After Four Years of 'the Resistance,' Trump Is Right to Challenge the Election Results." *The American Spectator*, 15 Nov. 2020, spectator.org/trump-challenge-election-results/?fbclid=IwAR2GSxBM9u_6At4-WzmAdzCyI6sA_LYByWB6eavhyBDbqofNcDkppXjy0D4.

Kotkin, Stephen. "Communism's Bloody Century ." *The Wall Street Journal*, 3 Nov. 2017, kickthemallout.com/article.php/Communisms_Bloody_Century.

Krause, Paul. The NSBA's fake apology." *American Thinker*, 26 Oct. 2021, www.americanthinker.com/blog/2021/10/the_nsbas_fake_apology.html.

Kupelian, David. "The biggest election fraud of all." *WND*, 8 Dec. 2020, www.wnd.com/2020/12/biggest-election-fraud/?fbclid=IwAR3sqDGtj6BPxBYfOq9rXhuiiuSCSshl4-Zu8KhEsR6rhvZtDlZINmYynGQ.

LaChance, Mike. "Democrat Senator Speaks At Awards Ceremony For The Communist Party (VIDEO)." *The Gateway Pundit*, 15 Dec. 2021, www.thegatewaypundit.com/2021/12/democrat-senator-speaks-awards-ceremony-communist-party-video/.

LaChance, Mike. "Wow. FBI Admits They Don't Track Violence Of Radical Left Antifa (VIDEO)." *Gateway Pundit*, 5 Oct. 2021, www.thegatewaypundit.com/2021/10/fbi-admits-dont-track-violence-radical-left-antifa-video/.

Laila, Cristina. "Antifa Members Who Brutally Beat, Robbed Two Latino Marines Will Get No Jail Time – All Felony Charges Dropped by Soros-Backed Philly DA." *Gateway Pundit*, 13 June 2022, www.thegatewaypundit.com/2022/06/antifa-members-beat-two-latino-marines-will-get-no-jail-time-felony-charges-dropped-soros-backed-philly-da/.

Laila, Cristina. "Antifa Member Who Shot Proud Boy Tusitala 'Tiny' Toese Unmasked, Identified and Charged with First-Degree

Assault While Armed with a Deadly Weapon." *Gateway Pundit*, 27 September 2021, www.thegatewaypundit.com/2021/09/antifa-member-shot-proud-boy-tusitala-tiny-toese-unmasked-identified-charged-first-degree-assault-armed-deadly-weapon/.

Laila, Cristina. "FBI Director Wray Echoes AG Garland, Condemns 'Attacks on the Integrity of the FBI'." *Gateway Pundit*, 11 Aug. 2022, www.thegatewaypundit.com/2022/08/fbi-director-wray-echoes-ag-garland-condemns-attacks-integrity-fbi/.

Laila, Cristina. "Minneapolis BLM Leader Says He Quit After Learning 'Ugly Truth' About Marxist Organization's Priorities (VIDEO)." *Gateway Pundit*, 1 June 2021, www.thegatewaypundit.com/2021/06/minneapolis-blm-leader-says-quit-learning-ugly-truth-marxist-organizations-priorities-video/.

Laila, Cristina. "REPORT: Milley Told China in Secret Phone Call He Would Give the CCP Advance Warning if US Was Ever Going to Attack." *Gateway Pundit*, 14 Sept. 2021, www.thegatewaypundit.com/2021/09/report-milley-told-china-secret-phone-call-give-ccp-advance-warning-us-ever-going-attack/.

Laila, Cristina. "Sidney Powell: We Are Living Under a Communist Totalitarian Regime (AUDIO)." *Gateway Pundit*, 5 May 2021, www.thegatewaypundit.com/2021/05/sidney-powell-living-communist-totalitarian-regime-audio/.

LaRouchPac. "President Trump Invokes Constitution Against Election Fraud Amid Psyop Campaigns to Derail the Fight." 3 Dec. 2020. larouchepac.com/20201203/president-trump-invokes-constitution-against-election-fraud-amid-psyop-campaigns-derail

LaRouchePAC. "President Trump: Who Has The Courage... To Save The Republic?" *LaRouchePAC*, 9 Dec. 2020, larouchepac.com/20201209/president-trump-who-has-courage-save-republic.

Leach, Matt, and Paul Steinhauser. "Trump says if he's right about election fraud, 'Biden can't be president'." *Fox News*, 2 Dec. 2020, www.foxnews.com/politics/trump-charges-if-hes-right-about-election-fraud-biden-cant-be-president.

Lechter, Lynne. "Dems Double Down on Election Misdeeds." *American Thinker*, 9 Oct. 2021, www.americanthinker.com/blog/2021/10/dems_double_down_on_election_misdeeds.html.

Lemon, Jason. "'Trump Will Be Charged,' Kirschner Concludes After AG Garland's Remarks." *Newsweek*, 10 Mar. 2022, www.newsweek.com/trump-will-charged-kirschner-concludes-after-ag-garlands-remarks-1686912.

Lennox, Stacey. "There Are Already Laws on the Books That Ban Critical Theories in Schools: Time for Parents to Get Busy." *PJ Media*, 10 Jun. 2021, pjmedia.com/columns/stacey-lennox/2021/06/10/removing-curriculum-based-on-critical-theories-from-k-12-should-be-uncontroversial-n1453259.

leohohmann. "2nd Retired General Calls on Trump to Crush Coup Plotters: 'This Is More Dangerous Than the Civil War'." *LeoHohmann.com*, 13 Dec. 2020, leohohmann.com/2020/12/13/2nd-retired-general-calls-on-trump-to-crush-coup-plotters-this-is-more-dangerous-than-the-civil-war/?fbclid=IwAR3OZeUpT1gaxpDv1Ggkz3guw3I0BWQ4WEI8fS37MYVByd7NkSuVRNcyi-M.

Lewis, Jeff M. "They Intend to Destroy America." *American Thinker*, 23 Sept. 2021, www.americanthinker.com/articles/2021/09/they_intend_to_destroy_america.html.

Liberato, Frank. "Our administrative state and military have become dangerously partisan." *American Thinker*, 21 Sept. 2021, www.americanthinker.com/blog/2021/09/our_administrative_state_and_military_have_become_dangerously_partisan.html.

Linge, Mary Kay and Jon Levine. "Twitter censoring Post's Hunter Biden exposé is 'election interference': GOP leaders." *New York Post*, 17 Oct. 2020, nypost.com/2020/10/17/twitter-censoring-posts-biden-expose-is-election-interference-gop/?utm_source=facebook_sitebuttons&utm_medium=site%20buttons&utm_campaign=site%20buttons&fbclid=IwAR0MVFPbM2wuZF10ytsfsgpEas9UhZSuhtVw8FrJRlOho8_eB_A0MTw_I-A.

Lively, Scott. "5 Steps to Survive the Marxist Purge." *WND*, 11 Jan. 2021, www.wnd.com/2021/01/5-steps-survive-marxist-purge/?utm_source=facebook&utm_medium=wnd&utm_campaign=dlvrit&utm_content=2021-01-11&fbclid=IwAR2tL73-OGfhTqDPsqjaDb-DG1UM3O0bzd9bU_-9DVeJnMfKxTX0tPdmI0c.

Livshitz, Felix. "America's 'Ministry of Truth' hasn't gone away: Official Washington hasn't abandoned its plan to control social networks" *RT*, 10 Nov. 2022, www.rt.com/news/566038-us-ministry-of-truth/.

Livshitz, Felix. "Be careful what you post: How Facebook and the US government have united against Americans with the 'wrong' views" *RT*, 6 Oct. 2022, www.rt.com/news/563670-big-brother-watches-your-messages/.

Livshitz, Felix. "How the 'Twitter Files' have exposed a senior FBI official's role in manipulating the outcome of the 2020 US election." *RT*, 9 Dec. 2022, www.rt.com/news/567844-twitter-files-senior-fbi-officials/.

"London mayor calls for censorship." *RT*, 22 Nov. 2022, www.rt.com/news/566962-london-khan-trump-twitter/.

Lott, John R. Jr. "Voting Fraud Is a Real Concern. Just Look Around the World | Opinion." *Newsweek*, 4 Aug. 2020, www.newsweek.com/voting-fraud-real-concern-just-look-around-world-opinion-1522535?fbclid=IwAR21TLPGWoeeuo8-6hWnM3LOLVjVFmbDaT9aI6-XhWJZKIJVdj4OfqUF3n4.

Lott, Maxim. "BLM Clenched-Fist Symbol Has Little-Known Communist History, Critics Say." *Fox News*, 15 Apr. 2021, www.foxnews.com/politics/black-lives-matter-antifa-clenched-fist-symbol-communist-history.

Lucas, Fred. "3 Things to Know as 2020 Election Challenge Moves to Congress." *The Daily Signal*, 14 Dec. 2020, www.dailysignal.com/2020/12/14/3-things-to-know-as-2020-election-challenge-moves-to-congress/?utm_source=rss&utm_medium=rss&utm_campaign=3-things-to-know-as-2020-election-challenge-moves-to-

congress&fbclid=IwAR05uKABxnl5TO756k7h6pNukxvlV9D
ke9Vywle9so2si8Q4BZ0cvCJU6Eg.

Lucas, John. "Did You Miss The Chairman Of The Joint Chiefs Of Staff Labeling Trump Voters Enemies Of The State?" *The Federalist*, 2 July 2021, thefederalist.com/2021/07/02/did-you-miss-the-chairman-of-the-joint-chiefs-of-staff-labeling-trump-voters-enemies-of-the-state/.

Ludwig, E. Jeffrey. "Decades of Communist Pushing Will Get You a Communist America." *American Thinker*, 12 Dec. 2021, www.americanthinker.com/articles/2021/12/decades_of_communist_pushing_will_get_you_a_communist_america.html.

Ludwig, E. Jeffrey. "The UN Wants to Be Our World Government By 2030." *American Thinker*, 27 Oct. 2018, www.americanthinker.com/articles/2018/10/the_un_wants_to_be_our_world_government_by_2030.html.

Luther, Daisy. "An American Manifesto: Don't Let Everything for Which This Republic Stands Be Destroyed." *NOQ Report*, 23 Oct. 2021, noqreport.com/2021/10/23/an-american-manifesto-dont-let-everything-for-which-this-republic-stands-be-destroyed/.

MacDonald, Brad. "The Election Exposes the Radical Left's Rolling Coup." *The Trumpet*, 5 Nov. 2020, www.thetrumpet.com/23120-the-election-exposes-the-radical-lefts-rolling-coup.

Madsen, Wayne. "Soros's 'Purple Revolution' Brewing for Trump Presidency." *Wayne Madsen Report*, 11 Nov. 2016, stateofthenation2012.com/?p=56078.

"Major Development in Lawsuit Against Dominion Voting Systems." *Diamond and Silk*, 28 Dec. 2021, www.diamondandsilk.com/major-development-in-lawsuit-against-dominion-voting-systems/.

"Majority Staff Report Supplemental." *Committee on Finance, Committee on Homeland Security and Governmental Affairs*, 18 Nov. 2020, www.finance.senate.gov/imo/media/doc/2020-11-18%20HSGAC%20-%20Finance%20Joint%20Report%20Supplemental.pdf.

Malloch, Theodore Roosevelt. "How to End the Deep State." *American Greatness*, 13 Oct. 2021, amgreatness.com/2021/10/13/how-to-end-the-deep-state/.

Maresca, Suzanne. "Chair of the Federal Election Commission Drops Bombshell Announcement." *Golden Age of Gaia*, 11 Nov. 2020, goldenageofgaia.com/2020/11/11/chair-of-the-federal-election-commission-drops-bombshell-announcement/.

Margolis, Matt. "5 Reasons I'll Always Resist Joe Biden and the Democrats (and You Should Too)." *PJ Media*, 24 Dec. 2020, pjmedia.com/news-and-politics/matt-margolis/2020/12/24/5-reasons-ill-always-resist-joe-biden-and-the-democrats-and-you-should-too-n1231571?fbclid=IwAR2PKI8enN-9z2H8rrZVXnnzGUPTgCTWpYzLGeEDeQhtFyFTuCtMkH53nDQ.

Margolis, Matt. "Sen. Hawley Perfectly Explains Why You Should Never Feel Bad About Questioning the Election." *PJ Media*, 21 Dec. 2020, pjmedia.com/news-and-politics/matt-margolis/2020/12/21/sen-hawley-perfectly-explains-why-you-should-never-feel-bad-about-questioning-the-election-n1222277?fbclid=IwAR3LD1jCKDhz9TZ_38w4foFwIwNg36PJ7JOgJ7yoAjZCpqGAxJbUUwLvU8A.

Marsden, Rachel. "US cyber agency keeps the work of the 'Ministry of Truth' alive, leak shows." *RT*, 3 Nov. 2022, www.rt.com/news/565829-us-cybersecurity-agency-censorship/.

Mastrangel, Alana. "The Who's Roger Daltrey Slams 'The Woke Generation': They're Creating a 'Miserable World for Themselves,' 'We've Seen the Communist System Fail.'" *Breitbart*, 7 May 2021, www.breitbart.com/entertainment/2021/05/07/the-whos-roger-daltrey-slams-the-woke-generation-theyre-creating-a-miserable-world-for-themselves-weve-seen-the-communist-system-fail/.

McBroom, Douglas. "Why it must be Trump in 2024." American Thinker, 11 Jan. 2022, www.americanthinker.com/blog/2022/01/why_it_must_be_trump_in_2024.html#ixzz7HhdkLlE3.

McCann, Steve. "So Much Evidence that January 6, 2021 was a Calculated Set-Up." *American Thinker*, 13 July 2021, www.americanthinker.com/articles/2021/07/so_much_evidence_that_january_6_2021_was_a_calculated_se tup.html.

McCarthy, Andrew C. "Trump raid not about classified documents — it's about Jan. 6." *New York Post*, 9 Aug. 2022, nypost.com/2022/08/09/trump-raid-not-about-classified-documents-its-about-jan-6/.

McCarthy, Charlie. "McLaughlin Poll: 64% Say Biden Won't Run in 2024, Trump Beats Harris." *Newsmax*, 19 May 2021, www.newsmax.com/newsfront/trump-harris-biden-mclaughlin/2021/05/19/id/1021965/.

McDonough, Richard. "AOC's Logical Stumbles Criticizing Capitalism." *The American Thinker*, 26 Feb. 2022, www.americanthinker.com/blog/2022/02/aocs_logical_stumbles_criticizing_capitalism.html.

McManus, John F. "Socialist Strategy Against America: Pressure From Above and Below." *The New American*, 19 Dec. 2018, thenewamerican.com/socialist-strategy-against-america-pressure-from-above-and-below/

McMurray, Patty. "Alan Dershowitz First Guest On Mike Lindell's 'FRANK' Social Media Platform Drops Bombshell... Announces $1.6 Billion Lawsuit Against Dominion: 'It is our right to look at Dominion's source codes'." *Gateway Pundit*, 19 Apr. 2021, www.thegatewaypundit.com/2021/04/alan-dershowitz-first-guest-mike-lindells-frank-social-media-platform-drops-bombshellannounces-1-6-billion-lawsuit-dominion-right-look/.

McSwain, William M. 9 Jun. 2021, cdn.donaldjtrump.com/djtweb/general/Letter_to_President_Trump.pdf?_ga=2.246608324.1559950344.1626544612-1756619748.1626544612.

"Meet Norm Eisen: Legal Hatchet Man and Central Operative in the 'Color Revolution' Against President Trump." *Revolver*, 9 Sept. 2020, www.revolver.news/2020/09/meet-norm-eisen-legal-

hatchet-man-and-central-operative-in-the-color-revolution-
a g a i n s t - p r e s i d e n t - t r u m p / ?
fbclid=IwAR1DxDKIPyELnujkR0cRDgjYVlGBJyBHbKhn_M
MAjEiu1jsRApK4jHVebSU.

Memoree, Joelle. "Conservatives and moderates need to build a parallel
economy in the US." *RT*, 9 Oct. 2022, www.rt.com/news/
563807-conservatives-party-economy-us/.

Michelle, Lindsey. "Update: 93 Legislators From Multiple States Call
For 50-State Audit & Decertification Where Appropriate." *The
Freedom Times*, 4 Oct. 2021, www.thefreedomtimes.com/
2021/10/04/update-93-legislators-from-multiple-states-call-
for-50-state-audit-decertification-where-appropriate/.

"Military must be 'apolitical' – top US general." *RT*, 28 May 2022,
www.rt.com/news/556270-milley-military-apolitical-trump/.

Miller, Alex. "White House Shell-Shocked After El Salvador President
Brings The Receipts Exposing Biden Corruption." *Patriot
Newsfeed*, 13 Dec. 2021, patriotnewsfeed.com/white-house-
shell-shocked-after-el-salvador-president-brings-the-receipts-
exposing-biden-corruption/.

Moore, Mark. "DHS warns against mistrust of US government in latest
terror bulletin." *New York Post*, 9 Feb. 2022, nypost.com/
2022/02/09/homeland-security-labels-conspiracy-theories-a-
terror-threat/.

Moorhead, Richard. "Democratic Prosecutor Drops Murder Charge
Against Left-Wing Security Guard Who Shot Conservative
Protester." *Western Journal*, 11 March 2022,
www.westernjournal.com/democratic-prosecutor-drops-murder-
charge-left-wing-security-guard-shot-conservative-protester/?
utm_source=mewe&utm_medium=westernjournalism&utm_co
ntent=2022-03-11&utm_campaign=manualpost.

Morgan, Ryan. "Now 2,750 New Active-Duty Troops Deployed in DC,
Adding to 25,000 Nat'l Guard for Biden Inauguration."
American Military News, 19 Jan. 2021,
americanmilitarynews.com/2021/01/now-2750-new-active-
duty-troops-deployed-in-dc-adding-to-25000-natl-guard-for-
b i d e n - i n a u g u r a t i o n / ?

utm_source=fbchat&utm_campaign=alt&utm_medium=facebo
ok?%20.

Morgan, Ryan. "Ret. Gen Flynn warns of unelected 'tyrants,' says 'time
for God-fearing Americans to fight.'" *American Military News*,
14 Dec. 2020, americanmilitarynews.com/2020/12/ret-gen-
flynn-warns-of-unelected-tyrants-says-time-for-god-fearing-
a m e r i c a n s - t o - f i g h t / ?
utm_campaign=alt&utm_medium=facebook&utm_source=amn
&fbclid=IwAR3_cFqNLwek7OhkUYXPIMc_lINJ-4Vlc78k3E
8gYSIJtPT5nvfNKSuWGGU

Morgan, Ryan. "Twitter Erupts over Milley's 'Fight Trump from Inside'."
A m e r i c a n   M i l i t a r y   N e w s,   9   A u g .   2 0 2 2 ,
americanmilitarynews.com/2022/08/twitter-erupts-over-
milleys-fight-trump-from-inside/.

"MUST WATCH: Military Intelligence Exposes Massive Fraud in 49/50
States." *Freedom Headlines*, freedomheadlines.com/freedom-
wire/must-watch-military-intelligence-exposes-massive-fraud-
in-49-50-states/.

"Nancy Pelosi confident Biden will be president 'whatever the end count
is' on Election Day." *RT*, 29 Oct. 2020, on.rt.com/atn4.

"National Election Fraud During the 2020 Election Fraud During the
2020 Presidential Race." *Blacklisted News*, 15 Nov. 2020,
www.blacklistednews.com/article/78561/national-election-
f r a u d - d u r i n g - t h e - 2 0 2 0 - p r e s i d e n t i a l . h t m l ?
f b c l i d = I w A R 2 E f I 7 F e V -
zklwZ65juBPPle3VbHJS0G0WvpRZffanAB7miVEy-
NHq_Okg.

Natural News. "With Vote Theft: Biden Wins with 304 Electoral Votes.
CAUGHT! Election Data Analyzed, Producing Detailed List of
over 500,000 Votes Switched from Trump to Biden via Voting
Machine Software Theft, with Heavy Fraud Focused on Swing
States." *Natural News*, 11 Nov. 2020, www.naturalnews.com/
2020-11-11-election-data-analyzed-votes-switched-biden-
software.html#.

Nelson, Steven. "Guatemala's prez blames Biden for border crisis as
protesters tell Kamala Harris 'Trump won.'" *New York Post*, 7

Jun. 2021, nypost.com/2021/06/07/guatemala-protesters-tell-kamala-harris-trump-won/.

"New grand jury seated for next stage of Trump investigation." *Fox News*, 25 May 2021, www.foxnews.com/us/new-york-grand-jury-trump-investigation.

"New World Order: 37 Quotes on The New World Order, One-World Government and One-World Religion." *End Times Prophecy Report*, 8 Aug. 2018, endtimesprophecyreport.com/2013/06/05/new-world-order-37-quotes-on-the-new-world-order/.

"Newly released docs shed light on attempts to influence Twitter." *RT*, 20 Dec. 2022, www.rt.com/news/568579-twitter-files-fbi-pressure/.

Newman, Alex. "UN-Backed 'Great Reset' to Usher in New World Order." *The New American*, 15 July 2020, www.thenewamerican.com/world-news/europe/item/36379-un-backed-great-reset-to-usher-in-new-world-order?fbclid=IwAR20CLmHQsrwV0V7dk46O5yT2KjetreQXYFIivnu-wJa8YRevNaUz5A16Bw.

News Editors. "America's 'Night of the Long Knives' under Biden and Democrats MUST be repelled – they're readying 'their bloody purge' of Christians and Conservative Americans." *Natural News*, 3 June 2022. www.naturalnews.com/2022-06-03-americas-night-of-long-knives-must-be-repelled.html

News Editors. "Critical Race Theory may violate Civil Rights Act, the Constitution: Dr. Carol Swain." *Natural News*, 23 June 2021, www.naturalnews.com/2021-06-23-critical-race-theory-may-violate-civil-rights.html.

"Newsmax: Confident the Election Was Stolen from President Donald Trump, Former Democrat Strategist and White House Adviser-Turned-Author Dick Morris...Is Not Confident It Can Be Fixed." *DrewBerquist.com*, 17 Nov. 2020, www.drewberquist.com/2020/11/dick-morris-says-election-stolen-and-little-chance-of-changing-it/?fbclid=IwAR14EkX2E9PTUGBklxFAI8gPrYGt_QrknrN45VaV7n16GYxR29d-JaCpt4c.

NewsNation Prime. "'Being a White Supremacist Is Not a Mental Illness, It's a Crime': Former FBI." *YouTube*, uploaded by NewsNation Prime, 28 Aug. 2023, www.youtube.com/watch?v=-IZ8MD9k_78 at 1:30.

'Next Time I'm in the White House": Trump Issues Epic Response to Facebook's 2 Year Ban.' *We Love Trump*, 4 June 2021, welovetrump.com/2021/06/04/next-time-im-in-the-white-house-trump-issues-epic-response-to-facebooks-2-year-ban/?utm_source=newsletter_ssp&utm_medium=email&utm_campaign=ssp."

Nicholas, James. "Sidney Powell: "They Ought to Have to Give Us Our President Back, Because We the People Know Trump Won." *The Freedom Times*, 26 Jun. 2021, www.thefreedomtimes.com/2021/06/26/sidney-powell-they-ought-to-have-to-give-us-our-president-back-because-we-the-people-know-trump-won/.

Nolte, John. "Nolte: Left-wing Thugs Brutally Assault Man They Believe Is Andy Ngo." *Breitbart*, 2 Jun. 2021, www.breitbart.com/the-media/2021/06/02/nolte-left-wing-thugs-brutally-assault-man-they-believe-is-andy-ngo/.

"Number of Americans willing to take up arms revealed." *RT*, 1 Jul. 2022, www.rt.com/news/558193-americans-arms-against-government/

Nwo Report. "Google Whistleblower: 'We Rewrote Our Algorithm To Censor Conservatives & Stop Trump From Winning.'" *Nwo Report*, 14 Aug. 2021, nworeport.me/2021/08/14/google-whistleblower-we-rewrote-our-algorithm-to-censor-conservatives-stop-trump-from-winning/.

Olson, Tyler. "Guatemala protesters display signs telling Harris to 'mind your own business'." *Fox News*, 8 June 2021, www.foxnews.com/politics/guatemala-protesters-harris-signs-trump-won.

O'Neil, Tyler. "Trump Taps Conservative Giants to Lead 1776 Commission." *PJ Media*, 18 Dec. 2020, pjmedia.com/news-and-politics/tyler-o-neil/2020/12/18/trump-taps-conservative-giants-to-lead-1776-commission-n1219741?

fbclid=IwAR3DYR4ESSmPv_imuMm5MKU3Zl6vnMR8-
fM9zpeTtGLWCuQxgNwlwWcq2_U.

"Officers Reveal Problems with US Army Recruiting." *RT*, 27 Jun. 2022,
www.rt.com/news/557944-army-recruiting-shortage-pentagon/.

Olson, William J. "The Viral Memo Changing the Trump Legal
Strategy." *The Western Journal*, 23 Nov. 2020,
thefederalistpapers.org/us/viral-memo-changing-trump-legal-
s t r a t e g y ? f b c l i d = I w A R 0 -
wRCPb1h7tQnaGJNwdofHoyigEMtT4iH4woTjyLtS-
W6RHm7H7WcW4uI.

"On The Shocking 2025 'Deagel' Forecast: War, Population Reduction, &
The Collapse Of The West." *Alogora Blog*, 21 April 2021,
www.algora.com/Algora_blog/2021/04/21/on-the-
shocking-2025-deagel-forecast-war-population-reduction-the-
collapse-of-the-west.

Orlando, Robert. "Donald Trump: The Reincarnation of George S
Patton?" *Townhall*, 9 Jun. 2021, townhall.com/columnists/
robertorlando/2021/06/09/donald-trump-the-reincarnation-of-
george-s-patton-n2590689.

"OVERTHROW IMMINENT! American Republic Under Withering
Assault by Communist Coup Plotters." *State of the Nation*, 31
Oct. 2019, stateofthenation2012.com/?p=131044.

Palmieri, Jacob. "Perhaps Should Be Impeached, Or Court-Martialed" -
Trump Unloads On General Milley, Fake Books." *Palmieri
Report*, 16 July 2021, thepalmierireport.com/impeached-or-
court-martialed-trump-unloads-on-general-milley/.

Palmieri, Jacob. "Sidney Powell: We Have Video And Photo Evidence Of
Election Fraud...Crosses Party Lines." *Palmieri Report*. 20
Nov. 2020, thepalmierireport.com/sidney-powell-we-have-
video-and-picture-evidence-of-election-fraud-crosses-party-
lines/.

Parker, Alex. "Ivy League School Gives Birth to the 'Columbia
Communism Club'." *Red State*, 21 May 2021, redstate.com/
alexparker/2021/05/21/ivy-league-school-gives-birth-to-the-
columbia-communism-club-n384621.

Pearce, Tim. "17 State AGs Condemn DOJ Targeting School Board Meetings: Trying To 'Chill Lawful Dissent By Parents." *DailyWire.com*, 18 Oct. 2021, www.dailywire.com/news/17-state-ags-condemn-doj-targeting-school-board-meetings-trying-to-chill-lawful-dissent-by-parents.

Pearce, Tim. "Pollsters Admit 'Major Errors' In 2020, 'Egregiously' Undercounted GOP Support." *DailyWire.com*, 14 Apr. 2021, www.dailywire.com/news/pollsters-admit-major-errors-in-2020-egregiously-undercounted-gop-support? utm_source=facebook&utm_medium=social&utm_campaign=b enshapiro&fbclid=IwAR2wpMiRDDPSFOyxaHQRFllZHFrUF nqrBa1FrHJDyfO6F84bGa8kIyWnbjE.

Penley, Taylor. "District Attorney: 2 PA Women Face Voter Fraud Charges for Casting Dead Mothers' Ballots." *The Western Journal*, 4 May 2021, www.westernjournal.com/district-attorney-2-pa-women-face-voter-fraud-charges-casting-dead-mothers-ballots/? ff_source=mewe&ff_medium=westernjournalism&ff_campaign =manualpost&ff_content=2021-06-15.

Perazzo, John. "Yes, It Was a Stolen Election." *FrontPageMag*, 23 Dec. 2020, www.frontpagemag.com/fpm/2020/12/yes-it-was-stolen-election-john-perazzo/? fbclid=IwAR2Dpq_eONssRRf_lWo7Kyl_nvHFieCopV0-FsM1Ay82R1T1K8rKPXs3hMo.

Phillips, Morgan and Cavallier, Andrea. "Now the FBI SUBPOENAS Republican state lawmakers for information on Rep. Scott Perry: Bureau's bid for GOP members to turn on Congressman after his phone was confiscated while he was with his family and Mar-a-Lago was raided." *Daily Mail*, 10 Aug. 2022, www.dailymail.co.uk/news/article-11100863/Now-FBI-delivers-SUBPOENAS-Pennsylvania-lawmakers-confiscated-Rep-Scott-Perrys-phone.html.

Pollak, Joel B. "Left-Wing Rioters Attack Trump Supporters Leaving Minneapolis Rally." *Breitbart*, 10 Oct. 2019, www.breitbart.com/2020-election/2019/10/10/left-wing-rioters-attack-trump-supporters-leaving-minneapolis-rally/#.

"Pollster says Biden election victory is not 'statistically impossible' but 'statistically implausible.'" *Washington Examiner*, 6 Dec. 2020, www.washingtonexaminer.com/news/pollster-says-biden-election-victory-is-not-statistically-impossible-but-statistically-i m p l a u s i b l e ? fbclid=IwAR3amVrwXdh49AuiZRtNlrbmYIP5jry5faDzhoDE AS4X727jw_YJFn1I8a8.

Porter, Jeremy. "Joe Biden & Merrick Garland Go Into Hiding After 'KGB Style' FBI Raid On Trump's Mar-a-Lago [VIDEO]." *Lifezette*, 11 Aug. 2022, www.lifezette.com/2022/08/joe-biden-merrick-garland-go-into-hiding-after-kgb-style-fbi-raid-on-trumps-mar-a-lago-video/?utm_source=redvoicemedia.com.

Posobiec, Jack. "EXCLUSIVE: Leaked State Department Memo Indicates Official Support for BLM Agenda." *Human Events*, 24 May 2021, humanevents.com/2021/05/24/breaking-news-leaked-state-department-memo-indicates-official-support-for-blm-agenda/.

Powe, Alicia. "DHS: Extremists Against COVID Vaccines, Stolen Election Pose National Security Threat Ahead of 9/11." *Gateway Pundit*, 14 Aug. 2021, www.thegatewaypundit.com/2021/08/dhs-extremists-covid-vaccines-stolen-election-pose-national-security-threat-ahead-9-11/.

Powe, Alicia. "EXCLUSIVE | Gen. Mike Flynn: 'The Constitution Itself Is At Risk', The Patriot Act Must Be 'Constantly Reviewed' Or 'R e m o v e d.'" *G a t e w a y P u n d i t*, 2 A u g. 2 0 2 2, www.thegatewaypundit.com/2022/08/exclusive-gen-mike-flynn-constitution-risk-patriot-act-must-constantly-reviewed-r e m o v e d / ? utm_source=Gab&utm_campaign=websitesharingbuttons.

Powe, Alicia. "MUST SEE: Mom From Soviet Union Destroys Marxist Critical Race Theory: This 'Equity For All' Propaganda 'Quickly Ended With Nothing To Eat'." *Gateway Pundit*, 19 June 2021, www.thegatewaypundit.com/2021/06/must-see-mom-soviet-union-destroys-marxist-critical-race-theory-equity-propaganda-quickly-ended-nothing-eat.

Powell, Scott S. "Remedy for Election Irregularities and Vote Fraud is Found in the Constitution." *Discovery Institute*, 19 Nov. 2020, www.discovery.org/a/remedy-for-election-irregularities-and-v o t e - f r a u d - i s - f o u n d - i n - t h e - c o n s t i t u t i o n / ?

fbclid=IwAR3uKnLCU7Q7sbykNLQ-2RoRRZEKg-
l6_zGPRKqGE2chsry2-NRvxk_QY-0.

"President Trump: Who Has The Courage... To Save The Republic?"
LaRouchePac, December 9, 2020, larouchepac.com/20201209/
president-trump-who-has-courage-save-republic

"Purported purpose of Trump FBI raid revealed." *RT*, 12 Aug. 2022,
www.rt.com/news/560687-trump-fbi-raid-nuclear-weapons/.

Quill, Vince. "Sidney Powell Is In Some Hot Water—An Update On The
Kraken." *We Love Trump*, 27 Aug. 2021, welovetrump.com/
2021/08/27/sidney-powell-is-in-some-hot-water-an-update-on-
t h e - k r a k e n / ?
utm_source=newsletter_ssp&utm_medium=email&utm_campai
gn=ssp.

Rabil, Dan. "Biden's Great Leap Forward: A split second in Wisconsin."
American Thinker, 14 Nov. 2020, www.americanthinker.com/
b l o g / 2 0 2 0 / 1 1 /
bidens_great_leap_forward_a_split_second_in_wisconsin.html.

Ratcliffe, John. "China Is National Security Threat No. 1." *The Wall
Street Journal*, 3 Dec. 2020, www.wsj.com/articles/china-is-
n a t i o n a l - s e c u r i t y - t h r e a t - n o - 1 - 1 1 6 0 7 0 1 9 5 9 9 ?
mod=opinion_lead_pos5.

Ratcliffe, John. "Ratcliffe - Views on Intelligence Community Election
Security Analysis." 7 Jan. 2021, www.scribd.com/document/
491038048/Ratcliffe-Views-on-Intelligence-Community-
Election-Security-Analysis#from_embed.

"Read the full transcript and listen to Trump's audio call with Georgia
secretary of state." *CNN Politics*, 3 Jan. 2021, www.cnn.com/
2021/01/03/politics/trump-brad-raffensperger-phone-call-
transcript/index.html.

"Rep. Matt Gaetz will challenge Electoral College votes." *World Tribune*,
20 Dec. 2020, www.worldtribune.com/rep-matt-gaetz-will-
c h a l l e n g e - e l e c t o r a l - c o l l e g e - v o t e s / ?
fbclid=IwAR1omJZKUQgI6DxqOCG06tmUQa_hQC_i5kI0kN
prYDwKMfQ0WnkDJwkZUHs.

"Report of the Commission on Federal Election Reform." *Building Confidence in U.S. Elections,* Sept. 2005, www.legislationline.org/download/id/1472/file/ 3b50795b2d0374cbef5c29766256.pdf.

"Republican senator predicts 'riots' if Trump charged." *RT*, 29 Aug. 2022, www.rt.com/news/561760-graham-predicts-trump-prosecution-riost/.

"Republicans vow to investigate FBI's Trump raid." *RT*, 9 Aug. 2022, www.rt.com/news/560553-republicans-blast-fbi-trump-raid/.

Revolver. "Democrat Hatchet Man Norm Eisen's Fingerprints Are All Over a Dark New Element of the Jan 6 Witch Hunt." *Revolver*, 18 June 2022, www.revolver.news/2022/06/norm-eisen-january-6-committee-benny-thompson-dark-conspiracy-against-president-trump/.

Riccardi, Nicholas. "Donald Trump banned from Colorado ballot in historic ruling by state's Supreme Court." *ABC News*, 19 Dec. 2023, abcnews.go.com/US/wireStory/colorado-supreme-court-bans-trump-states-ballot-constitutions-105793147.

Risk, R. Thomas. "Socialism Be Not Proud." *American Thinker*, 17 Sept. 2021, www.americanthinker.com/articles/2021/09/ socialism_be_not_proud.html.

Roberts, Paul Craig. "The Proof Is In: The Election Was Stolen." *PaulCraigRoberts.org*, 30 Nov. 2020, www.paulcraigroberts.org/2020/11/30/the-proof-is-in-the-election-was-stolen/? fbclid=IwAR3IaxP1zLIz3tdfTlAVeT2Fm_5fX8Gy1VafwqkT7 NCqRoI3swesA7Qosfo.

Rodack, Jeffrey. "Trump Spokeswoman Warns: No 'Next Election' Without Repairing 2020 Contest." *Newsmax*, 20 July 2021, www.newsmax.com/politics/harrington-election-trump-warning/2021/07/20/id/1029260/.

Rooslet, David III. "Missouri House of Representatives Declare No Confidence in Presidential Election." *America's Tribune*, 9 Dec. 2020, www.americastribune.com/post/missouri-house-of-representatives-declare-no-confidence-in-presidential-election?

fbclid=IwAR3PRWX4JGedz2rqVHVSBaWPVReh39WU4JUN
jDp2ma4XGW-vrKU-9leVPy4.

Ross, Chuck. "Blumenthal Speaks at Communist Party Awards Ceremony." *The Washington Free Beacon*, 14 Dec. 2021, freebeacon.com/democrats/blumenthal-speaks-at-communist-party-awards-ceremony/.

Rucker, J.D. "As Cubans Take to the Street to Protest Socialism, the Biden Regime Pretends They're Demanding Vaccines." *The Liberty Daily*, 11 Jul. 2021, thelibertydaily.com/as-cubans-take-to-the-street-to-protest-socialism-the-white-house-pretends-theyre-demanding-vaccines/.

Rufful, David. "Michigan Armed Protesters Wearing Antifa, Black Lives Matter Attire Stun Many As They Chant: We Support Karl Marx Not Biden." *Analyzing America*, 24 Dec. 2020, m.analyzingamerica.org/2020/12/613246/? fbclid=IwAR0FHhchxvb3P4dpraDyibDcO7OEd8M0Q95YjXb m3RhrRjycD5Cd4d5QYoU.

Rugg, Colin. "80 Million Votes": Sidney Powell Drops Bombshell Prediction About the Finalized 2020 Election." *Trending Politics*, 18 Nov. 2020, archive.is/wip/UhmAb.

Rugg, Collin. "Fox's Maria Bartiromo Sounds the Alarm, Alleges 'An Intel Source Told Me President Trump Did, in Fact, Win the Election.'" *Trending Politics*. Jan. 2021, trendingpolitics.com/ fox-s-maria-bartiromo-sounds-the-alarm-alleges-an-intel-source-told-me-president-trump-did-in-fact-win-the-election/? utm_source=collin&utm_medium=instagram&fbclid=IwAR3w ksuV46_77c3pJjr0WvpTGQucR2fLjWFmJp-icQzJyrE57g32uMQca2o.

Rugg, Colin. "May Have to Get Witness Protection": Sidney Powell Gives Big Update On Election Investigations." *Trending Politics*, 21 Nov. 2020, archive.is/wip/qXV9k.

Ruiz, Michael. "Virginia mom who survived Maoist China eviscerates school board's critical race theory push." *Fox News*, 10 Jun. 2021, www.foxnews.com/us/virginia-xi-van-fleet-critical-race-theory-china-cultural-revolution-loudoun.

"Russia Calls America a 'Liberal Totalitarian State' with a 'Monopoly on the Media' and 'Irremovability of Oligarchic Elites'." *Big League Politics*, 26 Jun. 2021, bigleaguepolitics.com/russia-calls-america-a-liberal-totalitarian-state-with-a-monopoly-on-the-media-and-irremovability-of-oligarchic-elites/.

Saavedra, Ryan. "126 Ex-Generals, Admirals Warn About Biden: U.S. In 'Deep Peril,' Health A Concern, 7 Red Flags Emerging." *DailyWire.com*, 13 May 2021, www.dailywire.com/news/126-ex-generals-admirals-warn-about-biden-u-s-in-deep-peril-health-a-concern-7-red-flags-emerging.

Saavedra, Ryan. "Details Emerge About What FBI Agents Were Searching For In Raid On Trump Home, Report Says." *DailyWire.com*, 8 Aug. 2022, www.dailywire.com/news/breaking-details-emerge-about-what-fbi-agents-were-searching-for-in-raid-on-trump-home-report-says.

Sacchetti, Cesare. "Italiagate: il governo Conte accusato di essere responsabile della frode elettorale contro Trump." *City of Genova News*, 24 Mar. 2021, citygenova.com/italiagate-il-governo-conte-accusato-di-essere-responsabile-della-frode-elettorale-contro-trump/.

Sadler, Ashley. "Trump tells Fox News US is in 'very dangerous' place following FBI raid of Mar-a-Lago residence." *LifeSite*, 15 Aug. 2022, www.lifesitenews.com/news/trumps-first-post-fbi-raid-interview-terrible-things-will-happen-if-we-dont-de-escalate-tensions/?utm_source=digest-freedom-2022-08-22&utm_medium=email

Sánchez, Mario. "Socialism Has Ruined Cuba, And It Seeks To Engulf The United States." *The Federalist*, 21 Jul. 2021, thefederalist.com/2021/07/21/socialism-has-ruined-cuba-and-it-seeks-to-engulf-the-united-states.

Saunders, Joe. "Declassified Doc Ties Obama, Brennan to Hillary's Russia 'Collusion' Plot Against Trump." *The Federalist Papers*, 10 Dec. 2020, thefederalistpapers.org/us/uh-oh-declassified-doc-ties-obama-brennan-hillarys-russia-collusion-plot-trump?fbclid=IwAR2mt-oj-BuBsruljGr_oYwH6_1l7Z3oXzU5weoTyi7Mc6nO3m1rjI5bBTc.

Saunders, Joe. "Survivor of Communism Slams Down Democratic Rep for Claiming 'White Nationalism' Is More Dangerous than Communism.' *The Western Journal*, 30 Jun. 2021, www.westernjournal.com/survivor-communism-slams-democratic-rep-claiming-white-nationalism-dangerous-c o m m u n i s m / ? ff_source=mewe&ff_medium=westernjournalism&ff_campaign =manualpost&ff_content=2021-07-07.

"Senate security chief on January 6 dies before surprise hearing." *RT*, 28 June 2022, www.rt.com/news/557995-january6-senate-sergeant-dead/.

Saxena, Vivek. "Gingrich on vote anomalies: 'It looks like 2020 may be the biggest Presidential theft since … 1824.'" *BPR*, 29 Nov. 2020, www.bizpacreview.com/2020/11/29/gingrich-on-vote-anomalies-it-looks-like-2020-may-be-the-biggest-presidential-theft-since-1824-1000534/.

Saxena, Vivek. "Michael Flynn speaks out after pardon: 'This is still a coup in progress.'" *BPR*, 29 Nov. 2020, www.bizpacreview.com/2020/11/29/michael-flynn-speaks-out-after-pardon-this-is-still-a-coup-in-progress-1000723? fbclid=IwAR3TTAEVkmFXAD4nry5Z0uJPUk3M2UTwzcGa OTSACW3cwBffP0NW3TRhDBo.

Schnell, Mychael. "New York Supreme Court Suspends Giuliani's Law License." *The Hill*, 24 June 2021, thehill.com/homenews/state-watch/560046-new-york-supreme-court-votes-to-suspend-giulianis-law-license.

Seagray, Louis. "Key to Absolute Power: Brand EVERYONE that you Disagree with as a 'Terrorist'." *Big League Politics*, 26 Feb. 2022, bigleaguepolitics.com/key-to-absolute-power-brand-everyone-that-you-disagree-with-as-a-terrorist/.

Sharp, Keely. "WATCH: Mike Lindell Declares Trump Will be Reinstated on August 13." *Think Americana*, 6 July 2021, thinkamericana.com/watch-mike-lindell-declares-trump-will-be-reinstated-on-august-13/.

Shepherd, Igor, Dr. "Covid-19: A Psychological Military Operation, Part I." *Lewrockwell.com*, 13 Oct. 2021, www.lewrockwell.com/

2021/10/dr-igor-shepherd/covid-19-a-psychological-military-operation-part-i/.

Shelley, Susan. "Missouri v. Biden: A Victory for Free Speech." *Los Angeles Daily News*, 9 July 2023, www.dailynews.com/2023/07/09/missouri-v-biden-a-victory-for-free-speech/.

Shiver, Phil. "Army officer resigns, gives up pension in protest of Biden's 'tyrannical' vaccine mandate, 'Marxist takeover of the military'." *Blaze Media*, 14 Sept. 2021, www.theblaze.com/news/army-officer-resigns-covid-vaccine-mandate.

"Shocking Claim: Michigan Senate Majority Leader Mike Shirkey – Jan. 6th Was Staged to Impeach Trump." *TCPov*, 13 June 2022, tcpov.com/politics-government/shocking-claim-michigan-senate-majority-leader-mike-shirkey-jan-6th-was-staged-to-impeach-trump/.

Shurk, J.B. "The Biden Regime Has Made Us All Enemies of the State." *American Thinker*, 18 July 2021, www.americanthinker.com/articles/2021/07/the_biden_regime_has_made_us_all_enemies_of_the_state.html.

"SICK: Obama Calls For The Eradication of Trump Supporters [VIDEO]." *Freedom Clash*, freedomclash.com/sick-obama-calls-for-the-eradication-of-trump-supporters-video/?utm_source=BS-Mailer-FC&utm_medium=email&utm_content=subscriber_id:71132098&utm_campaign=%23sick-obama-NK. Accessed 24 June 2023.

"Sidney Powell: America is now a 'Communist regime.'" *Natural News*, 7 May 2021, www.naturalnews.com/2021-05-07-sidney-powell-america-now-a-communist-regime.html#.

"Sidney Powell: Smartmatic, Dominion Stole Millions of Votes from Trump - Smartmatic is a Crown Jewel of the British Empire." *LaRouchePac*, 16 Nov. 2020, larouchepac.com/20201116/sidney-powell-smartmatic-dominion-stole-millions-votes-trump.

Skurkiss, Peter. "If America's Going to Split Apart, Here's What Will Happen to You." *American Thinker*, 6 Oct. 2021, www.americanthinker.com/blog/2021/10/ if_americas_going_to_split_apart_heres_what_will_happen_to_ you.html.

Slag, Molly. "No, 'capitalism' and 'socialism' don't define economic systems." *American Thinker*, 21 Feb. 2022, www.americanthinker.com/blog/2022/02/ no_capitalism_and_socialism_dont_define_economic_systems. html.

Smith, Brandon. "In A Civil War The Authoritarian Left Would Be Easily Beaten – But It Won't End There." *Alt-Market.us*, 1 Oct. 2021, alt-market.us/in-a-civil-war-the-authoritarian-left-would-be-easily-beaten-but-it-wont-end-there/.

Smith, Brandon. "Is The Cloward-Piven Strategy Being Used To Destroy America?" *State of the Nation*, 4 Jul. 2014, stateofthenation2012.com/?p=6175.

Smith, Brandon. "Oregon Is Proof That Leftist Politics Ultimately Lead To Tyranny And Decay." *Alt-Market.us*, 28 May 2021, alt-market.us/oregon-is-proof-that-leftist-politics-ultimately-lead-to-tyranny-and-decay/.

Smith, Brandon. "There Will Never Be A 'Woke' US Military – Here Are The Reasons Why." *Alt-Market.us*, 20 May 2021, alt-market.us/ there-will-never-be-a-woke-military-here-are-the-reasons-why/.

Smith, E.J. "WHOLE FOODS CEO: 'Socialists Are Taking Over'." *Your Survival Guy*, 11 Aug. 2022, www.yoursurvivalguy.com/ personal-security/the-great-reset/whole-foods-ceo-socialists-are-taking-over/? utm_source=MeWe&utm_medium=Social&utm_campaign=8-1 1-22&utm_id=Social.

Smith, Justin O. "Willing to Risk Everything for Freedom: All Eyes Are On Cuba and America." *The Blue State Conservative*, 15 Jul. 2021, thebluestateconservative.com/2021/07/15/willing-to-risk-everything-for-freedom-all-eyes-are-on-cuba-and-america/.

Snyder, Tarra. "BLM Activists Seize Control of George Floyd Square Again, Put Barriers Back Up." *The Western Journal*, 8 June 2021, www.westernjournal.com/blm-activists-seize-control-george-floyd-square-put-barriers-back/?utm_source=mewe&utm_medium=westernjournalism&utm_content=2021-06-08&utm_campaign=manualpost.

Snyder, Tara. "'Black Lives Matter' Founder Builds Expensive Wall Around Newly Purchased Upscale House: Report." *The Western Journal*, 11 Jun. 2021, www.westernjournal.com/black-lives-matter-founder-builds-expensive-wall-around-newly-purchased-upscale-house-report/?utm_source=mewe&utm_medium=westernjournalism&utm_content=2021-06-11&utm_campaign=manualpost.

"Soros's 'Purple Revolution' brewing for Trump presidency." *Wayne Madsen Report*, 11 Nov. 2016, stateofthenation2012.com/?p=56078.

"Space Force Commander Dismissed for Criticizing 'Neo-Marxist' Critical Race Theory in the US Military." *RT*, 16 May 2021, www.rt.com/usa/523950-space-force-commander-fired-diversity-extremism/.

Spencer, Robert. "Biden: 'Terrorism from white supremacy is the most lethal threat to the homeland today.'" *PJ Media*, 1 June 2021, pjmedia.com/news-and-politics/robert-spencer/2021/06/01/biden-wants-us-to-watch-out-for-white-guys-no-not-antifa-n1451371.

Sperry, Paul. "How Obama Is Scheming to Sabotage Trump's Presidency." *New York Post*, 11 Feb. 2017, nypost.com/2017/02/11/how-obama-is-scheming-to-sabotage-trumps-presidency/.

Sperry, Paul. "OFA has raised more than $40 million in contributions and grants." *New York Post*, 11 Feb. 2017, nypost.com/2017/02/11/how-obama-is-scheming-to-sabotage-trumps-presidency/.

Spiering, Charlie. "Criminal Investigation of Donald Trump Heats up as He Plans Political Future." *Breitbart*, 8 Jun 2021, www.breitbart.com/politics/2021/06/08/criminal-investigation-of-donald-trump-heats-up-as-he-plans-political-future/.

Spitzer, Glenn. "The connection between Kyle Rittenhouse's trial and Julius Caesar's rise." *American Thinker*, 20 Nov. 2021, www.americanthinker.com/blog/2021/11/the_connection_between_kyle_rittenhouses_trial_and_julius_ca esars_rise.html.

Spitzer, Glenn. "Thirty years: Good riddance to the USSR!" *American Thinker*, 1 Jan. 2022, www.americanthinker.com/blog/2022/01/thirty_years_good_riddance_to_the_ussr.html#ixzz7GwodJO6L.

"Stalin-era mass grave found in Ukraine." *BBC*, 26 Aug. 2021, www.bbc.com/news/world-europe-58340805.

Stanford, Stefan. "Remember That 'ALL Totalitarian Regimes Control People Through Protein Starvation' As These 'Two Most Precious Commodities For The Coming Months' Come Under 'Attack.'" *All News Pipeline*, 2 Jun. 2021, allnewspipeline.com/ALL_Totalitarian_Regimes_Control_People_Through_Protein_Starvation.php.

Shurk, J.B. "The Biden Regime Has Made Us All Enemies of the State." *American Thinker*, 18 July 2021, www.americanthinker.com/articles/2021/07/the_biden_regime_has_made_us_all_enemies_of_the_state.html.

Staff Writers. "Trump Jr. blasts NY investigators 'political' motivations." *The American Digest*, 3 June 2021, americandigest.com/trump-j-blasts-ny-investigators-political-motivations/.

Starnes, Todd. "CNN Director Admits Network's Focus was to 'Get Trump Out'." Apr 13, 2021, www.toddstarnes.com/media/cnn-director-admits-networks-focus-was-to-get-trump-out/?fbclid=IwAR2-wJLUQ2xE-WPGZInf5T5AYjKootuRoS1NmVY_QAmyUjcOJ5MwECRL73s

"Statement by Donald J. Trump, 45th President of the United States of America, on Radical Left New York Political Prosecutors." *Save America*, 28 June 2021, www.donaldjtrump.com/news/statement-by-donald-j-trump-45th-president-of-the-united-states-of-america-on-radical-left-new-york-political-prosecutors-06.28.21-02.

"Statement by Donald J. Trump, 45th President of the United States of America." *Save America*, 30 June 2021, www.donaldjtrump.com/news/statement-by-donald-j-trump-45th-president-of-the-united-states-of-america-06.30.21-03

"Statement by Donald J. Trump, 45th President of the United States of America." *Save America*, 7 July 2021, www.donaldjtrump.com/news/statement-by-donald-j-trump-45th-president-of-the-united-states-of-america-07.07.21-2.

Stauffer, Elizabeth. "Dems Leave Out Trump's Call to 'Peacefully and Patriotically Make Your Voices Heard' During Impeachment Opening." *The Western Journal*, 10 Feb. 2021, www.westernjournal.com/dems-leave-trumps-call-peacefully-patriotically-make-voices-heard-impeachment-opening/?ff_source=mewe&ff_medium=westernjournalism&ff_campaign=manualpost&ff_content=2021-06-08.

Sun, Melanie. "Michael Flynn Says Coup Against Trump Still In Progress In First Public Remarks Since Pardon." *The Epoch Times*, 29 Nov. 2020, archive.is/lotKt.

Sundance. "Attorney General Merrick Garland Pre-Positioning Assets Against Looming Election Audit Results and Voter Data Forensics." *The Last Refuge*, 14 Jun. 2021, theconservativetreehouse.com/blog/2021/06/14/attorney-general-merrick-garland-pre-positioning-assets-against-looming-election-audit-results-and-voter-data-forensics/.

Sundance. "FBI Triggers Politically Strategic Narrative, Highlights Q-Anon Supporters as Domestic Violent Extremists." *The Last Refuge*, 14 June 2021, theconservativetreehouse.com/blog/2021/06/14/fbi-triggers-politically-strategic-narrative-highlights-q-anon-supporters-as-domestic-violent-extremists/.

Sundance. "Joe Biden Begins Using FBI to Arrest Political Opposition from Prior Administration." *The Last Refuge*, 3 June 2022, theconservativetreehouse.com/blog/2022/06/03/joe-biden-begins-using-fbi-to-arrest-political-opposition-from-prior-administration/.

Sundance. "Nancy Pelosi Directs Capitol Hill Security Police Units to Regional Offices in California and Florida, Future Locations Coming." *The Last Refuge*, 6 July 2021, theconservativetreehouse.com/blog/2021/07/06/nancy-pelosi-directs-capitol-hill-security-police-units-to-regional-offices-in-california-and-florida-future-locations-coming/.

Swier, Dr. Rich. "Is America Headed Toward a Second Civil War?" 26 July 2021. drrichswier.com/2021/07/26/is-america-headed-toward-a-second-civil-war/.

Swier, Dr. Rich. "Trevor Loudon's 2020 List of 65 Communists, Socialists and Security Risks in Congress." 1 Septe. 2020, drrichswier.com; trevorloudon.com.

T, Brett. "Squad, Bernie hardest hit: President Biden denounces communism, says socialism isn't a very useful substitute." *Twitchy*, 15 Jul. 2021, twitchy.com/brettt-3136/2021/07/15/squad-bernie-hardest-hit-president-biden-denounces-communism-says-socialism-isnt-a-very-useful-substitute/.

Taibbi, Matt. "We're in a permanent coup." *TK News*, 11 Oct. 2019, taibbi.substack.com/p/were-in-a-permanent-coup.

Taylor, Kristinn. "Dark Brandon Returns: Biden to Give Speech Tonight on 'Threat of Election Deniers' and Political Violence." *Gateway Pundit*, 2 Nov. 2022, www.thegatewaypundit.com/2022/11/dark-brandon-returns-biden-give-speech-tonight-threat-election-deniers-political-violence/.

Taylor, Kristinn. "Poll: 35 Percent Want 2020 Presidential Election Overturned; Only 39 Percent Definitely Believe Election Was 'Free and Fair.'" *Gateway Pundit*, 27 Oct. 2021, www.thegatewaypundit.com/2021/10/poll-35-percent-want-2020-presidential-election-overturned-39-percent-definitely-believe-election-free-fair/.

Terrell, Rebecca. "Fraud and Future Elections." *The New American*, Aug. 2022, thenewamerican.com/fraud-and-future-elections/.

"Texas claims victory in censorship fight." *RT*, 17 Sept. 2022, www.rt.com/news/562980-texas-big-tech-censorship/.

"Texas Republicans declare Biden 'not legitimately elected.' *RT*, 19 June 2022, www.rt.com/usa/557457-texas-republicans-biden-election-stolen/.

"The American 'Cassandra Prophecy': Everything Changes After Election Day 2020." *State of the Nation*, 28 Nov. 2019, stateofthenation.co/?p=211.

The Associated Press. "Amazon Asks Federal Judge to Dismiss the FTC's Antitrust Lawsuit Against the Company." *ABC News*, 8 Dec. 2023, abcnews.go.com/Technology/wireStory/amazon-asks-federal-judge-dismiss-ftcs-antitrust-lawsuit-105512882.

"The Communist *Purple Revolution* Rages Inside the Beltway." *State of the Nation*, 24 Oct. 2019, stateofthenation2012.com/?p=130471.

The DC Patriot. "WATCH: Project Veritas EXPOSES Democrat U.S. Senate Candidate Who Pushed for 'Secret Sleepers' to Run as Conservatives." 28 June 2022, thedcpatriot.com/watch-project-veritas-exposes-democrat-u-s-senate-candidate-who-pushed-for-secret-sleepers-to-run-as-conservatives/.

"The Democrat-Run COMMUNIST TAKEOVER PLOT Is About Ready To Go Prime Time." *The Millennium Report*, 30 Oct. 2020, themillenniumreport.com/2020/10/the-democrat-run-communist-takeover-plot-is-about-ready-to-go-prime-time/

"The FBI's Trump residence raid could mean he can't run in 2024 – and his militant followers will rise up." *RT*, 11 Aug. 2022, www.rt.com/news/560615-fbis-trump-residence-raid/.

"The Greatest Act of Collective Treason in U.S. History." *State of the Nation*, 26 Dec. 2018, stateofthenation2012.com/?p=112038.

"The longer Trump is out of office the more people realize how right he was on a number of issues." *Right News Wire*, 2 Jun. 2021, rightnewswire.com/the-longer-trump-is-out-of-office-the-more-people-realize-how-right-he-was-on-a-number-of-issues/?

utm_source=rnwnl&utm_medium=ong&utm_campaign=12904 68231.

"The Media's Meltdown Over Durham Revelations Directly Refutes Years of Prior Coverage, According to Liberal Law Professor." *The Gateway Pundit,* Feb. 2022, www.thegatewaypundit.com/ 2022/02/liberal-law-professor-medias-meltdown-durham-revelations-directly-refute-years-prior-coverage/? utm_source=Gab&utm_medium=PostTopSharingButtons&utm _campaign=websitesharingbuttons.

"The Military Has Gone 'Woke'" The Editorial Board. *The Wall Street Journal*, 25 June 2021. www.wsj.com/articles/has-the-military-gone-woke-11624660049?mod=itp_wsj.

"The New World Order and the United States of America." *Philadelphians.50megs.Com*, philadelphians.50megs.com/nwo-us.html.

"The Scheme to Terminate the American Republic Exposed." *The Millennium Report*, 28 July 2020, themillenniumreport.com/ 2020/07/super-secret-globalist-scheme-to-terminate-the-american-republic-exposed/.

"The Wretched Xavier Becerra Wants to Control Your Life." *Washington Examiner*, 10 July 2021, www.washingtonexaminer.com/ opinion/editorials/the-wretched-xavier-becerra-wants-to-control-your-life.

Tillison, Tom. "'Brilliant' thread capturing the justified fury and cynicism of MAGA mindset earns resounding accolades." *BPR*, 9 July 2021, www.bizpacreview.com/2021/07/09/brilliant-thread-capturing-the-justified-fury-and-cynicism-of-maga-mindset-earns-resounding-accolades-1101272/.

Toledo, Arsenio. "Political correctness and indoctrination in American universities no different from BRAINWASHING in North Korea, says defector." *Natural News*, 30 June 2021, www.naturalnews.com/2021-06-30-political-correctness-indoctrination-america-same-as-north-korea.html.

"Transition Integrity Project: Is this Soros-Linked Group Plotting a 'Color Revolution' Against President Trump?" *Revolver*, 4 Sept.

2020, www.revolver.news/2020/09/transition-integrity-project-is-this-soros-linked-group-plotting-a-color-revolution-against-president-trump/.

Trejo, Shane. "Anti-American 'Orders Project' is Encouraging Military to Stand Down to Leftist Terrorists After the Election." *Big League Politics*, 24 Oct. 2020, bigleaguepolitics.com/anti-american-orders-project-is-encouraging-military-to-stand-down-to-leftist-terrorists-after-the-election/.

"Troops Accuse Pentagon of 'Religious Purge'." *RT*, 29 Apr. 2022, www.rt.com/news/554699-pentagon-purge-vaccine-mandate/.

"Trump accuses Democrats of plot." *RT*, 14 Jun. 2022, www.rt.com/news/557118-trump-democrats-capitol-probe/.

"Trump ally says FBI seized cell phone." *RT*, 10 Aug. 2022, www.rt.com/news/560563-fbi-seize-republican-phone/.

"Trump brands Biden 'enemy of the state' *RT*, 4 Sept. 2022, www.rt.com/news/562137-trump-biden-enemy-of-state/.

"Trump describes shock FBI raid as 'political persecution.'" *RT*, 9 Aug. 2022, www.rt.com/news/560498-fbi-raid-trump-florida/.

Trump, Donald. "Statement by Donald J. Trump, 45th President of the United States of America." *Save America*, 16 Feb. 2021, www.donaldjtrump.com/news/statement-by-donald-j-trump-45th-president-of-the-united-states-of-america.

Trump, Donald. "Statement by Donald J. Trump, 45th President of the United States of America." *Save America*, 4 Mar. 2021, www.donaldjtrump.com/news/statement-by-donald-j-trump-45th-president-of-the-united-states-of-america_2.

Trump, Donald. "Statement by Donald J. Trump, 45th President of the United States of America." *Donaldtrump.com*, 5 Mar. 2021, www.donaldjtrump.com/news/statement-by-donald-j-trump-45th-president-of-the-united-states-of-america-05.03.21.

Trump, Donald. "Statement by Donald J. Trump, 45th President of the United States of America." *Save America*, 7 May 2021, www.donaldjtrump.com/news/statement-by-donald-j-trump-45th-president-of-the-united-states-of-america-05.07.21-3.

Trump, Donald. "Statement by Donald J. Trump, 45th President of the United States of America." *Save America*, 15 May 2021, www.donaldjtrump.com/news/statement-by-donald-j-trump-45th-president-of-the-united-states-of-america-05.15.21-2.

Trump, Donald. "Statement by Donald J. Trump, 45th President of the United States of America." *Save America*, 27 Jun. 2021, www.donaldjtrump.com/news/statement-by-donald-j-trump-45th-president-of-the-united-states-of-america-06.27.21-02.

Trump, Donald J. "Statement by Donald J. Trump, 45th President of the United States of America." *Save America*, 12 May 2021, www.donaldjtrump.com/news/statement-by-donald-j-trump-45th-president-of-the-united-states-of-america-05.12.06.

Trump, Donald J. "Statement by Donald J. Trump, 45th President of the United States of America." *Save America*, 15 July 2021, www.donaldjtrump.com/news/statement-by-donald-j-trump-45th-president-of-the-united-states-of-america-07.15.21-07.

Trump, Donald J. "Statement by Donald J. Trump, 45th President of the United States of America." *Save America*, 1 Aug. 2021, www.donaldjtrump.com/news/news-qvb8wmvsyn0.

"Trump has only ONE response to the ongoing soft coup being run by rogue elements within the U.S. Intelligence Community A Military Response." *State of the Nation*, 29 Nov. 2017, stateofthenation2012.com/?p=90049.

"Trump hints at possible dirty FBI trick." *RT*, 10 Aug, 2022, www.rt.com/news/560607-trump-fbi-raid-planted/.

"Trump hints at using FBI to prosecute opponents." *RT*, 11 Nov. 2023, www.rt.com/news/587056-us-trump-prosecute-opponents/.

"Trump issues statement over Hunter Biden Twitter files." *RT*, 4 Dec. 2022, www.rt.com/news/567649-trump-election-deception-claim/.

"Trump lashes out at new probe." *RT*, 19 Nov. 2022, www.rt.com/news/566801-trump-lashes-out-probe/.

"Trump leading Biden in poll – WaPo." *RT*, 7 May 2023, www.rt.com/news/575938-trump-leading-biden-poll/.

"Trump makes prediction on potential indictment." *RT*, 15 Sept. 2022, www.rt.com/news/562889-donald-trump-indictment-election/.

"Trump may have more classified docs – NYT." *RT*, 7 Oct. 2022, www.rt.com/news/564231-trump-more-classified-documents/.

"Trump pushes back on DOJ accusation." *RT*, 31 Aug. 2022, www.rt.com/news/561922-trump-denies-doj-allegations/.

"Trump raid makes US 'banana republic' – governor." *RT*, 9 Aug. 2022, www.rt.com/news/560503-desantis-biden-banana-republic/.

"Trump responds to 'insurrection' referrals." *RT*, 20 Dec. 2022, www.rt.com/news/568558-trump-january6-committee-insurrection/.

"Trump says Republicans must fight the 'radical left's crusade against our culture'." LifeSite, 22 Jun. 2022, https://www.lifesitenews.com/news/trump-says-republicans-must-fight-the-radical-lefts-crusade-against-our-culture/.

"Trump sees one way to end his 'persecution'." *RT*, 23 Jul. 2022, www.rt.com/news/559529-trump-claims-persecution/.

"Trump should be barred from White House – lawmakers." *RT*, 23 Dec, 2022, www.rt.com/news/568815-capitol-riot-final-report/.

"Trump trial begins in New York." *RT*, 31 Oct. 2022, www.rt.com/news/565683-trump-organization-fraud-trial/.

TTN Staff. "The Nation Reacts to FBI Raiding President Trump's Mar-a-Lago Home." *TTN*, 9 Aug. 2022, trumptrainnews.com/

2022/08/09/the-nation-reacts-to-fbi-raiding-president-trumps-mar-a-lago-home/.

Tuccille, J.D. "American Revolution Images Might Reveal You as a 'Violent Extremist,' Says the FBI." *Reason*, 8 Aug. 2022, reason.com/2022/08/08/american-revolution-images-might-reveal-you-as-a-violent-extremist-says-the-fbi/.

"Tucker: Why is Mark Milley still in command of US military?" *Fox News*, 17 Jul. 2021, www.foxnews.com/transcript/tucker-why-is-mark-milley-still-in-command-of-us-military.

"Twitter blocks Russian diplomats over US Covid claim." *RT*, 9 Aug. 2022, www.rt.com/news/560555-twitter-suspends-russian-foreign-ministry/.

"Twitter cracks down on radical Antifa-affiliated accounts." *RT*, 28 Nov. 2022, www.rt.com/news/567332-twitter-suspends-antifa-accounts/.

"Twitter files unveil more FBI collusion." *RT*, 10 Dec. 2022, www.rt.com/news/567991-twitter-files-fbi-collusion/.

"Twitter reveals how it banned Trump." *RT*, 9 Dec. 2022, www.rt.com/news/567990-twitter-files-trump-ban/.

"Twitter's 'secret blacklists' exposed." *RT*, 9 Dec. 2022, www.rt.com/news/567931-twitter-secrets-blacklist-exposed/.

Unruh, Bob. "Big Tech Could Ruin U.S. Elections, Huge Majority Believes." *WND*, 8 July 2021, www.wnd.com/2021/07/big-tech-ruin-u-s-elections-huge-majority-believes/?utm_source=Email&utm_medium=wnd-breaking&utm_campaign=breaking&utm_content=breaking&ats_es=b57b07e04c3cd981482b12794bc1313a.

Unruh, Bob. "Head of Joint Chiefs called out for naming Trump supporters as 'enemies'." *WND*, 2 July 2021, www.wndnewscenter.org/head-of-joint-chiefs-called-out-for-naming-trump-supporters-as-enemies/.

Unruh, Bob. "Lindell Sues Dominion, Smartmatic for RICO Violations." *WND*, 3 June 2021, www.wnd.com/2021/06/lindell-sues-d o m i n i o n - s m a r t m a t i c - r i c o - v i o l a t i o n s / ? u t m _ s o u r c e = E m a i l & u t m _ m e d i u m = w n d - breaking&utm_campaign=breaking&utm_content=breaking&at s_es=e4ceb773ae56eafbb7bcab59cacf4964.

Unruh, Bob. "New report finds 2020 presidential election abuses Dems scuttled voter ID rules, flooded mailboxes with ballots, restricted integrity rules." *WND*, 19 Aug. 2021, www.wnd.com/ 2021/08/new-report-confirms-2020-presidential-election-a b u s e s / ? f f _ s o u r c e = E m a i l & f f _ m e d i u m = w n d - breaking&ff_campaign=breaking&ff_content=breaking.

"US attorney general faces impeachment push over Trump house raid." *RT*, 13 Aug, 2022, www.rt.com/news/560754-us-impeachment-attorney-general/.

"US cybersecurity chief assesses 'integrity' of midterms." *RT*, 10 Nov. 2022, www.rt.com/news/566248-cisa-midterm-elections-security/.

"US Federal Election Commission Chairman Says 2020 US Election Is Illegitimate Due To Widespread Fraud." *Great Game India*, 13 Nov. 2020, greatgameindia.com/us-elections-illegitimate/.

"US names war crimes prosecutor to investigate Trump." *RT*, 18 Nov. 2022, https://www.rt.com/news/566796-trump-special-counsel-smith/.

"US Republican explains Biden impeachment move." *RT*, 18 May, 2023, w w w . r t . c o m / n e w s / 5 7 6 5 3 7 - r e p u b l i c a n - m t g - b i d e n - impeachment/.

"US Republicans slam 'woke' military leadership." *RT*, 22 Nov. 2022. www.rt.com/news/566998-us-republicans-woke-pentagon/.

Van Drew, Jeff. "VAN DREW: Why I'll vote against certifying the Electoral College results." *Save Jersey*, 30 Dec. 2020, savejersey.com/2020/12/van-drew-electoral-college-results/? fbclid=IwAR1b1UkugCLcGEH-8UQICVW4lTvZI30ZJOew9O IZS7kYx0wzj6Mld3r2Pqo.

Veltmeyer, James. "The Cultural Marxist attack on Western society." *The Washington Times*, 29 Nov. 2019, stateofthenation.co/?p=252.

Vince. "Steve Cortes: A Biden Win Was Statistically 'Impossible.'" *We Love Trump*, 11 Jun. 2021, welovetrump.com/2021/06/11/steve-cortes-a-biden-win-was-statistically-impossible/?utm_source=newsletter_vm&utm_medium=email&utm_campaign=vm.

"Vladimir Lenin Quotes." *Brainy Quote*, www.brainyquote.com/quotes/vladimir_lenin_136421.

Walker, David N. "Demise of a Great Nation." 27 Dec. 2016. *David N. Walker*, davidnwalker.com/2016/12/27/demise-of-a-great-nation/.

Walsh, Martin. "Boebert Unleashes on Biden: 'Rules For Thee But Not For My Crackhead Parmesan-Smoking Gun Criminal Son'." *Conservative Brief*, 7 July 2021, conservativebrief.com/boebert-unleashes-44507/?utm_source=CB&utm_medium=ABC.

Walsh, Martin. "Pirro: Deep State Didn't Just Steal Election from Trump, They Stole It From You — 'You Never Mattered Because It Was Never About You.'" *CB*, 14 Dec. 2020, conservativebrief.com/maga-1555-gfvds-30836/?fbclid=IwAR0Go86q-PNeEa-reik_5Y58zVh8N8owIpxkzQjazyynpscZDqwjzkFKkGE.

Warren, Ben. "Trump Says We'll Fight Back Against Election Fraud in Fireside Chat." *InfoWars*, 23 Dec. 2020, www.infowars.com/posts/trump-says-well-fight-back-against-election-fraud-in-fireside-chat/?fbclid=IwAR20sRebGYznjhrLKzfM7kNew4oiC0i8cN0VMmKeuHmI3lrTGqpvCsSHT7o.

"WATCH: Dr. Shiva, official involved in Maricopa audit, highlights key findings, concerns." *DML*, 15 Oct. 2021, dennismichaellynch.com/watch-dr-shiva-official-involved-in-maricopa-audit-highlights-key-findings-concerns/?fbclid=IwAR2fCPGBHJmwcHs-TFa_UyABBaak8qR1EdERSGCjCJNCIjfuQAsn9d6Dhlk.

"Watch: Tucker Carlson Ties It All Together, Lays Out the Undeniable Truth of the 2020 Election Elizabeth Stauffer." *The Western Journal*, 10 Jul. 2021, www.westernjournal.com/watch-tucker-

carlson-ties-together-lays-undeniable-truth-2020-election/?
utm_source=facebook&utm_medium=huckabee.

Watson, Steve. "Video: Sen. Cotton Reveals Details Of 'Anti-American Indoctrination' In U.S. Military." *InfoWars*, 14 June 2021. www.infowars.com/posts/video-sen-cotton-reveals-details-of-anti-american-indoctrination-in-u-s-military/.

Weiss, Rusty. "Obama Gloats: Biden Is 'Finishing the Job' I Started." *The Political Insider*, 1 June 2021, thepoliticalinsider.com/obama-gloats-biden-is-finishing-the-job-i-started/?utm_campaign=TPI06012021BR1&utm_source=criticalimpact&utm_medium=email&utm_content=c49c051d9b3705f9a6473c7b9fa19141&source=TPICI.

Weiss, Rusty. "President Trump Hosts Meeting With House Republicans To Discuss Challenging Election." *Political Insider*, 22 Dec. 2020, thepoliticalinsider.com/president-trump-hosts-meeting-with-house-republicans-to-discuss-challenging-election/?fbclid=IwAR3RVOQDn4xTikIsen7O1i0WPhnEE_g0vyrMf2VAFnqcNQMRoRLpTz92QK0.

Wells, S.D. "4-Stage Brainwashing Process That Turns America Communist." *Natural News*, 28 May 2021, www.naturalnews.com/2021-05-28-4-stage-brainwashing-con-turning-america-communist.html.

West, Andrew. "Trump Tells Acquaintances That He'll Be 'Reinstated' by August." *Flag and Cross*, 1 Jun. 2021, flagandcross.com/trump-tells-acquaintances-that-hell-be-reinstated-by-august/.

Wetmore, Ben. "Exclusive: FBI Agents and National Archives Goon Are Harassing 2020 Michigan Trump Electors." *The Gateway Pundit*, 22 June 2022, www.thegatewaypundit.com/2022/06/exclusive-fbi-national-archives-goon-harassing-2020-michigan-trump-electors/?ff_source=Gettr&ff_campaign=websitesharingbuttons.

Wheeler, Scott. "EXCLUSIVE: Former FBI Assistant Director Says 'Handful in Leadership' Are Politicizing Bureau, Following Mar-a-Lago Raid." *The Epoch Times*, 12 Aug. 2022, www.theepochtimes.com/exclusive-former-fbi-assistant-director-says-handful-in-leadership-are-politicizing-bureau-following-mar-a-lago-raid_4660458.html? utm_source=partner&utm_campaign=ZeroHedge.

Whitehead, John & Nisha. "Federal Bureau of Intimidation: The War on Political Freedom." *Off-guardian.org*, 5 Oct. 2022, off-guardian.org/2022/10/05/federal-bureau-of-intimidation-the-war-on-political-freedom/.

"White House deems Trump supporters 'extremist threat.'" *RT*, 31 Aug, 2022, www.rt.com/news/561932-maga-republicans-threat-democracy-biden/.

"White House dodges question about FBI interference." *RT*, 20 Dec. 2022, www.rt.com/news/568569-fbi-twitter-white-house/.

Whiton, Christian. "Trump Remains the Key to Republican Election Victories." *The National Interest*, 20 May 2021, nationalinterest.org/feature/trump-remains-key-republican-election-victories-185655.

Wickert, David. "Georgia headed toward yet another presidential election review." *The Atlanta Journal-Constitution*, 21 May 2021, www.ajc.com/politics/georgia-headed-toward-another-presidential-election-audit/ O6WU557RGZACJL3PUHVNKIP57M/.

Widburg, Andrea. "The false claim that Trump was in wrongful possession of confidential documents." *American Thinker*, 19 Feb. 2022, www.americanthinker.com/blog/2022/02/ the_false_claim_that_trump_was_in_wrongful_possession_of_ confidential_documents.html.

Widburg, Andrea. "The 'smartest man in the room' has joined Sidney Powell's team." *American Thinker*, 28 Nov. 2020, www.americanthinker.com/blog/2020/11/ the_smartest_man_in_the_room_has_joined_sidney_powells_te am.html#ixzz6qRkT0OFw.

Widburg, Andrea. "Tucker Carlson warns that Biden is actively criminalizing political opposition." *American Thinker*, 13 Sept. 2022. Accessed 28 Sept. 2022. www.americanthinker.com/blog/ 2022/09/

tucker_carlson_warns_that_biden_is_actively_criminalizing_po
litical_opposition.html#ixzz7esKuwFGS.

Willoughby, Rick. "Margaret Thatcher on Socialism." *Rickety.us*, 15 Jan.
2012, www.rickety.us/2012/01/margaret-thatcher-on-socialism/.

Wilsey, John. "Alexis de Tocqueville, socialism, and the American Way."
Acton.org, 17 Oct. 2018, www.acton.org/pub/commentary/
2018/10/17/alexis-de-tocqueville-socialism-and-american-way?
fbclid=IwAR0x_dLzfjopIcWB5WPkMR0HqXonzrTUUt-
fbgSanSyZaMyegn4Cy7fZzyo.

"Winston S. Churchill > Quotes > Quotable Quote." *Goodreads*,
www.goodreads.com/quotes/10838424-the-schemes-of-the-
international-jews-the-adherents-of-this.

Winters, Natalie. "UNSEEN VIDEO: BLM Founder Says Her Book Is
Like Mao's Red Book." *The National Pulse*, 6 May 2021,
thenationalpulse.com/breaking/blm-founder-compares-book-to-
maos-red-book/.

Widburg, Andrea. "Tucker Carlson warns that Biden is actively
criminalizing political opposition." *American Thinker*, 13 Sept.
2022, www.americanthinker.com/blog/2022/09/
tucker_carlson_warns_that_biden_is_actively_criminalizing_po
litical_opposition.html#ixzz7esKuwFGS.

"Will an American Spring take place in 2017? If so, the Trump
Movement needs to lead the way.." *State of the Nation*, 17 Feb.
2017, stateofthenation2012.com/?p=66275.

WND News Services. "15 million votes in 2020 election not accounted
for, report finds." *WND*, 19 Aug. 2021, www.wnd.com/
2021/08/15-million-votes-2020-election-not-accounted-report-
finds/.

WND Staff. "Ex-FEC member profiles case alleging fraud changed
election outcome." *WND*, 24 Aug. 2021, www.wnd.com/
2021/08/ex-fec-member-profiles-case-alleging-fraud-changed-
election-outcome/?
utm_source=add2any&utm_medium=PostBottomSharingButto
ns&utm_campaign=websitesharingbuttons.

Wolf, Mark. "Texas GOP Openly Declares Biden an Illegitimate President, Rejects Certified 2020 Results." *Long Island, NY*, 20 June 2022, www.longisland-ny.com/2022/06/20/texas-gop-openly-declares-biden-an-illegitimate-president-rejects-certified-2020-results/.

Woltz, Howell. "Did President Trump Just Go Nuclear?" *The Richardson Post*, 5 Dec. 2020, richardsonpost.com/howellwoltz/19243/did-president-trump-just-go-nuclear/?fbclid=IwAR2Sxvtc4e7QVtgGxC-pgz06eppXQbV4KGC47W1ZKiKamk68fjS7si0fW1Q.

Wong, Kristina. "Adviser to Pentagon Counter-Extremism Group Warns of Protected Speech Crackdown." *Breitbart*, 29 Jun. 2021, www.breitbart.com/politics/2021/06/29/adviser-to-pentagon-counter-extremism-group-warns-of-protected-speech-crackdown/#.

Wong, Kristina. "Declassified CIA Documents Reveal Brennan Briefed Obama on Clinton's Plan to Tie Trump to Russia." *Breitbart*, 6 Oct. 2020, www.breitbart.com/politics/2020/10/06/declassified-cia-documents-reveal-brennan-briefed-obama-on-clintons-plan-to-tie-trump-to-russia/.

Wong, Kristina. 'This Fight Is Inside the Gates Today': Pompeo Warns Lawmakers of the Chinese Communist Party." *Breitbart*, 11 Jan. 2021, www.breitbart.com/politics/2021/01/11/this-fight-is-inside-the-gates-today-pompeo-warns-lawmakers-of-the-chinese-communist-party/?fbclid=IwAR1Aphr-hMdh_LEYH13OyUXEZupOAGIITtBNjSP7njRCBS6h1zELtnYSXW0.

"Wow: 40 Percent Of Republicans Voted For Joe Biden In Pima County, Arizona?" *US Politics And News*, 22 Oct. 2021, www.conservativeworldnews.com/wow-40-percent-of-republicans-voted-for-joe-biden-in-pima-county-arizona/.

Xu, Kenny. "Critical Race Theory's Poisonous Roots Trace Back To Harvard University." *The Federalist*, 9 June 2021, thefederalist.com/2021/06/09/critical-race-theorys-poisonous-roots-trace-back-to-harvard-university/?utm_campaign=ACTENGAGE.

"Yes, President Trump Won: The Case, Evidence, & Statistical Receipts: Volume Three of the Navarro Report." *Natural News*, www.naturalnews.com/files/The-Navarro-Report-Volume-III.pdf.

Young, Richard C. "BECK: The Democrats' Dangerous FBI Raid Endgame." *Richardyoung.com*, 11 Aug. 2022, www.richardcyoung.com/politics/trump-administration/beck-the-democrats-dangerous-fbi-raid-endgame/?utm_source=MeWe&utm_medium=Social&utm_campaign=8-11-22&utm_id=Social.

Young, Richard. "NY Times Ignores Reality While Explaining Falling Support for BLM." *Richardyoung.com*, 24 May 2021, www.richardcyoung.com/politics/culture-wars/ny-times-ignores-reality-while-explaining-falling-support-for-blm/?utm_source=MeWe&utm_medium=Social&utm_campaign=5-25-21.

Young, Richard C. "NY Times Ignores Reality While Explaining Falling Support for BLM." *Richardyoung.com*, 24 May 2021, www.richardcyoung.com/politics/culture-wars/ny-times-ignores-reality-while-explaining-falling-support-for-blm/?utm_source=MeWe&utm_medium=Social&utm_campaign=5-25-21.

Young, Richard C. "'Part of the Club': Joe Biden Bows to Globalism." 18 June 2021, *Richardyoung.com*, www.richardcyoung.com/politics/foreign-policy-politics/part-of-the-club-joe-biden-bows-to-globalism/?utm_source=MeWe&utm_medium=Social&utm_campaign=6-18-21%20RCY.

Zempel, Kylee. "FBI: Lincoln Project Never Trumpers Peddled Iranian Disinformation Meant To Help Biden." *The Federalist*, 21 Oct. 2020, thefederalist.com/2020/10/21/fbi-lincoln-project-never-trumpers-peddled-iranian-disinformation-meant-to-help-biden/?fbclid=IwAR0LuSUJD_l0vbrWAYpgzEUwExFoJbVn1xGLCZHkNkBL2oeoBJBE_0z7Qdo#.X5D_1-IVVKY.facebook.

Zilber, Ariel and Ronny Reyes. "GOP Colorado Rep. Lauren Boebert demands Justice Department explain why Capitol rioters are being charged and jailed while BLM rioters who attacked federal buildings are NOT." *Daily Mail*, 21 Jul. 2021, www.dailymail.co.uk/news/article-9809941/Lauren-Boebert-demands-DOJ-explain-Capitol-Hill-rioters-treated-differently-BLM-rioters.html.

Zukerman, David. "Putin's Remarks About 'Woke' Culture Deserve Serious Consideration." *American Thinker*, 31 Oct. 2021, www.americanthinker.com/blog/2021/10/putins_remarks_about_woke_culture_deserve_serious_consideration.html.

ABOUT THE AUTHOR

Cynthia F. Hodges, JD, LLM, MA, is a multifaceted professional known for her accomplishments across various fields, including writing, law, translation, and equestrian pursuits. Her educational journey boasts a Doctor of Jurisprudence from South Texas College of Law in Houston, Texas, an LLM in Environmental Law from Lewis & Clark Law School in Portland, Oregon, and a BA and an MA in Germanic Studies from the University of Texas at Austin.

An active member of the Washington State Bar Association, Hodges has maneuvered through diverse legal terrains, focusing on animal and environmental law. Her commitment to justice shines through her contributions, highlighted by several law review articles published by Michigan State University's Animal Law Center.

Beyond the legal realm, Hodges devoted almost two decades to the training and showing of dressage horses, displaying expertise in the equestrian field. Proficient in German, Hodges has skillfully translated several books on dressage theory, demonstrating her profound understanding of horsemanship.

Hodges literary repertoire includes compelling works such as *Zion's Legacy: The Nakba Catastrophe and the Israeli-Palestinian Conflict, Downsized: The Deindustrialization of America, CODE RED: The Secret Communist Takeover of America, Den of Vipers: Central*

Banks & the Fake Economy, 5 Easy Ways to Promote Your Book Online, and *Leadership by George: The Leadership Principles of George Washington* (co-author). Her influence as an author spans diverse genres, blending imaginative storytelling with insightful analysis. Her political commentaries, notably *Code Red,* challenge established narratives, encouraging readers to reexamine their preconceptions. Across disciplines, Hodges inspires readers and makes a lasting impact, showcasing her resolute commitment to uncovering the truth.

For more information, visit cynthiahodges.com.

Made in United States
North Haven, CT
27 March 2024

50587498R00402